Medical Patent Law – The Challenges of Medical Treatment

Medical Patent Law – The Challenges of Medical Treatment

Dr Eddy Ventose

Senior Lecturer in Law and Head, Intellectual Property Unit, Faculty of Law, University of the West Indies, Cave Hill Campus, Barbados

Edward Elgar

Cheltenham, UK • Northampton, MA, USA

Published by

Edward Elgar Publishing Limited
The Lypiatts
15 Lansdown Road
Cheltenham
Glos GL50 2JA
UK

Edward Elgar Publishing, Inc.
William Pratt House
9 Dewey Court
Northampton
Massachusetts 01060
USA

A catalogue record for this book
is available from the British Library

Library of Congress Control Number: 2011926838

MIX
Paper from responsible sources
FSC® C018575

ISBN 978 1 84980 171 3

Typeset by Columns Design XML Ltd, Reading
Printed and bound by MPG Books Group, UK

Contents

List of abbreviations viii
Foreword x
Preface xi
Table of cases xiii
Table of national and international legislation xxii

1. Introduction 1
   - A General 1
   - B The arguments 2
   - C The EPO jurisprudence 5
   - D The question of patentability 6
   - E The future of medical patents 7

2. Arguments for patent protection 9
   - A Introduction 9
   - B Incentive to disclose 11
   - C Incentive to invent/innovate 14
   - D The prospect theory 23
   - E Rent dissipation theory 27
   - F Reward/desert 31
   - G Liberty/autonomy 34
   - H Conclusion 39

3. Arguments against patent protection 41
   - A Introduction 41
   - B Methods and products 43
   - C Public health implications 45
   - D Physician liberty and autonomy 58
   - E Physician/patient relationship 60
   - F The Hippocratic Oath/sharing norm 61
   - G Other incentive structures 66
   - H Breach of patient's privacy 68
   - I Conclusion 69

4. Therapeutic methods 71
- A Introduction 71
- B Legislative history 73
- C Defining therapeutic methods 75
- D Medical treatment and implantable devices 78
- E Involvement of medical practitioners 88
- F Cosmetic methods 89
- G Contraceptive methods 97
- H Animals 101
- I New medical technology 112
- J Conclusion 116

5. Surgical methods 117
- A Introduction 117
- B Legislative history 119
- C The referral to the EBA 123
- D Defining surgical methods 124
- E MEDI-PHYSICS/treatment by surgery 138
- F Cosmetic methods 148
- G Other considerations 153
- H An excluded surgical step 158
- I Disclaimers 168
- J Conclusion 183

6. Diagnostic methods 184
- A Introduction 184
- B Legislative history 187
- C The narrow approach 189
- D The broad approach 196
- E Reconciling the two approaches 201
- F Application of principles 208
- G New medical technology 218
- H Conclusion 228

7. Second and further medical uses 229
- A Introduction 229
- B Legislative history 230
- C The origin of second medical uses 234
- D Requirements of Swiss-type claims 237
- E Extending the reach of the EISAI principle 244
- F Second medical uses of devices and instruments 246
- G Reform of the EPC 254

H	Dosage or treatment regimes	255
I	New medical technology	285
J	Conclusion	286
8.	Manner of new manufacture	287
A	Introduction	287
B	Nature of the exclusion	288
C	The rationale for the exclusion	295
D	Contraceptive methods	315
E	The Commonwealth	321
F	Conclusion	330
9.	United Kingdom Patents Act 2004	332
A	Introduction	332
B	Comparison with pre-1977 law	333
C	Application of the exclusion	338
D	Second and further medical uses	345
E	Dosage regimes	356
F	Conclusion	372
10.	United States of America	374
A	Introduction	374
B	Initial judicial determination	375
C	Legislative intervention	382
D	The constitutional power	392
E	Conclusion	431
11.	Conclusion	433
A	Judicial determination of the exclusion	433
B	European patent office jurisprudence	436
C	The arguments for and against patent protection	443
Bibliography		448
Index		457

List of abbreviations

Courts and Tribunals

Court of Appeal of England and Wales	CA
Enlarged Board of Appeal of the European Patent Office	EBA
Federal Court of Australia	FCA
High Court of Australia	HCA
High Court of England and Wales	HC
New Zealand Court of Appeal	NZCA
Patent Appeal Tribunal	PAT
Patent Office Board of Appeal (US)	POBA
Technical Board of Appeal	TBA

Legislation and Conventions

United Kingdom Patents Act 1977	1977 Act
European Patent Convention 1973	EPC 1973
Trade Related Aspects of Intellectual Property Rights	TRIPs
Medical Procedures and Affordability Act 1996	MPAA
Patent Convention Treaty	PCT
Genomic Research and Diagnostic Accessibility Act	GRDA

Organisations and Bodies

America Medical Association	AMA
European Patent Office	EPO
US Patent and Trademark Office	USPTO
World Medical Association	WMA

Others

Cornish, Llewellyn and Aplin, *Intellectual Property: Patents, Copyright, Trademarks and Allied Rights* (7th edn, Sweet and Maxwell, London 2010)	Cornish, Llewellyn and Aplin, *Intellectual Property*
Bently & Sherman, *Intellectual Property Law* (3rd edn, Oxford University Press, Oxford 2008)	Bently & Sherman, *Intellectual Property*
Base Proposal on the Revision of the European Patent Convention Munich (29 Nov 2000) MR/3/00 Rev	Base Proposal 2000
EC Directive on the Legal Protection of Biotechnological Inventions 98/44/EC of 6 July 1998, (1998) OJ L213/13	Biotech Directive

Foreword

Since its inception in the Statute of Monopolies, modern patent law has been remarkably adroit in adapting to the changing needs of inventors and industry. But changes in innovation and in the developed economies over the last 50 years have arguably put more acute pressures on the conceptual framework of the law than any it has encountered in its history. Those pressures have revealed how fragile are some of the distinctions – such as that between invention and discovery – that patent law has always taken for granted. They have pushed policy makers and lawyers back to the much contested, and often contradictory, justifications for the grant of the patent monopoly, even though those justifications have often had to be retrofitted onto the existing structures of the law.

One of the interesting things about those pressures is that they have often brought into the spotlight curious byways of the law; they have made issues that might once have been thought to be of merely scholarly interest commercially vital. It is in the consideration of these issues that the contradictions of patent law and policy have often become most plain.

In this way, enormous changes in the economics of the health system, in the way in which doctors regard their professional calling, and in patterns of healthcare innovation, together with contemporary expectations that all (or at least most) innovation should be rewarded, have put huge strain on the exclusion from patentability (however technically it may be achieved) of methods of medical treatment. The conceptual basis of that exclusion, while not robust, draws upon many other fundamental assumptions in the law of patents and, properly examined, opens up many of those assumptions themselves for further consideration.

This book is a careful, timely, and thorough treatment of what is therefore a question, not only of increasing commercial importance, but also of enormous intellectual interest. As its author teases out the policy underpinnings of the exception and the arguments against it, we get not only a helpful guide to this area of the law and its development, but a deeper understanding of patent law as a whole. I have no doubt that it will be of great interest not only to researchers and academics, but to practitioners and policy makers as well. Dr. Ventose is to be congratulated on a significant contribution to a growing and complex area of the law.

Dr. Michael Spence
The Vice-Chancellor and Principal
University of Sydney

Preface

The idea that the issue of excluding methods of medical treatment from patent protection could have generated enough material on which to write a thesis, let alone a book, would have startled anyone 10 or so years ago. But the question of patent protection for methods of medical treatment, which comprises therapeutic methods, surgical methods and diagnostic methods, has been debated and resolved with different results in Europe, the United States and some Commonwealth countries. The rationale for the exclusion from patent protection – one might say justifiably so – is to ensure that the activities of physicians when they treat their patients are not hampered by patents. The notion of a physician being able to secure a patent on a life-saving medical treatment has perhaps most potently put the idea of patent protection for such treatments beyond question. The exclusion for methods of medical treatments in Europe is seemingly here to stay, whereas in the United States the courts have revived the debate of whether they should be excluded from patent protection.

This book is divided into 11 chapters. Chapter 1 is the introduction. Chapters 2 and 3 examine the arguments of principle and policy that are usually made for and against patent protection for methods of medical treatment. What then marks the difference between the availability of patent protection in some countries and the lack thereof in others? Article 27(3)(a) of the Trade Related Aspects of Intellectual Property Rights (TRIPs) Agreement provides that Members may exclude from patent protection diagnostic, therapeutic and surgical methods for the treatment of humans or animals. So either way, there would be compliance with this agreement. Sitting on the fence on this important issue is not comforting for those medical or veterinary practitioners, patients, inventors and pharmaceutical companies who all have a vested interest in the patentability or otherwise of methods of medical treatment. The arguments made in these two chapters put the debate in an appropriate context.

Chapters 4–6 deal with the exclusions from patentability under the European Patent Convention (EPC), namely, therapeutic methods, surgical methods and diagnostic methods respectively. It is in these three chapters that the fascinating legal framework for the exclusion of methods of medical treatment, which is found in a single provision, Article 53(c) EPC, is to be found. The scope of the exclusion and how it is to be interpreted in light of competing considerations have, therefore, taken centre stage in Europe. The Technical Board of Appeal (TBAs) of the EPC have been delineating the scope of the exclusion in the last 38 years and the Enlarged Board of Appeal of the European Patent Office (EBA) has had to intervene in delineating the scope of the exclusion on four occasions: 1985 (second medical uses); 2004 (diagnostic methods); 2010 (surgical methods); 2010 (dosage regimes), with the effect that many of the troubling issues have been laid to rest by these decisions. Chapter 7 follows suit with an examination of the vexed question of patent protection for second and further medical uses, including that relating to dosage or treatment regimes under the EPC. Where appropriate, these chapters will also examine the exclusion in light of new technological advancements in medical treatments and considers other EPC exclusions that might be implicated in respect of these new technologies.

Chapter 8 considers the historical basis for the exclusion in the United Kingdom before 1977, examining its jurisprudential bases over the years, concluding with an examination of the position in New Zealand and Australia whose patent legislation is still based on pre-1977 UK patent law. Chapter 9 continues the examination of UK law by examining how UK courts have applied the decisions of the TBAs and the EBA relating to the exclusions (therapy, surgery and diagnosis), second and further medical uses and, most recently, dosage or treatment regimes. Chapter 10 considers the position in the United States of America, namely of the US Patent and Trademark Office (USPTO), legislative intervention and recent examination of the issue of patenting diagnostic methods by the Federal Circuit and the Supreme Court.

This book originated from my thesis completed as part of my doctorate at the University of Oxford between 2001 and 2004. The thesis has now been substantially expanded, revised and completely reworked to form this book. I wish to thank the Clarendon Fund Scholarship which funded my doctoral research. I am grateful for my supervisor, Dr Michael Spence, Vice-Chancellor and Principal of the University of Sydney, for his excellent supervision and my examiners, Dr Justine Pila and Dr Jenifer Davis, for their constructive comments. Special thanks to Chantal, Dimitrios, Faye, Gareth and Matt, for their unfailing support and encouragement throughout.

Eddy D. Ventose
Faculty of Law, UWI, Cave Hill Campus
March 2011

Table of cases

Australia

Anaesthetic Supplies Pty Ltd v Rescare Ltd (1994) 50 FCR 1 **4, 41, 44, 55, 64, 313, 322, 323, 334**

Bristol-Myers Squibb Co. v FH Faulding & Co. Ltd (2000) 97 FCR 524; (2000) FCA 316 **311, 321, 322, 323, 334**

Joos v Commissioner of Patents (1972) 126 CLR 611 **312, 313, 322, 323, 434**

National Research Development Corporation v Commissioner of Patents (1959) 102 CLR 252; (1961) RPC 134 **299, 322**

Maeder v Busch (1938) 59 CLR 684 **298, 302, 322, 323**

Wellcome Foundation Ltd (Hitching's) Application [1980] RPC 305 **322**

Wellcome v Commissioner of Patents (1980) 30 ALR 510 **322**

Canada

Tennessee Eastman Co v Commissioner of Patents (1974) 30 DLR (3rd) 459 **325**

Israel

Wellcome Foundation Ltd v Plantex Limited [1974] RPC 514 **44, 46, 297, 330**

New Zealand

Pfizer Inc v Commissioner of Patents [2004] NZCA 104 **2, 311, 324**

Pfizer Inc v Commissioner of Patents [2005] NZLR 362 **334**

Pharmaceutical Management Agency Ltd v Commissioner of Patents [2000] 2 NZLR 529 **321, 322, 324, 327, 328, 329**

Swift and Company v Commissioner of Patents [1960] NZLR 775 **322**

Wellcome Foundation v Commissioner of Patents [1979] 2 NZLR 591; [1983] NZLR 385 **55, 447**

Swift and Company's Application [1961] RPC 147 **294, 295**

Swift & Co Application [1960] NZLR 775 **324**

United Kingdom

A & H's Application (1927) 44 RPC 298 **308**

Actavis UK Limited v Merck & Co Inc. [2008] EWCA Civ 444; [2008] RPC 26 **25, 185, 255, 271, 282, 357, 361, 362, 365, 371, 372, 442**

American Home Products v Novartis [2001] RPC 8 **354, 355**

Bayer AG (Meyer's) Application [1984] RPC 11 **346**

Bio-Digital Sciences Incorporated's Application [1973] RPC 668 **291, 324, 336, 337**
Blendax-Werke's Application [1980] RPC 491 **319, 320**
Biogen Inc. v Medeva Plc [1997] RPC 1 **25, 114, 355**
Boulton v Bull (1795) 126 ER 651 **287**
Bristol-Myers Squibb Co v Baker Norton Pharmaceuticals Inc [1999] RPC 253 **10, 44, 50**
Bristol-Myers Squibb v Baker Norton Pharmaceuticals Inc [2001] RPC 1 **185, 357**
C & W's Application (1914) 31 RPC 235 **289, 333**
Calmic Engineering Co. Ltd's Application [1973] RPC 684 **290, 291**
Canterbury Agricultural College's Application [1958] RPC 85 **288, 293, 294, 304, 306**
Ciba-Geigy AG (Durr's) Application [1977] RPC 83 **318**
Consultants Suppliers Ltd's Application [1996] RPC 348 **355**
Darcy v Allen (1602) 77 ER 1260 **287, 321**
Douglas v Hello! Ltd [2001] QB 967 **68**
Dow Corning Corp. (Bennett's) Application [1974] RPC 235 **319**
Eli Lilly & Company's Application [1975] RPC 438 **291, 311–313, 333, 334, 434**
GEC's Application (1942) 60 RPC 1 **297, 298**
Gillick v West Norfolk and Wisbech Area Health Authority [1986] 1 AC 112 **59**
Hoerrmann's Application [1996] RPC 341 **355**
Hunter v Mann [1974] QB 767 **69**
Imperial Chemical Industries Ltd (Richardson's) Application [1981] RPC 609 **355**
John Wyeth and Brothers Ltd's Application and AG's Schering Application [1985] RPC 545 **240, 338, 362**
L'Oreal's Application [1970] RPC 565 **318**
Lee Pharmaceutical's Application [1978] RPC 51 **290, 334**
London Rubber Industries Ltd's Patent [1968] RPC 31 **301, 303, 305, 316, 317, 319, 320**
McManus Application [1994] FSR 558 **355**
Merrell Dow Pharmaceuticals v N H Norton [1996] RPC 76 **349**
Monsanto & Company v Merck & Co. Inc [2000] RPC 77 **353, 354**
NV Phillips' Gloelampenfabrieken's Application (1954) 71 RPC 192 **294**
Neva Corporation's Application [1968] RPC 481 **290, 302, 334**
Organon Laboratories Ltd's Application [1970] RPC 574 **288, 317, 319, 320**
Palmer's Application [1970] RPC 597 **290, 302, 303, 334**
Pfizer Ltd's Patents [2001] FSR 16 **355**
Prendergast's Applications [2000] RPC 446 **355**
Puharich and Lawrence's Application [1965] RPC 395 **290, 291**

R (on the application of Quintavalle) v Secretary of State for Health [2002] 2 All ER 625 **222**
Re Cementation Co Ltd (1945) 62 RPC 151 **307**
Roussel-Uclaf v GD Searle and Co Ltd [1977] FSR 125 **55**
Schering AG's Application [1971] RPC 337 **2, 45, 288, 292, 294, 300, 301, 305, 306, 309–311, 313, 316, 317, 319, 333–336, 338, 340, 434**
Sopharma SA's Application [1983] RPC 195 **346, 347**
Stafford Miller Ltd's Applications [1984] FSR 258 **324**
Swift and Company's Application [1961] RPC 129 **294, 295**
Swift and Company's Application [1962] RPC 37 **295**
Teva Industries Ltd v Instituto Gentili SpA [2003] EWHC Civ 5; [2003] FSR 29 **10, 339, 352, 353, 357, 360**
Unilever Ltd's (Davis's) Application [1983] RPC 219 **340, 342**
United States Rubber Company's Application [1964] RPC 104 **289, 294**
Upjohn Company (Robert's) Application [1977] RPC 94 **291, 305, 310, 312, 313, 333, 334**
Virginia-Carolina Chemical Corporation's Application [1958] RPC 35 **305**
Visx v Nidex Co. Ltd [1999] FSR 405 **338**
Welcome Foundation Ltd (Hitchings's) Application [1980] RPC 305 **322**
Young v Bristol Aeroplane Company [1944] KB 718 **371**

United States

Abele, In re 684 F.2d 902 (Fed. Cir. 1982) **395**
Adler v Montefiore Hospital Association (1973) 453 Pa 60 **59**
Ariad Pharmaceuticals Inc. v Eli Lilly and Co. 560 F 3d 1366 (Fed. Cir. 2009) **409**
Association of Molecular Pathology v US Patent and Trademark Office US District Court (Southern District of New York, 09 Civ 415, 29 March 2010) **413**
AT&T Corp. v Excel Communications Inc. 172 F. 3d 1352 (Fed. Cir. 1999) **409**
Bilski, In re 545 F.3d 943 (Fed. Cir. 2008) (en banc) **395, 400, 402, 404, 407–409, 413, 415, 416**
Bilski v Kappos 130 S. Ct. 3218; 177 L. Ed. 2d 792 (2010) **7, 374, 375, 394, 409,–413, 415, 416, 422, 423, 430, 431, 432, 435**
Brinkerhoff, Ex parte (1883) reprinted in 27 JPOS 797 (POBA (1945) **375, 377–381, 431, 435**
Classen Immunotherapies, Inc. v Biogen Idec 2006 U.S. Dist. LEXIS 98106 (D.Md., 16 August 2006) **402–404**
Classen Immunotherapies, Inc. v Biogen Idec 304 Fed. Appx. 866 (Fed. Cir. 2008) **375, 412, 414, 416, 417, 430–432, 435**
Cochrane v Deener 94 U.S. 780 (1954) **378**
Diamond v Chakrabarty 447 U.S. 303 (1980) **3, 219, 393, 445, 446**
Diamond v Diehr 450 U.S. 175 (1981) **393, 397, 410, 418**

Dick v Lederle Antitoxin Laboratories 43 F 2d 628 (DC SDNY (1930)) **378**

Funk Bros. Seed Co. v Kalo Inoculant Co. 333 U.S. 127 (1948) **416, 417**

Gottschalk v Benson 409 U.S. 63 (1972) **416**

Grams, In re 888 F.2d 835 (Fed. Cir. 1989) **394, 408, 414, 422, 424, 428**

Griffin, In re 285 F.3d 1029 (Fed. Cir. 2002) **395, 414**

Kettering, Ex parte 35 USPQ 342 (POBA (1936)) **375, 381**

Laboratory Corporation v Metabolite Labs 548 U.S. 926; 126 S. Ct. 2976; 165 L. Ed. 2d 990 (2006) **374, 393, 394, 396–402, 405–407, 414, 416, 417, 420, 430, 432, 435**

Martin v Wyeth 96 F Supp 689 (DC DM (1951)) **379, 380, 431**

Meyer, In re 688 F.2d 789 (Fed. Cir. 1982) **395, 414**

Morton v New York Eye Infirmary 17 F Cas 879 (CC SDNY (1982)) **29, 375, 377, 378, 380**

Pallin v Singer 36 USPQ 2d 1050 (US DCDY (1995)) **22, 374, 381, 382, 432, 435**

Parker v Flook 437 U.S. 584 (1978) **7, 412, 416–419, 423, 427**

Prometheus Laboratories Inc. v Mayo Collaborative Services (Invalidity Opinion, 2008 WL 878910) **405**

Prometheus Laboratories Inc. v Mayo Collaborative Services 581 F.3d 1336 (Fed. Cir. 2009) **375, 404, 407, 412, 414–416, 422, 423, 430–432, 435**

Prometheus Laboratories Inc. v Mayo Collaborative Services (No. 2) (dated 17 December, 2010) (Fed. Cir. 2010) **415, 422, 423, 425, 431, 432, 435**

Roe v Wade 410 U.S. 113 (1973) **68**

Scherer, Ex parte 103 USPQ 107 (POBA (1954)) **374, 375, 378, 380, 381, 431, 435**

Schloendorff v Society of New York Hospital 105 NE 92 (1914) **59**

State Street Bank & Trust Co. v Signature Financial Group Inc. 149 F. 3d 1368 (Fed. Cir. 1998) **399, 409**

Wappler, Ex parte 26 USPQ 191 (POBA (1934)) **378**

Zuckerberg v Blue Cross and Blue Shield 487 NYS 2d 595 (CC DNY (1985)) **59**

European Patent Office

ABBOTT LABARATORIES/Multiplex sensor and method of use (T 0330/03) **209, 211**

ABBOTT RESPIRATORY/Dosage Regime (G 02/08) **256, 259, 271, 275, 283, 284, 286, 441**

AEROCRINE AB/Evaluation of a respiratory function (T 0125/02) **213, 214**

ALINOMOTO/Feed for sows (T 1223/01) **110**

ARS/Infertility (T 1074/06) **268**

ASTA/Cytostatic Combination (T 09/81) [1979–85] EPOR B303 **235**

BAYER AG (T 774/89) **76, 104, 105**

BAYER/Immunostimulant (T 780/89) [1993] EPOR 377 **97, 107–109, 111**
BAYER/Nimodipin (I) (T 17/81) [1979–85] EPOR B320 **235**
BAXTER/Blood extraction method (T 0329/94) [1998] EPOR 363 **84, 85, 88, 153, 163, 165, 191, 193, 199**
BETH ISRAEL HOSPITAL ASSOCIATION/Method for diagnosing Alzheimer's disease (T 0143/04) **212, 215–217, 344**
BIOTRONIC/Heart monitoring apparatus and method (T 0598/07) **192**
BRUKER/Non-invasive measurement (T 385/86) [1988] EPOR 357 **186, 189–198, 200, 204, 205, 209, 218, 344**
BRITISH TECHNOLOGY GROUP/Contraceptive method (T 74/93) [1995] EPOR 279 **98–100**
CAMTECH AS (T 0005/04) **129, 162**
CANADY JEROME/Surgical coagulation device (T 1138/09) **72**
CODMAN/Second surgical use (T 0227/91) [1995] EPOR 82 **247–250, 343**
CSIR/Appetite suppressant (T 0543/04) **173, 174**
CYGNUS/Diagnostic method (G 01/04) [2006] EPOR 15 **73, 89, 96, 107, 123, 125, 127, 130, 133, 136–139, 144, 148, 154–157, 160, 161, 164–167, 175, 178, 179, 185, 186, 196, 201, 202–205, 207–210, 213–218, 220, 228, 276, 283, 343, 344, 370, 413, 414, 420, 439–441**
CYGNUS/Diagnostic method (T 964/99) [2002] EPOR 272 **186, 189, 195–200, 203–205**
DU PONT/Appetite suppressant (T 144/83) [1987] EPOR 6 **75, 76, 90–95, 97, 100, 107**
DUPHAR/Pigs II (T 19/86) [1988] EPOR 10 **76, 77, 244,–246, 265**
DURAMED PHARMACEUTICALS/ Method of oral contraception (T 1063/04) **98**
EISAI/Medicament for gastritis (T 913/94) [2001] EPOR 362 **241**
EISAI/Second medical indication (G 05/83) [1979–85] EPOR 241 **6, 26, 75, 76, 78, 90, 117, 126, 165, 171, 185, 230, 235, 236, 238, 240–245, 247, 248, 250–257, 259–268, 273, 74, 277–286, 321, 325–329, 345, 347–351, 354–357, 359, 360, 362, 364, 366–368, 371, 372, 440, 441**
ELA MEDICAL/Therapeutic method (T 789/96) [2003] EPOR 23 **82–84**
ELAN CORPORATION/Use of nicotine (T 0584/97) **247, 264, 267**
ELI LILLY/Serotonin receptor (T 241/95) [2001] EPOR 292 **240**
EURO-CELTIQUE/ Thiazide diuretics (T 56/97) **247, 267**
EXERGEN CORPORATION/ Radiation detector (T 1255/06) **209**
EXOMIS/Haloperoxide (T 0292/04) **239, 247**

EXPANDABLE GRAFTS/Surgical device (T 0775/97) [2002] EPOR 24 **134, 152, 240, 249, 250**
GENENTECH INC/IGF-1 to improve the neural condition (T 0486/01) **245**
GENENTECH INC/Intrapulmonary delivery (T 0138/95) **238, 252, 253**
GENENTECH INC/Method of administration of IGF-I (T 1020/03) **255, 259, 270,357, 364, 365, 371, 372, 442**
GEORGETOWN UNIVERSITY/Pericardial access (T 35/99), [2001] EPOR 169 **118, 124, 130–132, 134, 135, 137–139, 147, 157, 160, 162, 343**
GENERAL ELECTRONIC COMPANY (T 0530/93) **190**
GENERAL HOSPITAL/Contraceptive method (T 820/92) [1995] EPOR 446 **76, 97, 171**
HARVARD/Onco-mouse (T 19/90) [1990] OJ EPO 476 **315**
HOWARD FLOREY INSTITUTE/Relaxin (T 272/95) [1995] EPOR 541 **221**
ICI/Cleaning plaque (T 290/86) [1991] EPOR 157 **76, 93, 94, 97, 107, 108, 265**
INTRAVASCULAR RESEARCH METHOD (T 0948/95) **78**
KANEGAFUCHI KAGAKU KOGYO KABUSHIKI KAISHA (T 0138/02) **238**
KIRIN-AMGEN/Erythropoietin (T 0787/00) **238, 258**
KONINKLIJKE PHILIPS ELECTRONICS NV/Medical diagnostic imaging (T 09/04) **86, 135, 159, 162, 164**
KONINKLIJKE PHILIPS ELECTRONICS NV/Determining a dimension from density distribution (T 0504/03) **210**
KOS LIFE SCIENCES INC/Dosage regimen (T 1319/04) **255, 256, 269, 372**
L'OREAL/Cosmetic method (T 1077/93) **152**
L'OREAL/Procédé et appareil pour la détermination de caractéristiques d'un produit cosmétique (T 0619/03) **210**
LEO PHARMACEUTICALS PRODUCTS LTD/EDTA-free heparins (T 0532/96) **236, 160, 165, 213**
LEXION/Method for conditioning gas (T 0238/06) **160, 165, 213**
LONZA/L-carnitine (T 80/96) [2000] EPOR 323 **235, 241**
MACRI/Down's syndrome screening method (T 0310/99) **200**
MAI/Trigonelline (T 143/94) [1996] EPOR 613 **242**
MAQUET CRITICAL CARE AB/Method for determining a transfer function (T 1102/02) **86, 135, 162, 165, 212**
MAX-PLANCK/BDP1 Phosphate (T 0870/04) **222**
MEDCO RESEARCH/Adrenaline (T 0233/96) **245, 246**
MEDI-PHYSICS/Treatment by surgery (G 01/07) **85–88, 111, 115, 119, 120, 123, 127, 133, 137, 138, 140, 146, 148, 153, 155, 158, 161, 166, 168, 169, 175, 177, 180, 182,183, 220, 343, 344, 354, 438**

MEDI-PHYSICS/Treatment by surgery (T 0992/03) [2007] EPOR 32 **91, 118, 119, 137–139, 154, 157, 165, 169, 183**
MEIJI/Feeds (T 438/91) [1999] EPOR 333 **76, 109**
MELLES/Vital dyes for vitreo-retinal surgery (T 0566/07) **236**
MIT/Perception of fatigue (T 0469/94) **78, 245, 246**
MOBIL/Friction reducing additive (G 02/88) [1990] EPOR 73 **131, 248, 252, 327**
NATIONAL DEVELOPMENT CORPORATION/Method of producing image information (T 400/87) **186, 193, 194**
NATIONAL RESEARCH COUNCIL OF CANADA/Method of assessing tissue viability (T 0041/04) **210**
NESTEC SA/High fibre composition (T 1002/09) **235, 284**
NESTEC/Probiotics (T 0515/06) **247, 268**
NEXINS RESEARCH/Apoptotic cells (T 1038/00) **193**
NIPRO/Combined anti-inflammatory agent (T 0292/99) **241**
NOGIER/Magnetic therapy (T 30/83) [1979–85] EPOR C755 **72, 76**
NOVARTIS/Method of improving immune response (T 0485/99) **247, 265, 267**
NOVARTIS/Transgenic plant (T 1054/96) **173**
NOVARTIS/Transgenic plant (G 01/98) [2000] EPOR 303 **170, 177, 178**
NYCOMED AS/Contrasting agent for NMR imaging (T 665/92) [1998] EPOR 206 **186, 193**
OPTIMATA/Optimized drug delivery (T 1873/06) **82**
PHARMA MAR/Aplidine (T 0385/07) **240, 255, 259**
PHILIPS/Diagnostic method (T 45/84) [1979–85] C937 **192**
PLANT GENETIC SYSTEMS/Plant cells (T 0356/93) **315**
PPG/Disclaimer (G 01/03) [2004] EPOR 33 **168, 169, 173–177, 180–183, 439**
PRAECIS/GnRH Antagonists (T 0380/05) **247**
PROCTOR & GAMBLE/ Gastrointestinal compositions (T 317/95) [1999] EPOR 528 **247, 261, 267**
QUEEN'S UNIVERSITY KINGSTON/Controlling bleeding (T 893/90) **245**
REDEKEN LABOARATORIES/ Chelating (T 0453/95) **92**
REICHART/Anti-snoring means (T 584/88) [1989] EPOR 448 **94**
RORER/Dysmenorrhoea (T 81/84) [1988] EPOR 297 **77, 240**
RHOMED INC/Radiolabeled antibodies (T 0606/96) **79**
ROUSSEL-CULAF/Thenoyl peroxide (T 36/83) [1987] EPOR 1 **97, 235**
ROUSSEL-UCLAF/ Tetrahydropyridinyl-Indole Derivatives (T 43/82) [1979–85] EPOR B448 **235**
SALMINEN/Pigs III (T 58/97) [1989] EPOR 125 **76, 109, 275**

SCHERING/Combination therapy HCV (T 0036/04) **247, 268**
SEE-SHELL/Blood flow (T 182/90) [1994] EPOR 320 **118, 127–132, 134, 135, 138, 139, 143, 148, 150, 151, 160, 163, 343**
SEQUUS/Lipsome composition (T 04/98) [2002] EPOR 371 **247, 263, 267**
SERENO/HCG (T 51/93) **247, 265**
SEPRACOR INC/Method and composition for treating hypertension (T 1031/00) **246**
SIEMENS/Diagnostic method (T 83/87) [1988] EPOR 365 **186, 190, 195, 199**
SIEMENS/Flow measurement (T 245/87) [1989] EPOR 241 **80, 81, 83, 85, 88, 171**
SIEMENS/Pacemaker (T 0426/89) [1992] EPOR 149 **81, 83**
SMITHKLINE BEECHAM CORPORATION/Treatment of ovarian cancer (T 1001/01) **268, 269**
STERLING/S(+)ibuprofen (T 315/98) [2000] EPOR 401 **241**
STIMTECH/Transcutaneous electrical nerve stimulation (T 94/83) [1979–85] EPOR C811 **79**
SQUIBB/Prostaglandin analogs (T 0825/94) **241**
TEIJIN LIMITED/Bone evaluation method (T 0775/92) **193**
TELECTRONICS/Pacer (T 82/93) [1996] EPOR 409 **80, 82, 158–160**
TEXAS/Amendments (J 10/84) [1979–85] EPOR A213 **72, 76**
THE AUSTRALIA NATIONAL UNIVERSITY/Method and apparatus for early detection of glaucoma (T 1197/02) [2007] EPOR 9 **165**
THE GENERAL HOSPITAL CORPORATION/Hair removal method (T 383/03) **134, 135, 139–143, 149, 159, 343**
THE PRESIDENT AND FELLOWS OF HARVARD COLLEGE/ Method for producing transgenic animals (T 315/03) (OJ 2006, 15) **223**
THERAPEUTIC SUBSTITUTES/Anti-tumoural agent (T 958/94) [1997] EPOR 417 **242, 243**
THERMAGE/Apparatus for skin resurfacing (T 1172/03) **129, 133, 135, 136, 142, 151, 152, 251, 252**
THOMPSON/Cornea (T 24/91) [1996] EPOR 19 **76, 88, 89, 154, 159, 172**
THOMPSON-CSF/ Tomodensitometry (2) (T 208/83) [1979–85] EPOR C917 **192**
THOMPSON-CSF/ Tomodensitometry (1) (T 61/83) [1979–85] EPOR C763 **192**
ULTRAFEM/Feminine hygiene device (T 1165/97) [2002] EPOR 384 **76, 97, 99, 100, 136, 154, 200**
UNIVERSITY OF CALIFORNIA/Lung cancer dated (T 629/98) **238, 258**
UNIVERSITY OF MANITOBA/Lung ventilator device (T 0592/98) **76**

UNIVERSITY OF TEXAS/DNA damaging agents (T 0036/04) **247, 285**
UNIVERSITY OF UTAH/Breast and ovarian cancer (T 1213/05) **222, 224, 227**
UNIVERSITY OF UTAH/Method of diagnosis (T 0080/05) **220, 222, 227**
UNIVERSITY OF UTAH/Mutation (T 0666/05) **219, 220, 226**
UROLOGIX INC/Apparatus for surgical treatment (T 0634/02) **79**
VERICORE/Sea lice infestation (T 0708/02) **242, 246, 47, 268**
WAVE ENERGY SYSTEMS/Mycobactericide (T 0051/99) **76**
WARF/Stem cells (T 1374/04) [2006] EPOR 31 **222**
WARF/Use of embryos (G 02/06) [2009] EPOR 15 **127**
WEIGHT WATCHERS/Slimmer's calculator (T 0537/04) **173**
WELLCOME/Pigs I (T 116/85) [1988] EPOR 1 **76, 97, 103, 110, 197, 202**
WISCONSIN ALUMNI RESEARCH FOUNDATION/ Rapid acquisition resonance imaging (T 0266/07) **86, 87**
ZAIDAN/Benanomicin A (T 0853/94) **243**
ZYMOGENETICS/ Hematopoietic receptor (T 0898/05) **222**

European Court of Justice

C-428/08 Monsanto Technology LLC v Cefetra BV and others (Argentine State intervening) [2010] All ER (D) 65 (Jul) **219**

Table of national and international legislation

United Kingdom

Patent and Designs Act 1907
s. 75 **308**
Patents Act 1949
s. 32(1)(d) **307**
s. 101
Patents Act 1977
s. 2(6) **345–347, 353, 357, 358, 362, 372**
s. 4(2) **334–338, 342, 345, 347, 351, 353, 358, 359**
s. 4(3) **345, 347, 358**
s. 4A(2) **345, 358**
s. 4A(3) **355**
s. 4A(4) **356**
s. 36 **38**
s. 37 **38**
s. 48(1)(a) **54**
s. 48(1)(b) **55**
s. 48(2)(a) **55**
s. 48(1)(c) **55**
s. 48(2)(a) **55**
s. 48(3)(a) **55**
s. 48(3)(d) **55**
s. 48(3)(e) **55**
s. 60 **65, 68, 307**
s. 60(5) **13**
s. 60(5)(a) **68**
s. 60(5)(b) **13, 68**
s. 72(1) **307**
s. 91(1) **348**
s. 130(7) **332, 333**

Statute of Monopolies
s. 6 **7, 287, 289, 296, 298, 299, 301, 304, 305, 311, 313, 314, 322, 330, 333, 434**

European Patent Convention
Art. 4(3) **96**
Art. 52(1) **95, 96, 101–103, 191, 202–204, 241, 420**
Art. 52(2)(a) **203**
Art. 52(4) 1973 **2, 71, 87, 227, 252**
Art. 52(4) **71, 72, 76–82, 86, 88–91, 93–98, 101, 102, 104–106, 108–110, 114, 117, 122–125, 127,–129, 131–141, 144, 149–155, 157–164, 166, 170–174, 177–179, 185, 186, 189, 190, 192–194, 196–201, 203–208, 210, 212, 215–217, 228, 235–240, 242, 249–252, 256–258, 261–264, 266, 267, 280, 285, 286, 325, 327, 328, 335, 343, 354, 433**
Art.53(a) **8, 113, 115, 177, 223–227, 314, 438, 440**
Art. 53(c) **2, 71 86–88, 95, 102, 103, 106, 113, 114, 115, 117, 122, 126, 134, 140,141, 143–146, 155, 161, 162, 167, 168, 176–178, 180–184, 192, 202, 219, 220, 229, 255, 259, 261, 269–275, 277, 280, 281, 282, 285, 343, 354, 372, 385, 433, 437–440**

Art. 54(4) **6, 229, 240, 253, 254, 259, 260, 268, 271–274, 276–278, 281–284, 441**
Art. 54(5) 1973 **6, 115, 229, 230, 234, 235, 237, 239, 240,247, 251–254, 256–262, 268, 273, 274, 276, 278, 280, 281, 283, 284, 286, 327, 328, 345, 346, 350,354, 372,441**
Art. 54(5) **6, 115, 185, 229, 240, 253–255, 259–261, 268–286, 347, 356, 372, 441, 442**

United States

Patent Law 35 U.S.C.
s. 101 **374, 392–395, 403, 404, 407, 409–411, 413,415–418, 420, 422–426, 431, 432, 435**
s. 103(b) **386**
s. 271(a) **390**
s. 271(b) **398**
Medical Procedures and Affordability Act
s. 287(c) **384, 385**
s. 287(c)(1) **384, 386**
s. 287(c)(2) **384, 386, 391**
s. 287(c)(2)(A) **384**
s. 287(c)(2)(B) **384**
s. 287(c)(2)(b)(ii) **389**
s. 287(c)(3) **291**
s. 287(c)(3)(A) **385, 386**
s. 287(c)(3)(A)(i) **387**
s. 287(c)(3)(B) **386**
s. 287(c)(3)(B)(i) **384, 386**
s. 287(c)(3)(B)(ii) **384, 386, 387**
s. 287(c)(3)(B)(iii) **384, 386, 387**
s. 287(c)(3)(C)(i) **385, 386**
s. 287(c)(3)(C)(ii) **385, 386**
s. 287(c)(3)(D) **385, 388, 389, 390**
s. 287(c)(3)(E) **385, 391**
s. 287(c)(3)(F)(i) **386**
s. 287(c)(3)(F)(ii) **386**
s. 287(c)(4) **385, 391**
Genomic Research and Diagnostic Accessibility Act
s. 2(1) **391**
s. 3(a)(1) **391**
s. 3(a)(3) **391**
s. 3(b) **391**
s. 3(c) **392**

European Union

Biotech Directive 1998
R. 16 **115**
R. 20 **115**
R. 21 **155**
R. 22 **115**
R. 23 **115**
R. 24 **115**
R. 26 **224**
R. 35 **122, 221**
R. 36 **222**
R. 37 **222**
R. 38 **222**
R. 39 **222**
R. 40 **222**
R. 41 **115**
R. 42 **221**
R. 45 **221**
Art. 5(1) **222**
Art. 5(2) **222**
Art. 5(3) **26, 222**
Art. 6(1) **222**
Art. 6(2) **222, 223**
Art. 9 **222**

International

TRIPs Agreement
Art. 27(3) **47**

Other

AMA's Code of Medical Ethics, E-9.08 New Medical Procedures **62**
Declaration on the TRIPs Agreements and Public Health **47**

International Code of Medical Ethics **62, 67**

World Association International Code of Medical Ethics **62**

1. Introduction

A GENERAL

This book will examine the scope of patent protection for methods of medical treatment,[1] focusing on the exclusion of therapeutic, surgical and diagnostic methods in Europe, the United States of America and some Commonwealth countries. The focus on medical treatments is important in light of its exclusion from patent protection in most of the jurisdictions covered by this book, particularly in light of new developments in technology, including gene therapy, genetic diagnostic testing and stem cell therapy. Although the exclusion in the United Kingdom, for example, has been in existence for approximately 95 years, it was only in 1973, with the coming into force of the European Patent Convention (EPC), that the exclusion had a firm legal basis in most European countries. However, while in Europe the emphasis is on delineating the scope of the exclusion in decisions of the Technical Boards of Appeal (TBAs) and the Enlarged Board of Appeal (EBA) of the European Patent Office (EPO), other countries, for example, the United States, are still struggling with the issue of whether medical procedures are excluded from patent protection.

The question of whether patents should be granted for methods of medical treatment is still a live issue in some Commonwealth countries, in particular, in New Zealand where only six years ago, its Court of Appeal ruled that such methods are not patentable. However, in Australia, patent protection is available. In the United States, the issue of patentability was once thought settled and that methods of medical treatment were allowable was not questioned, especially in light of the Medical Procedures and Affordability Act 1996 (MPAA) which provided physicians with immunity from infringement suits relating to patent for methods of medical treatment. Recently, however, the question has arisen as to whether such treatments, in particular, diagnostic methods, are patentable and in 2006 the Supreme Court refused to rule on the issue. But, recently, the Federal Circuit has been examining the issue with inconsistent rulings on the

[1] The term 'methods of medical treatment' will be used interchangeably with 'medical procedures'.

question of whether methods of medical treatment are excluded from patent protection. It will not be long before the Supreme Court finally rules on the issue of patentability of methods of medical treatment, in particular, diagnostic methods.

Notwithstanding that the exclusion in Europe was etched in stone in Article 53(c) EPC 2000 (previously, Article 52(4) EPC 1973), some academics and judges in the United Kingdom have questioned the rationale and the logic of the exclusion. In 1999, for example, Jacob J., as he then was, stated that '[t]he thinking behind the exception [for methods of medical treatment] is not particularly rational: if one accepts that a patent monopoly is a fair price to pay for the extra research incentive, then there is *no reason* to suppose that that would *not also apply* to methods of treatment'.[2] In 1971, 28 years earlier, Whitford J. in *Schering A G's Application* stated that it was 'difficult to see any logical justification for the practice [of not granting patents] in relation to the processes for medical treatment, if the object of the system is in truth to give hope of a reward to people whose research and industry results in valuable products or processes.'[3]

These statements create more problems than they solve. They do not identify *why* patenting methods of medical treatment would serve the public interest or whether there exist other public policy considerations that are stronger than those currently made against patenting methods of medical treatment. This book will seek to determine whether there is a coherent rationale for the exclusion of methods of medical treatment from patent protection and, in the process, outline the main arguments for and against patent protection for methods of medical treatment. A similar approach to, and consideration of, the issues relating to methods of medical treatment to be examined in this book was applied by Hammond J. in *Pfizer Inc v Commissioner of Patents*.[4]

B THE ARGUMENTS

The question of patenting methods of medical treatment is one that is multi-faceted because many arguments can be and are made either way for and against patent protection. The question of whether patent protection should be allowed or, in some jurisdictions, be removed is one that does not lend itself to an easy answer. This is evident in the different approaches of the Australian and New Zealand courts to the issue even when similar

---

2 [1999] RPC 253 (emphasis added).

3 [1971] RPC 337 (PAT) 343.

4 (2004) NZCA 104 (28 June 2004) [95]–[135].

statutory provisions were considered. In the United Kingdom, the then judicially-created exclusion is now in statutory form and is here to stay for the foreseeable future. This is so because the revision of the EPC in 2000 has kept the exclusion in its current form. An examination of the arguments made for and against patenting methods of medical treatment revealed that the question of which set of arguments should prevail cannot solely be answered at a theoretical level. Due weight must be given to empirical evidence, if any, of the impact of medical procedures on society in general, because without such evidence pointing in any particular direction, any attempt at coming to a firm conclusion on whether patents should be granted for methods of medical treatment would be unconvincing.

Where a change in the law would have serious implications for public health a cautious approach is needed. And, if there is to be any change in Europe, it should only be achieved if there are strong arguments (supported by empirical evidence) that that should be done. It has often been stated that the judicial branch is unable to accede to requests for changes in the law that have significant public policy implications. In the period before 1977, it was said that, if UK law were to change, it would be a matter for Parliament and not the courts, implying that such policy decisions were not the province of the courts. Similarly, in *Diamond v Chakrabarty*,[5] where the issue was whether a live, human-made micro-organism was patentable subject matter, the Supreme Court stated that:[6]

> What is more important is that we are without competence to entertain these arguments – either to brush them aside as fantasies generated by fear of the unknown, or to act on them. The choice we are urged to make is a matter of high policy for resolution with the legislative process and after the kind of investigation, examination, and study that the legislative bodies can provide and the courts cannot. The process involves the balancing of competing values and interests, which in our democratic system is the business of elected representatives. Whatever their validity, the contentions now pressed upon us should be addressed to the political branches of Government, the Congress and the Executive, and not to the courts.

This speaks directly to the issue that we are similarly confronted with here. The robust examination, investigation and study of the issue of whether patents should be granted for methods of medical treatment cannot be, and will not be, achieved within the pages of this book alone. The modest aim of chapters 2 and 3 is to outline and examine the various arguments that are

---

5 447 U.S. 303 (1980).
6 Ibid, at 318.

made for and against patent protection for methods of medical treatment. This exercise is important since it will provide, among other things: (a) an insight into the various considerations (including ethics and morality) that the UK courts in the period before 1977 were hinting at but never fully explored; and (b) a more in-depth examination of the possible rationale for the exclusion of methods of medical treatment from patent protection.

To achieve this, the book will first consider, in chapter 2, the arguments that are made for patent protection for methods of medical treatment. Secondly, to ensure that the arguments are balanced, it will examine in chapter 3 the arguments that are made against patent protection of methods of medical treatment. Wilcox J. in *Anaesthetic Supplies v Rescare*[7] observed that '[p]olicy arguments may be made, *each way*, upon the question whether the law should permit [patents for methods of medical treatment]'.[8] The examination of these will show that the issue of patent protection for medical procedures is not as simplistic as it may initially seem and that a resolution of the various issues is only possible when evidence points directly to a certain impact on public health.

The arguments that are made against patent protection that will be examined include: (a) public health implications; (b) physician liberty and autonomy; (c) physician/patient relationship; (d) the Hippocratic Oath/sharing norm; (e) other incentive structures; and (f) breach of patient's privacy. The arguments that are made for patent protection that will be examined include: (a) incentive to disclose; (b) incentive to invent/innovate; (c) prospect theory; (d) rent dissipation theory; (e) reward/desert; and (f) liberty/autonomy.

The arguments that are made for patent protection for methods of medical treatment may apply equally to pharmaceutical products. Therefore, no attempt will be made to analyse this aspect in this book. However, those who argue against patent protection for methods of medical treatment do not take into account that some of these same arguments equally apply to pharmaceutical products. Patent protection is available in most countries for pharmaceutical products and substances but not medical procedures. Why then is there a distinction between the two? When examining the arguments that are made against patent protection for methods of medical treatment, this book will attempt to highlight, where necessary, the differences between the two. The issue, as the Australian Federal Court in *Bristol-Myers Squibb Co v F H Faulding & Co. Ltd*[9] saw it, was 'the insurmountable

---

7 (1994) 50 FCR 1 (FCA).

8 Ibid, at 42 (emphasis added).

9 (2000) FCA 316.

problem, from a public policy viewpoint, of drawing a logical distinction which would justify allowing patentability for a *product* for treating the human body, but deny patentability for a *method* of treatment'.[10]

It is arguable that the issue is one of direct control over the supply of the patented invention. In the case of pharmaceuticals, the patentee can limit supply and increase the price but, in most cases, it would not be in their interests to do so. Similarly, with methods of medical treatment, the patentee physician can also restrict supply of the necessary or potentially life-saving procedure by denying others the right to use it or by not performing it herself – which would be contrary to the public good. The consequences for the public seem to be worse in the case of the medical treatment since the procedure/process is unlike a drug which can be manufactured and distributed to millions of people. If licences are not readily made available by the patentee, one method by which this question of access to the medical treatment may be resolved is to subject it to a compulsory licensing regime. That approach also has limitations and, without empirical evidence concerning its economic impact on public health, one cannot come to a firm conclusion on whether it achieves an optimum balance.

C THE EPO JURISPRUDENCE

In exploring the issues to be resolved in this field, an examination of the jurisprudence of the European Patents Office (EPO) will be undertaken to assist in delineating the rationale for the exclusion of methods of medical treatment from patentability. This exercise will examine how the Technical Boards of Appeal (TBAs) and the Enlarged Board of Appeal of the European Patent Office (EBA) have interpreted the exclusion for methods of medical treatment in Europe, and, in the process, enable some conclusions to be made concerning how the exclusion came about, why, if at all, the exclusion should be maintained, and, importantly, what considerations the TBAs and the EBA have taken into account in making sense of the exclusion from patent protection of methods of medical treatment. Each method of medical treatment, namely, therapeutic methods (chapter 4), diagnostic methods (chapter 5) and surgical methods (chapter 6) will be examined in detail to determine: first, how they are each defined by the TBAs and the EBA; secondly, what limitations, if any, have the TBAs and the EBA accepted that would influence how each of the exclusions are to be

---

[10] Ibid, at [15] (emphasis in original).

defined; thirdly, what factors or considerations have the TBAs and the EBA taken into account in interpreting the exclusions; fourthly, whether there is any consistency in the broad approach to the interpretation of the exclusion by the TBAs and the EBA; and fifthly, whether a distinction is properly made in the jurisprudence of the TBAs and the EBA between treatment of animals and humans when interpreting the exclusion. This book will also examine the legislative history of the EPC in relation to each of the three exclusions to see what light, if any, it sheds on the rationale for the exclusion and, indeed, the manner in which they are to be interpreted.

Of critical importance too will be the examination in chapter 7 of the issue of second medical use patents under the EPC to determine: first, what do Articles 54(4) and 54(5) EPC 2000 really say; secondly, why was it necessary for the EBA to interpret Article 54(5) EPC 1973 to include second and further medical uses, contrary to its ordinary meaning; thirdly, what exactly did the EBA in *EISAI/Second medical indication* decide; and fourthly, whether the TBAs were correct in expanding this decision to other areas where, arguably, it was not intended. A related but important issue is that concerning patenting dosage regimes. Numerous issues are ripe for consideration, the first of which is whether the decision of the EBA in *EISAI/Second medical indication* compels the result in the recent decision of the EBA in *ABBOTT RESPIRATORY/Dosage regime*; secondly, whether Articles 54(4) and 54(5) EPC 2000 can properly be interpreted to provide patent protection for dosage regimes; thirdly, whether such protection is justified as a matter of principle or policy.

The application of the principles derived from the interpretation of the exclusion by TBAs and the EBA by the UK courts will also be examined in chapter 9 in light of the requirement that UK courts should ensure consistency with the approach of the EPO. The pre-1977 law will be briefly compared to the position under the UK Patents Act 1977 (the 1977 Act), followed by an examination of how the UK courts have applied the principles emerging from the EPO in respect of the matters considered in chapters 4–7.

D THE QUESTION OF PATENTABILITY

The issue of whether patent protection was available for methods of medical treatment was still debatable in the United Kingdom until the early 1970s. Although the courts and the Patent Appeal Tribunal (PAT) were agreed that the exclusion existed, its jurisprudential foundations were very precarious. The jurisprudence in the United Kingdom prior to 1977 will be examined in chapter 8 to determine what light, if any, it sheds on the subsequent UK interpretation of the 1977 Act, which incorporated the EPC 1973. The New Zealand and Australian approaches will also be considered in that section in light of their historical origins – s 6 of the Statute of Monopolies. However, although sharing a common ancestry, the courts in Australia have allowed patent protection for methods of medical treatment, whereas the courts in New Zealand have rejected such protection. These decisions will be examined to determine why this was the case. This chapter will also explore the issue of why the New Zealand Court of Appeal applied an EBA decision relating to second and further medical uses, notwithstanding that that decision originated from a totally different statutory framework than that which obtains in New Zealand.

The courts in the United States and the US Patent and Trademark Office (USPTO) were of the clear view that patents were available for methods of medical treatment. That this was so was evident by the fact that there was actual litigation relating to infringement of a medical procedure patent, which created a firestorm in a teacup in the United States. Swiftly following the litigation, Congress enacted the MPAA, which provided immunity to physicians when using medical procedure patents. Chapter 10 will consider the decisions of the USPTO, relating to exclusion, and also examine the legislative history and provisions of the MPAA. In addition, it will also consider whether the question of patentability of medical procedures, in particular, diagnostic methods, can be answered using Supreme Court jurisprudence relating to patentable subject matter, namely, *Benson*, *Flook* and *Diehr* and as recently rearticulated in *Bilski v Kappos*. In light of its decision in the latter case, the Supreme Court vacated two decisions of the Federal Circuit relating to diagnostic methods. However, since at least two decisions are making their way back to the Federal Circuit for reconsideration, and another for consideration, it is opportune that the book also examines the jurisprudence of the Federal Circuit and the Supreme Court to articulate an approach to resolve the issue of patenting diagnostic methods that are in line with Supreme Court jurisprudence.

E THE FUTURE OF MEDICAL PATENTS

It is apt that a book dealing with medical procedure patents should also examine the possible application of the exclusion of methods of medical treatment to the new technologies currently being applied to treat and diagnose illnesses. The medical treatment exception, as interpreted by the various TBAs and the EBA, will be examined to determine the extent to which it may limit the patenting of new treatments such as genetic therapy, stem cell therapy and genetic diagnostic testing. The complex nature of such treatments and the technologies involved may implicate other areas, and the Biotech Directive will be evaluated in light of the issues to be discussed. Also important will be the examination of Article 53(a) EPC 2000 relating to morality and *ordre public* to determine to what extent the new treatments impact on that exclusion. In order to properly apply the relevant jurisprudence to the new medical treatments, these issues will be considered in the chapters dealing with the various methods of medical treatments, chapters 4–7.

2. Arguments for patent protection

A INTRODUCTION

The importance of public health to a country's welfare and economy is such that governments usually spend considerable amounts of money in ensuring that there is an adequate supply of medical services and that medical research continues unabated.[1] Ensuring that public health is not unnecessarily compromised by patent law should, therefore, be a legitimate goal of government. According to Dworkin, it is competent for governments to pursue arguments in favour of public health and to adopt programs and strategies that are generated by such arguments.[2] But, before any government can make an informed decision either way on the patentability of methods of medical treatment, it should ensure that there is sufficient evidence of the impact that they have on public health. It must also ensure that due consideration is given to the types of arguments that will be considered in this chapter.[3]

There was no major debate in Europe when the methods of medical treatment were excluded from patent protection under the European Patent Convention (EPC) in 1973. However, in the United States, the Medical Procedures and Affordability Act 1996 (MPAA) was preceded by a significant amount of debate both inside and outside Congress.[4] The main arguments *for* patenting methods of medical treatment are based on various rationales that have been used to explain the patent system: namely, the incentive to disclose; the incentive to invent/innovate; the prospect

---

[1] For example, in the United States, $488.8 billion was allocated to the Department of Health and Human Service (http://www.hhs.gov/budget/pdf/hhs2003bib.pdf) (accessed on 15 April 2011). Six years later, this amount doubled to $911 billion being allocated for the fiscal year 2011. (http://www.hhs.gov/asrt/ob/docbudget/2011budgetinbrief.pdf) (accessed 15 April 2011).

[2] R. Dworkin, *Taking Rights Seriously* (Duckworth, London 1996), p. 83.

[3] See A. Odell-West, 'A Proposal to Amend the Medical Exclusion within Patent Law to Provide for Patentability of Certain Methods of Treatment' [2007] EIPR 492.

[4] See Chapter 10.

theory; and the rent dissipation theory. Professor Cornish adequately summarises the debate although he was speaking about a slightly dissimilar area:[5]

> *The main purpose of the patent system is unquestionably economic*. The system is to be judged by whether it does lead to earlier and wider productivity of new technology at an effective rate, taking into account the effects of early publication of the invention in the patent specification. *This implies comparisons*. Is it significantly more effective than other schemes for enticing invention? What about government subsidies, grants and tax remits, the research side of universities, support from charities and other foundations? *That is an extraordinarily difficult calculation to make, but it is one that we should continue to attempt*.

In this chapter I will, first, outline the main arguments for patent protection and, secondly, determine the extent to which these arguments support a case for patent protection of methods of medical treatment.

Approximately 40 years ago, patent protection for methods of medical treatment was rejected because 'the whole subject matter [was] conceived as *essentially non-economic*'.[6] However, in recent times, Jacob J. (as he then was) has asserted that the 'thinking behind the exception is not particularly rational because if one accepts that a patent monopoly is a *fair price to pay for the extra research incentive*, then there is, *no reason* to suppose that it would not *apply* to methods of medical treatment'.[7] Jacob J. seemed to be making a general statement about methods of medical treatment that has no specific basis in fact and is not supported by empirical evidence. The economic incentives *may* apply to some medical procedures but that alone, it is suggested, is not sufficient to warrant a change in the current law.

He expressed similar sentiments in *Teva Industries Ltd v Instituto Gentili SpA*,[8] where he asserted that since 'patents are provided to encourage research … there would be less of a research incentive to find such methods' if new treatment regimes are not, in principle, patentable.[9] This is a more limited criticism to the effect that treatment regimes do need the incentives of the patent system to further research into more efficient methods of administering drugs to patients.

---

[5] W.R. Cornish, *Intellectual Property: Omnipresent, Distracting, Irrelevant?* (Clarendon Lecture Series, OUP, Oxford 2004), pp. 9–10 (emphasis added).

[6] *National Research Development Corporation's Application* (1961) RPC 134 (HCA) 145 (emphasis added).

[7] *Bristol-Myers Squibb v Baker Norton* [1999] RPC 253 (Pat Ct) 274 (emphasis added).

[8] [2003] EWHC Civ 5; [2003] FSR 29.

[9] Ibid, at [80].

B INCENTIVE TO DISCLOSE

1 Outline

The requirement of disclosure is the *quid pro quo* for the grant of the patent monopoly.[10] Without patent protection, inventors may keep their inventions secret either through actual secrecy or through legal trade secrecy.[11] The inventor may make her invention freely available to all persons who may wish to use it, she may either keep it secret, or use the patent system where disclosure is mandatory. The incentive to disclose theory 'presumes a bargain between the inventor and society, the former surrendering the possession of the secret knowledge in exchange for protection of a temporary exclusivity in its industrial use'.[12] Sustained growth, it has been suggested, cannot be obtained in a system that is dominated by trade secrets keeping new technology from the public domain.[13] It is, therefore, in society's interest to offer the inventor 'exclusive patent rights in return for the public disclosure of the invention'.[14] Trade secrecy would not further the public good, because the owner would have, in perpetuity, a complete monopoly over the invention and its development. Trade secret protection is therefore the antithesis of patent protection. Patent protection would be an incentive for inventors to disclose their inventions rather than keep them secret.[15] Therefore, the reward is seen as an incentive for continued innovation and investment in research and development (R&D).

2 Methods of Medical Treatment

One of the main arguments against patent protection for methods of medical treatment is that it adversely interferes with the free flow of

---

[10] M. & R.J. Staaf, 'Patents, Coprights and Trademarks: Property or Monopoly?' (1990) Harv JL & Pub Pol'y 911 and W.F. Baxter, 'Legal Restrictions on the Exploitation of the Patent Monopoly' (1966) 76 Yale LJ 267.

[11] R.S. Eisenberg, 'Proprietary Rights and the Norms of Science in Biotechnology Research' (1987) 97 Yale LJ 177, 191.

[12] F. Machlup, *An Economic Review of the Patent System* (Study of the Subcommittee on Patents, Trademarks and Copyrights of the Committee of the Judiciary, United States Senate 85th Congress, Study No 15, 1958), p. 21.

[13] Ibid.

[14] Ibid.

[15] K.W. Dam, 'The Economic Function of Patent Law' (1994) 23 JLS 247, 270–71.

information in the medical community.[16] This argument is somewhat misleading, because it does not appreciate that, rather than interfering with the disclosure of information, the patent system may actually encourage it. Patent disclosure facilitates this free flow of information when the claims and specifications are published. Disclosure in the patent specification is the *quid pro quo* for the patent grant. The sharing norm is important to ensure the free flow of information within the medical profession, and applies equally to physicists, chemists, engineers and scientists working in the biotech and pharmaceutical industries.[17] However, similar arguments are not brandished with such vigour as they are with regard to the patenting of medical procedures.

The essential difference between the two remains that the medical profession is governed by a code of ethics which clearly outlines the obligations of physicians and the fiduciary duties they owe to their patients. Secrecy, therefore, is contrary to the sharing norm and is vividly illustrated in the example of the Chamberlain Family.[18] In the past, many women and babies died in childbirth. However, the invention which then revolutionised and, more than any other, has made childbirth safer, was kept secret for over 100 years.[19] The Chamberlains were a family of male midwives who fled to England from France in 1569 to escape religious persecution and changed their name to Chamberlain.[20] The success of their invention, the forceps, soon became known. They did many things to keep the invention secret including: (a) carrying their instruments around in a wooden chest; (b) blindfolding the women in labour; (c) keeping everyone outside the surgery room when they operated; and (d) banging sticks and ringing bells to hide the clink of metal.[21] The family became wealthy but did not give away their secret until the last of them died in 1728 and, in 1733, Edmund Chapman published the first detailed description of forceps.[22] This example shows how society could be deprived of useful medical treatments when inventions are kept secret. This arguably would not have happened if the inventors had used the patent system to protect their invention.

---

16 American Medical Association Principles of Medical Ethics. See also American Medical Association 'Ethical Issues in the Patenting of Medical Procedures' (1998) Food & Drug LJ 341.

17 R.S. Eisenberg, 'Proprietary Rights and the Norms of Science in Biotechnology Research' (1987) 97 Yale LJ 177, 181–84.

18 http://en.wikipedia.org/wiki/Forceps_in_childbirth (accessed 21 April 2011).

19 Ibid.

20 Ibid.

21 Ibid.

22 Ibid.

The disclosure requirement of the patent system guarantees that information about new procedures is made available to the public which ensures that other physicians have access to the most recent and probably more effective/efficient procedures that could best treat their patients. Although not a perfect system, the methods of disclosure, through publication in journals and at conferences, have always been seen as the hallmark of the medical profession, and are also effective methods of disclosure to the individuals who are best placed to make use of the new medical procedures. However, as was pointed out by the Federal Court of Australia in *Bristol-Myers Squibb Co v F H Faulding & Co. Ltd*:[23]

> [o]n the issue of disclosure it has been a feature of the patent system since its inception that full disclosure of the invention is required as the consideration for the grant. Indeed publication with a specification of the means of working a patent may in many respects result in a much wider dissemination of the information therein contained than would be the case if the same information is published in a medical journal or at a medical convention.[24]

When a medical procedure is patented, a physician will not be able to use the method of medical treatment disclosed in the patent specification without infringing the patent. She will have to secure a licence to use the procedure. However, the disclosure in the patent specification would provide information to enable researchers to continue research and further development of the invention. Section 60(5)(b) of the UK Patents Act 1977 (the 1977 Act) ensures that the grant of patents does not hinder research into ways of improving any invention.[25] It may be argued that this means that patents on methods of medical treatment would not prevent continued research into the various procedures covered by the patent. Some disclosure, it might be argued, is better than no disclosure at all. Further, the patent monopoly lasts only 20 years, after which the information becomes part of the public domain and could then be used by anyone.

---

[23] (2000) FCA 316.

[24] Ibid, at [138].

[25] Section 60(5) of the 1977 Act provides that an act which, apart from the subsection, would constitute an infringement of a patent for an invention shall not do so if (b) it is done for experimental purposes relating to the subject matter of the invention. See W.R. Cornish, 'Experimental Use of Patented Inventions in European Community States' (1998) IIC 735.

C INCENTIVE TO INVENT/INNOVATE

1 Outline

Classical economic theorists saw the reward theory as a sufficient justification for the patent system. The grant of a patent monopoly was considered as a just method to reward the inventor for his R&D costs.[26] The patent system was seen as instrumental to provide 'protection against imitators'.[27] Society would benefit from any new inventions and disclosures made in the patent specification because, *inter alia*, other inventors may use the information in the specification to improve the invention. The argument, therefore, is based on utilitarian principles.

Kitch thought that the reward theory offered an incomplete view of the patent system, but he did not seek to question it on its own terms.[28] Grady and Alexander had no problem with what they termed the weak version of the reward theory – one that stresses that the basic purpose of patent law is to reward and, thus, to stimulate inventive activity.[29] Pires de Carvalho was of the opinion that three factors indicated that the function of the patent system was not solely to reward inventors, namely: (a) patents represented a technical evaluation that an invention satisfied the requirements of patentability; (b) patents were subject to identical standards regardless of the field of technology and irrespective of the technical merits of their subject matter; and (c) the laws of some countries, namely, the United States, expressly established that patents further social goals rather than reward individuals.[30] The essential question concerning patents was the manner in which the patent system could work in order to make it more socially efficient.[31]

Another limitation of the reward theory is that the patent term does not correspond with the technical contribution and economic value of the

---

[26] A. Smith, *The Wealth of Nations* (J.E.T. Rogers (ed), 2nd edn, Clarendon Press, Oxford 1880) p. 189.

[27] J. Bentham, 'A Manual of Political Economy' in *The Works of Jeremy Bentham* (J. Bowring edn 1962), p. 71.

[28] E.W. Kitch, 'The Nature and Function of the Patent System' (1977) 20 JL & Econ 265, 266.

[29] M.F. Grady and J.I. Alexander, 'Patent Law and Rent Dissipation' (1992) 78 Va L Rev 305, citing W.S. Bowman *Patent and Anti-trust Law: A Legal and Economic Appraisal* (1973).

[30] N.P. De Carvalho, 'The Primary Function of Patents' (2001) JL Tech and Pol'y 25.

[31] M.S. Hart, 'Getting Back to Basics: Reinventing Patent Law for Economic Efficiency' (1994) IPJ 216.

patent. Such a position would be unattainable because this would require the impossibility of an *ex ante* economic valuation of the patent.[32] If patents were simply rewards for inventive effort, the various forms of patent legislation would not make it mandatory that the patentee make the invention available to consumers.[33] Failure to do this would result in a successful bid by someone claiming a compulsory licence. Professor Dam recognised that the primary problem the patent system solved was the 'appropriability problem' which exists when an inventor is unable to recover the costs of the invention if the information were available to all and sundry – the result of which would be a lower or sub-optimal level of innovation.[34] Patent law solves this problem 'by creating property rights in inventions'.[35] These reasons are similar to the incentive to invent theory.

The incentive to invent theory is based on the recognition that the inventor should be compensated for her R&D costs. It recognises that without this input of capital the invention would not have been created. The prospect of being able to secure a monopoly on all aspects of her invention would provide the necessary incentive to inventors to invest in developing new inventions. However, some inventions 'are made by accident, for the most part no doubt as the chance by-product of activity directed to some other purpose'.[36] It would be contrary to common sense if a physician were able to secure a patent by making simple and obvious improvements to existing techniques and procedures. The doctrine of obviousness in patent law would, however, provide sufficient armoury against patenting these medical treatments. Simple and non-obvious inventions would, of course, still be patentable.

2 Methods of Medical Treatment

It is arguable that methods of medical treatment that are complex should be treated differently. The incentive to invent would be stronger where the R&D costs of the invention were high.[37] The patentee should be assured of

---

32 Ibid.

33 Ibid.

34 K.W. Dam, 'The Economic Underpinning of Patent Law' (1994) 23 JLS 247.

35 Ibid.

36 A.S. Plant, 'The Economic Theory Concerning Patents for Inventions' in A.S. Plant *Selected Economic Essays and Addresses* (Routledge & Kegan Paul Ltd, London 1974), p. 39.

37 A similar point was made by Beata Gocyk-Farber, below, where she argued that high cost inventions would enhance the general welfare of the nation whilst low cost inventions would not. One agrees with her that low development cost inventions do not sit comfortably with the incentive to invent.

the possibility of a reasonable return on her investment so that she may continue research in improving the invention. The same argument would also apply to inventors who have made significant improvements to the invention and have incurred a high cost in doing so. The incentive to innovate theory is based on a similar premise as the incentive to invent theory. Simply stated, it posits that the grant of a patent monopoly would ensure that inventors invest the necessary capital in R&D on existing inventions. This is of particular significance to the pharmaceutical industry which spends vast amounts of capital on not only developing new drug therapies, but also on researching new uses of known substances and pharmaceutical products. The patent system prevents others from reaping the benefits where they have not invested in the creation of the invention and assists in the promotion of R&D.[38]

The paradox is obvious. If patents are needed to recoup R&D costs, the 'elimination of patents on certain types of medical inventions will mean that some medical inventions will not be made'[39] which will result in a net loss to society. Noonan observed that to 'the extent that the availability of patent protection serves as an incentive to invest in costly clinical research, it becomes a condition of the very existence of the procedure in controversy'.[40] In *Bristol-Myers Squibb Co v F H Faulding & Co. Ltd*,[41] the Federal Court of Australia stated that:

> [o]n the other side of the debate is the underlying objective of patents, namely the promotion of science and the advancement of the arts for the general welfare of the State. As a general principle there can be no doubt that patent protection is desirable to encourage new medicines and surgical methods. It is an inescapable fact that inducement is necessary to encourage the great expense that is now required to evaluate and investigate the utility of many new medical processes and surgical methods.[42]

This begs the question as to whether the dual incentives of innovation and invention are needed for methods of medical treatment. The exclusion for methods of medical treatment does not cover: drug therapies, products or substances used in medical treatments; biomedical, genetic or embryonic methods of treatment; or equipment used in surgery, therapy or diagnosis. Once it is appreciated that the scope of the exclusion is very narrow, it seems

---

38 K.W. Dam, 'The Economic Underpinnings of Patent Law' (1994) 23 JLS 247.

39 W.D. Noonan, 'Patenting Medical and Surgical Procedures. (1995) 77 J Pat and Trademark Off Soc'y 651, 656.

40 Ibid.

41 (2000) FCA 316.

42 Ibid, at [136].

that what effectively remains are actual methods of medical treatment of patients by physicians.

Medical research is expensive and Governments have usually subsidised it. In 2003, the head of the Medical Research Council (the 'MRC'), Prof. Colin Blakemore, stated that the amount spent on medical research in the United Kingdom should be increased to one billion pounds.[43] In 2003, the MRC had an annual budget of £416m, but in 2010, only seven years later, this almost doubled to over £700m.[44] However, the amount of money spent on medical research is not sufficient and, in comparison to other developed countries, the United Kingdom spends less on public research[45] and, with recent cuts, this will further deteriorate and precipitate a brain drain.[46] Although a significant amount of money is spent on medical research, these figures do not indicate the exact amount spent on the development of medical procedures as opposed to bio-medical or genetic solutions. What is certain is that governments usually spend a considerable amount of their annual budget on the provision of health care and medical research.

The application of the incentive to invent/innovate theory to methods of medical treatment is not without its shortcomings. There is a notable lack of empirical evidence to show that the incentives of the patent system are needed to ensure the continued creation of methods of medical treatment. A similar point was made by the drafters of the *Discussion Document* in New Zealand where it was stated that '[t]here appears to be *no empirical evidence* to suggest that this acts as a disincentive to medical research in New Zealand (or anywhere else)'.[47] It is, therefore, not surprising that Davis has stated that '[t]he question whether patents are also *necessary* to *encourage* investment in innovation has been *hotly* debated and the *evidence is unclear*'.[48] The economic incentives may not apply in equal strength to all

---

43 D. MacLeod, 'Raise investment to £1bn, medical research chief tells MPs' *The Guardian* Online (London, 9 December 2003) http://education.guardian.co.uk/higher/research/story/0,9865,1103199,00.html (accessed 15 April 2011).

44 M. Henderson, 'Post-election budget squeeze may bring about cuts in health research' (*The Times*, London 11 January 2010) http://www.timesonline.co.uk/tol/life_and_style/health/article6982918.ece (accessed 15 April 2011).

45 P. Curtis, 'Britain struggling in medical research stakes' (*The Guardian* Online London 8 December 2003) http://education.guardian.co.uk/higher/research/story/0,9865,1102451,00.html (accessed 15 April 2011).

46 P. Hutchison, 'Government cuts "will trigger brain drain" ' (Daily Telegraph, London 1 October 2010) http://www.telegraph.co.uk/news/newstopics/politics/8035993/Government-cuts-will-trigger-brain-drain.html (accessed 15 April 2011).

47 Review of the Patents Act 1953: Boundaries to Patentability, March 2002, para. 225.

48 J. Davis *Intellectual Property Law* (Butterworths, London 2001), p. 23 (emphasis added).

methods of medical treatment and 'there appears to be no empirical data to support [the] argument'[49] that it would apply at all. Therefore, the incentive to invent/innovate theory, as applied to methods of medical treatment, rests on certain assumptions of behaviour which means that the evaluation is conducted *ex ante*. Without a study which examines the actual economic impact and extent of patent protection, and the impact of methods of medical treatment on society, any analysis of the economics of patenting methods of medical treatment is bound to be limited. However, as argued below, the SET patent illustrates, albeit limitedly, the issues and potential economic need of the patent system in this field.

3 Methods of Medical Treatment: the SET Patent

The patent system should be able to provide incentives to the researcher and, importantly, to investors. It is vital that this distinction is appreciated because researchers, although willing, are sometimes unable to continue further research because of the prohibitive costs. Institutional investors are, therefore, needed to ensure that, where necessary, sufficient funds are made available to researchers to continue or pursue new research projects. Those investors, therefore, need the assurance of strong patents to ensure that they can secure a return on their investment.

The Surrogate Embryo Transfer (SET) procedure has been cited as an example of a procedure that would not have existed without the dual incentives of invention and innovation.[50] This procedure has been very successful and one of the most popular procedures ever invented. Dr John E. Buster invented the SET in 1984, and on 28 March 1989, the USPTO issued patent number 4,816,257 to Dr Buster and James Simon.[51] The invention claimed '[a] method for producing, in a functionally agonadal human female body, an environment suitable for the implantation, nutrition, and development of an embryo, comprising the placement of at least one carrier containing at least one releasable steroid hormone into the vagina of the human female'. The patent was for the creation of proper conditions for the implantation of a fertilised egg of one female into the womb of another female. It is without question that the SET is a method of medical treatment: the treatment of infertility in women.

---

[49] Review of the Patents Act 1953: Boundaries to Patentability, March 2002, para. 228.

[50] B. Gocyk-Farber, 'Patenting Medical Procedures: A Search for a Compromise between Ethics and Economics' (1997) 18 Cardozo L Rev 1527, 1342–3.

[51] United States Patent, Method of producing in an in vivo environment suitable for human embryo transfer, Patent No. 4, 816, 257.

The procedure was an expensive one to make so the inventors sought public funding to develop the invention. They were turned down by the National Institute of Health.[52] They then sought and received private funding from the Fertility and Genetics Research Inc. to the tune of US$500,000.[53] The private organisation would not have agreed to fund the research without the knowledge that its investment would be protected with the strength of patent rights. It is clear that without this funding the research and development of the medical procedure would not have taken place. This serves to illustrate the potency of patent law to encourage invention and provide the necessary incentives for researchers to embark on costly and high-risk medical procedures.

Funding is not only necessary for the development of the invention, it is also needed in the post-developmental stage where high research cost would be 'incurred in perfecting [the] invention for commercial exploitation'.[54] The costs of marketing the product and making it available for commercial sale are also significant factors to be considered. Trade secrecy is always an option for the inventor provided she is able to keep the invention a secret.[55] The law of confidence would also provide some protection for an inventor who has a trade secret.[56] Society as a whole would not benefit when inventions are kept secret, so the patent systems provide sufficient protection to the inventor whilst ensuring that information about the invention is made available to the public.

The argument has been proffered that, without the incentives of the patent system, some methods of medical treatment would not exist and that researchers would be unwilling to undertake the necessary and costly research without having the surety of the patent system to prevent others from using the invention without paying. Simply put, it would prevent

---

52 B. Gocyk-Farber, 'Patenting Medical Procedures: A Search for a Compromise between Ethics and Economics' (1997) 18 Cardozo L Rev 1527, 1543.

53 Ibid.

54 E. Kaufer *The Economics of the Patent System* (Harwood Academic Publishers, Switzerland 1989), p.19.

55 C.J. Katopis, 'Patients v. Patents?: Policy Implications of Recent Patent Legislation' (1997) 71 St. John's L Rev 329, 339. Methods of medical treatment provide the most fertile area where trade secrets may be used. It would, however, be contrary to the public interest and the Hippocratic Oath for a physician to engage in such a practice.

56 W. Cornish, D. Llewelyn and T. Aplin, *Intellectual Property: Patents, Copyrights, Trademarks and Allied Rights* (7th edn, Sweet & Maxwell, London 2010), p. 331 and Bently and Sherman, *Intellectual Property Law* (3rd edn, OUP, Oxford 2008), p. 1036.

'others from imitating [the] inventor's invention'.[57] The SET patent is one clear example where the incentives of the patent system directly contributed to the creation of an invention. However, on the whole, it has not been shown conclusively that the lack of patent protection is hindering research into various other methods of medical treatment. Empirical evidence has to be adduced before any firm conclusion can be made concerning the significance of the patent system to the development of medical procedures. This contrasts with drug therapies where explicit exceptions were grafted on to the 1977 Act and the EPC to ensure that: (a) substances and compositions of matter; (b) their use for medical treatments; (c) their first known medical use; and, recently, (d) their second and further medical uses were all capable of being patented – testimony to the lobbying power of the pharmaceutical industry and the significant influence of the incentives of the patent system.

4 High Development Cost Inventions

The case for patent protection is *a fortiori* when the invention has a high developmental cost. Without the incentives of the patent system and the recovery of R&D costs, research into finding possible cures for diseases would arguably be hindered. Although this view seems to be a correct one, the majority of research that currently takes place in the medical field is either biomedical or genetic in nature so their patenting, as will be shown in chapters 4 and 6, would not implicate the exclusion for methods of medical treatment. Understanding the causes and finding methods of diagnosing illnesses have become increasingly sophisticated with the employment of genetic technology in diagnostic methods. They are not medical procedure patents that restrict the actions of practitioners when treating their patients. There is a whole range of methods of medical treatment that have high ongoing research and developmental costs. Examples include a method for treating impotence in men,[58] a method of testing for the predisposition to

---

[57] B. Gocyk-Farber, 'Patenting Medical Procedures: A Search for a Compromise between Ethics and Economics' (1997) 18 Cardozo L Rev 1527, 1543.

[58] United States Patent No. 4,127, 118: Method of Effecting and Enhancing an Erection. The Description read as follows: 'The invention is a method of treating impotence by effecting and enhancing an erection of the penis without physiologic nervous stimulation. Preferably, the method is injection into the corpora cavernosa of the penis a predetermined amount of an appropriate vasodilator, including a sympathomimetic amine or an adrenergic blocking agent.'

certain cancers[59] and detecting whether children born of certain women will have Down's syndrome.[60] The R&D costs of the major pharmaceutical companies and research laboratories are great. There is no question that substantial investment is needed for continued research into finding new cures for diseases and new uses for current drug therapies. These examples do not fall under the exclusion of methods of medical treatment because they can be patented as substances, products or compositions of matter.

The need to have patent protection for high cost inventions is evident in the solution suggested by Gocyk-Farber who argued that the United States Patent Act should be amended to include a provision that placed the burden on the patentee to demonstrate that the invention would not have been developed without substantial expense for R&D.[61] Inventions that have high developmental costs are presumed to need the incentives that the patent system provides. According to her, the 'net social gain of patenting medical procedures is most questionable in cases of low development cost procedures'[62] than it is in cases of inventions with high developmental cost. However, it is suggested that the question of whether an invention is regarded as having a low or a high developmental cost should be divorced from the question of the societal and welfare benefits that they provide. It is arguable that low developmental cost inventions may not necessarily need the incentives of the patent system, but this is different from arguing that there is *little* social gain in low developmental cost inventions.

Gocyk-Farber argued that, in cases of low developmental cost inventions, the 'patents have a detrimental net effect on society [versus] the benefit of having a new procedure which could have been developed in the absence of patent protection'.[63] Her analysis misses the crucial factor, which involves an appreciation of the actual benefits derived from the invention in question, because it assumes that society would *only* benefit when the procedure *is* a high developmental cost one. The social benefit,

---

59 United States Patent No. 4,582,787: Method of testing a patient for predisposition to lung cancer, certain other cancers, neurofibromatosis and certain other hereditary disorders.

60 United States Patent No. 4, 874, 693: Method for assessing placental dysfunction.

61 B. Gocyk-Farber, 'Patenting Medical Procedures: A Search for a Compromise between Ethics and Economics' (1997) 18 Cardozo L Rev 1527, 1559. Subsection (3) of this proposal provides that 'in no case can an inventor be denied a patent for lack of substantial expense if he demonstrates that the developmental costs of the procedure were equal to or exceeded $100,000'.

62 B. Gocyk-Farber, 'Patenting Medical Procedures: A Search for a Compromise between Ethics and Economics' (1997) 18 Cardozo L Rev 1527, 1550.

63 Ibid, at 1555.

according to Gocyk-Farber, occurs when the 'advancement [in the] new medical processes [would] never have been developed in the absence of patent protection'[64] and the net social benefit of an invention is dependent on its importance in terms of public health. Patent protection would be *more* justifiable if the invention was important, significant and lead to *greater* societal benefit. Gocyk-Farber, therefore, assumes incorrectly that net social benefit would only accrue with inventions that have a high developmental cost.

Contrary to Gocyk-Farber's view, the cost-benefit analysis of methods of medical treatments is not a function of the developmental cost of the invention. The issues are complex and the analysis is not as straightforward, because any cost-benefit analysis will have to take into account the cost of developing the invention and the nature of the invention itself. Similarly, it is not correct to assume that an invention that has a low developmental cost is not worthy of patent protection. It may not have been created because of the incentives of the patent system but, depending on its nature, the invention may need the continued incentives of the patent system to ensure that research continues into developing and perfecting it. Developmental research is not needed when the invention is a simple one, for example, the medical suture in the *Pallin v Singer* case because the whole 'technology' would have been created. Where such inventions are simple ones that have the potential for development there would be a strong case for patent protection at the creative or the developmental stage.

With the mapping of the human genome in 2001 there was a marked shift in emphasis in medical research to the biomedical sciences and genetics which both have high developmental costs. Using various methods including '[m]olecular biology techniques, computer power, and robotics', scientists are now able to 'move from studying one gene or one protein at a time to studying entire sets of genes and proteins, and figuring out how they interact'.[65] Medical science is now much broader and interacts with other disciplines such as 'imaging, chemistry, computer science, mathematics, and informatics, which uses computer and statistical techniques to manage extensive amounts of data'.[66] This effectively means that there is an increased emphasis on methods of treating, diagnosing and preventing diseases that are highly technology intensive. These methods are, correctly,

---

64 Ibid.

65 United States, National Institute of Health, 'Investments, Progress, and Plans Selected, Examples from FY 1999–2003' http://www.nih.gov/about/investments.htm (accessed 15 April 2011).

66 Ibid.

outside the scope of the exclusion of methods of medical treatment from patent protection.

D THE PROSPECT THEORY

1 Outline

Professor Edmund Kitch, of the University of Chicago Law School, articulated his theory of the patent system.[67] He began by redefining the function of the patent system, which he claimed was to increase output from resources used for technological innovation.[68] The patent system was seen as a crucial element in technological innovation by providing protection for 'an array of prospects'. A prospect is defined as the 'opportunity to develop a known technological opportunity' and, to be effective, the theory needs a system for the allocation of resources to the most efficient producer and communicator of that information.[69] Kitch thought that the prospect theory was best explained through the patent system. He accepted that the reward theory, which was 'not questioned on its own terms', played a role in explaining the patent system but claimed that it 'offers an incomplete view of the functions of the patent system'.[70] The prospect theory therefore explains why it is possible to claim a workable prototype of the invention that will be infringed by later and superior inventions. The patentee is allowed to patent her invention as early as possible even if the patented invention is not seen as an end in itself, but rather the first step in the 'developmental process'.[71] The theory rests on the footing that the patent system allows the patentee to patent an invention that works, rather than one that is 'fully developed and or in a commercially valuable form'.[72]

The prospect theory would therefore support patent protection for an invention in its early stages of development, thereby providing the patentee with a monopoly over all possible uses of the technology. When this happens, in Kitch's opinion, the 'matrix of technological possibilities' shifts and 'dwarfs the original invention'.[73] The benefits of the patent system,

---

67 E.W. Kitch, 'The Nature and Function of the Patent System' (1977) 20 JL & Econ 265.
68 Ibid.
69 Ibid, at 266.
70 Ibid.
71 Ibid, at 269.
72 Ibid, at 270.
73 Ibid, at 271.

according to Kitch, include: (1) an increased efficiency in investment innovation; (2) the incentive to invest in inventions not easily appropriated by competitors; (3) a lower cost of negotiating contracts with potential competitors; (4) the signal function which reduces duplications in investment innovation; (5) reduction in the cost of policing the technology; and (6) improvements to the structure of the returns to innovation.[74]

According to Kitch, the question was not whether the invention was worth the patent monopoly but whether the information was sufficiently significant that it should be investigated.[75] The prospect theory saw patents as prospects which should be developed by the inventor who was most able to do so. The patent system facilitated the process by granting a monopoly to the first person to patent the invention. The prospect theory, therefore, rested on the assumption that R&D would continue in the period after the patent was granted. The grant of the patent was seen as a prospect that created the right to develop the invention which, according to Kitch, was the most efficient method of developing any form of technology. Innovation was achieved through collaboration with other inventors because simultaneous innovative efforts lead to an inefficient allocation of resources. The collaboration is manifested in the co-ordination of licences of various parts of an invention if different inventors have patents on them. In other words, '[r]ivalry is avoided [and] [p]lanning is possible'.[76]

One significant limitation of the prospect theory was its reliance on analysis derived from mineral claims.[77] It has been argued that the prospect theory failed to 'foresee the impact the exploitation of that prospect will have on the behaviour of other prospectors'[78] which includes innovation in the area of technology and increased activity to produce compatible technology.[79] However, since 'no one knows for sure what the possible inventions are in the technological pool'[80] the prospect theory, it has been

---

74 Ibid, at 275–80.

75 Ibid, at 284. He continued by arguing that this 'turns not upon the size of the firm, but on its dominance over a fruitful technological prospect'.

76 R.P. Merges and R.R. Nelson, 'On the Complex Economics of Patent Scope' (1990) 90 Colum L Rev 839, 872.

77 M.F. Grady and J.I. Alexander, 'Patent Law and Rent Dissipation' (1992) 78 Va L Rev 305, 316.

78 S.E. Cohen, 'To Innovate or not to Innovate, That is the Question: The Functions, Failures and Foibles of the Reward Function Theory of Patent Law in Relation to Computer Software Platforms' (1998) 5 Mich Telecom & Tech L Rev 1.

79 Ibid, at 19.

80 R.P. Merges and R.R. Nelson, 'On the Complex Economics of Patent Scope' (1990) 90 Colum L Rev 839, 873.

argued, offered an incomplete view of the patent system[81] and that the 'patent law favors not just invention, but *early* invention'.[82]

2 Methods of Medical Treatment

At the initial stages of development of any invention research costs would usually be high. However, in the case of medical procedures, R&D should continue to ensure that alternative methods of treatment are found. The case for developing a synthetic drug, if the natural chemical substance were limited in supply, is even stronger.[83] Therefore, the development of one invention may signal various other possibilities for future R&D. This facilitates harmless competition in the medical research field since society benefits when a new cure or procedure is developed. The prospect theory and its emphasis on co-ordinated development can be used to justify some medical patents, especially pharmaceutical products. If a prospect is an opportunity to develop a known technological opportunity, then the invention must be one that lends itself to further development before it can be patented. Treatment regimes can be readily explained using this method of analysis since the prospect theory is also based on a system that allows for the efficient allocation of resources to the inventor who is most efficient in the production of an invention and the communication of that information.

Treatment regimes consist of the method of administering the product to the patient. In 1999, the Court of Appeal held in *Bristol-Myers Squibb* that the treatment regime in that case, although clothed in the Swiss form of claim, which is allowable, were in fact methods of medical treatment and therefore excluded from patent protection.[84] In 2008, however, a differently constituted Court of Appeal in *Actavis UK Limited v Merck & Co Inc.*,[85] with Jacob L.J. giving the leading judgment, has reversed *Bristol-Myers Squibb* holding that treatment regimes are patentable under UK patent law.

Research continues unabated into finding the most efficient manner of administering drugs and drug therapies to humans. If one accepts that patent protection should be available for inventions that are sufficiently important that research should continue on them, and that treatment regimes are part of the efficient development and administration of drug therapies, then a case for patent protection would have been made. The

81 Ibid.
82 Ibid, at 879 (emphasis in original).
83 *Biogen Inc. v Medeva Plc* [1997] RPC 1.
84 [2001] RPC 1 (CA) 21.
85 [2008] EWCA Civ 444; [2008] RPC 26.

manufacturer of the drugs is, arguably, most able to conduct intensive research into finding the most efficient treatment regime. However, this would not exclude other research laboratories from engaging in the same research. Since duplication is to be avoided, collaborative research efforts are to be encouraged to prevent inefficient allocation of resources.

The manufacturer of the drug would control the means of developing that procedure, allowing other researchers to 'redirect their work so as not to duplicate work already done',[86] preventing waste and an inefficient allocation of resources. Developments in the field of gene therapy and embryonic cloning are perfect examples where the use of collaborative research efforts has shown immense potential. Second and further medical uses of known substances fit neatly into this category since the scope for finding second or further medical uses of known substances usually exists. It was the potential of these new discoveries, and the possibility that significant research and new drug treatments may be undiscovered, that led the EPO in *EISAI/Second medical indication*[87] to allow patents for second and further medical indications to the *chagrin* of many European states.

Simple methods of medical treatment, which would include some of the medical procedures that are usually carried out by some physicians or surgeons, may not have the potential to signal further development. Where the medical treatment is one that has potential for future development, it would, arguably, be explained by the prospect theory. These may include bone marrow transplantation and its usefulness in treating leukaemia, sickle cell and anaemia. The potential for gene therapy and embryonic cloning to eliminate many of the currently incurable diseases is vast. The requirement of utility[88] in the patenting of ESTs was an attempt to ensure that the patentee 'had unearthed enough to justify a "prospect" patent'.[89] The standard to be attained has not yet been set as the disclosure of the specific treatment itself. Indeed, patenting ESTs at such an early stage shows that the patentees see the discovery/invention[90] as having *some potential* to be used for the treatment of some diseases even if the specific treatments are still hitherto unknown.

---

[86] R.P. Merges and R.R. Nelson, 'On the Complex Economics of Patent Scope' (1990) 90 Colum L Rev 839, 873.

[87] (G 05/83) [1979–85] EPOR 241.

[88] Biotech Directive, Article 5(3).

[89] W.R. Cornish, *Intellectual Property: Omnipresent, Distracting, Irrelevant?* (Clarendon Lecture Series, OUP, Oxford 2004) at 19.

[90] The Nuffield Bioethics Report 2002 was not convinced that the identification of the structure of genetic material should be considered as an invention but more appropriately a discovery.

E RENT DISSIPATION THEORY

1 Outline

The most comprehensive and elaborate theory to attempt an explanation of the nature and function of the patent system is the rent dissipation theory articulated by Grady and Alexander in their seminal article, 'Patent Law and Rent Dissipation'.[91] It 'seeks to identify an underlying unity that explains the seemingly disorderly patent results'[92] and posits that patent protection should be available for 'inventions that *signal* large possibilities for improvement relative to the rent the patent gives to the inventor'.[93] The aim of the patent system is to reduce rent dissipation which was achieved: (a) in the developmental stages where the invention is created; (b) when the invention is created and other inventors are attempting to improve on it; and (c) when the inventor is deciding whether or not to protect the invention by keeping it secret.[94]

The rent dissipation theory 'posits that society profits from innovations, often realising benefits far in excess of the inventor's development costs'.[95] The inventor should receive the difference between what society is willing to pay and the development costs of the invention. This takes the 'form of a monopoly right; otherwise competition by imitators would discourage innovation by making it unprofitable'.[96] When an invention is on the market and 'signals ways in which [it] might be improved'[97] other inventors might seek to find ways of improving it. When this happens, according to Grady and Alexander, there will be a waste of efforts, which justifies the grant of a monopoly because 'it eliminates the incentive to engage in *wasteful* improvement efforts'.[98]

Similarly, when inventors over-invest in keeping their inventions secret it also leads to rent dissipation. Grady and Alexander asserted that rent dissipation theory 'predicts that the courts will enforce a patent when the size of the patent rent is proportionate to the rent dissipation that the

---

91 M.F. Grady and J.I. Alexander, 'Patent Law and Rent Dissipation' (1992) 78 Va L Rev 305.

92 Ibid, at 309.

93 Ibid (emphasis in original).

94 R.P. Merges, 'Rent Control in the Patent District: Observations on the Grady-Alexander Thesis' (1992) 78 Va L Rev 359.

95 M.F. Grady and J.I. Alexander, 'Patent Law and Rent Dissipation' (1992) 78 Va L Rev 305, 308.

96 Ibid.

97 Ibid.

98 Ibid (emphasis added).

inventor's technological signal would otherwise induce. ... Otherwise, broad patent protection is unwise'.[99] To the extent that rent dissipation theory accepts that 'the benefit to society of an invention is dissipated when there are redundant development efforts ...'[100] it comes very close to the prospect theory. Central co-ordination, however, they argued, 'neither dispenses with all rent dissipation nor explains many patent decisions'.[101] The inventions that are '[m]ost likely to receive patent protection are inventions that, although of comparatively small value signal a large potential for improvement'.[102] In such a case, rent dissipation is reduced. Grady and Alexander explained the essence of their theory in the following manner:[103]

> Inventions with little potential for further development are less likely to receive patents because the prospect of a rent-dissipating race among improvers is unlikely. The worst patent case is a valuable innovation that cannot be improved upon; here, a patent would clearly induce more rent dissipation than it would avoid.

There is an obvious bias against patents that do not signal any improvements. Patent protection would, therefore, not be available for simple inventions that do not have any prospect of being further developed.

Merges pointed out that rent dissipation theory, although making a profound contribution to the field,[104] does have its shortcomings. The first is that the actual decisions in the cases turned on the particular doctrinal underpinning of the concept used and that '[o]nly in retrospect does rent dissipation explain the outcomes'.[105] Secondly, the doctrine explained cases that were decided under old doctrines that are no longer relevant and this 'comes perilously close to prescribing a normative theory'.[106]

2 Methods of Medical Treatment

Grady and Alexander have argued that the rent dissipation theory 'seems to explain actual patent rulings better than the rules and tests applied by the

---

99 M.F. Grady and J.I. Alexander, 'Patent Law and Rent Dissipation. (1992) 78 Va L Rev 305, 321.

100 Ibid.

101 Ibid, at 318.

102 Ibid.

103 Ibid (emphasis added).

104 R.P. Merges, 'Rent Dissipation in the Patent District: Observations on the Grady-Alexander Thesis' (1992) Va L Rev 359.

105 Ibid, at 366.

106 Ibid.

courts'.[107] Some cases that considered the issue of patent protection for methods of medical treatment may be explained using the rent dissipation theory. One such case is *Morton v New York Eye Infirmary*.[108] The claimed invention was for a process of anaesthetising patients with ether. The patent was invalidated by the court because it lacked novelty. The use of ether was well known and the effect of the increased quantities was not new. The invention was simply for the use of an old substance (the ethers), in an old way (by inhalation), for inducing insensitivity in mammals (old purpose). This, the court held, was not sufficient to confer novelty on the invention. Grady and Alexander pointed out that the reward theory could *not* explain the *Morton case*. This observation, at first blush, seems unassailable as the court pointed out that the invention was one of the '*great* discoveries of modern times'.[109] However, on a closer analysis it is appreciated that the invention was not invalidated *because* it was a discovery but because it was already part of the state of the art.

Grady and Alexander re-examined the *Morton case* through the lenses of rent dissipation theory. They argued that 'the key to [the] *Morton* [*case*] is that the invention of anaesthesia was enormously valuable relative to the signal that it offered for further improvements'.[110] The limitation of the patent in the *Morton case* was that the idea was too good and too simple[111] and it had no potential to signal improvements. Such inventions were termed 'elegant' because the inventors had 'invented the whole technology' which meant that '[n]o patent was needed to stave off a race to improve'.[112] However, some medical procedures patents may not have the potential for improvement as such, for example, Keratotomy, which is the surgical incision of the cornea of the eye. They may not be explained by rent dissipation theory since it is not applicable when the whole technology (or procedure, in the case of methods of medical treatments) is invented.

Where there is potential for improvement, as in the case of some medical procedures, it is usually achieved through trial and error, or through physicians experimenting with more efficient procedures. This was the case with open heart surgery. In the earlier years many patients died during heart surgery but, as the years progressed and surgeons improved their technique,

---

107 Ibid, at 323.
108 17 F Cas 879 (CC SDNY 1982).
109 Ibid, at 883 (emphasis added).
110 M.F. Grady and J.I. Alexander, 'Patent Law and Rent Dissipation' (1992) 78 Va L Rev 305, 326.
111 Ibid.
112 Ibid, at 327.

the procedure became quite safe.[113] The first successful operation was in 1952 when surgeons realised that if the body temperature reached 81 degrees F, the patient could survive without a pumping heart for ten minutes. However, ten minutes was not sufficient for major heart defects and complications. In 1958, an injection was developed which stopped the heart from beating during surgery.[114] After the first successful kidney transplant in 1963, it was a matter of time before the technique would be used for heart transplants. This was first done in 1967 but the lives of patients were usually short-lived. Many heart transplant units closed as a result.[115] However, one surgeon, Dr. Norman Shumway, continued the work and attempted to solve the problems that persisted. It was found that, by feeding a catheter into the heart and removing a piece of heart muscle for examination, rejection attacks would be detected. It was only when signs of rejection were noticed that doses of the dangerous immuno-suppressive drugs could be increased.[116] At about the same time, in Norway, a fungus was found which contained a compound called cyclosporin, which had immuno-suppressant properties (controlling organ rejection without knocking out all the resistance to infection). With that discovery heart transplantation became commonplace and more effective than before. Surgeons are still continuing to find ways of surgically solving the problem of heart failure.[117] In the case of heart surgery there is still the potential for development of the procedure to make it safer, which makes it the type of invention that the rent dissipation theory attempts to explain.

Similarly, treatment regimes could possibly be explained using the rent dissipation theory, since they would normally have potential for further development. This, however, is subject to an optimal level at which the patient would not benefit from further changes in the level of administration of the drug or treatment provided. Therefore, rent dissipation theory would explain patent protection of treatment regimes up to the optimal level. After the optimal level, the invention would have little, if any, potential for further development, and would be less likely to receive a patent. In any event, patent protection may not be sought since the net benefit to society or the net gain would not be sufficient for the patentee to seek patent protection. It may be argued that consumers would not purchase any medical product that does not provide a higher marginal rate of

---

113 Pioneers of Heart Surgery: http://www.pbs.org/wgbh/nova/heart/pioneers.html (accessed 15 April 2011).

114 Ibid.

115 Ibid.

116 Ibid.

117 Ibid.

benefit than a previous one. Therefore, the incentive to continue research in the post optimal stage would be minimal, inefficient and may lead to diminishing returns.

F REWARD/DESERT

1 Outline

John Stuart Mill was of the opinion that the patent monopoly should not be condemned and that the inventor 'ought to be both compensated and rewarded'.[118] However, the reward theory is not based on the utilitarian concept that underlies the classical economic argument. It is based on the argument that the inventor deserves to be rewarded because she has created a valuable tangible or intangible. Locke's theory, a stronger version of the reward theory,[119] 'implies something stronger – that this reward ought to be given and that the labourer is entitled to it'.[120] The question ultimately becomes a consideration of the reasons why her 'creation' justifies rewarding her with a property right in the form of the patent monopoly – the creator of the invention is rewarded because she deserves it. The reward is not seen as part of any additional incentive to innovate and invent. Becker[121] identified three justifications for the claim of an inventor/creator to the property that he has created: (a) that his effort in creating the product of his labour 'exemplifies human excellence'; (b) he has created a public benefit and therefore derives a 'fitting and proportional benefit in return'; and (c) that certain factors create 'special needs' in the creator that 'can appropriately be met by the award of property rights'.[122]

The desert argument for intellectual or other property rights raises more questions than it answers. This was appreciated by Waldron when he asked three questions: '(1) What makes the [creation] a good [creation]? (2) Why should it be rewarded (as opposed to merely noted, praised or approved)?; and (3) What reward is appropriate?'[123] He answers the first question by using the Lockean theory, stating that 'labouring is good because it makes a

---

118 J.S. Mill, *A Manual of Political Economy* (D Appleton & Co 1901), p. 548.

119 Locke's theory is better explained as part of the liberty/autonomy theory of property rights.

120 J.S. Mill, *A Manual of Political Economy* (D Appleton & Co 1901), p. 548.

121 L.C. Becker, 'Deserving to Own Intellectual Property' (1993) Chi-Kent L Rev 609, 618–29.

122 Ibid, at 626.

123 J. Waldron, *The Right to Private Property* (Clarendon Press, Oxford 1988), p. 202.

useful contribution to the wealth and prosperity of mankind',[124] and that it encourages the creator and others to act in a similar way in the future. Waldron makes the point that not all morally good acts ought to be rewarded and that compensation payable for labour is a reward for the 'unpleasant' nature of labouring.[125] He accepts that the reward 'amounts to full and exclusive property rights in the resources one has worked on'.[126] As for the third question, he wonders why the entire property right in the creation is awarded to the creator when his contribution should be for the benefit of mankind. According to him, the 'putative reward represents a cost to everyone but the person rewarded'.[127] Everyone, apart from the person rewarded, is worse off than they were before the value was given to the labourer.[128] Locke's theory, according to Waldron, implies that the 'reward *ought* to be given and that the labourer is *entitled* to it'.[129]

The argument for desert is not generally used to justify intellectual property rights as such. One cannot but agree with Spence that '[g]iven the general philosophical difficulties with the concept of desert ... it is not surprising that it has been the least important in ... the discussion of intellectual property rights generally'.[130] The reward theory is often misunderstood. It is frequently stated that it rests on the premise that 'justice requires that [the inventor] receive reward for [her invention] in proportion to [its] usefulness to society' and that 'society must secure [her] that reward'.[131] This argument may be useful in explaining why the inventor is able to secure a reward beyond her R&D costs. However, it is limited insofar as it does not appreciate that technological innovation does not stop at the grant of the patent but it continues in the post-grant period to enable the patentee to improve the invention. Society would benefit if the inventor were able to improve the invention which would necessitate further capital for R&D that the grant of the patent monopoly may secure.

---

124 Ibid.

125 Ibid.

126 Ibid.

127 Ibid, at 205.

128 Ibid.

129 Ibid (emphasis in original).

130 M. Spence, 'Passing Off and the Misappropriation of Valuable Intangibles' (1996) LQR 472, 486–87.

131 F. Machlup *An Economic Review of the Patent System* (Study of the Subcommittee on Patents, Trademarks and Copyrights of the Committee of the Judiciary, United States Senate 85th Congress, Study No 15 1958).

2 Methods of Medical Treatment

The application of the desert/reward[132] theory to methods of medical treatment and drug therapies is suitable but unfortunately is of limited scope. The creators of medical procedures and drug treatments would, according to the theory, deserve the reward of the patent grant. The tripartite formula that Becker articulated above provides a good test to determine whether or not the property right in medical treatments and drug therapies can find justification based on the arguments from desert. The first of these seems clear. Both methods of medical treatment and drug therapies include some element of human excellence in their creation that occurs when it 'exceeds human achievements – perhaps by being exceedingly original, or difficult, or brave or beautiful'.[133] The requirement of novelty and non-obviousness in patent law are apt to illustrate this concept. Since the standards are high, it seems that any patent that satisfies this criterion would be justified on the basis of human excellence.

For example, it could be said that the development of endocrine therapy, or hormonal therapy, which is treatment that adds, blocks, or removes hormones, would count as part of human excellence.[134] It is used in many areas of medicine and is sometimes the best hope of a cure that patients have. It is useful for some serious medical conditions, for example, diabetes or menopause or certain thyroid conditions where hormones are given to adjust low hormone levels.[135] Sometimes it is provided to patients to slow or stop the growth of certain cancers, such as prostate and breast cancer: in these instances, hormones may be given to block the body's natural hormones. In other patients, surgery is needed to remove the source of hormones.[136]

The second argument is not based on the excellence of the producer's activity but, rather, on the value of the product to society which necessitates an assessment of the value of the creation.[137] In reality this concept is difficult to apply and does not represent what happens in practice. Patent

---

132 The form of title 'reward/desert' is derived from M. Spence, 'Passing Off and the Misappropriation of Valuable Intangibles' (1996) LQR 472, 486–87 and M. Spence, 'Justifying Copyright' in D. McLean and K. Schubert (eds) *Dear Images: Art, Copyright and Culture* (Ridinghouse, London 2002).

133 L.C. Becker, 'Deserving to Own Intellectual Property' (1993) 68 Chicago-Kent LR 609, 623.

134 Endocrine therapy http://www.health-news-and-information.com/4civista/libv/g07.shtml#link_e (accessed 15 April 2011).

135 Ibid.

136 Ibid.

137 Ibid.

rights are granted irrespective of the value of the invention to the public and impose the same obligation on the public not to use, dispose or reproduce the patent without authority from the patentee. It is not obvious that medical treatments, as a class of patentable subject matter, are less valuable than drug therapies. They both seek the same objective – the maintenance and enhancement of public health. In the same way it could not be said conclusively that surgery is a more valuable method of treating cancer than chemotherapy, radiation therapy, biological therapy or vice versa. Their use may be more efficient depending on the cancer in question, for example, radiation therapy is usually used for cancers of the tongue, uterus or cervix; and for many cancer patients, a combination of these treatments may be used.[138]

According to Becker, need, the third in his tripartite formulation, is generated by dependency through the connectedness of the product with the identity of the creator, which creates a social need for the welfare of the products or sustained through social norms.[139] The notion of need as a justification for the award of patent rights for drug therapies or medical treatments is riddled with difficulty. Need, as a justification for intellectual property rights, would hardly explain or rationalise the actions of patentees and all physicians in the medical field. The argument is even stronger since the motive for patent protection is usually economic. When a creator creates a work, for example, Michelangelo's David, it would not be surprising that there would be a high degree of dependency originating from his connectedness with the work. Therefore, Michelangelo would need social norms to protect the welfare of his work. This may seem inapplicable to drug therapies insofar as there may exist many researchers at any one time responsible for the final product so that such 'need' is not generated.

G LIBERTY/AUTONOMY

1 Outline

Some theories of intellectual property rest on the necessity of property for the development of one's personality and usually begin with the theory of the person as the foundation of their arguments.[140] The classic exposition

---

138 Ibid.

139 L.C. Becker, 'Deserving to Own Intellectual Property' (1993) 68 Chicago-Kent LR 609, 617.

140 See M. Spence, 'Justifying Copyright' in D. McLean and K. Schubert (eds), *Dear Images: Art, Copyright and Culture* (London, Ridinghouse 2002).

of this theory (the liberty/autonomy theory[141]) is to be found in the writings of Locke in his *Two Treatises of Government*[142] and Hegel in his *Philosophy of Right*.[143] The theory is based on the notion that every person has a property right in his own person and his labour.[144] This makes personality and labour indivisible insofar as anything created by labour is a reflection, if not part, of personality. Margaret Jane Radin has offered a comprehensive exposition of this theory,[145] explaining that conservatives rely on an absolute conception of property as sacred to personal autonomy, communitarians believe that changing conceptions of property reflect and shape the changing nature of persons and communities, while welfare rights liberals find entitlement to a minimal level of resources necessary to the dignity of persons even when their entitlement might curtail the rights of others.[146]

Locke's theory of property takes as its starting point the fact that all property was part of the commons.[147] He then asserted that 'every Man has a Property in his own Person' which lead him to conclude that '[t]he labour of his Body, and the Work of his hands … are properly his'.[148] The use of labour to create something made that thing his property:[149]

> Whatsoever, then, he removes out of the state that Nature hath provided and left it in, *he hath mixed his labour with it*, and joined to it something that is his own, and thereby makes it his property. It being by him removed from the common state Nature placed it in, *it hath by this labour something annexed to it that excludes the common right of other men*. For this 'labour' being the unquestionable property of the labourer, no man but he can have a right to what that is once joined to, at least where there is enough, and as good left in common for others.

---

141 The form of title 'liberty/autonomy' is derived from M. Spence, 'Passing Off and the Misappropriation of Valuable Intangibles' (1996) LQR 472, 486–87 and M. Spence 'Justifying Copyright' in D. McLean and K. Schubert (eds), *Dear Images: Art, Copyright and Culture* (London, Ridinghouse 2002).

142 J. Locke, *Two Treatises of Government* (M Goldie (ed) 1993).

143 G.W.F. Hegel, *Philosophy of Right* (S.W. Dyde (tr) 1996).

144 See M. Spence, 'Justifying Copyright' in D. McLean and K. Schubert (eds) *Dear Images: Art, Copyright and Culture* (London, Ridinghouse 2002).

145 M.J. Radin, 'Property and Personhood' (1982) 34 Stan L Rev 957. J.W. Harris, *Property and Justice* (OUP, Oxford 1996) doubts whether the ' "personhood" argument' is the same as the 'Hegelian property-freedom argument' although it is 'frequently so termed' since it 'would not yield to full-blooded ownership … [and] is incompatible with freedom to transmit' (at p. 221).

146 M.J. Radin, 'Property and Personhood' (1982) 34 Stan L Rev 957, 959.

147 J. Locke, *Two Treatises of Government* (M. Goldie (ed) 1993), p. 127.

148 Ibid, at 128.

149 Ibid.

If she owns that thing the only way to reward her, as the argument runs, was to protect her property (the manifestation of her labour in the tangible or intangible object) through intellectual property or other property rights. The labour that is used and applied to the commons is reduced to private ownership by that fact alone. As Locke succinctly stated, since God 'has given to us all things richly,'[150] 'he cannot be supposed he meant that it should always remain common'.[151] To the contrary, he intended that each person takes 'as much as he may by his labour fix a property in'.[152] This indicates that a person's right to take as much property as she can was subject only to the limitation that she must be able to fix it to make it her own.

Hegel also viewed property rights as based on a conception of persons from the standpoint of their free will and autonomy.[153] Property rights are justified purely on the basis of the subjectivity of personality since:

> [a] *person must translate his freedom into an external sphere in order to exist as Idea*. Personality is the first, still wholly abstract, determination of the absolute and infinite will, and therefore this sphere distinct from the person, *the sphere capable of embodying his freedom, is likewise determined as what is immediately different and separable from him.*[154]

The existence of this right begins when '[his] will acts on the external world'. In other words, '[t]he person must give its freedom an external sphere in order to exist as an Idea'.[155] Property, therefore, 'is the first embodiment of freedom and so is in itself a substantive end'.[156] The justification of property rights is seen in terms of the will, freedom and right.[157] The free will can be seen as the origin and the basis of the right insofar as the mind objectifies itself in a system of right that gives expression to freedom, which Hegel claims was the goal and substance of the right itself.[158]

Property rights are needed to allow individuals to sustain and develop their abilities and self-conceptions which are definitive of their status as

---

150 J. Locke, *Two Treatises of Government* (M. Goldie (ed) 1993), p. 130.
151 Ibid, at 131.
152 Ibid, at 130.
153 G.W.F. Hegel, *Philosophy of Right* (SW Dyde (tr) 1996).
154 Ibid, at 41 (emphasis added).
155 Ibid.
156 Ibid.
157 Ibid.
158 Ibid.

persons.[159] The freedom of their personalities needs to be embodied in external objects, so that their conception of themselves as persons ceases to be purely subjective and becomes concrete and recognisable to themselves and others in the public and the external world.[160] The processes by which such rights are created are twofold. There must be: (i) an interaction between the external object and ones personality, which are then (ii) concretised in that object in a manner that is recognised by others. In other words, the 'Hegelian argument sees property not only as a necessary condition for this development, but as the manifestation of this development itself'.[161]

Radin claims that the two main functions of any property theory are the general justification of property rights and their delineation. She summarises her position as follows:[162]

> (1) At least some conventional property interests in society ought to be recognized and preserved as personal.
> (2) Where we can ascertain that a given property right is personal, there is a prima facie case that that right should be protected to some extent against invasion by government and against cancellation by conflicting fungible property claims of other people. This case is strongest where without the claimed protection of property as personal, the claimants' opportunities to become fully developed persons in the context of our society would be destroyed or significantly lessened, and probably also where the personal property rights are claimed by individuals who are maintaining and expressing their group identity.
> (3) Where we can ascertain that a property right is fungible, there is a prima facie case that that right should yield to some extent in the face of conflicting recognized personhood interests, not embodied in property. This case is strongest where without the claimed personhood interest, the claimants' opportunities to become fully developed persons in the context of our society would be destroyed or significantly lessened.

The creation of any intellectual property might be justified on these approaches to property rights. If society is to value the liberty/autonomy of the individual it must grant the creator some control over his creations.

---

159 J. Waldron, *The Right to Private Property* (Clarendon Press, Oxford 1988), p. 253.

160 Ibid.

161 T.G. Palmer, 'Are Patents and Copyrights Morally Justified? The Philosophy of Property Rights and Ideal Objects' Harv J Law & Publ Pol'y 13, no 3 (Summer 1990) 818, 837.

162 M.J. Radin, 'Property and Personhood' (1982) 34 Stan L Rev 957, 1014–15.

2 Methods of Medical Treatment

The patenting of methods of medical treatment may be justified on the liberty/autonomy argument insofar as individuals usually create them. Although individuals employed by a medical laboratory, a research hospital or the national health services would usually create inventions, the invention would be patented in the name of employer and not the individual researcher or research team. Therefore, the application of the liberty/autonomy argument to methods of medical treatment does not seem totally appropriate. The argument becomes more tenuous for drug therapies because individuals who are employed by pharmaceutical companies generally create them. It would be difficult to justify why pharmaceutical companies are the ones that obtain patent protection when their employees are the ones 'most intimately associated' with the invention. The liberty/autonomy argument, as a justification for intellectual property rights, does not explain the *degree* of association that is necessary before any property rights are vested in the creator.

Another conceptual difficulty with the application of the liberty/autonomy argument in the medical field is that most inventions, especially in the pharmaceutical field, are collaborative research efforts. For example, a team of researchers from Oxford University, funded with a £95,000 grant from Action Medical Research and working in conjunction with colleagues at Cambridge University, were looking at how conditions in the body's circulation cause sickle cell crises, and how the use of drugs can prevent the condition by stopping the rogue red cells from changing shape.[163] If this team were successful it would be difficult to determine which part of the invention that each individual had created. It also means that necessary close association, which is essential to the liberty/autonomy argument, would be difficult to prove when the patentee (usually the University in the previous example) has not actually created anything.

Similarly, identifying the creators for the purposes of determining association is problematic and is manifested in the different approaches to joint authorship and ownership that obtain in the United Kingdom[164] and the

---

[163] http://www.action.org.uk/touching_lives/2004/autumn/sickle_cell_treatments (accessed 15 April 2011).

[164] Section 37 of the 1977 Act defines the circumstances under which the controller may have jurisdiction to determine questions relating to the ownership of a patent. Section 36 outlines the rights of joint owners of the patent in question. The court will identify the inventive elements of the invention then determine the contribution that each of the inventors made.

United States.[165] Locke's approach to this is intimately associated with mixing labour. Although a difficult concept to grasp, the idea of mixing labour with one's personality simply means the creation of an object where the individual intellectual effort contributes significantly to the end result. In light of that, one can certainly disagree with Nozick when he argued that 'if I mix my tomato juice with the sea, I lose my tomato juice'. This is not an argument that defeats the one based on mixing labour. Rather, it simply shows that, if ones efforts or labour were not enough to dominate the object created, then it would not be sufficient to justify the grant of a property right in the thing created.

This liberty/autonomy argument for patent protection of methods of medical treatment, as with any other justification for intellectual property rights, focuses on the rights of the creator of the invention at the expense of the public who are deprived of the use of the invention unless they pay for using it. Any argument which exalts the rights of one party, without having regard to the corresponding loss and consequences to society would not be able to withstand scrutiny. However, the application of the liberty/autonomy argument may not be appropriate given the manner in which medical procedures are created. Medical procedures are usually the result of trial and error by physicians or researchers over a period of time and would vary depending on the complexity of the procedure in question. Where a group of researchers invents treatments in the form of drug therapies, locating the nexus of association may prove elusive when the patentee *is* the pharmaceutical company itself.

H CONCLUSION

The incentives that the patent system provides for innovation and invention are not questioned. Undoubtedly, the economic incentives that have traditionally and historically been at the foundation of the patent system still retain the vigour that fuelled the industrial revolution. However, the broadening of patentable subject matter meant that some of the inventions may not necessarily need the incentives of the patent system for their R&D. It is arguable that the economic incentives – the foundation of modern patent law – may not be generally applicable to all methods of medical treatment. However, it was shown that there exist specific examples of methods of medical treatment, for example, the SET patent which might need the

---

165 The position in the United States does not differ fundamentally when determining whether a co-ownership exists: see U.S.C. 116 Inventors. Patent Laws, s. 35.

incentives that the patent system provides. This seems to be more of the exception than the norm.

Similarly, the prospect and rent dissipation theories are also applicable to treatment regimes. The prospect theory is based on a system that allows for the efficient allocation of resources to the inventor who is most efficient in the production of an invention and the communication of that information. Based on this analysis, the inventor who has found the most efficient administration method should obtain patent protection. Therefore, the rent dissipation theory would explain patent protection of treatment regimes up to the optimal level, after which the invention would have little or no potential for further development, and would, therefore, be less likely to receive any patent protection.

It may be argued that physicians do not depend entirely on the patent system for continued research and development of medical procedures. The evidence is not available to show or prove *convincingly* that methods of medical treatment need the incentives of the patent system to thrive. Although it has been argued that patenting treatment regimes can be explained by one or more of the economic theories of patent law which, alone, is not sufficient to warrant patent protection of all methods of medical treatment. Important medical and scientific research continues into understanding and finding the cures for various diseases, and the emphasis on biomedical and genetic solutions to the concerns in the medical community means that there may be little economic incentive for developing non-scientific methods of medical treatment.

3. Arguments against patent protection

A INTRODUCTION

It is understandable that, in a debate concerning patent protection for methods of medical treatment, emotive arguments would be invoked because they relate to an aspect of public life that inevitably evokes strong feeling. As Lockhart J. puts it in *Anaesthetic Supplies v Rescare*:[1]

> Some people have a *deep seated feeling* or view that the art of a physician or a surgeon in alleviating human suffering does *not* belong to the area of economic endeavour of trade and commerce; and there is need for care lest a restriction on the freedom of action of those who treat patients endangers human life or health.

A similar view was expressed by Professor Vaver when he stated that the exclusion for methods of medical treatment 'springs from the *ethical* and *emotional* reasons based on a desire not to hamper the saving of life and the alleviation of suffering'.[2] Where does this deep seated feeling originate? This chapter examines the arguments that are made against patent protection for methods of medical treatment that may form the underlying rationale for the exclusion of methods of medical treatment from patent protection.[3]

An emotive argument may arise from one's view of what intuitively feels right. However, it still begs the question of the actual justification of that view. In *Bristol-Myers Squibb Co v F H Faulding & Co. Ltd*,[4] it was stated that '[t]he opponents to the grant of a monopoly in respect of medical and surgical processes raise objections that can be put into two broad groups: (i) the adverse effects on the provision of medical care; and (ii) the adverse effects on medical progress and education'. And, that '[i]n addition there is

1 (1994) 50 FCR 1 (FCA) 18 (emphasis added).
2 D. Vaver, *Intellectual Property Law* (Concord, Ont., Irwin Law 1997), p. 131 (emphasis added).
3 See A. Sims, 'The Case against Patenting Methods of Medical Treatment' [2007] EIPR 43.
4 (2000) FCA 316.

the related "ethical" question whether a medical practitioner (medical and surgical processes are usually invented by a medical practitioner) should be entitled to patent her invention consistent with her obligation to provide medical services to humanity'.[5]

The arguments *against* patenting methods of medical treatment include the negative impact they may have on public health and quality/access to health care; the possible negative consequences for the physician/patient relationship; and the availability of other incentive structures that may possibly motivate physicians to develop new procedures. Some of the arguments considered in this chapter are based on the identity of the patentee.[6] It has been argued that for a physician to act as an inventor in seeking patents for her invention may make her: (a) breach the Hippocratic Oath; and (b) act contrary to the sharing norm that has characterised the medical profession. It is not without sound reason, therefore, that legislators have attempted to ensure that the activities of physicians are not limited by patents and the courts in the United Kingdom and Technical Boards of Appeal (TBAs) and the Enlarged Board of Appeal of the European Patent Office (EBA) have made it clear that the rationale for the exclusion for methods of medical treatment is to ensure that physicians are not hindered by patents in the practice of medicine. The right to health, patient privacy and to the autonomy of both physician and patient are arguably compromised when methods of medical treatment are patented. The potential impact and possible implications that patenting medical procedures may have on these rights will be examined briefly.

The arguments that are made against patent protection that will be considered in this chapter include: (a) public health implications; (b) physician liberty and autonomy; (c) physician/patient relationship; (d) the Hippocratic Oath/sharing norm; (e) other incentive structures; and (f) breach of patient's privacy. Similar arguments may also be made against the patenting of drug therapies. In the process of delineating the arguments against patent protection for methods of medical treatment, I will also attempt to indicate, where necessary, where they differ from patenting drug therapies. This is done to show that, although many of the arguments are similar, there are some that are specific to medical procedure patents that *may* provide another explanation for the different approaches to patentability between them and drug therapies. There is the possibility that licences may solve the problem of access to and control over the supply of

[5] Ibid, at [133].

[6] J.M. Reisman, 'Physicians and Surgeons as Inventors: Reconciling Medical Process Patents and Medical Ethics' (1995) 10 High Tech LJ 355.

medical procedures, and, if it cannot satisfactorily do so, a compulsory licensing regime may be suitable. Indeed, the recent struggle of Third World countries to manufacture generic drugs for HIV patients is testimony to this ongoing debate.[7]

B METHODS AND PRODUCTS

The question has been asked: since methods of medical treatment and drug therapies both relate to the same subject matter – methods by which the human body may be treated – why then is patent protection provided for one and not the other? The answer to this question is not an easy one because the arguments against patent protection for methods of medical treatment that are considered in this chapter, with subtle differences in some places, may similarly be made against patenting drug therapies. It was no surprise that, in holding that methods of medical treatment were patentable under Australian law, the Australian Federal Court in *Bristol-Myers Squibb Co v F H Faulding & Co. Ltd*[8] stated that it was 'fortified by two considerations' one of which was the 'insurmountable problem, from a public policy viewpoint, of drawing a logical distinction which would justify allowing patentability for a product for treating the human body, but deny patentability for a method of treatment'.[9] The second was the limited manner in which the Parliament dealt with patents with respect to the human body when it enacted the Australian Patent Act 1990.[10]

In *Bristol-Myers Squibb Co v F H Faulding & Co. Ltd*, it was also pointed out that there seemed to be a general consensus around the world that pharmaceutical products are patentable, but that this was 'notwithstanding the fact that many patients (perhaps millions around the world) are denied access to new pharmaceuticals, because of the price charged by the monopolist or its licensee'.[11] The court continued that:[12]

> No doubt it is the ever-increasing cost of developing new and more effective pharmaceuticals and surgical products that underlies the support for medical

[7] South Africa and India are examples where legislation allowed pharmaceutical companies to produce generic drugs to combat the AIDS crisis. See also P.L. Wojahn, 'A Conflict of Rights: Intellectual Property under TRIPs, the Right to Health and AIDS Drugs' (2001) UCLA Journal of International Law and Foreign Affairs 464; and M.T. Griffin, 'AIDS Drugs and the Pharmaceutical Industry: A Need for Reform' (1991) 17 Am. J.L. & Med. 363, 393–97.

[8] (2000) FCA 316.

[9] Ibid, at [15].

[10] Ibid, at [16].

[11] Ibid, at [132].

[12] Ibid.

> and surgical product patents. That is to say, the investment needed for the research and development of these products justifies patent protection. The support may also be explained, in part at least by the fact that it is usually a commercial organisation rather than a physician that is the inventor of pharmaceuticals and surgical products.

The court was simply trying to underscore the point that although pharmaceutical products and medical procedures both need the incentives of the patent system (because of the cost of developing such inventions), the distinction between the two may be explained on the basis that, in the case of drug therapies, the exploitation of the invention is by an organisation and not a physician.

Lockhart J. in *Anaesthetic Supplies Property Limited v Rescare Ltd*[13] quoted[14] Davison C.J., at first instance, in the New Zealand case of *Wellcome Foundation v Commissioner of Patents*[15] where he stated that '[t]he law permits the granting of a patent for a drug. The inventor has his rights to it protected and it can be employed in medical treatments only if made available to the medical profession by reason of licensing or compulsory licensing. If a process for a medical treatment is invented can that not be licensed in the same way and cannot the legislature amend the statute if it is thought desirable to do so? *Is any member of the public going to be deprived of the treatment more than he might be deprived of a drug under existing law?*'[16] These views, however, were not endorsed by the Court of Appeal.[17]

In *Wellcome Foundation Ltd v Plantex*,[18] Witkon J. stated that '[t]here is no logic in such exclusion as long as it is lawful to obtain a patent on a pharmaceutical product, since in both cases there is an equal need for patent protection'.[19] The argument is that if there is no distinction between the objectives of medical procedures and drug therapies, then there is no reason why patents should be available for one and not the other. Jacobs J., as he then was, made a similar point in *Bristol-Myers Squibb v Baker Norton* where he stated that '[t]he thinking behind the exception [for methods of medical treatment] is not particularly rational: if one accepts that a patent monopoly is a fair price to pay for the extra research incentive, then there is *no reason* to suppose that that would *not also apply* to methods

13 [1994] 50 FCR 1.
14 Ibid, at [72].
15 [1979] 2 NZLR 591.
16 Ibid, at 620 (emphasis added).
17 [1983] NZLR 385.
18 [1979] RPC 514.
19 Ibid, at 536.

of treatment'.[20] A similar sentiment was also echoed 28 years earlier, in 1971, when Whitford J. in *Schering A G's Application* pointed out that it was 'difficult to see any logical justification for the practice [of not granting patents] in relation to the processes for medical treatment, if the object of the system is in truth to give hope of a reward to people whose research and industry results in valuable products or processes'.[21]

It is, of course, true that one of the justifications for the patent system is the economic reward for the inventor who has created a patentable invention (whether valuable or not). It would then be necessary to show that the incentives of the patent system are also applicable to medical procedures to justify patent protection. But, arguably, this should not be the only question asked and, in the medical field, it is legitimate to consider other factors that may be affected when some patents are granted. As we shall see in this chapter, there are public health and other considerations that might be taken into account when deciding whether or not patent protection should be made available for medical procedures and, by extension, drug therapies.

C PUBLIC HEALTH IMPLICATIONS

1 Introduction

The debate over patenting methods of medical treatment has traditionally focused on the ethical considerations and their consequences. The courts and legislators initially used ethical considerations as *the* possible policy justification for excluding methods of medical treatment from patent protection. The conference papers of the EPC 1973 did not indicate that the drafters of the EPC had explicitly accepted ethical considerations as *the* justification for the exclusion. Methods of medical treatment were excluded because they were deemed not subject to industrial application. However, the drafters of the EPC 2000 appreciated that this was a fiction and asserted that it was *undesirable* to uphold that fiction because methods of medical treatment were *only* excluded from patent protection '*in the interests of public health*'.[22] This shows an acceptance of a policy-based rationale for the exclusion of methods of medical treatment from patent protection. The public health aspect of methods of medical treatment is usually seen as one of the many policy-based arguments *against* patents for methods of medical treatment.

---

20 [1999] RPC 253 (emphasis added).

21 [1971] RPC 337 (PAT), at 343.

22 Base Proposal for the Revision of the European Patent Convention, 2002 (emphasis added).

The negative public health consequences of granting patents for methods of medical treatment have been exhaustively dealt with in the literature.[23] In *Wellcome Foundation Ltd v Plantex Ltd*,[24] Khan J. stated that '[t]here exist *grave* reasons against the creation of a monopoly by a patent in respect of medical treatment. We are concerned here with *saving human life or alleviating human suffering* and one should take great care lest a restriction on the freedom of action of those who treat, caused by patents, would affect human life or health'.[25]

2 The Right to Health

During the debate concerning patentability in the medical field, the moral right to health was used to justify excluding patents from the medical field.[26] The right to health would be an important consideration for various reasons. First, it would provide an interpretative guide for the courts in deciding cases concerning patenting methods of medical treatment. Secondly, it would be an important factor in determining whether a State should exclude methods of medical treatment from patent protection. Thirdly, patenting medical procedures or drug therapies would have a negative impact on access to health care, limiting their availability to treat patients, therefore, directly impacting the right to health.

Intellectual property protection in the medical field is bound to raise questions concerning public health. The arguments are usually very emotive and divisive. Such was its importance that in 2001 the *Declaration on*

---

[23] See generally B.G. Alten, 'Left to One's Own Devices: Congress Limits Patents on Medical Procedures' (1998) 8 Fordham Intell. Prop. Media & Ent. LJ 837; S.L. Nichols, 'Hippocrates, the Patent-Holder: The Unenforceability of Medical Procedure Patents' (1997) 7 Geo. Mason L Rev 227; C.J. Katopis, 'Patients v. Patents?: Policy Implications of Recent Patent Legislation' (1997) 71 St. John's L Rev 329; W.W. Yang, 'Patent Policy and Medical Procedure Patents' (1995) 1 B U J Sci & Tech L 5; R.M. Portman, 'Legislative restriction on Medical and Surgical Procedure Patents Removes Impediments to Medical Progress' 4 (1996) U Balt Intell Prop LJ 91; S.D. Anderson, ' A Right Without a Remedy: The Unenforceable Medical Procedure Patent' (1999) 3 Marq Intell Prop L Rev 117; W.E. Havins, 'Immunising the Medical Practitioner "process" Infringer: Greasing the Squeaky wheel, Good Public Policy or What?' (1999) 77 Uni Det Mercy L Rev 51; W.B. Lafferty, 'Statutory and Ethical Barriers in the Patenting of Medical and Surgical Procedures' (1996) 29 J Marshall L Rev 891 and B.J. Meier, 'The New Patent Infringement Liability Exception for Medical Procedures' (1997) 23 J Leg 265.

[24] [1979] RPC 514.

[25] Ibid, at 540 (emphasis added).

[26] C.A. Maddren, 'AIDS Vaccines: Balancing Human Rights with Public Health' (2003) 17 Temp Int't & Comp LJ 277.

the TRIPs Agreements and Public Health was adopted by the World Trade Organisation.[27] It may be argued that this gave expression to the concept of a right to health which, inevitably, raises questions concerning the scope of the right and the content of the right itself.[28] I am not concerned here with delineating or considering the scope of the right to health argument but, rather, with examining it as another way of recasting the public health argument where the focus is on the individual right rather than on the collective goal of society. Although various versions of the 'right to health' claims exist, at a very basic level it includes a right to a decent minimum of health care.

In the United Kingdom, the right to health, in either its legal or moral formulation, should inform the enactment of legislation implementing Article 27(3) of the TRIPs Agreement.[29] A State that respects the rights of its citizens would take the right to health in consideration when deciding whether to exclude methods of medical treatment from patent protection. Article 27(3) of the TRIPs Agreement provides that states *may* exclude methods of medical treatment from patentability.[30] This is a curious formulation, since there is *no mandate* to exclude methods of medical treatment from patentability but simply a requirement – *a strong moral requirement* – that this should be so. A State that allows patent protection for methods of medical treatment would be fulfilling its obligations under the TRIPs Agreement but may not be respecting the right to health. If due consideration is given to the right, then patent protection would not be provided in the medical field unless the economic incentives are applicable. The United Kingdom, along with other European countries, has excluded methods of medical treatment from patent protection, which is in line with the requirement of Article 27(3) of the TRIPs Agreement.

Any argument based on the right to health would not support restrictions on the availability of medical procedures or drug therapies to patients. If patenting medical procedures leads to limited access to medical procedures/drug therapies, or very expensive ones (unless this reflects the cost of the procedure with a reasonable profit margin), it is arguable that the right to health would be infringed. The right to health would, therefore, be conflicting with the right of the patentee to exploit her invention. Alternatively, patent protection for methods of medical treatment may have

---

27 WT/MIN (01)/DEC/1, 20 November 2001.

28 A.E. Buchanan, 'The Right to Decent Minimum of Health Care' (1984) 13 Phil & Pub Aff 55.

29 P.L. Wojan, 'A Conflict of Rights: Intellectual Property under TRIPs, the Right to Health and AIDS Drugs' (2002) 6 UCLA J Int'l & Foreign Aff 463.

30 TRIPs Agreement, Article 27(3).

a positive impact on the right to health if it leads to the creation of more efficient and cost effective medical procedures or drug therapies.

Patents in the medical field, especially the biomedical and pharmaceutical research areas, have had enormous success in providing more effective drug treatments. The right to health would be implicated in the same manner irrespective of whether one is considering a method of medical treatment or drug therapy. Since the effect of patent protection is to limit the availability of the medical treatments, it would have negative consequences for public health and, consequently, the right to health would therefore be infringed. However, in the case of drug therapies the competing arguments of policy, in particular the economic arguments, may be, and seem to be, strong enough to counter any right to health argument. Therefore, it is arguable that the right to health is compatible with patents in the medical field since, without it, the much-needed incentives for inventing drug therapies would not exist. Indeed, facilitating medical treatments in this manner may be even more effective guarantee of the right to them. This, in turn, depends on where the balance lies between the public health arguments against patenting methods of medical treatment and the economic arguments for patenting methods of medical treatment (provided, of course, there is empirical evidence to support the case).

3 Access to Medical Procedures

(a) Methods of medical treatment

The patent grant creates a monopoly over the patented procedure which may restrict the availability of methods of medical treatment to other physicians to treat their patients. Access to medical procedures would be severely limited if patentees were to either set unreasonably high licensing fees for performing them or did not perform them themselves. It would be contrary to common sense if a patent on a method of treatment prevented a physician from using a particular procedure to save a patient's life. As Professor Cornish puts it:[31]

> The spectre of a single doctor reserving the performance of the most satisfactory, possibly life-saving, operation to his or her own team and extracting therefrom monopoly profits on the scale of a successful pop-star seemed to *put the matter beyond argument*.

That would be the one of the most potent arguments against patent protection for methods of medical treatment. It is at this juncture that the

---

[31] Cornish, Llewelyn and Aplin, *Intellectual Property*, pp. 237–38 (emphasis added).

arguments of the right to health activists find currency. It was, therefore, not surprising that in *Bristol-Myers Squibb Co v F H Faulding & Co. Ltd*[32] the Federal Court of Australia pointed out that:

> [p]erhaps the most powerful argument against patenting is the idea that a patient may be denied medical treatment that she needs. *It is certainly the most emotive of the arguments*. It presumes that a medical practitioner may be unable to obtain the right to use a particular process, or may not be able to do so within due time, and therefore will be unwilling to undertake the process on her patients for fear of legal action.[33]

Access to health care has a myriad of meanings. It has been argued that it means that an individual cannot legitimately be prevented from obtaining health care. This is effectively a negative freedom, meaning that the State, or other persons endowed by law with coercive powers, should not restrict access to health care by exploiting the patent system or through secrecy. However, this definition does not explain or allow one to determine who is to provide the necessary health care; neither does it dictate that the State or others should provide health care or distributable health care.[34] The question of access to health care is dependent on the choices available in society and whether the available services are affordable and may well lie outside of the factors considered in this chapter. The right to health, arguably, requires everyone to have equal access to all treatments that are reasonably available to anyone in society.[35]

Patent protection for a medical procedure means that if anyone uses it without paying they would be liable for patent infringement. There is the possibility that a licence may be negotiated between the patentee and the would-be user to procure the use of the procedure. Failing that, a compulsory licensing regime, if made available, should ensure that there is adequate access to the necessary medical procedures. Any unnecessary limitation on access to treatments that are necessary to save a patient's life is troubling. The limitation on access to methods of medical treatment is a real possibility if unqualified patent protection for methods of medical treatment is provided. It is not sufficient to counter argue, as Jacob J. has done, that where 'any such exception has gone, … no-one, so far as I know,

---

32 (2000) FCA 316.

33 Ibid, at [134] (emphasis added).

34 T.L. Beauchamp and J.F. Childress, *Principles of Biomedical Ethics* (5th edn, OUP, Oxford 2001), p. 244.

35 Ibid.

suggests that its removal has caused any trouble'.[36] Arming patentees with the potential for disrupting the medical profession and the health care system (if they were not to use or grant licences to use the medical procedures) does not find justification with an argument that acknowledges the possibility exists, but discounts it on the basis that it has not 'caused any trouble'.

The case against patent protection is even stronger when the method of treatment is an essential one[37] (needed to save the patient's life) or where there are no effective substitutes available to the patient. The definition of essential medicines accepted by the WHO is '*those that satisfy the priority health care needs of the population*, are intended to be available within the context of functioning health systems at all times in adequate amounts, in the appropriate dosage forms, with assured quality, and at a price the individual and the community can afford'.[38] This definition is very broad and recognises that: (a) public health is a vital consideration; (b) a good quality of health care should be provided; (c) medicines should be affordable; (d) there should be adequate access to medicines that satisfy the priority health care needs of the population; and (e) there should be an adequate supply of essential medicines.

(b) The question of control

It is arguable that the question of control is one of the pillars upon which the distinction between patent protection for pharmaceutical products and the lack thereof for methods of medical treatment rests. A pharmaceutical company ('Company A') is able to control the supply of the drug in that it may limit the supply to increase prices so that it can earn supernormal profits. This may not always happen for the following reasons: (a) there is the possibility that another company ('Company B') could produce generic drugs that would compete directly with Company A's drug. However, Company A may speculate and decide that it would not matter much in the long run because: (i) start-up costs for Company B may be high and serve as a deterrent to others like it operating in the market; and (ii) the goodwill that Company A may have developed and the brand may be strong enough to keep customers during the period in which Company B's product is on the market or after the expiration of the patent; (b) if Company A is not a

---

36 *Bristol-Myers Squibb v Baker Norton Inc.* [1999] RPC 253 (Pat Ct), at 274.

37 K.A. Friedgen, 'Rethinking the Struggle between Health and Intellectual Property: Proposed Framework for Dynamic rather than absolute Patent Protection of Essential Medicines' (2002) 16 EMORYILJ 689.

38 WHO Policy Perspective on Medicine, The Selection of Essential Medicines, WHO, Geneva, 2002 (emphasis added).

monopolist it would not risk limiting its supply in the market which may decrease its profits; and (c) a decrease in the market share may result if there is fierce competition therein.

Since the pharmaceutical industry is highly competitive it would not make economic sense to limit supply which may decrease profits and may result in a loss of market share. Company A may license its patent to other companies to produce the drug to ensure that it has or continues to have a market lead in the area. The manufacture by one company of a pharmaceutical drug would reach millions of people who are then able to purchase the drug at their pharmacy (provided, of course, they are able to afford it). However, supply to the patient is only limited insofar as there may be an inadequate supply of the drug on the market. The patentee/manufacturer cannot refuse the supply of the drug to any particular patient. Even if it refuses to grant a licence to another company, that would not necessarily mean that a decrease in the supply of the drug would result, because the patentee may well have the capacity to fulfil the needs of the market itself. As was stated by the Australian Federal Court, '[t]he support [in terms of the grants of patent protection for pharmaceutical products] may also be explained, in part at least by the fact that it is usually a commercial organisation rather than a physician that is the inventor of pharmaceuticals and surgical products'.[39]

In the case of methods of medical treatment, however, the dynamics of demand and supply, arguably, operate differently. There is no empirical evidence to support the following claims but they are not unreasonable assumptions given the nature of medical procedures. The physician/patentee would control the supply of the medical procedure, and it is arguable that without licensing the procedure to other physicians it may not be available to all those people who need it. She could either use the patented procedure herself or similarly license the procedure to other physicians. But the question of whether it would restrict supply would significantly depend on the demand for the treatment in question. Assuming, for present purposes, there is a high demand for a particular medical procedure, it is possible that: (a) the physician may not be able to meet that demand herself since she cannot be more than one place at any one time; or (b) licences provided to other physicians may solve the problem of access because a greater number of physicians would be able to carry out the medical procedure.

For example, with hysterectomy it is essential that it should be done by a gynaecologist with the necessary expertise and experience. A hysterectomy

[39] *Bristol-Myers Squibb* (2000) FCA 316, at [132].

is the removal of the uterus which results in a woman's inability to menstruate or have children.[40] Data from the US Centre for Disease Control and Prevention shows that annually over half a million hysterectomies are performed in the United States. This makes it the second most frequently performed major surgical procedure among reproductive-aged women in the United States.[41] Since there is a high demand for this surgical procedure, there exists a possibility that if one surgeon had a patent on the surgical treatment and did not license it to others, a serious crisis would ensue. Given the statistics above, it is clear that no surgeon would be able to satisfy the demand for the procedure and, therefore, the possibility for exploiting that monopoly is rife. The only effective way to ensure that the demand is met is to license the procedure to other physicians making it available to a greater number of women than would otherwise be the case.

If the physician/patentee decides not to license the procedure (or does not use it at all), or even refuses to license it to a particular physician, it is arguable that she effectively controls, even more intimately, the supply of the medical procedure to the public. It is this power to directly control supply of medical procedures that (arguably) lies at the heart of the issue of access to methods of medical treatment and has troubled legislatures and the courts. Professor Cornish put the issue rather succinctly when he stated '[t]he spectre of a single doctor reserving the performance of the most satisfactory, possibly life-saving, operation to his or her own team and extracting therefrom monopoly profits on the scale of a successful pop-star seemed to *put the matter beyond argument*'.[42] If patents for medical procedures were allowed it would need to be supplemented with a regime that effectively accommodates this issue of access and control.

4 Increased Costs of Health Care

Licence fees paid for using medical procedures would be an additional cost to the already high costs of health care. Research and development of some methods of medical treatment may be costly and the price of the service may simply reflect this. However, when such costs are low, the prices that one may have to pay for a medical procedure may be artificially inflated. Without any empirical data to determine the actual costs involved in creating a method of medical treatment, the argument concerning

---

40 Hysterectomy, http://www.health-news-and-information.com/4civista/libv/w14.shtml (accessed 18 April 2011).

41 Ibid.

42 Cornish, Llewelyn and Aplin, *Intellectual Property*, pp. 237–38 (emphasis added).

increased costs is mere conjecture. This argument does, however, appreciate that patentees may inflate the costs of the particular patent to earn supernormal profits. If the increases are not exorbitant, and simply reflect the market value of the improvement, the argument lacks potency.

The government may subsidise the cost of providing medical treatments to make them more affordable and, therefore, accessible to the public.[43] But it is not the function of the marketplace to subsidise goods and services to the public; rather, it is done through governmental policy and initiatives. There are, however, other factors that contribute to the increase in the costs of health care and are not necessarily criticised, namely, insurance costs and the costs of medicine.[44] This is not intended to be a counter argument but, simply, to put the debate in an appropriate context showing that, in some areas, there is little debate where the consequences for public health are the same.

If patients or other physicians are not charged unreasonable prices or high licence fees for using medical procedure patents by patentee-physicians then the argument concerning increased costs would be surmountable. The increase in the costs of medical treatments may restrict access to affordable health care. This occurs when the patent holder charges exorbitant prices for licensing the treatment or where she refuses to license the treatment to other physicians. If the costs of some treatments are prohibitive it would have an overall impact on the quality of public health.

5 Compulsory Licences

(a) Introduction

Compulsory licensing is defined as the practice of governments to compel the transfer, from a patent holder to a third party, of some or all of the patent holder's right to produce a patented product or use a patented process.[45] The different reasons why compulsory licences are employed include: (i) where a dependent patent is being blocked by a patent holder; (ii) where an invention is not being worked by the patentee; and (iii) where there are public interest considerations. The question of whether compulsory licences should be granted in any field is a question of policy, which is best decided by the policy-makers, that is the legislature. Professor Cornish

---

43 For example, the UK National Health Service.

44 D.S. Lee, 'Pharmaceutical Manufacturers: Players or Pariah in Health care reform?' (1993) 3 Kan J L & Pub Pol'y 89.

45 M. Halewood, 'Regulating Patent Holders: Local Working Requirements and Compulsory Licences at International Law' (1997) 35 Osgoode Hall LJ 243, 260.

noted '[i]f there were to ever be a change, there would be a strong case for subjecting methods of medical treatment to compulsory licensing'.[46] It is arguable that one of the ways to counter the potential negative consequences of granting patents on methods of medical treatment is to impose a system of compulsory licensing.

Intellectual property rights, including patent rights, confer on the owner an exclusive right to its creation[47] and cover the commercial value inherent in the application of ideas and information.[48] Expressed differently, intellectual property rights regulate the creation, use and exploitation of mental or creative labour.[49] Compulsory licences, therefore, mitigate the negative consequences inherent in the patent monopoly.[50] The use of compulsory licences is coercive and Professor Cornish rightly noted that they '*prevent* the patentee from acting as sole producer'.[51] Since patents for methods of medical treatments raise important questions of public health, especially concerning the question of access to medical procedures including significantly life-saving medical treatments, the case for compulsory licensing is *a fortiori*.

(b) The 1977 Act

The 1977 Act provides for the grant of compulsory licences.[52] A person is entitled to apply for a compulsory licence after the expiration of three years from the date of the patent grant.[53] This is an effective limitation on the usefulness of the compulsory licences under the 1977 Act for methods of medical treatment. If there were an urgent need to use the patent in question, the time limit would render its application to medical procedures meaningless. It may well be suitable for other kinds of inventions where the limitations on the use of a patent may not have such dire consequences for the individual.

A person may apply, on one or more of the relevant grounds, to the comptroller for a licence[54] or for an entry to the register enabling licences

---

46 Cornish, Llewelyn and Aplin, *Intellectual Property*, p. 243.

47 F.-K. Beier, 'Exclusive Rights, Statutory Licences and Compulsory Licences in Patent and Utility Model Law' (1999) 30 IIC 251.

48 Cornish, Llewelyn and Aplin, *Intellectual Property*, p. 6.

49 Bently and Sherman, *Intellectual Property Law*, p.1.

50 TRIPs Agreement, Article 30.

51 Cornish, Llewelyn and Aplin, *Intellectual Property*, p. 317.

52 Section 48 of the 1977 Act.

53 Section 48(1) of the 1977 Act.

54 Section 48(1)(a) of the 1977 Act.

under the patent to be available as of right.[55] If the applicant satisfies the relevant grounds for the grant of the patent, the comptroller may grant the licence on such terms that she thinks fit.[56] The relevant grounds that would enable the comptroller to exercise her discretion under s. 48(4)(a)–(c) of the 1977 Act are outlined in s. 48(3) of the 1977 Act and include: (a) when the patentee is not working the invention;[57] and/or (b) has imposed unreasonable terms on the grant of licenses;[58] and/or (c) has made any unreasonable conditions.[59]

(c) Compulsory licences and public health

It would be remiss of legislatures if they did not provide the necessary safeguards against the potential abuses and unintended effects of the patent system.[60] It has been stated that the patent monopoly should 'be carefully limited to resolving only the identified market failure and the resulting distortion of incentives to desirable innovation which justifies its existence'.[61] The supply of affordable medical healthcare is essential if a decent standard of public health is to be preserved. If, as argued above, the most vexed issue is the possibility that a physician/patentee may limit access to medical treatments, it seems sensible, in the interests of public health, that compulsory licences should be used to ensure that patients have access to life-saving treatments[62] and affordable medical procedures. When the procedure is necessary to save a patient's life the case is *a fortiori*.[63] One cannot but agree with Davison C.J., at first instance, in the New Zealand case of *Wellcome Foundation v Commissioner of Patents*,[64] where he stated that:

> '[t]he law permits the granting of a patent for a drug. The inventor has his rights to it protected and it can be employed in medical treatments only if made

---

[55] Section 48(1)(b) of the 1977 Act: A Governmental department may also apply for a compulsory licence under the Act: s 48(1)(c) of the 1977 Act.

[56] Section 48(2)(a) of the 1977 Act.

[57] Section 48(3)(a) of the 1977 Act.

[58] Section 48(3)(d) of the 1977 Act.

[59] Section 48(3)(e) of the 1977 Act.

[60] F.-K. Beier, 'Exclusive Rights, Statutory Licenses and Compulsory Licenses in Patent and Utility Model Law' (1999) 30 IIC 251.

[61] V. Chiapetta, 'Defining the Proper Scope of Internet Patents: If We Don't Know Where We Want to Go, We're Unlikely to Get There' (2001) Mich Telecomm Tech L Rev 289.

[62] Compulsory licences would allay the fears of Sheppard J. in *Anaesthetic Supplies v Rescare* (1994) FCR 1 (HCA) where is stated that the denial of a patent of a method of medical treatment 'might mean death or unnecessary suffering of countless people' (at p. 41).

[63] *Roussel-Uclaf v GD Searle and Co Ltd* [1977] FSR 125.

[64] [1979] 2 NZLR 591.

> available to the medical profession by reason of licensing or compulsory licensing. *If a process for a medical treatment is invented can that not be licensed in the same way and cannot the legislature amend the statute if it is thought desirable to do so?* Is any member of the public going to be deprived of the treatment more than he might be deprived of a drug under existing law?'[65]

The response would not be a straightforward yes, but, as argued below, one that inevitably would have to take into account the economic effects of compulsory licensing in the area of public health before a final answer could be provided.

The use of compulsory licensing has been accepted as the best possible way to deal with the issue of medical procedure patents.[66] Professor Cornish rightly observed that 'if there were to ever be a change, there would be a *strong case* for subjecting methods of medical treatment to compulsory licensing'.[67] The same view was echoed, albeit indirectly, by Davison C.J. in *Wellcome Foundation v Commissioner of Patents*[68] where he stated that '[i]f a process for medical treatment is invented can that not be patented in the same way and cannot the legislature amend the statute *to provide for compulsory licences* if it is thought desirable to do so?'[69] However, compulsory licences would not solve all the issues that may arise with patents for methods of medical treatment.[70] The grant of compulsory licences for methods of medical treatment is based on the acceptance that there are particular methods of treatment that should be available for public use, taking into account particular health considerations.[71] A compulsory licence should be granted when the method of medical treatment has no equally efficacious substitutes and the medical procedure is needed to save a patient's life. The use of compulsory licences, however, is arguably the most sensible option to deal with the question of access to methods of medical treatment.

---

65 Ibid, at 620 (emphasis added).

66 G.F. Burch, 'Ethical Consideration in the Patenting of Medical Processes' (1987) 65 Tex L Rev 1139, 1166.

67 Cornish, Llewelyn and Aplin, *Intellectual Property*, p. 243 (emphasis added).

68 [1979] 2 NZLR 591 (NZSC).

69 Ibid, at 620 (emphasis added).

70 W.W. Yang, 'Patent Policy and Medical Procedure Patents' (1995) 1 B U J Sci & Tech L 5, 68 (observing that licensing only solves the enforcement and accessibility problems and does not address the related issues of distortion of the rational norms of research and adverse effects on the physician-patient relationships).

71 T. Cook, C. Doyle and D. Jabbari, *Pharmaceuticals, Biotechnology & the Law* (Macmillan Publishers Ltd 1991).

(d) Limitations

The use of compulsory licensing for any public interest objective is bound to provoke considerable hostility from the affected industry. The aim of compulsory licensing is usually to ensure that there is an adequate supply of the patented product or method. As the argument runs, compulsory licensing is diametrically opposed to incentives of the patent system to further innovation and invention.[72] At first blush, the argument seems plausible but, on a closer analysis, it does not withstand scrutiny. Compulsory licences derogate from the patent grant and would only be granted in exceptional circumstances if there is a sufficiently strong public interest rationale. Similarly, the argument does not consider the role of the comptroller in determining the fair and reasonable price that should be paid for the patent in question. It is accepted that, if the issue relates to the cost of using the patented medical procedure, the comptroller would have to determine what the reasonable price is.[73]

The implementation of a compulsory licensing regime would mean that patients or medical practitioners would have to seek approval from the courts or licensing tribunal to force the patentee to grant a licence on specific terms. Therefore, the costs of applying for a licence and the time within which the applicant, if successful, receives the licence would be relevant considerations in determining whether a compulsory licensing regime would be effective in alleviating the concerns relating to access to medical procedures. The position would differ according to the applicant and the urgency of the medical treatment needed. The physician or medical authority would *not* usually seek the licence at the latest possible time. The possibility that the applicant may use the invention and pay the cost *ex post* reduces the risk of high initial transaction costs. However, this is not a usual feature of compulsory licensing provisions. Determining whether the physician has used the patented procedure would be a difficult task in most cases since patient files are confidential. Compulsory licensing, it may be argued, attempts to achieve a socially optimal level of patent protection by creating a balance between providing effective access to patented methods of medical treatments and the incentives of the patent system.

However, the transaction costs associated with applying for a compulsory licence should be minimal to ensure greater access to the relevant medical procedure. If applicants are unable to use the courts due to prohibitive costs then the purpose of having a compulsory licensing regime

---

[72] A.M. Fisch, 'Compulsory Licensing of Pharmaceutical Patents; An Unreasonable Solution to an Unfortunate Problem' 34 (1994) Jurimetrics J 295, 303.

[73] See generally P. Tandon, 'Optimal Patents with Compulsory Licenses' (1982) 90 J of Pol Econ 470, 471.

would be defeated. Whether compulsory licensing in the medical field actually provides the necessary socially beneficial optimal level of patent protection generally, or specifically with regard to medical procedure patents, is a question that cannot be answered without empirical evidence pointing one way or the other. Similarly, the transaction costs involved with compulsory licensing need to be evidenced to show that they are low and do not place an additional burden on the applicant. These issues of economics and policy are, however, beyond the scope of this book.

D PHYSICIAN LIBERTY AND AUTONOMY

The grant of the patent restricts the actions of others unless they seek a licence to use the patented subject matter. Patents on methods of medical treatment would directly affect the actions of physicians since they usually perform medical procedures. As Palmer puts it, '[the] intellectual property right is a claim of a right over how another person uses her body'.[74] The same issue does not arise in the context of patents for drug therapies since the actions of the physician are not *directly* limited by patenting pharmaceuticals. The patent creates a monopoly over the supply and the creation of drug therapies but they are not directly inaccessible to patients except when they have prohibitive prices. If the patient is able to afford the drug, she may be able to purchase it at numerous pharmacies. However, the actions of medical practitioners are, arguably, directly limited when medical treatments or treatment regimes are patented. The physician who wants to use the patented procedure will not be able to use it without infringing the patent. However, the physician may license the patented medical treatment from the owner so that she would not infringe. It is when this licence is not forthcoming, or the unavailability of any form of compulsory licences, that the limitation becomes an issue. Although both drug therapies and medical procedures are both methods of medical treatment, they do not necessarily invoke the same arguments in respect of patent protection.

Since the physician may not be able to use a particular method of medical treatment, patient care and public health would inevitably suffer. The same argument could be made for patenting pharmaceuticals as this, also, may conceivably affect public health insofar as the much-needed drug therapies would be beyond the reach of many patients because of prohibitive prices. However, it may be argued that this could be offset by the R&D

---

[74] T. Palmer, 'Are Patents and Copyright Morally Justified? The Philosophy of Property Rights and Ideal Subjects' in A. D. Moore (ed.), *Information Ethics: Privacy, Property, and Power* (Seattle, University of Washington Press 2005), p. 131.

that is generated and, in the long run, the creation and availability of new drug therapies that are more efficient and cost effective. Inextricably linked to the limitation on the treatments available for use on patients are the restrictions placed on the autonomy of the physician who is bound to act in the best interests of the patient. In other words, there would be limitations on the availability of medical procedures used by physicians because patents would place restrictions on what treatments physicians can perform without infringing the medical procedure patent. These considerations affect the physician's judgement as to the appropriate treatment required for the patient.[75] Since the physician cannot use the procedure without infringing (and is in the long run unable to get a licence for the procedure) he would not be acting in the best interests of the patient if a potentially more efficient and effective procedure is not used. A solution to this would be to make an application for a licence to use the procedure from the patentee but, when this licence is refused, it is then that the full impact of patent protection of medical procedures is appreciated.

However, there may be other limitations on the actions of physicians when they treat their patients. The other factors which exist that may also affect the judgement of the physician include: (a) the terms of the physician's contract with an employer hospital;[76] (b) clauses in a patient's insurance policy;[77] (c) the role of informed consent;[78] and (d) the question of capacity.[79] Whether medical procedure patents would be more intrusive on the personal autonomy of the physician than the intrusions mentioned above is an important question to be answered.[80] There does not seem to be any basis to suggest that the limitations which may be placed on the actions of physicians as a result of medical procedure patents are more intrusive than those mentioned above. The inability to treat a patient who, for example, does not have insurance or is a minor is, arguably, no different in effect from the limitations which may result if medical procedures are patented even if different principles underlie each of them.

It is, therefore, not productive to make an in-depth comparison between the various limitations. Proper patient care demands that the physician

---

75 G.F. Burch, 'Ethical Considerations in the Patenting of Medical Processes' (1987) 65 Tex Law Rev 1139, 1152.

76 *Adler v Montefiore Hospital Association* (1973) 453 Pa 60, 75.

77 *Zuckerberg v Blue Cross and Blue Shield* 487 NYS 2d 595 (CC DNY 1985) 598.

78 *Schloendorff v Society of New York Hospital* 105 NE 92 (1914).

79 *Gillick v West Norfolk and Wisbech Area Health Authority* [1986] AC 112 (HL).

80 G.F. Burch, 'Ethical Considerations in the Patenting of Medical Processes' (1987) 65 Tex Law Rev 1139, 1154.

should be allowed the full measure of authority in determining what lawful treatment the patient should receive. Therefore, no major limitations should be placed on the physician's efforts to find the best possible lawful treatment for her patient. It seems evident that the liberty/autonomy of the physician is not directly limited when patents are granted for drug therapies. The physician is still able to prescribe appropriate drugs for her patient although, in such a case, her role is limited to just that. However, when one is dealing with methods of medical treatment her *actions* are limited, because she cannot treat her patient without infringing the patented procedure unless she seeks a licence to perform it.

E PHYSICIAN/PATIENT RELATIONSHIP

The physician is bound to act in the best interests of the patient and must use 'that method of treatment which according to [her] ability and judgment, [she] consider for the *benefit* of [the] patient and abstain from whatever is harmful or mischievous'.[81] Similarly, any research carried out on patients must be with their valid informed consent based on the 'understanding that research must have as its purpose the furtherance of the health of that individual', and that she will act 'for the benefit of the sick and will abstain from every voluntary act of mischief or corruption'.[82]

When patentees or licensees use the patented or licensed medical procedures to the exclusion of more efficient or equivalent cheaper alternatives, there is the possibility that they could be in breach of their fiduciary duties to the patient. The costs of performing the medical procedure will be borne by the patient irrespective of whether: (a) it is covered by a licence or (b) the physicians own the patented procedure. In both cases, they have a vested economic interest in using that medical procedure so that they can recover the costs of purchasing the licence or the R&D costs of the patent. The intuitive view that the economic interest of a physician/patentee in the patent necessarily implies a conflict of interest needs to be jettisoned. Such conflict only arises when this economic interest clouds her judgement concerning what is the best lawful treatment for her patient. The use of a less efficient and less effective procedure (whether patented or licensed), to the exclusion of another, will create a conflict of interest and result in an overall decrease in the quality of health care provided to patients. When the physician is aware that alternative lawful procedures exist she should be

---

[81] Hippocratic Oath (current version).

[82] Ibid.

bound to use them if they are more efficient and would lead to greater benefits to the patients. This avoids any breach of her fiduciary duty to her patient. Whether she owns a patent on the procedure or had licensed it would matter little because of the overriding consideration to act in the best interests of the patient.

There are other factors that could also affect a physician's choice of treatments including: (a) the policy of the physician's employer if she is an employee; and (b) inadequate training or experience with the new procedure. Similarly, a physician may simply have a personal preference for a particular method, which would operate outside the scope of the conflict-of-interest considerations. This may be the result of years of using a particular procedure and/or simply a distrust of the new procedure.

F THE HIPPOCRATIC OATH/SHARING NORM

1 Code of Ethics

Since the 5th Century BC, the Hippocratic Oath has been the foundation of medical practice throughout western civilization.[83] The original version mandated that physicians should 'impart [the] knowledge of the Art to … to disciples bound by a stipulation and oath according the law of medicine'.[84] The modern version of the oath is in similar terms but also imposes an obligation on physicians to 'continue with diligence to keep abreast of advances in medicine'.[85] It states that the physician should respect the hard-won scientific gains of those other physicians and gladly share new knowledge with others as it is as much his as it is the next generation of physicians.[86] This long-established tradition has found its way to the various codes of medical ethics in the United States and the United Kingdom. A more comprehensive mandate is provided in the American Medical Association (AMA) Code of Medical Ethics.[87] This reflects the medical profession's adherence to the sharing norm.

This view was reiterated by the AMA's code of ethics which accepted that the role of the physician was 'that of a teacher who imparts knowledge to

---

[83] See, generally, R. Porter, *The Greatest Benefit to Mankind: A Medical History of Humanity from Antiquity to the Present* (HarperCollins Publishers 1997).

[84] Hippocratic Oath (classical version).

[85] Hippocratic Oath (modern version) (Written in 1964 by Louis Lasagna, Academic Dean of the School of Medicine at Tufts University).

[86] Ibid.

[87] 'A physician shall make relevant information available to patients, colleagues, and the public, obtain consultation, and use the talents of other health professionals when indicated': Principles of Medical Ethics, Para. V, 2001.

colleagues'.[88] It placed much emphasis on the obligation of physicians to share knowledge and skills and to report the result of clinical and laboratory research to the rest of the medical profession.[89] This approach, the code continued, 'enhances patient care and leads to early evaluation and dissemination of new techniques'.[90] It strongly condemns the intentional withholding of new medical knowledge, skills, and techniques from colleagues for reasons of personal gain.[91] It proclaimed that the 'essential elements in the foundation of good medical care includes the prompt presentation before scientific organizations and timely publication of clinical and laboratory research in scientific journals'.[92] These can be seen as strong arguments against the patenting of methods of medical treatment because they would be contrary to the tenets of the medical profession as expressed in the various codes of medical ethics. The AMA has specifically pointed out that the patenting of medical treatments would undermine the coherence of the profession[93] since the patent system, with its emphasis on individual reward and ownership, is diametrically opposed to the principles on which the medical profession rests.[94] The World Medical Association International Code of Medical Ethics also emphasised that physicians shall not permit motives of profit to influence their free and independent exercise of professional judgement on behalf of patients.[95]

2 Sharing Norm

The traditional norms of scientific and medical research have been eroding over the years as the gains from the patent system have eclipsed the once sacred norms of the scientific and medical community.[96] The sharing norm can be conceived as the dissemination of techniques or best practices in the

---

[88] AMA's Code of Medical Ethics, Opinion 9.08.

[89] AMA's Code of Medical Ethics, E-9.08 New Medical Procedures (I).

[90] Ibid, (II).

[91] Ibid, (III).

[92] Ibid, (IV).

[93] American Medical Association, Council on Ethical and Judicial Affairs, 'Ethical Issues in the Patenting of Medical Procedures' 53 Food & Drug LJ 341, 342.

[94] Ibid.

[95] World Association International Code of Medical Ethics, Adopted by the 3rd General Assembly of the World Medical Association, London, England, October 1949 and amended by the 22nd World Medical Assembly Sydney, Australia, August 1968 and the 35th World Medical Assembly Venice, Italy, October 1983. Physicians must also abide by the Declaration of Geneva (1949).

[96] R.S. Eisenberg, 'Proprietary Rights and the Norms of Science in Biotechnology Research' (1987) 97 Yale LJ 177.

medical profession or the sharing of scientific and technical knowledge in the scientific community. In both cases, the obligation is to share the knowledge and information in the individual's field of expertise so that there can be a greater dissemination of information for the public benefit. The notion of 'open science'[97] is under constant pressure and the challenge is to maintain an appropriate balance so that the sharing norm is not rendered obsolete. The sharing norm in the medical profession is expressed as part of the Hippocratic Oath which governs the actions of physicians.

3 Methods of Medical Treatment

In the academic and medical community, there is a tradition of sharing knowledge and information. Patents for methods of medical treatment would be outside the scope of peer reviews as other physicians would not be able to access the information without having to first pay the licensing fee.[98] It is common practice for employees to own the inventions that they create using their individual labour and inventive effort.[99] However, of all existing professionals, the medical profession's members are the only ones limited by the Hippocratic Oath and its constituent fiduciary duties that bind them to act solely in the interests of their patients. Patent protection for methods of medical of treatment would be diametrically opposed to the time honoured tenets of the medical profession as expressed in the various codes of medical ethics. The medical practitioner, like any other, would have the same professional incentives to perform her duty. The physician is not duty bound to invent any medical procedure that may benefit her patients, but, when she creates a medical procedure she must, acting consistently with the code of medical ethics, use it for their benefit and share it with colleagues, but not patent it. The relevant issues were succinctly summarised by the Federal Court of Australia in *Bristol-Myers Squibb Co v F H Faulding & Co. Ltd*[100] when it was stated that:[101]

---

97 *Keeping Science Open: The Effects of Intellectual Property Policy on the Conduct of Science* Royal Society's Report 2003.

98 The US Food and Drug Administration regulate drugs and medical devices and ensure that the quality and safety standards are maintained. However, this quality assurance is not available to patented procedures. If the invention meets the statutory requirements of patentability it would be protected, but the patent grant does not guarantee the quality and safety of any new procedure.

99 Sections 39–41 of the 1977 Act and W.R. Cornish, 'Rights in Employee Inventions: The UK Position' (1990] 21 IIC 290.

100 (2000) FCA 316.

101 Ibid, at [135].

> It is also said that the traditional commitment of medical practitioners to develop, share and disseminate new knowledge will be repressed. That is to say, the medical practitioner who is seeking to discover a new medical or surgical process will deliberately withhold new medical knowledge from her colleagues so as to protect her discovery and enhance her ability to obtain patent protection for financial reward. Another aspect of this argument is the potential conflict of interest which could arise when a medical practitioner has an economic interest in a patent: a conflict that might result in the practitioner not acting in the best interests of her patient. A further aspect of this argument is the suggestion that the existence of a patent is a disincentive to further invention.

Since the Hippocratic Oath is specific to the medical profession the duties it imposes do not affect patent protection for drug therapies because pharmaceutical companies create and patent them. However, since they involve intensive scientific research, they may similarly impact on the sharing norm of the scientific community. The sharing norm of the medical profession has some similar characteristics to the traditional view of the norms of science. Professor Eisenberg, in her influential article,[102] argued that universities, where much research is conducted, did not seek patents on inventions because it was thought contrary to scientific norms to claim exclusive rights to research discoveries.[103] The patent system, she argued, distorts the traditional norms of research which derive from the belief that new discoveries should be made available to the scientific community, *a fortiori*, when it is necessary to save a patient's life.[104] The reward for the sharing/disclosing of information, she argued, is professional recognition by the scientific community which fuels a race to be the first to publish scientific discoveries and facilitates and ensures that the claims are validated and verified by the scientific community.[105]

Sheppard J., dissenting, in *Anaesthetic Supplies v Rescare*,[106] accepted a similar view of the sharing norm.[107] Medical colleges and most professions, he accepted, involve research and teaching and their members have a willingness to share information about new discoveries and new methods of medical treatment. Irrespective of the nature of the treatment, 'members of the medical profession and those associated with them learn as they go

---

[102] R.S. Eisenberg, 'Proprietary Rights and the Norms of Science in Biotechnology Research' (1987) 97 Yale LJ 177.

[103] Ibid, at 183.

[104] Ibid.

[105] Ibid.

[106] (1994) FCR 1 (FCA).

[107] Ibid, at 40–41.

along and thus develop and improve the quality of medical treatment in the community'.[108] As Sheppard J. puts it:[109]

> Commonly, important research or discoveries become the subject of learned papers or articles or even text books which are public throughout the medical world. *In this way there is wide dissemination of knowledge*. This occurs when doctors, as they commonly do travel from one country to another to attend conferences or witness methods of medical treatment of patients in their own countries. Not infrequently knowledge is disseminated to medical practitioners in countries less fortunate than our own. These are sometimes visited by doctors so that they may teach local practitioners about these matters and many others.

It is, therefore, of paramount importance to the medical profession that knowledge be disseminated to a wide audience. This is seen as the best way to ensure that the majority of physicians are able to know of, and therefore use, new and improved medical procedures to treat their patients.

However, patenting methods of medical treatment may not lead to a *total* erosion of the 'sharing norm'.[110] The disclosure requirement in patent law means that there will be full disclosure of the invention to the public. This publication in patent law is achieved when the application is filed which, in the United Kingdom, is done as early as possible so that the applicant can establish title and priority. Subject to the right of research found in s. 60 of the 1977 Act, the disclosure in the patent specification, although available to the public, cannot be used without a licence from the patentee. However, this general restriction only lasts 20 years when the patent expires and the information enters the public domain and can then be used by anyone. In a report, *Keeping Science Open* 2003, it was emphasised that '[t]he evidence received during our study indicates that patenting rarely delays publication significantly'.[111] Therefore, the argument that publication in a medical journal is more effective than disclosure in the patent specification will withstand scrutiny only if it can be proven that publication in a journal reaches a greater number of physicians and other persons in the medical profession. In any event, the patentee may still publish the details about the procedure in a medical journal after she has received the patent. Some form of disclosure is certainly better than none.

---

108 Ibid, at 41.

109 Ibid (emphasis added).

110 W.D. Noonan, 'Patenting Medical and Surgical Procedures' (1995) 77 J Pat and Trademark Off Soc'y 651.

111 *Keeping Science Open* 2003 (v).

4 Conclusion

The rationale for the various medical codes of ethics is based on the thinking that patent protection of methods of medical treatment contradicts the sharing norm that ensures the free dissemination of information within the medical community. However, it may be argued that the disclosure requirement of the patent system assists in allaying the fears of those who argue that it erodes the sharing norm. The medical profession finds itself in a unique position because it forms part of the scientific community where innovation is encouraged, but, it also specifically imposes a code of ethics on its members prohibiting them from patenting medical procedures. It differs from other research-based professions because its members are also bound by fiduciary duties to their patients which limit their actions. The norms of the medical profession, as expressed in the Hippocratic Oath and other medical codes of ethics, mandate that physicians share medical knowledge for the benefit of their patients and not for personal gain.

G OTHER INCENTIVE STRUCTURES

It has been argued that the existence of other incentive structures in the medical profession means that there is no need for them to be supplemented by the economic incentives of the patent system. The reward structure inherent in the medical profession includes the recognition provided thorough tenure, publication in medical journals, and grants for further research. In the *Discussion Document* of the New Zealand Parliament it was stated that:[112]

> In any case, financial rewards may not be the only incentives to innovation in the field of medical treatment, particularly where the innovator is a doctor or other medical practitioner. Rewards such as prestige, peer recognition, and respect by society may be other drivers of innovation. Some doctors may be motivated to develop new medical treatments by the need to improve the health or quality of life of their patients rather than by any desire for personal advancement.

It also has been argued that the exclusion of patents for methods of medical treatment is 'like professional individual skills that are, or should not be

---

[112] *Review of the Patents Act 1953: Boundaries to Patentability* March 2002, para. 229.

"susceptible of industrial application" '.[113] Professional skills, it may be argued, are no different from the other skills inherent in business method patents[114] or sports moves.[115] The only difference is that they operate in different spheres. If there were to be an argument for rejecting methods of medical treatment it cannot be that they are unpatentable subject matter. That notion has long since been rejected as is implicit in the reformulation of the exclusion by the European Patent Convention (EPC) 2000.

Professor Vaver observed that '[p]rofessionals, moreover, do not need the spur of the patent to do the best for their client; professional codes of conduct require that of them in any event. Nor should they be prevented by a patent from acting in the best interests of the client or patient – particularly when life-saving surgery is being undertaken'.[116] This statement is important since it implies that individuals in any profession, especially the medical one, should not be able to patent their services. Moreover, the view that such professionals do not need the incentives of the patent system to act in the best interest of the patient, because their codes of conduct already require that of them, accommodates the argument that alternative incentive structures may work together to stimulate invention.

Similarly, Hettinger pointed out that the alternative incentives to the patent system that are available to professionals include 'fees, awards, acknowledgement, gratitude, praise, security, power, status and public financial support'.[117] In 1999, the WMA accepted a policy statement condemning the practice of patenting medical procedures that outlined the existing incentives that are available to physicians, particularly those who work in research institutions. These include professional reputation, professional advancement and ethical and legal obligations to provide competent medical care.[118] The policy statement made it clear that physicians were already paid for these activities, and that public funding is available for

---

[113] D. Vaver, 'Defining and rewarding invention: a review and a modest proposal for patent law' in Mirfin and Smith (eds) *Essays for Colin Tapper* (Butterworths London 2003).

[114] M. Spence and M. Molineaux, *The First Mover Monopoly: A Study on Patenting Business Methods in Europe* (Olswang and Oxford Intellectual Property Research Centre, Oxford University 2001).

[115] J.A. Smith, 'It's your move – No its not! The Application of Patent Law to Sports Moves' (1999) U of Colorado Law Review 1051.

[116] D. Vaver, 'Defining and rewarding invention: a review and a modest proposal for patent law' in Mirfin and Smith (eds) *Essays for Colin Tapper* (Butterworths, London 2003).

[117] E.C. Hettinger, 'Justifying Intellectual Property' (1989) 18 Philosophy and Public Affairs 31, 41.

[118] International Code of Medical Ethics, 17.A.

medical research which covers the cost of clinical trials and other regulatory costs.[119] These incentives, it has been stated, are sufficient to ensure that methods of medical treatment are discovered or invented, and, therefore, the incentives of the patent system are not necessary to induce invention.

It has also been argued that since methods of medical treatment are part of the liberal arts, and as professionals, physicians already benefit from state-granted monopoly to practise their skills, so they should not seek to enclose their skills through monopoly or other means, but should rather share them as widely as possible for the public benefit.[120] This is correct because only registered medical practitioners are legally able to practise medicine in the United Kingdom. To allow them to patent their procedures would be to confer a second monopoly over the skill that they have, which should be used for the benefit of the public.

H BREACH OF PATIENT'S PRIVACY

Another concern arising from the grant of patents for methods of medical treatment is that the enforcement of patent rights will have the adverse effect of encroaching on the privacy of patients.[121] In order to prove infringement, the claimant would have to search through the private and confidential files of patients which do not arise during infringement proceedings for patents of drug therapies.[122]

The right to privacy has been judicially recognised in the United States,[123] but the UK courts have been hesitant to develop such a right, despite the enactment of the Human Rights Act 1998.[124] The right to privacy is an integral part of the physician/patient relationship. It is one of

---

119 Ibid.

120 D. Vaver, 'Defining and rewarding invention: a review and a modest proposal for patent law' in Mirfin and Smith (eds) *Essays for Colin Tapper* (Butterworths, London 2003), p. 186.

121 J.A. Taylor, 'Medical Process Patents and Patient Privacy Rights' (1995) 14 J Marshall J Computer & Info L 131.

122 The nature of the product does not involve any use of patient files, since patients are used for clinical trials for pharmaceutical products, but their use does not raise the same issues as the enforcement of medical procedure patents. In any event, this is less likely to happen since the 1977 Act contains s. 60, which excludes acts that are done 'privately and for purposes that are not commercial' (s. 60(5)(a)) and those that are 'done for experimental purposes relating to the subject-matter of that invention' from liability for infringement (s. 60(5)(b)).

123 *Roe v Wade* 410 U.S. 113 (1973).

124 *Douglas v. Hello! Ltd* [2001] Q.B. 967 (CA).

strict confidence because 'the doctor is under a duty not to disclose, without the consent of the patient, information which he, the doctor has gained in his professional capacity'.[125] There is a distinction however, between the confidence required of the physician and that required generally. The confidential nature of the relationship is required to ensure that trust is maintained between the physician and her patient. Without this trust, the patient will not be able to communicate effectively with the physician. The physician is bound to respect the patient's privacy based on the patient's right to be immune from incursions into her personal life which means that, unless there is an overriding public policy objective, or she is required by law to do so, the information that she shares with the physician should only be used for the purposes of her treatment.

To the extent that disclosure of a patient's treatment is necessary to prove patent infringement, patent protection of methods of medical treatment would breach the patient's right to privacy. It does not seem correct to argue that the existence of other 'invasions' on the patient's medical records should provide support to the argument that *such* a breach should be tolerated for the purposes of enforcement of patent rights.[126] Limitations on the right of patient privacy should only be allowed where there is a justifiable reason for it. If patient privacy is not guaranteed in the physician/ patient relationship its very foundation would be severely compromised and the essence of the relationship would be eroded.

I CONCLUSION

The arguments that are made against patent protection considered in this chapter included (a) public health implications; (b) physician liberty and autonomy; (c) physician/patient relationship; (d) the Hippocratic Oath/ sharing norm; (e) other incentive structures; and (f) breach of patient's privacy. These are crucial factors that need to be considered when the question of patenting methods of medical treatment is considered. Some of these arguments may also be made against patenting drug therapies. Many of the arguments considered relate to the impact of medical procedure patents on society and the question of whether they should prevail in the debate cannot be answered without regard to empirical evidence of the impact that they would have on society. It has been suggested that the reason why patent protection is not available for medical procedures when

---

125 *Hunter v Mann* [1974] QB 767, 772.

126 G.F. Burch, 'Ethical Considerations in the Patenting of Medical Processes' (1987) 65 Tex Law Rev 1139, 1155.

it is available for drug therapies revolves primarily around the question of control over the supply of the medical procedure. Where the patentee does not license the procedure, it is arguable that a compulsory licensing regime would resolve the issue of access to such procedures. However, given the economic uncertainty of implementing that regime, only a more in-depth study would provide a final answer.

4. Therapeutic methods

A INTRODUCTION

Article 53(c) of the European Patent Convention (EPC) did not fundamentally change the substance of the exclusion of methods of medical treatment from patent protection found in Article 52(4) EPC.[1] Article 53(c) EPC, like Article 52(4) EPC, includes an exclusion relating to a 'method for treatment of the human or animal body by ... *therapy*'.[2] This exclusion does not apply to products used in any of the excluded methods of medical

[1] This article was previously Article 52(4) EPC 1973. With the entry into force of the EPC 2000, on 13 December 2007, Article 52(4) EPC has been replaced by Article 53(c) EPC 2000. The content of the exclusion of methods of medical treatment remains unchanged, but the juridical basis of the exclusion found in Article 52(4) EPC has been excised from the new formulation of the exclusion found in Article 53(c) EPC. The drafters of the EPC 2000 made it clear that '[a] change in the EPO's current practice regarding these inventions is not envisaged' as a result (The Basic Proposal for the Revision of the European Patent Convention, 13 October 2000, Article 53 EPC, Explanatory Remarks, at para. 3). The juridical basis of the exclusion as lacking industrial application is notably absent in Article 53(c) EPC. So, although the previous legal basis of the exclusion has been excised, the jurisprudence relating to Article 52(4) EPC will, for the most part, remain applicable under the new Article 53(c) EPC. For ease of reference and to avoid confusion, this chapter will refer to Article 52(4) EPC where the decision of the Technical Boards of Appeal (TBAs) or the Enlarged Board of Appeal of the European Patent Office (EBA) was based on that Article.

[2] See, A. W. White, 'Patentability of Medical Treatment Welcome Foundation (Hitching's Application)' [1980] EIPR 364; P. Pennant, 'Patentability of Medical Treatment' [1981] EIPR 64; Y. Cripps, 'The Refusal of Patents of Methods of Medical Treatment – A Preference for Parliamentary Guidance' [1983] EIPR 173; A. White, 'Patentability of Medical Treatment Claims – The Nimodipin Cases' [1984] EIPR 38; P. Lancon, 'Patentability in the Field of Therapy and Diagnosis' (1991) 22 IIC 893; W. De Smet, 'Patentability in the Area of Therapy and Diagnosis under Belgian Law' 22 IIC 888 (1991); K. E. Panchen, 'Patentability in the Field of Therapy and Diagnosis' (1991) 22 IIC 879; R. Moufang, 'Methods of Medical Treatment under Patent Law' (1993) 24 IIC 18; D. Kell, 'Expanding the Frontier of Patentability: Methods of Medical Treatment of the Human Body' [1995] EIPR 202; D. Thums, 'Patent Protection for Medical Treatment – A Distinction Between Patent and Medical Law' (1996) 27 IIC 423; A. Feros, 'Patentability of Methods of Medical Treatment' [2001] EIPR 79; J. Pila, 'Methods of Medical Treatment within

treatments.[3] The early decisions of the TBAs of the European Patent Office (EPO) did not engage a discussion of the relevant principles, since it was so obviously clear that a claim worded in the form whereby a process 'is suitable for the treatment of living organisms' was a method of treatment by therapy.[4] One TBA, therefore, had no hesitation in rejecting such a claim as an excluded method of treatment of the human body by therapy.[5] However, in most cases, it was not immediately clear whether the claimed method actually related to a method of treatment of the human or animal body by therapy. The TBAs have, therefore, sought to shed some much-needed light on the exception and, in the process, have delineated the boundaries of the exclusion to provide the necessary certainty that is all too important in this area of the law. Although the TBAs have examined the scope of this exclusion more than any other[6] they have, however, been unable to find concrete solutions to all the issues that have arisen before them. There are still some troubling areas.

The definition of 'treatment by therapy' seems now to be well-settled. The issues which now face the TBAs concern the application of that definition in various contexts including: (a) whether a claim is patentable if

---

Australian and United Kingdom Patents Law' (2001) 24 UNSW Law Journal 420; D. Thomas, 'Patentability Problems in Medical Technology', (2003) 34 IIC 847; E. Verkey, 'Patenting of Medical Methods – Need of the Hour' [2007] JIPLP 104. The ideas in this chapter have been derived, in part, from the following: E Ventose: ' "Farming" out an Exception to the Exclusion of Methods of Medical Treatment under the European Patent Convention' (2008) EPIR 509; 'New Developments in Patent Protection for the Myriad's BRAC 1 Gene at the European Patent Office' (2009) JIPLP 771; and 'Patent Protection for Therapeutic Methods under the European Patent Convention' (2010) EIPR 120.

[3] By way of compensation, Article 52(4) EPC further provides that this provision shall not apply to products, in particular substances or compositions, for use in any of these methods: see, *SIMTECH/Trancutaneous electrical nerve stimulation* (T 94/83) [1979–85] EPOR C811 at para. 3. So, although methods of medical treatments are excluded from patent protection, products for use in those methods are not: *CANADY JEROME/Surgical coagulation device* (T 1138/09) at para. 4.3.

[4] For example, *NOGIER/Magnetic therapy* (T 30/83) [1979–85] EPOR C755 at para. 2. See also, *TEXAS/Amendments* (J 10/84) [1979–85] EPOR A213 where the applicant, on realising that its claims related to a method of treatment of the human body by therapy, sought to amend the claims, and requested that they be incorporated into the application immediately upon dispatch of the report. The amended claims were not published. The TBA set aside the decision, holding that it was contrary to the principles of good faith that govern relations between applicant and the EPO for the applicant's request to have been disregarded by the EPO.

[5] *NOGIER/Magnetic therapy* (T 30/83) [1979–85] EPOR C755 at para. 2.

[6] This exclusion was specifically considered in R. Moufang, 'Methods of Medical Treatment under Patent Law' (1993) 24 IIC 18, 40–45 and D. Thomas, 'Patentability Problems in Medical Technology' (2003) 34 IIC 847, 865–878.

the therapeutic aspect of that claim is merely incidental; (b) what exactly are the boundaries between 'methods for treatment by therapy' and devices used to treat the human or animal body; (c) whether treatment by therapy on the animal body deserves differential treatment from that relating to humans; (d) whether claims to cosmetic methods that also have therapeutic value are patentable; and (e) the scope of protection for contraceptive methods. This chapter explores the definitional issues that lie at the heart of this exclusion and provides possible solutions to reconcile the inconsistent application of the exclusion of methods of treatment of the human or animal body by therapy found in the jurisprudence of the TBAs. It is essential that the boundaries of the exclusion be properly delineated to ensure that patentees are well aware of which claims are acceptable to the EPO and which are not. This provides the necessary certainty that is important for patentees – a critical point which has only recently been emphasised by the EBA of the EPO in *CYGNUS/Diagnostic method*.[7]

B LEGISLATIVE HISTORY

The 1965 version of the draft Convention established by the EEC 'Patent' Working Party provided that 'inventions within the meaning of paragraph 1 shall in particular exclude (e) *medical treatments*, including methods of diagnosis'.[8] An amendment to the preliminary draft Convention under the heading 'Patentable Inventions' provided, in Article 9(2), that 'the following in particular shall not be regarded as inventions within the meaning of paragraph 1 (e) *methods of therapy*, including diagnostic methods'.[9] The differences are noteworthy – the former refers to 'medical treatments', whereas the latter is directed at 'methods of therapy'. This shows that the drafters were attempting to introduce specificity in the provisions of the Convention, because a 'method of therapy' is one method of medical treatment of the human or animal body. By 1969, the exclusion related to 'therapeutic' 'methods for treatment of the human or animal body'.[10] 'Methods of therapy' and 'therapeutic methods' seem indistinguishable, but the 1969 draft clearly indicated that the therapeutic method

---

7 (G 01/04) [2006] EPOR 15. See Chapter 6.

8 Draft Convention established by the EEC 'Patents' Working Party, 1965 (emphasis added).

9 Amendments to the Preliminary Draft Convention relating to European Patent Law Patents, Working Party I, II, III, and IV, 22 January 1965 (emphasis added).

10 First Preliminary Draft of a Convention Establishing a European System for the Grant of Patents, Brussels, 21 December 1970.

excluded related to those 'for treatment on the human or animal body'. That limitation was not expressed in previous drafts of the exclusion. In 1971, the text of the exclusion remained substantially the same except that the words 'or animal' were placed in square brackets.[11] By May 1972, the exclusion was for '*methods for treatment of the human [or animal] body by* surgery or *therapy* and diagnostic methods practised on the human [or animal] body'.[12] This change was merely cosmetic.

Now that the wording of the exclusion relating to therapeutic methods was settled, it was left to the various delegations and organisations to spell out what they thought it meant. Some organisations argued that the exclusion of methods for treatment of the human body by therapy 'should be excluded from patentability only in the case of physical treatment';[13] others proposed 'to exclude specifically "*physical methods*" of treatment by therapy'.[14] The Conference noted that some delegations proposed that the last suggestion should be adopted in the Convention leaving it open to the jurisprudence of the EPO to decide on non-physical treatment by therapy and new therapeutic applications of known substances.[15] Consequently, the Conference directed Working Party I to re-examine that proposal.[16] In the end, the limitation to 'physical treatment' did not find expression in further drafts of the Convention. At the Munich Diplomatic Conference in

[11] Article 9(e), Second Preliminary Draft of a Convention Establishing a European System for the Grant of Patents, 1971. This reflects the same position at the stage reached on 29 January 1971 in relation to the First Preliminary Draft Convention Establishing a European System for the Grant of Patents, Brussels, 15 February 1971 (Stage reached on 29 January 1971). The Document correcting the Second Preliminary Draft Convention Establishing a European System for the Grant of Patents, Brussels, 6 December 1971 was to the same effect except that the square brackets were removed (Stage reached on 26 November 1971).

[12] Draft Convention Establishing a European System for the Grant of Patents (Stage reached on 20 May 1972) (emphasis added).

[13] Minutes of the 5th Meeting of the Inter-Governmental Conference for the Setting up of a European System for the Grant of Patents, Part II, Hearing of the Non-Governmental Organisations on the Second Preliminary Draft Convention Establishing a European System for the Grant of Patents, Luxembourg, 26 January to 1 February 1972, at para. 17.

[14] Minutes of the 5th Meeting of the Inter-Governmental Conference for the Setting up of a European System for the Grant of Patents, Parts I and III, Luxembourg, 24 to 25 January and 2 to 4 February 1972, at para. 33 (emphasis in original).

[15] Ibid.

[16] Ibid.

1973, the text of the exclusion, now found in Article 50(2)(d), did not change from the text which had by then been settled. It read as follows:[17]

> The following in particular shall not be regarded as inventions within the meaning of paragraph 1: methods for treatment of the human or animal body by surgery or therapy and diagnostic methods practised on the human or animal body.

The UK delegation was of the opinion that they understood the word 'therapy' to be 'concerned with the treatment of illness or disease'.[18] The Swiss delegation 'suggested that methods for prophylactic treatments should also be mentioned explicitly under [Article 50(2)(d)]'[19] and that 'in many cases prophylactic treatments could be treated similarly to surgical or therapeutic treatments'.[20] However, the Conference thought that these issues should be left to the jurisprudence of the EPO to determine on a case-by-case basis.[21]

C DEFINING THERAPEUTIC METHODS

1 The Scope of the Exclusion

The exclusion from patentability of methods of medical treatment is to be construed narrowly, which means that it is not applicable to treatments that are not therapeutic in nature.[22] The consistent application of this exclusion demanded that an exact meaning be given to the word therapy. Therapy, the

---

17 Draft Convention, Munich Diplomatic Conference for the Setting up of a European System for the Grant of Patents, Munich, 10 September to 6 October 1973.

18 Comments by the UK Government on the preparatory documents for the Munich Diplomatic Conference, at para. 6.

19 Minutes of the 6th Meeting of the Inter-Governmental Conference for the Setting up of a European System for the Grant of Patents, Luxembourg, 19 to 30 June 1972, at para. 28.

20 Ibid.

21 Ibid.

22 *DU PONT/Appetite suppressant* (T 144/83) [1987] EPOR 6 at para. 3; and *EISAI/Second medical indication* (G 05/83) [1979–85] EPOR 241. Interestingly, another TBA held that therapy should not be defined narrowly: *ROKER/Dysmenorrhoea* (T 81/84) [1988] EPOR 297 at para. 3. In that decision, the TBA held that the treatment of menstrual discomfort manifesting itself in intense headaches was a method of treatment of the human body by therapy, because it thought that it was impossible to make a distinction between basic and symptomatic therapy – the healing or cure, or the mere relief.

TBA held, 'cover[ed] any non-surgical treatment which is designed to cure, alleviate, remove or lessen the symptom of, or prevent or reduce the possibility of contracting any malfunction in the human body'.[23] The TBA also pointed out that therapy 'also relates to the treatment of a disease in general or to a curative treatment in the narrow sense, as well as the alleviation of the symptoms of pain and suffering'.[24] The definition of therapy was not limited to the curing of diseases,[25] but covered any treatment, which 'was designed to cure, alleviate, remove or lessen the symptoms of, or prevent or reduce the possibility of contracting any disorder or malfunction of the human or animal body,'[26] or prophylactic treatment aimed at maintaining health by preventing ill effects that would otherwise have arisen.[27] The exclusion applied equally to the treatment of ectoparasites as it did to endoparasites.[28]

The definition of the exclusion of treatment by therapy accepted in these decisions was applied in *UNIVERSITY OF MANITOBA/Lung ventilator device*,[29] where the TBA opined that '[t]he term "therapy" within the meaning of Article 52(4) EPC is not restricted to curing a disease or to removing its causes but it covers also any treatment designed to alleviate or reduce the symptoms of any malfunction of the human body'.[30] In that decision, the claims related to a method for delivering pressure assist ventilation to a patient in response to respiratory efforts of that patient. This, the TBA held, was a method of treatment by therapy, because '[t]he claimed method and use are designed to alleviate breathing insufficiency by providing pressure ventilation proportional to the ongoing effort of the

---

23 *SALMINEN/Pigs III* (T 58/97) [1989] EPOR 125 at para. 2.

24 Ibid. This definition was first articulated in *DU PONT/Appetite suppressant* (T 144/83) [1987] EPOR 6 at para. 3. The same point was also made by the TBA in *ULTRAFEM/Feminine hygiene device* (T 1165/97) [2002] EPOR 384 at para. 4.2.

25 *TEXAS/Amendments* (J 10/84) [1979–85] EPOR A213 at para. 2.

26 *THOMPSON/Cornea* (T 24/91) [1996] EPOR 19 at para. 2.7. In that decision, the TBA held that the claimed method, which related to a method of treatment of a patient's eye, which effectively removes myopia, hyperopia and astigmatism, was a therapeutic method and was, consequently, excluded from patent protection (at paras. 2.6 and 2.7). See also, *NOGIER/Magnetic therapy* (T 30/83) [1979–85] EPOR C755 at para. 1 and *BAYER AG* (T 774/89).

27 *EISAI/Second medical indication* (G 05/83) [1979–85] EPOR 241; *DUPHAR/Pigs II* (T 19/86) [1988] EPOR 10; *ICI/Cleaning plaque* (T 290/86) [1991] EPOR 157; *MEIJI/Feeds* (T 438/91) [1999] EPOR 333; and *GENERAL HOSPITAL/Contraceptive method* (T 820/92) [1995] EPOR 446 at para. 5.2. See also *WAVE ENERGY SYSTEMS/Mycobactericide* (T 0051/99) at para. 2.

28 *WELLCOME/Pigs I* (T 116/85) [1995] EPOR 1 at para. 4.3.

29 (T 0592/98).

30 Ibid, at para. 2.

patient throughout inspiration'.[31] The TBA explained that the rationale for Article 52(4) EPC was 'to prevent any obstacle to the freedom to choose the best medical treatment to be applied to a patient and to avoid any delay in the application of such medical treatment' and that '[s]uch obstacles or delays could arise if a medical treatment were the subject of an exclusive patent right'.[32] The claim was, therefore, rejected as an excluded method of treatment by therapy contrary to Article 52(4) EPC.

2 Restoration and Maintenance of Health

One consistent theme that is evident in the application of the exclusion for methods of treatment by therapy is that a particular method will not be considered as a medical one if it is not *directly related* to the maintenance or restoration of the patient's health. Consequently, the TBA in *DUPHAR/Pigs II* held that the prophylactic and curative treatment of disease should be regarded as therapeutic treatment because both are directed to the maintenance or restoration of health.[33] Treatment by therapy included the provision of medicaments for the alleviation of pain and discomfort from menstruation, and the origin of the pain was irrelevant for the purpose of determining whether the claim was directed at therapeutic treatment.[34] For example, in *RORER/Dysmenorrhea*,[35] the claimed method related to a method for relieving the discomfort of a human female, attendant to menstruation, which comprised administering to the human female an effective amount of a substance. The question, as the TBA saw it, was whether the character of menstrual discomfort, manifesting itself, for instance, in intensive headaches and other painful symptoms, was such that its treatment should fall under the category of therapeutic treatment.[36]

The TBA was of the opinion that the concept of therapy should not be confined narrowly and that it would be 'impossible and undesirable to distinguish between basic and symptomatic therapy, that is, healing or cure and mere relief' from pain.[37] The mere fact that the pain was caused by a naturally occurring function of the female body was an irrelevant criterion

---

31 Ibid.

32 Ibid. See the recent study entitled: 'The Exclusion of Surgical, Therapeutic and Diagnostic Inventions from Patentability Under Article 52(4) of the European Patent Convention' dated February 2008 prepared on behalf of the Intellectual Property Institute by Florian Levere and Jeremy Phillips.

33 *DUPHAR/Pigs II* (T 19/86) [1988] EPOR 10 at para. 7.

34 *RORER/Dysmenorrhoea* (T 81/84) [1988] EPOR 297 at para. 3.

35 Ibid.

36 Ibid, at para. 3.

37 Ibid.

when determining whether the treatment was of a therapeutic nature. This was because '[t]he use of medicaments may be called for whenever the human body is suffering from a disease, illness, pain or discomfort or incapacity, and the administration thereof could provide or contribute to either full or partial healing, or relief or restoration of fitness'.[38] It would, therefore, be impossible to claim a method of treating pain when caused by a disease and not otherwise. Attention, therefore, must necessarily focus on the end result – the pain – rather than its cause when the issue of patent protection is being considered. Moreover, according to the TBA, activities, such as relieving pain, 'are part of the everyday therapeutic activities of the medical profession'.[39] The claimed method was, therefore, held to be an excluded method of treatment of the human body by therapy. It was not surprising, therefore, that in *MIT/Perception of fatigue*,[40] the TBA held that the treatment for 'reducing the perception of fatigue is not even comparable with the relief of pain, discomfort and incapacity',[41] because 'pain or serious suffering do not appear to be manifestations of fatigue'.[42] It was simply 'a transitory physiological condition caused by natural circumstances and removable by simple rest'.[43] The claim was, therefore, held not to amount to an excluded method of treatment by therapy.[44]

D MEDICAL TREATMENT AND IMPLANTABLE DEVICES

1 Introduction

Out of an abundance of caution,[45] the second sentence to Article 52(4) EPC, in effect, provides that the exclusion from patent protection of methods of medical treatment shall not apply to products, in particular, substances or compositions for use in any of these methods.[46] It is

38 Ibid.
39 Ibid, at para. 4.
40 (T 0469/94).
41 Ibid, at para. 4.2.
42 Ibid.
43 Ibid.
44 Ibid, at para. 4.4.
45 *EISAI/Second medical indication* (G 05/83) [1979–85] EPOR 241 at para. 14.
46 For example, in *INTRAVASCULAR RESEARCH METHOD* (T 0948/95) a claim for a method and apparatus for the examination and treatment of internal organs was allowed because the claim no longer contained any feature which could

self-evident that the prohibition on patenting methods of medical treatments would not prevent the patentability of products, including substances or compositions, even if they are used in such excluded methods.[47] This meant that where claims were for a product, namely, a combination of TENS apparatus and an anaesthetic agent, they did 'not cover methods which are unpatentable by virtue of Article 52(4) EPC'.[48] Where, however, a claim covers the actual use of a device in the treatment of a patient, it becomes necessary to determine whether or not that device is patentable, notwithstanding the exclusion of methods of treatment by therapy from patent protection. Arguably, the exclusion for methods of medical treatment begins to bite when the claim is for a device 'when used' in a method of medical treatment such as by therapy, surgery or of diagnosis.[49] This means that while patent protection is available for medical devices, they cannot derive novelty from the way they are intended to be used in the excluded method of treatment.[50] These claims are, therefore, not excluded from patent protection by virtue of Article 52(4) EPC.[51] In this section, the decisions of the TBAs concerning methods of operating devices implanted on the human body will be examined with a view to understanding this complex area in the jurisprudence of the EPO.

2 The Need for a Functional Link or Nexus

The use of a device may be indicative of whether a method is actually a method of medical treatment. To fall within the scope of the exclusion, the use of the device must be so intimately connected to the human or animal body that its character changes and it effectively becomes an excluded method of medical treatment. That change in character necessarily depends on the degree of connectedness or nexus with the human or animal

---

be construed as a method of treatment of the human or animal body by therapy (at para. 6). Such claims are not, therefore, excluded from patent protection by virtue of Article 52(4) EPC.

47 A similar point is made by Moufang who argues that 'there is no doubt as to the patentability of such devices due to the second sentence of the exclusion clause …' (R. Moufang, 'Methods of Medical Treatment under Patent Law' (1993) 24 IIC 18, 43–44).

48 *STIMTECH/Transcutaneous electrical nerve stimulation* (T 94/83) [1979–85] EPOR C811 at para. 3.

49 The question of whether an apparatus for the surgical treatment of treatment of tissues by hyperthermia, preferably the prostate, with cooling means, was not even raised in *UROLOGIX INC/Apparatus for surgical treatment* (T 0634/02).

50 See the UK decision of *Visx v Nidex* [1998] FSR 405.

51 *RHOMED INC/Radiolabeled antibodies* (T 0606/96) at para. 4.

body. In *SIEMENS/Flow measurement*,[52] for example, the claim was for a method of measuring the flow rate of small quantities of liquid passing through a tubular element which was then used as a method of supplying insulin to the human body through a pump of an implantable device. The claimed method was, therefore, for a method of measuring the efficiency of the pump fitted in the device[53] which, the TBA held, was clearly unconnected with either a surgical device or a diagnostic method.[54] The invention did not provide a sufficient *nexus* with the human body to make it a process directed to a therapeutic purpose, because the method 'only involve[d] measuring the volume of the drug solution flowing into the body per unit of time and the flow itself is not affected'.[55] The claimed method only provided 'information on the current working order of the device, and the body in which the device is implanted is not affected'.[56] The TBA opined that it mattered little that the flow was being timed in an implanted device, because that action was not sufficient, on its own, to justify a finding that the flow timing was therapeutic in nature. For the timing of the flow to have any therapeutic effect, it 'would have to influence the quality and quantity of the drug flow'.[57] Therefore, the TBA has accepted that only if the human or animal body is affected, that is to say, if the claimed device in any way affects the quantity or quality of the flow of the substance to the patient, (and it produces a therapeutic effect), would it be possible to argue that the claimed method amounts to a method of treatment of the human body by therapy.

3 Implantable Devices Not Patentable

Where a claim relates to a method of operating a pacer in accordance with a required cardiac output, it will be considered as a therapeutic method of treatment of the human body.[58] In *TELECTRONICS/Pacer*, the TBA reiterated that, in its view, 'a claim is not allowable having regard to Article 52(4) EPC if it includes at least one feature defining a physical activity or action (e.g. a method step), and if such activity or action constitutes a "method for treatment of the human body by therapy"'.[59] In

52 (T 245/87) [1989] EPOR 241.
53 Ibid, at para. 3.2.1.
54 Ibid, at para. 3.
55 Ibid.
56 Ibid.
57 Ibid.
58 *TELECTRONICS/Pacer* (T 82/93) [1996] EPOR 409.
59 Ibid, at para. 1.4.

that decision, the claims related to a method of operating a pacer in accordance with the required cardiac output while a person is exercising. This type of claim was characterised by the TBA as a 'hybrid claim'.[60] The TBA noted that, on the facts, there was 'a functional link between the value which is measured and the therapeutic treatment which is applied',[61] because 'the use of a sensed pressure value derived from a particular part of the human body for quantitatively controlling the output of the pacer which is applied to the human body in order to obtain a therapeutic effect'.[62] The claim, in the opinion of the TBA, defined 'the use of the pacer to carry out physical actions which constitute a method of treatment by therapy' that was excluded from patent protection by virtue of Article 52(4) EPC.[63] This result can be contrasted with the holding in *SIEMENS/Flow measurement*,[64] where the claim, which was directed at measuring the blood flow through an instrument, was not actually used for administering and monitoring the dosage. That claim was, therefore, not considered by the TBA as a therapeutic method of treatment.

4 Implantable Devices Patentable

If a claimed method relates only to the technical means by which a device is used and if, in the process, that method explains how those technical means interact with the human body, the question becomes the extent to which that method should be excluded from patent protection for embracing an excluded method of treatment of the human body by therapy. In *SIEMENS/Pacemaker*,[65] claim 1 related to a method of operating a pacemaker for arresting tachycardia. The TBA stated that it did not agree with the respondent's arguments that any method for the operation of a device must necessarily be a technical method which was not covered by the exclusion of methods of treatment of the human or animal body by therapy. The TBA noted that 'an actual operating method for a pacemaker for arresting tachycardia would necessarily [amount to] a method for treating the human (or animal) body by therapy using a pacemaker', which would not be patentable by virtue of Article 52(4) EPC.[66] The respondent argued that the claim referred to process steps in a technical method, which

[60] Ibid, at paras. 1.3 and 1.5.
[61] Ibid.
[62] Ibid.
[63] Ibid.
[64] (T 245/87) [1989] EPOR 241.
[65] (T 0426/89) [1992] EPOR 149.
[66] Ibid, at para. 2.1.

did 'not define a method of treatment but rather [defined], in functional terms, the structural features of a pacemaker'.[67] The TBA agreed, accepting that, if properly interpreted, the claimed method did not define a method, 'but rather an apparatus (pacemaker) in terms of the function of its components'.[68] This meant that the exclusion of methods of medical treatment under Article 52(4) EPC did 'not prejudice the patentability of the subject matter of the [claim]' under consideration.[69] However, by the time the TBA heard the appeal, the claims were amended by the respondent so as not to refer to a 'method for the operation of a pacemaker', but only to a 'pacemaker'.[70] Although the claims used the words 'method' for the operation of the pacemaker, they did 'not define an act to be performed with the pacemaker itself or during its manufacture'.[71] Therefore, the claimed method, in the opinion of the TBA, was merely 'a functional definition of a pacemaker and the claim itself, therefore, as a product claim'.[72] Consequently, the TBA held that Article 52(4) EPC was not implicated because the patent now clearly related to a product, namely, a pacemaker for arresting a tachycardia.[73]

The decision of the TBA in *TELECTRONICS/Pacer* was distinguished by another TBA in *ELA MEDICAL/Therapeutic method*[74] on the basis that the claims in *TELECTRONICS/Pacer* had revealed 'a functional link between the value which is measured and the therapeutic treatment which is applied'.[75] The claims in *ELA MEDICAL/Therapeutic method* related to a method for controlling stimulation energy in a pacemaker, the purpose of the method being to solve the technical problem of reducing the energy of each stimulating pulse without losing efficiency, and thereby prolonging the life or reducing the size of the pacemaker battery. The Examining Division held that since the method produced cardiac stimulations, it was a method of treatment of the human or animal body by therapy.[76] The TBA disagreed, arguing that, while it was true that 'a method involving the use of a device having an effect on the heart is in principle a method of treatment by

---

67 Ibid.
68 Ibid. See also, *OPTIMATA/Optimized drug delivery* (T 1873/06) at para. 3.
69 (T 0426/89) [1992] EPOR 149 at para. 2.1.
70 Ibid, at para. 3.1.
71 Ibid, at para. 2.2.
72 Ibid.
73 Ibid, at para. 3.2.
74 (T 789/96) [2003] EPOR 23.
75 Ibid, at para. 2.2.2.3, citing *TELECTRONICS/Pacer* (T 82/93) [1996] EPOR 409, at para. 1.5.
76 *ELA MEDICAL/Therapeutic method* (T 789/96), at para. 2.2.2.

therapy', the claimed method was actually 'directed not to cardiac stimulation, but to "controlling stimulation energy in a pacemaker"'.[77] According to the TBA, the method was, in effect, 'designed to optimise a pacemaker's energy consumption'.[78] This, the TBA noted, gave 'special relevance' to the point made by the TBA in *SIEMENS/Flow measurement* that a method would not be considered a method of treatment by therapy if there is no functional link between the steps in the device and the therapeutic effect produced on the body by that device.[79] Referring to *SIEMENS/Pacemaker*, the TBA in *ELA MEDICAL/Therapeutic method* accepted that the programming of a pacemaker does not *per se* amount to a method of treatment by therapy because it is simply an act performed on an apparatus.[80]

The TBA in *ELA MEDICAL/Therapeutic method* was of the opinion that the method in question was 'not used to regulate the amplitude, the stimulation frequency or any other value acting *directly* on the heart',[81] which meant that there was 'no corresponding functional link'.[82] The method was used exclusively 'to minimize the energy needed for cardiac stimulation' and it 'neither positively nor negatively' affected or influenced the therapeutic effect of that stimulation.[83] The TBA then distinguished the decision of the TBA in *TELETRONICS/Pacer*, stating that the present decision 'differs completely from the facts' therein, because, in that decision, the TBA had found a functional link between the value measured and the therapeutic treatment which is applied.[84] The TBA, therefore, concluded that the claimed method was not a method of treatment by therapy, because, first, '[t]he patient fitted with a pacemaker functioning only as per the said method could die because the method is activated only periodically (e.g. every 6 or 24 hours) when he might need uninterrupted cardiac stimulation';[85] and, secondly, the pacemaker 'operates automatically, "using a computer program", without a doctor being involved'.[86] The TBA noted that a method involving the use of a pacemaker will not be considered a method of medical treatment unless the method was refined to have the effect of treating or preventing a pathological condition.[87] So, for

---

77 Ibid, at para. 2.2.2.1.
78 Ibid.
79 Ibid.
80 Ibid, at para. 2.2.2.2.
81 Ibid, at para. 2.2.2.3 (emphasis in original).
82 *ELA MEDICAL/Therapeutic method* (T 789/96) at para. 2.2.2.3.
83 Ibid.
84 Ibid.
85 Ibid, at para. 2.2.2.4.
86 Ibid.
87 Ibid.

example, a method of controlling the stimulation energy in the pacemaker, without losing efficiency, and thereby prolonging the life or reducing the size of the pacemaker battery, was not considered a method of medical treatment, because the 'therapeutic effect *does not depend* on the steps claimed'.[88] Therefore, the TBA further concluded by stating that:[89]

> a method applied to the human or animal body involving the use of a pacemaker with a therapeutic effect is not a therapy within the meaning of Article 52(4) EPC if the invention consists in refining said method but the refinement does not have the effect of preventing or treating a pathological condition.

Patent protection is available for a device irrespective of its intended purpose, but patentees will not be allowed to patent devices directed at a *particular* therapeutic purpose. This was explained further by the TBA in *BAXTER/Blood extraction method*[90] where the claimed method was for a blood assistance method that facilitated sustained venous blood flow through a human limb towards a venous blood extraction point that involved the use of limb stimulus means. After an examination of the relevant principles established by the jurisprudence of the EPO, the TBA concluded that, first, it was 'appropriate therefore to refuse protection for a blood extraction method considered per se, since otherwise a large part of medical activities would be hampered'; and, secondly, that the withdrawal of blood would be considered as 'a step of a method for treatment by therapy, for example in connection with a dialysis method or with a retransfusion of blood after cleaning …'.[91] The TBA was of the opinion that, in order to determine whether a claimed method is an excluded one, the purpose of the claimed method must first be determined in accordance with the patent application, as understood from the drawings and the description.[92] The object of the claimed method was held principally to facilitate sustained venous blood flow to a blood extraction point located in the vein of a human upper limb by alerting the blood donor.[93] This was designed 'to help in maintaining the desired blood flow through selective automated tactile stimulus'.[94] To be patentable, the claimed subject matter must actually be confined to the operation of an apparatus for performing

---

88 Ibid (emphasis in original).
89 *ELA MEDICAL/Therapeutic method* (T 789/96) at para. 2.2.3.
90 (T 0329/94) [1998] EPOR 363.
91 Ibid, at para. 4.
92 Ibid, at para. 5.
93 Ibid.
94 Ibid.

the method, with the technical aim of facilitating blood flow towards a blood extraction point, whereby the operating method has no therapeutic purpose or effect on the human body.[95]

The TBA in *BAXTER/Blood extraction method* then held that the claimed method was already covered by claim 1 (a device claim) which was directed at the apparatus for carrying out that same method. The TBA held the invention patentable, because the claim actually related to a method of operating a blood extraction assist apparatus.[96] The claimed method was not considered as a method of treatment of the human body by therapy,[97] because, first, it did not 'produce any therapeutic or prophylactic effect on the donor himself, this is with a view to maintaining or restoring his health by preventing or curing diseases';[98] secondly, there was 'no functional link or physical causality between the measure implemented and any therapeutic effect produced on the body to which this measure is applied';[99] and, thirdly, 'the purpose of the claimed blood extraction assistance method is not of therapeutical or surgical, but merely of a technical nature, with the sole aim of improving the efficiency of taking blood from a donor'.[100]

5 The Enlarged Board of Appeal

The EBA in *MEDI-PHYSICS/Treatment by surgery* stated that a typical class of cases in which the invention would be fully defined without requiring the presence of the potentially surgical step as a positive feature of the claim would be cases in which the invention only concerns the operating of a device.[101] With respect to such inventions, it continued, the TBAs have constantly held that a method which is only concerned with the operating of a device without any functional link between the claimed method and the effects produced by the device on the body does not qualify

---

95 Ibid, at para. 5. The TBA noted that the claim under consideration 'most resembles the one reviewed in [*SIEMENS/Flow measurement*] where the 'board found that the miniaturisation of a system for monitoring a device to ensure that it was in working order had to do exclusively with the production of an effect on the structure of the device and was not itself influenced by the effects produced by the device on the body. The steps claimed thus had no therapeutic effect in themselves and the method claim was accepted' (at para. 5).

96 *BAXTER/Blood extraction method* (T 0329/94) at para. 6.

97 Ibid, at para. 9.

98 Ibid, at para. 7.

99 Ibid.

100 Ibid, at para. 8.

101 (G 01/07), at para. 4.3.2.

at all as a method for treatment within the meaning of Article 52(4) EPC.[102] If, on the contrary, there is such a functional link the method is excluded from patentability. These principles, the EBA reiterated, have been acknowledged in cases in which the device was for use in a therapeutic treatment but also to the extent that the application of the device as such needed a surgical step to be practised on the body and, where the operating of the device as such comprised making use of a surgical step, expressions like 'predelivered' or 'preimplanted' have been allowed to make clear that the feature pertaining to that step was not part of the claimed invention.[103]

The EBA claimed that while formally supporting the position adopted in decision *THE GENERAL HOSPITAL CORPORATION/Hair removal method*[104] as regards the limitation of the exclusion to surgical methods for a therapeutic purpose, the TBA decisions of *MAQUET Critical Care AB*[105] and *KONINKLIJKE PHILIPS ELECTRONICS NV*[106] cited by the referring TBA also fell in the category of inventions having been considered as purely technical methods. This principle, the EBA continued, was also acknowledged by practice.[107] Importantly, the EBA claimed that the approach adopted in that jurisprudence was not questioned in the proceedings before it and it also saw no reasons for doing so, accepting that methods which are merely directed to the operating of a device without themselves providing any functional interaction with the effects produced by the device on the body are teachings in which the performance of a physical activity or action that constitutes a method step for treatment of a human or animal body by surgery or therapy is not required in order for the teaching of the claimed invention to be complete.[108] The EBA continued that even if in such a case the use of the device itself requires the application of a surgical step to the body or is for therapeutic treatment the same does not apply to the claimed method for operating the device.[109]

The EBA in *MEDI-PHYSICS/Treatment by surgery* therefore concluded that it was correct to say that, first, such inventions are not methods for treatment of the human or animal body within the meaning of Article 53(c) EPC and that the distinction made in the jurisprudence of the TBAs

---

[102] Ibid.
[103] Ibid.
[104] (T 383/03).
[105] (T 1102/02).
[106] (T 09/04).
[107] See the EPO Guidelines for Examination, C-IV, 12.
[108] *MEDI-PHYSICS/Treatment by surgery* (G 01/07), at para. 4.3.2.
[109] Ibid. See *WISCONSIN ALUMNI RESEARCH FOUNDATION/Rapid acquisition resonance imaging* (T 0266/07), at para. 4.4

properly delimits patentable methods of a merely technical nature from such inventions as fall within the exclusion under Article 53(c) EPC; and, secondly, whether or not a claimed invention only concerns the operation of a device, without any functional link to the effects of the device on the body, is not an issue of law but requires an evaluation of the overall technical circumstances of the case and is therefore a matter to be determined by the Examiners and the TBAs in the individual cases under consideration before them.[110]

In *WISCONSIN ALUMNI RESEARCH FOUNDATION/Rapid acquisition resonance imaging*,[111] the Examining Division held that the claimed method of producing a magnetic resonance angiogram (MRA) implicitly included the invasive step of introducing – by injection – a contrast agent into the vasculature of a patient to be examined, and refused the claims under Article 52(4) EPC 1973 on the grounds that the method had a surgical character. On appeal, the TBA disagreed with that finding.[112] The TBA then quoted the statement of the EBA in *MEDI-PHYSICS/Treatment by surgery* above and held that the claimed method was directed to the operating of a magnetic resonance imaging (MRI) system.[113] It continued that although the presence of a contrast agent was indeed obligatory for the imaging method defined in claim 1, the method for operating the MRI device was not functionally related to the actual administration of the contrast agent. The TBA noted that claim 1 must be interpreted as only covering the production of an MRA of a vasculature into which a contrast agent has already been introduced.[114] It further noted that the actual step of introducing the contrast agent into the vasculature is not included within the scope of the method claim. The TBA reasoned that when this interpretation was invoked the method represented a technical method for producing an MRA of a selected vasculature by means of a magnetic resonance imaging system, and not a surgical method.[115] Consequently, the TBA concluded that the claimed method was not concerned with a method of surgical treatment of the human or animal body within the meaning of Article 53(c) EPC and was, therefore, not excluded from patentability.[116]

---

110 Ibid.
111 (T 0266/07).
112 Ibid, at para. 4.1.
113 Ibid, at para. 4.3.
114 Ibid.
115 Ibid, at para. 4.4.
116 Ibid.

6 Conclusion

The TBAs have had to consider whether a claimed method that includes a device which was implanted in the human body was a method of treatment of the human body by therapy. In respect of such claims, the TBAs have made it clear that, first, there should not be any therapeutic effect produced on the human body, that is with a view to maintaining or restoring the health of the human body or curing diseases; secondly, there should be no nexus or functional link between the device claimed and any therapeutic effect produced on the human body to which it is applied; and, thirdly, the claim must only relate specifically to the functional or technical features of the device claimed. If all these conditions are satisfied, the claimed method will not amount to an excluded method of treatment of the human or animal body by therapy contrary to Article 53(c) EPC 2000. This jurisprudence has received the approval of the EBA in *MEDI-PHYSICS/Treatment by surgery*.

E INVOLVEMENT OF MEDICAL PRACTITIONERS

The actions of the medical (or veterinary) practitioner in relation to the claimed method was considered by the TBAs in determining the question of whether a claimed method was a method of treatment of the human or animal body by therapy. The previously accepted view was that any intimate involvement by a medical (or veterinary) practitioner in the process, either actively or through the supervision of others, was indicative of whether the process was excluded under Article 52(4) EPC.[117] This reasoning was rejected in *BAXTER/Blood extraction method*[118] where the TBA pointed out that it mattered little whether the method was performed by: (a) a medical practitioner; or (b) another person having medical knowledge;[119] or (c) under the supervision of such a person or medical practitioner.[120] However, the medical competence of the practitioner may be a useful – though not a conclusive – indication of whether the treatment in

[117] *THOMPSON/Cornea* (T 24/91) [1996] EPOR 19, at para. 2.4.

[118] (T 0329/94) [1998] EPOR 363.

[119] In *SIEMENS/Flow measurement* (T 245/87) [1989] EPOR 241, the claim was for a method of measuring the flow rate of small quantities of liquid passing through a tubular element. The TBA held that a claim to a method which monitored the operation of the device 'requires no medical knowledge whatsoever as regards the behaviour of the body into which the device is introduced' (at para. 3.1).

[120] *BAXTER/Blood extraction method* (T 0329/94) [1998] EPOR 363, at para. 5.

question is regarded as a method of medical treatment.[121] The exclusion in Article 52(4) EPC was invoked when there was a serious health risk involved with the specific treatment of the patient which had to be performed by a physician or by someone under her supervision.[122] Where the procedure is complicated and can only be carried out by someone trained in the medical field, a strong case would be made for it to be considered as a medical one; for example, a delicate process for correcting a patient's vision required an ophthalmologist to carry it out, and, the actual curing of an eye defect meant that the method was considered to be quintessentially therapeutic in nature.[123]

In *CYGNUS/Diagnostic method*, the EBA decisively rejected the previously accepted approach, stating emphatically that:[124]

> whether or not a method is a diagnostic method within the meaning of Article 52(4) EPC should neither depend on the participation of a medical or veterinary practitioner, by being present or by bearing the responsibility, nor on the fact that all method steps can also, or only, be practised by medicinal or non-medicinal support staff, the patient himself or herself or an automated system.

Notwithstanding the fact that this statement was made in the context of the exclusion of diagnostic methods, the need for consistency in the interpretation of the exclusions means that it should also be applicable to methods of treatment of the human or animal body by therapy.

F COSMETIC METHODS

1 Introduction

It would be surprising, indeed, if the question of the scope of patent protection for substances or compositions that have both a cosmetic and a therapeutic effect had not arisen for consideration by the TBAs. Inventors are continuously seeking new properties of known substances and compositions and have sought to push the boundaries of patentability to breaking point. However, in this context, the issue relates primarily to determining where the boundaries of the exclusion of methods of treatment by therapy

---

121 Ibid.
122 *THOMPSON/Cornea* (T 24/91) [1996] EPOR 19, at para. 2.4.
123 Ibid.
124 (G 01/04) [2006] EPOR 15, at para. 6.3.

begin and end; in particular, whether a claimed method that is directed at a cosmetic purpose, but which also has a therapeutic effect, is patentable. This topic has been the subject of considerable debate in relation to methods of treatment of the human or animal body by surgery. Cosmetic treatment was defined by the TBA as a process 'designed to beautify hair, skin, complexion etc ... or intended to improve appearance'.[125] A literal reading of this definition might lead one to assume that cosmetic treatments would fall outside the scope of the Article 52(4) EPC. Arguably, such methods are, in principle, not to be included in the definition of methods of treatment of the human body by therapy.[126]

2 Cosmetic Methods Patentable

In some decisions, the TBAs have had to consider the question of whether a cosmetic method that also has a therapeutic effect is excluded from patent protection on the basis that the claimed method, as a whole, can be considered as an excluded method of treatment of the human or animal body by therapy. This was vividly illustrated in the decision of the TBA in *ROUSSEL-CULAF/Thenoyl peroxide*[127] where the applicant discovered that thenoyl peroxide (a known compound) had both a cosmetic as well as a therapeutic purpose (treating acne). The issue was whether the cosmetic indication was distinct from the medical indication, and therefore patentable.[128] The TBA accepted that the cosmetic treatment, according to the application, may also incidentally involve a medical treatment[129] and that the activity of skin cleansing clearly belonged to the field of non-medical body hygiene rather than that of therapy.[130] Consequently, it emphasised that the benefits gained by this activity in a cosmetic indication should not, therefore, be considered as being excluded from patentability under Article 52(4) EPC.[131] The TBA was of the opinion that an applicant who has discovered a new medical and non-medical use should be provided with patent protection for, first, the new medical use if claimed as a second/further medical use in accordance with the decision of the EBA in *EISAI/*

---

[125] *DU PONT/Appetite suppressant* (T 144/83) [1987] EPOR 6, at para. 3, citing Concise Oxford Dictionary's 10th Impression 1980.

[126] R. Moufang, 'Methods of Medical Treatment under Patent Law' (1993) 24 IIC 18, 42.

[127] (T 36/83) [1987] EPOR 1.

[128] Ibid, at para. 6.

[129] Ibid, at para. 6.1.

[130] Ibid, at para. 6.2.

[131] Ibid.

Second medical indication;[132] and, secondly, the cosmetic method because it 'is one falling within the general field of patentable inventions'.[133] The TBA emphasised that 'it would have been possible to envisage the exclusion of the non-patentable invention within the meaning of that article by means of a *disclaimer*'.[134] However, the use of the word 'cosmetic' by the applicant was considered by the TBA to be sufficiently precise to avoid any possible conflict with Article 52(4) EPC.[135]

Since the exclusion for methods of medical treatment should be narrowly construed,[136] a method for achieving a loss of weight was not excluded from patent protection.[137] This also means that the exclusion 'should not apply to treatments which are not therapeutic in character'.[138] In *DU PONT/Appetite suppressant*, the claimed method related to a method of improving the bodily appearance of a non-opiate-addicted mammal that comprised of orally administering to that mammal naltrexone or a pharmaceutically effective salt in a dosage effective to reduce appetite, and repeating that dosage until a cosmetically beneficial loss of body weight had occurred.[139] The TBA held that the claims clearly covered 'a method of cosmetic use and is unrelated to the therapy of human or animal body in the ordinary sense', because the 'loss of weight, like gain of weight, is normally not dictated as a desirable effect by medical considerations at all'.[140] The TBA noted that cosmetic treatments of the human or animal body are sometimes 'adjoined to the therapeutic use without a sharp distinction in some cases'.[141] It is usually difficult to determine what parts of a claim relate to either the therapeutic aspect or the cosmetic aspect. As the TBA further noted, it 'may even be difficult to distinguish between the cosmetic and therapeutic effect, i.e. losing weight and curing obesity'.[142] The difficulty in distinguishing cosmetic and therapeutic treatments, the TBA held, should not 'be allowed to work to the disadvantage of an applicant who, according to the wording of her claims, seeks patent

---

132 (G 05/83) [1979–85] EPOR 241.

133 *ROUSSEL-CULAF/Thenoyl peroxide* (T 36/83), at para. 6.3.

134 Ibid, at para. 6.4. See the recent referral by the TBA to the EBA in *MEDI-PHYSICS/Treatment by surgery* (T 0992/03) [2007] EPOR 32.

135 *ROUSSEL-CULAF/Thenoyl peroxide* (T 36/83) at para. 6.4. See also, R. Moufang, 'Methods of Medical Treatment under Patent Law' (1993) 24 IIC 18, 42.

136 *DU PONT/Appetite suppressant* (T 144/83) [1987] EPOR 6, at para. 3.

137 Ibid.

138 Ibid.

139 Ibid, at para. I.

140 Ibid.

141 Ibid, at para. 4.

142 Ibid.

protection for cosmetic treatment but not for the therapeutic treatment as such'.[143] The TBA made it clear that the fact that a chemical product has both a cosmetic and a therapeutic effect when used to treat the human or animal body does not render the cosmetic treatment unpatentable.[144]

Therefore, where a claim, properly construed, covers only a cosmetic method, it would not be excluded from patent protection.[145] Moufang claimed that the conclusion in *DU PONT/Appetite suppressant* seems problematic, because there 'is a difference whether the cosmetic and therapeutic kinds of use of a method can be applied alternatively or are necessarily combined'.[146] In that latter case, he argued, the prohibition against patenting should apply.[147] Pagenberg, however, argues differently, observing that the distinction between cosmetic and therapeutic methods seems to be artificial and that obesity can be caused by an illness.[148] Arguably, patent claim construction must provide an understanding of what the patentee meant by the words used in the claim. If the Examining Officer, correctly guided, has come to the view that the claims, properly construed, only cover a cosmetic product, then it matters little that there might be some instances where that claim may also incidentally have a therapeutic effect. Surely, the scope of the exclusion cannot be construed so broadly that it would cover a claim that does not directly embrace a method of treatment by therapy but might do so in the rarest of cases – contrary to the received wisdom emanating from the jurisprudence of the EPO. That could not have been the intention of the drafters of the exclusion of methods of medical treatment from patent protection. Further, it matters little in such marginal cases, because the TBA has stated explicitly that patentees can overcome that hurdle by simply disclaiming the therapeutic aspect of the claim.[149]

---

143 Ibid.

144 Ibid.

145 *REDEKEN LABORATORIES/Chelating agent* (T 0453/95), at para. 3. In that decision, the claim was for a method for reducing normal average daily hair loss by distributing a substance on the scalp of such a person. The TBA, agreeing with the Examining Officer, held that the claimed subject matter was not excluded from patent protection, because it did not include any therapeutic treatment.

146 R. Moufang, 'Methods of Medical Treatment under Patent Law' (1993) 24 IIC 18, 43.

147 Ibid.

148 J. Pagenberg, 'Appetite Suppressant' (with case comment) (1987) 18 IIC 258, 261.

149 *ROUSSEL-CULAF/Thenoyl peroxide* (T 36/83), at para. 6.4.

3 Cosmetic Methods Not Patentable

The issue of patenting cosmetic methods again arose directly for consideration in *ICI/Cleaning plaque*[150] where the claim was for a method of cleaning plaque using water-soluble lanthanum salts. The question for the TBA was whether the claimed method was an excluded method of treatment of the human body by therapy contrary to Article 52(4) EPC.[151] The applicant argued that the claimed method was a cosmetic one, because the removal of plaque from a person's teeth has a clear cosmetic aspect insofar as the resulting cleaner teeth improve the appearance of that person.[152] The TBA was not convinced, noting that, generally, the prevention of tooth decay is the prevention of a disease,[153] so the claim was obviously for a therapeutic method of treatment.[154] The TBA distinguished *DU PONT/Appetite suppressant*, pointing out that, in that decision, the invention as claimed was for treating someone with obesity which, on a proper construction of the claims, did not cover an excluded method of treatment by therapy but was directed solely to a cosmetic method of treatment.[155] The claims in the instant decision, the TBA clarified, would 'always inevitably have a therapeutic effect[,]... as well as a cosmetic effect',[156] which meant that the claimed method was not directed solely to a cosmetic treatment but also defined a treatment of the human body by therapy as well.[157] The TBA further noted that, in contrast, in *DU PONT/Appetite suppressant*, the:[158]

> cosmetically beneficial loss of weight caused by treatment in accordance with the claimed invention of a person who is not suffering from obesity in the medical sense would not necessarily be beneficial to the health of that person, and therefore would not be a therapeutic treatment of that person.

---

150 (T 290/86) [1991] EPOR 157.
151 Ibid, at para. 3.
152 Ibid, at para. 3.1.
153 The TBA also pointed out that: 'The fact that tooth decay and periodontal diseases do not arise in the usual interval between cleaning the teeth but only become apparent over a longer time span does not render the removal of plaque a purely cosmetic treatment, since the presence of plaque on the teeth for any length of time is a detrimental factor in relation to tooth decay and periodontal diseases' (at para. 3.3).
154 *ICI/Cleaning plaque* (T 290/86), at para. 3.1.
155 Ibid.
156 Ibid.
157 Ibid.
158 Ibid, at para. 3.2.

The claim was, therefore, rejected on the basis that it was not directed *solely* to a cosmetic treatment but also covered a defined treatment of the human body by therapy.[159]

Moufang claimed that this decision is to be welcomed, since it revealed a clear disassociation with the decision of the TBA in *DU PONT/Appetite suppressant*.[160] However, this argument misses the critical distinction between the two decisions. The TBA in *ICI/Cleaning plaque* accepted that the method in question would always have a therapeutic effect; whereas, the TBA in *DU PONT/Appetite suppressant* accepted that the claimed method would not always have a therapeutic effect but that any such effect would depend on the person who actually took the substance. Therefore, far from being a disassociation with *DU PONT/Appetite suppressant*, the TBA in *ICI/Cleaning plaque* was merely distinguishing that decision in order to reach its decision, which does not in any way conflict with the previous one. The difficulty in such cases is admittedly determining *where* the line is to be drawn. In *REICHART/Anti-snoring means*, for example, it was not easily ascertainable whether the snoring was merely troublesome or harmful to health.[161] In that decision, the claims were directed to the use of a substance for manufacturing an agent for the treatment of snoring. The claim was allowed because snoring was generally considered troublesome rather than a pathological phenomenon.[162] Regard, therefore, will be had to the nature of the problem itself to determine whether it is considered a pathological one. This meant that the claimed method was not an excluded method of treatment of the human body by therapy.

4 Industrial Application

Article 57 EPC provides that an invention shall be considered as susceptible of industrial application if it can be made or used in any kind of industry, including agriculture. It was not surprising that the TBAs have also had to decide whether cosmetic methods satisfied the requirements of industrial application in accordance with the jurisprudence of the EPO relating to Article 57 EPC. That approach is understandable in light of the then formulation of the exclusion of methods of medical treatment from patent protection, as lacking industrial application. If a claimed method was a method of medical treatment, then, according to Article 52(4) EPC, that

159 Ibid.
160 R. Moufang, 'Methods of Medical Treatment under Patent Law' (1993) 24 IIC 18, 43.
161 *REICHART/Anti-snoring means* (T 584/88) [1989] EPOR 448, at para. 4.
162 Ibid.

method would lack industrial application and would, therefore, not be patentable. Article 53(c) EPC does not mention industrial application at all.[163] The framers of the EPC 2000 were of the opinion that methods of medical treatment were excluded for public health reasons and rejected the fiction of industrial application which was the juridical basis for the exclusion in Article 52(4) EPC.[164] However, the requirement for industrial application is nonetheless one of the requirements for patentability in Article 52(1) EPC.[165] This means that any method that is not excluded by virtue of Article 53(c) EPC would still need to satisfy the requirement of industrial application to be patentable. Consequently, Article 57 EPC was used to justify the patenting of appetite suppressants because they satisfied the requirement of industrial application when used in cosmetic salons and beauty parlours.[166]

5 Acceptable Form of Claim

The TBAs have made it clear that when considering claims to cosmetic methods, the actual wording of the claims is particularly important. The TBA in *ROUSSEL-CULAF/Thenoyl peroxide* accepted that an applicant who has discovered various uses of a known substance has a right, subject to the provisions of the EPC, to have those uses protected.[167] The TBA noted that where an applicant has discovered two uses of a known substance – one, an excluded method, and the other a non-medical method of

---

163 Article 53(c) EPC 2000 provides that 'European patents shall not be granted in respect of methods for treatment of the human or animal body by surgery or therapy and diagnostic methods practised on the human or animal body; this provision shall not apply to products, in particular substances or compositions, for use in any of these methods'.

164 The Basic Proposal for the Revision of the European Patent Convention, 13 October 2000, Article 53 EPC, Explanatory Remarks, at para. 3.

165 Article 52(1) EPC 2000 now provides that 'European patents shall be granted for any inventions, *in all fields of technology*, provided that they are new, involve an inventive step and are susceptible of industrial application'. There was not any significant change to the previous Article 52(1) EPC in the EPC 2000, except for the inclusion of 'in all fields of technology'.

166 *DU PONT/Appetite suppressant* (T 144/83) [1987] EPOR 6 at para. 3.2. The term 'industry' was given a wide definition to include any activity carried out continuously, independently and for financial gain. The TBA then cited another decision of a TBA, which had already decided that 'the professional use of such inventions in a cosmetic salon is an industrial application in the sense of Article 57 EPC' (at para. 5, citing *ROUSSEL-CULAF/Thenoyl peroxide* (T 36/83) [1987] EPOR 1).

167 *ROUSSEL-CULAF/Thenoyl peroxide*, at para. 6.3.

treatment, only the excluded method is unpatentable.[168] A claimed method in the form: 'use as a cosmetic product of [X substance or composition]' is, therefore, acceptable to avoid the exclusion found in Article 52(4) EPC.[169] As mentioned above, the TBA in *ROUSSEL-CULAF/Thenoyl peroxide* observed that, in order to avoid any possible conflict with the provisions of Article 52(4) EPC in a use or indication claim, 'it would have been possible to envisage the exclusion of the non-patentable invention within the meaning of that article by means of a *disclaimer*'.[170]

6 Conclusion

It is sometimes conceptually difficult to distinguish which claims should be patentable if they relate to both a therapeutic and cosmetic treatment. The TBAs have attempted to provide some guidance when such questions arise for consideration, seemingly emphasising the important principle that generally patents should be granted, subject, of course, to the exclusion of methods of medical treatment.[171] Various principles may be extrapolated from the decisions of the TBAs in this area. First, if the two purposes are distinct and the patentee claims only the cosmetic indication, then patent protection should be available for the cosmetic indication. However, two conditions must be satisfied, namely, the therapeutic effect must be either (a) incidental to the cosmetic effect; or (b) only arise in some instances (either in relation to the subject to which it is applied, or by its nature). Secondly, where the claimed method would always have a therapeutic effect, it would not be patentable notwithstanding the secondary cosmetic indication. In other words, the therapeutic effect should not be an inevitable consequence of carrying out the claimed method. Thirdly, to specifically exclude any therapeutic aspect of the claimed method from the ambit of the claims, applicants can use a disclaimer.

---

168 Ibid.

169 Ibid.

170 Ibid, at para. 6.4 (emphasis added).

171 In *CYGNUS/Diagnostic method* (G 01/04) [2006] EPOR 15 at para. 6, the EBA stated that 'According to Article 4(3) EPC, it is the general task of the EPO to grant European patents. Moreover, Article 52(1) EPC lays down *the fundamental maxim of a general entitlement to patent protection* to the effect that, as a matter of principle, a European patent is to be granted for an invention which meets the requirements of that provision' (emphasis added).

G CONTRACEPTIVE METHODS

1 Whether a Method of Treatment by Therapy

One of the other major questions that faced the TBAs was the extent to which patent protection should be provided for contraceptive methods. In *GENERAL HOSPITAL/Contraceptive method*,[172] the claim was for a method for preventing pregnancy in a female mammal by the administration of an LHRH composition. Not only was LHRH composition administered to the female mammal, she was also to be administered oestrogenic and progestational steroids which were meant to counteract the various side-effects of the administration of the LHRH composition.[173] The TBA held that this latter step was a method of treatment by therapy contrary to Article 52(4) EPC.[174] The applicants argued that the claim should be read as a whole, as being directed to a method of contraception, drawing on the jurisprudence relating to Article 52(2) EPC, wherein the claimed subject matter may not be patented *as such*.[175] This argument was rejected by the TBA which noted that 'the critical question is whether there is any disclosure of a method none of whose steps fall under the prohibition of Article 52(4) EPC'.[176]

The TBA, applying the decisions of *ICI/Cleaning plaque*, *BAYER/Immunostimulant* and *WELLCOME/Pigs I*, noted that in all these decisions the appellants had failed to satisfy the TBA that the methods were not directed to a method of treatment by therapy contrary to Article 52(4) EPC.[177] It also noted that in the cosmetic method decisions, namely, *ROUSSEL-UCLAF/Thenoyl peroxide* and *DU PONT/Appetite suppressant*, the TBA was satisfied that the claims, properly construed, did not cover a method of treatment by therapy.[178] In other words, to be excluded from patent protection the claimed method had to be for a curative purpose.[179] The TBA then stated that, in respect of a claim for a method involving administration of two or more substances, the question for the purposes of Article 52(4) EPC is not whether the main or even the only

---

172 (T 820/92) [1995] EPOR 446.
173 Ibid, at para. 5.2.
174 Ibid.
175 Ibid, at para. 5.4.
176 Ibid, at para. 5.5.
177 Ibid, at para. 5.6.
178 Ibid, at para. 5.7.
179 *ULTRAFEM/Feminine hygiene device* (T 1165/97) [2002] EPOR 384, at para. 4.2.

reason for carrying out the whole of the claimed method is non-therapeutic.[180] However, a claim would offend Article 52(4) EPC 'if the administration of one of the substances is a treatment by therapy, and the administration of this substance is a feature of the claim'.[181] The TBA, therefore, concluded that since the claim method included a treatment by therapy, the claim was not patentable for offending the prohibition on patentability set out in Article 52(4) EPC.[182] In recent years, the question of whether such claims are methods of treatment by therapy is no longer entertained or even argued at all.[183]

2 Whether Susceptible to Industrial Application

Although the decision of the TBA in the *GENERAL HOSPITAL/Contraceptive method* had to address the question of whether a contraceptive method was a method of treatment by therapy, it was left to the TBA in *BRITISH TECHNOLOGY GROUP/Contraceptive method*[184] to deal with the issue of whether the specific claims in that decision were industrially applicable. In that decision, the claim was for the use of a composition for application to the cervix of a female mammal capable of conception. The Examining Division had objected to the aspect of the claim whereby the contraceptive was applied to the cervix of a human female on the basis that it was for a purely personal use which did not meet the requirement of industrial application in Article 57 EPC.[185] Pregnancy, the TBA held, was not an illness so its prevention was not therapeutic in nature which meant that a claimed contraceptive method was not, *per se*, excluded from patent protection by virtue of Article 52(4) EPC.[186] There can be no doubt concerning the veracity of that statement in light of the obvious nature of what a pregnancy entails.

The essential question in this context was whether the invention could be used in industry according to the dictates of Article 57 EPC. The TBA reiterated that the claimed method was intended for application by the woman herself.[187] The appellants argued that the claimed method was

---

[180] *GENERAL HOSPITAL/Contraceptive method* (T 820/92), at para. 5.9.

[181] Ibid.

[182] Ibid, at para. 5.10.

[183] See *DURAMED PHARMACEUTICALS/Method of oral contraception* (T 1063/04).

[184] (T 74/93) [1995] EPOR 279.

[185] Ibid, at para. 2.2.

[186] Ibid, at para. 2.2.3.

[187] Ibid, at para. 2.2.4.

industrially applicable, since it could be used in industry, and gave the example of a prostitute, and nurse.[188] The question, in the view of the TBA, was not 'whether a prostitute's profession is an industry, but whether the application by a prostitute of a contraceptive method to the cervix is part of an industry'.[189] The appellant's argument was rejected by the TBA as 'unconvincing'[190] on the basis that, first, 'the mere motive for using a contraceptive is of minor importance for the question of industrial application';[191] and, secondly, 'the fact that for some women contraception is connected with professional activities does not give an act, which is in essence private and personal, an industrial character'.[192] The TBA noted that the particular contraceptive method, as claimed, was not patentable because it could *not* be used in industry.[193] This approach adopts a very sensible view of what constitutes industry for the purposes of Article 57 EPC. In respect of the use of the contraceptive by a nurse on a disabled patient, the TBA claimed that this did not alter the legal position, because the 'fact that this person acts professionally is not sufficient to make the application of the contraceptive an industrial activity'.[194] The TBA further observed that the 'nurse does not offer the contraception to the disabled patient as an industry but to help her satisfy her strictly personal needs'.[195]

It was not long before the vexed issue of industrial application again arose for consideration. In *ULTRAFEM/Feminine hygiene device*,[196] the claim was for a method of placing a vaginal discharge collector, holding it in place in the vaginal canal of a woman, collecting discharge in the collector, retrieving it and disposing of the collector after a single use. The TBA accepted that the claim satisfied the requirements of Article 57 EPC if it was imaginable that these steps were carried out as a paid service and were not exclusively dependent for their execution on the instructions of the woman in question.[197] The TBA also made it clear that:[198]

---

188 Ibid.
189 Ibid, at para. 2.2.5.1.
190 Ibid, at para. 2.2.5.
191 Ibid.
192 Ibid, at para. 2.2.6. The TBA also made it clear that '[i]t has to be stressed that this does not apply to contraception in general, but to the specific type of application of a composition as claimed in Claim 5' (at para. 2.2.6).
193 *BRITISH TECHNOLOGY GROUP/Contraceptive method* (T 74/93), at para. 2.2.6.
194 Ibid, at para. 2.2.5.2.
195 Ibid.
196 (T 1165/97) [2002] EPOR 384.
197 Ibid, at paras. 3.1–3.2.
198 Ibid, at para. 3.1.

> Such a method can be performed by an enterprise of which the object is to assist women in collecting a sample of their vaginal discharge, eg for subsequent visual, chemical or bacterial inspection or for extraction of one or more of its components for use in industrial preparation of pharmaceutical compositions.

The TBA held that it did not matter that the service was non-existent because what mattered for the purposes of Article 57 EPC was that there exists a 'possibility that such a service may be offered by an enterprise'.[199] The TBA explained that, currently, laboratories take samples of bodily fluids, for example, blood, for further analysis for financial gain.[200] It also pointed out that such:[201]

> services are performed for a fee and are run on a commercial basis, which meant that it was not inconceivable that such services might be extended to the provision and placement of a vaginal discharge collector, collection of vaginal discharge therein and the retrieval and subsequent disposal of the collector.

The TBA distinguished *BRITISH TECHNOLOGY GROUP/Contraceptive method* on the basis that, in that decision, '[t]he service of applying the contraceptive method was not offered as an industry but to satisfy the strictly personal needs of the [patient]'.[202] It did not matter that the activity was not exercised by the patient but by an assistant following her instructions.[203] However, in the instant case, the TBA noted that: (a) 'it can be foreseen that application and retrieval of the discharge collector is performed by a professional in the service of an enterprise';[204] (b) 'the service is not one satisfying only the strictly personal needs of the woman in question';[205] and (c) the person taking the sample generally will not be acting on the instructions of the woman in question, 'but rather on the basis of the instructions supplied with the collector itself' or otherwise, if necessary.[206] The TBA also noted that the claimed method was not a method of treatment by therapy because it did not have as its object the curative or preventative treatment of an illness or the alleviation of the symptoms of pain and suffering.

---

199 Ibid, at para. 3.1.

200 Ibid, at para. 3.1, citing *DU PONT/Appetite suppressant* (T 144/83) [1987] EPOR 6, at para. 5.

201 *ULTRAFEM/Feminine hygiene device* (T 1165/97), at para. 3.2.

202 Ibid.

203 Ibid.

204 Ibid.

205 Ibid.

206 Ibid.

H ANIMALS

1 Introduction

Notwithstanding that the exclusion of methods of medical treatment found in Article 52(4) EPC relates to: (a) methods for treatment of the human or *animal* body by (i) therapy; and (ii) surgery; and (b) diagnostic methods practised on the human or *animal* body, the TBAs and the EBA have hardly engaged in any detailed analysis of the application of the exclusion with respect to animals.[207] It would be readily appreciated that the jurisprudence relating to methods of medical treatment of the human body and diagnostic methods practised on the human body would be similarly applicable to animals. However, this is not always the case. On a few occasions, the TBAs have had to consider the scope of the exclusion only in relation to animals. This section will consider the application of the exclusion of methods of medical treatment as it relates to animals, focusing on the considerations that the TBAs have had to grapple with when considering such patent applications. It will also briefly examine the preparatory documents relating to the EPC to, first, find out whether they can throw any light on the rationale for and interpretation of the exclusion from patent protection of methods of medical treatment of animals, and, secondly, determine whether the approach taken by the TBAs mirrors the intention of the drafters of the EPC.

2 Industrial Application

(a) Introduction

Article 52(1) EPC provides that 'European patents shall be granted for any inventions which are *susceptible of industrial application*, which are new and which involve an inventive step' – all of which are the essential conditions which must be satisfied for patentability.[208] Article 57 EPC states that an

[207] 'Examination Guidelines for Patent Applications relating to Medical Inventions in the UK Intellectual Property Office' June, 2007 provides invaluable guidance in respect of the jurisprudence on methods of medical treatment, in particular treatment of stock animals, in the United Kingdom and the European Patent Office.

[208] Article 52(1) EPC 2000 now provides that 'European patents shall be granted for any inventions, *in all fields of technology*, provided that they are new, involve an inventive step and are susceptible of industrial application'. There was not any significant change to this article in the EPC 2000, except for the inclusion of 'in all fields of technology'.

invention shall be considered as susceptible of industrial application if it can be made or used in any kind of industry, including agriculture. Article 52(4) EPC, in effect, provides that methods of medical treatment shall not be regarded as inventions which are susceptible of industrial application within the meaning of para. 1. It must be noted that the other exclusions contained in Article 52(2) EPC are excluded on the basis that they shall not be regarded as inventions within the meaning of para. 1. The TBA in *WELCOME/Pigs I* explained the difference in the wording of these provisions as follows:[209]

> The subject-matters which are set out in [Article 52(2) EPC] are excluded primarily because they have traditionally been regarded within national patent laws as more in the nature of ideas than industrial manufactures. In contrast, the methods which are set out in [Article 52(4) EPC] are excluded from patentability, even though such methods are capable of being applied industrially, as a matter of policy. Thus the wording of [Article 52(4) EPC] is implicitly recognizing that such methods are susceptible of industrial application as a matter of reality, but provides that they 'shall not be regarded as' inventions which are susceptible of industrial application, by way of legal fiction.

The TBA has stated that: (a) 'the scheme of Articles 52 to 57 … makes it quite clear that even though agricultural methods in general are potentially patentable subject matter, the particular methods defined in Article 52(4) EPC are excluded from patentability';[210] and (b) 'for the particular methods defined in Article 52(4) EPC, Article 52(4) takes precedence over Article 57 EPC'.[211] This clearly means that even if a method of medical treatment can be used as part of agriculture (and would, therefore, satisfy the requirements of Article 57 EPC), its exclusion in Article 52(4) EPC means that it cannot be patented.

The nexus between the requirement for industrial application in Article 52(1) EPC, which is defined in Article 57 EPC, and the method of medical treatment exclusion found in Article 52(4) EPC has now been jettisoned as a result of the EPC 2000. Article 53 EPC relates to the exceptions to patentability. In particular, Article 53(c) EPC provides that 'European patents shall not be granted in respect of methods for treatment of the human or animal body by surgery or therapy and diagnostic methods practised on the human or animal body; this provision shall not apply to products, in particular substances or compositions, for use in any

---

209 (T 116/85) [1988] EPOR 1, at para. 3.3.
210 Ibid.
211 Ibid, at para. 3.5.

of these methods'. Article 53(c) EPC, importantly, makes no mention of industrial applicability – methods of medical treatment are simply not patentable.[212] The drafters of the EPC 2000 were of the view that methods of medical treatment are excluded from patentability in the interests of public health and rejected as undesirable the previous fiction of lacking industrial application.[213] That is not to say, however, that the issue of industrial application is no longer relevant to the determination of whether such medical procedure inventions that relate to animals are patentable. As mentioned above, it is still important, because an invention that is not an excluded method of medical treatment would still need to satisfy the requirements of Article 52(1) EPC, namely, whether it is, among other things, susceptible of industrial application.

(b) Application by the TBAs

One of the first decisions of the TBA to examine the exclusion of therapeutic methods in the context of a patent relating to animals was *WELLCOME/Pigs I*.[214] In that decision, the claims related to a method for the control of ectoparasitic infestations of pigs, comprising the application, to a localised area of the pig's body surface, of a pesticidal composition comprising a pesticide admixed with an aliphatic hydrocarbon oil, to substantially prevent systemic action of the pesticide. The main problem for the TBA was that the method, as defined by the claims, could be applied both to an individual animal and to a herd of animals.[215] The TBA observed that when the method was applied to an individual animal 'it has the nature of a veterinary treatment, and when applied to herds of animals it also has the nature of an industrial activity'.[216] The TBA accepted that the rearing of animals is a farming activity and, as such, can be said to be part of an industry for the purposes of Article 57 EPC.[217] However, the TBA clarified that 'any therapeutic treatment of a farm animal can also be considered as an industrial activity', because, first, 'farming is clearly an industrial activity' and, secondly, 'the medical treatment of disease in both

212 E. Ventose 'Patent Protection for Methods of Medical Treatment in the United Kingdom' [2008] IPQ 58, 61.

213 Basic Proposal for the Revision of the European Patent Convention, 13 October 2000, Article 53 EPC, Explanatory Remarks, at para. 3.

214 (T 116/85) [1988] EPOR 1.

215 Ibid, at para. 4.1.

216 Ibid.

217 Ibid.

individual farm animals and herds of farm animals is intended to increase the efficiency of such industrial activity'.[218]

The TBA, therefore, concluded that 'if a claimed method requires the treatment of the animal body by therapy, it is a method which falls within the prohibition on patentability set out in Article 52(4) EPC'.[219] In respect of the interaction of these provisions, the TBA further concluded that:[220]

> It is not possible as a matter of law to draw a distinction between such a method as carried out by a farmer and the same method as carried out by a veterinarian, and to say that the method when carried out by a farmer is an industrial activity and therefore patentable under Article 57, and when carried out by a veterinarian is a therapeutic treatment not patentable under Article 52(4).

The TBA also made it clear that it was not possible, as a matter of law, to distinguish between the use of such a method for the treatment of ectoparasites and endoparasites.[221] Where, however, a method of treatment relates to a production process (that excludes any therapeutic purpose), it seems that the TBA will not invalidate the patent on the basis that it amounts to a curative treatment of the animal body. This was the case in *BAYER AG*[222] where the TBA allowed claims which were directed at medication for increasing milk production in cows, because: (a) the success of the medication did not depend on the health of the cow; and (b) the applicant had inserted a disclaimer in the claims in the form of the term 'non-therapeutic', which the TBA accepted was sufficient to exclude the therapeutic effect of the medication.[223]

(c) Legislative history

The interpretation by the TBAs of the exclusion of methods of medical treatment of animals is in line with the accepted view of the drafters at the

---

[218] Ibid. The TBA also pointed out that '[t]o prevent the death of a farmyard pig from disease by a medical treatment, or to cure it of a disease by such a treatment and thus to increase its yield of meat, is in each case both an industrial activity and a therapeutic treatment. Clearly the therapeutic treatment of animals is commonly an aspect of agriculture'.

[219] *WELCOME/Pigs I* (T 116/85) at para. 4.3.

[220] Ibid.

[221] Ibid.

[222] (T 774/89).

[223] Case Law of the Boards of Appeal of the European Patent Office, Fifth Edition, December, 2006, at 28.

negotiating stage of the EPC.[224] The drafters of the EPC clarified that the intention behind the text was 'merely to exclude from patentability *all therapeutic treatment practised on animals*, the aim of this provision being to exclude from patentability treatments falling within the meaning of treatment intended to cure or alleviate the suffering of animals'.[225] In the same vein, the Main Committee at the Munich Diplomatic Conference endorsed the United Kingdom's interpretation of the exclusion that it would only include treatments on animals that had a purely therapeutic purpose, and would *not cover* treatments effected with a view to increasing the quantity or quality of the production of an animal product.[226] This view was echoed by the Netherlands' delegation on numerous occasions.[227] This approach makes it quite clear that, first, only therapeutic treatment of animals was to be excluded from patent protection and, secondly, treatments that increased the quantity or quality of the animal product were thought patentable and not excluded, by virtue of the exclusion, from patent protection of methods of medical treatment of animals. The value of the *travaux preparatoires* was not lost on the TBA in *WELCOME/Pigs I* where it:[228]

> considered the various preparatory documents which led to the EPC. The interpretation of the Articles 52 and 57 EPC set out above appears to be fully consistent with such documents, in that the object of the provision of Article 52(4) EPC was to exclude from patentability 'treatment intended to cure or alleviate the suffering of animals' (see in particular Conference document BR/219/72, paragraph 27).

Therefore, *WELCOME/Pigs I* can be explained on the basis that it was directed at a therapeutic treatment; whereas *BAYER AG* was directed at a treatment effected with a view to increasing the quantity or quality of the production of the animal product (that is, milk).

---

[224] See J. Pila, 'Article 52(2) of the Convention on the Grant of European Patents: What did the Framers Intend? A Study in the *Travaux Preparatoires*' (2005) 36 IIC 755 for a brief history of the legislative history of the exclusion of methods of medical treatment of animals.

[225] Minutes of the 6th Meeting of the Inter-Governmental Conference for the Setting up of a European Patent System for the Grant of Patents, Luxembourg, 19 to 30 June 1972, at para. 27 (emphasis added).

[226] Minutes of the Munich Diplomatic Conference for the Setting up of a European Patent System for the Grant of Patents, Munich, 10 September to 5 October 1973, at para. 23.

[227] Minutes of the 6th Meeting of the Inter-Governmental Conference for the Setting up of a European Patent System for the Grant of Patents, Luxembourg, 19 to 30 June 1972, at para. 27.

[228] *WELCOME/Pigs I* (T 116/85), at para. 3.8.

(d) Conclusion

Methods of medical treatment of the human or animal body were excluded from patent protection under Article 52(4) EPC on the basis that they lacked industrial application. Farming is clearly part of the agricultural industry. The policy considerations inherent in preventing physicians from patenting methods of medical treatment are not evident when a farmer performs a similar procedure on animals. The inconsistency is manifestly evident, since a farmer who carries out the same procedure would be caught by that provision, because Article 52(4) EPC applies to *any person* who carries out the medical treatment. Patentees have argued that any therapeutic treatment of animals that increases the quality or quantity of any animal product should be patentable. The TBAs have made it absolutely clear that no distinction should properly be made between the activities of a farmer and a veterinary practitioner when they carry out such treatment on animals.

As mentioned above, the reformulation of the exclusion now found in Article 53(c) EPC will not relieve the TBAs and practitioners of the need to consider whether any such invention is susceptible of industrial application. In the context of medical treatment patents relating to animals, the issue will normally arise for consideration because, in most cases, the inventor will argue that the invention does not actually relate to a method of medical treatment but, rather, is of an industrial character in the farming industry. The above decisions show that the TBAs have been reluctant to countenance such an argument – and quite rightfully so. It is unlikely that there will be any change to the EPC to accommodate the farming industry in light of the recent revisions in 2000 that did not change the substance of the exclusion of methods of medical treatment from patent protection. Moreover, the interpretation given to the exclusion by the TBAs sits comfortably with the intention of the drafters of the EPC insofar as it excludes purely therapeutic treatment of animals from patent protection, whereas treatments that are designed to increase the quantity or quality of the animal product are allowable.

3 Incidental and Other Objectives

(a) Introduction

Scientists are continually trying to find means of treating animals to improve their meat yields or by the administration of substances or compositions to accelerate the growth in those animals.[229] The issue, therefore, that deserves some consideration is whether a claim that embraces a therapeutic method of treatment of animals is excluded from patent protection if there is some other beneficial effect on the animals, for example, by increasing the production of meat or milk, resulting from such treatment – and the patentee claiming that aspect as such. A similar question arose in the context of cosmetic methods where the TBAs had to determine whether the therapeutic use of a substance could be distinguished from the non-therapeutic (cosmetic) use.[230] The desire to ensure consistency in the application of the exclusion demands that the TBAs apply the same principles to ensure legal certainty for patentees and to avoid a fragmentation of the jurisprudence relating to the exclusion of methods of medical treatment from patent protection.[231]

(b) Legal analysis

Immunostimulation, irrespective of its intended purpose, was considered by the TBA as a therapeutic method of treatment.[232] In *BAYER/Immunostimulant*, the claim was for the use of certain compounds as an immunostimulant in poultry for an increase in meat production. The TBA, after considering various decisions of the TBA, noted that, first, if a method constitutes a method of treatment by therapy it cannot be patented and, secondly, a claimed method must be specifically directed at the non-therapeutic effect of the claim for it to be patentable.[233] The TBA, citing *DU PONT/Appetite suppressant*,[234] observed that '[i]f the properties of a product did not differ, however, the claim was not considered grantable since the therapeutic use could not be distinguished from the non-therapeutic use'.[235] This means that the critical factor is whether the method actually claims two uses that can be distinguished and claimed separately. If they can be distinguished, and the patentee specifically claims the non-therapeutic aspect (and, for completeness, disclaims the therapeutic one), there is no reason, in principle, why she should not be granted patent protection for that aspect of the claim.

---

229 'Examination Guidelines for Patent Applications relating to Medical Inventions in the UK Intellectual Property Office', June 2007, at para. 41.

230 See *ROUSSEL UCLAF/Thenoylperoxide* (T 36/83) [1987] EPOR 1; *DU PONT/Appetite suppressant* (T 144/83) [1987] EPOR 6; and *ICI/Cleaning plaque* (T 290/86) [1991] EPOR 157.

231 The need for legal certainty was at the core of the recent decision of the EBA in *CYGNUS/Diagnostic method* (G 01/04) [2006] EPOR 15.

232 *BAYER/Immunostimulant* (T 780/89) [1993] EPOR 377, at para. 7.

233 Ibid, at para. 4.

234 (T 144/83) [1987] EPOR 6.

235 *BAYER/Immunostimulant* (T 780/89), at para. 3.3.

The question for consideration, as the TBA saw it, was whether a compound which had therapeutic effects also had other effects on the immune system of poultry and mammals that were unconnected with this therapeutic treatment.[236] The TBA accepted that, although immunostimulation was not always employed to prevent a specific disease, it did not follow that it was not a therapeutic method of treatment, because it generally served to 'prevent or alleviate potential ailments'.[237] Consequently, the claimed method was to 'be classified as a therapeutic measure, since all prophylaxis serves to maintain health and therefore comes under the provisions of Article 52(4) EPC'.[238] In the opinion of the TBA, such measures which serve to stimulate the body's own defences are always 'accompanied *simultaneously* by specific prophylactic measures against infection with coccidiosis and toxoplasmosis'.[239] This reasoning is not dissimilar to that found in the decision of the TBA in *ICI/Cleaning plaque*[240] where the TBA accepted that a method for cleaning plaque using water-soluble lanthanum salts would inevitably have a therapeutic effect as well as a cosmetic effect.[241] Consequently, that claimed method was rejected by the TBA on the basis that it was not directed at a cosmetic method but that it also defined a therapeutic method of treatment as well.[242]

The applicant in *BAYER/Immunostimulant* asserted that the immunostimulation increased meat production which, in its view, meant that the claim was not directly related to a therapeutic method but had, as its primary objective, the increasing of meat production. In rejecting this argument, the TBA pointed out that:[243]

> If true, however, that would still not alter the legal position, since even if more meat is produced because fewer animals become sick or die the method for which patent protection is claimed remains a therapeutic treatment. The increase in meat production is merely a consequence of the therapeutic treatment. A purely secondary effect of successful therapeutic treatment does not deprive the latter of its character as a therapeutic treatment within the meaning of Article 52(4) EPC.

It seems incredulous that such an argument could be made in the face of the plain effect of the claims: you treat the animals with the medicament and

---

236 Ibid, at para. 5.
237 Ibid, at para. 6.
238 Ibid.
239 Ibid (emphasis added).
240 (T 290/86) [1991] EPOR 157.
241 Ibid, at para. 3.1.
242 Ibid, at para. 3.2.
243 *BAYER/Immunostimulant* (T 780/89), at para. 7.

their health is improved as a result; therefore, less die or fall ill. That the consequential increase in meat production is of immense benefit to the farmer matters little. The treatment is therapeutic, plain and simple; and such treatment is clearly excluded from patent protection. Similarly, in *MEIJI/Feeds*,[244] the claims were, in effect, for a method of breeding domestic animals that remedied scours and increased the weight of the animals being bred.[245] The TBA reiterated that in considering whether a claim is allowable in light of the exclusion in Article 52(4) EPC, 'the critical question is whether there is any disclosure of a method falling under the prohibition of the said provision'.[246] If that is the case, 'such a method cannot be subject matter or part of the subject matter covered by a method claim'.[247] The question presented on the facts was whether the method for breeding domestic animals related to either therapeutic or prophylactic treatment.[248] The TBA considered the wording of the claims in the specification and noted that the 'general tenor of the disclosure [was] contrary to the respondents argument that the [weight increase in the animals being bred was] the main effect and [the remedying of scours] the secondary one and that they [were] separable'.[249] The TBA held that the applicant's intention, as derived from the wording of the claims, was to treat animals suffering from scours (treatment by therapy) *and* to prevent that complaint in those that did not already have it (treatment by prophylaxis).[250] The TBA emphasised that, contrary to the respondent's argument that increasing the animal's weight was the primary effect, it was clear that the respondent's intention was to achieve both results *simultaneously*.[251] Therefore, the patent was not granted.

(c) Method of treatment by therapy?

In some instances, the question is not whether a method of treatment of the animal body by therapy is patentable in light of its application to animals generally (and, by extension, its usefulness in the farming industry) as was the case in *BAYER/Immunostimulant* but, rather, whether the claimed subject matter is a method of treatment by therapy at all. In *SALMINEN/*

---

244 (T 438/91) [1999] EPOR 333.
245 Ibid, at para. 3.1.3.
246 Ibid, at para. 3.1.1.
247 Ibid.
248 Ibid, at para. 3.1.3.
249 Ibid.
250 Ibid.
251 Ibid.

Pigs III,[252] for example, the claims related to a method of preventing piglets from suffocation under a dam in the brooding pen, by blowing air under the standing dam thus creating unpleasant conditions for the piglets.[253] The TBA defined therapy as either: (a) any non-surgical treatment which is designed to cure, alleviate, remove or lessen the symptom of, or prevent or reduce the possibility of contracting any malfunction of the animal body; or (b) the treatment of a disease in general or curative treatment in the narrow sense as well as the alleviation of the symptoms of pain and suffering.[254] The TBA claimed that the action of blowing air under the standing dam, which was practised on the bodies of the piglets, could not reasonably be called therapy within the meaning of Article 52(4) EPC.[255] Agreeing with the Opposition Division, the TBA accepted that the invention was 'concerned with preventing accidents, analogous to a method of preventing a worker from trapping his hand in machinery'.[256] The prevention of accidents was not considered as a method of treatment by therapy because, although aimed at the prevention of harm to the animal, it was not of such a nature as to fall under the rubric of methods of medical treatment[257] – that is to say, it was not curative in nature. As a result, the claimed method was not excluded from patent protection. Clearly, if the method related to an additive for use in feed for sows and feed for sows, it would not offend Article 52(4) EPC.[258]

(d) Conclusion

As mentioned above, in *WELLCOME/Pigs I*, the claimed method, which was for the use of a pesticidal composition to treat pigs and to remove ectoparasites, was held to be a method of treatment of the animal body by therapy even if general agricultural uses were considered as patentable subject matter.[259] The question in such cases inevitably becomes whether the incidental objectives are separable. If they are, then the existence of a possible therapeutic use would not usually be a bar to patent protection. For example, a substance for the stimulation of the body's defences is a therapeutic treatment and its secondary beneficial effect would not be

---

252 (T 58/87) [1989] EPOR 125.
253 Ibid, at para. 2.3.
254 Ibid, at para. 2.2.
255 Ibid.
256 Ibid.
257 Ibid, at para. 3.
258 *ALINOMOTO/Feed for sows* (T 1223/01), at para. 2.
259 (T 116/85) [1988] EPOR 1, at para. 4.3.

sufficient to alter this.[260] If a claim method, properly construed, embraces a therapeutic method, it will be excluded from patent protection.[261] Where the industrial benefit of such treatment on animals is the result of the therapeutic treatment, the claimed method would be unpatentable.[262]

4 The Enlarged Board of Appeal

The EBA in *MEDI-PHYSICS/Treatment by surgery* claimed that in the following deliberations on the draft EPC a long discussion developed around the reference of the exclusion to 'animals', claiming that it was suggested from various sides that that reference be deleted on the grounds: first, that it would be difficult to distinguish between methods of breeding in animals and methods protecting animals from disease; secondly, the difficulty of distinguishing between strictly veterinary methods of treatment and other methods, concerning stock-raising or sterilisation of certain species of insects, for example, which would be clearly of a more industrial nature; thirdly, to enable jurisprudence to make a distinction between veterinary treatment and cases which were more typically industrial.[263] The EBA concluded that it appeared that the question of the patentability of certain kinds of treatments of animals was perceived as being more generally concerned with finding an appropriate distinction between methods for the industrial exploitation of animals, which should be patentable, and methods for the therapeutic treatment of animals which were to be excluded from patentability on humanitarian grounds and in the interest of public health.[264]

The EBA added that while, with respect to animals, it could be an *a priori* defendable concept to regard surgical methods like organ transplantation, embryo transfer, sterilisation and castration as methods of industrial exploitation which might be patentable, the situation under the EPC nevertheless remains that the legislator has decided otherwise.[265] It pointed out that, after long discussions, the drafters of the EPC decided, for reasons

---

260 *BAYER/Immunostimulant* (T 780/89) [1993] EPOR 377, at para. 7.

261 See *FUJISAWA PHARMACEUTICAL CO/Antimicrobial agent* (T 0150/95) where the TBA noted that '[t]he Appellant has thus ignored the comment by the Board that if he wishes to cover non-therapeutic uses of [the substance] as an antimicrobial agent, a different claim formulation should be used' (at para. 2). The claim was, therefore, rejected.

262 'Examination Guidelines for Patent Applications relating to Medical Inventions in the UK Intellectual Property Office', June 2007, at para. 41.

263 (G 01/07), at para. 3.3.2.2.

264 Ibid.

265 Ibid, at para. 3.3.7.

of public health, to extend the exclusion from patentability to animals based on the same criteria applied to humans and more recent discussions on that subject in the context of drafting the Biotech Directive have still led to the same result.[266] Therefore, the EBA held that no distinction can be made between humans and animals when the scope of the exclusion is interpreted.[267] The teething issues that are raised in this context were not addressed by the EBA, since this was not the question about which it was primarily concerned.

5 Conclusion

The TBAs have had to steer a course between ensuring that the exclusion from methods of medical treatment was not rendered meaningless on the basis that such treatments can be part of the farming industry and, therefore, should fall outside the scope of the exclusion. Not surprisingly, they have maintained that although the exclusion should be narrowly construed, it cannot be interpreted in such a way that medical treatments for use in commercial farming are allowable, whereas other medical treatments are not. There was no intention by the drafters of the EPC to make such a distinction in the application of the exclusion, and none can reasonably be interpreted into the exclusion. It is quite clear that non-therapeutic treatments of animals were, undoubtedly, intended by the drafters of the EPC to fall outside the scope of the exclusion from patent protection of methods of medical treatment. The TBAs, in line with the jurisprudence of the EPO relating to cosmetic methods, have accepted that where a claimed method, on a proper construction of the claims, inevitably covers a method of treatment of the animal body by therapy, it will be excluded from patent protection even if the claimed method also has a non-therapeutic effect.

I NEW MEDICAL TECHNOLOGY

The application of scientific principles to medical treatments finds expression in new forms of medical treatment *viz.* gene therapy and therapeutic cloning. These developments are not surprising given the recently completed quest to map the human genome. Numerous incurable diseases still exist today and governments should either fund such endeavours or provide

---

266 Ibid.
267 Ibid.

the incentives to physicians/researchers to secure the necessary funding to continue work in this field. The incentives should be in the form of patent protection where the patentee can reap a sufficient return so that she can continue R&D. The importance of providing the necessary incentives for R&D cannot be underestimated. The aim of this section is merely to highlight the issues that arise in the context of patenting these new technologies and how they interact with the medical treatment exclusion found in Article 53(c) EPC and the exclusion based on morality or ordre public found in Article 53(a) EPC. The exhaustive policy-based arguments are considered elsewhere and will not be rehearsed here.[268]

Gene therapy and therapeutic cloning are of particular significance as they have provided, and have the ability to provide, cures to diseases that are incurable according to previous and current scientific knowledge, for example, cystic fribrosis, muscular dystrophy, cancer and heart disease. Gene therapy is able to provide, not only the cure, but it can also determine whether an individual carries the gene of a particular disease. Gene therapy is valued not only for its therapeutic purpose but, similarly, for its diagnostic capabilities, in particular, for gene-based diagnostic kits.[269]

Gene therapy is essentially the application of DNA technology to the treatment and alleviation of diseases.[270] Recombinant DNA technology allows scientists to cut pieces of DNA which are then placed in bacteria

---

[268] IPI (Intellectual Property Institute), 'Patents for genetic sequences: The competitiveness of current UK law and practice', http://www.berr.gov.uk/files/file10475.pdf (accessed 18 April 2011); Nuffield Council on Bioethics, 'The ethics of patenting DNA: a discussion paper' London, United Kingdom: Nuffield Council on Bioethics, 2002, http://www.nuffieldbioethics.org/sites/default/files/The%20ethics%20of%20patenting%20DNA%20a%20discussion%20paper.pdf (accessed 22 April 2011); Australian Law Reform Commission, 'Report 99—genes and ingenuity: gene patenting and human health', Sydney, Australia: Australian Law Reform Commission, 2004, http://www.austlii.edu.au/au/other/alrc/publications/reports/99/ (accessed 18 April 2011); Ontario Ministry of Health, 'Genetics, testing and gene patenting: charting new territory in healthcare', Toronto, Canada: Ontario Ministry of Health 2002, http://www.health.gov.on.ca/english/public/pub/ministry_reports/geneticsrep02/report_e.pdf (accessed 18 April 2011); Secretary's Advisory Committee on Genetics, Health, and Society, Meeting transcript, Washington, DC: SACGHS, 2009, http://oba.od.nih.gov/SACGHS/sacghs_past_meeting_documents.html#oct2009 (accessed 18 April 2011).

[269] See A. Odell-West, 'The legacy of Myriad for gene-based diagnostic: a new policy and regulatory option' (2009) JIPLP 267 and M. Rimmer, 'Myriad Genetics: Patent Law and Genetic Testing' [2003] EIPR 20.

[270] See, generally, N. Jain, 'To Patent or not to Patent: Gene Therapy in the European Union and the United States' (1996) Cardozo J Int'l & Comp L 103; J. Bradshaw, 'Gene Patent Policy: Does Issuing Gene Patents accord with the purposes of the US Patent System?' (2001) Willamette L Rev 637.

where they multiply rapidly. In other words the DNA of a cell is altered to produce a protein which, in nature, occurs in another organism.[271] Although experimentation began as early as 1970, it was not until 22 May 1989 that the first successful experiment was carried out. There are two types of gene therapy, namely, somatic and germline gene therapy.[272] Somatic gene therapy exists where the gene expression in cells is manipulated in such a way that it corrects the defect in the patient, and it has the effect where this correction is not inherited by the next generation. Somatic gene therapy is further classified in three categories, namely: (1) *ex vivo* where the cells are removed from the human body, combined with a vector then returned to the human body; (2) *in situ* where the vector is placed directly into the human tissue without having to remove it from the human body; and (3) *in vivo*, where the vector is inserted directly into the bloodstream.[273] Germline therapy involves the genetic modification of cells so that correction will be passed on to the next generation.[274]

One important feature of the Biotech Directive is that it excludes germline therapy from patent protection. This was based on the consensus within the Community that such a process offends against *ordre public* and public morality. This exclusion was based on the recommendation of the Group of Advisers on the Ethical Implications of Biotechnology of the European Commission.[275] Without becoming embroiled in the continuing discussion over the 'patenting of life', it is suggested that the drafters of the Biotech Directive acted precipitously in excluding germline therapy from patent protection. The question is whether this exclusion is justified on moral grounds in light of its substantially beneficial use for a therapeutic purpose. Answers to such questions will be attempted in this section.

Somatic gene therapy, however, *is* patentable. The process of inserting the vector would hardly offend Article 52(4) EPC as it would not be considered as a method of medical treatment. However, the claim could be directed at the manufacture of the medicament for the therapeutic purpose. This would result in a product patent. Questions concerning second medical use are likely to arise since the significant aspect of gene therapy is

---

[271] *Biogen Inc. v Medeva Plc* [1997] RPC 1 (HL) 32.

[272] J. Anderson, 'Human Gene Therapy' (1999) http://www.ndsu.edu/pubweb/~mcclean/plsc431/students99/anderson.htm (accessed 1 June 2011).

[273] Ibid.

[274] 'Should Genetic Manipulation of Human Genes that Affect Future Offspring be Allowed?' http:/www.angelfire.com/hi3/germline/ (accessed 1 June 2001.

[275] Opinion of the Group of Advisors on the Ethical Implications of Biotechnology of the European Commission No. 7 (1996), point 1.4 and 1.7 http://ec.europa.eu/european_group_ethics/docs/opinion7_en.pdf (accessed 22 April 2011).

identification of the relevant gene and its use for a method of treatment of the human or animal body by therapy. Gene therapy hardly would be excluded under Article 53(c) EPC which prohibits patents on methods of treatment for therapy and surgery, and for diagnosis, since its patenting does not offend the *ratio legis* of the exclusion from patent protection of methods of medical treatment. The physician or veterinary practitioner is in no way inhibited in the method by which she chooses to treat her patients by allowing patents on these new technologies. It is also likely that since gene therapy is so specific, there would be no need to find protection under Articles 54(5) or 54(5) EPC, which protects first and second and further therapeutic uses, respectively. This does not mean that, if necessary, these two provisions cannot be used by a patentee to secure patent protection. However, unlike the traditional methods of medical treatment contemplated by the drafters of the EPC, genetic-based treatments and diagnoses present distinct problems that will be examined in chapter 6.[276]

In relation to methods for the treatment of the human body by therapy under Article 53(c) EPC, as was noted above, the TBAs have defined therapy as being not limited to the curing of diseases but that it covered any which was designed to cure, alleviate, remove or lessen the symptoms of, or prevent or reduce the possibility of contracting any disorder or malfunction of the human or animal body. There is, therefore, no question that the methods of treatment exclusion is implicated in relation to these new technologies but, it must be noted that Article 53(c) EPC goes further and provides that 'this provision shall not apply to products, in particular substances or compositions, for use in any of these methods'. As was noted before, it is self-evident that the prohibition of methods procedure patents would not prevent the patentability of products, including substances or compositions, even if they are used in such excluded methods of medical treatment. Therefore, it is unlikely that such new therapies, such as stem cell therapy, and gene therapy, would offend the exclusion from patent protection of methods for treatment of the human or animal body by therapy. The application of the method of medical treatment exclusion to the new technologies outlined above is apt. In answering the question of whether any of the new technologies relating to any of the methods of medical

---

[276] The issue of morality has found its place in Article 53(a) EPC. In relation to stem cells, see G. Laurie, 'Patenting Stem Cells of Human Origin' [2004] EIPR 59; H. Vogelsang-Wenke, 'Patenting of Stem Cells and Processes Involving Stem Cells According to the Rules of the European Patent Convention' (2004) 23 Biotechnology Law Report 155, 156; and see A. Agovic, 'Stem cell patents on a knife edge' (2008) JIPLP 718, 719. See also Recitals 16 and 41 and 20–24 (relating to genes) of the Biotech Directive.

treatment are patentable, the *ratio legis* of the exclusion must first be examined. The EBA in its decision in *MEDI-PHYSICS/Treatment by surgery* reiterated that the real reason for excluding the defined methods from patentability were socio-ethical considerations and considerations of public health.[277] Consequently, it argued that medical and veterinary practitioners should be free to use their skills and knowledge of the best available treatments to achieve the utmost benefit for their patients, uninhibited by any worry that some treatment might be covered by a patent.

J CONCLUSION

The TBAs have been fairly consistent in defining the exclusion of methods of treatment of the human or animal body by therapy, stating that it not only covers curing a disease or removing its causes, but that it also covers treatments which are meant to alleviate or reduce the symptoms of any malfunction of the human body. As a result, they have held that contraceptive methods are not excluded from patent protection since they do not fall within that broad definition. They have exalted the principle that patents should be granted, and that the exclusion should be narrowly construed, ensuring that cosmetic methods are patentable even if they might incidentally have some therapeutic effect. With similar boldness, they have allowed patents for implantable devices in the human body only where there is no relationship between the device and the therapeutic benefit on the human body to which it is applied. The patenting of methods that involve animals for industrial purposes has proved troubling and the TBAs have still to establish some clear rules relating to this. The potential for the exclusion to become an unruly horse has been tamed, ensuring that the exclusion only applies where it relates specifically to a therapeutic method of treatment.

---

[277] (G 01/07), at para. 3.3.6.

5. Surgical methods

A INTRODUCTION

Article 53(c) of the European Patent Convention (EPC) excludes, *inter alia*, 'methods of treatment of the human and animal body by *surgery*' from patent protection.[1] This exclusion, more so than any of the other methods of medical treatment exclusions, arguably, cuts right at the heart of why the exclusion exists in the first place. The Technical Boards of Appeal (TBAs) have stated that generally the exclusion exists to free from restraint the activities of physicians (and, of course, veterinary practitioners) by patent monopolies when they treat their patients.[2] If one accepts this, then, the case is *a fortiori* for excluding methods of treatment by surgery from patent protection, because it is difficult to conceive of a surgical treatment that does not actively require the presence and, of course, intimate involvement of a surgeon (or surgeons) in the surgical procedure.[3]

---

[1] See generally, D. Thomas, 'Patentability Problems in Medical Technology' (2003) 34 IIC 847 and R. Moufang, 'Methods of Medical Treatment under Patent Law' (1993) 24 IIC 18. See also, A. Odell-West, 'Protecting Surgeons and their Art. Methods for Treatment of the Human Body by Surgery under Article 52(4) EPC' [2008] EIPR 102. The ideas in this chapter have been derived, in part, from the following: E. Ventose, 'Exclusion of methods of treatment of the human or animal body by surgery from patent protection' (2007) JIPLP 574; 'Patent Protection for Surgical Methods Under the European Patent Convention' (2008) 39 IIC 58; 'Disclaiming Methods of Medical Treatment from Patent Protection Under the European Patent Convention' (2009) JIPLP 706; 'The Enlarged Board of Appeal rules on the scope of the exclusion from patent protection for methods for treatment of the human or animal body by surgery' (2010) JIPLP 393; and 'Patenting Surgical Methods in Europe after *MEDI-PHYSICS/Treatment by surgery*' (2011) JIPLP 108.

[2] This was first articulated by the TBA in *WELCOME/Pigs I* (T 116/85) [1988] EPOR 1 at para. 3.7. The EBA in *EISAI/Second medical indication* (G 05/83) [1979–85] 241 also pointed out that the intention behind the exclusion was only to prevent non-commercial and non-industrial medical and veterinary activities from being limited by patent monopolies (at para. 22).

[3] See generally, P. Lancon, 'Patentability in the Field of Therapy and Diagnosis' (1991) 22 IIC 893; W. De Smet, 'Patentability in the Area of Therapy and Diagnosis under Belgian Law' 22 IIC 888 (1991); K.E. Panchen, 'Patentability in the Field of

However, inventors have still sought to patent surgical procedures notwithstanding the existence of the exclusion.[4] The thorny issues relating to methods of treatment by surgery inevitably revolve around a consideration of whether the following, among other things, are excluded from patent protection: (a) a method of treatment that involves the death of the subject; (b) second medical uses of surgical instruments; (c) surgical methods of treatment which are directed at primarily a cosmetic purpose (where the therapeutic aspect of the claim is only incidental); and (d) a claim which merely contains or recites a surgical feature. The issues, therefore, focus on the fringes of what is protected and what is not. Where the line is to be drawn has occupied the time of the TBAs in the various decisions that will be considered in due course. Consequently, the TBAs have had to engage in legal gymnastics to try to give some measure of consistency in the interpretation of the exclusion, ensuring that statements made in one context do not undermine principles enunciated elsewhere. That consistent approach has evaded them, as will be apparent in due course.

It was hardly surprising, therefore, that a recent decision of the TBA in *MEDI-PHYSICS/Treatment by surgery*[5] referred three questions relating to the scope and definition of the exclusion of methods of treatment of the human or animal body by surgery from patent protection to the Enlarged Board of Appeal of the European Patent Office (EBA) for its consideration. Much has happened[6] since the decision of the TBA in *GEORGETOWN UNIVERSITY/Pericardial access* which had, only six years earlier, refused to refer four questions relating to the scope of the exclusion to the EBA. This was because it thought that the facts did not raise any new point of law which 'could not have been decided in conformity with the comprehensive and uniform jurisprudence which exists on the question posed by the applicant'.[7]

This chapter will not only examine the nature and scope of the exclusion of methods of treatment of the human or animal body by surgery, but it will also examine the issues that lie at the heart of this new referral by the

Therapy and Diagnosis' (1991) 22 IIC 879; P. Pennant, 'Patentability of Medical Treatment' [1981] 2 EIPR 64 and D. Thomas, 'Patentability Problems in Medical Technology' (2003) 34 IIC 847.

4 R. Moufang, 'Methods of Medical Treatment under Patent Law' (1993) 24 IIC 18, 36–40.

5 (T 0992/03) [2007] EPOR 32.

6 In particular, see the 2004 decision of the TBA in *THE GENERAL HOSPITAL CORPORATION/Hair removal method* (T 0383/03) and subsequent decisions that have rejected the learning in *SEE-SHELL/Blood Flow* (T-182/90) and *GEORGETOWN UNIVERSITY/Pericardial access* (T-35/99).

7 (T 35/99) [2001] EPOR 169 at para. 11.

TBA in *MEDI-PHYSICS/Treatment by surgery*. Importantly too, this chapter will consider the decision of the EBA in *MEDI-PHYSICS/Treatment by surgery*[8] where it answered the questions referred to it by the TBA and brought some clarity to this area of the law, but left some issues unresolved. An attempt will be made at reconciling the seemingly irreconcilable decisions of the TBAs. It is important to have a symmetry in any approach that is adopted to ensure consistency giving effect to a necessary seamless web that is integral throughout the jurisprudence of the TBAs in this area. This chapter will also examine the areas where the EBA could have provided more guidance and the inconsistencies that are inherent in its reasoning as well as the salient points made therein.

B LEGISLATIVE HISTORY

The early drafts of the exclusion for methods of medical treatment did not make any reference to surgical methods. However, in 1969, the exclusion for methods of medical treatment was broadened to include 'surgical methods'.[9] By 1970, the exclusion related to 'surgical methods for treatment of the human or animal body'[10] and in 1971 it was for 'methods for treatment of the human [or animal] body by surgery'.[11] The change in the wording between the drafts of 1970 and 1971 was merely cosmetic. Similarly, with therapeutic methods the exclusion of methods of treatment of the human

---

8 (G 01/07).

9 Article 9(2) provided that: 'Inventions within the meaning of paragraph (1) shall in particular exclude: (e) therapeutic or *surgical methods* for treatment of the human or animal body, and diagnostic methods' (Preliminary Draft Convention for a European System for the Grant of Patents, Inter-Governmental Conference for the Setting up of a European System for the Grant of Patents, Minutes of the Working party, Luxembourg, 8 to 11 July, 1969) (emphasis added).

10 First Preliminary Draft of a Convention Establishing a European System for the Grant of Patents, Brussels, 21 December 1970.

11 Article 9(e), Second Preliminary Draft of a Convention Establishing a European System for the Grant of Patents, 1971. This reflects the same position at the stage reached on 29 January 1971 in relation to the First Preliminary Draft Convention Establishing a European System for the Grant of Patents, Brussels, 15 February 1971 (Stage reached on 29 January 1971). The Document correcting the Second Preliminary Draft Convention Establishing a European System for the Grant of Patents, Brussels, 6 December 1971 was to the same effect except that the square brackets were removed (Stage reached on 26 November 1971).

or animal body by surgery remained unchanged in May 1972[12] and formed part of the text which was tabled at the Munich Diplomatic Conference in 1973.[13]

The *travaux préparatoires* did not contain copious explanations by the delegations of the meaning of the exclusion of surgical methods from patent protection. There were only a few instances in the *travaux préparatoires* where there was a clear articulation of the rationale for the exclusion of methods of medical treatment of humans from patent protection. At one meeting, the Working Party considered the issue of whether surgical treatment for destructive purposes, for example, the sterilisation of insects, should be explicitly excluded from the provision.[14] The Working Party was of the view that treatment of this kind was not intended to be included in the exclusion but considered it unnecessary to draft a text stating this explicitly.[15] It seems clear, therefore, that the drafters of the Convention were convinced that the exclusion of surgical methods from patent protection would not apply only to those treatments which were destructive in nature. During discussions at an Inter-Governmental Conference, concerning whether the exclusion should also apply to animals, the Conference emphasised that the intention behind the text was merely to exclude from patentability all therapeutic treatment practised on animals. The aim of the exclusion was to exclude from patentability treatments intended to cure or alleviate the suffering of animals.[16] This indicated a clear policy objective behind the exclusion of therapeutic treatment of animals from patent protection.

The EBA in *MEDI-PHYSICS/Treatment by surgery* considered the legislative history of the provisions of the EPC in order to determine whether it provided any guidance on the question whether only surgical methods of a curative nature were excluded from patent protection under the EPC, noting that before it could embark on a definition of the term 'surgery', it was useful to investigate the legislative history and the purpose

[12] Draft Convention Establishing a European System for the Grant of Patents (Stage reached on 20 May 1972).

[13] Draft Convention, Munich Diplomatic Conference for the Setting up of a European System for the Grant of Patents, Munich, 10 September to 6 October 1973.

[14] Minutes of the 11th Meeting of the Working Party I held in Luxembourg from 28 February to 3 March 1972, at para. 9(d).

[15] Ibid.

[16] Minutes of the 6th Meeting of the Inter-Governmental Conference for the Setting up of a European Patent System for the Grant of Patents, Luxembourg, 19 to 30 June 1972, at para. 27.

of the insertion of the term 'surgery' in the EPC 1973.[17] Observing that little by way of explanation may be gleaned from the EPC 2000, the EBA clarified that it is the preparatory work to the EPC 1973 which it must consider when looking for the 'right' meaning to be given to the term 'treatment by surgery'.[18]

After examining the two documents, relied on by the TBA in *THE GENERAL HOSPITAL CORPORATION/Hair removal method*,[19] for the view that it was the intention of the legislator only to exclude from patentability those treatments by surgery which concern curative activities,[20] the EBA claimed that when the first document relied on by the TBA was drawn up, an exclusion for surgical methods from patentability had not yet been considered and the statement in the document concerned the suggested incorporation in the then Article 9 of an exclusion from patentability of therapeutic and diagnostic methods only. The EBA continued that it was in this context that that document was to be placed and no conclusion as regards any meaning the legislator wanted to give to the later incorporated term 'treatment by surgery' can be derived from these remarks.[21] The EBA stated that the exclusion from patentability of treatments by surgery was only incorporated into draft Article 9(2) during the meeting of Working Party I in order to bring it into conformity with the corresponding draft Rule 39.1 of the Patent Convention Treaty (PCT), but no further information as to how the European drafters understood the term 'treatment by surgery' was apparent from this document.[22] In relation to Rule 39.1 PCT, the EBA continued that the Records of the Washington Diplomatic Conference on the PCT, 1970, showed that the reason for introducing such a rule was the fear that International Searching Authorities would have difficulties in searching prior art for subject matter that was unpatentable under national law.[23]

Notwithstanding its statements above, the EBA went on to state that the only document explicitly addressing the issue as to whether surgical treatment of animals not intended for therapeutic purposes, but, on the contrary, for destructive purposes (e.g. the sterilisation of insects) was included in Article 9(d).[24] The drafters of the Convention said that: 'The Working

---

[17] (G 01/07) at para. 3.3.1.
[18] Ibid, at 3.3.2.1.
[19] (T 0383/03).
[20] (G 01/07) at para 3.3.2.2.
[21] Ibid.
[22] Ibid.
[23] Ibid.
[24] Ibid.

Party was of the opinion that treatment of this kind was not in fact intended to be included in this provision, but did not consider it necessary to draft a text stating this explicitly.'[25] As a result, the EBA concluded that neither document BR/177/ e/72 nor any other document from the *travaux préparatoires*, including the document cited by the TBA in *THE GENERAL HOSPITAL CORPORATION/Hair removal method*, reflected the general view that only such surgical methods of a therapeutic nature, were intended by the legislator to be excluded from patentability by the words used in Article 52(4) EPC.[26]

Curiously, the EBA also considered the legislative history of an altogether different area, biotechnology, claiming that the President of the EPO reported that the first draft of the Biotech Directive contained an 'interpretation rule' stating that the exclusion from patentability, or from industrial applicability, of methods practised on the animal body for the purpose of surgical treatment or diagnosis only apply if such methods are practised for therapeutic purposes, based on the consideration that the legislator had insufficiently foreseen the development of surgical methods that were not therapeutic in nature, but industrial.[27] The EBA further noted that the Biotech Directive did only apply to animals, but said that the said rule was contained neither in the second draft of the Biotech Directive nor in the adopted version. It continued that Recital 35 of the Biotech Directive only stated that the Biotech Directive is without prejudice to the provisions of national patent law, whereby processes for treatment of the human or animal body by surgery or therapy and diagnostic methods, practised on the human or animal body, are excluded from patentability. It explained that in addition the EPC legislators did not take up this issue when revising the EPC in November 2000, but left the substance of Article 52(4) EPC untouched, it being their declared intention to maintain the current practice of the EPO while transferring the substance of the provision to the list of exceptions from patentability.[28]

The EBA then asked what would be the normal reading of the wording of Article 53(c) EPC as a provision containing three alternatives, that is, that these alternatives are different in scope?[29] It replied that, as a consequence, the exclusion of 'treatments by surgery' cannot be seen as limited to surgery which is performed for a therapeutic purpose. This was because it would already be entirely covered by the exclusion of therapeutic methods

25 Ibid.
26 Ibid, at 3.3.2.3.
27 Ibid, at 3.3.2.4.
28 Ibid.
29 Ibid.

from patentability which was supported by the course of the preparatory work for the EPC 1973 and by the outcome of later legislative initiatives.[30]

C THE REFERRAL TO THE EBA

In *MEDI-PHYSICS/Treatment by surgery*, the application related to the following methods: (a) a method of magnetic resonance for imaging the pulmonary and/or cardiac vasculature and evaluating blood flow using dissolved polarized 129Xe; (b) a method for determining a spectroscopic signal representative of a blood volume or blood flow of a subject; and (c) a cardiac imaging method.[31] Each of these methods comprised a step of delivering the polarised 129Xe to the subject, in particular, via inhalation. Claim 17, in particular, comprised a step of delivering the polarized 129Xe 'to the region of the heart such as via injection and the like into the left ventricle'.[32] The injection of the polarized 129Xe into the patient's heart, in the view of the TBA, represented 'a substantial physical intervention on the body which entails a health risk and requires professional medical expertise to be carried out'.[33] For reasons, which will be examined in due course, the TBA decided to refer the following questions for the consideration of the EBA:

1. Is a claimed imaging method for a diagnostic purpose (examination phase within the meaning given in [*CYGNUS/Diagnostic method*[34]]), which comprises or encompasses a step consisting in a physical intervention practised on the human or animal body (in the present case, an injection of a contrast agent into the heart), to be excluded from patent protection as a 'method for treatment of the human or animal body by surgery' pursuant to Article 52(4) EPC if such step does not per se aim at maintaining life and health?
2. If the answer to question 1 is in the affirmative, could the exclusion from patent protection be avoided by amending the wording of the claim so as to omit the step at issue, or disclaim it, or let the claim encompass it without being limited to it?
3. Is a claimed imaging method for a diagnostic purpose (examination phase within the meaning given in [*CYGNUS/Diagnostic method*]) to be considered as being a constitutive step of a 'treatment of the human or animal

---

30 Ibid, at 3.3.2.5.
31 (T 0992/03) at para. 4.1.
32 Ibid.
33 Ibid, at para. 4.2.
34 (G 01/04) [2006] EPOR 15.

> body by surgery' pursuant to Article 52(4) EPC if the data obtained by the method immediately allow a surgeon to decide on the course of action to be taken during a surgical intervention?

The issues of fundamental importance raised by this decision will be explored in the appropriate sections of this chapter, namely: first, whether the definition of a 'method of treatment by surgery' should embrace only the purpose of the method to the exclusion of its nature; secondly, whether the existence of a surgical step in a claimed method makes that method an excluded method of treatment by surgery; and, thirdly, whether disclaimers can legitimately be used to prevent a claim from being excluded as a surgical method.

In addition, although the TBA in *GEORGETOWN UNIVERSITY/Pericardial access* did not refer to the EBA any of the questions raised by the applicants, it might be fitting, in light of this current referral and the subsequent inconsistent decisions of the TBAs on the scope of the exclusion, that those unanswered questions are also attempted in this chapter, namely:

(a) Does a method of treatment of the human or animal body mean any non-insignificant intervention performed on the human or animal body?
(b) If yes, what is a non-insignificant intervention?
(c) If no, what is the definition of a method of treatment?
(d) For a claim to be excluded under Article 52(4) EPC, does it have to relate in its entirety to a method of treatment?
(e) Whether the presence of a surgical step means that the claim is automatically excluded under Article 52(4) EPC.[35]

D DEFINING SURGICAL METHODS

1 Introduction

Inevitably, before one considers the scope of any exclusion, one must first determine what exactly is protected and what is not; therefore, the definition of 'methods of treatment of the human or animal body by surgery' would obviously assist. The TBAs have not been able to delineate the scope of the exclusion with any measure of consistency. This gives rise to

[35] (T 35/99) at para. VII.

attendant consequences, especially when other TBAs have come to determine what exactly is excluded by that definition. This problem is highlighted with the myriad definitions of the term 'surgery' adopted by the TBAs. An expansive definition might, contrary to the spirit of the exclusion, exclude claims which should not realistically be covered; whereas, a narrow one might allow the patenting of surgical procedures that should properly be excluded from patent protection. A balance must necessarily be struck when defining the exclusion to ensure that legitimate research and development in the medical field is not stifled, while, at the same time, ensuring that the actions of physicians and veterinary practitioners are not limited by patent monopolies. It is also important that any interpretation given to the exclusion for surgical methods is not narrower than that of the other methods of medical treatment exclusions, for example, methods of treatment by therapy and diagnostic methods practised on the human or animal body.[36] The need for legal certainty, of course, lies at the heart of these arguments.[37]

The exclusion of methods of medical treatment in Article 52(4) EPC specifically excludes from patent protection methods for 'treatment of the human or animal body by *surgery*'. The analysis of this exclusion by an examination of its constituent parts, as was done by the TBA in *SEE-SHELL/Bloodflow*,[38] seems appropriate. In that decision, the TBA first defined 'treatment'; secondly, 'surgery'; and, thirdly, 'treatment by surgery', before it could provide any conclusion on the meaning of that particular exclusion in Article 52(4) EPC. A cursory reading of this provision suggests that the exclusion is limited only to those surgical methods which are meant for the *treatment* of the human or animal body. What, therefore, does 'treatment', in the ordinary sense of the word, add to the term 'surgery'? The question of whether the word 'treatment' necessarily involves some therapeutic purpose becomes a pressing one. Arguably, this cannot be so, since the exclusion in Article 52(4) EPC would not have specifically excluded methods of treatment of the human or animal body by *therapy* from patent protection. The TBAs have, however, disagreed. In the process of defining which surgical methods are excluded from patent protection, the TBAs have come to accept, with some reluctance, that they usually relate to methods that have the aim of maintaining the health of the human person or animal, implying that the therapeutic purpose of the surgery is of

---

36 The need for consistency in the approach of the various TBAs when interpreting the exclusion was emphasised by the EBA in its recent decision of *CYGNUS/Diagnostic method* (G 01/04) at para. 1.

37 *CYGNUS/Diagnostic method* (G 01/04) at para. 3.

38 (T 182/90) at para 2.1.

particular relevance. The troubled journey by which this conclusion was arrived at will be explored in this chapter.

2 A Narrow Interpretation

In answering the questions referred to it by the TBA, the EBA in *MEDI-PHYSICS/Treatment by surgery* was of the opinion that it was established in the jurisprudence of the EBA, ever since the EBA decision in *EISAI/Second medical indication*, that the principles of interpretation of Articles 31 and 32 of the Vienna Convention were to be applied to the interpretation of the EPC even though its provisions do not apply to the EPC *ex lege*.[39] It continued that, according to Article 31(1) of the Vienna Convention, a treaty shall be interpreted in good faith in accordance with the ordinary meaning to be given to the terms of the treaty in their context and in the light of its object and purpose.[40] As a result, the EBA concluded that no general principle of narrow interpretation of exclusions from patentability, which would be applicable *a priori* to the interpretation of any of the EPC exclusions, can be derived from the Vienna Convention.[41] Rather, it continued, the general rule in Article 31 that a treaty shall be interpreted, in good faith in accordance with the ordinary meaning to be given to the terms of the treaty in their context and in the light of its object and purpose must, apply to the exclusions contained in the EPC.[42]

Moreover, the EBA clarified that if the interpretation of Article 53(c) EPC, in light of these principles of interpretation, leads to the result that a narrow interpretation was the right approach then, and only then, such restrictive meaning is to be given to it.[43] The EBA accepted that when it came to considering the impact of the context of a provision, the fact that an exclusion was at issue was important, in relation to its interpretation, but this was only one of the factors in determining what the right interpretation of the provision concerned should be. It continued that, in addition to the ordinary meaning to be given to the provision, it must be interpreted in such a manner that achieves the purpose for which it was designed.[44] This, the EBA argued, must apply to an exclusion from patent protection in the same manner as to any other requirement for patentability.[45] The EBA then

39 (G 01/07) at 3.1.
40 Ibid.
41 Ibid.
42 Ibid.
43 Ibid.
44 Ibid.
45 Ibid.

cited *CYGNUS/Diagnostic method* observing that the EBA, in that decision, came to its conclusion that the exclusion of diagnostic methods was indeed to be interpreted narrowly only after a thorough investigation of the wording and the purpose of the exclusion clause concerned.[46] It then examined *WARF/Use of embryos*[47] noting that the EBA, in that decision, did not mention the existence of a principle of narrow construction of exceptions from patentability at all. The EBA clarified that, instead, as a method for interpreting the extent of the prohibition, the EBA in *WARF/Use of embryos* went directly to the rules of interpretation laid down in the Vienna Convention, that is, it looked at the terms of the provision and its object and purpose. The EBA acknowledged that no mention was made, in *WARF/Use of embryos*, of any narrow or restrictive view which would have to be taken because it was there dealing with an exclusion from patentability and that, in *MEDI-PHYSICS/Treatment by surgery*, it will proceed in the same way.[48]

3 Nature of the Intervention

(a) Only the nature of intervention relevant

The first decision of the TBA to examine exhaustively the scope of the exclusion of methods of treatment of the human or animal body by surgery is *SEE-SHELL/Bloodflow*.[49] In that decision, the method in question related to the use of labelled micro spheres of a size adapted to follow through the circulatory system of the animal but to be trapped in the capillaries of the tissue. After the introduction of the micro spheres, the animal was sacrificed and the trapped micro spheres were then counted. The question was whether these steps represented a method of treatment of the animal body by surgery. The TBA first defined the term 'treatment' and accepted that the term:[50]

> 'medical treatment' means any non-insignificant intentional physical or psychic intervention performed directly or indirectly by one human being – who need not necessarily be a medical practitioner – on another (or, by analogy, on animals) using means or methods of medical science.

It also pointed out that the word 'treatment', as it appears in Article 52(4) EPC, was 'not restricted to methods serving a direct therapeutic purpose

---

46 Ibid.
47 (G 02/06) *Official Journal* EPO 5/2009, 306.
48 (G 01/07) at 3.1.
49 *SEE-SHELL/Blood flow* (T 182/90) [1994] EPOR 320.
50 Ibid.

(including prophylactic) purpose'; noting that such purpose 'is introduced by the express reference to "therapy" in Article 52(4) EPC'.[51] In light of the above definition, the TBA emphasised that:[52]

> the term 'medical treatment' may also include treatments for other, non-curative purposes such as cosmetic treatment, the termination of pregnancy, castration, sterilisation, artificial insemination, embryo transplants, treatments for experimental and research purposes and the removal of organs, skin or bone marrow from a living donor.

The TBA then proceeded to define the term 'surgery', observing that '[t]he Guidelines for Examination in the European Patent Office (cf. C-IV, 4.3) state that the term "surgery" defines the *nature* of the treatment rather than its *purpose*. This may, however, not be true in all cases'.[53] The exception to this accepted by the TBA will be explored in the next section. The TBA then examined various definitions of surgery, the first being the 'practice of medicine that deals with the diagnosis and correction of bodily defects resulting from injury or disease and the relief of suffering by manual and instrumental procedures'. That approach also embraces 'closed surgery', which is defined as the 'manipulation of a part, organ, or tissue without making a skin incision'.[54] The second defined surgery as 'the branch of medicine concerned with the healing of disease, accidental injury or bodily defects by operating on the living body', and includes 'conservative (non-invasive) procedure (sic) such as repositioning, and the far more numerous operative (invasive) procedures using instruments'.[55] The third, the TBA noted, defined surgery as 'an operation as direct or indirect treatment of any kind performed on the structure of an organism',[56] and includes 'endoscopy, puncture, injection, excision, and opening of the bodily cavities. Catheter insertion is also considered as an intensive surgical technique'.[57]

The TBA emphasised that the 'reference to healing in some of the preceding definitions of "surgery" appears to be inconsistent with the fact

---

[51] Ibid, at para. 2.2.

[52] Ibid.

[53] Ibid, at para. 2.3 (emphasis added).

[54] *SEE-SHELL/Blood flow* (T 182/90) at para. 2.3, citing 'International Dictionary of Medicine and Biology', Vol. III (John Wiley & Sons, 1986), p. 2762.

[55] *SEE-SHELL/Blood flow* (T 182/90) at para. 2.3, citing *Brockhaus Enclyopadie* (19th edn, Vol 4, 1987).

[56] *SEE-SHELL/Blood flow* (T 182/90) at para. 2.3, citing M. Reifferscheid and S. Weller 'Chirurgie' ('Surgery'), (8th edn, Georg Thieme Verlag Stuttgart-New York 1989), pp. 131, 132).

[57] Ibid.

that, in today's medical and legal linguistic usage, the non-curative treatments [such as cosmetic surgery] are, if carried out by surgery, regarded as surgical treatments'.[58] The term 'treatment by surgery', the TBA clarified, had undergone a change insofar as it now comprised of particular treatments that are not directed to the preservation of the health of the human or animal body.[59] Generally, the exclusion of methods of treatment of the human or animal body by surgery was initially interpreted to embrace surgical methods by which the body was cured from: (a) disease; (b) accidental injury; and (c) bodily defects. Based on the foregoing, the TBA accepted that: (a) the definition of surgery embraced only the nature of the treatment itself and not its purpose; and (b) treatments that are not based solely on preserving the health of the human and animal body are also caught by the exclusion.

Following the decision of the TBA in *SEE-SHELL/Bloodflow*, a surgical method has been defined as 'any method comprising a non-insignificant intentional physical intervention performed directly or indirectly by one human being on another by manual or instrumental procedures'.[60] This definition, it must be noted, first, did not contain any reference to the purpose for which the 'intentional physical intervention' was performed on the human or animal body. Secondly, the use of the phrase 'non-insignificant' is quite problematic, since it is not altogether clear how that would be applied in practice by the TBAs. In order for a method to be excluded from patent protection under Article 52(4) EPC, it is not necessary that the intervention on the human or animal body be invasive or that the tissue be penetrated.[61] At this juncture, the definition of methods of treatment by surgery seems to be very broad and covers all physical interventions on the human or animal body irrespective of their intended purpose.[62] The sole qualification related only to whether the intervention was 'non-insignificant'. What is immediately clear is that this definition would cover cosmetic methods which do not form part of any medical treatment of the human body.

---

58 Ibid, at para. 2.4.

59 Ibid.

60 *THERMAGE/Apparatus for skin resurfacing* (T 1172/03) at para. 2.1, citing *SEE-SHELL/Bloodflow* (T 182/90).

61 *CAMTECH AS* (T 05/04) at para. 2. In that decision, the TBA noted that what actually counts for the assessment under Article 52(4) EPC was that the sensors are placed inside the body and that feature is part of the method as claimed.

62 See R. Moufang, 'Methods of Medical Treatment under Patent Law' (1993) 24 IIC 18, 38–39.

The TBA in *GEORGETOWN UNIVERSITY/Pericardial access* accepted wholeheartedly the various statements made by the TBA in *SEE-SHELL/Blood flow*, stating that it saw 'no reason to deviate from the above view'.[63] It further expanded on these definitions by examining two categories of physical interventions on the human or animal body.[64] The first, it noted, embraced 'interventions which, *whatever their specific purpose*, give priority to maintaining life or health of the human or animal body on which they are performed'.[65] This definition was seemingly accepted by the EBA in *CYGNUS/Diagnostic method* but without the limitation 'whatever their specific purpose'.[66] The TBA was of the opinion that this definition applied to both healing and cosmetic surgery, and to all physical interventions which were aimed at altering the functions of the living body (for example, castration to bring about changes in the body linked to sex) as well as the removal of body parts (for example, for the purposes of transplantation).[67] But, if the TBA actually intended to disavow any reliance on the 'purpose' of the claimed method, then the statement that such physical interventions 'give priority to maintaining life or health of the human or animal body on which they are performed' is clearly contradictory. The second category of physical interventions on the human or animal body examined by the TBA comprised those that end in the death of the living beings.

The requirement that the surgical method must relate to some therapeutic treatment of the human or animal body was expressly rejected by the TBA in *GEORGETOWN UNIVERSITY/Pericardial access* where it emphasised that the clear and deliberate choice of the legislator to use the terms 'treatment' and 'surgery' '*cannot* be considered as constituting two distinct requirements for the exclusion'.[68] The TBA explained that for a particular patient 'the optimal or only available treatment could not be administered if even a single part or step thereof – and most treatments comprise several steps – were covered by patent protection'.[69] This was because: (a) the intentions of the user are not a feature of claims in patent

---

63 (T 35/99) at para.3.

64 *GEORGETOWN UNIVERSITY/Pericardial access* (T 35/99) [2001] EPOR 169.

65 Ibid, at para. 4.1 (emphasis added).

66 (G 01/04) at para. 6.2.1.

67 *GEORGETOWN UNIVERSITY/Pericardial access* (T 35/99) at para. 4.1, [2001] EPOR 169. See R. Moufang, 'Methods of Medical Treatment under Patent Law' (1993) 24 IIC 18, 39.

68 *GEORGETOWN UNIVERSITY/Pericardial access* (T 35/99) at para. 7 (emphasis added).

69 Ibid.

law;[70] (b) of the impossibility of defining what a complete or insignificant surgical method is.[71] If these criteria were applicable under the jurisprudence of the EPC, they 'would run counter to clarity and legal certainty'.[72] Where the procedure ends in the death of the animal, it is clearly one that is non-therapeutic. The TBA, therefore, concluded that the wording of the exclusion means 'any (by its nature) surgical ... method which can be carried out ... as such on the human or animal body'.[73]

(b) The exception

The scope of the exclusion was further limited by the interpretation given to the definition of surgery by the various TBAs. They were at pains to point out that there was general agreement that treatments may be excluded from patentability only if they were carried out on a *living* human or animal body.[74] No authority, however, was cited for this proposition. The TBA in *SEE-SHELL/Blood flow* claimed that the issue was considered at the preparatory stage of the EPC, where '[i]t was agreed that these methods were not to be excluded from patentability and that, however, there was no need to expressly mention this in the Article'.[75] The TBA further claimed that a method which includes a surgical step practised on a living laboratory animal and, in addition, a step of sacrificing the said animal, which is necessary to carry out the method, cannot be regarded in its entirety as a method of treatment by surgery in the sense of Article 52(4) EPC.[76] In other words, a claimed method, when considered in its entirety, would not be considered as a method of treatment of the animal or human body by surgery, because the conscious ending of life cannot be a method of surgical treatment.[77] That might be true, but it must not be confused with an acceptance that the claimed method was neither surgical nor a 'surgical method' – the claimed method was simply not a 'method of *treatment* by surgery', as the TBA rightly held.

This reasoning was, apparently, in accordance with the primary purpose of Article 52(4) EPC, which was to achieve an improved state of health of

---

[70] *Cf MOBIL/Friction reducing additive* (G 02/88) [1990] EPOR 73.

[71] *GEORGETOWN UNIVERSITY/Pericardial access* (T 35/99) at para. 7.

[72] Ibid.

[73] Ibid, at para. 8.

[74] See also R. Moufang, 'Methods of Medical Treatment under Patent Law' (1993) 24 IIC 18, 38.

[75] (T 182/90) at para. 2.5.2.

[76] Ibid. The TBA also held that for this same reason, the claimed method did not constitute a diagnostic method, since the animal body on which it is practised does not survive (at para. 2.6).

[77] *SEE-SHELL/Bloodflow* (T 182/90) at para. 2.6.

the human or animal body and not the destruction thereof.[78] Surgery, whether therapeutic or cosmetic, normally involves the enhancing of the quality of human or animal life and would necessarily exclude surgery that involves the conscious ending of human or animal life. In *GEORGETOWN UNIVERSITY/Pericardial access*, the TBA saw no reason to deviate from the views expressed in *SEE-SHELL/Blood flow*, noting that 'it believes that the exclusion of "destructive treatments" from the scope of Article 52(4) is perfectly consistent with, and therefore imposes no limits on, the concept that "surgery" defines the *nature* of the treatment rather than its intended *purpose*'.[79] Therefore, '[m]ethods consciously ending in the treated subject's death are not *in their nature* methods of surgical treatment ... irrespective whether they comprise one or more surgical steps'.[80]

4 The Purpose of the Intervention

(a) Introduction

A comprehensive definition of surgical methods cannot be undertaken without an understanding of the rationale behind the exclusion of methods of medical treatment, in particular, surgical methods under Article 52(4) EPC. This would inform any such definition, and the various TBAs would need to have them in mind when interpreting and delineating the scope of the exclusion. For example, in *GEORGETOWN UNIVERSITY/Pericardial access*, the TBA stated that legislators have ensured that a regime was in place to deal with all aspects in the medical sphere, for example, strict regulations relating to the use of medical treatments and criminal liability for injury caused by such treatments, and penalties for medical misuse.[81] Given that framework, the TBA asked how far patent protection should cover medical procedures. It reiterated that the policy behind the exclusion of methods of medical treatment from patent protection was clearly to ensure that those who carry out such methods as part of the medical treatment of human or the veterinary treatment of animals should not be hampered by patents.[82]

(b) The 'ratio legis' of the exclusion

To properly interpret the exclusion, including methods of treatment by surgery, it is necessary to understand what is meant by the term 'the *ratio*

---

78 Ibid.
79 (T 35/99) at para. 3 (emphasis added).
80 Ibid.
81 Ibid, at para. 5.
82 Ibid.

legis of Article 52(4) EPC'.[83] The TBA in *THE GENERAL HOSPITAL CORPORATION/Hair removal method* thought that to answer any question relating to the scope of the exclusion of methods of treatment by surgery from patent protection, in particular, the definition of the phrase 'treatment by surgery', it was 'necessary to refer to the *ratio legis* of Article 52(4) EPC'.[84] It noted that the '*Travaux préparatoires* [show that] the intention of the legislator was to exclude from patentability curative methods[85] of human or veterinary medicine including diagnostic methods'.[86] The TBA further noted that the jurisprudence of the TBAs have 'repeatedly confirmed this *ratio legis* of Article 52(4) EPC stating that the policy behind the exclusion of the methods set out in Article 52(4) EPC was clearly to ensure that those who carry out such methods as part of the medical treatment of humans or the veterinary treatment of animals should not be inhibited by patents'.[87] Essentially, the question is not only whether that approach is the correct one, but whether it is the *only* one which defines the nature of the exclusion of methods of treatment by surgery. As the TBA in *THERMAGE/Apparatus for skin resurfacing* explained, the definition of the word 'surgery' 'must be adapted to the current situation keeping in mind the aim of the legislator when he wrote the law, the so called "*ratio legis*" '.[88] The TBA continued by stating that '[t]his adaptation is particularly important in a field such as patent law, in which the technology is rapidly developing so that the legislator could never foresee all the possible applications of the law'.[89]

The EBA in *MEDI-PHYSICS/Treatment by surgery*, as noted above, claimed that the exclusion of 'treatments by surgery' could not be seen as limited to surgery which was performed for a therapeutic purpose since it was already covered by the exclusion of therapeutic methods from patentability. This, it noted, was not in conflict with, but, rather, supported

---

83 *THE GENERAL HOSPITAL CORPORATION/Hair removal method* (T 0383/03) at para. 3.2.

84 Ibid.

85 The TBA defined curative activities as 'those activities aimed at maintaining and restoring the health, the physical integrity, and the physical well being of a person (and also preventing diseases). The same applies to activities performed on animals' (ibid, at para. 3.2).

86 *THE GENERAL HOSPITAL CORPORATION/Hair removal method* (T 0383/03) at para. 3.2. This view was reiterated by the EBA in *CYGNUS/Diagnostic method* when it pointed out that '[f]rom the fact that Article 52(4) EPC further refers to methods of surgery and therapy it can be inferred that these diagnostic methods serve *curative purposes* ...' (at para. 6.4).

87 *THE GENERAL HOSPITAL CORPORATION/Hair removal method* (T 0383/03) at para. 3.2.

88 *THERMAGE/Apparatus for skin resurfacing* (T 1172/03) at para. 2.1.

89 Ibid.

travaux préparatoires of EPC 1973 and by the outcome of later legislative initiatives.[90] The EBA claimed that, in relation to the exclusion for methods of medical treatment found in Article 53(c) EPC, it was commonly accepted that the real reason for excluding the defined methods from patentability were socio-ethical considerations and considerations of public health.[91] It continued that, previously, the legislative mechanism by which methods of medical treatment were excluded from patent protection was on the basis of the legal fiction that they were not to be regarded as inventions susceptible of industrial application. The EBA emphasised that medical and veterinary practitioners should be free to use their skills and knowledge of the best available treatments to achieve the utmost benefit for their patients uninhibited by any worry that some treatment might be covered by a patent.[92] By incorporating Article 52(4) EPC into Article 53(c) EPC, the EBA clarified that the legislator of the EPC 2000 had brought out this idea and rationale much more clearly.[93]

(c) Only the purpose of the intervention relevant

Some decisions of the TBA have rejected the notion that surgical procedures that do not have a therapeutic purpose are excluded from patent protection. The first to do so was the decision of the TBA in *THE GENERAL HOSPITAL CORPORATION/Hair removal method*. There, the claim related to a cosmetic method for the simultaneous removal of a plurality of hairs from a skin region, each hair being in a follicle extending into the skin from a skin surface. The TBA, after considering the decisions of *SEE-SHELL/Blood flow*,[94] *GEORGETOWN UNIVERSITY/Pericardial access*[95] and *EXPANDABLE GRAFTS/Surgical device*,[96] stated that, although 'methods of treatment which are not directed at improving or maintaining the health of the human being or animal may be patentable, the case is not so clear where the treatment involves manual and/or instrumental procedures', for example, methods of treatment by surgery.[97] Therefore, the TBA thought that it was necessary to examine, first, 'whether

---

90 Ibid, at 3.3.2.5.
91 Ibid, at 3.3.6.
92 Ibid.
93 Ibid.
94 (T 182/90) [1994] EPOR 320.
95 (T 35/99) [2002] EPOR 169.
96 (T 0775/97) [2002] EPOR 24.
97 *THE GENERAL HOSPITAL CORPORATION/Hair removal method* (T 0383/03) at para. 3.1.

Article 52(4) EPC intends to exclude from patentability this type of intervention as such';[98] or, secondly, 'whether a therapeutic effect plays a decisive role in determining which interventions are excluded from patentability'.[99] The answer to those questions, the TBA continued, were 'all the more important since the term "surgery" [had] undergone a change in meaning as explained in [*SEE-SHELL/Blood flow*]'.[100]

Such methods, it has been stated, are 'in principle excluded from patentability unless they are clearly neither suitable nor potentially suitable for maintaining or restoring the health, the physical integrity, and the physical well being of the human being'.[101] This definition was first articulated by the TBA in *THE GENERAL HOSPITAL CORPORATION/Hair removal method*[102] and has since been used by various TBAs to determine which claims are actually directed at methods of treatment by surgery.[103] After examining the legislative rationale behind the exclusion of methods of medical treatment and the reasons given by the EBA in *EISAI/Second medical indication*[104] for the exclusion, the TBA in *THE GENERAL HOSPITAL CORPORATION/Hair removal method* concluded that:[105]

> It follows that the intention of the legislator was that only those treatments by therapy or surgery are excluded from patentability which are suitable for or potentially suitable for maintaining or restoring the health, the physical integrity, and the physical well being of a human being or an animal and to prevent diseases.

The TBA was very much aware that its interpretation was contrary to the received view of the TBAs in *SEE-SHELL/Blood flow* and *GEORGETOWN UNIVERSITY/Pericardial access*. However, it was made clear that:[106]

---

[98] Ibid.
[99] Ibid.
[100] Ibid.
[101] *THERMAGE/Apparatus for skin resurfacing* (T 1172/03) at para. 2.1.
[102] (T 0383/03) at para. 3.2.
[103] *See also KONINKLIJKE PHILIPS ELECTRONICS NV* (T 09/04) at para. 6; *THERMAGE/Apparatus for skin resurfacing* (T 1172/ 03) at para. 6; and *MAQUET Critical Care AB* (T 1102/02) at para. 3, all applying the test articulated in *THE GENERAL HOSPITAL CORPORATION/Hair removal method* (T 0383/03).
[104] (G 05/88) [1979–85] EPOR 241.
[105] *THE GENERAL HOSPITAL CORPORATION/Hair removal method* (T 0383/03) at para. 3.2.
[106] Ibid, at para. 3.

> Even if in medical linguistic usage the term 'treatment by surgery' nowadays also comprises treatments which are not directed to the health of human beings or animals, they do not fall within the exclusion from patentability if they are not covered by the *ratio legis* of Article 52(4) EPC.

The TBA reiterated that a 'claimed method is patentable only if it is clearly not potentially suitable for maintaining or restoring the health, the physical integrity, and the physical well-being of a human being or an animal'.[107] The TBA defined curative activities as those 'activities aimed at maintaining and restoring the health, the physical integrity, and the physical well being of a person (and also preventing diseases)', and accepted that the same applies to 'activities performed on animals'.[108] Therefore, based on the foregoing, surgical methods were defined by the TBAs as those methods of treating the human or animal body which might be useful for maintaining or restoring the: (a) health; (b) physical integrity; and/or (c) physical well-being of the human being or animal and (d) to prevent diseases. The TBA reasoned that, in accordance with the jurisprudence of the EPO whereby treatments without a surgical step but having only a cosmetic step are not excluded from patent protection, methods for the treatment of the animal or animal body by surgery that are 'clearly neither suitable nor potentially suitable for maintaining or restoring the health, the physical integrity, or the physical well being of human beings or animals do not fall within the exclusion from patentability of Article 52(4) EPC'.[109] On that basis, cosmetic methods would clearly be patentable.

5 The EBA in CYGNUS/Diagnostic Method

The EBA in *CYGNUS/Diagnostic method* did not explicitly adopt the new approach outlined above primarily because that was not the issue it had to grapple with. However, it observed that '[m]ethods of surgery within the meaning of Article 52(4) EPC include any physical interventions on the human or animal body in which maintaining the life and health of the subject is of *paramount importance*'.[110] It also pointed out that, '[f]or

[107] Ibid, at para. 4.

[108] Ibid, at para. 3.2. *Cf THERMAGE/Apparatus for skin resurfacing* (T 1172/03) at para. 2.1.

[109] Ibid, at para. 3.4. In *ULTRAFEM/Feminine hygiene device* (T 1165/97), the TBA emphasised that '[a] prerequisite therefore (sic) is the act of surgery or the curative or preventive treatment of illness or the alleviation of the symptoms of pain and suffering, which is not the case with the method of the invention' (at para. 4.2).

[110] (G 01/04) at para. 6.2.1.

example, within the meaning of Article 52(4) EPC, a claim including the feature "performing a lumbar puncture to deliver epidural injections" is to be considered to relate to a method of surgery'.[111] It is this last-mentioned *obiter* statement made by the EBA in *CYGNUS/Diagnostic method*, among other things, that caused the TBA in *MEDI-PHYSICS/Treatment by surgery* to raise 'the question whether the claimed method, insofar as they encompassed the step of delivering polarized 120Xe via injection, might be considered as treatments by surgery excluded from patent protection under Article 52(4) EPC'.[112]

The EBA in *MEDI-PHYSICS/Treatment by surgery* pointed out that in *CYGNUS/Diagnostic method* the EBA was primarily concerned with defining the meaning of the exclusion from patentability of diagnostic methods under Article 52(4) EPC 1973 and not with giving a definition of the term 'treatment by surgery'.[113] As a result, the EBA explained that the considerations of the EBA in *CYGNUS/Diagnostic method* on methods of surgery or therapy only served the purpose of delimiting the diagnostic methods as being multistep methods. The EBA continued that in addition the use of the word 'including' in the sentence above indicated that the EBA in *CYGNUS/Diagnostic method* did not intend to give an exhaustive definition of the term 'methods of treatment by surgery'.[114] It noted that saying that treatments by surgery *included* any physical interventions on the human or animal body 'in which maintaining the life and health of the subject is of paramount importance' was not equivalent to saying that the term 'treatment by surgery' *was* limited to therapeutic methods. The EBA further noted that it was evident that in all but destructive surgical methods, for example, cosmetic surgery, organ removal, embryo transfer etc., but also in the imaging methods claimed in the application underlying the referral, in particular, when involving potentially risky interventions like an injection into the heart, maintaining the life and health of the subject is of paramount importance.[115] As a result, the EBA held that the definition given by the EBA in *CYGNUS/Diagnostic method* cannot be understood in the sense that the EBA endorsed the view that the term 'treatment by surgery' is limited to therapeutic surgery. On the contrary, the EBA held that definition accepted by the EBA in *CYGNUS/Diagnostic method* fitted in very well with the previously established jurisprudence, namely *SEE-SHELL/Blood flow* and *GEORGETOWN UNIVERSITY/Pericardial*

[111] Ibid.
[112] (T 0992/03) at para. VI.
[113] (G 01/07) at para. 3.3.5.
[114] Ibid.
[115] Ibid.

access, which held that the term surgical treatment embraced those interventions which, whatever their specific purpose, give priority to maintaining life and health of the human or animal body on which they are performed. The TBA continued that these decisions also accepted that, because it was the purpose of the exclusion to apply in the medical sphere, it could not be so broadly construed as to include destructive treatments, that is such procedures whose conscious (deliberate or incidental) end result is the death of the living being 'under treatment'.[116] Such procedures, the EBA clarified, did not qualify as methods in which 'maintaining the life and health of the subject is of paramount importance'. The EBA held that the definition given by the EBA in *CYGNUS/Diagnostic method* therefore cannot be interpreted as going beyond the approach adopted by the TBA in *SEE-SHELL/Blood flow* and *GEORGETOWN UNIVERSITY/Pericardial access*.[117]

Similarly, the EBA continued, the example of the lumbar puncture given in that context cannot be interpreted as expressing the EBA's position that 'treatments by surgery' are only those methods pursuing a therapeutic purpose. It explained that the fact that therapeutic surgery was considered excluded from patentability told nothing about what would be the EBA's position with respect to non-therapeutic surgery.[118]

E MEDI-PHYSICS/TREATMENT BY SURGERY

1 The Decision of the TBA

The question of whether the claimed imaging methods, 'insofar as they encompassed the step of delivering polarized 129Xe via injection, might be considered as treatments by surgery excluded from patent protection under Article 52(4) EPC' arose for consideration by the TBA in *MEDI-PHYSICS/Treatment by surgery*, because of an *obiter* statement made by the EBA in *CYGNUS/Diagnostic method*.[119] The TBA also noted that the question of whether 'the claimed methods as a whole should be regarded as constituting an element of treatment by surgery', because statements made in the description in the patent specification whereby 'the imaging methods

[116] Ibid.
[117] Ibid.
[118] Ibid.
[119] Ibid.

of the invention provided real-time feedback during surgery to verify success of treatment'.[120]

The TBA in *MEDI-PHYSICS/Treatment by surgery* examined the decisions of the TBA in *SEE-SHELL/Blood flow*, *GEORGETOWN UNIVERSITY/Pericardial access*, *THE GENERAL HOSPITAL CORPORATION/Hair removal method* and the decision of the EBA in *CYGNUS/Diagnostic method.* The TBA in the instant decision was very cautious. It explained the inconsistent definitions, as outlined above, noting that the jurisprudence of the TBAs relating to surgical treatments 'identifies two aspects in the definition of surgery, namely the nature of the physical intervention on the one hand and its purpose on the other hand'.[121] It emphasised that they 'have drawn different conclusions in respect of the exclusion under Article 52(4) EPC depending on whether the emphasis was put on the former or the latter aspect'.[122] The TBA also pointed out that the jurisprudence relating to the interpretation of the exclusion for methods of treatment by surgery by the various TBAs 'does not appear to be consistent', explaining that:[123]

> Whereas one approach is based on an assessment of the nature of the physical intervention on the body, the other concentrates on whether the physical intervention is suitable for maintaining or restoring the health, the physical integrity or the physical well-being of a person or an animal.

Then, with little analysis, the TBA concluded that 'the approach based on the purpose may give rise to opposing judgements as to the exclusion from patent protection of one and the same physical intervention'.[124] This was because:[125]

> For example, an injection of a medicament for treating a disease would be excluded but an injection of a substance reducing wrinkles for cosmetic purposes might not be considered to constitute a treatment by surgery within the meaning of Article 52(4) EPC because it is not suitable for maintaining or restoring health. In both cases, the physical intervention on the body would be substantially the same, i.e. an injection.

The TBA concluded that it was necessary to make the reference to the EBA because it considered that a decision was required: (a) to ensure uniform

---

120 Ibid.
121 (T 0992/03) at para. 4.5.
122 Ibid.
123 Ibid, at para. 4.5.1.
124 Ibid.
125 Ibid.

jurisprudence of the law; or (b) if an important point of law arises.[126] In respect of the former, the TBA noted that '[d]ifferent definitions of the term "surgery" have been identified in the jurisprudence of the boards of appeal', namely, one focusing on 'the nature of the physical intervention on the one hand or its purpose on the other hand'.[127] This, the TBA thought, 'might result in different conclusions on patentability under Article 52(4) EPC'.[128] Importantly, the TBA noted that the 'application of other approaches [to the interpretation of the exclusion] may not be excluded'.[129] It was, therefore, necessary for the EBA to clarify how the exclusion is to be interpreted. In any event, the TBA emphasised that the 'issue of which interpretation to take is an important point of law', which serves, *inter alia*, to determine 'the extent of an area of activities exempt from patent protection',[130] since 'the scope of the exclusion [of methods of medical treatment under Article 52(4) EPC] is materially dependent upon the interpretation of the expression "*treatment by surgery*" '.[131]

2 The Decision of the EBA

(a) A literal interpretation

The EBA in *MEDI-PHYSICS/Treatment by surgery* claimed that in order to be patentable a claimed invention must fulfil all of the requirements for patentability and must not be excluded from patent protection by any of the exclusions in the EPC. It noted that the three alternative exclusions in Article 53(c) EPC are thus cumulative requirements, which meant that in order to be patentable a claimed method must neither be a therapeutic nor a surgical nor a diagnostic one.[132] Consequently, the EBA noted that although the invention at issue was excluded from patent protection as a diagnostic method, it could, nevertheless, still be excluded from patent protection as a surgical method if *THE GENERAL HOSPITAL CORPORATION/Hair removal method* limiting the exclusion to treatments for a therapeutic purpose was not to be followed.[133]

The EBA explained that the fact that the exclusion of methods of treatment by surgery from patentability is one of three alternative exclusion

---

126 Ibid, at para. 6.
127 Ibid.
128 Ibid.
129 Ibid.
130 Ibid.
131 Ibid (emphasis in original).
132 Ibid at para. 3.3.
133 Ibid.

conditions *prima facie* indicated that the situations covered by each of the alternatives were not meant to be identical, since the inclusion of the term 'by surgery' in Article 53(c) EPC would be pointless if the meaning of that alternative was already entirely contained in the exclusion from patentability of the other alternative, that is the 'treatments by therapy'.[134] In this context, the EBA continued, it was noteworthy that the exclusion condition referring to 'surgery' was not initially contained in the draft EPC but was introduced later than the exclusions relating to therapeutic and diagnostic methods.[135]

(b) The 'ratio legis' of the exclusion

The EBA explained that, at least with respect to humans, a limitation of the exclusion to such surgical methods which serve a therapeutic purpose did not take full account of and did not give full effect to the purpose of the exclusion.[136] The EBA explained that in relation to serious and risky surgical interventions, for example, in cosmetic surgery, organ transplantation, embryo transfer, sex change operations, sterilisation and castration (surgical methods which require considerable professional medical expertise to be carried out and involve serious health risks even when carried out with the required professional care and expertise), the *ratio legis* of the exclusion (to free practitioners from being potentially hampered by patents in the application of the best possible treatment on their patients) did apply, was important and called for their exclusion from patentability.[137]

The EBA pointed out that, for three reasons, the approach adopted by the TBA in *THE GENERAL HOSPITAL CORPORATION/Hair removal method* created discrepancies between the definition of what is to be understood as therapeutic in the context of a 'treatment by therapy' and in the context of a 'treatment by surgery'.[138] The first was that, while for 'treatment by therapy' it was recognised that symptomatic therapy which cured a symptom but not the underlying disease fell under the exclusion, that did not appear to be recognised, at least not to the same extent, with respect to a potentially surgical method.[139] Secondly, it appeared from that definition that, according to the TBA in *THE GENERAL HOSPITAL CORPORATION/Hair removal method*, which accepted the purpose/related construction of Article 52(4) EPC, only aspects relating to physical

134 (G 01/07) at 3.3.1.
135 Ibid.
136 Ibid, at para. 3.3.7.
137 Ibid.
138 Ibid, at para. 3.3.8.
139 Ibid, at para. 3.3.8.1.

health should be taken into consideration but the term 'treatment by therapy' also included treatments aimed at maintaining or restoring the mental health of the subject.[140] Thirdly, in relation to surgical treatments, which may be carried out for therapeutic purposes or for non-therapeutic ones, for example, for aesthetical or other personal reasons, it would have to be established in each case whether or not the non-therapeutic effect was distinguishable from the therapeutic effect. If it was not distinguishable, the EBA reasoned that the claimed method would have to be excluded from patentability.[141]

The EBA emphasised that by contrast to the decision in *THE GENERAL HOSPITAL CORPORATION/Hair removal method* in which the therapeutic and the surgical character of curing a symptom (excess hair) was denied, although it was acknowledged that excess hair may be a symptom of a disease, in *THERMAGE/Apparatus for skin resurfacing* the therapeutic and surgical character of the method claimed as a cosmetic method for tightening the skin's surface by delivery of electromagnetic energy through the skin surface and the epidermis to a deeper collagen containing tissue site was acknowledged.[142] The reason why this latter decision was so decided was because the claimed method could be used for several therapeutic purposes including the application on the face or neck for reconstructive purposes.[143] It continued, stating that by comparing the cases underlying the decisions in *THERMAGE/Apparatus for skin resurfacing* and *THE GENERAL HOSPITAL CORPORATION/Hair removal method*, it was not *prima facie* evident why removing excess hair would not be a therapeutic treatment even if the cause for the excess hair is a disease and it would then be the symptom of a disease which is cured, and why, on the other hand, 'altering the consistency and geometry of soft tissue' is excluded from patentability – even if limited to cosmetic methods – for the sole reason that it can be used for reconstructive (that is, therapeutic) purposes.[144]

Consequently, the EBA held that the comparison between *THERMAGE/Apparatus for skin resurfacing* and *THE GENERAL HOSPITAL CORPORATION/Hair removal method* shows how inconsistent the decisions to be made could become, if the term 'treatment by surgery' was seen as limited to therapeutic surgery only.[145] Admittedly, the EBA continued, it was often also difficult to precisely delimit excluded therapeutic from

---

140 Ibid, at para. 3.3.8.2.
141 Ibid, at para. 3.3.8.3.
142 Ibid, at para. 3.3.8.4.
143 Ibid.
144 Ibid, at para. 3.3.8.5.
145 Ibid, at para. 3.3.8.6.

patentable cosmetic treatments.[146] It accepted that this problem could not be avoided because the express wording of Article 53(c) EPC states that only therapeutic methods are excluded from patentability (and thus cosmetic methods are not) and the exclusion could not be extended to treatments which are not therapeutic in character.[147] As a result, the EBA concluded that the *ratio legis* of the exclusions from patentability in Article 53(c) EPC justified a limitation of the term 'treatment by surgery' to curative surgery, contrary to what the ordinary meaning of the word 'surgery' implied and contrary to the fact that Article 53(c) EPC defined three separate alternative exclusions suggesting that these were not merely identical in scope.[148] It further concluded that the meaning of the term 'treatment by surgery' was not to be interpreted as being confined to surgical methods pursuing a therapeutic purpose.[149]

(c) A broad or narrow construction of the exclusion

The EBA stated that the broad approach to the types of interventions considered as surgical accepted by the TBA in *SEE-SHELL/Blood flow* was not challenged by the TBA in *THE GENERAL HOSPITAL CORPORATION/Hair removal method* and the later decisions following it have simply additionally required a therapeutic purpose in order for the exclusion to apply.[150] The EBA agreed with the appellant that the broad approach was and had become overly broad when considering today's technical reality.[151] The EBA claimed that advances in safety and the now routine character of certain, albeit invasive techniques, at least when performed on uncritical parts of the body, mean that many of those techniques are now generally carried out in a non-medical, commercial environment such as in cosmetic salons and in beauty parlours.[152] The EBA, therefore, ruled that it was now hardly justified to exclude such methods from patent protection.[153] It then said that examples of such techniques include tattooing, piercing, hair removal by optical radiation, micro abrasion of the skin.[154] The EBA continued that, in light of this technical reality, 'excluding from patentability such safe routine techniques,

146 Ibid.
147 Ibid.
148 Ibid, at para. 3.3.10.
149 Ibid.
150 Ibid, at para. 3.4.2.1.
151 Ibid, at para. 3.4.2.2.
152 Ibid.
153 Ibid.
154 Ibid.

even when of invasive nature, appeared to go beyond the purpose of the exclusion of treatments by surgery from patent protection in the interest of public health.'[155] The EBA then concluded that, insofar as the definition given by the EBA in *CYGNUS/Diagnostic method* that ' "any physical intervention" on the human or animal body ...' was a method of surgery within the meaning of Article 52(4) EPC, it appeared too broad.[156]

The EBA reasoned that a narrower understanding of what constituted, by its nature, a 'treatment by surgery' within the meaning of Article 53(c) EPC was required and that any such meaning must allow the purpose of the exclusion to be effective but it must also not go beyond it.[157] It explained that the exclusion served the purpose of, in the interests of public health and of patients, specifically freeing the medical profession from constraints which would be imposed on them by patents granted on methods for surgical or therapeutic treatment. Therefore, the EBA held that any definition of the term 'treatment by surgery' must cover the kind of interventions which represent the core of the medical profession's activities, that is the kind of interventions for which their members are specifically trained, and for which they assume a particular responsibility.[158] The EBA stated that these were the physical interventions on the body which required professional medical skills to be carried out and which involved health risks even when carried out with the required medical professional care and expertise. It noted that it was in this area that the *ratio legis* of the provision to free the medical profession from constraints by patents came into play.[159] This narrower understanding, the EBA emphasised, ruled out from the scope of the application of the exclusion clause uncritical methods involving only a minor intervention and no substantial health risks, when carried out with the required care and skill, while still adequately protecting the medical profession.[160]

(d) Redefining methods of treatment by surgery

The EBA was of the opinion that it was not possible for it, in the context of the referral when trying to redefine the meaning of the term 'treatment by surgery', to give a definition which would, once and for all, also delimit the

---

155 Ibid.
156 Ibid.
157 Ibid, at para. 3.4.2.3.
158 Ibid.
159 Ibid.
160 Ibid.

exact boundaries of such a new concept with respect to the whole comprehensive body of technical situations which might be concerned by it.[161] The EBA added that the required new direction was that the exclusion from patentability should not be applied to methods where the interests of public health, protection of patients and freedom of the medical profession to apply the treatment of choice to their patients, did not call for their exclusion from patentability.[162] The EBA explained that the Examining Division and the TBAs were much better suited to define the boundaries of a more narrowly construed concept of 'treatment by surgery' in future cases.[163] The factors they were to take into account included: (i) required medical expertise; (ii) health risks involved; and (iii) degree of invasiveness or complexity of the operation performed.[164] It noted that, although it appeared likely that interventions involving a high degree of complexity and/or a high degree of invasiveness would normally require professional medical expertise and entail health risks even when carried out with the required care and expertise, it did not wish to rule out from the outset that, depending on the circumstances of the individual case under consideration, other criteria could not also determine that a physical intervention on the human or animal body is a 'treatment by surgery' within the meaning of Article 53(c) EPC.[165]

The EBA explained that another reason why it could not give an authoritative once and for all definition of what the term 'treatment by surgery' may comprise was that, in the ever changing technical and medical reality, the term 'surgery' did not have a fixed meaning either.[166] It stated that there was no general common concept for the acts which were commonly regarded as surgical in the medical sense but that what was to be understood by 'surgery' in the medical sense was, to a large extent, a matter of convention.[167] Thus, the EBA reasoned that in order to be surgical it was not necessary that the intervention be invasive or that tissues be penetrated.[168] The EBA, nonetheless, readily admitted that in many situations it would not be an easy task to determine whether or not an invasive step constituting a substantial physical intervention on the body, comprised or encompassed by a claim, required professional medical skills to be carried

161 Ibid, at para. 3.4.2.4.
162 Ibid.
163 Ibid.
164 Ibid.
165 Ibid.
166 Ibid, at para. 3.4.2.5.
167 Ibid.
168 Ibid.

out and involved a substantial health risk even when carried out with the required care and expertise.[169]

The EBA claimed that although legal certainty was important in order to enable persons to assess in advance what could be patented and what was excluded, it emphasised that it was equally important to give these inventions the protection they deserve and to come to a balanced system of exclusion, on one hand, and patentability on the other hand.[170] It explained that where a new direction was taken in interpreting a requirement for patentability, be it in the form of an exclusion or in the form of a positive requirement, it was normal and unavoidable that practice and jurisprudence need time and the handling of a number of cases in order to develop a line which would then create a new uniform system of applying a new concept.[171] However, in light of the fact that the field of methods which potentially involve surgical steps was vast, the EBA pointed out that each category of cases will have to be assessed on its own merits and that this could, however, not be a reason for not opting for new solutions, as the old approach was considered unsatisfactory.[172]

(e) Legal analysis

The implications of this decision for those who are engaged in research relating to cosmetic method and devices are vast. The previous decisions of the TBAs, arguably, allowed patent protection for such methods which did not have a curative purpose but simply had a cosmetic or industrial purpose. However, the decision of the EBA in *MEDI-PHYSICS/ Treatment by surgery* has now closed the gap in the jurisprudence of the TBAs. The EBA stated clearly that some methods, namely, uncritical methods involving only a minor intervention and no substantial health risks, when carried out with the required care and skill, while still adequately protecting the medical profession, would not be excluded from patent protection under Article 53(c) EPC. It explained that some invasive techniques, for example, tattooing, piercing, hair removal by optical radiation, micro abrasion of the skin, which are now safe and of routine character, nowadays are generally carried out in a non-medical, commercial environment such as in cosmetic salons and beauty parlours and, as such, it is hardly still justified to exclude them from patentability.[173]

---

169 Ibid, at para. 3.4.2.6.
170 Ibid.
171 Ibid.
172 Ibid.
173 Ibid, at para. 3.4.2.2.

But the reasoning of the EBA is suspect – whereas it interpreted the exclusion of 'treatment by surgery' as not limited to those for a curative purpose, it went on to accept that the term 'surgery' was regarded as too broad and that there existed some types of surgery, because of their routine nature, should hardly be excluded from patentability. The EBA is not saying that these are not 'surgical' methods per se, but that, given that they are routinely performed, they do not need the expertise of the medical practitioner to perform them and, as such, do not impact on the *ratio legis* of the exclusion which is to ensure that there are no restrictions on the ability of medical or veterinary practitioners to practise medicine. The clear objective of the EBA was to provide an interpretation of the exclusion that accommodates new technologies, but in the process, the EBA may very well have left open the possibility for patentees to attempt to patent certain medical methods. This reasoning, nonetheless, fits well with the EBA's view that such methods do not affect the interests of public health or the protection of patients and, importantly, do not impact on the *ratio legis* of the exclusion, which was to protect the medical practitioner's freedom to apply the treatment of their choice to their patients.

There exists a significant limitation of the test(s) accepted by the EBA to determine whether a method should be regarded as a method of treatment by surgery, namely, whether that method includes an invasive step representing a substantial physical intervention on the body which requires professional medical expertise to be carried out, and which entails a health risk even when carried out with the required professional care and expertise. This test is vague and, as I argued elsewhere, that type of question would receive different answers depending on who is asked.[174] Even the TBA in *GEORGETOWN UNIVERSITY/Pericardial access* had rejected this argument, stating that 'it would be quite difficult if not impossible to define clearly whether a surgical method is complete or a non-insignificant treatment per se, or as carried out in an individual case'.[175] The Examiners and TBAs of the EPO will have the burden of deciding, on a case-by-case basis, whether a method is uncritical and involves only a minor intervention on the human body, and has no substantial health risks, when carried out with the required skill and care – in which case it would not be excluded from patent protection. There is bound to be another referral to the EBA in due course!

The difficulty of, first, providing tests/guidelines which rest on such subjective criteria; secondly, dictating that the Examiners and TBAs take into consideration other criteria which are also arguably subjective; and,

---

174 Ventose, (2008) 39 IIC 58, 72.

175 (T 0992/03) at para. 4.5.2.

thirdly, saying that other criteria are not foreclosed in determining what amounted to a method of treatment by surgery, means that the EBA has not conformed with its own self-professed aim of providing legal certainty. It was at great pains to emphasise this requirement when interpreting the exclusion for diagnostic methods practised on the human or animal body in *CYGNUS/Diagnostic method.*[176] The EBA responded to this criticism by stating that although legal certainty is important in order to enable persons to assess in advance what could be patented and what is excluded, it emphasised that it was equally important to give these inventions the protection they deserve and to come to a balanced system of exclusion, on one hand, and patentability, on the other hand.[177] It emphasised that where a new direction is taken in interpreting a requirement for patentability, be it in the form of an exclusion or in the form of a positive requirement, it is normal and unavoidable that practice and jurisprudence need time and the handling of a number of cases in order to develop a line which then creates a new uniform system of applying a new concept.[178] Notwithstanding the EBA's retort, patentees are not provided with any concrete test to determine what would amount to a surgical method. It merely clarified that this would be difficult since the definition of surgery may change with time and that it was unable to provide a comprehensive test. The clear implication is that the TBAs will be responsible for making sense of the decision of the EBA in *MEDI-PHYSICS/Treatment by surgery* and I am sure that, in time, a further reconsideration of the exclusion of surgical methods from patent protection will be necessary in light of the interpretation of this decision by the TBAs.

F COSMETIC METHODS

1 Introduction

As was seen above, the definition of surgery has a direct impact on whether cosmetic methods that are carried out through surgical procedures are patentable. It seems to be generally understood that cosmetic methods by surgery are unpatentable.[179] The TBA in *SEE-SHELL/Blood flow* had

---

176 *CYGNUS/Diagnostic method* (G 01/04) [2006] EPOR 15 at para. 6.2.

177 (G 01/07) at para. 3.4.2.6.

178 Ibid.

179 R. Moufang, 'Methods of Medical Treatment under Patent Law' (1993) 24 IIC 18, 39. In the UK, this casuistry was accepted, albeit *obiter*, by Falconer J. in *Uniliver Ltd's (Davis's) Application* [1983] RPC 219, 228.

made it clear that the definition of surgery was wide enough to cover all surgical methods, irrespective of the intended purpose, and specifically identified cosmetic methods as an example of a type of treatment that is covered by the term 'medical treatment' and, therefore, would be excluded from patent protection.[180] However, this view has not found favour with some TBAs. The rationale for this view, in Moufang's opinion, was that it 'follows from the semantics of the legislation, which lists surgical methods as an independent alternative category and not as a sub-category of therapeutic methods'.[181] However, an attempt will be made, in this section, using the example of patenting surgical methods which have only a cosmetic purpose, to show why the definition of the exclusion of methods of treatment of the human or animal body by surgery could perhaps embrace the purpose and not merely the nature of the surgical treatment.

2 Application of the Purpose Test to Cosmetic Methods

As mentioned previously, the TBAs had redefined the definition of surgical methods to embrace only those methods that have a therapeutic or curative purpose. Consequently, this definition impacted directly on the question of whether cosmetic methods would be excluded from patent protection. In *THE GENERAL HOSPITAL CORPORATION/Hair removal method*, the claim was for a cosmetic method involving the simultaneous removal of a plurality of hairs from a skin region.[182] The TBA noted that the exclusion of methods of treatment by surgery, like that relating to therapy, should be narrowly construed, and that no difference should be made between the two.[183] The TBA stated that even if the medical linguistic use of the term 'treatment by surgery' comprised treatments that were not directed to the health of human beings or animals, because 'they do not fall within the exclusion from patentability if they are not covered by the *ratio legis* of Article 52(4) EPC',[184] which 'was clearly to ensure that those who carry out such methods as part of the medical treatment of humans or the veterinary treatment of animals should not be inhibited by patents'.[185]

The TBA claimed that, by analogy with the decisions of the TBAs on substances and compositions that have both a cosmetic and therapeutic

---

[180] (T 182/90), at para. 2.2 and para. 2.4.

[181] R. Moufang, 'Methods of Medical Treatment under Patent Law' (1993) 24 IIC 18, 39.

[182] (T 0383/03) at para. 2.

[183] Ibid, at para. 3.3.

[184] Ibid.

[185] Ibid, at para. 3.2.

effect, patent protection should be available for surgical methods that do not relate to or are not suitable for the well-being of human beings or animals. Consequently, the TBA accepted that a 'claimed method is patentable only if it is clearly not potentially suitable for maintaining or restoring the health, the physical integrity, and the physical well-being of a human being or an animal'.[186] It emphasised that it did *not* share the view expressed in *SEE-SHELL/Blood flow* that 'medical treatments also encompass treatments by surgery for non-curative purposes such as cosmetic methods'.[187]

The claimed method, in the instant decision, was for removing hair using optical radiation. The TBA noted that, while excess hair may be a disease, the 'excess hair itself is not harmful and its removal does not treat the underlying causes of the unwanted hair'.[188] The TBA further noted that it was not 'relevant to the physical health of the treated person, the treatment merely results in an aesthetic improvement of the appearance of the person'.[189] The claim was, therefore, a quintessential cosmetic method which was aimed primarily at improving the aesthetic appearance of the individual treated rather than to cure the underlying malady.[190] The TBA also pointed out that the 'underlying medical condition of itself is not a sufficient ground for classifying the method as a method of medical treatment'.[191] In any event, the TBA concluded that, although the claimed method involved a non-insignificant intentional physical intervention which was to be regarded as a surgical operation, it was 'clearly neither suitable nor potentially suitable for maintaining or restoring the health, physical integrity, or physical well being of a person'.[192] Such a method, the TBA further concluded, 'is not to be considered as falling under the exclusion of protection foreseen in Article 52(4) EPC'.[193]

The method, according to the TBA, fell into the category of methods whose only object was to beautify the human body, for example tattooing and piercing, which are used by enterprises such as cosmetic salons or beauty parlours. These *differed* from treatments, which, although cosmetic, 'may also be used to restore the physical integrity of the body, such as a method of breast enlargement by surgery (following a cancer operation, for

---

186 Ibid, at para. 4.
187 Ibid, at para. 4.1.
188 Ibid.
189 Ibid.
190 Ibid.
191 Ibid.
192 Ibid, at para. 4.2.
193 Ibid.

example) or a correction of the shape of the nose (after a car accident, for example)'.[194] Therefore, on the basis of this decision, where a claimed method is not so suitable, or potentially suitable, for maintaining or restoring the health, physical integrity, or physical well-being of a person, and the method is only suitable or directed at aesthetic purposes (and could not be used for medical reasons), the method would not be excluded from patent protection.[195] The TBA embraced the approach based on the purpose of the intervention, and not its nature. The claimed method did not contravene the *ratio legis* of Article 52(4) EPC and was, therefore, patentable. This approach accords with common sense and is in line with Panchen's view that the interpretation of the exclusion of methods of medical treatment should 'avoid exclusions from patentability [including surgical methods] from going beyond their proper limits'.[196]

3 Technical Features of the Claims

The claim in *THERMAGE/Apparatus for skin resurfacing*[197] related to a cosmetic method of tightening a skin surface overlying a collagen containing tissue site. The method involved an intentional physical intervention by an instrumental procedure *viz.* the application of electromagnetic energy through the skin surface of the body to a collagen-containing tissue site, in order to achieve controlled contraction of collagen and skin tightening. The TBA pointed out that the intervention on the human body was non-insignificant, since the skin was burned.[198] The claimed method had many therapeutic purposes, for example, application to the face or neck for reconstructive purposes, which meant that it was suitable for maintaining or restoring the health, physical integrity and physical well-being of the human being.[199] Consequently, the TBA concluded that the claimed method was a method of treatment by surgery and therapy, and was therefore excluded from patent protection for contravening Article 52(4) EPC.

The TBA was reluctant not to follow the interpretation given to the exclusion by the TBA in *SEE-SHELL/Blood flow*.[200] In respect of the

---

194 Ibid.
195 Ibid.
196 K.E. Panchen, 'Patentability in the Field of Therapy and Diagnosis' (1991) 22 IIC 879, 880.
197 (T 1172/03).
198 Ibid, at para. 2.1.
199 Ibid.
200 Ibid.

interface between therapeutic and cosmetic methods, the TBAs have accepted that patent protection of a cosmetic use of a substance was allowable if the cosmetic effect was a technical feature of the treatment, but disallowed the claim if the cosmetic effect of the method was actually caused by, or was not distinguishable from, the therapeutic effect.[201] In other words, the cosmetic effect of the claimed method must be a 'functional or technical feature defining the method', which would distinguish the cosmetic method from the therapeutic method, so that 'in fact the word "cosmetic" in the claim should not be necessary'.[202] The appellant argued that, therefore, in accordance with the jurisprudence of the EPO relating to cosmetic and therapeutic methods, the same criteria should be applied to surgical methods.[203]

However, the TBA was of the opinion that a claim should be judged for the purpose of the exclusion in Article 52(4) EPC 'on the basis of substantive and not formal aspects of the claim', noting that the exclusion of methods of medical treatment 'cannot be simply avoided by a wording of the claims defining the method as a cosmetic method in a formal way, if in substance the method is a therapeutic one'.[204] The TBA, therefore, rejected the appellant's argument, stating that:[205]

> It follows that, applying the criteria used by the boards for the cosmetic use of substances, patentability must be excluded if the cosmetic use is not expressed as a technical feature inherent in the claimed method, but only expressed in the claim as a mere intention of the applicant.

The TBA further held that the cosmetic treatment was not distinguishable from the therapeutic one.[206] The claims in respect of the method of treatment of laxity and wrinkling of the face and neck for cosmetic purpose did not affect the reconstructive effect of the method. This meant that the method could also be regarded as a method of restoring the patient's physical integrity. The TBA, therefore, concluded this was 'not a technical feature of the method which renders it cosmetic and different from a therapeutic method, but only the intention of the person using the method for cosmetic purposes'.[207] As a result, the TBA asserted that this was

---

201 Ibid, at para. 2.2.
202 Ibid.
203 Ibid.
204 Ibid, citing *EXPANDABLE GRAFTS/Surgical device* (T 775/97) [2002] EPOR 24 and *L'OREAL/Cosmetic method* (T 1077/93).
205 *THERMAGE/Apparatus for skin resurfacing* (T 1172/03) at para. 2.1.
206 Ibid, at para. 2.3.
207 Ibid.

'clearly neither a functional nor a technical feature inherent to the method',[208] which meant that the claimed method was still excluded from patent protection for contravening Article 52(4) EPC.

4 The EBA in MEDI-PHYSICS/Treatment by Surgery

As was noted above, the reasoning of the EBA in *MEDI-PHYSICS/Treatment by surgery* would have ruled out the possibility that cosmetic methods were patentable under the EPC since it accepted that it was not the purpose of the surgical treatment that was important but the nature of the treatment in question. Therefore, cosmetic methods cannot be patentable by the fact alone that they are not curative in nature – that view which had been espoused by the TBAs has now been jettisoned by the EBA in *MEDI-PHYSICS/Treatment by surgery*. The focus should now be on whether a claimed method is a method of treatment by surgery, not whether its purpose is curative. Therefore, cosmetic methods do not now have any special significance in delineating the scope of this exclusion than was hitherto the case.

G OTHER CONSIDERATIONS

1 Involvement of Medical Practitioners

The question of whether the role of a physician, in respect of the claimed method, is a factor that should be taken into account in determining whether or not it is a surgical method has engaged the attention of the TBAs from time to time.[209] There has been an explicit acceptance by the TBA that where a claimed method requires a physician to perform it, or is one that a physician can also perform, the method would be excluded from patent protection on the basis that it would be contrary to what was perceived as the public policy rationale for the exclusion, *viz.* that the

---

208 Ibid.

209 The TBA in *BAXTER/Blood extraction method* (T 0329/94) has made it clear that the need for a medical practitioner to perform a measure on the human body or supervise such an operation is not the sole criterion by which a method step has to be assessed with regard to the exclusion of subject matter from patenting under Article 52(4) EPC. The purpose and inevitable effect of the step at issue are much more important.

activities of physicians, and veterinary practitioners, should not be hampered by patent monopolies when they treat their patients.[210] This much was reiterated by the TBA in *THOMPSON/Cornea* when it opined that, in light of the health risks connected with such a treatment, where 'a claimed method for treatment has to be performed by a physician or under his supervision, it will *normally* fall within the exclusion of the first sentence of Article 52(4) EPC'.[211] The TBA rejected the appellant's argument that the process was actually carried out by a technician having no medical training rather than by a physician, emphasising that:[212]

> Since the physician is bound to exercise extreme care both during the medical treatment and during the use of medical technical apparatus and, moreover, is responsible for the surveillance of his medical and non-medical staff, the Board is convinced that the claimed process is and has to be carried out by the ophthalmologist or ophthalmic surgeon himself or at least under his supervision. This fact indicates that the claimed process falls under the exclusion of Article 52(4) EPC.

Since the recent decision of the EBA in *CYGNUS/Diagnostic method*, any such requirement must surely be doubted. In that decision, the EBA stated emphatically that:[213]

> whether or not a method is a diagnostic method within the meaning of Article 52(4) EPC should neither depend on the participation of a medical or veterinary practitioner, by being present or by bearing the responsibility, nor on the fact that all method steps can also, or only, be practised by medicinal or non-medicinal support staff, the patient himself or herself or an automated system.

Although this statement was made in the context of the exclusion of diagnostic methods, the need for consistency in the interpretation of the exclusion of methods of medical treatment means that it is also applicable to methods of treatment of the human or animal body by surgery. Similarly, the TBA in *MEDI-PHYSICS/Treatment by surgery* also examined other approaches to the interpretation of the exclusion of methods for treatment of the human or animal body by surgery, *viz*. that relating to the nature of the medical risk involved in the physical intervention.[214] That

---

[210] *ULTRAFEM/Feminine hygiene device* (T 1165/97) at para. 4.2.
[211] (T 0024/91) at para. 2.4 (emphasis added).
[212] Ibid, at para. 2.5.
[213] (G 01/04) at para. 6.3.
[214] (T 0992/03) at para. 4.5.2.

risk, the TBA noted, 'is linked to the further issue of whether a medical or veterinary practitioner should be responsible for carrying out such steps'.[215] The TBA further noted that, in that regard, the approach based only on the nature of the physical intervention appears to be more suitable than one based only on its purpose, at least, it argued, for those methods that could only be performed by a physician or veterinary practitioner.[216] This approach, the TBA thought (and rightly so), should be jettisoned because the EBA in *CYGNUS/Diagnostic method*, as mentioned above, eschewed any reliance on the involvement of a medical practitioner in the determination of whether a method can fall under Article 52(4) EPC.

The EBA in *MEDI-PHYSICS/Treatment by surgery* stated that the question of the involvement of a medical or veterinary practitioner had been comprehensively dealt with and answered by the EBA in *CYGNUS/Diagnostic method*, and, consequently, it saw no need to go into detail again, while reiterating that whether or not a method was excluded from patentability under Article 53(c) EPC cannot depend on the person carrying it out.[217] The EBA clarified that, although the findings of the EBA in *CYGNUS/Diagnostic methods* relate to diagnostic methods, they dealt with the exclusion from patentability under Article 52(4) EPC and are, therefore, equally valid for the other exclusion in Article 53(c) EPC.[218]

2 Other Interpretative Criteria

Moufang, in explaining that 'only operations of a certain significance can be considered as surgical', noted that 'administering an injection, taking blood and tattooing can hardly be classified as a surgical method'.[219] He pointed out that operations such as ear-piercing and cutting of the nails 'clearly lie at the borderline to be drawn here'.[220] Histolytic operations, he explained, would be placed above this borderline if they only serve to remove warts and moles.[221] Moufang opined that that borderline is 'drawn less precisely in the field of dental treatment methods, for example those concerning teeth extraction or treatment of teeth by means of drilling or

---

215 Ibid.

216 Ibid.

217 (G 01/07) at para. 3.4.1.

218 Ibid.

219 R. Moufang, 'Methods of Medical Treatment under Patent Law' (1993) 24 IIC 18, 37. This point was also made by K.E. Panchen, 'Patentability in the Field of Therapy and Diagnosis' (1991) 22 IIC 879, 880.

220 R. Moufang, 'Methods of Medical Treatment under Patent Law' (1993) 24 IIC 18, 37.

221 Ibid.

filling holes therein'.[222] It is not immediately clear what types of operations can be considered as significant or not. Also, it is not advisable to interpret the exclusion in such a vague manner such that the question of whether an invention is patentable rests on such subjective criteria.

Panchen made similar observations, noting that 'operations':[223]

> such as giving an injection, taking a blood sample, piercing ears, or tattooing which are performed on the body but which in general would not be regarded as surgery by the UK Patent Office, the test applied being whether or not the skill or knowledge of the physician is required.

The first remark outlines the previous position of the UK Patent Office which cannot now be considered as correct in light of their acceptance of the decision of the EBA in *CYGNUS/Diagnostic method*.[224] But, critically, he makes a crucial distinction between: (a) the fact that it is usually a surgeon who carries out the surgical treatment; and (b) the rationale for the exclusion of surgical methods from patent protection. This clearly shows that the interpretation of the exclusion must take into account the rationale of the exclusion of surgical methods from patent protection. This serves as a boundary beyond which any interpretation must not exceed and would provide the necessary legal certainty allowing patentees to know, with clarity, what inventions are actually excluded from patent protection. Panchen then remarked that this approach is consistent with the intention of the drafters of the EPC to free from restraint the activities of physicians when they treat their patients, observing, importantly, that the '[i]nterpretation of the provision should avoid the exclusions from patentability from going beyond their proper limits'.[225]

Thomas, however, has observed that, in general, 'all methods that intervene on the structure of the organism have been classified as surgery', and that they 'range from endoscopy to puncture, injection and excision, to the opening of the body cavities and the insertion of catheters'.[226] He continued by stating that there should 'rightly be no distinction between major

---

[222] Ibid.

[223] K.E. Panchen, 'Patentability in the Field of Therapy and Diagnosis' (1991) 22 IIC 879, 880.

[224] Examination Guidelines for Patent Applications relating to Medical Treatments in the UK Patent Office, March 2006, at para. 61.

[225] K.E. Panchen, 'Patentability in the Field of Therapy and Diagnosis' (1991) 22 IIC 879, 880.

[226] D. Thomas, 'Patentability Problems in Medical Technology' (2003) 34 IIC 847, 861.

and minor surgery'.[227] There is enormous sympathy for this second view because, if that distinction were to be adopted, it would involve the importation of the subjective element of determining which operations are major or minor into the interpretation of the exclusion. Questions which might inevitably arise include whether the surgery is major/minor dependent on: (a) the degree of intervention on the human or animal body; (b) the degree of complexity of the operation; (c) whether it is so defined by the surgeon; and (d) whether it is significant in terms of its value to save the patient's life. These questions will receive different answers depending on who is asked. However, Moufang's view that 'in accordance with the general use of language, only operations of a certain significance can be excluded as surgical' cannot be dismissed altogether since it clearly evidences that opinions will always be divided on such issues.

The TBAs have also opined on the use of such criteria in interpreting the exclusion of surgical methods from patent protection. In *GEORGETOWN UNIVERSITY/Pericardial access*, for example, in answering the question of whether a surgical method relates only to those methods which are non-insignificant, and if so, what does non-insignificant in the context of the exclusion mean, the TBA pointed out that 'it would be quite difficult if not impossible to define clearly whether a surgical method is a complete or a non-insignificant treatment per se, or as carried out in an individual case'.[228] Such an approach, the TBA noted, 'would run counter to clarity and legal certainty'.[229] Similarly, the TBA in *MEDI-PHYSICS/Treatment by surgery*, in its quest to find some solution to the manner by which the exclusion of surgical methods should be defined, mentioned, albeit rather briefly, other approaches, namely those relating to 'the degree of invasiveness or the operative complexity of the physical intervention'.[230] The TBA did not explain in any detail what its views on these were, but merely opined that it 'is aware of the difficulty of defining interpretative criteria for the exclusion under Article 52(4) EPC on the basis of such factors'.[231] These views indicate the paucity of support for such an approach primarily because, if adopted, it might prove very difficult to implement in actual cases and would, moreover, lack clarity and legal certainty – factors which have only just recently been highlighted by the EBA in *CYGNUS/Diagnostic method*.

---

227 Ibid.
228 (T 35/99) at para. 8.
229 Ibid.
230 Ventose, (2007) JIPLP 574, 575.
231 (T 0992/03) at para. 4.5.2.

H AN EXCLUDED SURGICAL STEP

1 Introduction

It seems to be trite law, according to the jurisprudence of the TBAs of the EPO, that, where a claim comprises one or more steps that can be considered as surgical, the claim will be excluded from patent protection on that basis alone.[232] This approach has been followed in many decisions of the TBAs. However, recently, some TBAs have attempted to make artificial distinctions in order to evade the rule relating to one surgical step, as just outlined. Claims are not usually directed at a surgical method *per se*. As will be seen, the approach of the TBAs was that, if a claimed method contained any step which was either surgical or was of a surgical nature, the claim would offend Article 52(4) EPC. The problem arises, in particular, where the claim is for a device that has a feature which necessitates some interaction with the human or animal body.[233] Where that interaction is of a surgical nature, as is sometimes the case, the issue for the TBA is whether that surgical element excludes the entire claim from patent protection. One way in which the TBAs have tried to determine whether a claimed method is excluded on that basis is to determine, first, whether any of the steps in the claim interacts with the human or animal body and, secondly, whether any of those steps can be considered as a surgical method. The decisions of the TBAs have not always been consistent on this issue and there seems to be some disquiet relating to the application of that approach. They have, therefore, sought to limit its reach by various means.

The following sections will: first, delineate the issue relating to 'surgical steps' in the jurisprudence of the EPO; secondly, analyse the decisions that have held that the mere presence of a surgical step in a claimed method is sufficient to exclude the entire claim as an excluded method of treatment by surgery; thirdly, examine the decisions that have sought to limit the reach of that approach and, in the process, elucidate on the ways in which this was done, thereby providing patentees, yet again, with another means by which to ensure that their claims fall outside the scope of the exclusion; and, fourthly, examine the decision of the EBA in *MEDI-PHYSICS/Treatment by surgery* which has answered definitively this question that has plagued the TBAs for a number of years.

---

[232] *TELECTRONICS/Pacer* (T 82/93) [1996] EPOR 409 at para. 1.1.

[233] R. Moufang, 'Methods of Medical Treatment under Patent Law' (1993) 24 IIC 18, 37 has argued that using instruments for surgery is not patentable.

2 The Existence of Surgical Steps in a Claim

As mentioned above, the claim in *SEE-SHELL/Blood flow* was for a method of measuring the blood flow of a specific tissue in an experimental animal by injecting micro spheres into its left atrium.[234] The TBA held that '*[n]ormally* the presence of the surgical step in a multi-step method for the treatment of the human or animal body confers a surgical character on that method'.[235] What is immediately clear is that, ordinarily, a surgical step in a claim that consisted of many steps would necessarily confer a surgical character on that method. However, the TBA further pointed out that when considered as a whole, the claimed method under consideration could not be regarded solely as a method of treatment of an animal by surgery, because it ended in the laboratory animal's death.[236] Notwithstanding its view that surgical treatments are not limited only to those for curative purposes, the TBA was of the opinion that 'the distinction between surgical and non-surgical procedures could not be so broadly drawn that 'surgical treatment' includes any kind of manual or instrumental intervention by one human being on another, or on an animal'.[237] Consequently, where a surgical method contains a step that has the consequence of consciously ending of an animal's life, that method would not be considered as a method of treatment by surgery.

This means that the identification of a surgical step in a claimed method was sufficient to exclude the claim from patent protection and it was of no consequence that there were also non-surgical steps extant in the process.[238] For example, in *TELECTRONICS/Pacer*, the TBA stated that 'a claim is not allowable having regard to Article 52(4) EPC if it *includes at least one feature defining a physical activity or action* (for example, a method step), and if such activity constitutes a "method for treatment of the human body by therapy"'.[239] In *THE GENERAL HOSPITAL CORPORATION/ Contraceptive method*, it was pointed out that:[240]

> The decided cases show that in considering whether a request for a particular set of claims is allowable under Article 52(4) EPC, the critical question is whether

---

234 (T 182/90) [1994] EPOR 320.

235 Ibid, at para. 2.5.1. See also *KONINKLIJKE PHILIPS ELECTRONICS NV* (T 09/04) at para. 6.

236 (T 0182/90) at para. 2.5.3.

237 Ibid, at para. 2.5.2.

238 *THOMPSON/Cornea* (T 24/91) [1996] EPOR 19.

239 Ibid, at para. 1.4 (emphasis added).

240 (T 0820/92) at para. 5.5 (emphasis added). This paragraph was cited with approval by the TBA in *TELECTRONICS/Pacer* (T 82/93) [1996] EPOR 409 at para. 1.4.

> there is any disclosure of a method *none of whose steps fall under the prohibition of Article 52(4) EPC*, i.e. none of whose steps are either a method for the treatment of the human or animal body by therapy or surgery, or a diagnostic method practised on the human or animal body.

The TBA in *GEORGETOWN UNIVERSITY/Pericardial access*,[241] asserted, citing the 'uniform jurisprudence' emanating from *SEE-SHELL/Blood flow*, *GENERAL HOSPITAL/Contraceptive method*,[242] and *TELECTRONICS/Pacer*,[243] that patent protection would not be available if a claim contained 'at least one feature defining a physical activity or action (*e.g.* a method step) which constitutes [a surgical method]'.[244] According to the TBA, it did not matter that the method could have been carried out in isolation or in combination with other methods of treatment which together achieved the same intended medical effect.[245] What mattered was the actual existence of a step which was of a surgical nature in the claimed method.[246]

If there was any doubt as to the correctness of this approach, the EBA in *CYGNUS/Diagnostic method* reiterated its efficacy. While discussing the question of whether diagnostic methods practised on the human or animal body within the meaning of Article 52(4) EPC related only to those methods containing: (a) all the procedural steps to be carried out when making a medical diagnosis; or (b) one procedural step that can be used for diagnostic purposes or relates to the diagnosis, the EBA stated that:[247]

> According to the established jurisprudence of the boards of appeal, a method claim falls under the prohibition of Article 52(4) EPC if it includes *at least one feature* defining a physical activity or action that constitutes a method step for treatment of the human or animal body by surgery or therapy. … It follows that the surgical or therapeutic nature of a method claim can perfectly be established by *a single method step* without contravening Article 84 EPC. Diagnostic methods, however, differ in this respect from the methods of surgery and therapy.

All this analysis would be of little significance if it is not determined with clarity what exactly amounts to a method of treatment of the human or animal body by surgery. Article 52(4) EPC properly relates to 'method of

---

241 (T 35/99) [2001] EPOR 169.
242 (T 182/90) [1994] EPOR 320.
243 (T 82/93) [1996] EPOR 409.
244 Ibid, at para. 8.
245 Ibid.
246 *LEXION/Method for conditioning gas* (T 0238/06) at para. 4.4.
247 (G 01/04) at para. 6.2.1 (emphasis added). This was reiterated at para. 6.2.2.

treatment of the human or animal body by surgery' – it does not mention a surgical step at all. The focus should, naturally, be on the text of the provision of Article 52(4) EPC.[248] The presence of the latter seems to be fatal to the question of whether a claimed method is excluded from patent protection on the basis of being a method of treatment by surgery.

3 The 'Ratio Legis' of the Exclusion

The EBA in *MEDI-PHYSICS/Treatment by surgery* argued that even though it may not be entirely unreasonable to assume that a practitioner, practising a single therapeutic or surgical step of a multi-step method, would not normally infringe a patent claim directed to that multi-step method, any issues of infringement ultimately depended on the construction of the applicable national laws.[249] It continued that it was also common ground that the socio-ethical consideration underlying the exclusion of therapeutic, surgical and diagnostic methods from patentability, to free the medical profession from possible constraints imposed on them by patents, was of relevance for the interpretation of Article 53(c) EPC.[250] Moreover, the EBA accepted that there was no term in Article 53(c) EPC which would allow concluding that hampering of the practitioner's freedom was a prerequisite for the exclusion to apply in the individual case considered. It was of the view that the only condition defined in Article 53(c) EPC for a claim to be excluded from patentability was that it contained subject matter being a method for treatment of the human or animal body by surgery or therapy or a diagnostic method.[251] If that were the case, the EBA concluded that the claimed method would be excluded from patentability and it was then irrelevant whether, in the individual situation under consideration, a medical practitioner would or could infringe the claim.[252]

The EBA clarified that the drafters of the EPC deliberately maintained the exclusions under Article 52(4) EPC in the now Article 53(c) EPC.[253] As

---

[248] For example, the EBA in *CYGNUS/Diagnostic method* had pointed out that '[t]he provision *does not make reference* to particular steps pertaining to such methods, *nor does it contain* a wording such as "relating to diagnosis" or "of value for diagnostic purposes". Thus, the *text of the provision itself* already gives an indication towards a narrow interpretation in the sense that, in order to be excluded from patentability, the method is to include all steps relating to it'. (at para. 6.1 (emphasis added)).

[249] (G 02/07) at 3.2.3.2.

[250] Ibid.

[251] Ibid.

[252] Ibid.

[253] Ibid.

a result, the EBA stated that the principle has been confirmed that medical and veterinary practitioners' freedom to use the best available treatments to the benefit of their patients uninhibited by any worry that some treatment might be covered by a patent was protected by excluding these activities from patentability.[254] It continued that also excluding from patentability multi-step methods which comprise or encompass a therapeutic or a surgical step serves to give full effect to that legislative purpose. Therefore, the EBA claimed that the principle developed in the EPO jurisprudence, that the presence of one therapeutic or surgical step in a multi-step method excludes that method from patentability, was not only formally justified by the fact that the exclusion under Article 53(c) EPC did not contain any limitation as to the defined methods being excluded only when claimed as such.[255] More importantly, the EBA acknowledged, that view was also justified as to substance, that is, it served to enable achieving the legislative purpose served by the exclusion.[256]

4 Surgical Steps Defined as Excluded Surgical Treatments

The TBA has recently noted that mere catheterisation or the insertion of components of a device into the body was already prohibited by Article 52(4) EPC as constituting a surgical step.[257] However, this is not always the case, as the TBA in *KONINKLIJKE PHILIPS ELECTRONICS NV* has recently pointed out.[258] Other decisions have not, however, challenged the previous learning.[259] In *GEORGETOWN UNIVERSITY/Pericardial access*,[260] the claim was for a method for transvenously accessing the pericardial space between a heart and its pericardium in preparation for a medical procedure. This was done by introducing a catheter and/or electrodes into the pericardial space for delivery of electricity to treat muscle and/or for introducing pharmacologic agents directly into the pericardial sac.[261] TBA held that the claimed methods related to a method of treatment by surgery, because they involved catheterisation as part of the medical

---

[254] Ibid.

[255] Ibid.

[256] Ibid.

[257] *CAMTECH AS* (T 05/04) at para. 2, citing *GEORGETOWN UNIVERSITY/Pericardial access* (T 35/99). *Cf KONINKLIJKE PHILIPS ELECTRONICS NV* (T 09/04) at para. 6.

[258] *CAMTECH AS* (T 05/04) at para. 2.

[259] *MAQUET CRITICAL CARE AB* (T 1102/02) at para. 3.

[260] (T 35/99) [2001] EPOR 169.

[261] Ibid, at para. 9.

process and, consequently, were excluded from patent protection. It was also pointed out that:[262]

> It is also evident that the claims do not relate to any technical feature of a particular device for practising the claimed method, in particular not to catheters or electrodes, in contrast to the subject matter in question in decision [*BAXTER/Blood extraction method*], which was confined to a method for operating a particular device.

The claim in *BAXTER/Blood extraction method*[263] comprised a blood extraction assistance method for facilitating sustained venous blood flow through a human limb towards a venous blood extraction point. The TBA stated that the withdrawal of blood in the claimed method *might* fall under the exclusion of medical treatment by surgery when considering that the taking of blood requires the use of surgical instruments and the operation is performed on the structure of the organism.[264] However, the TBA found that the purpose of the blood extraction assistance method was not of a therapeutic or surgical nature, but merely of a technical nature with the sole aim of improving the efficiency of taking blood from a donor.[265]

This point was reiterated by the TBA in *LEXION/Method for conditioning gas* where the claim related to a method of heating and humidifying insufflation gases prior to passage of the gases into the patient.[266] The TBA pointed out that '*[i]f* those methods involve purely technical steps and do not include any interaction with the body or the actual step of delivery of the pulse or the mixture to the body, they may be patentable under Article 52(4) EPC'.[267] The TBA stated that '[i]n the present case, were the step of flowing the gas into the patient to be included in claim 1, then the method would relate to a surgical method since the purpose of the gas is to inflate body cavities to create space for medical instruments, or a therapeutic method'.[268] However, that final step was not actually included in claim 1. Therefore, the claim was not considered as either a surgical or therapeutic method of treatment of the human body, excluded from patent protection under Article 52(4) EPC. A similar conclusion was reached in *CAMTECH*[269] where the claimed method related to the internal registration of gas, air and

---

262 Ibid, at para. 10.
263 (T 0329/94) [1998] EPOR 363.
264 Ibid, at para. 4, citing *SEE-SHELL/Blood flow* (T 182/90).
265 (T 0329/94) [1998] EPOR 363 at para. 8.
266 (T 0238/06).
267 Ibid, at para. 4.3 (emphasis added).
268 Ibid, at para 4.4.
269 (T 05/04).

other fluid flows in the human body and the use of pressure sensors for such registration. The TBA stated that '[w]hat actually counts for the assessment of Article 52(4) EPC is that the sensors are placed inside the body and that this feature *is* part of the method *as claimed*'.[270] Therefore, following *SEE-SHELL/Blood flow*, the claimed method as a whole was considered an excluded method of treatment by surgery, contrary to Article 52(4) EPC,[271] because it contained a feature which was of a surgical nature.

5 Surgical Steps Not Defined as Excluded Surgical Treatments

The purely formalistic approach outlined above has not met with universal approval by other TBAs; so, they have sought to limit its application in some recent decisions. In *KONINKLIJKE PHILIPS ELECTRONICS NV*,[272] the application was based on the technical problem of how to organise exchange of a patient's identification data when different images need to be taken of the patient. The solution, as defined in claim 11, involved producing diagnostic images of the patient with each of the first imaging and second equipments. The TBA asked whether the claimed method fell within the definition of a surgical method accepted by recent TBAs.[273] It then pointed out that:[274]

> With respect to this question the fact must be considered that the method according to claim 11 represents a technical method for exchanging a patient's identification data when different images of the patient are taken, and that claim 11 does not include or inevitably require any surgical steps which may be necessary for placing a catheter, etc.

The TBA further pointed out that '[t]he examining division's argument that the claimed method may involve the placement of a catheter, for example, and therefore has a surgical nature is *not sound*'.[275]

Since the claims must be narrowly construed, as dictated by the EBA in *CYGNUS/Diagnostic method*, the TBA concluded that the instant claim must be 'interpreted as *only* covering the production of diagnostic images

---

270 Ibid, at para. 2 (emphasis added).
271 Ibid.
272 (T 09/04).
273 That surgical methods are, in principle, excluded from patentability unless they are clearly neither suitable nor potentially suitable for maintaining or restoring the health, the physical integrity, and the physical well being of the human being.
274 (T 09/04) at para. 6.
275 Ibid (emphasis added).

and not any preliminary steps necessary for facilitating the image production [which might include a surgical step]'.[276] In other words, if any of the preliminary steps in a claimed method is of a surgical nature, then, they would not be considered as part of the claim itself. There was no need, therefore, to consider whether they were methods of treatment by surgery. This reasoning also logically applies to steps which are incidental with respect to the claimed method, and would be in line with the reasoning of the TBA in *THE AUSTRALIA NATIONAL UNIVERSITY/Method and apparatus for early detection of glaucoma*.[277] In that decision, the TBA held, applying the decision of the EBA in *CYGNUS/Diagnostic method*, that the criterion 'practised on the human or animal body' did not apply to intermediate steps of a technical nature, and those steps 'are to be ignored when assessing the diagnostic character of the method'.[278]

Additionally, the claim must specifically contain a feature which describes how the patient is connected to the system itself for it to be excluded from patent protection.[279] For example, in *MAQUET CRITICAL CARE AB*,[280] in respect of a claim directed to a method and apparatus for determining a transfer function for a connection system in a ventilator system, the TBA stated that 'the claim does not contain any feature describing how the patient is connected to the connection system' and that the particular method 'as a whole represents a technical method for determining a system parameter (the transfer function) which is then used to adjust the functioning of the ventilator system'.[281] That much was previously accepted by the TBA in *BAXTER/Blood extraction method* where it held that the purpose of the blood extraction assistance method was of a technical nature with the sole aim of increasing the efficiency of taking blood from the donor.

6 MEDI-PHYSICS/Treatment by Surgery

(a) The decision of the TBA

The TBA in *MEDI-PHYSICS/Treatment by surgery*[282] was of the opinion that since the claimed method contained a step that included the delivery of

---

276 Ibid (emphasis added).
277 (T 1197/02).
278 Ibid, at para. 2.2.
279 *MAQUET CRITICAL CARE AB* (T 1102/02) at para. 3.
280 (T 1102/02).
281 Ibid, at para. 3. *See also LEXION/Method for conditioning gas* (T 0238/06) at para. 4.3.
282 (T 0992/03).

the polarized 129Xe to the patient via injection, it could be regarded as a method of treatment of the human or animal body by surgery. However, it qualified that statement by noting that the intervention on the human body 'does not aim in itself at maintaining life and health but constitutes a prerequisite for the collection of data in the course of an examination of a medical diagnosis'.[283] Therefore, according to the TBA, the question was whether the claimed method which contained 'a [surgical] step would fall under the prohibition of Article 52(4) EPC, although they do not in themselves provide any curative effect'.[284] The TBA noted that it was important that, in the specification, the application 'repeatedly refers to the usefulness of the inventive imaging methods during a surgical intervention'.[285] The images produced by the claimed method enabled 'a surgeon to decide on the course of action to be taken'.[286] In other words, the question was whether the claimed method 'should as a whole be considered a constitutive element or step of such [surgical] treatment', because it provided information of diagnostic value when used during a method of treatment by surgery.[287]

(b) The decision of the EBA

The EBA in *MEDI-PHYSICS/Treatment by surgery* began its discussion of the issue by noting that it was clear from question one, and the claims at issue, that the step potentially to be considered as a surgical step was only one step in a multi-step method and the claimed imaging method was not directed to surgery as such.[288] As a result, the EBA accepted that if the answer to the above question was no, then referred question one would also have to be answered in the negative.[289] The EBA noted in the passage quoted earlier, the EBA, in *CYGNUS/Diagnostic method*, clearly and explicitly approved that jurisprudence in relation to method steps for treatment by surgery or therapy. It argued that whether an *obiter dictum* or not, the above-mentioned passage was drafted in such clear terms as to leave no doubt that the EBA in *CYGNUS/Diagnostic method* endorsed the principle developed in the jurisprudence of the TBAs, that a method claim falls under Article 52(4) EPC if it included at least one feature defining a physical activity or action that constituted a method step for treatment of a

---

283 Ibid, at para. 4.2.
284 Ibid.
285 Ibid, at para. 4.3.
286 Ibid.
287 Ibid.
288 (G 01/07) at para. 3.2.
289 Ibid.

human or animal body by surgery or therapy.[290] The EBA argued that since this principle was, by now, a long-established principle in the jurisprudence of the EPO, it was irrelevant whether it was first acknowledged in *SEE-SHELL/Blood flow*, noting that this decision was not mentioned by the EBA in *CYGNUS/Diagnostic method*.[291]

The EBA then examined the *ratio legis* of the exclusion, as outlined above, and concluded that there was no good reason not to uphold the principle confirmed in *CYGNUS/Diagnostic method*, and underlying EPO practice and jurisprudence, that a method claim fell under the prohibition of patenting methods for treatment by therapy or surgery under Article 53(c) EPC if it comprised or encompassed at least one feature defining a physical activity or action that constituted a method step for treatment of the human or animal body by surgery or therapy.[292]

(c) Legal analysis

There is no difficulty with the central ruling of the EBA that if a claimed method contained a method step that amounts to a surgical step then that claim is consequently excluded from patent protection. The problem arises in the determination of whether a particular step is indeed a surgical one; or, in other words, whether the step is a method of treatment of the human or animal body by surgery, because it is that determination that is fatal to the claimed method that contains a surgical step. Elsewhere, I have argued that if it is accepted, which the EBA did not, that surgical method needs to be for a curative purpose, it would follow then that any such method step must first be for a curative purpose for it to be excluded from patent protection.[293] Having jettisoned the requirement that a surgical method must be for a curative purpose for it to be excluded from patent protection under Article 53(c) EPC, the EBA must necessarily apply its broader definition of what methods amount to a method for 'treatment by surgery', namely, whether it comprises or encompasses an invasive step representing a substantial physical intervention on the human or animal body, which requires professional medical expertise to be carried out, and which entails a substantial health risk even when carried out with the required professional care and expertise. Appreciating, of course, that this definition would cover 'minor' surgical procedures, the EBA quickly asserted that routine and safe procedures may not be considered as surgical methods and would, therefore, be patentable. The extent to which this determination

---

290 Ibid.
291 Ibid.
292 Ibid, at para. 3.2.5.
293 Ventose, (2008) 39 IIC 58, 80.

becomes problematic would depend, to a great extent, on whether the Examiners and TBAs have any difficulty applying the criteria outlined by the EBA in *MEDI-PHYSICS/Treatment by surgery*.

I DISCLAIMERS

1 Introduction

It is of critical practical importance to patentees (and patent practitioners) to use disclaimers properly because, if they are not used as intended, or at all, it is possible that their invention would not be patentable as offending one or more of the exclusions from patent protection. Disclaimers are useful tools which provide patentees with powerful armoury during prosecution and opposition proceedings at the EPO. The use of disclaimers under the EPC by patentees has been given the nod of approval by the EBA in *PPG/Disclaimer*.[294]

Whether the use of disclaimers addresses the concerns relating to methods of medical treatment has yet to be ironed out by the EPO. Not surprisingly, before the decision in *PPG/Disclaimer*, the TBAs of the EPO addressed, in an *ad hoc* way, the question of what is the acceptable form of claim where a patentee seeks protection for a patentable invention but the claim embraces an excluded method, in particular, a method of medical treatment. Article 53(c) EPC excludes from patent protection 'methods for treatment of the human or animal body by surgery or therapy and diagnostic methods practised on the human or animal body'. In some decisions the TBA has stated explicitly that patentees may evade the exclusions from patentability, including methods of medical treatment, by using disclaimers without any specific guidance on how this might be achieved generally.[295]

In relation to disclaimers generally, the TBAs can find limited guidance in *PPG/Disclaimer*[296] where the EBA accepted that disclaimers are allowable in respect of exclusions under the EPC, including methods of medical treatment. More important is the decision of the EBA in *MEDI-PHYSICS/Treatment by surgery*, which has answered the three questions relating to the scope of the exclusion of method of treatment of the human or animal body by surgery, including the use of disclaimers for methods of treatment of the human or animal body by surgery, which had been referred to it by the TBA. This section will explore the use of disclaimers in

294 (G 01/03) [2004] EPOR 33.

295 *ROUSSEL-CULAF/Thenoyl peroxide* (T 36/83) [1987] EPOR 1.

296 (G 01/03) [2004] EPOR 33.

respect of methods of medical treatment, in particular, it will examine: first, the decision of the TBA in *MEDI-PHYSICS/Treatment by surgery*, which has referred questions relating to the use of such disclaimers to the EBA; secondly, the decisions of the TBAs that have considered, or made reference to, disclaimers for methods of medical treatment to determine what light they shed on answering the question posed; and thirdly, examine:

(a) the juridical basis for such disclaimers in excluded methods generally;
(b) other such methods which might achieve the same objective;
(c) the limitations of both (a) and (b); and
(d) the decision of the EBA in *MEDI-PHYSICS/Treatment by surgery* to find out how it has answered the question referred to it by the TBA.

2 The Issue

As stated above, in *MEDI-PHYSICS/Treatment by surgery*, the TBA decided to refer, *inter alia*, the following question for consideration by the EBA:

> 2. If the answer to question 1 is in the affirmative, could the exclusion from patent protection be avoided by amending the wording of the claim so as to omit the step at issue, *or disclaim it*, or let the claim encompass it without being limited to it?

The question of the use of disclaimers for excluded methods of medical treatment is still an important one even if *MEDI-PHYSICS/Treatment by surgery* could, arguably, be decided without a consideration of that issue. Its importance is underscored by decisions of the TBA which have explicitly sanctioned the use of such disclaimers to avoid the exclusion of: (a) methods of treatment of the human or animal body by (i) therapy and (ii) surgery and (b) diagnostic methods practised on the human or animal body. In *MEDI-PHYSICS/Treatment by surgery*, the TBA noted that if the first question was answered in the affirmative, 'the question arises of whether such an exclusion might be avoided either by omitting this step from the claim wording or *by disclaiming it*', which could be achieved by making it clear that the steps precede but do not form part of the claimed method.[297] The appellant relied on two EBA decisions. The first was *PPG/Disclaimer*[298] in support of its argument that such disclaimers are allowable in respect of any subject matter which, under Articles 52 to 57

[297] (T 0992/03) at para. 5.1 (emphasis added).
[298] (G 01/03) [2004] EPOR 33.

EPC, was excluded from patent protection for non-technical reasons.[299] The second was *NOVARTIS II/Transgenic plant*[300] for the view that 'a claim of a higher level of abstraction embracing subject matter excluded from patent protection without explicitly claiming it should be allowed'.[301] Therefore, the TBA reasoned that 'a claim including the step of "administering a contrast agent", leaving open in which way the administration step was to be performed, should be allowed at least if uncritical methods for administration of the contrast agent, as by inhalation or orally, were disclosed or available'.[302] The TBA offered no view as to which approach it thought acceptable in the circumstances.

3 Methods of Medical Treatment and Disclaimers

The TBAs have also had to consider the question of whether a cosmetic method that also had a therapeutic effect was excluded from patent protection on the basis that the claimed method, as a whole, could be considered as an excluded method of treatment of the human or animal body by therapy. This was vividly illustrated in *ROUSSEL-CULAF/Thenoyl peroxide*[303] where the applicant discovered that thenoyl peroxide (a known compound) had both a cosmetic as well as a therapeutic purpose (treating acne). The issue was whether the cosmetic indication was distinct from the medical indication.[304] The TBA accepted that the cosmetic treatment, according to the application, may also incidentally involve a medical treatment,[305] and that the activity of skin cleansing clearly belonged to the field of non-medical body hygiene rather than that of therapy.[306] Consequently, the TBA emphasised that the benefits gained by this activity in a cosmetic indication should not therefore be considered as being excluded from patentability under Article 52(4) EPC.[307] The TBA concluded that an applicant who discovered a new medical and non-medical use should be provided with patent protection for, first, the new medical use if claimed as a second/further medical use in accordance with the decision of the EBA in

---

[299] Ibid.
[300] (G 01/98) [2000] EPOR 303.
[301] (T 0992/03) at para. 5.2.
[302] Ibid.
[303] (T 36/83) [1987] EPOR 1.
[304] Ibid, at para. 6.
[305] Ibid, at para. 6.1.
[306] Ibid, at para. 6.2.
[307] Ibid.

EISAI/Second medical indication[308] and, secondly, the cosmetic method, because it is one falling within the general field of patentable inventions.[309]

The TBA observed that, when considering such claims, the actual wording of the claims is important, and that an applicant who discovered various uses of a known substance has a right, subject to the provisions of the EPC, to have those uses protected.[310] The TBA emphasised that to avoid any possible conflict with Article 52(4) EPC in a use or indication claim, it would have been possible to envisage the exclusion of the non-patentable invention within the meaning of that article 'by means of a *disclaimer*'.[311] However, the use of the word 'cosmetic' by the applicant was considered 'sufficiently precise' to avoid any possible conflict with Article 52(4) EPC.[312] In other words, the TBA 'treated the use of the word "cosmetic" in the context of this application as sufficient to exclude therapeutic uses, without the need for a specific disclaimer of such uses'.[313] Importantly, the TBA accepted that patentees could disclaim the subject matter of the claim if it was for a method of medical treatment. For that approach to be acceptable, the medical treatment aspect of the claim must not be a critical part of the claim as whole. In any event, the claim in *ROUSSEL-CULAF/Thenoyl peroxide* itself was a use claim – it is easier to disclaim the *use* of a substance for a method of medical treatment when patent protection is sought solely for the non-medical use.

The TBA has suggested that disclaimers might be used. In *SIEMENS/Flow measurement*,[314] for example, the claim was for a method of measuring the flow rate of small quantities of liquid passing through a tubular element, which was then used as a method of supplying insulin to the human body through a pump of an implantable device. The claimed method was, therefore, a method of measuring the efficiency of the pump fitted in the device,[315] which was 'clearly unconnected with either a surgical device or a diagnostic method'.[316] The invention provided insufficient *nexus* to the human body to make it a process directed to a therapeutic purpose because the method 'only involve[d] measuring the volume of the drug solution flowing into the body per unit of time and the flow itself is not

308 (G 05/83) [1979–85] EPOR 241.
309 (T 36/83) [1987] EPOR 1 at para. 6.3.
310 Ibid.
311 Ibid, at para. 6.4 (emphasis added).
312 Ibid.
313 *GENERAL HOSPITAL/Contraceptive method* (T 820/92) [1995] EPOR 446.
314 (T 245/87) [1989] EPOR 448.
315 Ibid, at para. 3.2.1.
316 Ibid, at para. 3.

affected'.[317] The claimed method only provided 'information on the current working order of the device and the body in which the device is implanted is not affected'.[318] The TBA stated that it mattered little that the flow was being timed in an implanted device because that was not sufficient, on its own, to justify a finding that the flow timing was therapeutic in nature. For the timing of the flow to have any therapeutic effect, it 'would have to influence the quality and quantity of the drug flow'.[319] The TBA, therefore, concluded that it was satisfied that the subject matter of the claims met 'the requirements of Article 52(4) EPC without limitation, either verbal or substantive or both, and without a *disclaimer* in Claim 1'.[320] Although a disclaimer was not actually used in respect of the claim in this decision, the EBA clearly thought that, if necessary, a disclaimer could have properly limited the scope of the claims in question.

Where disclaimers are used, the TBA has declined to address the question of whether they are effective to limit the scope of the claims in relation to the exclusion of method of treatment of the human body by surgery. In *THOMPSON/Cornea*,[321] the claim covered a method of ablating by laser predetermined portions of the anterior surface of a synthetic lenticule secured to the cornea of the human eye for correcting vision. It was pointed out that '[b]oth the lens and the lenticule form a unit with the patient's cornea and serve to correct the patient's refractive error'.[322] The TBA held that the claimed treatment of the patient's eye, which effectively removes myopia, hyperopia and astigmatism, was a therapeutic method and was thus excluded from patent protection.[323] The TBA noted that:[324]

> The wording of claim 1 thus indicates, *by using what the appellant considers a disclaimer*, that the claimed teaching does not cover the steps of securing the synthetic lenticule to the cornea of the human eye and of removing the epithelium grown over the lenticule, which steps have been admitted by the appellant to be surgical and have necessarily to be carried out before reprofiling the secured lenticule.
>
> *Whether or not such a disclaimer is effective for the decision on exclusions under the first sentence of Article 52(4) EPC can be left undecided* in the present case in

---

317 Ibid, at para. 3.2.
318 Ibid.
319 Ibid.
320 Ibid, at para. 6 (emphasis added).
321 (T 24/91) [1996] EPOR 19.
322 Ibid, at para. 2.6.
323 Ibid, at paras. 2.6 and 2.7.
324 Ibid, at para. 2.2 (emphasis added).

> view of the findings set out in the following points that the claimed process falls within the exclusion of this article.

The TBA specifically declined to consider whether the use of a disclaimer, which sought to disclaim any method of medical treatment that might be embraced by the claims in question, was allowable. This is regrettable since it would have provided clear *ratio* rather than the *obiter* statements concerning disclaimers made by previous TBAs. The TBA had yet another occasion to consider the effect of a disclaimer, albeit in the context of Article 53(b) EPC, but it was of the opinion that the issue was not relevant to any of the claims in the application, or to any of the questions referred, so no comment was required.[325] In *CSIR/Appetite suppressant*,[326] the TBA stated that:[327]

> In order to disclaim subject-matter which, under Article 52(4) EPC, is excluded from patentability for non-technical reasons, the method of claim 14 has been defined as being a 'non-therapeutic' method. Such disclaimer, although not having a basis in the application as published, is allowable and does not contravene the requirements of Article 123(2) EPC according to [the EBA in *PPG/Disclaimer* at para.2.4].

As a result, the TBA held that the claims: (i) met the requirements of Article 123(2) EPC;[328] (ii) were clear and supported by the description; and (iii) were unobjectionable under Article 84 EPC.[329] The applicability of disclaimers in the context of the exclusion of methods of medical treatment from patent protection is without doubt because the TBA accepts that the decision of the EBA in *PPG/Disclaimer* applies to the exclusion of methods of medical treatment from patent protection. There was no insistence that specific words be used for a valid 'disclaimer' because, in *CSIR/Appetite suppressant*, the words 'non-therapeutic' sufficed.

The question whether the term 'non-therapeutic' was sufficient to disclaim the therapeutic aspect of a claim was considered in *WEIGHT WATCHERS/Slimmer's calculator*.[330] The claimed method was for a

---

325 *NOVARTIS/Transgenic plant* (T 1054/96) (OJ 11/1998, 511) at para. 22.
326 (T 0543/04).
327 Ibid, at para. 1.
328 A European patent application or a European patent may not be amended in such a way that it contains subject matter which extends beyond the content of the application as filed.
329 The European patent application must disclose the invention in a manner sufficiently clear and complete for it to be carried out by a person skilled in the art.
330 (T 0537/04).

method of non-therapeutic slimming comprising allocating a maximum daily calorie target to a person and that person ingesting food, in accordance with that target, so as to effect a bodily size reduction.[331] The appellant argued that: (i) claim 1 had technical character as a whole because it was directed to the technical process of reducing the weight of a person and involved the technical step of ingesting food; (ii) by means of the disclaimer, the claim was directed to 'non-therapeutic' slimming and was thus not a therapy; and (iii) the outcome of the algorithm of the method was actively used to achieve the technical effect of weight loss.[332] The TBA doubted:[333]

> that the use of such a disclaimer limits the method to cosmetic purposes in order to fulfill the requirement of Article 52(4) EPC, in the light of decision T 1172/03 (not published in OJ EPO) and of the fact that the method steps specifying the claim define measures usually used for a therapeutic purpose.

In this decision, contrary to the TBA's views in *CSIR/Appetite suppressant*, the TBA doubted whether such a disclaimer, which sought to limit the claims only to cosmetic purposes so as not to offend the prohibition on patentability of methods of medical treatment, was acceptable. This decision is opposed to another decision of the TBA in *ROUSSEL-CULAF/Thenoyl peroxide* which stated that disclaimers are allowable in respect of claims relating to non-therapeutic uses of substances. The TBA in *ROUSSEL-CULAF/Thenoyl peroxide* had accepted that a claim which was directed at a 'cosmetic' purpose was sufficient to disclaim the additional therapeutic purpose of the substance in question. This meant that there was no need for the appellant in *CSIR/Appetite suppressant* to have used a disclaimer. The decision of the TBA in *WEIGHT WATCHERS/Slimmer's calculator* is, therefore, contrary to the weight of authority emanating from the EPO, namely, *ROUSSEL-CULAF/Thenoyl peroxide*, and, more importantly, the recent decision of *CSIR/Appetite suppressant* that specifically referred to *PPG/Disclaimer* as the authority for allowing disclaimers for methods of medical treatment.

The decisions of the TBAs before *PPG/Disclaimer* vacillated on the issue of whether disclaimers can effectively be used to disclaim an excluded method of medical treatment. The TBA first accepted that it was possible to use such disclaimers but generally avoided addressing the issue specifically. However, since *PPG/Disclaimer*, one TBA has accepted that the

331 Ibid, at para. VII.
332 Ibid, at para. VIII.
333 Ibid, at para. 15.

decision of the EBA in *PPG/Disclaimer* is determinative of the issue and that such disclaimers are allowable, whereas another TBA, without referring to *PPG/Disclaimer,* accepted the contrary view. I have noted elsewhere that, 'Legal certainty is important in patent law where legal rules should be as clear as possible to better enable inventors to assess whether they are able to gain patent protection for their inventions'.[334] This much was emphasised by the EBA in *CYGNUS/Diagnostic method.*[335] The definitive answer given by the EBA in *MEDI-PHYSICS/Treatment by surgery* will be examined below.

4 Form of Admissible Claim

(a) Disclaimers

The subject matter of a claimed invention is defined by the positive features found in the claims in the patent specification.[336] However, the extent of the monopoly claimed may be limited by means of a disclaimer, which effectively is a negative limitation on the claimed invention, that ensures that the excluded subject matter does not form part of the scope of the claims. To be effective, disclaimers must conform to the requirements laid down by the EBA in *PPG/Disclaimer,*[337] when it considered whether disclaimers were allowable under the EPC. It concluded that disclaimers are allowed in order to: (i) restore novelty by delimiting a claim against state of the art under Article 54(3) and (4) EPC[338]; (ii) restore novelty by delimiting a claim against an accidental anticipation under Article 54(2) EPC (an anticipation is accidental if it is so unrelated to, and remote from, the claimed invention that the person skilled in the art would never have taken it into consideration when making the invention)[339] and (iii) to disclaim subject matter which, under Articles 52 to 57 EPC, is excluded from patentability for non-technical reasons.[340] The EBA also pointed out that a disclaimer should not remove more than is necessary to disclaim subject matter

---

[334] Ventose, (2007) 38 IIC 884, 886–887.
[335] (G 01/04) at para. 3.
[336] See, Guidelines for Examination in the European Patent Office 2007, Chapter III, Part C at 4.20.
[337] (G 01/03) [2004] EPOR 33.
[338] Ibid, at Order 2.1.
[339] Ibid.
[340] Ibid.

excluded from patentability for non-technical reasons and a claim, containing a disclaimer, must meet the requirements of clarity and conciseness of Article 84 EPC.[341]

While delineating the uses of disclaimers, the EBA stated that they could also be used in respect of the exceptions to patentability, including methods for medical treatment under Article 53(c) EPC. In such cases, the EBA noted 'it may happen that a general claim comprises embodiments which fall under the exception, whereas the rest are patentable'.[342] According to the EBA in *PPG/Disclaimer*, the excluded subject matter must be disclaimed for non-technical reasons. In other words, the use of disclaimers for things excluded from patent protection only extends to inventions that are excluded from patent protection for reasons other than technical aspects, for example, for public health reasons (methods of medical treatment). Such disclaimers are useful where, for example, a claim embraces a therapeutic method but the patentee wants patent protection only for a cosmetic (or other) method. In such a case, the patentability issue relates to the unpatentability of therapeutic methods derived from Article 53(c) EPC.

To avoid this exclusion, the patentee might simply use words indicating that only the cosmetic (or other) method is claimed, by actually saying so, because the use of the word 'cosmetic' has been held sufficient to disclaim a therapeutic method extant in the claimed method. Similarly, the patentee might simply refer to the 'non-therapeutic' use in the claims. Either way, the excluded subject matter is disclaimed either directly or indirectly. Support for the use of disclaimers for methods of medical treatment is found in the Patent Office Manual of Patent Practice where it is stated that:[343]

> Where the method set out in the claim is itself patentable but could also cover non-patentable embodiments, for example, a method for increasing weight-gain in animals by the addition of substances such as antibiotics to their feedstuffs where, it is known that the substance has therapeutic activity, a claim must be clearly limited (*e.g. by a disclaimer*) to methods which are patentable, and there must be support in the description for a non-therapeutic method. *If necessary, the description should be amended to clarify that therapeutic methods do not form the invention.*

Where, however, the invention is excluded for technical reasons, for example, computer programs, disclaimers cannot be used. There is no longer any

341 Ibid, at Order 2.2.

342 Ibid, at para. 2.4.1.

343 United Kingdom *Manual of Patent Practice*, Section 4A: Methods of treatment or diagnosis at 4A.03.3 (emphasis added).

debate as to whether such disclaimers are allowable for excluded methods of medical treatment. Indeed, before *PPG/Disclaimer*, patentees were already making use of disclaimers but, as noted above, they were not always successful because some TBAs thought disclaimers were, in principle, not allowed for such claims. Now that disclaimers are allowed, it is expected that the TBAs will be consistent in their use until the decision of the EBA in *MEDI-PHYSICS/Treatment by surgery* which, it is hoped, will provide much needed guidance and clarity on the use of such disclaimers in the context of the exclusions from patent protection, in particular, methods of medical treatment.

(b) A higher level of abstraction

In *NOVARTIS II/Transgenic plant*, the EBA held that a claim, wherein specific plant varieties are not individually claimed, is not excluded from patentability under Article 53(b) EPC even though it may embrace plant varieties.[344] This principle was articulated in the context of an exclusion from patent protection, namely, plant varieties. Such claims are product claims whereas methods of medical treatment are process/method claims. Therefore, the principle articulated in *NOVARTIS II/Transgenic plant*, which are applicable product claims, namely, plant varieties, arguably has no place in relation to process claims, namely, methods of medical treatment.

The EBA in *MEDI-PHYSICS/Treatment by surgery* stated that it was established in the jurisprudence of the TBAs that a claim encompassing an embodiment, which was excluded from patentability under now Article 53(c) EPC, could not be left unamended.[345] It noted that the examples given by the EBA in *NOVARTIS II/Transgenic plant*, to show that the rule accepted therein by the referring TBA was not without exception, did not address Article 52(4) EPC but concerned Article 53(a) EPC and Article 83 EPC. In relation to Article 53(b) EPC, the EBA opined that the idea underlying the provision was not that there should be no patent protection for plant varieties but the exclusion in the EPC should correspond to the availability of protection in UPOV, so that the two forms of protection would constitute a single comprehensive system of industrial property protection for plant innovations permitting neither overlapping nor gaps in the protection of eligible subject matter.[346]

---

344 (G 01/98) at paras. 3.1 and 3.8.
345 (G 01/07) at para. 4.1.
346 Ibid.

In this respect, the EBA accepted that the purpose of Article 53(b) EPC was quite different from the purpose of Article 52(4) EPC.[347] Therefore, the EBA concluded that the findings of the EBA in *NOVARTIS II/Transgenic plant* did not doubt but actually confirmed the principle that a claim which encompasses an embodiment, which is excluded from patentability under Article 53(c) EPC, could not be left to encompass that embodiment.[348]

5 Implications of Using Disclaimers

In *CYGNUS/Diagnostic method*, the EBA considered when essential features of claims might be excluded from the claim in question. In that decision, the EBA held that:[349]

> [A]ccording to the established jurisprudence of the EPO, it is accepted that the method steps to be carried out when making a diagnosis as part of the medical treatment of humans or the veterinary treatment of animals for curative purposes include: (i) the examination phase involving the collection of data, (ii) the comparison of these data with standard values, (iii) the finding of any significant deviation, i.e. a symptom, during the comparison, and (iv) the attribution of the deviation to a particular clinical picture, i.e. the deductive medical or veterinary decision phase.

Since all the steps in a diagnostic method must be contained in the claims for it to be rejected by the EPO as an excluded diagnostic method, it is necessary that an applicant outlines the specific steps in the patent specification including the claims. Article 84 EPC states that the claims must define the subject matter for which patent protection is sought, and that they must also be clear. The EBA reasoned that this meant that an independent claim 'should explicitly specify all the essential features needed to define the invention, and that the meaning of these features should be clear for the person skilled in the art from the wording of the claim alone'.[350] This principle was held also to apply to diagnostic methods, which 'serve[d] the overriding purpose of legal certainty'.[351] The EBA added that, if diagnosis as the deductive medical or veterinary decision phases is a purely intellectual exercise, the feature pertaining to the diagnosis for curative purposes and the features relating to the preceding steps,

---

347 Ibid.
348 Ibid.
349 Ibid, at para. 5.
350 Ibid, at para. 6.2.
351 Ibid.

which are constitutive for making diagnosis, represent the essential features of a diagnostic method within the meaning of Article 52(4) EPC.[352] This, according to the EBA, meant that any claim, in order to satisfy the requirement of Article 84 EPC, must include these features.[353]

The possibility that applicants might circumvent the exclusion by not including in the claims any essential feature of a diagnostic method, the EBA explained, did not seem to pose a real risk having regard to the well-established jurisprudence of the EPO in respect of Article 84 EPC, which requires that, in order to be patentable, an independent claim must recite all the essential features which are necessary for clearly and completely defining a particular invention.[354] This means that even the last step – the diagnosis *stricto sensu*, which is a purely intellectual exercise (unless it is carried out by a device) – must also be included as an essential feature in the independent claim.[355] The same principle applied to the preceding steps whether or not they were of a technical or non-technical nature. With regards to the features of the claim which were of a non-technical nature, they were to 'be included as an essential feature in the respective independent claim if its essentialness is unambiguously inferable from the respective European patent application or European patent as whole'.[356] Thus a patentee who decides to disclaim any excluded method (including a method of medical treatment) must be careful to ensure that any disclaimed aspect of the claim is not an essential feature of the claimed invention. Even where the essential feature is a technical or non-technical aspect of the claim, it should be included if it is necessary for clearly and completely defining the invention. If the disclaimed aspect amounts to an essential feature of the claimed method as a whole it would offend Article 84 EPC, and would, in accordance with *CYGNUS/Diagnostic method*, not be patentable.

In addition, the EPC Guidelines for Examination state that the replacement or removal of a feature from a claim does not violate Article 123(2) EPC if the skilled person would directly and unambiguously recognise that: (i) the feature was not explained as essential in the disclosure; (ii) the feature is not, as such, indispensable for the function of the invention in the light of

---

352 Ibid, at para. 6.2.3.
353 Ibid.
354 Ibid, at para. 6.2.4.
355 Ibid.
356 Ibid.

the technical problem the invention serves to solve; and (iii) the replacement or removal requires no real modification of other features to compensate for the change.[357] In addition, when a disclaimer is introduced to a claim, any such subject matter that is covered by the claims is necessarily excluded. This does not mean that in every case there would be an issue relating to whether the claims, as they now stand, would not be supported by the description. That might be a consequence, so patentees and patent practitioners might very well anticipate that and ensure that what is disclaimed does not prejudice Article 84 EPC. Arguably, in most cases the disclaimer would either be a negative limitation or a positive limitation on the claims and, as such, would not affect the description at all – for example, where a claim relates to the 'cosmetic', or 'non-surgical' or 'non-therapeutic' aspect of the claim, it is unlikely that such a disclaimer would affect the description in any significant way. Where, however, the disclaimer does affect the scope of the claims, patentees and patent practitioners should be cognisant of the possibility that the EPO might reject the claim as offending against Article 84 EPC.

6 The Enlarged Board of Appeal

(a) Disclaimers

The EBA in *MEDI-PHYSICS/Treatment by surgery* stated that, in accordance with the decision of the EBA in *PPG/Disclaimer*, the term 'disclaimer' means an amendment to a claim resulting in the incorporation therein of a 'negative' technical feature, typically excluding from a general feature specific embodiments or areas.[358] It also stated that the use of terms like 'pre-delivered' and/or 'pre-implanted' was not a disclaimer within the meaning of *PPG/Disclaimer* but was a form of omitting the step from the claim by making it clear that the step did not form part of the claimed method.[359] In responding to question 2 of the referring TBA decision, which asked whether the exclusion from patent protection under Article 53(c) EPC can be avoided by amending the wording of the claim so as to disclaim the step at issue, the EBA replied that it appeared difficult for it to imagine how there could still be a problem under Article 53(c) EPC if the claimed invention no longer contained any subject matter excluded from

[357] Guidelines for Examination in the European Patent Office, Part C, Chapter VI, 5.3.10.
[358] (G 01/07) at para. 4.2.1.
[359] Ibid.

patentability under that article, as a result of the surgical subject matter having been disclaimed.[360]

The EBA clarified that any problems arising from such disclaimers would relate to the conditions for them to be compatible with the remaining requirements of the EPC, in particular, with Article 84 EPC.[361] It argued that Articles 56 and 83 EPC may, however, also be concerned, for example, in a case in which the only example for carrying out the method would be the disclaimed surgical one.[362] Therefore, it held that the answer to question 2 was that the exclusion from patentability under Article 53(c) EPC could be avoided by disclaiming an embodiment or embodiments which are methods of treatment by surgery within the meaning of Article 53(c) EPC, but the overall patentability of any such claim depended on the remaining requirements of the EPC, and, where applicable, the conditions as defined in *PPG/Disclaimer* also being fulfilled.[363] The EBA further clarified that whether or not this was the case was to be decided in each case, individually, and that this applied also to the question of which form the disclaimer can or must take, that is whether (only) a particular embodiment can or must be disclaimed or whether a disclaimer can and/or must take a more general form by using the word 'non-surgical'.[364]

(b) Omission of the step

The EBA noted that Article 84 EPC in conjunction with Rule 43 EPC required that the claims shall define the matter for which protection is sought; so that a claim should explicitly specify all of the essential features needed to define the invention and it must be clear.[365] The EBA stated that, under Article 84 EPC, whether or not a step being or encompassing a surgical step excluded from patentability can be omitted either by using positive wording for such omission like 'pre-delivered' or by simply leaving it out from the claim, depended on whether the claimed invention was fully and completely defined by the features of the claim without that step.[366] That, the EBA noted, required an assessment of the individual case under consideration. The EBA continued that, when omission of a step from a claim was being considered, the remaining requirements of the EPC for allowing such omission and the patentability of a claim, not containing the

360 Ibid, at para. 4.2.2.
361 Ibid.
362 Ibid.
363 Ibid.
364 Ibid.
365 Ibid, at para. 4.3.1.
366 Ibid.

omitted feature, must also be fulfilled.[367] These included Article 123(2) EPC and, in opposition proceedings, Article 123(3) EPC, but Articles 83 or 56 EPC might also come into play, for example, if, as a result of the omission, the claimed invention could no longer be carried out over the whole breadth of the claim or the problem was not so solved.[368]

7 Legal Analysis

Where a patentee seeks patent protection for a cosmetic (or other) method, but the invention also embraces a surgical or therapeutic method, a disclaimer might be a useful tool in limiting the claims to only the cosmetic (or other) aspect by using such words as 'non-surgical' or 'non-therapeutic'. This should be a sufficient disclaimer unless the cosmetic (or other) purpose arises directly from the medical purpose. The focus should not be on the form that the disclaimer should take. Specific words should not necessarily be made a strict requirement for disclaimers. Patentees should simply be allowed to use clear words to disclaim any excluded method of medical treatment. The decisions of the TBA that have considered the issue of whether disclaimers are permissible for methods of medical treatment have been inconsistent, with some TBAs claiming that they are allowable, whereas others make it clear that they are not. The EBA in *PPG/Disclaimer* made it abundantly clear that under the EPC such disclaimers are, in principle, allowed. It means, therefore, that the question of whether they should be allowed is now a moot one.

The reasoning of the EBA in *MEDI-PHYSICS/Treatment by surgery* suggests that an applicant may use terms such as 'previously obtained', 'previously injected', or 'pre-delivered contrast agent' in the specification of their patent application which would enable patentees to disclaim the surgical method/step so that the claim as a whole would not be excluded from patent protection by virtue of Article 53(c) EPC. There is no argument that the EBA's reasoning on this point is correct insofar as it accepts, in line with an established line of authority from the TBAs, that disclaimers may legitimately be used to disclaim not only surgical methods but therapeutic methods and diagnostic methods as well, provided that the other requirements of the EPC are satisfied, namely, Articles 56, 83 and 84 EPC, and that the specific requirements of *PPG/Disclaimer* are also followed.

---

[367] Ibid, at para. 4.3.3.
[368] Ibid.

J CONCLUSION

The TBAs had not been able to articulate a clear definition of surgical treatment. They have adopted a myriad of meanings, namely, that relating to the physical intervention itself, and those that broadly have, as their primary function, the maintenance of the life and well being of the human or animal body. This issue, finally, has now been determined by the EBA after consideration of the three questions referred to it by the TBA in *MEDI-PHYSICS/Treatment by surgery*. The debate concerning the scope of the exclusion of method of treatment of the human or animal body by surgery has now been settled. The EBA, although declining to give a definitive and comprehensive definition of 'treatment by surgery', has ruled that the definition of surgical methods does not embrace methods that are for a curative purpose and that neither the ordinary reading nor the intention of the drafters of the EPC 1973 compels one to that conclusion. It asserted that the exclusion for surgical methods, and indeed the other medical treatment methods under Article 53(c) EPC, namely therapeutic and diagnostic methods, should not be applied to methods in respect of which the interests of public health, protection of patients and freedom of the medical profession to apply the treatment of choice to their patients does not mean that they should be excluded from patent protection – the so called 'new direction'. Importantly too, the EBA, agreeing with the established jurisprudence of the TBAs, reiterated that a claimed method is excluded under Article 53(c) EPC if it comprises or encompasses at least one feature defining a physical activity or action that constitutes a method step for treatment of the human or animal body by surgery or therapy. The EBA also formally accepted that disclaimers may be used in claims in respect of the exclusions under Article 53(c) EPC, provided that they satisfy the requirements in *PPG/Disclaimer* and conform to the requirements of Articles 83 and 84 EPC.

In essence, the decision of the EBA in *MEDI-PHYSICS/Treatment by surgery* has broadened the interpretation of what can be considered 'treatment by surgery' by accepting that it is not limited to methods that have only a curative purpose. This, arguably, would be a disappointment to applicants of cosmetic methods that may involve some surgical element. However, the EBA acknowledged that, with the increase in surgical research and advances made therein, some uncritical methods involving minor interventions may not fall under the exclusion from patentability under Article 53(c) EPC.

6. Diagnostic methods

A INTRODUCTION

Article 53(c) of the European Patent Convention (EPC) also excludes from patent protection '*diagnostic methods* practised on the human or animal body'. Although not specifically a method of medical treatment, the exclusion of diagnostic methods is found in what is termed the 'methods of medical treatment exclusion' found in Article 53(c) EPC. This chapter will consider the scope of the exclusion of diagnostic methods and its necessity in light of the rationale for the exclusion of methods of medical treatment from patent protection.[1] With the increasing complexity and technical sophistication associated with medical treatments, and by extension diagnostic methods, in this technologically advanced age, it is important that the exclusion in Article 53(c) EPC is not construed in a manner that stifles appropriate research and development in this vital and essential area. The new age of technological advancement in the medical field, using genetic testing and gene therapy, would not be sustainable if an appropriate balance is not struck when interpreting the exclusion.[2] Therefore, it was not surprising that the recent revisions to the EPC in 2000 confirmed that the exclusion for methods of medical treatment is here to stay,[3] while, at the same time, providing a new statutory basis for second medical use patents.[4]

---

[1] See generally, P. Lancon, 'Patentability in the Field of Therapy and Diagnosis' (1991) 22 IIC 893, W. De Smet, 'Patentability in the Area of Therapy and Diagnosis under Belgian Law' (1991) 22 IIC 888, K.E. Panchen, 'Patentability in the Field of Therapy and Diagnosis' (1991) 22 IIC 879; P. Pennant, 'Patentability of Medical Treatment' [1981] 2 EIPR 64; and D. Thomas, 'Patentability Problems in Medical Technology' (2003) 34 IIC 847. The ideas in this chapter have been derived, in part, from the following: E. Ventose, 'Patent Protection for Diagnostic Methods Under the European Patent Convention' (2007) 38 IIC 884; 'Making Sense of the Decision of the Enlarged Board of Appeal in *CYGNUS/Diagnostic method*' (2008) EIPR 145; and 'In the Footsteps of the Framers of the European Patent Convention: Examining the *Travaux Preparatoires*' (2009) EIPR 353.

[2] W.R. Cornish, *Intellectual Property: Omnipresent, Distracting, Irrelevant?* (Oxford, Oxford University Press, 2004) pp. 10–26.

[3] The drafters of the EPC 2000 were of the opinion that the previous formulation of the exclusion of methods of medical treatment from patent protection was

In *CYGNUS/Diagnostic method*,[5] the Enlarged Board of Appeal of the European Patent Office (EBA) has restated the law relating to diagnostic methods after a spate of differing decisions of the TBA and confirmed the necessity of granting patents in the medical field, and specifically made it clear that the exclusion of diagnostic methods should be narrowly construed in a manner which preserves the principle that patents should generally be available, while, at the same time, ensuring that medical and veterinary practitioners are not hampered in their practice of medicine.[6] We have seen this pragmatism before: in *EISAI/Second medical indication*,[7] where the EBA accepted that the Swiss type claim was sufficient to gain patent protection for second medical uses. The English Courts have duly followed suit.[8]

The issue relating to the scope of the exclusion of diagnostic methods arose for consideration at the EBA in *CYGNUS/Diagnostic method* because the President of the European Patents Office (EPO), on 29 December 2003, referred the following questions, among others, to the consideration of the EBA:[9]

(i) Whether diagnostic methods practised on the human or animal body within the meaning of Article 52(4) EPC relate only to those methods containing:
  (a) all the procedural steps to be carried out when making a medical diagnosis; or
  (b) one procedural step that can be used for diagnostic purposes or relates to the diagnosis;

---

indeed a 'fiction', and that the exclusion seems to be grounded in public health. In any event, the EPO and the UK courts were always of the opinion that the exclusion was based on public health considerations.

4 Article 54(5) EPC 2000 which provides that paras 2 and 3 shall also not exclude the patentability of any substance or composition referred to in para. 4 for any specific use in a method referred to in Article 53(c), provided that such use is not comprised in the state of the art.

5 (G 01/04) [2006] EPOR 15.

6 Ibid, at para. 4.

7 (G 05/83) [1979–85] EPOR 241.

8 The Patents Court, sitting *en banc*, in *John Wyeth and Brothers Ltd's Application and AG Schering's Application* [1985] RPC 545 and the decision of the Court of Appeal in *Bristol-Myers Squibb v Baker Norton Pharmaceuticals* [2001] RPC 1. However, the UK Court of Appeal has taken a different approach to this issue: *Actavis UK Limited v Merck & Co Inc* [2008] EWCA Civ 444; [2008] RPC 26. See F. Ch'en and I. Karet, 'Court of Appeal can overrule itself to follow the EPO: UK adopts EPO stance on second medical use claims' [2008] JIPLP 543.

9 See also S.J.R. Bostyn, 'No Cure without Pay? Referral to the Enlarged Board of Appeal Concerning the Patentability of Diagnostic Methods' [2005] EIPR 412.

(ii) Whether a claimed method is a 'diagnostic method' if it contains at least one procedural step requiring participation by a physician (by being present or bearing the responsibility); and
(iii) Whether the requirement 'practised on the human or animal body' in Article 52(4) EPC meant that all or only one step must be practised on the body in order that the method can be said to have the character of a diagnostic method.

These questions which were put to the EBA reflected differing views of various Technical Boards of Appeal (TBAs) on the question of the proper scope of Article 52(4) EPC. In particular, it reflected concerns relating to the decision of the TBA in *CYGNUS/Diagnostic method* in 2002[10] which rejected the established learning found in a 1987 decision of another TBA, in *BRUKER/Non-invasive measurement*,[11] and the subsequent cases that followed it.[12] It was not surprising that this referral to the EBA was made since there were conflicting decisions on the scope of the exclusion from patent protection of diagnostic methods. Legal certainty is important in patent law where legal rules should be as clear as possible to better enable inventors to assess whether they are able to gain patent protection for their inventions. Understandably, the EBA in *CYGNUS/Diagnostic method* was at pains to point out the need for legal certainty when interpreting the provisions of the EPC.[13]

To set the scene for the analysis of the decision of the EBA in *CYGNUS/Diagnostic method*, this chapter will, first, analyse the decision in *BRUKER/Non-invasive measurement* with a view to understanding what it decided, including an examination of the subsequent cases to determine the extent to which they have applied it, or have attempted to limit its reach; and secondly, analyse the decision of the TBA in *CYGNUS/Diagnostic method* to properly understand why it came to an opposite conclusion relating to the scope of the exclusion, as compared to the decision in *BRUKER/Non-invasive measurement.* This chapter will then examine the decision of the EBA *CYGNUS/Diagnostic method* to delineate the current state of the law relating to the scope of the exclusion for diagnostic methods and determine whether the decision was justified as a matter of principle or policy.

---

[10] (T 964/99) [2002] EPOR 272.

[11] (T 385/86) [1988] EPOR 357.

[12] *GENERAL ELECTRONIC COMPANY* (T 0530/93); *NATIONAL DEVELOPMENT CORPORATION/Method of producing image information* (T 400/87); *NYCOMED AS/Contrasting agent for NMR imaging* (T 665/92); and *SIEMENS/Diagnostic method* (T 83/87) [1988] EPOR 365.

[13] *CYGNUS/Diagnostic method* (G 01/04) at para. 6.2.

B LEGISLATIVE HISTORY

Although surgical methods were included in the exclusion as late as 1969, the decision to insert 'diagnostic methods' in Article 9(2) was made as early as 1964 at the 15th meeting of the Working Party.[14] The fact that diagnostic methods were patentable in Germany was explained on the basis that chemical products were not patentable in Germany.[15] As a result, the Working Party instructed the Drafting Committee to take into account its decision when drawing up Article 9(2) 'in order to indicate the exclusion of methods for treating the human body or animals, *including diagnostic methods*'.[16] An early draft of the Convention excluded 'methods of therapy, *including* diagnostic methods'.[17] As mentioned above, the 1965 version of the Draft Convention, as established by the EEC 'Patent' Working Party, excluded 'medical treatments, *including* methods of diagnosis'.[18] By 1970, the exclusion related to 'therapeutic or surgical methods for treatment of the human or animal body, *and* diagnostic methods'.[19] In 1971, the text of the exclusion was for 'methods for treatment of the human [or animal] body by surgery or therapy, *as well as* diagnostic methods'.[20] The early drafts of the exclusion mentioned diagnostic methods but merely as part of 'therapeutic methods' evidenced by the use of the word 'including'. However, later drafts marked a significant shift from the use of the word 'including' to

---

[14] Minutes of the Proceedings of the 15th meeting of the Patents Working Party held in Brussels from 19–26 October 1964.

[15] Ibid.

[16] Ibid.

[17] Amendments to the Preliminary Draft Convention relating to European Patent Law, Brussels, 22 January 1965 (emphasis added).

[18] Draft Convention established by the EEC 'Patents' Working Party, 1965 (emphasis added).

[19] First Preliminary Draft of a Convention Establishing a European System for the Grant of Patents, Brussels, 21 December 1970 (emphasis added).

[20] Article 9(e), Second Preliminary Draft of a Convention Establishing a European System for the Grant of Patents, 1971. This reflects the same position at the stage reached on 29 January 1971 in relation to the First Preliminary Draft Convention Establishing a European System for the Grant of Patents, Brussels, 15 February 1971 (Stage reached on 29 January 1971). The Document correcting the Second Preliminary Draft Convention Establishing a European System for the Grant of Patents, Brussels, 6 December 1971 was to the same effect except that the square brackets were removed (Stage reached on 26 November 1971) (emphasis added).

the use of 'and' and 'as well as'. This meant that diagnosis was given its independent status and not simply included as part of the definition of therapy.[21]

Some organisations 'expressed reservations' about the inclusion of 'diagnostic methods' in the exclusion, pointing out that '[d]evelopments in technology had been seen with regard to diagnostic methods which were not specifically medical in nature', for example, the use of equipment to determine the blood group of a patient.[22] As a result, the Inter-Governmental Conference instructed the Working Party to examine these concerns.[23] Some interested parties thought the exclusion of methods of medical treatment from patent protection should not extend to 'processes and laboratory equipment for the purpose of diagnosis'.[24] The Working Party rejected that proposal, because, first, 'in so far as the processes involved treatment by doctors, this would not be patentable anyhow';[25] and, secondly, 'laboratory equipment could be dealt with under the ordinary rules of patentability'.[26]

In 1972, a compromise was eventually reached on the wording of the exclusion of diagnostic methods: the Working Party accepted the French government's proposal to qualify the exclusion of diagnostic methods by adding the words 'applied to the human or animal body'.[27] Presumably, this was done to ensure that diagnostic methods, which were not applied to the human or animal body, for example, those that were carried out in laboratories, were not covered by the exclusion. The Working Party agreed that

---

[21] Article 9(2) provided that: 'Inventions within the meaning of paragraph (1) shall in particular exclude: (e) therapeutic or surgical methods for treatment of the human or animal body, and diagnostic methods' (Preliminary Draft Convention for a European System for the Grant of Patents, Inter-Governmental Conference for the Setting up of a European System for the Grant of Patents, Minutes of the Working Party, Luxembourg, 8–11 July 1969).

[22] Minutes of the 5th Meeting of the Inter-Governmental Conference for the Setting up of a European System for the Grant of Patents, Part II, Hearing of the Non-Governmental Organisations on the Second Preliminary Draft Convention establishing a European System for the Grant of Patents, Luxembourg, 26 January–1 February 1972, at para. 17.

[23] Minutes of the 5th Meeting of the Inter-Governmental Conference for the Setting up of a European System for the Grant of Patents, Luxembourg, 24–25 January and 2–4 February 1972, at para. 34.

[24] Minutes of the 9th meeting of Working Party I held from 12–22 October, 1971, in Luxembourg, para. 93.

[25] Ibid.

[26] Ibid.

[27] Minutes of the 11th meeting of the Working Party I held in Luxembourg from 28 February–3 March 1972, at para. 9(c).

'this specification in no way implied that psychological procedures or autopsies were not referred to, and that diagnostic apparatus would in principle be patentable'.[28] In accordance with the French proposal, the exclusion was reformulated to exclude only 'diagnostic methods practised on the human [or animal] body'[29] and formed part of the text tabled at the Munich Diplomatic Conference in 1973.[30]

C THE NARROW APPROACH

1 Introduction

In *BRUKER/Non-invasive measurement*, the TBA had to consider the scope of the exclusion of diagnostic methods from patent protection. The claim was for the non-invasive determination of chemical and/or physical conditions inside a living animal or human body using local magnetic resonance. After examining the legislative history of the exclusion, the TBA concluded that the purpose of Article 52(4) EPC was to ensure that physicians would not be hampered in the practice of medicine by patent legislation.[31] The TBA then examined: first, the definitional issues relating to diagnostic methods; secondly, whether such methods would be unpatentable if they could only be carried out by a doctor in the exercise of his healing skills; and, thirdly, the scope of the limitation 'practised on the human or animal body'. The decision is of some significance since it is the first reported decision to consider the exclusion for diagnostic methods and establish that a diagnostic method must 'give reference to the diagnosis to be made'.[32]

2 Defining Diagnostic Methods

The TBA had first to define 'diagnostic methods' before it could consider the second issue of whether the claimed methods were in fact diagnostic methods. It was only then that the TBA could properly assess the invention to determine whether or not it was excluded from patent protection. The

---

28 Ibid.

29 Draft Convention Establishing a European System for the Grant of Patents (Stage reached on 20 May 1972).

30 Draft Convention, Munich Diplomatic Conference for the Setting up of a European System for the Grant of Patents, Munich, 10 September–6 October 1973.

31 *CYGNUS/Diagnostic method* (T 964/99) at para. 3.1.

32 P. Lancon, 'Patentability in the Field of Therapy and Diagnosis' (1991) 22 IIC 893, 907.

TBA was of the opinion that 'the only diagnostic methods to be excluded from patent protection are those whose results immediately make it possible to decide on a particular course of medical treatment'.[33] This meant that, to be excluded from patent protection, the diagnostic method must enable the physician to decide immediately on the course of treatment for the patient. According to the TBA, methods providing only interim results were not diagnostic methods within the meaning of Article 52(4) EPC, first sentence, even if they could be utilised in making a diagnosis.[34] Interim results are clearly not definite, and more testing and analysis would usually have to be carried out to confirm them. In answering the question whether a method was a diagnostic one, it was necessary to ascertain whether the method claimed contained all the steps involved in reaching a medical diagnosis.[35]

The steps leading to diagnosis, in the view of the TBA, included: (1) examination and data gathering; (2) comparison of the data with normal values; (3) recording any significant deviation; and (4) attributing the deviation to a particular clinical picture.[36] In other words, diagnosis comprised the period in which information is gathered, compared, recorded and then attributed to a particular medical condition. This four-pronged test provided a useful one which enabled the TBA to determine what would qualify as a method of diagnosis. This meant that all the steps must be present in the claimed method for it to be excluded from patent protection; if only one step was missing, the claim would not be a diagnostic method but, according to the TBA, at best, a method of data acquisition or data processing that could be used in a diagnostic method.[37]

This four-pronged test to determine whether a method was a diagnostic one was criticised by Moufang who observed that '[t]his strict interpretation is very problematic',[38] because, first, it expanded the definition of diagnostic methods to include not only the purely deductive step – the

---

[33] *BRUKER/Non-invasive measurement* (T 385/86) at para. 3.1; and *SIEMENS/Diagnostic method* (T 83/87) [1986] EPOR 365.

[34] Ibid. See also *GENERAL ELECTRONIC COMPANY* (T 0530/93) at para. 4.

[35] Ibid.

[36] *BRUKER/Non-invasive measurement* (T 385/86) at para. 3.3.

[37] Ibid. This was the case in *NATIONAL DEVELOPMENT CORPORATION/Methods of producing image information from objects* (T 400/87) where the claimed method related only to the examination and data gathering phase, which meant that there was no diagnostic method, since all four of the steps were not extant in the claimed method in question.

[38] R. Moufang, 'Methods of Medical Treatment under Patent Law' [1993] 24 IIC 18, 46.

diagnosis *stricto sensu* – but also the examination and data gathering phases. Secondly, the inevitable consequence of an acceptance of this test meant that: (a) where any of the steps are missing there would be no diagnostic method; and (b) where the method only produced interim results it would not be patentable. The definition of 'diagnostic methods' was very narrow, which, arguably, allowed patentees to patent methods which, otherwise, would not have been patentable. It seems, therefore, that Moufang's issue with the decision in *BRUKER/Non-invasive measurement* related actually to its narrow nature, preferring instead the approach of the German and Swedish case law, which, in his words, 'clearly reveal an effort not to permit a complete drainage of the meaning of the exclusion clause'.[39]

It is suggested that it must be correct that 'diagnostic methods' cannot simply comprise the diagnosis *strictu sensu*, since they would relate to methods, which, 'as mere instructions to the human intellect, do not constitute technical rules for controlling natural forces and which therefore are not patentable from the outset'.[40] Therefore, quite sensibly, the TBA in *BRUKER/Non-invasive measurement* interpreted the exclusion to include the preceding steps necessary for making the diagnosis. That approach is to be commended for the following reasons: first, the exclusion would not have been drafted in the manner which implicitly recognised 'diagnostic methods' as inventions within the meaning of Article 52(1) EPC; secondly, it would have been superfluous to exclude diagnostic methods on the basis of lacking industrial application if it was actually an intellectual exercise more properly excluded on the basis of Article 52(2) EPC; and, thirdly, there would have been no need for the EPC to explicitly state that only diagnostic methods 'practised on the human and animal body' are excluded from patent protection, because, if the alternative argument is right, diagnostic methods would be an intellectual exercise and, therefore, incapable of being practised, as such.

The steps in the instant claim resulted in the obtaining of a specific value for body temperature which, by itself, could not determine the presence or absence of a particular disease.[41] The method, according to the TBA, was simply a 'technical method of measurement which might be useful *inter alia* in diagnosis';[42] it did not, therefore, satisfy the requirement that they must

---

39 Ibid.

40 Ibid, at 47.

41 See, for example, *BAXTER/Blood extraction method* (T 329/94) [1998] EPOR 363 where the blood was taken from the human body with a view to finding out the cause of the disease.

42 *BRUKER/Non-invasive measurement* (T 385/86) at para. 3.6.

immediately result in the making of a medical diagnosis. The diagnosis itself had also to be *clearly identifiable* before a claim could be rejected as an excluded method of treatment.[43] This deductive decision phase is the most crucial aspect of the diagnostic method since it is the conclusion reached by the medical or veterinary practitioner, after successfully completing the preceding steps.[44] If it is not clearly identifiable, it would suggest either: (a) more information might be needed to make an accurate diagnosis; or (b) that there might be more than one possible diagnosis based on the current information that the preceding steps provided. Therefore, the requirement that the claims in the patent specification must be enabled would not be satisfied.[45]

3 Involvement of Medical Practitioners

Even without any explicit rationale emerging from its examination of the *travaux préparatoires* of the EPC, the TBA was confident to assert that the first sentence of Article 52(4) EPC was intended to exclude from the possibility of patent protection only methods of treatment by therapy, so that no one could be hampered in the practice of medicine by patent legislation.[46] After defining diagnostic methods, and concluding that the claimed method did not satisfy the requirement therein outlined, the TBA then considered whether, assuming that the exclusion was 'intended to prevent a doctor being hampered in the practice of medicine by patent legislation', the claimed methods 'define[d] methods which cannot be considered susceptible of industrial application because they can only be carried out by a doctor in the exercise of his healing skills'.[47]

The claimed method, which was of a technical nature, did not require a physician to perform it or include any measures having the character of medical treatment. The TBA confirmed that it was a technician who, using the claimed method, was able, quite independently from any physician, to

---

[43] *THOMPSON-CSF/Tomodensitometry (2)* (T 208/83) [1979–85] EPOR C917, 919, *THOMPSON-CSF/Tomodensitometry (1)* (T 61/83) [1979–85] EPOR C763, 766, *PHILIPS/Diagnostic method* (T 45/84) [1979–85] C937, 938–9.

[44] In *BIOTRONIC/Heart monitoring apparatus and method* (T 0598/07), the TBA held that the claimed method did not include a step relating to the diagnosis for curative purposes *strictu sensu* representing the deductive medical or veterinary decision phase, so it did not fall under the exclusion of Article 53(c) EPC (at para. 5).

[45] Article 84 EPC.

[46] *BRUKER/Non-invasive measurement* (T 385/86) at para. 3.2.

[47] Ibid, at para. 3.5.

produce a working basis for the doctor's subsequent activity of diagnosis.[48] The TBA observed that since the examination phase did not need the presence of a physician, and that the physician had at his disposal equipment detached from the living body, the claimed method was susceptible to industrial application in the same way as laboratory tests carried out on blood or tissue samples taken from the human or animal body.[49] The TBA, therefore, concluded that '[a] claimed method involving interaction with the human or animal body is susceptible to industrial application if it can be used with the desired result by a technician without specialist knowledge and skills'.[50] It would not matter either if only the final diagnostic activity was performed by a physician if the skilled person was previously responsible for carrying out and controlling the other parts of the diagnostic method.[51]

Therefore, a claimed method would be patentable if it could not be performed by a physician, or if it could be performed by a technician without any specialist medical knowledge.[52] This gloss on the exclusion of diagnostic methods meant that the TBAs were now to engage in an inquiry of whether a physician could perform the procedure, as outlined in the claims.[53] It can readily be appreciated why the TBA came to that conclusion since it accepted that the rationale of the exclusion was to ensure that physicians are not prevented from practising medicine by patent legislation. This limitation does not find itself in the text of Article 52(4) EPC, which does not mention this requirement at all, or require any indication of the identity of the person performing the method of diagnosis as a necessary element of the exclusion. This approach sowed the seeds of the later confusion that confronted other TBAs.

The TBAs that followed *BRUKER/Non-invasive measurement* did not heed the words of caution given by the TBA in *BAXTER/Blood extraction*

---

48 Ibid, at para. 3.5.2.

49 Ibid. See *NEXINS RESEARCH/Apoptotic cells* (T 1038/00) where the TBA held that a method for detecting and/or quantifying and/or separating apoptotic cells in or from a sample was not a method of diagnosis practised on the human or animal body (at para. 6).

50 *BRUKER/Non-invasive measurement* (T 385/86) at para. 3.5.2

51 *NYCOMED AS/Contrast agent for NMR imaging* (T 0655/92) at para. 5.3.

52 This requirement was again reasserted by the TBA in *NATIONAL DEVELOPMENT CORPORATION/Methods of producing imagine information from objects* (T 0400/87) where it was made clear that the effects of the continuous magnetic field do not leave any harmful side-effects in the living matter, which meant that the claimed method could be implemented without specialist medical knowledge or skills (para. 3.2). See also: *TEIJIN LIMITED/Bone evaluation method* (T 0775/92) at para. 10.

53 *NYCOMED AS/Contrast agent for NMR imaging* (T 0655/92) at para. 5.3.

method,[54] where it had to consider a claimed extraction assistance method for facilitating sustained venous flow through a human limb towards a venous extraction point. Given the purpose of the invention, the TBA noted that:[55]

> [I]t matters little whether the measure is performed by a medical practitioner or another person having medical knowledge or under the supervision of such a person … *This sole criterion is not sufficient to decide whether the method step is objectionable under Article 52(4)*, though the medical competence of the practitioner may be, at first sight, a useful indication. Much more important are the purpose and inevitable effect of the feature under consideration.

4 Practised on the Human or Animal Body

Quite sensibly, the exclusion of diagnostic methods in Article 52(4) EPC is couched in terms which require that the claimed method be practised on the human or animal body to be excluded from patent protection. This specific requirement is in line with the rationale of the exclusion, which is to free from restraint the activities of medical and veterinary practitioners when they treat their patients. The TBA in *BRUKER/Non-invasive measurement* was of the opinion that the Examining Division did not engage the question whether the claimed method was practised on the human or animal body, presumably because it assumed that this was so (because of the magnetic fields' effect of producing magnetic resonance on the body) without any discussion of whether that actually was the case.[56] The TBA felt that this was not the correct approach. It explained that since Article 52(4) EPC is an exclusion clause it should be narrowly construed, which, according to it, meant that both the examination and deviation measured from the norm must be carried out on a living human or animal body.[57]

Based on the facts of the case, it was held that the steps described in the claims resulted in a measured value which was only visible outside the body in a high-resolution resonance spectrum that appeared on a screen or

---

[54] (T 0329/94).

[55] Ibid, at para. 5 (emphasis added).

[56] *BRUKER/Non-invasive measurement* (T 385/86) at para. 4.

[57] Ibid, at para. 4.1. In *NATIONAL DEVELOPMENT CORPORATION/Methods of producing imagine information from objects* (T 0400/87), the TBA held that the measures claimed in the invention resulted in diagrams which show a two-dimensional spin-density distribution in selected planes. It therefore concluded that a possible deviation from the norm is discerned from these diagrams and not from the human body itself (at para. 3.3).

plotter page in the final stage of the diagnostic apparatus.[58] The information was gathered using technical measures performed outside the human body and that information was, subsequently, displayed on a data carrier which was detached from the human body. Therefore, the TBA concluded that the claim did not define a method that was practised on the human body.[59] The TBA then stated that 'the practice of a diagnostic method on the human or animal body in the meaning of Article 52(4), first sentence, EPC presupposes that even a deviation from a norm that must be regarded as a symptom is directly discernable on the body itself'.[60] This meant that: (a) the symptom must be discernable from the human or animal body itself; and (b) there must be no additional step which takes place outside the body that determines the deviation itself – '[t]he condition ascertained must of itself demonstrate the pathological deviation'.[61] This requirement further narrows the scope of the exclusion because not only must the excluded method include all of the steps mentioned above, the TBA has now stipulated that each of those steps, including the diagnosis *strictu sensu*, must be practised on the human or animal body. Therefore, quite sensibly, if the diagnostic method is practised on human or animal tissue, organs or liquids after they have been removed permanently from the subject, it would not be excluded from patent protection.[62]

Again, Moufang, has noted his disquiet about this aspect of the reasoning of the TBA in *BRUKER/Non-invasive measurement*. He did not appreciate why it had accepted this restrictive interpretation whereby the exclusion for diagnostic methods would only bite where the preceding steps leading to the diagnosis *strictu sensu* had to be practised on the living human or animal body.[63] As a result, he concluded, the approach to the interpretation of the exclusion of diagnostic methods adopted by the TBA in *BRUKER/Non-invasive measurement* amounted to a 'practical dissolution of the legislative exclusion of diagnostic methods'.[64] However, this reasoning rests on the assumption that all methods, which even relate to diagnosis should be unpatentable, a view that cannot be right, since the

---

58 *BRUKER/Non-invasive measurement* (T 385/86) at para. 4.2.
59 Ibid.
60 Ibid, at para. 4.3.
61 Ibid, at para. 4.3.2.
62 *SIEMENS/Diagnostic method* (T 83/87); and see R. Moufang, 'Methods of Medical Treatment under Patent Law' [1993] 24 IIC 18, 45.
63 R. Moufang, 'Methods of Medical Treatment under Patent Law' [1993] 24 IIC 18, 47.
64 Ibid. These paragraphs were cited by the TBA in *CYGNUS/Diagnostic method* (T 964/99) (at para. 3.6) as an indication of academic disquiet about the decision in *BRUKER/Non-invasive measurement* (T 385/86).

limitation that such methods be 'practised on the human or animal body' evidences a clear intention by the drafters of the EPC that not all diagnostic methods should be excluded from patent protection. That view has been rejected by the EBA in *CYGNUS/Diagnostic method.*

D THE BROAD APPROACH

1 Introduction

The approach of the TBA in *BRUKER/Non-invasive measurement* was not without its difficulties. First, there was no explanation of why *all* of the steps involved in reaching a medical diagnosis were required for a method to be excluded from patent protection. Secondly, it was not immediately clear why the presence or involvement of a medical practitioner was at all relevant to the question whether a method was a diagnostic one.

2 Defining Diagnostic Methods

Since the TBA's decision in *BRUKER/Non-invasive measurement*, it was settled law that, among other things, a claim would offend Article 52(4) EPC 'only if it contained *all the steps involved in reaching a medical diagnosis* (emphasis added)'.[65] However, the TBA in *CYGNUS/Diagnostic method* questioned the correctness of that approach and challenged many of the propositions articulated in *BRUKER/Non-invasive measurement.* In this decision, the claims related to a method of iontophoretically sampling a substance from the living animal body for diagnostic purposes. The TBA did not accept that the expression 'diagnostic methods practised on the human or animal body' could be equated with the conventional meaning of the word 'diagnosis', which included 'activities which are not normally practised on the body but predominantly involve *mental acts*,[66] i.e. activities of a non-technical nature performed by a medical professional, such as the steps of comparing the data with normal values and recording any significant deviation and attributing the deviation to a particular clinical picture'.[67] This interpretation, in the TBA's view, amounted to 'setting a different standard for diagnostic methods than that established for methods of surgery or therapy, the latter being excluded from patent protection

---

65 *CYGNUS/Diagnostic method* (T 964/99) at para. 3.4 (emphasis added).

66 See s. 1(2)(c) of the Patents Act 1977 ('the 1977 Act'), which excludes 'a scheme, rule or *method for performing a mental act*, playing a game or doing business, or a program for a computer' (emphasis added).

67 *CYGNUS/Diagnostic method* (T 964/99) at para. 3.5.

if they comprise only a single step of surgical or therapeutic nature'.[68] This view reflected a misunderstanding of the scope of the exclusion. Only a single step of a surgical or therapeutic nature was sufficient to exclude a claim on the basis that it was an excluded method of treatment by surgery or therapy. However, this is not sufficient in relation to the exclusion for diagnostic methods because of the multi-step nature of such methods.

Using the Oxford English Dictionary's meaning of both 'diagnosis' and 'diagnostic', the TBA hastily concluded that the straightforward meaning of 'diagnostic methods', based on these meanings, would be 'methods pertaining to, or of value for the purposes, of diagnosis'.[69] Therefore, it opined that 'any medical activity concerning the gathering of information in the course of establishing a diagnosis qualifies as a diagnostic method',[70] noting that 'Article 52(4) EPC is meant to exclude from patent protection all methods *practised on the human or animal body* which *relate to diagnosis or which are of value for the purposes of diagnosis*'.[71] Although the term 'diagnostic' (as such) may be interpreted as encompassing all steps required for reaching a medical diagnosis, 'it can also define an individual step of a diagnostic examination when used in the expression "*methode de diagnostic*".'[72] Therefore, *a* single step relating to diagnosis is now sufficient to exclude any claimed method if it is performed on the human or animal body. This interpretation, the TBA thought, was also reflected in the corresponding meanings given to the words 'diagnosis' and 'diagnostic' in Germany and France,[73] and was in line with the narrow interpretation given to surgery and therapy in the jurisprudence of the EPO.

3 Involvement of Medical Practitioners

The TBA in *CYGNUS/Diagnostic method* also accepted that the purpose of the exclusion was 'clearly to ensure that those who carry out such methods as part of the medical treatment of humans or the veterinary treatment of animals should not be inhibited by patents'.[74] The TBA stated, as mentioned above, that the interpretation given to the phrase 'diagnostic method' by the TBA in *BRUKER/Non-invasive measurement* covered

68 Ibid, at para. 3.6.
69 Ibid.
70 Ibid.
71 Ibid, at para. 4.4 (emphasis in original).
72 Ibid, at para. 4.2.
73 Ibid.
74 Ibid, at para. 3.1, citing *WELLCOME/Pigs I* (T 116/85) [1988] EPOR 1 at para. 3.7.

activities of a non-technical nature performed by a medical professional. It also stated that it would go against the spirit of the exclusion to interpret the exclusion in such a way that those manual procedures of a physical examination, essential for making a diagnosis, and executed by a medical practitioner, would not constitute an exception to patentability.[75]

The TBA in this case was not as equivocal as the TBA in *BRUKER/Non-invasive measurement* in stipulating that the involvement of a medical practitioner was fatal to the question of whether the method was a diagnostic one. However, it emphasised that the interpretation given to the exclusion by the TBA in *BRUKER/Non-invasive measurement* might cover diagnostic methods that were usually performed by medical practitioners. The TBA was of the opinion that, in respect of the instant claim, 'the *crucial* step of diagnostic character is the extraction of a body substance for *diagnostic purposes*, which is to be considered as constituting an elementary diagnostic activity performed under the *ultimate responsibility* of a *physician*'.[76] This interpretation, however, did not affect the practice of allowing patents for methods of diagnosis when they are isolated and *then* practised outside the human or animal body.

4 Practised on the Human or Animal Body

Since any diagnostic method would be excluded from patent protection if practised on the human or animal body, the essential question which faced the TBA was what degree of interaction with the human body was necessary to satisfy that requirement. Critically, the TBA opined that:[77]

> Diagnostic methods can be classified in two categories: those which are practised *on the living body* and those whose performance takes place *outside the body*. It appears from the wording of Article 52(4) EPC that the legislator intended to exclude from patent protection only methods 'practised on the human or animal body', whereas for example extra-corporal laboratory tests would be patentable.

Therefore, if the method takes place in a laboratory, without being intimately related to the living human or animal body, it would be patentable. The TBA held that the claimed method was a diagnostic method because 'the claimed step of sampling a substance relates to diagnosis and constitutes in this context an essential diagnostic measure *practised on the living*

---

75 *CYGNUS/Diagnostic method* (T 964/99) at para. 3.5.
76 Ibid, at para. 6.2 (emphasis added).
77 Ibid, at para. 4.3 (emphasis in original).

human or animal body'.[78] It was immaterial that the patient could perform the claimed method, or that it would not have a significant impact on the body or involve a serious health risk. The decisive factor was 'the fact that all the method claims on file comprise the step of taking a body sample for the purpose of diagnosis and that such a step is to be regarded as an essential activity pertaining to diagnosis *and* practised on the living body'.[79] This conclusion was in line with the reasoning of the TBA that any step relating to diagnosis (more so, it seems, if the step was an 'essential one' pertaining to diagnosis) would, if practised on the human or animal body, amount to an excluded diagnostic method. The TBA opined that 'the taking of a body sample for the purpose of a medical examination belongs to a fundamental diagnostic activity, regardless of the means used, be it a spatula for taking a swab or smear, a syringe for taking a blood sample, or, as in the present case, an iontophoretic current forcing a substance though the skin'.[80] There can be no dispute that this relates to diagnosis since the sample would ordinarily be taken to determine whether the patient is suffering from any disease.

The previous cases, such as *SIEMENS/Diagnostic method* and *BAXTER/Blood extraction method*, were distinguished by the TBA in *CYGNUS/Diagnostic method* on the basis that they did not include any step that was practised on the human body and did not contain any claim stating explicitly that the sample was to be taken from the human body. The claim in *BAXTER/Blood extraction method* was excluded from patent protection because the blood was taken from the human body with a view to finding out the cause of the disease.[81] Moreover, the claimed method was also excluded because, first, there was no immediate diagnosis resulting from the preceding steps; and, secondly, the method was not practised on the human body, as it is obvious from a reading of the claims that the blood was extracted from the body and then tested. Therefore, the TBA correctly pointed out that the important question was the purpose and the inevitable effect of the feature under consideration.[82] Article 52(4) EPC specifically states that the diagnostic method has to be *practised* on the human or animal body, which was not the case where blood was extracted from the human body and *then* tested.

---

78 Ibid, at para. 5.2 (emphasis in original).
79 Ibid, at para. 6.1 (emphasis in original).
80 Ibid, at para. 5.2.
81 (T 329/94) [1998] EPOR 363.
82 Ibid, at para. 5.

5 Application of General Principles

The decision in *ULTRAFEM/Feminine hygiene device*[83] would be incorrect in light of the decision of the TBA in *CYGNUS/Diagnostic method.* The claimed method related to a vaginal discharge collector which was capable of being used to assist women in collecting a sample of their vaginal discharge, for example, for subsequent visual, chemical or bacterial inspection, or for the extraction of one or more of its components for use in the industrial preparation of pharmaceutical compositions. The TBA held that the steps of providing the collector, placing it, collecting discharge therein, retrieving and disposing it, did not contain all the steps involved in reaching a medical diagnosis because on the sample collected not even data was gathered.[84] This decision applies the requirement in *BRUKER/Non-invasive measurement* and is, therefore, in line with the decision of the EBA in *CYGNUS/Diagnostic method.* This case, however, can be distinguished from the decision of the TBA in *CYGNUS/Diagnostic method* on the basis that the invention was not related to a diagnostic purpose and, since the last element was missing, there was no diagnostic method. This view is to be eschewed, however, because the TBA in *CYGNUS/Diagnostic method* decided that 'the taking of a body sample for the purpose of medical examination *belongs* to a fundamental diagnostic activity, *regardless of the technical means used*'.[85] The vaginal discharge collector was an excluded diagnostic method for two reasons: first, according to the previous learning in *BRUKER/Non-invasive measurement*, no data was collected; and, secondly, it was practised on the human body.

In *MACRI/Down's syndrome screening method*,[86] the claimed method related to, *inter alia*, an *in vitro* screening method for determining if a pregnant woman was carrying a foetus with Down's syndrome comprising assaying a pregnant woman's blood for free beta human chorionic gonadotropin (hCG), the results of the assay being indicative of increased risk of foetal Down's syndrome. The TBA approved of the reasoning in *CYGNUS/Diagnostic method* that Article 52(4) EPC was meant to exclude from patent protection all methods practised on the human or animal body which relate to diagnosis or which are of value in diagnosis.[87] The claimed methods were not diagnostic methods, because: (a) they were not practised on the body of the pregnant woman but on a sample of her blood; (b) there was no

83 (T 1165/97) [2002] EPOR 384.
84 Ibid, at para. 4.3.
85 *CYGNUS/Diagnostic method* (T 964/99) at para. 5.2 (emphasis added).
86 (T 0310/99).
87 Ibid, at para. 12.

sampling step; (c) each of the claims contained an explicit mention that it related to an *in vitro* method;[88] and (d) their application did not require the presence or involvement of a physician. The TBA pointed out that 'the activities ... of assaying a blood sample for free beta hCG or alpha fetoprotein and of using computer means for comparing the measured levels to a set of reference data taking into account the gestinal age of the woman can undoubtedly be carried out by a laboratory assistant without requiring the actual intervention of a physician'.[89]

E RECONCILING THE TWO APPROACHES

1 Introduction

The EBA in *CYGNUS/Diagnostic method* had to reconcile those diverging views in both decisions in respect of: (a) the proper definition of diagnostic methods; (b) whether the involvement of the medical practitioner was necessary for the method to be excluded from patent protection; and (c) the degree of interaction necessary to satisfy the condition of the exclusion 'practised on the human or animal body'. The decision of the EBA, arguably, struck an appropriate balance between on the one hand, the protection of legitimate research and development of diagnostic methods and, on the other hand, preventing the patenting of medical procedures that would inhibit the activities of medical and veterinary practitioners when they treat their patients.

2 Defining Diagnostic Methods

(a) Rationale for the exclusion

The EBA thought that it must have regard to considerations relating to 'the object and purpose of the provision, the various interests associated with diagnostic methods, and legal certainty', because they 'constitute important aspects to be taken into consideration' before one can attempt a definition of diagnostic methods.[90] The EBA reiterated that the exclusion in Article 52(4) EPC was based on the legal fiction of not susceptible of

---

88 Ibid, at para. 13.

89 Ibid, at para. 14. The TBA did not consider the issue whether the use of the computer in relation to diagnosis was also excluded by virtue of Article 52(2) EPC. Cf K.E. Panchen, 'Patentability in the Field of Therapy and Diagnosis' (1991) 22 IIC 879, 887.

90 *CYGNUS/Diagnostic method* (G 01/04) at para. 3.

industrial application.[91] However, it stressed that the actual policy behind the exclusion 'seems actually to be based on socio-ethical and public health considerations'.[92] This meant that:[93]

> Medical and veterinary practitioners should be free to take the actions they consider suited to diagnose illnesses by means of investigative methods. Consequently, the policy behind the legal fiction referred to above appears to be aimed at ensuring that those who carry out diagnostic methods as part of the medical treatment of humans or veterinary treatment of animals are not inhibited by patents.

The EBA referred to the documents relating to the revision of the EPC in 2000 where the rationale for the exclusion of methods of medical treatment from patent protection was recast in terms, which emphasised the public health considerations as the reason why the exclusion exists.[94] Therefore, as the EBA put it, the exclusion, which is now Article 53(c) EPC, was the result of the 'realisation that these methods were excluded from patentability for reasons of public health and that, consequently, one should not base the argument on the lack of industrial applicability anymore'.[95]

(b) First principles

The EBA reiterated that 'Article 52(1) lays down the fundamental maxim of a general entitlement to patent protection to the effect that, as a matter of principle, a European patent is to be granted for an invention which meets the requirements of that provision'.[96] Although it accepted the salient principle that exclusions from patent protection are to be narrowly construed, the EBA noted that that principle did not apply without exception and that nonetheless, it applied to the scope of the exclusion for diagnostic methods.[97] Where the public policy consideration is sufficiently high, it would be sensible to interpret the exclusion narrowly and, thereby, limit the patentability of such medical treatment methods.

(c) Multi-step approach

The EBA was of the opinion that:[98]

---

[91] Ibid.
[92] Ibid, at para. 4.
[93] Ibid, citing *WELLCOME/Pigs I* (T 116/85) [1988] EPOR 1 at para 3.7.
[94] *CYGNUS/Diagnostic method* (G 01/04) at para. 10.
[95] Ibid.
[96] Ibid, at para. 6.
[97] Ibid.
[98] Ibid, at para. 5.

> [A]ccording to the established jurisprudence of the EPO, it is accepted that the method steps to be carried out when making a diagnosis as part of the medical treatment of humans or the veterinary treatment of animals for curative purposes include: (i) the examination phase involving the collection of data, (ii) the comparison of these data with standard values, (iii) the finding of any significant deviation, i.e. a symptom, during the comparison, and (iv) the attribution of the deviation to a particular clinical picture, i.e. the deductive medical or veterinary decision phase.

Therefore, it thought there was no reason to depart from that jurisprudence. Thus, the semantics engaged by the TBA in *CYGNUS/Diagnostic method* were avoided, although the EBA did address the issue of whether diagnostic methods referred to in Article 52(4) EPC related only to step (iv) above or the preceding steps (i) to (iii).[99] It stated that 'diagnosis in connection with the patent exemption for diagnostic methods practised on the human or animal body under Article 52(4) EPC is the determination of the nature of a medical or veterinary medicinal condition intended to identify or uncover a pathology. It includes a negative finding that a particular condition can be ruled out.'[100] The EBA emphasised that since diagnostic methods were inventions within that subsection, to be patentable, they must 'necessarily further include preceding steps of a technical nature, in order to satisfy the requirements' thereof.[101] Therefore, all of the preceding steps of a technical nature were required for a method to be considered as a diagnostic one, due to the multi-step nature of such methods.

(d) An intellectual exercise

Intellectual property laws have always sought to exclude from patent protection what are generally considered to be discoveries, abstract concepts, ideas and the laws of nature.[102] The EBA held that 'as the deductive or veterinary decision phase, diagnosis for curative purposes in itself is an intellectual exercise, unless, as a result of developments in the field of technology, a device capable of reaching diagnostic conclusions can be used'.[103] It was, therefore, not surprising that the EBA held that the

---

[99] Ibid.

[100] Ibid, at para. 5.1.

[101] Ibid, at para. 5.3. The TBA accepted that 'the subject matter of a claim including technical and non-technical features may satisfy the requirements of Article 52(1) EPC if the non-technical features interact with the technical features to bring about a technical effect' (ibid, at para. 3).

[102] See Article 52(2)(a) EPC.

[103] *CYGNUS/Diagnostic method* (G 01/04) at para. 5.2.

deductive medical or veterinary decision phase, as an intellectual exercise, was not a patentable invention within the meaning of Article 52(1) EPC.[104]

(e) Delineating the scope of the definition

Having accepted the definition of diagnostic methods enunciated in *BRUKER/Non invasive measurement*, the EBA now had to consider the limitations of accepting such a broad definition of the exclusion. The EBA noted that Article 52(4) EPC did not include or make reference to particular steps pertaining to such methods (*BRUKER/Non invasive measurement*), nor did it contain wording such as 'relating to diagnosis' or 'of value for diagnostic purposes' (*CYGNUS/Diagnostic method*).[105] It then stated that:[106]

> Thus, the text of the provision itself already gives an indication towards a narrow interpretation in the sense that, in order to be excluded from patentability, the method is to include all steps relating to it.

It is not immediately clear how the *text* of the exclusion provides any indication that the method was to include *all* steps relating to it. Perhaps, the EBA meant that there were no strong reasons why it should not accept that definition of diagnostic methods enunciated in *BRUKER/Non invasive measurement*. However, this was surely deficient because the EBA did not explain *why* the reasoning of the TBA in *CYGNUS/Diagnostic method* was incorrect. This was particularly necessary since that decision of the TBA had radically recast the scope of the exclusion of diagnostic methods and had called into question the various patents granted since 1987 on the basis of the learning in *BRUKER/Non invasive measurement*.

The EBA argued that, if one single step was lacking, there was no diagnostic method, 'but at best a method of data acquisition or processing that can be used in a diagnostic method'.[107] It observed that 'whilst the surgical or therapeutic nature of a method claim can be achieved by a single method step, … several method steps are required to define a diagnostic method within the meaning of Article 52(4) EPC due to the inherent and inescapable multi-step nature of such a method'.[108] Diagnostic methods, the EBA noted, 'differ in this respect from methods of surgery and

---

104 Ibid, at para. 5.5.

105 Ibid, at para. 6.1.

106 Ibid.

107 Ibid, at para. 6.2.2, citing *BRUKER/Non invasive measurement* (T 385/86) at para. 3.3.

108 *CYGNUS/Diagnostic method* (G 01/04) at para. 6.2.2.

therapy'.[109] This signalled the death-knell for the part of the reasoning of the TBA in *CYGNUS/Diagnostic method*, where it was of the opinion, wrongly according to the EBA, that the interpretation[110] given to diagnostic methods by the TBA in *BRUKER/Non invasive measurement* amounted to setting a different standard than that relating to therapy or surgery. According to the EBA, the restrictive interpretation of the patent exemption for diagnostic methods adopted by the TBA in *BRUKER/Non invasive measurement* did 'not amount to setting a different standard for diagnostic methods than that established for methods of surgery or therapy, as had been asserted by the [TBA in *CYGNUS/Diagnostic method*]'.[111]

(f) The essential features of the claims

Since all the steps in a diagnostic method must be contained in the claims for it to be rejected by the EPO as an excluded diagnostic method, it is necessary that an applicant outlines the specific steps in the patent specification including the claims. Article 84 EPC states that the claims must define the subject matter for which patent protection is sought, and that they must also be clear. The EBA reasoned that this meant that an independent claim 'should explicitly specify all the essential features needed to define the invention, and that the meaning of these features should be clear for the person skilled in the art from the wording of the claim alone'.[112] This principle was also to apply to diagnostic methods, which 'serve[d] the overriding purpose of legal certainty'.[113] The EBA further stated that 'if diagnosis as the deductive medical or veterinary decision phases is a purely intellectual exercise ... the feature pertaining to the diagnosis for curative purposes and the features relating to the preceding steps which are constitutive for making diagnosis represent the essential features of a diagnostic method within the meaning of Article 52(4) EPC'.[114] This, according to the EBA, meant that any claim, in order to satisfy the requirement of Article 84 EPC, must include these features.[115]

The possibility that applicants might circumvent the exclusion by not including in the claims any one of the essential features of a diagnostic

---

[109] Ibid, at para. 6.1.

[110] The requirement that all the method steps of a diagnostic nature in respect of a diagnostic method – as opposed to a single step in the case of therapy or surgery – had to be present for the claimed method to be excluded from patent protection.

[111] *CYGNUS/Diagnostic method* (G 01/04) at para. 6.2.2.

[112] Ibid, at para. 6.2.

[113] Ibid.

[114] Ibid, at para. 6.2.3.

[115] Ibid.

method, the EBA explained, did 'not seem to pose a real risk having regard to the well-established jurisprudence of the EPO in respect of Article 84 EPC, which requires that, in order to be patentable, an independent claim must recite all the essential features which are necessary for clearly and completely defining a particular invention'.[116] This means that even the last step – the diagnosis *stricto sensu*, which is a purely intellectual exercise (unless it is carried out by a device) – must also be included as an essential feature in the independent claim.[117] The same principle applied to the preceding steps whether (or not) they were of a technical or non-technical nature. With regards to the features of the claim which were of a non-technical nature, they were to 'be included as an essential feature in the respective independent claim if its essentialness is unambiguously inferable from the respective European patent application or European patent as whole'.[118]

3 Involvement of Medical Practitioners

In relation to this aspect, the EBA was particularly emphatic, stating that 'the qualification of an activity as having a diagnostic character may *not* depend on who is involved' and that '[t]he wording of Article 52(4) EPC is unequivocal in that the exclusion relates only to the method, and not to the person carrying out the method'.[119] The EBA was fortified in this conclusion because: (a) there was no evidence from the preparatory documents to the EPC indicating that the exclusion was to be so limited; and (b) defining a medical or veterinary practitioner at the European level was difficult, if not impossible. Therefore, it held that:[120]

> [W]hether or not a method is a diagnostic method within the meaning of Article 52(4) EPC should neither depend on the participation of a medical or veterinary practitioner, by being present or by bearing the responsibility, nor on the fact that all method steps can also, or only, be practised by medicinal or non-medicinal support staff, the patient himself or herself or an automated system.

The EBA also pointed out that 'no distinction should be made in this context between essential method steps having diagnostic character and

---

116 Ibid, at para. 6.2.4.
117 Ibid.
118 Ibid.
119 Ibid, at para. 6.3 (emphasis added).
120 Ibid.

non-essential method steps lacking it'.[121] The need for legal certainty was at the heart of this reasoning because the assessment of the factual and legal situation of such issues may change considerably in time, which means that the rules relating to them must be able to accommodate and, where necessary, adapt to these changes from time to time. The EBA stated that diagnostic methods were becoming increasingly complex and technically sophisticated, which meant that medical practitioners were less equipped to carry them out.[122] The EBA concluded that, as a result, it was 'difficult to see why applicants and inventors in the field of diagnostics should be deprived of *comprehensive* patent protection'.[123]

4 Practised on the Human or Animal Body

The EBA explained that, since Article 52(4) EPC further refers to methods of surgery and therapy, it can be inferred that these diagnostic methods must 'serve curative purposes and are thus meant to be practised on the living human or animal body'.[124] It concluded, therefore, that '[t]he criterion "practised on the human or animal body" was to be considered only in respect of method steps of a technical nature. Thus, it did not apply to the diagnosis for curative purposes *stricto sensu*, i.e. the deductive decision phase, which as a purely intellectual exercise cannot be practised on the human or animal body.'[125] The EBA pointed out that some of the preceding steps, for example, comparisons of the data collected, were non-technical and were not normally practised on the human or animal body.[126]

By way of qualification, the EBA made it clear that Article 52(4) EPC did not require a specific type and intensity of interaction with the human or animal body.[127] In respect of the preceding steps, which are constitutive for making a diagnosis for curative purposes, the EBA held that 'each and every one of these method steps satisfies the criterion "practised on the human or animal body" if its performance implies any interaction with the human or animal body, necessitating the presence of the latter'.[128] The EBA further held that, however, if any of those steps 'are carried out by a device without implying any interaction with the human or animal body,

121 Ibid.
122 Ibid, at para. 6.1.
123 Ibid (emphasis added).
124 *CYGNUS/Diagnostic method* (G 01/04) at para. 6.4.
125 Ibid, at para. 6.4.1.
126 Ibid.
127 Ibid, at para. 6.4.2.
128 Ibid.

for instance by using a specific software program, these steps may not be considered to satisfy the criterion "practised on the human or animal body", because their performance does not necessitate the presence of the latter'.[129] This criterion is obviously not complied with where the method steps are carried out in a laboratory, for example, DNA microarrays.[130] In any event, the EBA made it clear that the grant of such patents would not hamper medical or veterinary practitioners in the practice of medicine because: (a) 'it will normally be sufficient to produce the device in question in order to be entitled to carry out the method';[131] and (b) the same diagnostic conclusions can be attained by a method not including the use of the device.[132]

5 Conclusion

The EBA held that in order that the subject matter of a claim relating to a diagnostic method practised on the human or animal body falls under the prohibition of Article 52(4) EPC, the claim is to include the features relating to:[133]

(a) the diagnosis for curative purposes *stricto sensu* representing the deductive medical or veterinary decision phase as a purely intellectual exercise,
(b) the preceding steps which are constitutive for making that diagnosis, and
(c) the specific interactions with the human or animal body which occur when carrying those out among these preceding steps which are of a technical nature.

F APPLICATION OF PRINCIPLES

1 Defining Diagnostic Methods

(a) Introduction

The EBA in *CYGNUS/Diagnostic method* clarified and restated the definition of diagnostic methods that was to be used by the TBAs when they

---

129 Ibid.
130 Ibid, at para. 6.4.3.
131 Ibid, at para. 9.
132 Ibid.
133 Ibid, at para. 1 of the conclusion.

applied the exclusion from patent protection of diagnostic methods practised on the human or animal body. Diagnostic methods were to comprise the following steps: (a) examination and data gathering; (b) comparison of the data with normal values; (c) recording any significant deviation; and (d) attributing the deviation to a particular clinical picture (the deductive medical or veterinary decision phase[134] or the diagnosis for curative purposes *stricto sensu*). In addition any claimed method, to constitute a diagnostic method, must contain all of the four steps outlined above. And, to be excluded from patent protection, at least one step of a technical nature must be practised on the human or animal body. The last step, step (d), is clearly a defining feature of a diagnostic method; without it, the claim would, at best, relate to diagnosis but not comprise a diagnostic method. So strict is that requirement that any claim which does not clearly outline the actual diagnosis, and only leads to intermediate results, would not be patentable.[135] The TBAs have continued to reject patent applications relating to diagnostic methods for broadly the same reasons that they did before. The TBA decisions that have followed *CYGNUS/Diagnostic method* have not found any significant difficulty in applying the principles enunciated therein, in particular, the four-pronged definition of diagnostic methods.

(b) No diagnosis

In *ABBOTT LABORATORIES/Multiplex sensor and method of use*,[136] the TBA considered a patent application relating to a method for measuring one parameter of a biological sample, which, more specifically, was focused on determining the concentration of glucose in blood. After citing *CYGNUS/Diagnostic method*, the TBA held that although the claim may be performed on the human body, the information it yielded provided only intermediate results by measuring at least one parameter in the sample. The claimed method did not include the steps which were constitutive for making a diagnosis, which meant that it did not enable a decision to be made on any treatment necessary. Moreover, the claim did not contain the medical or veterinary decision phase as a purely intellectual exercise. As a result, the TBA held that the claimed method was not a method of diagnosis excluded from patent protection.[137]

---

134 *BRUKER/Non-invasive measurement* (T 385/86) at para. 3.3.
135 *CYGNUS/Diagnostic method* (G 01/04) at para. 6.2.3.
136 (T 0330/03).
137 See also *EXERGEN CORPORATION/Radiation detector* (T 1255/06) at para. 3.3.

(c) No diagnosis and not practised on the body

The TBA in *KONINKLIJKE PHILIPS ELECTRONICS NV/Determining a dimension from density distribution*[138] held, following *CYGNUS/Diagnostic method*, that claims, which related to a method of measuring a dimension of a detail of an object from a density distribution of the object obtained from a shadow image, and to a corresponding apparatus, did not: (a) include any feature relating to the diagnosis for curative purposes *stricto sensu*; and (b) contain any step of a technical nature that was practised on the human body. In the opinion of the TBA, the claimed method merely related to the 'analysis of data set and the information which it yielded provided intermediate results which, on their own, did not enable a decision to be made on the treatment necessary'.[139] Therefore, the claimed method was not considered as a diagnostic method practised on the human or animal body excluded from patent protection by virtue of Article 52(4) EPC.

(d) Only examination and data gathering phase present, and practised on the body

The claim in *NATIONAL RESEARCH COUNCIL OF CANADA/Method of assessing tissue viability*[140] related to a non-invasive method of measuring total haemoglobin, oxygen saturation and hydration of a compromised tissue portion of a patient which employed visible and near-IR spectroscopy. The claimed method was rejected because it did not fall within the definition of diagnostic methods accepted by the EBA in *CYGNUS/Diagnostic method*. The TBA concluded that:[141]

> The presently claimed method may be performed on a human body, but the information which it yields provides only *intermediate results* by measuring at least one parameter of a sample during an examination phase (step a). The claimed method does not include the comparison of this parameter with a standard value (step b), or the finding of any significant deviation (a symptom) during the comparison (step c), or the deductive medical or veterinary decision phase (step d). Therefore, according to the [EBA in *CYGNUS/Diagnostic method*], the claimed cannot be classified as a diagnostic method.

---

138 (T 0504/03).

139 Ibid, at para. 3. See also, *L'OREAL/Procédé et appareil pour la détermination de caractéristiques d'un produit cosmétique* (T 0619/03).

140 (T 0041/04).

141 Ibid, at para. 3.1 (emphasis added).

Similarly, in *KONINLKIJKE PHILIPS ELECTRONICS NV/Medical diagnostic imaging*,[142] the patent application was based on the technical problem of how to organise exchange of an object (a patient) identification date when different images needed to be taken of the patient. The solution, as defined in claim 11, involved producing diagnostic images of the patient with each of the first imaging and second equipments, for example, a CT scan, MRI or X-ray. The TBA held that the claimed method was not a diagnostic method practised on the human or animal body, noting that:[143]

> The presently claimed method may be performed on a human body, but the information which it yields provides only *intermediate results* (an image). It includes neither the comparison of this image with a standard, nor the finding of any significant deviation (a symptom) during the comparison ... The claimed method also does not include any features relating to the diagnosis for curative purposes *stricto sensu* representing the deductive medical or veterinary decision phase as a purely intellectual exercise ...

In *ABBOTT LABORATORIES/Multiplex sensor and method of use*,[144] the claim related to a method for measuring at least one parameter of a biological sample, for example, the concentration of an analyte in a biological sample. More specifically, the application concentrated on the determination of concentrations of glucose in blood.[145] The method involved illuminating a sample with light and investigating some property of the light after it irradiates and is influenced by the sample. The TBA, after examining the law relating to the exclusion of diagnostic methods from patent protection, pointed out that:[146]

> The presently claimed method may be performed on a human body, but the information which it yields provides only *intermediate results* by measuring at least one parameter of a sample. However, it includes neither the comparison of this parameter with a standard value, nor the finding of any significant deviation (a symptom) during the comparison ... Therefore, the claimed method does not enable a decision to be made on the treatment necessary. The claimed method does not include any features relating to the diagnosis for curative purposes *stricto sensu* representing the deductive medical or veterinary decision phase as a purely intellectual exercise ...

---

142 (T 09/04).
143 Ibid, at para. 5.2 (emphasis added).
144 (T 0330/03).
145 Ibid, at para. 3.
146 Ibid, at para. 4.1 (emphasis added).

For these reasons, the TBA held the claimed method was not a diagnostic method practised on the human or animal body excluded from patentability by virtue of Article 52(4) EPC.

These cases have reiterated the view that if a claimed method provides only intermediate results, it would not amount to a diagnostic method. Similarly, if a claimed method leads to an ambiguous result, it would not be excluded from patent protection, because the TBA in *BETH ISRAEL HOSPITAL ASSOCIATION/Method for diagnosing Alzheimer's disease*[147] has emphasised that:[148]

> The appellant's argumentation according to which the claimed method should not be regarded as a diagnostic method in the sense of Article 52(4) EPC, since it was not suitable, by itself, to unambiguously determine Alzheimer's disease, is not convincing. Neither Article 52(4) EPC nor [*CYGNUS/Diagnostic method*] requires that only reliable diagnostic methods which by themselves lead to an unambiguous result are excluded from patentability. Therefore the question whether or not a diagnostic method is absolutely reliable is not relevant for the assessment of patentability of the method with respect to Article 52(4) EPC.

(e) Only examination and data gathering phase present

The claims in *MAQUET CRITICAL CARE AB/Method for determining a transfer function*[149] defined a method for determining at least one transfer function designating how a respiratory system of a living creature (a patient) connected to a ventilator system influences a predefined gas flow pattern, that is the pressure and flow characteristics over time of the supplied gas. The TBA held that the purpose of the method was to compensate for the flow of the gas delivered to the patient with respect to the target value, without any relationship with a diagnostic method.[150] Importantly, the claim did not contain any of the essential steps which were necessary for a method to be considered as a diagnostic method, including the deductive or veterinary decision phase as a purely intellectual exercise, and the preceding steps which are of a technical nature and constitutive for making the diagnosis. Therefore, the method was clearly not a diagnostic method.[151]

---

147 (T 0143/04).
148 Ibid, at para. 3.4.
149 (T 1102/02).
150 Ibid, at para. 2.
151 Ibid.

2 Practised on the Human or Animal Body

(a) Introduction

The EBA in *CYGNUS/Diagnostic method* stated that, for a claim to be excluded from patent protection, any step of a technical nature from the 'preceding steps which are constitutive for making a diagnosis for curative purposes'[152] must be practised on the human or animal body. The EBA emphasised that no specific type and intensity of interaction with the human or animal body was required; the only requirement was that the performance of the step implied any interaction with the human or animal body necessitating its presence.[153] Therefore, the TBAs had to grapple with the issue of whether any such interaction was made in a myriad of circumstances. In the process, they have further clarified and explained the nature of this requirement.

(b) Interaction with the human or animal body

In most cases, the application of this requirement is rather straightforward. The claim in *LEXION/Method for conditioning gas*[154] related to a method of heating and humidifying insufflation gases prior to the passage of the gases into the patient. The method was used for a medical procedure which required the provision of heated and humidified gas. The TBA noted that the claim contained steps of a technical nature *viz.* directing the gas into a chamber, sensing its temperature, humidifying and heating the gas, then receiving the gas at the required temperature from the outlet of the chamber. Since these technical steps were 'performed in a chamber independently of the patient to which the gas [was] passed and not one of the steps require[d] any interaction with the patient necessitating the presence of the same',[155] the TBA concluded that the claimed method did not contain any step that was practised on the human or animal body. Consequently, the claimed method was not excluded from patent protection.

(c) Methodological issues: an early view

The TBA in *AEROCRINE AB/Evaluation of a respiratory function*[156] proceeded first, to examine whether the claimed method contained each of the steps that were constitutive of a diagnostic method, namely steps (a) to (d); secondly, to determine whether any of the steps were of a technical

152 *CYGNUS/Diagnostic method* (G 01/04) at para. 6.4.1.
153 Ibid, at para. 4 of the Conclusion.
154 (T 0238/06).
155 Ibid, at para. 4.2.
156 (T 0125/02).

nature; and, thirdly, to evaluate whether any of those steps of a technical nature were practised on the human body.[157] It seems clear that if any of the steps (a) to (d) were missing in a claimed method, there would be no diagnostic method; and, therefore, no need to continue the inquiry. Only if the claimed method is a diagnostic method would it be necessary to consider if any step of a technical nature from the 'preceding steps which are constitutive for making a diagnosis for curative purposes'[158] was practised on the human or animal body.

In the instant case, steps (a) to (d) were present in the claimed method. However, step (a) was practised on the human body because the phrase 'measuring … during one or more exhalation phases' implied the presence of the subject, and its 'connection to the device is necessary even if the measuring was to be performed on exhaled air removed from the body'.[159] This meant that the finding that step (a) – the examination phase – was practised on the human body was sufficient to exclude the diagnostic method from patent protection since the claim contained steps (b) to (d). This vividly illustrates the working of the exclusion – that notwithstanding a finding that the method amounted to a diagnostic method, and, therefore, still potentially patentable, it must be 'practised on the human or animal body' to be excluded from patent protection.

Logically, therefore, Examining Officers of the EPO, when examining claims relating to diagnostic methods, must, first, determine whether each of the four steps (steps (a) to (d)) is present; secondly, determine whether either step (a), (b) or (c) is of a technical nature; and, thirdly, evaluate whether that step of a technical nature is practised on the human or animal body according to the learning of the EBA in *CYGNUS/Diagnostic method.* A claim will be rejected if step (a), which necessarily has to be of a technical nature, is practised on the human or animal body making it unnecessary to consider whether the other steps for constituting the diagnosis *stricto sensu* are satisfied. However, the TBA in *AEROCRINE AB/Evaluation of a respiratory function* still went on to consider whether the claims comprised steps (b) to (d) notwithstanding a finding that step (a) was practised on the human body.

(d) Methodological issues: a more recent view

Some TBAs did not consider the caveat that the EBA in *CYGNUS/ Diagnostic method* had made with respect to the analysis relating to the

---

157 Ibid, at para. 2.2.
158 *CYGNUS/Diagnostic method* (G 01/04) at para. 6.4.1.
159 Ibid.

criterion 'practised on the human or animal body'. The EBA had noted that in respect of the 'preceding steps which are constitutive for making a diagnosis for curative purposes', namely, steps (a) to (c); step (b), which relates to the comparison of the data gathered from step (a), is 'predominantly of a non-technical nature, and in any event, [is] not normally practised on the human or animal body'.[160] Therefore, it was not surprising that the TBA in *THE AUSTRALIAN NATIONAL UNIVERSITY/ Detection of glaucoma*[161] reiterated the view that only the steps which are of a technical nature are to be evaluated to determine if they are practised on the human or animal body. In particular, it stated emphatically that:[162]

> The criterion 'practised on the human or animal body' is to be considered only in respect of method steps which are of a technical nature (points 6.4.1 and 6.4.4 of [*CYGNUS/Diagnostic method*]). Thus it neither applies to the deductive decision phase, nor to the above mentioned steps b) and c) which consist in comparing the data collected in the examination phase with standard values and in finding a significant deviation resulting from the comparison. These activities are principally of a non-technical nature and normally not practised on the human or animal body.
> It results therefrom that in most cases only step a) which refers to the examination phase and involves the collection of data can actually be of a technical nature and, therefore, concerned with the criterion 'practised on the human or animal body'.

Therefore, it was primarily with respect to step (a), which the TBA thought can actually be of a technical nature, that it would be necessary to determine whether the criterion, practised on the human body, was satisfied.[163] This approach, therefore, builds on that of the EBA in *CYGNUS/ Diagnostic method*, insofar as it emphasises that both step (b) (as the EBA had noted) and step (c) (the finding of a symptom during step (b)) were not usually of a technical nature, so that both steps would not *normally* be examined to determine whether they are practised on the human body. This

---

160 Ibid.

161 (T 1197/02) [2007] EPOR 9. See D. Rogers, 'Exclusion of patentability of diagnostic methods practised on the human body: Article 52(4) EPC' [2007] JIPLP 60; 'Glaucoma diagnostic invention ruling puts flesh on bones of G 0001/04' [2007] JIPLP 7; and E. Verkey, 'Patenting of medical methods – need of the hour' [2007] JIPLP 104.

162 *THE AUSTRALIAN NATIONAL UNIVERSITY/Detection of glaucoma* (T 1197/02) at para. 2.2.

163 Ibid. This approach was accepted as correct in *BETH ISRAEL HOSPITAL ASSOCIATION/Method for diagnosing Alzheimer's disease* (T 0143/04) at para. 3.1.

means that effectively only step (a), which can actually be of a technical nature, would, in most cases, be evaluated to determine whether it was practised on the human or animal body in accordance with the learning in *CYGNUS/Diagnostic method.*

(e) Intermediate steps

Steps which are incidental to steps (a) to (c) – the so-called 'additional, intermediate steps' – even if they are of a technical nature, 'are to be ignored when assessing the diagnostic character of the method'.[164] This is because they are 'not part of one of the steps a) to c) mentioned above, which are necessary for making the diagnosis'.[165] Such intermediate steps, which include 'the adjustment or preparation of the apparatus ... may be introduced into a method claim for completeness'.[166] The TBA in *THE AUSTRALIAN NATIONAL UNIVERSITY/Detection of glaucoma* made it clear that '[t]he issue of whether or not these intermediate features are of a technical nature and practised on the human or animal body is, therefore, irrelevant for this question'.[167] Therefore:[168]

> [I]t is not correct to require that all the steps pertaining to a claim to a diagnostic method, which are of a technical nature or are using technical means, fulfil the criterion 'practised on the human or animal body' in order to exclude the method from patentability.

The TBA concluded that:[169]

> Although they are of a technical nature, these intermediate steps are not part of the comparison per se and thus are of no relevance for making the diagnosis. As a consequence, they are not to be considered, for the question whether or not the claim refers to a diagnostic method in the sense of Article 52(4) EPC.

---

164 *THE AUSTRALIAN NATIONAL UNIVERSITY/Detection of glaucoma* (T 1197/02) at para. 2.2.

165 Ibid.

166 Ibid.

167 Ibid. This was accepted as correct by another decision of the TBA in *BETH ISRAEL HOSPITAL ASSOCIATION/Method for diagnosing Alzheimer's disease* (T 0143/04) at para. 3.2.

168 *THE AUSTRALIAN NATIONAL UNIVERSITY/Detection of glaucoma* (T 1197/02) at para. 2.2.

169 Ibid, at para. 2.3.

Consequently, the claim was rejected as an excluded diagnostic method practised on the human body.[170]

The claim in *BETH ISRAEL HOSPITAL ASSOCIATION/Method for diagnosing Alzheimer's disease*[171] related to a method of diagnosing Alzheimer's disease in a living subject. This was achieved, *inter alia*, by the following steps: (i) administering to the eye of the subject a neutral transmitter mediator; (ii) repeated and episodically imaging the subject's pupil; and (iii) measuring the pupil diameter with an automated apparatus. Step (a) of the four-pronged step accepted by the EBA in *CYGNUS/Diagnostic method* was achieved by steps (i) to (iii) found in the claims in the patent specification. The TBA noted that steps (i) and (ii), which were actually of a technical nature, required the presence of the patient, so the claimed method would satisfy the requirement of Article 52(4) EPC of being practised on the human body.[172] The TBA, following *THE AUSTRALIAN NATIONAL UNIVERSITY/Detection of glaucoma*, made it clear that:[173]

> [I]t is not correct to artificially dissociate the examination phase into a measuring step and a processing step, so as to further assert that the operation of processing the data with automated equipment does not require the presence of the patient and that, therefore, it is not practised on the human body.

The TBA further held that the data processing step using an automated apparatus was not part of the examination phase which involved the data collection phase, 'but it results from a subsequent, technical step, intermediate between the data collection and the comparison of these collected data with standard values'.[174] Such intermediate steps 'are not to be considered when assessing the diagnostic character of the method', because they are usually introduced for completeness in steps (a) to (d) of a diagnostic method.[175] It is only those latter steps that are essential for the purposes of identifying a diagnostic method and applying the jurisprudence relating to diagnostic methods articulated by the EBA in *CYGNUS/Diagnostic method*.[176] The TBA held that the claimed method contained all

170 Ibid.
171 (T 0143/04).
172 Ibid, at para. 3.2.
173 Ibid.
174 Ibid.
175 Ibid.
176 Ibid.

the features of a diagnostic method practised on the human or animal body, as defined by the EBA in *CYGNUS/Diagnostic method*.[177]

3 Conclusion

The EBA in *CYGNUS/Diagnostic method* has brought a measure of consistency to the approach to be used by the TBAs when they apply the exclusion of diagnostic methods from patent protection. The TBAs have not had any difficulty in applying the four-pronged test used to define diagnostic methods that was first articulated by the TBA in *BRUKER/Non-invasive measurement* and endorsed by the EBA in *CYGNUS/Diagnostic method*. However, the limitation that the diagnostic method must be practised on the human or animal body has been the subject of further clarification by the TBAs. First, following *CYGNUS/Diagnostic method*, it was held that only steps of a technical nature in steps (a) to (c) were to be examined to determine whether they were practised on the human body. Secondly, it was also decided that steps (b) and (c) would not usually be technical in nature; hence, in most cases, it was only with respect to step (a), which is usually of a technical nature, that it would be necessary to determine if it (step (a)) was practised on the human or animal body. Thirdly, it was decided that intermediate steps which form part of steps (a) to (c) are not to be examined to determine whether they are practised on the human or animal body and, consequently, are to be ignored for that part of the analysis.

G NEW MEDICAL TECHNOLOGY

1 Introduction

Advances in technology are having a significant impact on the medical profession. With this increasing technological revolution the boundaries of intellectual property law are constantly being expanded. Patent law is no exception.[178] Advancements in the scientific field have demanded that patent law respond to newly developed inventions and the application of various discoveries. Patent law has not been impotent to respond to various

---

177 Ibid, at para. 3.3.

178 See J. Pila, 'Bound Futures: Patent Law and Modern Biotechnology' (2003) 9 Bos UJSTL 326.

challenges.[179] Rather, biotechnological advances have illustrated the 'pragmatic nature of this expansive process',[180] and it is increasingly playing an important part in finding alternative medical treatments for patients. Judicial proclamation[181] or legislative intervention[182] has secured patent protection to various inventions relating to new technologies.[183] One hotly contested issue is the question of patent protection for genetic diagnostic testing. Patenting of the tests for BRCA1 and BRCA2 breast cancer has been contested in many jurisdictions worldwide. The term 'genetic diagnostic testing' covers many techniques including analysis of human DNA, RNA or protein.[184] Genetic tests are used as a health care tool to detect gene variants associated with a specific disease or condition, as well as for non-clinical uses such as paternity testing and forensics.[185] Genetic tests can be performed to confirm a suspected diagnosis, to predict the possibility of future illness, to detect the presence of a carrier state in unaffected individuals (whose children may be at risk), and to predict response to therapy.[186] They are also performed to screen foetuses, newborns or embryos used in *in vitro* fertilization for genetic defects.[187]

2 Genetic Diagnostic Testing and Methods of Medical Treatment

In two recent decisions concerning the BRAC 1 gene, the TBA considered whether the exclusion for methods of medical treatment under Article 53(c) EPC was implicated in relation to genetic diagnostic testing. In the first decision, *UNIVERSITY OF UTAH/Mutation*,[188] the TBA had to consider the question, *inter alia*, whether a method for diagnosing a predisposition for breast and ovarian cancer in humans was patentable. That method comprised determining whether there was germline alteration

---

179 This is evident in the case of patent protection for computer programs and business methods patents.

180 Cornish, Llewelyn and Aplin, *Intellectual Property*, p.217.

181 *Diamond v Chakrabarty* 447 U.S. 303 (1980).

182 EC Directive on the Legal Protection of Biotechnological Inventions 98/44/EC of 6 July 1998, (1998) OJ L 213/13. See also, *Monsanto Technology LLC v Cefetra BV and others (Argentine State intervening)* (C-428/08) [2010] All ER (D) 65 (Jul).

183 See, Examination Guidelines for Patent Applications relating to Biotechnological Inventions at the UK Patent Office (April 2009).

184 Genetic Testing, The National Human Genome Research Institute (http://www.genome.gov/10002335 (accessed 27 April 2010).

185 Ibid.

186 Ibid.

187 Ibid.

188 (T 0666/05).

185delAG -> ter39 in the BRCA1 gene in a human tissue sample, whereby any alteration indicated a predisposition to breast and ovarian cancer. In the second decision, *UNIVERSITY OF UTAH/Method of diagnosis*,[189] the TBA also had to consider the question, *inter alia*, whether a method for diagnosing a predisposition for breast and ovarian cancer in humans was patentable. In this method, the diagnosis comprised determining from a human tissue sample whether there was a germline alteration, which is a frameshift mutation in the sequence of the BRCA1 gene coding for a BRCA1 polypeptide altering the open reading frame for SEQ ID NO: 2, whereby any alteration indicated a predisposition to ovarian cancer. Both decisions were challenged on many (no less than 10) similar grounds, namely: (a) lack of clarity; (b) added subject matter; (c) extension of scope; (d) priority right; (e) novelty; (e) inventive step; (f) sufficiency of disclosure; (g) patentable invention; (h) excluded subject matter; and (i) industrial application.

In *UNIVERSITY OF UTAH/Mutation*, it was argued that methods for diagnosing a predisposition for breast and ovarian cancer in humans were excluded from patent protection in accordance with Article 53(c) EPC. The TBA held that Article 53(c) EPC, as interpreted by the EBA in *CYGNUS/Diagnostic method*, applies only if the method steps of a technical nature, belonging to the preceding steps which are constitutive for making a diagnosis as an intellectual exercise, are performed on a living human or animal body.[190] Since all the method steps of technical nature in the claimed invention were performed on a human tissue sample, the TBA held that the claimed method did not offend Article 53(c) EPC.[191] A similar argument was raised and rejected in *UNIVERSITY OF UTAH/Method of diagnosis* for the same reason.[192]

The application of the method of medical treatment exclusion to the new technologies outlined in this chapter is apt. In answering the question of whether any of the new technologies relating to any of the methods of medical treatment are patentable, the *ratio legis* of the exclusion must first be examined. The EBA in its decision in *MEDI-PHYSICS/Treatment by surgery* reiterated that the real reason for excluding the defined methods from patentability were socio-ethical considerations and considerations of public health.[193] Consequently, it argued that medical and veterinary practitioners should be free to use their skills and knowledge of the best

189 (T 80/05).
190 (T 0666/05) at para. 78.
191 Ibid, at para. 79.
192 (T 80/05) at paras. 62 and 63.
193 (G 01/07) at para. 3.3.6.

available treatments to achieve the utmost benefit for their patients uninhibited by any worry that some treatment might be covered by a patent.

3 EU Biotech Directive

(a) Introduction

The ethical considerations in relation to patenting these new technologies do exist and are of a serious nature. Specifically, they relate to the *subject matter* of the invention and the *process* by which it was achieved. Much ink has been spilt in Europe and in other jurisdictions concerning the ethical and moral issues relating to the patenting of genes, stem cells, ESTs and of biotechnological matter in general so they will not be rehearsed here.[194] This section will, however, discuss the solution to this issue which was arrived at in Europe. A compromise position has been developed, where the ethical considerations and moral arguments were balanced with the economic incentives, and a common ground found. This has resulted in the adoption of the Biotech Directive which is now the blueprint for the protection of biological subject matter in Europe. The United Kingdom has enacted the relevant legislation in the form of regulations to implement the Biotech Directive.[195] This directive is aimed at harmonisation of the law relating to biotechnological inventions, in particular, to the types of inventions that are the subject matter of this chapter.

(b) Methods of medical treatments

Recital 35 of the Biotech Directive preserves the national laws which exclude from patent protection processes for treatment of the human or animal body by surgery or therapy and diagnostic methods practised on the human or animal body. Recital 42 provides that, although uses of human embryos for industrial or commercial purposes must also be excluded from patentability, that should not affect the exclusion for therapeutic or diagnostic purposes which are applied to the human embryo and are useful to it. Recital 45 states that processes for modifying the genetic identity of animals which are likely to cause them suffering, without any substantial medical benefit resulting to man or animal in terms of research, prevention, diagnosis or therapy, must be excluded from patentability.

These recitals make it clear the intention was to preserve the exclusion of methods of medical treatment but that, where such new technologies are

---

[194] *HOWARD FLOREY/Relaxin* (T 74/91) [1995] EPOR 541.

[195] Sch. A2, para. 3(a) which was implemented by the Patents Regulations 2000 (SI 2000/2037).

useful in such methods, they are not to be considered as unpatentable subject matter. Indeed, recital 45 implicitly recognises the patentability of modifications to the genetic identity of animals provided that there is a substantial benefit in terms of diagnosis and therapy to man or animal.

(c) Morality

The most vexed issue relating to biotechnology is the question whether it should be excluded completely on the grounds of *ordre public* or morality. The provisions of the EPC, the Biotech Directive and the EPC Regulations govern the issue of new technologies and their relationship to the methods of medical treatment exclusion and the exclusion for *ordre public* and morality. However, the Biotech Directive covers aspects of the new technologies covered earlier in this chapter. The patenting of the human body, at the various stages of its formation and development, and the simple discovery of one of its elements is not possible.[196] On the other hand, an element isolated from the human body or otherwise produced by means of a technical process is patentable even if the structure of that element is identical to that of a natural element.[197] These must also satisfy the other requirements of patentability, in particular industrial application.[198]

Where the commercial exploitation of the invention would be contrary to *ordre public* or morality it will be considered as unpatentable.[199] Using this as justification, the Biotech Directive then adopts a policy position where it excludes processes for cloning humans from patent protection[200] and prohibits the use of human embryos for industrial or commercial purposes.[201] It must be emphasised that there was no outright ban on the use of human embryos. So this leaves open the door for the use of human embryos for therapeutic purposes and research on human embryos is now allowed in the United Kingdom.[202] The EBA in *WARF/Use of embryos*[203]

---

196 *Biotech Directive* Art 5(1).

197 *Biotech Directive* Art 5(2). See also Article 5(3) and Article 9.

198 *ZYMOGENETICS/Hematopoietic receptor* (T 0898/05); *MAX-PLANCK/BDP1 Phosphate* (T 0870/04); *UNIVERSITY OF UTAH/Method of diagnosis* (T 80/05); *UNIVERSITY OF UTAH/Breast and ovarian cancer* (T 1213/05); and *UNIVERSITY OF UTAH/Mutation* (T 0666/05). See also Rule 29(3) EPC.

199 Biotech Directive Art 6(1). See also Recitals 36–40 of the Biotech Directive.

200 Biotech Directive Art 6(2)(a).

201 Biotech Directive Art 6(2)(c).

202 *R (on the application of Quintavalle) v Secretary of State for Health* [2002] 2 All ER 625 (CA).

203 *WARF/Use of embryos* (G 02/06) [2009] EPOR 15. See also (T 1374/04) [2006] EPOR 31 and Examination Guidelines for Patent Applications relating to Biotechnological Inventions at the UK Patent Office (April 2009) at paras 103–113.

has considered the scope of patent protection for inventions that relate to methods that require the destruction of human embryos. In addition, the Biotech Directive also prohibits processes for modifying the germ line genetic identity of human beings[204] and processes for modifying the genetic identity of animals which are likely to cause them suffering without any substantial medical benefit to man or animal, and also animals resulting from such processes.[205]

4 Genetic Diagnostic Testing and Ordre Public and Morality

(a) Introduction

This section will examine the jurisprudence of the EPO as it relates to morality and *ordre public* and how that exception has been applied in relation to patenting the new technologies under consideration in this chapter. More importantly for our purposes, however, is what the TBA has said about the scope of this exclusion as it relates to the application of those new technologies in methods for the treatment of the human or animal body by therapy or surgery or diagnostic methods practised on the human or animal body. As mentioned above, since the coming into force of the Biotech Directive, Rules 23b–23e EPC concerning biotechnological inventions were also promulgated soon thereafter, to give effect to the Biotech Directive. The TBA has made it clear that these rules shall be used as supplementary means of interpretation of the EPC.[206]

(b) Ordre public and morality

Article 53(a) EPC excludes from patent protection inventions the publication or exploitation of which would be contrary to *ordre public* or morality, provided that the exploitation shall not be deemed to be so contrary merely because it is prohibited by law or regulation in some or all of the Contracting States of the EPC. It is not surprising that the issue of whether patenting methods of treatment by therapy that involve genes and stem cells has been the subject of considerations by the TBAs to determine whether they offend Article 53(a) EPC.[207] The Biotech Directive, and the manner in which it expanded upon Article 53(a) EPC to provide specific examples of things which were thought excluded pursuant to that Article, has already been examined. This section will consider the jurisprudence of

---

[204] Biotech Directive Art 6(2)(b).

[205] Biotech Directive Art 6(2)(d).

[206] *THE PRESIDENT AND FELLOWS OF HARVARD COLLEGE/Method for producing transgenic animals* (T 315/03) (OJ 2006, 15).

[207] See A. Agovic, 'Stem cell patents on a knife edge' (2008) JIPLP 718.

the EPO that has considered claims relating to medical treatments using the new technologies described above, and examine to what extent the TBAs have considered Article 53(a) EPC as a bar to patent protection.

(c) EPO Jurisprudence

The TBA in *UNIVERSITY OF UTAH/Breast and ovarian cancer*[208] had to consider whether a claim directed to a nucleic acid, which comprises a coding sequence for the human BRCA1 polypeptide, whereby the claimed product was defined by features of the polypeptide as well as by features of a process of genomic DNA and cDNA library screening, was excluded from patent protection under, *inter alia*, Article 53(a) EPC. Both Appellant II and Opponent 02 argued that the claimed subject matter was excluded from patentability under Article 53(a) EPC.[209] Appellant II submitted that no proof had been provided by Appellant I that the donors of the cells that had been critical to identify the BRCA1 gene had given a previous informed consent to the use of said cells.[210] In the opinion of Appellant II, such previous informed consent would have had to include an explicit consent to the commercial exploitation of the research results by patents, as well as a benefit sharing agreement, in particular with respect certain persons, the cell donations of which had been essential in arriving at the claimed invention. It continued that in the absence of such proof, it had to be assumed that the initial obtaining of these research results involved severe ethical violations, and thus a violation of *ordre public* or morality as referred to in Article 53(a) EPC.

The TBA observed that the EPC contained no provision establishing a requirement for applicants to submit evidence of a previous informed consent or a benefit sharing agreement. It noted that Rule 23b(1) EPC provides that the Biotech Directive shall be used as a supplementary means of interpretation of the relevant provisions of the Convention and of Chapter VI (Biotechnological inventions) of Part II of the Implementing Regulations. After quoting Recital 26 of the Biotech Directive, which relates to informed consent for use of biological material of human origin, the TBA further noted that the legislator had not provided for a procedure of verifying the informed consent in the framework of the grant of biotechnological patents under the EPC.[211] It concluded that it did not

208 (T 1213/05) at para. 62.
209 Ibid, at para. 46.
210 Ibid, at para. 47.
211 Ibid, at para. 49.

accept Appellant II's argument that the claimed subject matter was not patentable under Article 53(a) EPC.[212]

Opponent 02 argued that the socio-economic consequences of the patenting of the claimed subject matter should be considered by the TBA under Article 53(a) EPC, because these consequences touched ethical issues.[213] The patenting of the claimed subject matter, it argued, would not only result in increased costs for patients, but would also influence the way in which diagnosis and research would be organised in Europe which, clearly, would be to the detriment of patients and doctors.[214] It continued by stating that the fact that a particular group of patients, that is patients suspected to carry a predisposition to breast cancer, would be faced with severe disadvantages and would become dependent on the patent proprietor, was contrary to human dignity. Therefore, Opponent 02 claimed that the claimed subject matter constituted an exception to patentability under Article 53(a) EPC.

After examining Article 53(a) EPC, the TBA pointed out that it was important to note that Article 53(a) EPC referred to the 'exploitation of the invention', not the 'exploitation of the patent'.[215] It continued that the objections raised by Opponent 02 were directed to the possible consequences of the exploitation of the patent and that such an objection relating to the exploitation of the patent, and not to the exploitation of the invention, did not fall within Article 53(a) EPC. Consequently, the TBA rejected Opponent 02's objections under Article 53(a) EPC. Opponent 02 nonetheless argued that the exploitation of the patent, in this case, could be assimilated to the exploitation of the invention, and that the exploitation of the patent per se was contrary to *ordre public* and morality. It argued that the invention concerned breast and ovarian cancer and had a significant impact on public health, which meant that the TBA should apply Article 53(a) EPC to the exploitation of the patent.[216] The TBA rejected this reasoning, arguing that the possible consequences of exploitation of the patent identified by Opponent 02 were the result of the exclusionary nature of the rights granted by a patent. This included the right to stop competitors from using the invention and, in its view, such an objection applied to the exploitation of any patent, as the nature of the consequences of the exploitation of a patent (which derived from the exclusionary nature of

---

212 Ibid, at para. 51.
213 Ibid, at para. 52.
214 Ibid.
215 Ibid, at para. 53.
216 Ibid.

private property rights), was the same for all patents.[217] The TBA, therefore, rejected the objection on the basis of Article 53(a) EPC.

Opponent 02 impliedly argued that the correct implementation of the Biotech Directive required the importation of socio-economic concerns into the text of the Biotech Directive based on the claim that certain EU member states have adopted this approach to implementing the Biotech Directive.[218] The TBA rejected this, stating that the content of national legislation did not form part of the legal order established by the EPC and was irrelevant to the issue of how the EPC should be interpreted.[219] The TBA also rejected the view that the resolution of the European Parliament entitled 'Patents on biotechnological inventions' could be used to interpret the Biotech Directive which would, therefore, introduce socio-economic and ethical issues into the EPO's patent granting process.[220]

As a result, the TBA stated that there were no arguments or evidence to show that the publication or exploitation of the claimed probes, vectors and cells was contrary to *ordre public* or morality and that Rule 23e(2) EPC, which implemented Article 53(a) EPC, did not exclude the claimed invention from patentability under Article 53(a) EPC.[221] It therefore concluded that the subject matter of claims 1 to 3 was not excluded from patentability under Article 53(a) EPC.[222]

In *UNIVERSITY OF UTAH/Mutation*,[223] Opponent 04 argued that the subject matter of the claims contravened the requirements of Article 53(a) EPC. It also argued that if the patent was granted, patients would no longer be able to have their genetic information read and interpreted by the organisation of their choice and that there was no guarantee that criminal and medical gene databases were kept strictly separate, which was an accepted ethical principle in the member states of the EPC.[224] Opponent 06 argued that the socio-economic consequences of the patenting of the claimed invention should be considered by the TBA under Article 53(a) EPC because, in the present case, these consequences touched ethical issues. It claimed that the patenting of the claimed subject matter would not only result in increased costs for patients, but would also influence the way in which diagnosis and research would be organised in Europe which, clearly,

217 Ibid.
218 Ibid, at para. 55.
219 Ibid.
220 Ibid.
221 Ibid, at para. 56.
222 Ibid, at para. 57.
223 (T 0666/05).
224 Ibid, at para. 80.

would be to the detriment of patients and doctors. It asserted that the fact that a particular group of patients, that is patients suspected to carry a predisposition to breast cancer, would be faced with severe disadvantages and would become dependent on the patent owner, was contrary to human dignity. Therefore, Opponent 04 argued that the claimed subject matter constituted an exception to patentability under Article 53(a) EPC. A further indication that the legislator intended to enforce a critical examination of this aspect was seen in the transfer of Article 52(4) EPC 1973 to Article 53 EPC, referring to exceptions to patentability.[225] Since the TBA in *UNIVERSITY OF UTAH/Breast and ovarian cancer*[226] had dealt with the socio-economic and ethical consequences of the patenting of diagnostic methods involving the use of human genetic material, the TBA in the present case decided to follow that decision and, therefore, rejected the objection under Article 53(a) EPC.[227]

In *UNIVERSITY OF UTAH/Method of diagnosis*,[228] Respondent IV argued that the subject matter of the claims contravened the requirements of Article 53(a) EPC. They further argued that if the patent was granted, patients would no longer be able to have their genetic information read and interpreted by the organisation of their choice and it could not be guaranteed that criminal and medical gene databases were kept strictly separate, which was an accepted ethical principle in the member states of the EPO.[229] Since the TBA in *UNIVERSITY OF UTAH/Breast and ovarian cancer*[230] had dealt with the socio-economic and ethical consequences of the patenting of diagnostic methods involving the use of human genetic material, the TBA in this decision decided to follow it, and, consequently, rejected Respondent IV's objection under Article 53(a) EPC.[231]

(d) Conclusion

The TBAs in the decisions considered in this section did not find that Article 53(a) was a bar to patent protection for genetic diagnostic methods. The methods in question, specifically genetic diagnostic methods were not to be excluded from patent protection as being contrary to *ordre public* or morality. This is not to say, however, that this will be the approach of the EPO in all such cases, as these issues are usually decided on a case-by-case basis.

---

225 Ibid, at para. 81.
226 (T 1213/05) at para. 62.
227 Ibid, at para. 82.
228 (T 80/05).
229 Ibid, at para. 64.
230 (T 1213/05) at paras 52–53.
231 Ibid, at para. 65.

5 Conclusion

Genetic diagnostic testing has survived challenges based on the method of medical treatment exclusion, in particular, diagnostic methods and the exclusion for morality and *ordre public* under the EPC. Most of the issues relating to patent protection of the genes themselves were the subject of consideration by the Biotech Directive. Importantly too, the Directive makes it clear that methods of medical treatment, including diagnostic methods, continue to be patentable in relation to such new technologies.

H CONCLUSION

The decision of the EBA in *CYGNUS/Diagnostic method* has clarified the law relating to diagnostic methods under the EPC, and, in so doing, has made it clear that, generally, methods of medical treatment should be excluded from patent protection based only on the words used in the EPC. Foreign concepts and phrases should not be used to limit or expand the exclusion which should be construed narrowly. The EBA, therefore, quite rightly, rejected the notion that the presence or involvement of the medical or veterinary practitioner was at all relevant to the question of whether a method was a diagnostic one. The definition given to diagnostic methods is now reflective of the nature of such a multi-step method, so all its constituent steps must be present in a claim method to offend Article 52(4) EPC.

The decision should also be welcomed since it has recognised the potential of medical patents, and appreciates that, although the exclusion does serve a legitimate public health consideration, it should be malleable enough not to shut the door to new technologies, and, importantly, to much-needed research and development into improved and more sophisticated medical procedures.

7. Second and further medical uses

A INTRODUCTION

The drafters of the European Patents Convention (EPC) appreciated the importance of research and development to the pharmaceutical industry. However, for policy reasons, methods of medical treatment were excluded from patent protection in Article 53(c) EPC. Seemingly by way of compensation, the second sentence of Article 53(c) EPC provides that the methods of medical treatment exclusion shall not apply to products, in particular, substances or compositions, for use in any of these methods. In other words, substances used in treating patients remained patentable notwithstanding the medical treatment exclusion. A further and more important provision directly impacting the pharmaceutical industry was provided for in Article 54(5) EPC 1973[1] for medical uses of known substances and compositions. The inventive and innovative function of the patent system clearly is very pronounced in this field.[2] Research into further medicinal uses of current drugs and known substances will be enhanced, and any refusal to recognise second-use patents would deprive inventors of their just reward.

When a product is newly discovered, it can be claimed as a product and for that particular use. When a product is old, the exclusion of methods of medical treatment assumes particular significance because the claim would be for the product for use in a particular therapeutic method, that is a claim

---

[1] This is now found in Article 54(4) EPC 2000 (see also Article 54(5) EPC 2000). The ideas in this chapter have been derived, in part, from the following: E. Ventose, 'Patenting treatment or dosage regimes under Articles 53(c) and 54(5) of the European Patent Convention 2000' (2008) JIPLP 540; 'No European Patents for Second Uses of Devices or Instruments' (2008) EIPR 11; 'Patent Protection for Second and Further Medical Uses Under the European Patent Convention' (2009) SCRIPTed – A Journal of Law, Technology & Society 57; 'Patent Protection for Dosage Regimes under the European Patent Convention 2000' (2010) JIPLP 474; and 'Patent Protection for Dosage Regimes in Europe: A Dissenting View' (2011) JIPLP 238.

[2] See T. Scassa, 'Patents for Second Medical Indications and Their Potential Impact on Pharmacase in Canada' (2001) 9 Health Law Journal 23–59 for a detailed account of the law in Canada. See generally B. Domeij, *Pharmaceutical Patents in Europe* (Kluwer Law International, 2000).

to a method of medical treatment using the particular substance or composition. The EBA in *EISAI/Second medical indication*[3] was faced with the question of whether Article 54(5) EPC 1973 allowed second (and further) medical uses. This chapter aims to: first, examine the *travaux préparatoires* of the EPC to see what light they shed on the interpretation of Article 54(5) EPC 1973; secondly, explore the origins of second medical uses and the decision of the EBA in *EISAI/Second medical indication*; thirdly, delineate the requirements of the Swiss-type claim, including the form of claim; fourthly, examine the decisions applying *EISAI/Second medical indication* to find out whether they have extended that decision beyond its original parameters; fifthly, evaluate the recent changes heralded by the EPC 2000; and, sixthly, examine the issue of patenting dosage regimes under the EPC.

B LEGISLATIVE HISTORY

A limited exception for second medical use patents was made to the exclusion of methods of medical treatment.[4] Some organisations, for example, the EIRMA[5] and the PICPI,[6] proposed that 'new therapeutic applications of known substances should not be excluded from patentability',[7] and that rules should be adopted to encourage research into new therapeutic applications of known substances.[8] It was argued that '[w]ithout such incentive, the pharmaceutical industry might well concentrate its research efforts on entirely new products or compounds, which would be very costly to perfect'.[9] At a Working Party meeting in 1971, it was pointed out that interested parties 'had proposed that [the exclusion for methods of medical treatment] should not extend to "new therapeutic applications of

[3] (G 05/83) [1979–85] EPOR 241.

[4] See, for example, comments made at the 5th Meeting of the Inter-Governmental Conference for the Setting up of a European System for the Grant of Patents, Part II, Hearing of the Non-Governmental Organisations on the Second Preliminary Draft Convention establishing a European System for the Grant of Patents, Luxembourg, 26 January–1 February 1972, at para. 17.

[5] European Industrial Research Management Association.

[6] Fédération Internationale des Conseils en Propriété Industrielle.

[7] They also proposed that a method of interpreting the exclusion should be included in the Implementing Regulations. See the Minutes of the 5th Meeting of the Inter-Governmental Conference for the Setting up of a European System for the Grant of Patents, Part II, Hearing of the Non-Governmental Organisations on the Second Preliminary Draft Convention establishing a European System for the Grant of Patents, Luxembourg, 26 January–1 February 1972, at para. 17.

[8] Ibid.

[9] Ibid.

known substances"'.[10] The pharmaceutical industry, however, argued that 'in the interests of humanity, it was desirable to include such applications as patentable'.[11] The Working Party claimed that the reasons advanced were 'not sufficient to justify the claims by the pharmaceutical industry and it would be contrary to the common practice in most countries'.[12]

When the question of 'whether a new therapeutic use of a known substance should be included in the category of patentable inventions' was considered by the Working Party in 1972,[13] the majority were 'in favour of the Convention not specifying explicitly that such a thing was excluded'.[14] From the discussions held, one suggestion, which the Working Party considered 'more satisfactory',[15] was that patent protection might conceivably cover a substance for a specific indicated purpose.[16] The UK delegation expressed reservations on the very principle of patentability of new uses of known substances, and, finally, on the desirability of drawing a distinction between the first use and subsequent uses.[17] The United Kingdom, Danish and Netherlands delegations suggested replacing para. 2(d) of draft Article 50 with Article 52, para. 5, which read as follows:[18]

> Neither the provisions of this Article, nor those of Article 50, shall be interpreted as excluding the patentability of an invention consisting of a substance *per se* as a medicament provided that the state of the art does not include any such use of that substance.

---

[10] Minutes of the 9th meeting of Working Party I held from 12–22 October 1971, in Luxembourg, at para. 92. The Working Party observed that the amendment was 'based on the conception that, whereas new drugs were well protected by patents either in their processes or in respect of the products themselves, there was no economic incentive to invest in research involving new therapeutic uses of known substances as these are not patentable'.

[11] Ibid.

[12] Ibid.

[13] Minutes of the 11th Meeting of the Working Party I held in Luxembourg from 28 February–3 March 1972, at para. 9(a).

[14] Ibid.

[15] Ibid.

[16] Ibid. The first being the 'use of the substance for the purposes indicated could form the subject of the patent protection, on the understanding that the proprietor would institute proceedings only against an intermediary infringer (competing producer) and not against the real infringer, who would be the doctor'.

[17] Minutes of the 11th Meeting of the Working Party I held in Luxembourg from 28 February–3 March 1972, at para. 9(a).

[18] Minutes of a 3rd Meeting of the Co-coordinating Committee, Luxembourg, 23, 24 and 17 June 1972, at para. 5.

The word 'substance' was thought to be too restrictive especially in light of the fact that the text of Article 50(2)(d) referred to 'compounds'.[19] It was noted that, in a system which allowed the patentability of new substances, it was indispensable that this provision should refer specifically to known substances.[20] Since there was no dispute as to the 'justification for inserting a new provision of this nature in Article 52 on novelty', the Working Party wondered whether 'a provision along the same lines be inserted in Article 50 on patentability, in order to avoid any possible doubt'.[21] In the end, the Working Party decided that it was preferable to suspend examination of that point to 'enable the delegations to seek a solution', which would take into account all the points raised that might be submitted to the Conference.[22] Some interested parties proposed to allow the 'patentability of a new therapeutic application of already-known substances'.[23] The Conference noted that other delegations proposed that the last suggestion should at least be adopted in the Convention, leaving it open to the jurisprudence of the EPO to decide on treatment by therapy other than physical and on new therapeutic applications of known substances.[24] Consequently, the Conference directed the Working Party to re-examine that proposal.[25]

Some delegations were of the opinion that they interpreted draft Article 50(5) as not excluding the patentability of known substances or compositions, even if they are not used for the first time in an absolute sense for the purpose referred to in draft Article 50(2)(d).[26] Others made it clear that they would accept Article 50(5) if it was 'applicable only to the use for the first time in an absolute sense of any methods referred to in [draft Article 50(2)(d)]'.[27] The Conference concluded the discussion by observing that extending the scope of draft Article 50(5) beyond instances of use for the first time in an absolute sense comprised a modification of the compromise proposal contained in Working Document No. 28.[28] The Netherlands

---

19 Ibid.

20 Ibid.

21 Ibid.

22 Ibid.

23 Minutes of the 5th Meeting of the Inter-Governmental Conference for the Setting up of a European System for the Grant of Patents, Parts I and III, Luxembourg, 24–25 January and 2–4 February 1972, at para. 33.

24 Ibid.

25 Ibid.

26 Minutes of a 6th Meeting of the Inter-Governmental Conference for the setting up of a European System for the Grant of Patents, Luxembourg, 19–30 June 1972, at para. 31.

27 Ibid.

28 Ibid.

delegation proposed a change in the wording of the provision, which by now was draft Article 52(5), to read as follows:[29]

> The provisions of par. 1–4 shall not exclude the patentability of any substance or composition, disclosed as such in the state of the art, for use in a method referred to in article 50 par. 2(d), provided that its use for no such method has been disclosed in the state of the art.

There was no unanimity relating to the scope of the provision – some organisations supported the patenting of only the first medical use of substances or compositions.[30] Others, however, thought that the article could be clarified even further so as to emphasise that even a further new use of a substance or composition may be patented.[31]

At the Munich Diplomatic Conference, the Netherlands delegation wanted the wording of para. 5 improved, pointing out that on no account did they wish, with their proposal, to break away from the principle that only the first application in respect of the use of a known substance or composition in a method for the treatment of a human or animal body by surgery or therapy is patentable, and not the second and subsequent applications.[32] The Yugoslav delegation sought clarification on the meaning of the words 'even when the substance or composition in question is disclosed in the state of the art'.[33] The Chairman replied as follows:[34]

> [T]he aim in paragraph 5 was to make clear that a known substance (or a known composition) which, since it formed part of the state of the art, was no longer patentable, nevertheless could be patented for the first use in a method for treatment of the human or animal body by therapy; however, a further patent could not be granted if a second possible use were found for the same substance, irrespective of whether the human or animal body was to be treated with it.

---

29 Comments by the Netherlands Government on the proposed amendments concerning the draft convention and the draft implementing regulations, in particular, Article 52(5), Munich, 1 June 1973, at para. 9.

30 Comments by Standing Conference of the Chambers of Commerce and Industry of the European Economic Community on the proposed amendments concerning the draft convention and the draft implementing regulations, Munich, 1 June 1973, para. 4.

31 Comments by the *Comite pour la Protection de la propriété industrielle dan la Communaute Economique Européenne* on the preparatory documents for the Munich Diplomatic Conference, at para. 7 (30 March 1973).

32 Minutes of the Munich Diplomatic for the Setting up of a European System for the Grant of Patents, Munich 10 September–6 October, 1973, at para. 54.

33 Ibid, at para. 56.

34 Ibid.

The Chairman noted that his views were shared by the various Government delegations[35] and did not wish to endorse the view that the provision applied for the first medical use of the human body, and the first medical use of the animal body.[36]

There *travaux préparatoires* suggest that there was some controversy between member states concerning the meaning of the article. The majority were in favour of a restrictive interpretation, thereby excluding patent protection for second and further medical uses. Others, for example, the pharmaceutical industry, argued for patent protection to foster continued research and development in finding new uses of known drugs.

C THE ORIGIN OF SECOND MEDICAL USES

1 Initial Exclusion

Initially, the EPO was reluctant to grant patents for second (or further) medical uses based on a literal reading of the relevant articles. The TBA consistently reiterated that only the first medical use was protected under Article 54(5) EPC 1973. The issue first arose in *HOFFMAN-LA ROCHE/ Pyrrolidine derivatives*[37] where the claims covered known pyrrolidine derivatives whose pharmaceutical uses were not known. It was later found out that the derivatives were suitable for combating cerebral insufficiency and improving intellectual ability. The TBA accepted that Article 54(5) EPC 1973 introduced a special concept of novelty that was unknown in other technical fields and that the history of the EPC did not reveal any uniform idea on the breadth of the claim for pharmaceutical inventions.[38] The TBA noted that it was 'impossible to derive from the *travaux préparatoires* any arguments in favour of limiting claim scope'.[39] According to the TBA, the practice of the EPO indicated that claims for therapeutic compounds, not limited to specific indications, were allowed even though, as a rule, they were limited to only specific activities.[40] The principle of equal treatment, the TBA argued, meant that an inventor who had discovered a new therapeutic use of a known compound 'should be rewarded with a purpose-limited substance claim under Article 54(5) EPC [1973] to cover

35 Ibid, at para. 58.
36 Ibid, at paras. 29–60.
37 (T 128/82) [1979–85] EPOR 591.
38 Ibid.
39 Ibid.
40 Ibid, at para. 10.

the whole field of therapy'.[41] The TBA concluded that novelty was destroyed by the fact that the same therapeutic effect was already known in the prior art and the disclosure of any other specific therapeutic application.[42] This meant that the initial discovery of one therapeutic effect of a known substance or composition would give that patentee a monopoly over all future discoveries of new therapeutic effects. The term composition was to have a wider meaning which may legitimately cover a situation where the compounds are presented side by side, and not as a union.[43]

Whether a claim for the use of a substance or composition for therapy was admissible, given the prohibition in Article 52(4) EPC, was the issue for consideration in *BAYER/Nimodipin (I)*.[44] The TBA observed that, in view of the exclusion found in Article 52(4) EPC, it did not seem that use claims were allowable.[45] The TBA, therefore, referred a question to the EBA in accordance with Article 112(a) EPC in the following terms: 'Can [a] patent be granted for the use of a substance or composition for the treatment of the human or animal body by therapy?'[46] The EBA answered the question in the negative but sanctioned the use of claims in the Swiss form in its decision in *EISAI/Second medical indication*.[47]

2 EISAI/Second Medical Indication

The question of whether Article 54(5) EPC 1973 included second and further medical uses was answered in the affirmative by the EBA in *EISAI/Second medical indication*. The EBA was of the opinion that a claim to the use of a compound or composition for the therapeutic treatment of the human body was no different from a claim to a method of treatment by therapy of the human body with the substance or composition[48] – the only difference was one of form and it would be in conflict with Article 52(4) EPC.[49] The EBA held that 'use claims' were acceptable but that the particular claimed use must not be directed at one of the excluded methods

---

41 Ibid.

42 Ibid, at para. 13. This was accepted by the TBA in *ROUSSEL-UCLAF/Tetrahydropyridinyl-Indole Derivatives* (T 43/82) [1979–85] EPOR B448 and applied in *ROUSSEL-UCLAF/Thenoyl peroxide* (T 36/83) [1987] 1 EPOR 1, at para. 5.1.

43 *ASTA/Cytostatic Combination* (T 09/81) [1979–85] EPOR B303, B306.

44 (T 17/81) [1979–85] EPOR B320.

45 Ibid, at B321.

46 *BAYER/Nimodipin (I)* (T 17/81) [1979–85] EPOR B320, 322.

47 *LONZA/L-carnitine* (T 80/96) [2000] EPOR 323. See also *NESTEC SA/High fibre composition* (T 1002/09) at para. 3.2)

48 *EISAI/Second medical indication* (G 05/83) at para. 12.

49 Ibid, at para. 13.

found in Article 52(4) EPC.[50] Such 'use claims' are substantially equivalent to process claims.[51] The EBA opined that the inventor of a first medical use can obtain a purpose-limited product protection for a known substance or composition when the claim was in a form that was technically adapted to a specified therapeutic purpose.[52] This was contrary to the previous jurisprudence of the TBAs where the inventor of a first medical use would get a purpose-limited claim over the entire method in question. Claims that were directed to the use of a substance or composition for the treatment of the animal and human body by therapy were excluded from patent protection because they were 'in direct conflict with the provisions of Article 52(4)'.[53] This formulation, the EBA held, was no different from a claim directed to a method of medical treatment of the human or animal body by therapy with the substance or composition. The difference, the EBA asserted, was simply one of form.[54]

To circumvent that problem, the EBA accepted the practice of the Swiss Federal Intellectual Property Office,[55] which had sanctioned claims that were directed to the 'use of a substance or composition for the manufacture of a medicament for a specified (new) therapeutic application'.[56] This method, the EBA emphasised, meant that there may be problems relating to the novelty of the invention but it did not seem too concerned about this.[57] The claim, however, must be in the Swiss form to avail itself of such protection.[58] As I have stated elsewhere, 'the novelty of the medicament was derived from the new pharmaceutical use – not the product – since the product was old (the very reason for the origin of such use claims)'.[59] The EBA pointed out that claims that were in the Swiss-type of claim did not conflict with Article 52(4) EPC and that it was 'justifiable by analogy' with first medical uses to derive novelty for the new claim, notwithstanding the existence of a known pharmaceutical use.[60] The EBA argued that this was

---

50 Ibid, at para. 12.

51 *LEO PHARMACEUTICALS PRODUCTS LTD/EDTA-free heparins* (T 0532/96) at para. 2.2.3.

52 *EISAI/Second medical indication* (G 05/83) at para. 15.

53 Ibid, at para. 13.

54 Ibid. See also *LEO PHARMACEUTICALS PRODUCTS LTD/EDTA-free heparins* (T 0532/96) at para. 2.2.2.

55 [1984] OJEPO 581.

56 *EISAI/Second medical indication* (G 05/83) at para. 19.

57 Ibid, at para. 18.

58 *MELLES/Vital dyes for vitreo-retinal surgery* (T 0566/07) at para. 3.2.

59 Ventose [2008] IPQ 58, 71.

60 *EISAI/Second medical indication* (G 05/83) at para. 21.

possible because the exclusions existed to 'free from restraint non-commercial and non-industrial medical and veterinary activities'.[61] This was an ingenious way around the exclusion for methods of medical treatment found in Article 52(4) EPC because the novelty of such claims was derived not in the *substance* or its *use* but in the *new purpose* to which it was put. This applied even if the manner of manufacture did not differ from what was applied before using the same substance or composition. The EBA observed that there was no intention to exclude second and further medical indications and none can be deduced from the terms of the EPC or the legislative history of the relevant articles.[62] Consequently, the EBA reasoned that it was legitimate, *in principle*, to allow claims directed to the use of a substance or composition for the manufacture of a medicament for a specified new and inventive therapeutic application, even in a case in which the process of manufacture does not differ from known processes using the same active ingredient.[63]

The EBA correctly pointed out that it was legitimate, in principle, to allow such patents, given the rationale of the patent system to encourage research and development, in this instance to finding new uses of old substances and compositions. However, the question remained whether the rule articulated by the EBA was internally coherent. It was beyond doubt that Article 54(5) EPC 1973 allowed first medical use patents – the claim would provide purpose-limited patent protection for a known substance or composition. If, however, the substance or composition already has a known medical use then the exception begins to bite.[64] In the case of second medical use patents, the claim cannot be for the use of the substance or composition for any therapeutic purpose because it will offend against Article 52(4) EPC. To circumvent this, the EBA accepted the Swiss-type form of claim directed to the use of a new substance or composition for the manufacture of a medicament for a specified (new) therapeutic application.

D REQUIREMENTS OF SWISS-TYPE CLAIMS

1 Introduction

To secure patent protection, the Swiss-type claim must satisfy two criteria: (a) the manufacture of a medicament; and (b) a new 'therapeutic'

61 Ibid, at para. 22.
62 Ibid, at para. 23.
63 Ibid.
64 Cornish, Llewelyn and Aplin, *Intellectual Property*, p. 223.

application.[65] They are indispensable requirements of the Swiss-type claim and both have the functions of identifying novelty and defining the scope of the claim in question.[66]

2 Manufacture of a Medicament

The use of the Swiss-type claim, arguably, enabled patentees to circumvent the exclusion of methods of medical treatment in Article 52(4) EPC by claiming the manufacture of the medicament. The claim for the preparation of a medicament is an invention for a process, which means that the exact manner of manufacture must be clearly delineated in the claims. If the patent merely teaches how the invention is to be used, it will be a use claim and an excluded method of medical treatment.[67] This aspect of the Swiss form of claim has not been subject to detailed examination by the TBAs. Usually, that requirement does not get mentioned at all. However, this has changed with the decision of the TBA in *KANEGAFUCHI KAGAKU KOGYO KABUSHIKI KAISHA*[68] ("*KKKKK*") which focused on that aspect of the claim. The claim in *KKKKK* related to the use of an adsorbent which was claimed in the Swiss-type form. The question for the TBA was whether the different medical indications (the differences in the intended use of the adsorbent, characterised by the different proteins to be removed) could confer novelty on the claims in which further medical indications were stated.[69] The appellants argued that the claim for the adsorbent was directed at a new therapeutic application, because it consisted of removing at least one cytokine selected from a group from a patient's body fluid, which treated one of the diseases specified in the claims.[70] The TBA considered the decision of the EBA in *EISAI/Second medical indication*, and was of the opinion that the structure of the Swiss-type claim contained three elements, namely: (a) the use of a compound or composition; (b) for the manufacture of a medicament; and (c) for a therapy.[71] The TBA was of the opinion that conditions (a) and (c) were 'doubtlessly satisfied in the claims under examination'; however, it was 'not convinced that condition b) [was] met and, more specifically, that the

---

65 *KIRIN-AMGEN/Erythropoietin* (T 0787/00) at para. 8.
66 See *UNIVERSITY OF CALIFORNIA/Lung cancer* (T 629/98) at para. 2.
67 *GENENTECH INC/Intrapulmonary delivery* (T 0138/95).
68 (T 0138/02).
69 Ibid, at para. 2.1.
70 Ibid, at para. 2.4.
71 Ibid, at para. 2.5.

claims indeed relate to the manufacture of a medicament'.[72] The TBA thought it unnecessary to entertain all possible definitions of the term 'medicament', but was convinced that its use in the application did 'not meet at least one essential characteristic of a medicament', namely:[73]

> that it be administered to a patient's body in order to treat a disease. This means that the medicament is brought into contact with the body in order to deliver and apply a substance or composition in an effective form and dose for it to develop its therapeutic effects within the patient's body.

The TBA held that the porous adsorbent did not and could not be administered or applied directly to the human body.[74] The adsorbent was actually used in a cartridge (which is located in a circulation cycle outside the body) provided with a filter when the body fluid is passed through it.[75] The application resembled a membrane for blood dialysis.[76] The TBA argued that there was no analogy with an active carbon, which is taken orally to adsorb toxic species in their passage though the gastrointestinal ducts, because 'the active carbon is administered to the patient and develops its therapeutic effect within the patient's body, contrary to the present adsorbent'.[77] A change in the wording of the claim from 'adsorbent' to 'adsorbent medicament' did not change the substance of the claim, because 'the adsorbent does not become a medicament simply by calling it so'.[78] Therefore, the claimed method was not a medicament so the appellant could not rely on the jurisprudence of the EPO relating to second and further medical uses.

3 New Therapeutic Application?

The other distinct feature of the Swiss-type claim is that the claim must indicate a new therapeutic application.[79] Decisions of the TBAs have challenged this view of what is required of the Swiss type claim and indeed under Article 54(5) EPC. In this section, I will attempt first to articulate a

---

72 Ibid, at para. 2.6.
73 Ibid.
74 Ibid.
75 Ibid.
76 Ibid.
77 Ibid.
78 Ibid, at para. 2.8.
79 *EXOMIS/Haloperoxide* (T 0292/04) at para. 6 where the TBA rejected claims in the Swiss-type form which were directed to treatments other than those mentioned in Article 52(4) EPC.

view which shows that the EBA in *EISAI/Second medical indication* did, in fact, indicate that it was referring to a second therapeutic use, primarily because this was the medical treatment exclusion being considered there. This achieves the purpose of indicating that any interpretation of Article 54(5) EPC 1973 (and indeed Articles 54(4) and 54(5) EPC) should make reference back to the exclusions from patent protection for therapy, surgery and diagnostic methods. Secondly, this interpretation will form the basis upon which decisions of the TBAs will be evaluated to the extent to which they have moved away from that interpretation. Thirdly, it will also show that the focus should be on the particular medical treatment exclusion in question and that, although the EBA in *EISAI/Second medical indication* was primarily concerned with methods for treatment of the human and animal body, its decision should not be limited to that exclusion only, but that its reasoning should also apply to the other exclusions. While the focus now is on understanding the inner logic of the decision of the EBA in *EISAI/Second medical indication*, I will later consider and expand on the view that the EBA in that decision did not intend that its interpretation should relate to all the methods referred to in Article 52(4) EPC.

In other words, in relation to therapeutic methods, the claims must, first, provide for a therapeutic application; and, secondly, indicate that the therapeutic application is new.[80] This meant that the novelty of the claim should not reside in the *manner of use* but in the *new therapeutic* purpose to which the substance was put.[81] The manner of use would effectively be the method of treatment which could be evidenced by showing that there is no connection between the new use and any old uses.[82] As the EBA put it in *EISAI/Second medical indication*, the claim must be directed to a known medicament to treat an illness *not previously treated* by means of that substance, in order for it to be patentable.[83] The first point was emphasised by the TBA in *ELI LILLY/Serotonin receptor*[84] where the claims related to the use of (R)-fluoxetine for the preparation of a medicament for the treatment of certain conditions in mammals. The TBA reiterated that the

[80] See *RORER/Dysmenorrhea* (T 81/84) [1988] EPOR 297 and *REICHERT/Anti-snoring means* (T 584/88) [1989] EPOR 449.

[81] *EISAI/Second medical indication* (G 05/83) at para. 17.

[82] *John Wyeth & Brothers Ltd's Application and AG Schering's Application* [1985] RPC 545, 566.

[83] The determination of whether a claim satisfied the conditions of the Swiss-type formula meant that it was sensible to distinguish between methods of medical treatment by therapy and surgery: *EXPANDABLE GRAFTS/Surgical device* (T 775/97) [2002] EPOR 24, 30.

[84] (T 241/95) [2001] EPOR 292. See also, *PHARMA MAR/Aplidine* (T 0385/07) at para. 12.

applicant 'needed to find a *practical* application in the form of a defined, real treatment of a pathological condition for their discovery in order to make a technical contribution to the art'.[85] This reason is correct because one cannot determine whether or not the therapeutic application is new if one cannot first determine the exact nature of the treatment.[86] Therefore, the claims must define the subject matter specifically before it can claim protection under this method. For example, where claims merely stated that the use of hydroxyl sine or lysine when used in the preparation of medicaments could treat certain specified conditions, but did not provide the evidence of the effectiveness of this in the claims, they were denied patent protection.[87] Similarly, to be patented, it must be shown that an invention had actually been made, not a mere possibility that it could be made.

The decision of the TBA in *LONZA/L-carnitine*[88] has, however, cast doubt on the approach mentioned above. In that decision, the claim was for the use of L (-) carnitine, but the claims did not contain any specific therapeutic use. The substance was known to have therapeutic applications for a variety of illnesses. Therefore, in accordance with the received learning of the TBA, the claims should have been rejected on the basis that there was no specific therapeutic treatment. However, the TBA held that the use of a substance to make a new pharmaceutical product *without delimitation as to indication* does not contravene the requirements of Article 57 and Article 52(1) EPC.[89] A closer reading of the decision showed that the claim was not actually based on the Swiss-type claim alone but also consisted of a claim for the product itself. Where two diseases share a similar origin or causative factors, the second therapeutic application would be a reason to not find inventive step.[90] Where, however, the medical effect of the substance is uncertain, the claim will not amount to a second medical use in accordance with *EISAI/Second medical indication*; for example, in *STERLING/S(+)ibuprofen*,[91] where the claim was for a pharmaceutical composition containing S(+)ibuprofen substantially free of its R(-)antipode. The appellant argued that, in light of the decision of the EBA in *EISAI/Second medical indication*, the achievement of hastened onset of analgesia was novel because it was not made available to the public

---

[85] Ibid, at para. 3.1.2 (emphasis added).

[86] See also *NIPRO/Combined anti-inflammatory agent* (T 0292/99) at para. 3.3.

[87] *LONZA/L-carnitine* (T 80/96) [2000] EPOR 322 (emphasis added). See generally, *SQUIBB/Prostaglandin analogs* (T 0825/94).

[88] (T 80/96) [2000] EPOR 323.

[89] Ibid, at para. 2.

[90] *EISAI/Medicament for gastritis* (T 913/94) [2001] EPOR 362 at para. 3.3.6.

[91] (T 315/98) [2000] EPOR 401.

before the filing date.[92] The TBA held that it could agree that the achievement of an analgesic response in a human by using a specific pharmaceutical composition may represent a medical indication, but that it had:[93]

> strong doubts whether the mere reference in a claim to hasten onset of analgesia, if the analgesic effect of that composition is known the prior art, can be regarded as a second or further medical indication within the meaning of [*EISAI/Second medical indication*].

Claims would not be acceptable to the EPO if they simply provide increased information about an old therapeutic application or treatment. This was the case in *VERICORE/Sea lice infestation*[94] where the TBA clarified that increased information about the pathology would not render the claims patentable. The TBA argued that the mere explanation of an effect obtained when using a known substance, even if the explanation related to a pharmaceutical effect which was not known to be due to that substance, could not confer novelty on a known treatment if the skilled person was already aware of the occurrence of the desired effect when applying the known treatment. The TBA, therefore, concluded that the finding that cypermethrin was not only effective on the mature developmental stages of sea lice but also on immature developmental stages, such as the chalimus and copepodid phases, did not result in a different pathology being treated.

4 Acceptable Form of Claim

The TBA has emphasised that since Swiss-type claims do not conflict with Articles 52(4) and 57 EPC, and irrespective of the purpose they serve, 'no prior evidence of further medical use need to be submitted for this form of claim to be included in the patent application'.[95] In *THERAPEUTIC SUBSTITUTES/Anti-tumoural agent*,[96] the claim was for the use of a dextran derivative to manufacture an agent for inhibiting the growth of tumour cells. The derivative also had known uses as an anticoagulant and anti-inflammatory agent. The TBA emphasised that the EBA in *EISAI/Second medical indication* referred 'not to the formal aspect of the category of the claim but rather its substance, i.e. the definition of the claimed

---

92 Ibid, at para. 8.6.
93 Ibid, at para. 8.7.
94 (T 0708/02).
95 *MAI/Trigonelline* (T 143/94) [1996] EPOR 613 at para 3.2.
96 (T 958/94) [1997] EPOR 417.

invention in terms of its essential characteristics'.[97] This was because: first, such inventions could be claimed as either the application or use of a substance or composition to achieve a certain result or a method or process to achieve the same (both types of claim involve a sequence of steps giving rise to the final effect); secondly, a claim to the use of a substance or composition for therapeutic purposes is no different in substance from a claim to a method of medical treatment; and, thirdly, manufacturing a medicament. However, the TBA emphasised that, under *EISAI/Second medical indication*, both the use and method type of claim circumscribe in the same way the activity of formulating the medicament's active substance which constituted the process for obtaining the medicament. As a result, the TBA held that there can be no argument about the scope of protection conferred by use, or method claims under Article 64(2) EPC could be invoked solely in order to draw an *artificial substantive* distinction between the two.[98] This means that the form of claim can fall within any of those identified by the EBA in *EISAI/Second medical indication* as sufficient for protecting second and further medical uses.

In *ZAIDAN/Benanomicin A*,[99] the TBA considered the decision in *THERAPEUTIC SUBSTITUTES/Anti-tumoural agent* wherein the TBA accepted that Swiss-type claims may be claimed as either: (a) the use of the compound for the manufacture of a medicament for the therapeutic application; or (b) a process for the manufacture of a medicament for the therapeutic application characterised in the use of the compound.[100] In *ZAIDAN/Benanomicin A*, the claim related to the use of benanomicin A as an agent for inhibiting infection with a virus causative of acquired human immunodeficiency syndrome or for inhibiting syncytium formation of human T-cells induced by the same virus.[101] The TBA accepted the statement in *THERAPEUTIC SUBSTITUTES/Anti-tumoural agent* that there was no difference in substance whether the subject matter of the claimed invention is defined in accordance with the form and wording mentioned under (a) above, or in accordance with the wording and form mentioned under (b) above.[102] The TBA, therefore, concluded that there was no reason why these principles should not equally apply to the first and second sets of claims, noting that it considered these two sets of claims as equivalent. This meant that 'the subject matter of the second set of claims [was] also

---

97 Ibid, at para. 3.3.
98 Ibid, at para. 3.4.
99 (T 0853/94).
100 Ibid, at para. 3.3.
101 Ibid, at para. 3.2.
102 Ibid, at para. 3.3.

novel',[103] because 'of the hitherto undisclosed therapeutic application of benanomicin A'.[104]

E EXTENDING THE REACH OF THE EISAI PRINCIPLE

Unsurprisingly, the TBAs were burdened with considering which claims satisfied the requirements of the Swiss-type claim sanctioned by the EBA in *EISAI/Second medical indication*. As mentioned above, the Swiss-type claim must consist of a manufacture of a medicament and (in relation to therapeutic methods) a new therapeutic application of the medicament. However, the TBA in *DUPHAR/Pigs II* allowed claims that were directed at the administration of a vaccine to sero-positive pigs where the vaccine was not previously applied to that class of pigs.[105] The TBA observed that, in the case before it, there was no new therapeutic application of the vaccine of the kind that was before the EBA in *EISAI/Second medical indication*, namely an application to a different ailment.[106] Indeed, the novelty of the invention was that the known vaccine was effective on a new class of pigs – sero-positive pigs – that are maternally immune.[107] In the TBA's opinion, the question was whether the application of the vaccine to this new class of pigs can be considered a new therapeutic application from which novelty for the claims can be derived, in accordance with the principles enunciated by the EBA in *EISAI/Second medical indication*.[108] The TBA noted that:[109]

> The concept of patentability of the use of a substance or composition for the manufacture of a medicament for a new and inventive therapeutic application in accordance with the decision of the [EBA in *EISAI/Second medical indication*] even for a substance or composition, the use of which in therapy is known, should be broadly construed.

The TBA clarified that such a new use was not only valuable in cases where a novel area of therapeutic use, that is a novel medical indication, was

---

[103] Ibid, at para. 3.4.
[104] Ibid, at para. 3.2.
[105] *DUPHAR/Pigs II* (T 19/86) [1988] 1 EPOR 10.
[106] Ibid, at para. 6.
[107] Ibid.
[108] Ibid.
[109] Ibid, at para. 8.

provided but also in those cases where a novel class of animal, which previously did not respond to a medicament, was cured or protected against a disease.[110] This meant that:[111]

> The question whether a new therapeutic use is in accordance with the decision [EBA in *EISAI/Second medical indication*] should not be answered exclusively on the basis of the ailment to be cured but also on the basis of the subject (in the present case the new group of pigs) to be treated. A medical indication is incomplete if the subject to be treated is not identified; only a disclosure from which both the disease and the subject to be treated are clear represent a complete technical teaching.

This reasoning is dubious indeed. The *EISAI/Second medical indication* principle demanded that the medical purpose be novel. The fact that the class of animal treated was different is immaterial to the proper scope of the enquiry.[112] The TBA only had to find a *new* therapeutic application, *not* a new class of subject to which the substance or composition could *then* be applied.[113]

The issue was also considered in *MEDCO RESEARCH/Adrenaline*[114] where the claim related to the administration of adenosine to a human who was unable to exercise adequately. The TBA observed that the purpose of this feature was to confine the use of the diagnostic agent to an allegedly novel sub-group of patients as compared to the patients referred to in the closest prior art.[115] The TBA applied *DUPHAR/Pigs II* noting that, in its view, the position was that if the use of a compound was known in the treatment of a disease, the treatment of the same disease with the same compound could, nevertheless, represent a novel therapeutic or diagnostic application, provided that two conditions were satisfied.[116] The first was that the treatment must be carried out on a novel group of subjects which is clearly distinguishable with respect to its physiological or pathological

---

[110] Ibid.

[111] Ibid.

[112] See *MIT/Perception of fatigue* (T 0469/94) at para. 5.2.

[113] A similar argument was rejected in *GENENTECH INC/IGF-1 to improve the neural condition* (T 0486/01) at para. 11.

[114] (T 0233/96). See also *QUEEN'S UNIVERSITY KINGSTON/Controlling bleeding* (T 893/90) at para. 4.3.

[115] *MEDCO RESEARCH/Adrenaline* (T 0233/96) at para. 8.6.

[116] Ibid, at para. 8.7.

status from, and does not overlap with, the group previously treated.[117] In relation to the second, the TBA pointed out that:[118]

> [T]he choice of the new group, if distinguishable from the known one, must not be arbitrary, which means that there must exist a functional relationship between the particular physiological or pathological status of this new group and the therapeutic effect obtained. In other words, the peculiar feature identifying the new group of patients must have a real impact on the result of the treatment, since it is able finally to 'change' the treatment itself.

The TBA noted that these considerations applied to the use of a substance as a diagnostic agent, but that none of the above-mentioned conditions were satisfied in the case before it. In relation to the first condition, the TBA found that the limitation to patients who were unable to exercise adequately was too vague and general.[119] In respect of the second, the TBA held that no evidence or argument was produced by the appellant to show any interaction between the physical hindrance and the hyperaemic effect cause by adenosine.[120]

F SECOND MEDICAL USES OF DEVICES AND INSTRUMENTS

1 Not Analogous to New Therapeutic Uses

Claimants saw the utility of having the Swiss-type claims and were very quick to apply the formulation beyond its known parameters. It was not surprising, and even perhaps inevitable, that patentees would try to expand that logic to new 'things' or subject matter, as is currently in vogue,[121] to

---

[117] Ibid. This decision was applied in *VERICORE/Sea lice infestation* (T 0708/02) at para. 3.1.2.

[118] *MEDCO RESEARCH/Adrenaline* (T 0233/96) at para. 8.7.

[119] Ibid, at para. 8.8.

[120] Ibid. See also *SEPRACOR INC/Method and composition for treating hypertension* (T 1031/00) at para. 2.3.

[121] In particular, to a new: (a) class of subject matter: *DUPHAR/Pigs II* (T 19/86) [1988] EPOR 10 (pigs); *QUEENS UNIVERSITY KINGSTON/Controlling bleeding* (T 893/90) (non-haemophilic mammals); *MEDCO RESEARCH/Adrenaline* (T 0233/96) (patients who are unable to exercise adequately); *MIT/Perception of fatigue* (T 0469/94) (distinct group of persons) (the claim in *SOMERSET PHARMACEUTICALS/Deprenyl* (T 0863/96) failed because it was for the use of the same drug for the treatment of the same group of patients with the same application route with a drug having the same pharmaceutical effect); and

include devices or instruments that were actually used in the treatment of the human body by surgery. This was first attempted in *CODMAN/Second surgical use*,[122] where the claim was directed to an improvement of a device for use in laser surgery. The claimant argued that the claim for the new application of the surgical instrument should be accepted by the EPO, based on the decision of the EBA in *EISAI/Second medical indication*.[123] The TBA held that the actual indication of purpose of the surgical instrument, namely, intercepting the laser beam, was a characteristic of the surgical use of that instrument, and it did not affect the structure or composition of the entity itself.[124] The TBA further held that 'this kind of *functional reference* cannot normally impart novelty to an otherwise known article, unless the function implies a necessary modification of the article itself'.[125] It explained that the only exceptions recognised by the EPO are those based on Article 54(5) EPC 1973 and on any 'new therapy for a known medicament when the manufacture of the same is also characterised by the new use of the product' – second and further *medical* uses.[126] The surgical use of an instrument, the TBA emphasised, 'is not analogous to a therapeutic use [of substances or compositions] since the former is not consumed in the application and could be repeatedly used for the same or even other preparations as well. Medicaments, on the other hand, are expended in the process of use and only have a one-for-all utility'.[127] It further pointed out that '[a]ny new use [of a surgical device or instrument] is exactly correlated with a corresponding expansion of the manufacture of the entity for the purpose'.[128]

As a result, the TBA held that this approach 'rendered novelty for the new purpose acceptable in therapeutic cases' because 'any overlap with

VERICORE/Sea lice infestation (T 0708/02); and (b) mode of administration/ treatment regime: *SERENO/HCG* (T 51/93); *PROCTOR & GAMBLE/Gastro-intestinal compositions* (T317/95) [1999] EPOR 528; T (04/98) *SEQUUS/Liposome composition* [2002] EPOR 371; *EURO-CELTIQUE/Thiazide diuretics* (T 0056/97); *ELAN CORPORATION/Use of nicotine* (T 0584/97); *NOVARTIS/Method of improving immune response* (T 0485/99); *GENETECH INC/Method of administration of IGF-I* (T 1020/03); *EXOMIS/Haloperoxide* (T 0292/04); *PRAECIS/GnRH Antagonists* (T 0380/05); *SCHERING/Combination therapy HCV* (T 0036/04); *UNIVERSITY OF TEXAS/DNA damaging agents and p53* (T 0036/04); and *NESTEC/Probiotics* (T 0515/06).

122 (T 0227/91) [1995] EPOR 82.

123 Ibid, at para. 5.2.

124 Ibid.

125 Ibid (emphasis added).

126 Ibid.

127 Ibid.

128 Ibid.

existing or other uses for other purposes can be excluded', so that 'any confusion about the scope of the protection could be avoided'.[129] However, it reiterated that that approach would not apply to second surgical uses of instruments because of the possibility of repeated and even different uses.[130] At the manufacturing stage, the TBA reasoned, the purpose of the limitation becomes meaningless.[131] Consequently, the TBA rejected the claimed method for lack of novelty because it thought that 'the purpose of surgical use alone cannot render a subject-matter of a claim relating to the use of the components of a known instrument for its manufacture, that is, assembly, novel'.[132] The TBA was of the opinion that '[i]n view of the fact that the instrument itself was known together with its components, the claim to its manufacture must also be considered as lacking novelty'.[133] In any event, the TBA pointed out that the claimed method did not contain any novel technical feature[134] according to the learning in *MOBIL/Friction reducing additive*.[135] The claimed method was simply a claim for making a device defined by its process of manufacture, and not a genuine use claim.[136]

The TBA in *CODMAN/Second surgical use* attempted to explain, at various points in its decision, why the principle enunciated in *EISAI/Second medical indication* should not be applied to second surgical uses of an instrument. The reasons proffered for rejecting the patent application were based mainly on the differences between the subject matter of the Swiss-type claim, and surgical devices or instruments. They were: first, the purpose of the device or instrument does not affect the structure or composition of the entity itself; secondly, surgical devices or instruments are subject to repeated uses for same or other purposes, whereas medicaments are expended in the process of use; and, thirdly, the impossibility of excluding any overlaps of existing uses of devices or instruments for other purposes. Therefore, only second or further medical indications were caught by *EISAI/Second medical indication*, not surgical or other instruments. Patentees, surprisingly, interpreted the decision of the TBA in *CODMAN/Second surgical use* to mean that if these objections could be overcome, patent protection would then be available for second or further

---

129 Ibid.
130 Ibid.
131 Ibid.
132 Ibid.
133 Ibid.
134 Ibid, at para. 5.3.
135 (G 02/88) [1990] EPOR 73.
136 *CODMAN/Second surgical use* (T 0227/91) at para. 5.4.

uses of surgical devices or instruments.[137] The misunderstanding of what the TBA decided allowed for the continued uncertainty that clouded this issue for the next nine years.

2 Not Falling Within the 'Ratio Legis' of ESAI/Second Medical Indication

The TBA has now finally made it abundantly clear that Swiss-type claims were limited to process claims (that is the manufacture of the product (in this case, a medicament)) and were not applicable to the products themselves.[138] In *EXPANDABLE GRAFTS/Surgical device*,[139] the claimed method was for a surgical device comprising two tabular members which were united *in situ* within a body passageway, for example, a blood vessel, by a process of expansion/deformation so as to form a stent or graft. The appellant requested that the TBA refer the following questions to the EBA for consideration:

(a) Are purpose-related use claims in the 'second indication' format, which is standard for inventions relating to therapeutic products and functional combinations thereof, applicable to surgical products and functional combinations thereof? and
(b) Are product per se claims, limited to a construction which is only arrived at in the human or animal body following a surgical method step, allowable in view of Article 52(4) EPC?[140]

The TBA was of the opinion that, although both questions concern the scope of the exclusion of methods of medical treatment, and 'raise an important point of law', the 'issues in question can be decided upon on the basis of and in conformity with the comprehensive and uniform jurisprudence, including that of the [EBA]'.[141] This meant that there was no need to make any referral to the EBA.

---

[137] For example, the applicant in *EXPANDABLE GRAFTS/Surgical device* (T 0775/97) argued that 'the present case relates to a surgical device in which products known individually are combined for the purpose of a new medical use' (at para IX). It further argued that the 'device (the graft) being consumed in the medical use without the possibility of repeated use, the second indication claiming format is appropriate and allowable, in line with decision [of the TBA in *CODMAN/Second surgical use*]' (at para. IX).
[138] *EXPANDABLE GRAFTS/Surgical device* (T 0775/97) [2002] EPOR 24.
[139] Ibid.
[140] Ibid, at para. VI.
[141] Ibid, at para. 2.2.

In determining the issue of whether the claimed method amounted to a genuine second medical use claim, the TBA first examined the decision of the EBA in *EISAI/Second medical indication* to determine what exactly is caught by that decision. The TBA then compared the nature of the product in the claims under consideration to the Swiss-type claim, observing that an 'essential difference that is immediately evident' is that the 'medicament' that forms the basis of the Swiss-type claim is a 'finished product, i.e. it has the composition and shape in which it is ready to perform its therapeutic function without further modification' by virtue of 'an industrial ("non-medical") manufacturing process'.[142] Whereas, the TBA continued, the 'medicament' that formed part of the applicant's claim was not a finished product, but a surgical device which, in order to perform its function, was assembled and brought to its final form and position inside the human body by a surgical method.[143]

Therefore, the claim, according to the TBA, was actually directed to a surgical method which was characterised by the use of a known endoprotheses in a new way.[144] The TBA, echoing the views of the TBA in *CODMAN/Second surgical device*, held that no analogy could be made between the use of materials or devices in a surgical method, and the use of substances or compositions relating to second medical indications, as expounded in *EISAI/Second medical indication*.[145] This was because the 'use of a known material as, so to say, starting material for a medical activity, is *quite different* from the use of a known composition for manufacturing a medicament, which is an industrial process'.[146] Since it was the substance and not the form of the claim that mattered for the purposes of Article 52(4) EPC,[147] the TBA concluded by stating categorically that:[148]

> It follows that *no* European patent can be granted with claims directed to a new and even possibly inventive way of using materials or devices, in particular endoprotheses, involving a treatment by surgery. This is equally true in the case of product claims defined by a construction which is only arrived at in the human or animal body following a surgical method step.

---

142 Ibid, at para. 2.6.

143 Ibid. The claim was actually for a device for forming a bilateral passageway in a body passageway to repair the body passageway.

144 *EXPANDABLE GRAFTS/Surgical device* (T 0227/91) at para. 2.7.

145 Ibid. It is noteworthy that the TBA stated the decision in *CODMAN/Second surgical use*, on which the appellant relied, was not relevant in this context. This was primarily because the appellant sought to overcome the objections raised to argue that if that could be done, then patent protection should be available.

146 *EXPANDABLE GRAFTS/Surgical device* (T 0227/91) (emphasis added).

147 Ibid, at para. 2.6.

148 Ibid, at para. 2.8 (emphasis added).

These words speak loudly enough to say, quite unequivocally, that no patents are available under the EPC for second (or further) uses of instruments or devices, in particular devices used in methods of treatment of the human or animal body by surgery. It seems plain the rationale that underpinned the exception for second (and further) medical uses simply cannot be used to justify patents for second (or further) uses of surgical or other devices.

3 Not Applicable to Products which are not Medicaments

In *THERMAGE/Apparatus for skin resurfacing*,[149] where the claim related to a cosmetic method of tightening the skin surface overlying a collagen containing tissue site, the TBA was faced with similar arguments in respect of second medical uses of an apparatus. The TBA first explained that the EBA in *EISAI/Second medical indication* had accepted that there was no difference in substance between an activity claimed as a method of carrying out a particular activity and the use of a thing for that stated purpose; the difference being only in form, and they both would be in conflict with Article 52(4) EPC.[150] The TBA concluded that, therefore, 'the same [principle] applies to claims related to the use of an apparatus or of a device for the treatment of the human or animal body,' and that there were 'no legal reasons which would justify a different evaluation with respect to substances and other products in this respect'.[151] Although the TBA did not specify the nature of the treatment, one might reasonably assume that it was related to treatment by therapy or surgery in light of the wording of Article 52(4) EPC.

The TBA then examined the nature of the Swiss-type claim, explaining that the reason why they fell outside the scope of Article 52(4) EPC is 'the fact that the mere manufacturing of a product ... does not constitute a treatment of the [human or animal] body by therapy'.[152] This would still be the case, in the opinion of the TBA, even if the product manufactured is also a 'medicament', 'because of its capacity to produce certain effects on or in the human or animal body when administered to it, does not necessitate or comprise any action on an individual human or animal body'.[153] The TBA then claimed that the 'jurisprudence on "Swiss type claims" is based on Article 54(5) EPC [1973] which explicitly confers

[149] (T 1172/03).
[150] Ibid, at para. 3.1.
[151] Ibid.
[152] Ibid, at para. 3.2.
[153] Ibid.

novelty on medical products which are obtained through the use of known substances and compositions provided this use is new'.[154] The TBA further claimed that '[i]n this respect, a difference should be made between substances and other products because Article 54(5) EPC [1973] *only provides an exception for substances*, having regard to novelty. Exceptions must be construed narrowly and cannot be extended'.[155] The TBA then concluded that, therefore, 'the provision of Article 54(5) EPC [1973] *cannot be extended to other products*, such as an apparatus'.[156]

Since the use claims under consideration were 'medical in character', the TBA emphasised that it was governed by Article 52(4) EPC and Article 54(5) EPC 1973.[157] This was in line with the view that the decision of the EBA in *EISAI/Second medical indication* 'is essentially confined to the proper interpretation of Articles 52(4) and 54(5) EPC [1973] in their context'.[158] This, according to the TBA, meant that the decision of the EBA in *MOBIL/Friction reducing additive*, which related the questions regarding novelty and the new uses of a known compound under Article 54(5) EPC 1973, 'cannot be applied to the overriding questions of the medical or non-medical character of an invention'.[159] The reference to Article 54(5) 1973 EPC by the TBA must be an oversight, since the EBA itself made clear in *MOBIL/Friction reducing additive* that the claim it considered was 'not related to medical inventions but is of a general nature, being primarily concerned with the question of interpretation of Article 54(1) and (2) EPC'.[160] One might simply assume that the TBA in the instant case meant to cite Articles 54(1) and (2) EPC, and not Article 54(5) EPC 1973.

4 Are Claims to Second Uses of Devices and Instruments Really Allowable?

The decision of the TBA in *GENENTECH INC/Intrapulmonary delivery* stands out as an aberration, given the principled approach accepted by the TBA in the decisions just considered. In this decision, the main claim was drafted in the form of the Swiss-type claim, that is 'the "polypeptide selected from growth factors and cytokines" ... to be used for the manufacture of a medical device enabling its administration to patients via the intra

---

154 Ibid.
155 Ibid (emphasis added).
156 Ibid (emphasis added).
157 Ibid, at para. 4.
158 *MOBIL/Friction reducing additive* (G 02/88) at para. 6.1.
159 *THERMAGE/Apparatus for skin resurfacing* (T 1172/03) at para. 4.
160 Ibid.

pulmonary route'.[161] Another claim was similarly drafted: the polypeptide for the manufacture of a medicament in the form of a dispersion to be administered to patients via the intra pulmonary route.[162] The claims, although drafted in the Swiss-type claim were for the manufacture of: (a) a device; and (b) a medicament, for a particular purpose. As is obvious, the Swiss-type claim properly relates only to the manufacture of a medicament and not a device. In any event, the TBA in that decision did not actually rule on the question of whether the claim for the second use of device was patentable. The claim, as a whole, was found to be novel on the basis only that it related to a new method of administering the drug rather than to any new medical use of the known device.[163] This means that this decision can hardly be taken as an authority for the proposition that patent protection is available for second (or further) uses of devices or instruments. If the TBA meant to provide such protection, without any rigorous analysis, then, according to the principles found in *ESAI/Second medical indication*, and the previous decisions of the TBA that have actually ruled on the question, it should not be followed.

5 Recent Changes

The EPC 2000 has put the issue of second (and further) medical uses beyond doubt. First, the Article 54(5) EPC 1973 has been replaced by two articles: Article 54(4) EPC and 54(5) EPC. Article 54(4) EPC mirrors Article 54(5) EPC 1973 and provides patent protection only for first medical uses. Article 54(5) EPC codifies the *EISAI/Second medical indication* principle, allowing for a simpler method of allowing patent protection for second and further medical uses. Neither of these provisions speaks to the issue here under consideration, and a cursory reading of them suggests that no intention to include second medical uses of instruments or devices was envisaged by the drafters of these revised provisions.

6 Conclusion

Notwithstanding the anomalous decision of the TBA in *GENENTECH INC/Intrapulmonary delivery*, the above-cited decisions clearly show that, for various reasons, the TBA has stated, in no uncertain terms, that patents may not be granted for second surgical uses of instruments or devices.

---

161 (T 138/95) at para. 2.
162 Ibid.
163 Ibid.

Patentees should be well advised that the time has come to appreciate that although it is important to try to push the boundaries of patentable subject matter, the EPO will only be moved where there are clear reasons why such protection should be extended. There is little evidence to suggest that there exist any convincing policy or other reasons to justify the granting of such patents by the EPO. Before the decision of the EBA in *EISAI/Second medical indication*, the received view was that Article 54(5) EPC 1973 applied only to the first medical use of a substance or composition for use in a method of medical treatment. However, in that decision, the EBA made what many considered to be a policy decision that such protection should be extended to second (and further) medical uses. If that decision was based, arguably, on the need to foster research and development in finding new medicinal properties of known substances or compositions, even when they already had a known medical use, it seems very unlikely that that rationale can be applied to second surgical use of products. Therefore, any argument for patent protection for a second surgical (or even medical[164]) device is bound to fail. This is because the policy considerations inherent in the argument for patent protection for second (and further) medical uses of substances and compositions simply cannot be applied to any new things that are conceptually distinct from the type of product for which the EPC specifically provides an exception. Now that second (and further) medical uses have found their way to the EPC 2000, it seems more difficult to argue that it can apply to second surgical uses when the framers had no such intent.[165]

G REFORM OF THE EPC

The EPC 2000 has put the issue of second medical use patents beyond doubt. Article 54(5) EPC 1973 has become Article 54(4) EPC 2000 because of the deletion of the Article 54(4) EPC 1973. Article 54(4) EPC 2000 remains substantially the same as before, except that instead of providing that 'the provisions of paragraphs 1 to 4 shall not exclude the patentability of …', the new provision reads: 'the provisions of paragraphs 2 and 3 shall not exclude the patentability of …'. This does not change the substance of the provision, even though a new provision was added. The new Article 54(5) EPC 2000 provides that notwithstanding paragraphs (2) and (3), the provisions of this article shall not exclude the patentability of any

---

[164] D. Thomas, 'Patentability Problems in Medical Technology' (2003) 34 IIC 847, 883 argues for patent protection of second medical use of devices.

[165] Base Proposal for the Revision of the European Patent Convention 49.

substance or composition referred to in paragraph (4) for any specific use in any method referred to in Article 53(c), provided that such use is not comprised in the state of the art. This removes any doubt that second and further medical uses are patentable. The use that is now patentable must not have formed part of the prior art. This confirms *EISAI/Second medical indication* and reaffirms the salient principle found therein that it is only the new use that must be novel, although the substance or composition need not be.[166] The TBA in *KOS LIFE SCIENCES INC/Dosage regimen* has recently referred to the EBA (which the EBA has now answered)[167] three questions relating to the scope of Article 54(5) EPC 2000 for its consideration, in particular, whether dosage or treatment regimes are patentable under Article 53(c) and 54(5) EPC 2000.[168] This will be examined further in the next section.

H DOSAGE OR TREATMENT REGIMES

1 Introduction

One of the most controversial and much debated issues in patent law in recent years was the question of whether patent protection was available for dosage regimes under the EPC. The issue had been fought hard and patentees prevailed in the United Kingdom where the Court of Appeal of England and Wales, in *Actavis v Merck*,[169] overruled its previous decision of *Bristol-Myers Squibb v Baker Norton*[170] that had seemingly held dosage regimes were not patentable under the corresponding provisions of the 1977 Act. The battle for such protection came after patentees gained patent protection for second and further medical uses following the ruling by the EBA of the EPO in *EISAI/Second medical indication*.[171] While some TBAs were whittling away at what one thought was the central ruling in *EISAI/Second medical indication*, others had rejected the view that dosage regimes were patentable. It was not until the decision of the TBA in *GENENTECH INC/Method of administration of IGF-I*[172] that the TBAs explicitly accepted the patentability of dosage regimes under the EPC. This decision

166 See *PHARMA MAR/Aplidine* (T 0385/07) at para. 21.
167 (G 02/08).
168 (T 1319/04).
169 [2008] EWCA Civ 444; [2008] RPC 26.
170 [2001] RPC 1.
171 (G 05/83) [1979–85] EPOR 241.
172 (T 1020/03) [2006] EPOR 9.

was followed in many decisions of the TBAs but with a certain amount of disquiet, which resulted in the referral by the TBA in *KOS LIFE SCIENCES INC/Dosage regimen*[173] of three questions relating to patent protection of dosage regimes to the EBA for its consideration. The EBA in *ABBOTT RESPIRATORY/Dosage regime*[174] has now ruled decisively in favour of such protection. This section seeks to examine, first, the jurisprudential foundations of patenting dosage regimes found in the Swiss form of claims; secondly, the manner in which the TBAs had expanded the subject matter covered by those claims; thirdly, the jurisprudence of the TBAs both rejecting and accepting the patentability of dosage regimes; and, fourthly, the referring decision and the EBA decision in *ABBOTT RESPIRATORY/ Dosage regime*.

2 Second and Further Medical Uses

The question of whether Article 54(5) EPC 1973 included second and further medical uses was answered in the affirmative by the EBA in *EISAI/Second medical indication*.[175] To set the scene for the discussion to follow, it is first necessary to properly clarify what the EBA in *EISAI/ Second medical indication* decided. The EBA claimed that the question of law referred to it 'relates to *therapeutic use* claims for substances and compositions in general'.[176] It must be noted at the outset that there the EBA was concerned with the interaction of Article 54(5) EPC 1973 and Article 52(4) EPC, but the latter was in relation to therapeutic methods only. In interpreting Article 54(5) EPC 1973, the EBA stated that 'the inventor of a "*first medical indication*" can obtain purpose-limited product protection for a known substance or composition, without having to restrict himself to the substance or composition when in a form technically adapted to a specified therapeutic purpose'.[177] The sentence refers to medical indication, which meant that it refers not only to therapeutic methods, but the other medical treatments found in Article 52(4) EPC, namely surgical and diagnostic methods. The EBA reasoned that the appropriate type of protection in this example was, therefore, in its broadest form, a purpose-limited product claim. The first medical indication referred to by the EBA must, therefore, relate to any of the three 'medical'

173 (T 1319/04).
174 (G 02/08).
175 *EISAI/Second medical indication* (G 05/83) at para. 12.
176 Ibid, at para. 9.
177 Ibid, at para. 15 (emphasis added).

methods found in Article 52(4) EPC, namely, (a) therapeutic methods; (b) surgical methods; and (c) diagnostic methods.

The EBA drew a distinction between claims directed to substances for use in the excluded methods (a)–(c) and to the uses of substances or compositions, for the preparation of a pharmaceutical product, which are not excluded from patent protection.[178] As noted above, the EBA accepted claims that were directed to the 'use of a substance or composition for the manufacture of a medicament for a specified (new) therapeutic application'.[179] After noting that Article 54(5) EPC 1973 provided an exception to the general rule relating to novelty so far as the first use of medicaments was concerned, the EBA noted that 'the required novelty for the medicament which forms the subject-matter of the claim is derived from the *new pharmaceutical use*'.[180] Importantly too, the EBA claimed that it was 'justifiable by analogy to derive the novelty for the process which forms the subject-matter of the type of use claim now being considered from the new therapeutic use of the medicament and this irrespective of the fact whether a *pharmaceutical use* of the medicament was already known or not', and that it was 'to be clearly understood that the application of this special approach to the derivation of novelty can only be applied to claims to the use of substances or compositions intended for use in *a method* referred to in Article 52(4) EPC'.[181] The use of the words new pharmaceutical use must mean that the EBA had in mind a use which was related to the medical treatment methods in Article 52(4) EPC.

The EBA's statement that it did 'not deduce from the special provision of Article 54(5) EPC that there was any intention to exclude second (and further) medical indications from patent protection other than by a purpose-limited product claim'[182] cannot mean that the EBA had anything other than methods (a)–(c) above in mind when it referred to 'medical indications' in that sentence. The EBA continued that '[n]o intention to exclude second (and further) medical indications generally from patent protection can be deduced from the terms of the [EPC]: nor can it be deduced from the legislative history of the articles in question'.[183] The EBA reasoned that it was legitimate, *in principle*, to allow claims directed to the use of a substance or composition for the manufacture of a medicament for a *specified new and inventive therapeutic application*, even in a case in which

178 Ibid, at para. 16.
179 *EISAI/Second medical indication* (G 05/83) at para. 19.
180 Ibid, at para. 21 (emphasis added).
181 Ibid.
182 Ibid, at para. 22.
183 Ibid.

the process of manufacture does not differ from known processes using the same active ingredient.[184] That statement was made in the context of the medical treatment the EBA was there considering, namely therapeutic methods, and should not be taken to mean that the scope of the principle the EBA was articulating should be limited to a requirement relating to one method of medical treatment when three are found in Article 52(4) EPC. Therefore, to secure patent protection, the Swiss-type claim must satisfy two criteria: (a) the manufacture of a medicament; and (b) a new [therapeutic, surgical or diagnostic] application.[185] They are indispensable requirements of the Swiss-type claim and both have the functions of identifying novelty and defining the scope of the claim in question.[186]

Some observations are necessary at this juncture. First, the EBA accepted that the required novelty in respect of first medical uses was the first pharmaceutical use. The answer to the simple question of what are pharmaceuticals used for might throw some light on the appropriate answer to this question. Secondly, the use of 'medical indications' by the EBA in its reasoning, first, in relation to first medical uses, and secondly, in relation to second (and further) medical uses related to the therapeutic, surgical and diagnostic treatment methods. Thirdly, if the EBA intended that its analysis in relation to second and further medical uses should refer to something other than the therapeutic, surgical or diagnostic purpose to which the substance or composition is put, then its analysis is surely deficient. How could the second and further medical use be anything other than the type of use which was recognised as a first medical use? Surely the scope and content of the second and further medical uses must take its colour broadly from what the EBA accepted formed the first medical indication that is an excluded method of medical treatment. Fourthly, it follows, therefore, that while the novelty in relation to the first medical use was acknowledged, the EBA accepted, in principle that the first medical use does not exhaust the application of Article 54(5) EPC 1973, so that second and further medical uses were patentable, provided they were in the Swiss-type form of claim. In the case of second and further medical uses, the use cannot simply be the same as for the first (as it speaks to a general use in a method of medical treatment). The distinguishing factor then must be a different use from the first, or other known medical uses. In other words, the therapeutic, surgical or diagnostic purpose must be different from the first or other known medical uses of the substance or composition.

---

184 Ibid, at para. 19.
185 *KIRIN-AMGEN/Erythropoietin* (T 0787/00) at para. 8.
186 See, *UNIVERSITY OF CALIFORNIA/Lung cancer* (T 629/98) at para. 2.

In *EISAI/Second medical indication*, the EBA also stated, *obiter*, that where the medicament itself is novel in the sense of having novel technical features – for example, a new formulation, *dosage* or synergistic combination – the ordinary requirements of Article 54(1) to (4) EPC will be met and there will, in principle, be no difficulty over the question of novelty.[187] The TBA in *GENENTECH INC/ Method of administration of IGF-I* explained that it interpreted that statement as allowing Swiss form claims directed to the use of a composition for manufacture of a medicament for a specified new and inventive therapeutic application, where the novelty of the application might lie only in the dose to be used or the manner of application.[188] As will be examined in more detail below, the decision of the TBA in *GENENTECH INC/Method of administration of IGF-I*, therefore, paved the way for patent protection for treatment or dosage regimes. The question which remained was exactly what did the EBA in *EISAI/Second medical indication* decide?

3 European Patent Convention 2000

As mentioned above, the EPC 2000 has put the issue of second medical use patents beyond doubt. Article 54(5) EPC 1973 has become Article 54(4) EPC because of the deletion of the Article 54(4) EPC 1973. Article 54(4) EPC remains substantially the same as Article 54(5) EPC 1973 except that, instead of providing that 'the provisions of paragraphs 1 to 4 shall not exclude the patentability of …', the new provision reads: 'the provisions of paragraphs 2 and 3 shall not exclude the patentability of …'. This does not change the substance of the provision. Nevertheless, a new provision was added. The new Article 54(5) EPC provides that, notwithstanding paragraphs 2 and 3, the provisions of this article shall not exclude the patentability of any substance or composition referred to in paragraph 4 for *any specific use* in any method referred to in Article 53(c), provided that such use is not comprised in the state of the art. This removes any doubt that second and further medical uses are patentable. The specific use that is now patentable must not have formed part of the prior art. This confirms *EISAI/Second medical indication* and reaffirms the salient principle found therein that it is only the new use that must be novel, although the substance or composition need not be.[189] It is the proper interpretation of these provisions, and their interaction with Article 53(c) EPC, that lay at the heart of the decision of the EBA in *ABBOTT RESPIRATORY/Dosage regime*.

---

187 *EISAI/Second medical indication* (G 05/83) at para. 20.
188 (T 1020/03) [2006] EPOR 9 at para. 72.
189 See *PHARMA MAR/Aplidine* (T 385/07) at para. 21.

It is important to determine what these two provisions say. Article 54(4) EPC is in the same form as Article 54(5) EPC 1973, so the meaning remains the same viz, to provide an exception to the general rule relating to novelty so far as the first use of medicaments when used in any of the methods of medical treatments. The requirement in Article 54(5) EPC confirms *EISAI/ Second medical indication* in that it explicitly recognises second and further medical uses as patentable under the EPC. However, it goes further to distinguish the subject matter protected under Article 54(4) EPC (first use in therapeutic, surgical or diagnostic method generally) and Article 54(5) EPC, for specific uses in a therapeutic, surgical or diagnostic method. This means that, for example, whereas Article 54(4) EPC would be exhausted if a first therapeutic use of a known substance or composition is found, Article 54(5) EPC can, nonetheless, be used to patent further therapeutic uses provided they are specific and that they differ from known therapeutic uses. Indeed, the proposal by epi stated that any changes to Article 54(5) EPC 1973 'should indicate that protection could be obtained by a product claim limited by the specific use corresponding to the second or further medical use'.[190] They argued that second and further medical uses should be allowed 'in a case where a product is used in another way, for example to *cure a disease* which was not curable before'.[191] After noting the difficulties that national courts have in understanding clearly the decision of the EBA in *EISAI/Second medical indication*, they pointed out that 'this unclear situation is highly detrimental to the European industry and to the development of new means of *curing diseases*'.[192] The Swiss delegation at the Revision Conference stated succinctly that:[193]

> The new 54(5) EPC eliminates any legal uncertainty on the patentability of further medical uses. It unambiguously permits purpose-related product protection for each further new medical use of a substance or composition already known as a medicine. This protection is equivalent, as far as the further uses are concerned, to that offered by the 'Swiss type claim'. In contrast to previous Article 54(5), now Article 54(4) EPC, providing broad (generic) protection for use in a medical method for the inventor of such use for the first time, new

[190] Comments by the Institute of Professional Representatives before the European Patent Office (epi), at the 14th Meeting of the Committee on Patent Law dated 26 June 2000 (Info 1/PL 14 e).

[191] Final comments of epi at the Munich Diplomatic Conference to Revise the European Patent Convention dated 20 November 2000 (Info 9/MR 2000 e) (emphasis added).

[192] Ibid.

[193] Basic Proposal – Explanatory notes – Article 54(4) and Article 54(5) EPC – drawn up by the Swiss delegation, Munich, 21 November 2000 (MR/18/00 e).

> Article 54(5) is expressly limited to a specific use. This limitation is intended to match as closely as possible the scope of protection to the scope provided by a 'Swiss type claim'.

There is another difficulty with Article 54(5) EPC. It would be remembered that the EBA in *EISAI/Second medical indication* had said that a claim to the use of a compound or composition for the therapeutic treatment of the human body was no different from a claim to a method of treatment by therapy of the human body with the substance or composition[194] – the only difference was one of form and it would be in conflict with Article 52(4) EPC 1973.[195] Surely, this must mean also that Article 54(5) EPC would, therefore, be in conflict with Article 53(c) EPC.

4 Dosage or Treatment Regimes under the EPC 1973

(a) Dosage regimes not patentable

Under the EPC 1973, the issue first arose in *PROCTOR & GAMBLE/Gastrointestinal compositions*[196] as to whether a method of administration of a known drug was patentable. In that decision, claim 10 was for the use of two substances for the manufacture of a medicament for the treatment or prevention of gastrointestinal disorders in humans which comprised administering to the patient the two substances within five minutes of each other. The respondent argued that the claim lacked novelty because the concurrent administration of both the substances related to a method of treatment of the human or animal body by therapy and that, according to the established case law of the TBAs, it could not be relied upon to distinguish the alleged invention over the cited prior art.[197] They further argued that the sole difference between the prior art and the subject matter of claim 10 resided in the prescribed treatment regimen used for administering the two substances to individual patients in need of them.[198]

The TBA opined that the issue of novelty raised by the respondents essentially concerned the question of whether the mere difference in the course of the administration of the two drugs or, expressed differently, the difference in the prescribed regimen, could indeed confer novelty on claim 10.[199] The TBA, citing *EISAI/Second medical indication*, noted that,

---

194 *EISAI/Second medical indication* (G 05/83) at para. 12.
195 Ibid, at para. 13.
196 (T 317/95) [1999] EPOR 528.
197 Ibid, at para. 4.1.
198 Ibid, at para. 4.2.
199 Ibid, at para. 4.3.

therein, the EBA accepted that a further medical indication is the use of a substance, already known as a medicament, to treat an illness or disease not previously treated by means of that substance. However, it noted that, while the treatment of a different illness or disease was specifically recognised in *EISAI/Second medical indication* to represent a new therapeutic application (further medical indication) of a medicament known *per se*, this did not exclude the possibility of deriving a second or further medical indication (a new therapeutic application) of a substance or composition, already known as a medicament, likewise from some other previously unknown feature or embodiment (than treatment of a different illness or disease) associated with the use of that substance or composition in a method for the medical treatment of the human or animal body.[200] The TBA noted that since the invention which formed the subject matter of claim 10 involved the treatment of exactly the same category of patients by separately administering to them exactly the same two commercial drugs, in the same concentration, dosage and formulation, for the treatment of entirely the same illness or disease, with the sole exception that the prescribed regimen for this treatment was slightly modified, it was difficult to recognise it as a new field of therapeutic application or any further medical indication in general associated with the claimed combined use of both substances.[201]

The TBA claimed that in considering whether the instruction in claim 10 concerning the particular course of the administration of the two known drugs (that is the dosage regime) for the treatment of gastrointestinal disorders may be regarded as relating to a further medical indication, sight should not be lost of the reasons why the EBA in *EISAI/Second medical indication* allowed claims for a second or further medical indication by analogy to the fiction of novelty for first medical indications laid down in Article 54(5) EPC 1973. The EBA in *EISAI/Second medical indication* had stated, the TBA continued, that it was the purpose of the exclusion of medical treatments from patentability, according to Article 52(4) EPC, to free from restraint non-commercial and non-industrial medical and veterinary activities. The TBA clarified that to prevent the exclusion in Article 52(4) EPC from going beyond its proper limits, it seemed appropriate for the EBA to take a special view of the concept of the state of the art for second and further medical indications. The TBA explained that it was apparently the intention of the EBA to allow claims directed to a further medical indication in order to provide a certain compensation for the restriction on patent rights in the industrial and commercial field resulting

---

200 Ibid.
201 Ibid, at para. 4.4.

from Article 52(4) EPC, first sentence.[202] In the TBA's opinion, this suggested that, when it came to the assessment of the possible limits of what could indeed be recognised to be a further medical indication (new therapeutic application) within the meaning of the decision in *EISAI/Second medical indication*, it appeared appropriate to consider the question of whether the sole distinguishing feature, which was introduced in the claim directed to a further medical use for the purpose of delimiting the claimed subject matter from the prior art, related to non-commercial and non-industrial medical activities.[203]

In the instant case, the TBA stated that, before the priority date, the medical practitioner was aware of the possibility of treating gastrointestinal disorders using the particular combination of drugs defined in claim 10 and that similarly he was in a position to prescribe an effective regimen for treating each patient according to his individual needs.[204] The TBA proceeded to reject claim 10 for two reasons: first, based on its statements above, it noted that it appeared questionable whether the prescribing of a specific drug regimen for a basic known medical treatment could represent a further medical indication in accordance with the decision of the EBA in *EISAI/Second medical indication*. Secondly, it appeared questionable, too, whether this feature indeed reflected a medical activity in the industrial and commercial field not excluded from patentability within the terms of Article 52(4) EPC.[205] Surprisingly, the TBA then stated that since the claims were dismissed on the ground of lack of inventive step, there was no need to give a decision on the lack of novelty and non-patentability under the terms of Article 52(4) EPC.[206] This meant that its statements relating to whether dosage or treatment regimes were patentable are *obiter*.

In *SEQUUS/Liposome composition*,[207] claim 1 was for the use of a liposome composition effective to extend to at least 24 hours, to be administered intravenously in a therapeutically effective way, at a dose which contained an amount of the liposome-entrapped compound which was at least three times therapeutically effective. The TBA noted that, although the claims were all drawn up in the conventional 'second (further) medical use format', it had difficulties in accepting the opposition division's opinion that these claims reflected a second (further) medical use, and that the 'three times dosage' feature at the end of some claims, or the corresponding 'ten times dosage' feature, constituted a specified therapeutic

---

202 Ibid, at para. 4.5.
203 Ibid.
204 Ibid.
205 Ibid.
206 Ibid, at para. 4.6.
207 (T 04/98) [2002] EPOR 371.

application from which novelty for the claims can be derived in accordance with the principles of *EISAI/Second medical indication*.[208] The TBA claimed that the concept of 'therapy' or 'therapeutic application' included treatment of a particular illness or disease with a specified chemical substance or composition in a specified human or animal subject in need of such treatment. However, it continued that, by comparison, the 'three (or ten) times dosage' feature failed to provide any indication of at least: (i) the illness or disease to be treated or the ailment to be cured; (ii) the nature of the therapeutic compound used for treating or curing the disease; and (iii) the subject to be treated.[209] The TBA further noted that in the absence of the identification of any of these parameters (i) to (iii), the 'three times (or ten times) dosage' feature actually related to the intravenous (or subcutaneous) administration of an unspecified therapeutic compound in liposome-entrapped form in an amount, which is at least three (or ten) times the therapeutically effective amount of the unspecified therapeutic compound, for the treatment of an unspecified illness or disease in an unidentified patient or other human or animal subject.[210] Consequently, the TBA held that:[211]

> This being the case, the board fails to see how this feature could be construed as specifying a particular method of treatment or a therapeutic application within the meaning of Article 52(4) EPC. In accordance with the principles set out in [*EISAI/Second medical indication*] and the substantial body of case law which has been developed by the boards of appeal in this respect ... the concept of 'second (further) medical use' can only be applied to claims to the use of substances or compositions (here the liposome compositions defined in the claims) for the preparation of a medicament intended for use in a method referred to in Article 52(4) EPC.

For the above-mentioned reasons, the TBA concluded this was clearly not the case in relation to the claims under consideration. It also noted that, accordingly, the subject matter of the claims was to be understood as relating to a non-therapeutic technical activity (process) and that the 'three times (or ten times) dosage' feature can then only be construed as one of the process features characterising the claimed process.[212] The claim was, therefore, not patentable.

---

208 Ibid, at para. 8.
209 Ibid, at para. 8.1.
210 Ibid.
211 Ibid.
212 Ibid, at para. 8.2. This reasoning was applied by the TBA in *EURO-CELTIQUE/Thiazide diuretics* (T 56/97) at para. 2.5. See also, *ELAN*

(b) Dosage regimes patentable

In *SERENO/HCG*,[213] the claim was for the use of HCG for the manufacture of a non-depot medicament for use in the treatment, by subcutaneous administration, of infertility or male sexual disorders. The TBA accepted that the 'use' claim, as approved in *EISAI/Second medical indication*, emphasises that the intended use was a technical feature to be taken into account in assessing novelty and which limited the claim.[214] It continued that in the use claim, the wording 'for use in the treatment by subcutaneous administration ...' was to be treated in accordance with *EISAI/Second medical indication* as a technical feature capable of conferring novelty on the claim. The TBA claimed that this wording was not so treated in a process claim, which was established practice, as it gave applicants, where the process was novel, the opportunity of claiming protection for the process as such irrespective of intended uses of the product and, where the process was not novel, it gave them the opportunity of claiming the use of the product in the manufacture of a medicament for a novel medical treatment.[215]

The TBA noted that the treatment of the disease, cryptorchidism in boys, was a treatment of infertility or male sexual disorders using HCG by way of intramuscular injection. The claim, in its opinion, was not restricted to the medicament being manufactured in any particular concentration, dosage or formulation. This meant that the only difference between the invention, as claimed, and the disclosure in document (4) was that the claim was directed to an intended method of subcutaneous administration.[216] The TBA explained that the claim was drafted in the form approved in *EISAI/Second medical indication* for claims where the novelty was solely that of the intended therapeutic use, and that the only question was whether a difference in the mode of administration of a medicament can be treated as a new therapeutic use.[217] Applying *DUPHAR/Pigs II* and *ICI/Cleaning plaque*, the TBA concluded that it was sufficient for acknowledging novelty of the therapeutic treatment of the claim as a whole, if only one of the features of the treatment, namely, the mode of administration, was novel. It continued that the mode of administration may be a critical factor in a medical treatment, and saw no reason for any *a priori* bar to relying on this

---

CORPORATION/Use of nicotine (T 0584/97) and *NOVARTIS/Method of improving immune response* (T 0485/99).

[213] (T 51/93).

[214] Ibid, at para. 2.2.2.

[215] Ibid.

[216] Ibid, at para. 3.1.1.

[217] Ibid, at para. 3.1.2.

difference when distinguishing the prior art. Rather, patentability, the TBA emphasised, must be treated as depending only on whether this modification was in fact novel and inventive.[218]

(c) Dosage regimes: a new look

In *GENETECH INC/Method of administration of IGF-I*,[219] the claim was for the use of insulin-like growth factor-l in the preparation of a medicament for administering to a mammal in a specific discontinuous administration pattern. The TBA, after examining in detail the decision of the EBA in *EISAI/Second medical indication* stated that, rather, any use to which Article 52(4) EPC first sentence applied in circumstances where the composition had already been suggested for some therapeutic use, and would allow a further medical use claim to the preparation of the composition for that further medical use, irrespective of the detail in which the use was specified, subject to the use being novel and inventive.[220] It continued that a further medical use claim in the approved format (or formulated in the equivalent form of a claim directed to a process for the manufacture of the medicament using the substance) must be treated as complying with Article 52(4) EPC irrespective of the detail with which the therapy is specified. The contrary view, the TBA emphasised, would not be consistent with the reasoning in *EISAI/Second medical indication*.[221] The TBA explained that:[222]

> The [EBA's] decision certainly contains no guidance as to the specificity with which the therapy for a further medical indication has to be formulated, and its reasoning as to why a claim to the use of a composition for the manufacture of a medicament is allowable despite Article 52(4) EPC does not depend on any discrimination relating to the detail with which a therapy is stated.

The TBA claimed that the reasoning of the decision of the Examiner under appeal that there was some interference with the freedom of the physician to prescribe what he or she thought fit which conflicted with Article 52(4) EPC, seemed to miss the whole point of why the EBA in *EISAI/Second medical indication* decided that there was no conflict with Article 52(4) EPC, namely, because the patent proprietor would have a remedy only

---

218 Ibid.
219 (T 1020/03) [2006] EPOR 9.
220 Ibid, at para. 7.
221 Ibid, at para. 11.
222 Ibid.

against the maker or dealer in the composition.[223] Consequently, the TBA held that a claim such as those under consideration, which takes the form of use of a composition for the preparation of a medicament for a specified therapeutic use, would avoid being in conflict with Article 52(4) EPC, irrespective of the degree of detail with which the therapeutic use was stated.[224]

The TBA then claimed that the views expressed by the TBA in *PROCTOR & GAMBLE/Gastrointestinal compositions*,[225] *EURO-CELTIQUE/Thiazide diuretics*,[226] and *ELAN CORPORATION/Use of nicotine*[227] were *obiter*, and that the views on Article 52(4) EPC expressed in these decisions, along with *NOVARTIS/Method of improving immune response*,[228] and *SEQUUS/Liposome composition*,[229] have no proper basis in the EPC and were in conflict with *EISAI/Second medical indication*. Therefore, it was not prepared to follow the views in these decisions.[230] After examining each decision in detail, the TBA held that:[231]

> On the view taken by this Board there is a seamless fit, either a method of using a composition is not a treatment by therapy and therefore falls outside the provision of Article 52(4) EPC first sentence, and so is patentable subject to compliance with the other provisions of the EPC, or else a method is a treatment by therapy and therefore inside the provision of Article 52(4) EPC first sentence, and so not itself patentable, but use of a composition for making a medicament for use in such treatment by therapy is patentable for unspecified therapy as a first medical indication or for a specified therapy as a further medical indication, again subject to compliance with the other provisions of the EPC, in particular novelty and inventive step.

The TBA claimed that it could see no reason why the person who developed a novel therapy by looking for the most effective way in which a known composition can be administered should *a priori* be said to lack merit to such an extent that even the limited form of patent protection of the second medical use form can be denied without an examination of whether the

223 Ibid, at para. 17.
224 Ibid, at para. 18.
225 (T 317/95).
226 (T 0056/97).
227 (T 0584/97).
228 (T 0485/99).
229 (T 04/98).
230 *GENETECH INC/Method of administration of IGF-I* (T 1020/03) at para. 19.
231 Ibid, at para. 39.

therapy was indeed novel and inventive.[232] It further stated that the knowledge regarding the best treatments had to be gained somehow, from *in vitro* tests, *in vivo* tests on cells and animals, and clinical trials under specially supervised conditions. This, it continued, needed to be financed so that allowing second medical use patents served to increase the possibilities of someone undertaking the necessary research.[233] The TBA, therefore, held that if the possibility of obtaining a financial return was excluded less research was likely to take place.

After considering the new Articles 54(4) and 54(5) EPC[234] and the views of the courts in member states,[235] the TBA concluded that it interpreted *EISAI/Second medical indication* as allowing Swiss form claims directed to the use of a composition for manufacture of a medicament for a specified new and inventive therapeutic application, where the novelty of the application might lie only in the dose to be used or the manner of application.[236] The TBA clarified that the discussion in *EISAI/Second medical indication* concerning further medical indications did, indeed, refer to use for treating a new illness. However, it regarded this as significant only on the fact that most second or further medical use claims would refer to a new illness, since, in that case, novelty and inventive step are more likely to exist than in the case of a minor modification of the treatment known for an existing illness. The TBA also continued that the logic of *EISAI/Second medical indication* for allowing claims to further medical uses of known compositions, seems equally applicable to any use of such known composition for a new and inventive treatment which cannot be claimed as such because of Article 54(5) EPC 1973 first sentence.[237] The TBA also rejected a referral to the EBA.[238]

In *SMITHKLINE BEECHAM CORPORATION/Treatment of ovarian cancer*,[239] the TBA noted that, in *GENETECH INC/Method of administration of IGF-I*,[240] the TBA did not decide on the question relating to the novelty of dosage regimes. It argued this meant the notion that this decision

232 Ibid, at para. 43.
233 Ibid, at para. 46.
234 Ibid, at paras. 49–52.
235 Ibid, at paras. 56–68.
236 Ibid, at para. 72.
237 Ibid.
238 Ibid, at para. 78.
239 (T 1001/01).
240 This decision was followed by the TBAs in: (i) *NESTEC/Probiotics* (T 0515/06) at para. 4; (ii) *VERICORE/Sea lice infestation* (T 0708/02) at para. 3.1.2; (iii) *ARS/Infertility* (T 1074/06) at para. 14; and (iv) *SCHERING/Combination therapy HCV* (T 1399/04) at para. 21.

took a 'new approach to the concept of "new therapy"' was not relevant and the comments on the issue, in the absence of a conclusion by the TBA, meant they can only be taken as *obiter dicta*.[241]

5 Dosage or Treatment Regimes under the EPC 2000

(a) The decision of the TBA

The claimed method in *KOS LIFE SCIENCES INC/Dosage regimen* was for the use of nicotinic acid, or a compound metabolised to nicotinic acid by the body, chosen from a select group of substances for the manufacture of a sustained release medicament for use in the treatment by oral administration, once per day, prior to sleep of hyperlipidaemia. The claimed method was, in effect, for a treatment or dosage regime. After analysing the various issues, the TBA referred the following questions to the EBA for decision:

1. Where it is already known to use a particular medicament to treat a particular illness, can this known medicament be patented under the provisions of Articles 53(c) and 54(5) EPC 2000 for use in a different, new and inventive treatment by therapy of the same illness?
2. If the answer to question 1 is yes, is such patenting also possible where the only novel feature of the treatment is a new and inventive dosage regime?
3. Are any special considerations applicable when interpreting and applying Articles 53(c) and 54(5) EPC 2000?

The TBA in *KOS LIFE SCIENCES INC/Dosage regimen* observed that the legal question to be decided was whether a use, which differs from uses already part of the state of the art only in the dosage regimen for the substance to be administered to treat a particular medical condition, can be considered as a new specific use under Article 54(5) EPC. The TBA further observed that the language of Article 54(5) EPC was broad and does not, of itself, suggest that some specific uses should be treated differently from others.[242] The TBA was of the opinion that the previous decisions of the TBAs and the EBA dealing with this issue concerned uses of a known medicament to treat a new illness and that the EBA, therefore, had no particular need to distinguish between a case where the intended use was to

---

[241] *SMITHKLINE BEECHAM CORPORATION/Treatment of ovarian cancer* (T 1001/01) at para. 3.2.

[242] *KOS LIFE SCIENCES INC/Dosage regimen* (T 1319/04) at para. 3.

treat a different illness and a use to treat the same illness but under a different dosage regime.[243] The TBA stated that some TBAs have regarded the acceptance, in principle, of patentability as problematic where the specific therapeutic use differing from the prior art was a mere dosage regimen.[244]

The TBA noted that a long and detailed treatment of the issue was to be found in *GENENTECH INC/Method of administration of IGF-I* in which decision a pure dosage regimen was recognised for the first time as not excluded from patentability.[245] The TBA further noted that, however, a contrary view to that expressed in *GENENTECH INC/Method of administration of IGF-I* may be expressed in two ways.[246] The first was that for a therapy to be recognised as new, for the purposes of Articles 53(c) and 54(5) EPC, over a known therapy using the same substance or compound to treat the same disease, there must be some difference other than the dosage regime. The second was that a known therapy for using a substance to treat a disease must, for the purposes of Articles 53(c) and 54(5) EPC, be deemed to make known all possible dosage regimes using that known substance for treating that disease. In the TBA's opinion, the justification for either alternative way of expressing the view would be that assessing the right dosage was so much a question between physician and patient, the preservation of the physician's freedom to assess the right dosage must take precedence over any right to obtain a patent.[247]

Noting the question of whether medicaments, for use in methods of treatment by therapy where the only novel feature was a dosage regime, were patentable under Articles 53(c) and 54(5) EPC was an important point of law, the TBA emphasised that certainty required that the EBA give a ruling on this issue.[248] It noted that it was questionable whether regard should be paid to the following issues when considering the meaning of Articles 53(c) and 54(5) EPC, namely, that categorically denying patent protection for dosage regimes would: first, make it simpler to refuse patent applications or invalidate patents; and, secondly, avoid problems that courts might have in deciding on what evidence was satisfactory to show that an (old) medicament was being manufactured and/or marketed for use in a new dosage regime.[249] Curiously, the TBA noted that considerations of

243 Ibid, at para. 3.4.
244 Ibid, at para. 4.2.
245 Ibid, at para. 4.6.
246 Ibid, at para. 5.1.
247 Ibid.
248 Ibid, at para. 5.2.
249 Ibid, at para. 5.4.

public health, medical confidentiality to preserve the physician/patient relationship, or preserving the freedom of physicians to treat their patients in the best possible manner are primarily for the legislator in laying down the law and were not primarily considerations for interpreting the law; if they are to be relied on at all in interpreting the provisions of the EPC, it was best for the EBA to give authoritative guidance on how to do so.[250]

The need for legal certainty demanded that the EBA provides the necessary clarity relating to the scope of the interaction between Articles 53(c) and 54(5) EPC, in particular, an answer to the question of whether, in light of both these Articles, patent protection may be provided for treatment or dosage regimes. The desirability of the EBA determining the issue was even more pressing to avoid a fragmentation of European patent jurisprudence, especially in light of the recent Court of Appeal decision of *Actavis v Merck* allowing patent protection for such dosage regimes.

(b) The decision of the EBA

(i) Introduction The question for the EBA in *ABBOTT RESPIRATORY/Dosage regime*[251] was which of these above-mentioned opposing views relating to treatment regimes reflected a proper interpretation of Articles 54(4) and 54(5) EPC. The EBA stated that, based on a reading of Articles 31 and 32 of the Vienna Convention, the provisions of the EPC must first be construed according to the ordinary meaning of the terms in their context and in the light of their object and purpose. This meant that the judge was not entitled to depart from clear provisions of law, and that was supported by the requirement of good faith.[252] It continued that this also meant that preparatory documents were to be considered primarily in order to confirm a meaning or to determine a meaning if the first and ordinary means of construction would lead to ambiguity or to an absurd result.[253]

(ii) Relationship with the medical treatment exclusion Under the title 'Exceptions to patentability' Article 53 EPC provides that European patents shall not be granted in respect of: '(c) methods for treatment of the human or animal body by surgery or therapy and diagnostic methods practised on the human or animal body; this provision shall not apply to

250 Ibid, at para. 5.5.
251 (G 02/08).
252 Ibid, at para. 4.2.
253 Ibid.

products, in particular substances or compositions, for use in any of these methods'. It is clear that the first sentence embodies the exclusion for methods of medical treatment. Out of an abundance of caution, the second sentence provides that products, for use in methods mentioned in the first sentence, shall not be excluded from patent protection. The EBA clarified that Article 53(c) EPC was clear and unambiguous – it drew a borderline between unallowable method claims directed to a therapeutic treatment on the one hand and allowable claims to products for use in such methods on the other hand. It was, therefore, not permissible for the EBA, under the guise of interpretation, to extend the respective domains of the prohibition or the express permission found in Article 53(c) EPC. Consequently, the EBA held that it was improper to consider the second sentence of Article 53(c) EPC as a *lex specialis* to be interpreted narrowly; rather, it was appropriate to give both provisions the same weight, and draw the general conclusion that, in respect of claims directed to therapy, method claims were absolutely forbidden in order to leave the physician free to act unfettered, whereas product claims were allowable provided their subject matter is new and inventive.[254] That latter statement is important since it underscores the rationale for the exception which must be borne in mind when the provision is to be interpreted.

The EBA explained that the first sentence of Article 53(c) EPC, prohibiting patent protection for methods of treatment by therapy, was to be read and understood together with the provisions of its second sentence and with those of Articles 54(4) and 54(5) EPC respectively, so that, far from being mutually exclusive, they were complementary. It continued that by virtue of a legal fiction, Articles 54(4) and 54(5) EPC acknowledged the notional novelty of substances or compositions even when they were, as such, already comprised in the state of the art, provided they are claimed for a new use in a method which Article 53(c) EPC excluded (as such) from patent protection.[255] In such cases, the EBA noted, the notional novelty and, following it the non-obviousness, if any, was not derived from the substance or composition as such but from the purpose to which the claimed substance or composition was related, namely, its intended therapeutic use. The EBA clarified that such use can be either a new indication *stricto sensu* (in the sense of a disease not yet treated by the claimed substance or composition), or one or more steps pertaining, by their nature, to a therapeutic method which may not be claimed as such.[256] If, as argued

254 Ibid, at para. 5.7.
255 Ibid, at para. 5.9.10.
256 Ibid.

above, the subject matter protected under the first medical use related to, for example, a new therapeutic use, then the second and further therapeutic use must be just that – a further specific therapeutic use which is different from other known therapeutic uses of the same substance or composition. That way, the scope of protection for second and further medical uses under Article 54(5) EPC is broader, but consistent with the scope of protection for the first medical use.

The EBA further clarified that Article 54(5) EPC, however, refers to 'any specific use', holding that, on the basis of that wording in conjunction with the declared intention of the legislator to maintain the status quo of protection evolved in the case law of the TBAs under *EISAI/Second medical indication*, such use cannot be *ex officio* limited to a new indication *stricto sensu*.[257] While one cannot fault the EBA's reasoning that Article 54(5) EPC refers to any specific use, the language clearly suggests that, when applied to a therapeutic method, it should be restricted to only a new illness to be treated. This is because if the first use related to a use in a method of treatment by therapy, then the second and further use in a therapeutic method must also be so restricted to that extent, so that the further medical use must be for a new illness to be treated using the substance or composition. Indeed, the EBA's assertion, that this provision was intended to maintain the status quo as it relates to the jurisprudence under Article 54(5) EPC 1973, is correct, but it depends on the status quo to which one is referring. If it is referring to the decisions of the TBAs, then, arguably, it cannot be correct. However, if it is referring to the central ruling of the EBA in *EISAI/Second medical indication* that patent protection should be available under Article 54(5) EPC 1973, not only for first therapeutic uses, but further therapeutic uses of known substances or compositions, then clearly it could be supported.

(iii) First medical uses In respect of Article 54(4) EPC, the EBA accepted that no fundamental change from Article 54(5) EPC 1973 was intended. These provisions relate to the so-called first medical indication of a *per se* already known substance or composition.[258] In other words, either a product for use in a method under Article 53(c) EPC is new *per se* and can constitute the subject matter of a product claim under Article 53(c), second sentence, EPC, or a product (substance or composition) is already known *per se* but can nevertheless be patented provided, under Article 54(4) EPC, the product has not yet been used in a method under Article 53(c), first

257 Ibid.
258 Ibid, at para. 5.8.

sentence, EPC.[259] It must be remembered that Article 54(5) EPC 1973, like Article 54(4) EPC, makes special provision for the use of a substance when used in either a: (a) therapeutic method; (b) surgical method; or (c) diagnostic method. In other words, novelty is derived from the use of the product in either of those methods – nothing else! This point must be borne in mind when the scope of second medical uses under Article 54(5) EPC 1973 is examined.

(iv) Specific uses under EPC 2000 The EBA noted that in contrast to the absence of any provision relating to specific uses in the EPC 1973, Article 54(5) EPC now expressly allows further patent protection of substances or compositions already known as medicines provided their use in a method under Article 53(c) EPC be specific and not comprised in the state of the art. Thus, under the new law, the EBA continued, the lacuna in the former provisions, which had been filled in a praetorian way by the EBA in *EISAI/Second medical indication* and the case law based on that decision, no longer exists.[260] This lacuna was the lack of express protection under Article 54(5) EPC 1973 for second or further medical uses of substances and composition for use in therapeutic, surgical or diagnostic methods. It is that issue, which the EBA failed to grasp, and other TBAs have failed to appreciate, that has led to the decisions of the TBAs indicating that patent protection can be provided for anything, under these provisions, other than for a new specific therapeutic use, for example. The EBA emphasised that there are two critical points to note about Article 54(5) EPC. First, it did not define the nature of the further therapeutic use of a substance or composition already known as a medicine deserving protection, further than requiring that it must be specific. It is unclear why the *nature* of the use needs to be defined, as a proper reading of *EISAI/Second medical indication* shows that the EBA had in mind simply the use of the substance or composition in the new therapeutic method, for example. There is therefore *no* need to define the *nature* of the use as such, since the novelty clearly related to the new therapeutic method in which the substance was used, not the nature of the use *per se*. Secondly, the EBA claimed that Article 54(5) EPC did not define any degree of distinctiveness the new use would be required to have in order to qualify as a specific use.[261] Again, this second observation misses the critical point about what the EBA in *EISAI/Second medical indication* decided, and, moreover, does not necessarily result from the wording of Article 54(5) EPC itself.

---

[259] Ibid.
[260] Ibid, at para. 5.9.
[261] Ibid, at para. 5.9.1.

Moreover, the EBA claimed that the wording of Article 54(5) EPC stipulates that 'any' specific use, not comprised in the state of the art, may be eligible for patent protection under that article. While it is correct that Article 54(5) EPC so provides, it must be noted that the word 'any' used in that context related to any actual use of the substance or composition in any of the excluded methods, emphasising that any use would suffice so that no question of whether only second or further methods would be covered by the provision. It is doubtful whether the use of the word 'any' suggested that the drafters of EPC 2000 meant any *type* of use. In any event, even if that mattered at all, the question still is whether the substance is used in a new therapeutic method, for example. In other words, the Article 54(5) EPC should be read as stating 'any specific therapeutic use'. Clearly, if there was only one method of medical treatment then that simple route would have been taken. Since, however, there are three of such methods, namely therapeutic methods, surgical methods and diagnostic methods, then the wording of Article 54(5) EPC must be read with this in mind, and be interpreted to reflect the distinction between these methods.

The EBA then claimed that, for two reasons, Article 54(5) EPC should not be interpreted in a way that treated Article 53(c) EPC as the general prohibition and gave the provisions of Article 54(5) EPC only the status of a *lex specialis*, which is then interpreted narrowly in the sense that only a disease not yet treated by the known substance or composition can constitute a specific use.[262] But, this is not what was done. The TBA has defined therapy as 'the treatment of a disease in general or ... a curative treatment in the narrow sense, as well as the alleviation of the symptoms of pain and suffering'.[263] So, clearly, in relation to a therapeutic method, the use must be in relation to a curative treatment of the patient – in other words, the treatment of a new disease. That the interpretation of the Article 54(5) EPC, as it relates to therapeutic methods, leads to the conclusion that there must be a new disease to be treated does not lead to the conclusion that the scope of Article 54(5) EPC in its entirety must also be so limited. Other considerations may very well apply in determining the scope of Article 54(5) EPC as it relates to surgical or diagnostic methods. The first reason noted by the EBA was that it could not make that distinction where the provision, duly read in its context, makes none.[264] In its opinion, reading the term 'any specific use' as necessarily meaning treatment of another disease would amount to arbitrarily introducing a distinction the law does

262 Ibid.

263 *SALMINEN/Pigs III* (T 58/97) [1989] EPOR 125 at para. 2.

264 *ABBOTT RESPIRATORY/Dosage regime* (G 02/08) at para. 5.9.1.1.

not make in Article 54(5) EPC, which refers to 'any specific use' in a method of therapy. This, the EBA continued, would be at odds with the principle of good faith required by Article 31(1) of the Vienna Convention to give the term 'any specific use' a limited meaning contrary to its ordinary one.[265] In light of what was just examined, it seems plain that the ordinary meaning of Article 54(5) EPC as it relates to therapeutic methods compels the conclusion that it must relate to the treatment of a new disease to determine the novelty of the claimed substance for that new therapeutic use.

The second reason, according to the EBA, was that Articles 53(c), *in fine*, 54(4) and (5) EPC do not constitute exceptions to the absolute prohibition of patenting methods of therapy, but rather, enjoy an identical ranking which was aimed at allowing as a matter of principle, patent protection for products, substances or compositions for use in therapeutic methods.[266] It continued that to decide the contrary with respect to Article 54(5) EPC would unduly reduce the scope of the new provision of Article 54(5) EPC, and, to that extent, would not genuinely reflect the intention of the legislator and would be at odds with the hitherto understanding of Articles 52(4), second sentence and 54(5) EPC 1973. This analysis again misses the point that Article 54(5) EPC relates to three methods, and not only therapeutic methods, so its interpretation must be defined by the type of medical method at hand – in the case of therapeutic methods, the substance or composition must be used for the purpose of treating a new disease. It cannot be said that this can properly be applied to surgical or diagnostic methods. Indeed, the EBA in *CYGNUS/Diagnostic method* accepted that a diagnostic method is a multi-step method and recently, in *MEDI-PHYSICS/treatment by surgery*, clarified that surgical methods are not to be interpreted as relating to a therapeutic purpose.

The EBA explained that legislative history clearly illustrated the intention of the legislator who considered that the respective concepts of exclusion of therapeutic methods from patentability, on the one hand, and protection of products to be used in such methods, on the other hand, shared the same fate and ranking and therefore could not be either dissociated or mixed up.[267] The EBA continued that this also implied that precisely because they are complementary, none of these provisions needs to be treated as an exception. Moreover, the EBA reiterated that the revision of the EPC maintained a distinction between first and further medical uses of a known substance or composition reflected in the different wording of the

---

[265] Ibid.

[266] Ibid, at para. 5.9.1.2.

[267] Ibid, at para. 5.9.2.1.

provisions of Articles 54(4) and 54(5) EPC.[268] As a result, the EBA held that this indicated, beyond any reasonable doubt, that the drafters of the revision did not adopt the idea of having only equal use-limited protection scope both for the first therapeutic use as well as for any subsequent therapeutic use of a known substance or composition.[269] It is accepted that the exclusion for therapeutic methods should be interpreted in a way that ensures that the activities of physicians or veterinary practitioners are not hampered when they treat their patients. That also means that any protection for both Articles 54(4) and 54(5) EPC must not be so broad that it allows patent protection for subject matter properly excluded under Article 53(c) EPC. This would not be the case if it is appreciated that Articles 54(4) and 54(5) EPC make provision for patent protection for the substances or compositions *themselves*, and not for the underlying new therapeutic method they must be used in to get protection. The new therapeutic, surgical or diagnostic uses are referenced solely for the purpose of determining the novelty of the use claim.

(v) Swiss-type claims The EBA reformulated the question referred to it by the TBA as follows: Is a new use, deserving patent protection, of a *per se* known medicament, necessarily restricted to a disease not yet treated by said composition?[270] As argued above, the answer to this question is surely yes, if the question correctly asked referred specifically to a therapeutic method. The EBA then went on to say that the question of whether patent protection of new use of a *per se* known medicament (not necessarily restricted to treating a new disease) was mainly, although not unanimously, answered in the negative by the TBAs under the EPC 1973, provided the invention was claimed in the so-called Swiss-type format adopted by the EBA in *EISAI/Second medical indication*.[271] It is arguable, based on the reasoning above, that the TBAs that considered the issue simply got it wrong. The EBA explained that, in *EISAI/Second medical indication*, the EBA had filled a gap in the legal provisions and allowed claims concerning a second therapeutic indication of a known product, although not specifying whether such a second use could be something other than the treatment of another disease. But, properly construed, the application of Articles 54(4) and 54(5) EPC to therapeutic methods leads only to that conclusion. This was how the EBA in *EISAI/Second medical indication* saw the issue before it – as relating to therapeutic methods. Indeed, most of the

268 Ibid, at para. 5.9.2.2.
269 Ibid.
270 Ibid, at para. 5.10.
271 Ibid, at para. 5.10.1.

decisions considering Article 54(5) EPC were in the context of therapeutic methods. If that was realised and appreciated, it would seem obvious that this particular interpretation could not be applied generally to Article 54(5) EPC 1973 which related to three distinct methods. The jurisprudence of each of these methods shows that they have their distinct spheres of operation. Why then should Articles 54(4) and 54(5) EPC, which relate to specific medical methods, be defined only by its meaning as applied to therapeutic methods?

The EBA continued that under the new law, EPC 2000, the lacuna in Article 54(5) EPC 1973, which had been closed in a praetorian way by the decision of the EBA in *EISAI/Second medical indication* and the subsequent case law of the TBAs, no longer exists.[272] That lacuna, as mentioned above, was simply the lack of express provision for second or further medical uses. The EBA explained that it could not deduce from the wording of *EISAI/Second medical indication* that its ruling was to be restricted to a new indication in the sense of a new disease. Contrary to this conclusion, a reading of Article 54(5) EPC 1973 does lead to that conclusion if it related only to a therapeutic method; and the context of the decision of the EBA in *EISAI/Second medical indication* does confirm this interpretation. The EBA stated that Article 54(5) EPC now provides for patent protection of a known substance or composition for 'any specific use' of the said product in a method of therapy provided this use was not comprised in the state of the art and was inventive. Consequently, the EBA held that there could be only one sensible way of construing the requirement underlying the specificity of the use, namely, merely by contrast to the generic broad protection conferred by the first claimed medical application of a substance or composition, which is, in principle, not confined to a particular indication. Thus, the new use within the meaning of Article 54(5) EPC need not be the treatment of another disease.[273] The EBA misses the point here, because Article 54(5) EPC is intended to compensate for the lack of specificity and limited scope of Article 54(4) EPC, which provides only for the first use of the product in, for example, a therapeutic method. Article 54(5) EPC expands this to allow for any further specific therapeutic uses, intending to make it clear that, first, there was no limitation as to the number of therapeutic uses in which the product could be used and, secondly, that any new therapeutic use must be specific, so as to distinguish each use from the previous therapeutic one, indicating that there is no exhaustion of the therapeutic uses. In other words, as many as possible could be patentable as

---

[272] Ibid, at para. 5.10.2.
[273] Ibid, at para. 5.10.3.

long as they are specific, distinct from other such known uses and satisfy the other requirements for patentability.

The approach mentioned above, the EBA explained, was confirmed by the preparatory documents of the EPC 2000.[274] The EBA stated that from the very wording of decision *EISAI/Second medical indication*, it could not deduce that that ruling was to be restricted to a new indication in the sense of a new disease. The same, it clarified, held true for point 23 of the Reasons, reflected in point 2 of the Order of the EBA in *EISAI/Second medical indication*, which both mention 'a specified new and inventive therapeutic application' which does not necessarily correspond to a new indication being restricted to a 'new disease'.[275] However, a close reading of the decision of the EBA in *EISAI/Second medical indication* shows that this was what was intended in relation to second or further therapeutic uses.

(vi) Decisions of the TBAs The EBA made clear the view that the new indication was not restricted to a 'new disease' was reflected by the case law of the TBAs subsequent to *EISAI/Second medical indication* there was no reason to restrict the intention of the legislator that 'the case law evolved by the [EBA] should be enshrined in the Convention' to the sole teaching of *EISAI/Second medical indication*. Consequently, the EBA reasoned that the legislator could reasonably be deemed to have been aware of and have wished to include this later jurisprudence; in this respect, the terms 'case law evolved' also make more sense.[276] However, it must first be determined whether these decisions reflect a proper understanding of the scope of the decision of the EBA in *EISAI/Second medical indication*. It is doubtful that they do. However, the EBA noted that, under the EPC 1973, the jurisprudence of the TBAs had already acknowledged patentability of substances and compositions known in the prior art for use in the treatment by therapy of a particular disease, even if they were directed to the treatment of the same illness, provided this treatment was new and inventive.[277] It then gave examples of: (i) novel groups of subjects treated; (ii) new mode of administration; and (iii) differential technical effect leading to a new application. The EBA then concluded that since the legislator wished to maintain the status quo, as regards the availability of patent protection for further therapeutic uses, and insofar intended no change due to the introduction of the current provisions of Article 54(5) EPC, the principles established by

274 Ibid, at para. 5.10.4.
275 Ibid, at para. 5.10.5.
276 Ibid, at para. 5.10.6.
277 Ibid, at para. 5.10.7.

this case law still hold true.[278] This reasoning is not surprising since these decisions support the EBA's view that, under Article 54(5) EPC, something other than a new disease could provide the necessary novelty required for patentability of products, namely, substances and compositions for use in the excluded methods of medical treatments. But Article 54(5) EPC relates to each of the three methods contained in Article 53(c) EPC, so it is surprising that the EBA's interpretation does not make specific reference to the particular method at issue or recognise that distinction. In *EISAI/ Second medical indication*, the EBA noted this but was concerned mainly to delineate the scope of Article 54(5) EPC 1973 and, when it mentioned 'indication', it was merely referring back to the excluded methods found in Article 52(4) EPC. Therefore, the decisions of the TBAs referred to by the EBA were flawed in two respects. First, since the claimed methods considered usually related to therapeutic methods, this meant that the novelty should have resided only in a new illness to be treated. Secondly, these decisions are inconsistent with the reasoning and *ratio* of the EBA in *EISAI/Second medical indication* which sought to provide patent protection for second and further uses of products when used, for example, in new therapeutic methods.

(vii) Defining dosage regimes The EBA explained that the term 'dosage regime' may cover different acceptations that are normally reflected by corresponding features in the wording of the claim. However, it thought there was no need to define the term more precisely. Having accepted that 'any specific use' may reside in something other than the treatment of a different illness, the EBA held that there was no reason to give to a feature, consisting in a new dosage regime of a known medicament, a different treatment from the one given to any other specific use acknowledged in the case law.[279] Concerns regarding the extension of patent rights, the EBA thought, were accommodated by the rules relating to novelty and non-obviousness.[280] The EBA noted that, in particular, the claimed definition of the dosage regime must, therefore, not only be verbally different from what was described in the state of the art, but, must also reflect a different technical teaching.

The arguments made above show that patenting dosage regimes would not amount to a second medical use in accordance with neither the decision of the EBA in *EISAI/Second medical indication* interpreting Article 54(5)

278 Ibid, at para. 5.10.8.
279 Ibid, at para. 6.1.
280 Ibid, at para. 6.3.

EPC 1973 nor under Articles 54(4) and 54(5) EPC, properly construed. The EBA in *EISAI/Second medical indication* had interpreted Article 54(5) EPC 1973 in such a way to provide patent protection for second and further medical uses, contrary to its ordinary meaning which suggested that only a first therapeutic use was patentable. Its decision was a policy-based one and it has been accepted as such. However, a proper interpretation of Articles 54(4) and 54(5) EPC does not compel the conclusion that dosage regimes are patentable if one accepts the rationale for the decision of the EBA in *EISAI/Second medical indication* and that these new articles were simply to expressly provide for the patentability of second and further medical uses, rather than to continue to keep them grounded on the precarious reasoning of the EBA in *EISAI/Second medical indication*. If the EBA intended to make a policy decision that something else other than uses in the medical methods found in Article 53(c) EPC should be patentable, then it should say so expressly rather than to distort the ordinary meaning of the provision, in a similar way to the EBA in *EISAI/Second medical indication*.

(viii) New technical effect The EBA continued that the body of jurisprudence developed concerning the question as to when a technical effect of a claimed therapeutic application not previously described in the state of the art, can be recognised as conferring novelty on an application, continues to be applicable to the assessment of the individual cases under Article 54(5) EPC.[281] The EBA explained that, if the distinguishing feature of a claim, seeking patent protection for a known medicament to be used for a different treatment of the same illness, was a dosage regime, the new technical effect caused by that feature shall be considered when examining inventive step under Article 56 EPC. This would not apply if the distinguishing feature was a mere selection from a prior broader disclosure. The application of the jurisprudence concerning a new technical effect is not surprising since the EBA has now accepted that the actual method of treating the patient is patentable, rather than finding the product patentable based on the new therapeutic method in which it is used. One wonders whether the EBA fully considered the desirability, as a matter of principle and policy, of providing patent protection for dosage regimes in light of the exclusion for medical treatment methods in Article 53(c) EPC.

(ix) Differences between EPC 1973 and EPC 2000 After examining how courts of EPC contracting states have dealt with the question of patent

---

281 Ibid.

protection for dosage regimes, in particular, the decision of the UK Court of Appeal in *Actavis v Merck*, the EBA held that the patents underlying these decisions were under the ambit of the old law which did not contain any notional acknowledgement of novelty of a claim directed to a known product based on a feature relating to an intended further – therapeutic – use of that product.[282] The new provisions of Article 54(5) EPC, the EBA explained, were precisely intended to fill this lacuna. It continued that it appeared that the rights conferred on the patentee by the claim category under Article 54(5) EPC are likely broader, and could, in particular, lead to possible restrictions on the freedom of medical practitioners to prescribe or administer generics.[283] That is a startling admission indeed! Article 53(c) EPC was intended to exclude methods of medical treatment from patent protection, and to make it clear that products for use in those methods, however, remain patentable. The purpose or *ratio legis* of Article 53(c) EPC, as accepted by the EBA on three occasions, namely, *EISAI/Second medical indication* (1984); *CYGNUS/Diagnostic method* (2004) and *MEDI-PHYSICS/Treatment by surgery*, was to free from restraint non-commercial and non-industrial medical and veterinary activities. Articles 54(4) and 54(5) EPC relate only to the requirement of novelty, providing simply that products used in the excluded methods of medical treatment are patentable where, first, they are used for the first time in an excluded method; and, secondly, where there is a specific use of that product in those excluded methods. Nevertheless, the EBA claimed that, in view of the clear provisions of Articles 53(c) EPC, second sentence, and 54(5) EPC and the intention of the legislator, it had no power to broaden or reduce the scope of these provisions in a praetorian way, and that, if deemed necessary, the freedom of medical practitioners may be protected by other means on the national level.[284] Contrary to this point of view, it is indeed the function of the EBA to interpret the provisions in such a way that there is a clear demarcation between what is patentable and what is not, to ensure that excluded methods of medical treatments are not patented by the back door. For public health reasons, the drafters of the EPC maintained the medical treatment exclusion. The inclusion of Articles 54(4) and 54(5) in the EPC to provide protection for first and further medical uses should not, in any way, limit or negate the exclusion for methods of medical treatment found in Article 53(c) EPC.

(x) The end of Swiss-type claims The EBA accepted that since Article 54(5) EPC now permitted purpose-related product protection for any

---

[282] Ibid, at para. 6.4.
[283] Ibid, at para. 6.5.
[284] Ibid.

further specific use of a known medicament in a method of therapy, thereby closing the loophole in Article 54(5) EPC 1973, the effect of the EBA in *EISAI/Second medical indication* must also cease.[285] The EBA, therefore, ruled that where the subject matter of a claim was rendered novel only by a new therapeutic use of a medicament, such claim may no longer have the format of a so called Swiss-type claim as instituted by *EISAI/Second medical indication*.[286] Consequently, to ensure legal certainty and to protect legitimate interests of applicants, the EBA allowed a time limit of three months after publication of its decision in *ABBOTT RESPIRATORY/Dosage regime* for applicants to comply with the new law now declared by the EBA.[287]

(xi) Conclusions of the EBA In concluding, the EBA answered the questions referred to it by the TBA as follows:

1. Question 1: Where it is already known to use a medicament to treat an illness, Article 54(5) EPC does not exclude that this medicament be patented for use in a different treatment by therapy of the same illness.
2. Question 2: Such patenting is also not excluded where a dosage regime is the only feature claimed which is not comprised in the state of the art.
3. Question 3: Where the subject matter of a claim is rendered novel only by a new therapeutic use of a medicament, such claim may no longer have the format of a so called Swiss-type claim as instituted by decision G 5/83.

The first conclusion, as argued above, should have been limited in its scope if it is accepted that Articles 54(4) and 54(5) EPC relate to three distinct methods, and that *EISAI/Second medical indication*, with its emphasis on a new illness to be treated, was there dealing with a method of treatment of the animal body by therapy. It must mean, therefore, given that the excluded methods differ in their interpretation and scope, as has recently been held by the EBA in *CYGNUS/Diagnostic* method and *MEDI-PHYSICS/Treatment by surgery*, the proper interpretation of Article 54(5) EPC must relate to that particular exclusion only. In any event, the EBA also might not be correct to suggest that something else, other than a new

---

[285] Ibid, at para. 7.1.2.
[286] Ibid, at para. 7.1.3.
[287] Ibid, at para. 7.1.4.

illness to be treated, would suffice for the application of Articles 54(4) and 54(5) EPC. This reading of Articles 54(4) and 54(5) EPC necessarily means that, in relation to the second question, a dosage regime would not be included in the subject matter covered by these provisions, since they do not relate to a new illness but merely to new methods of administration of an old substance to treat an old illness. The third conclusion would necessarily follow from the inclusion of Article 54(5) in the EPC 2000. The EBA has therefore confirmed that patent protection is available for dosage regimes under the EPC, signalling in the process that the specific use referred to in Article 54(5) EPC is not limited to the treatment of a new disease, and confirming decisions of the TBAs that have accepted other new applications as patentable under Article 54(5) EPC 1973. As such, patentees no longer need to use the Swiss form of claim to gain patent protection for second or further medical uses, since this is specifically provided for in Article 54(5) EPC. The EBA also ruled that applicants would have a three-month limit to comply with the new requirement discussed by the EBA in its decision.

7 Conclusion

The demands of the pharmaceutical industry held sway and the EPO interpreted the EPC in light of the needs of the industry. The first occasion was the decision of the EBA in *EISAI/Second medical indication* to allow patent protection for second (and further) medical uses which was a watershed in the jurisprudence of the EPO. If there was any doubt as to the need of that incentive provided for by *EISAI/Second medical indication*, Article 54(5) EPC means that there is now a statutory basis for second (and further) medical uses under the EPC, so it will no longer be necessary to resort to the Swiss form of claim. The status quo as it relates to first medical uses is now found in Article 54(5) EPC.[288] In relation to second and further medical uses, Article 54(5) EPC, which was intended to codify *EISAI/Second medical indication*, the EBA in *ABBOTT RESPIRATORY/Dosage regime* has accepted that where it is already known to use a medicament to treat an illness, that Article did not exclude patent protection for a medicament for use in a different treatment by therapy of the same illness. In addition, the EBA held that patent protection was not excluded also where a dosage regime was the only feature claimed which was not comprised in the state of the art. In the same way that the EBA in *EISAI/Second medical indication* accommodated the needs of the pharmaceutical industry, the

---

[288] See *NESTEC SA/High fibre composition* (T 1002/09) at para. 3.2.

EBA, in the instant decision, did the same making a policy decision to allow patent protection for dosage regimes. The EBA's analysis does not distinguish between the three methods of medical treatment referred to in Article 54(5) EPC. As a result, it hastily concluded that a new disease is not required for the new specific use requirement but that it can reside in a new dosage regime. It is questionable too whether dosage regimes actually are medical treatment methods contrary to Article 53(c) EPC.

I NEW MEDICAL TECHNOLOGY

In *UNIVERSITY OF TEXAS/DNA damaging agents and p53*,[289] the claim was for the use of a p53 protein or gene in a pharmaceutically acceptable form for the preparation of a medicament to kill tumour cells which are located within an animal. The medicament was administered in combination with a DNA damaging agent selected from the group consisting of X-ray radiation, UV-radiation, γ- irradiation or microwaves. The tumour was first exposed to the DNA damaging agent and then contacted with the p53 protein or gene.[290] The claim, in essence, was drafted as referring to a second (or further) medical use of a p53 protein or gene.[291] The appellant argued that the use of a p53 protein or gene in cancer therapy was already known in the art. The TBA accepted that a claim referring to the use of this known compound for a known purpose, which claim was further characterised by a step of irradiation treatment, was excluded from patentability by virtue of Article 52(4) EPC.[292]

The TBA cited the decision of the EBA in *EISAI/Second medical indication* for the proposition that a claim which took the form of use of a composition for the preparation of a medicament for a specific therapeutic use, will avoid being in conflict with Article 52(4) EPC, irrespective of the degree of detail with which the therapeutic use is stated.[293] It continued that if the subject matter of a claim avoided the prohibited method of therapy of Article 52(4) EPC first sentence, as in its judgement was the case for claim 4 in the present case, which was in the approved 'Swiss-type' form, compliance with this provision did not need to be considered further. The decisive question, in the TBA's opinion, which needed to be answered in accordance with the decision in *EISAI/Second medical indication,* was whether the

---

289 (T 0036/04).
290 Ibid, at para. V.
291 Ibid, at para. 2.
292 Ibid.
293 Ibid, at para. 3.

intended method of treatment for which the medicament was manufactured was novel and inventive, and not any further considerations under Article 52(4) EPC. Consequently, the TBA rejected the appellant's arguments and found that the requirements of Article 52(4) EPC were met.[294]

J CONCLUSION

The demands of the pharmaceutical industry held sway and the EPO interpreted the EPC in light of the needs of the industry. The decision of the EBA in *EISAI/Second medical indication* to allow patent protection for second (and further) medical uses was a watershed in the jurisprudence of the EPO. Even if the decision was criticised because it did not result from the wording of Article 54(5) EPC 1973, and was contrary to the intentions of the drafter of the EPC, the result was a practical one. It provided patentees with the much-needed incentive of the patent system to justify continued research and development in finding new and further uses of substances and compositions. In the process, the EPO, arguably, carved a major exception to the exclusion for methods of medical treatment. Subsequent decisions of the TBAs have extended the *EISAI/Second medical indication* principle beyond its known parameters. If there was any doubt about the need of that incentive provided for by *EISAI/Second medical indication*, Article 54(5) EPC 2000 means that there is now a statutory basis for second (and further) medical uses under the EPC. Therefore, it will no longer be necessary to resort to the Swiss form of claim. The status quo as it relates to first medical uses is found in Article 54(5) EPC 2000.[295] In relation to dosage regimes, after much vacillation on the issue by the TBAs on whether dosage regimes are patentable under the EPC, the EBA in *ABBOTT RESPIRATORY/Dosage regime* has ruled that they are allowable, putting an end to the uncertainty that has plagued this question in the past.

---

[294] Ibid, at para. 4.
[295] Ibid.

8. Manner of new manufacture

A INTRODUCTION

In the period before 1977, the courts in the United Kingdom held that methods of medical treatment of the human body were unpatentable subject matter.[1] The exclusion was not based on strong policy considerations initially, but, rather, on an accepted construction of section 101 of the Patents Act 1949, which had codified section 6 of the Statute of Monopolies.[2] The patentability or otherwise of methods of medical treatment was based on whether they were compatible with the objects of the statute or considered a manner of manufacture. The concept of manufacture included a vendible machine or substance,[3] or mechanical or chemical objects.[4] It was not surprising that when the question of methods of medical treatment arose for consideration the courts were unable to find a satisfactory answer.

Some cases even accepted that the basis of the exclusion could be traced to Patent Office practice. The uncertainty of juridical origins allowed the courts to proffer differing rationales for the exclusion and then ultimately accepting a vague notion of public policy[5] as its underlying rationale. The failure of the courts in addressing this central question meant that they failed to articulate the proper role of such public policy considerations when determining patentability. They were also inconsistent in the use of various terminologies used to describe the exclusion. *Methods of medical treatment* of humans were excluded from patent protection and this view was not always consistently applied. The Patent Appeal Tribunal (PAT) in

[1] See generally J. Pila, 'Methods of Medical Treatment within Australian and United Kingdom Patents Law' (2001) 24 UNSW LJ 420 and R. Smither, *Patent Protection for Inventions Relating to Medical Treatment of Humans and Animals* (CLIP London 1993).

[2] 21 Jac I, c3, See *Darcy v Allen* (1602) 77 ER 1260 and for an exhaustive survey of the relevant case law see J. Pila, 'The Common Law Invention in its Original Form' [2001] IPQ 209.

[3] *Boulton v Bull* (1795) 126 ER 651, 660–1 (Rooke J).

[4] Ibid, at 664.

[5] The term public policy includes ethical considerations.

Schering A G's Application[6] doubted the logic of the exclusion but still maintained that it was sound. The PAT disregarded this specificity in *Organon Laboratories Ltd's Application* and held that a claim to a contraceptive device was excluded because it was a *method of treatment*.[7] This was corrected in *Schering A G's Application* where the PAT reiterated that only methods of medical treatment were excluded and that a method of contraception was not a *method of medical treatment* and, therefore, not excluded.[8] However, the courts and PAT maintained that all forms of *treatment*, including methods of medical treatment of animals, were excluded from patent protection.[9]

B THE NATURE OF THE EXCLUSION

1 Introduction

The nature of the exclusion for methods of medical treatment needed delineation. What exactly was being excluded? Was it the treatment of humans or animals for the purpose of curing or preventing disease, or was it any form of treatment irrespective of the intended purpose? In articulating the rationale for the exclusion, the courts used phrases such as 'methods of medical treatment', 'treatment of the human body' or 'treatment for the curing or preventing disease'. It is important that one gets a clear picture of the nature of the exclusion so that the underlying policy objective may be delineated. The Concise Oxford Dictionary defines medicine as 'the science or practice of diagnosis, treatment and prevention of disease, esp., as distinct from surgical methods'.[10] The definition of 'medical' refers to things that relate to the science of medicine in general.[11] One may accept a definition of medical treatment as including *treatment of the humans or animals that has the primary objective of diagnosing, treating and preventing disease*. This may include surgery but surgery is not considered a medical treatment unless it is directed to any one of the objectives of the science of medicine. A necessary corollary is that a method of treatment that does not have the objective of diagnosing, treating or curing disease would not be considered as a method of *medical* treatment.

---

6 *Schering A G's Application* [1971] RPC 337 (PAT), 344.
7 [1970] RPC 574 (PAT), 578.
8 *Schering A G's Application*, at 342.
9 *Canterbury Agricultural College's Application* [1958] RPC 85.
10 (9th edn (D Thompson (ed.)) Clarendon Press, Oxford 1995).
11 Ibid.

Therefore, therapy was the quintessential method of medical treatment excluded from patent protection. There were, however, other methods of treatment of humans and animals that were non-therapeutic in nature, namely some surgical, diagnostic and cosmetic methods. A definition that is not limited to *medical* treatment would have the effect of covering all types of treatment irrespective of its intended objective. It may be argued that the word *treatment* can cover therapy but the word treatment has a much wider meaning than that. Treatment was defined as 'a thing done to relieve or cure an illness or correct a problem'[12] and may cover therapeutic,[13] diagnostic,[14] surgical[15] and cosmetic[16] things done to the human or animal body. These considerations are not merely an exercise in futility because their indiscriminate use by the courts does not allow one to determine exactly what was excluded.

2 Treatment in Humans

The Solicitor-General in *C & W's Application*[17] did not define the treatment in question, which involved a process for removing lead from the human body. The question was whether the claimed invention was a 'manner of manufacture' as stated in section 6 of the Statutes of Monopolies. The Solicitor-General pointed out that the Patent Office had refused the application on the basis that it was for a *medical treatment* and that the medical profession prohibits patents for discoveries whose object is to alleviate human suffering.[18] The patent was clearly one that was directed at curing a human condition, namely lead poisoning and, therefore, can be classified as a therapeutic method of treatment of the human body. Another example of a case involving a method of medical treatment of humans was *United States Rubber Company's Application.*[19] In that decision, the claim was for a process for the prevention of malignant tumour cells and, more specifically, for the inhibition of mitosis in malignant tumour cells and the

---

12 *Concise Oxford Dictionary* (9th edn (D Thompson (ed.)) Clarendon Press, Oxford 1995).

13 Inducing fever to treat disease US Patent No. 2, 098, 295 1937.

14 Method of diagnosing colon lesions by introducing silicone rubber into the colon, allowing it to set, and removing it by defecation, US Patent No. 3, 247, 841 1966.

15 Surgical Method of cryonic cataract removal US Patent No. 3, 942, 519 1976.

16 Cosmetic surgery process of removing subcutaneous tissue and fat from redundant tissue, homogenising the tissue and fat, and injecting the mixture under tightened skin US Patent No. 3, 654, 914 1972.

17 (1914) 31 RPC 235.

18 Ibid, at 236 (emphasis added).

19 [1964] RPC 104.

prevention of synthesis of deoxyribonucleic acid. It was clear that this was a method of medical treatment. The Examining Officer recognised this, observing that it was 'unreasonable to think of a method of medical treatment of the human body as an invention within the meaning of s. 101 of the Act'.[20] The fact that the Examining Officer specifically referred to methods of medical treatment of the human body buttresses the point that *only* methods of *medical treatment* of humans were thought to be excluded from patent protection. The intention was not to cover *all* treatments of the human body but only the medical treatment thereof.

This reasoning meant that a claim for a device used to inject a substance into a person, as a means of defence, was not considered a method of medical treatment.[21] However, a method for repairing a defect in the surface of a tooth; the sealing and filling of developmental pits and fissures in tooth surfaces; and a method of drying hard tooth surfaces, were all claims to methods of medical treatment because they were related to the treatment of dental caries which is a disease.[22] Similarly, a patent for a method of inducing a state of reduced awareness in humans, by means of sound generated by a known machine, was held unpatentable because its usefulness was contingent on the interaction with the human brain.[23]

The question whether a machine that assisted hearing was a method of medical treatment arose for consideration in *Puharich and Lawrence's Application*.[24] Lloyd-Jacob J disagreed with the Examiner, pointing out

---

[20] Ibid, at 106.

[21] *Palmer's Application* [1970] RPC 597 (PAT).

[22] *Lee Pharmaceutical's Application* [1978] RPC 51, 52–53.

[23] *Neva Corporation's Application* [1968] RPC 481.

[24] [1965] RPC 395 (PAT). On the other hand, Lloyd-Jacob J. considered that the insertion of the receiver in the tooth could not be considered as a method of medical treatment as this would result in a wide exclusion sufficient to exclude even new materials for dental fillings. The Examining Officer in *Calmic Engineering Co. Ltd's Application* observed that the significance of this case was that it demonstrated the sanctioning of a claim to an apparatus, which, although intimately associated with the human body is nonetheless distinct from it. It was observed that if a claim were made to the process for making the cavity it would have had to be excluded as being a claim to a method of medical treatment. This is not necessarily correct as the making of the cavity would not have been made pursuant to a disease or rather the necessary surgery was not directly related to a disease. The analysis was continued when the examiner observed that there is a degree of intimate association between the dialysis apparatus and the human body in the normal use of such apparatus, which is comparable to the degree of association between the transmitter and the tooth in *Puharich and Lawrence's Application*. The analogy fails because the objective of placing the receiver in the tooth in *Puharich and Lawrence's Application* was merely incidental to the claim itself whereas the apparatus in *Calmic Engineering Co. Ltd's Application* was necessary to the working of the invention. In any event

that the method in question was not a method of medical treatment.[25] The actual justification for this reasoning is not obviously apparent. Deafness is defined as 'a condition in which the sense of hearing in both ears is *not functional* for ordinary purposes of life',[26] which means that a device that attempts to alleviate this condition is certainly a method of medical treatment. The logic of this reasoning was accepted in *Calmic Engineering Co. Ltd's Application*[27] when the PAT held that an apparatus for the purification of blood via dialysis for treatment of patients suffering from kidney disease was a method of medical treatment. Similarly, patent protection was available for new uses of old chemical compounds provided the new use was not directed to a method of medical treatment of the human body.[28]

The jurisprudence of the courts and the PAT in the pre-1977 period clearly showed that therapeutic methods of treatment of humans were outside the scope of patent protection. The courts now had to determine whether a particular method of treatment was a medical one and, therefore, excluded from patent protection. The Court of Appeal held that a claim which included a method for the reduction of gastric secretion was *not* patentable because it was directed to a method of treatment of a human ailment.[29] The exclusion of methods of medical treatment was interpreted narrowly to include *only* methods of treatment for the prevention or curing of a disease, which meant that it was not applicable to diagnostic methods.[30] The PAT in *Bio-Digital Sciences Incorporated's Application*[31] pointed out that the claim for a method of separating cells for evidence of disease was not directed at the prevention or curing of a disease since the whole process was carried out before considering whether any medical treatment was necessary.[32] This seems eminently sensible because the definition of a method of medical treatment would necessarily exclude diagnostic methods that do not directly involve interaction with the human or animal body. In that case, the diagnosis took place in a laboratory and did not directly

---

the surgery in the former was not directed to a therapeutic purpose whereas the apparatus had that objective at its core.

25 *Puharich and Lawrence's Application*, at 395.

26 Online Medical Dictionary: http://www.deafhub.com/infohub/spokes/deafness/ (accessed 8 May 2011).

27 [1973] RPC 684 (PAT), 686.

28 *Eli Lilly & Company's Application* [1975] RPC 438 (PAT).

29 *The Upjohn Company (Robert's) Application* [1977] RPC 94 (CA).

30 *Bio-Digital Sciences Incorporated's Application* [1973] RPC 668 (PAT).

31 Ibid.

32 Ibid, at 674.

involve the patient and was akin to scientific research. If diagnostic methods were held to be unpatentable, it would have closed the door to much-needed research in detecting and finding cures for diseases.

Where a claim covers a therapeutic and a cosmetic method of treatment, the latter would not prevent rejection of the claim as being directed to a method of medical treatment.[33] In *Oral Health Products Inc. (Halstead's) Application*, claims for a method of removing plaque from teeth (claim 33), preventing calculus (claim 34) and removing carious material from teeth (claim 35) were rejected. The PAT, reversing the Examining Officer, accepted that the prevention of caries was a disease so the claim directed at preventing it was a method of medical treatment.[34] However, claim 32, which was directed at cleaning (whitening) teeth, used the same material that formed the basis of claims 33–35. The PAT held that it was, therefore, legitimate to reject claims 33–35 as methods of medical treatment, but not claim 32, since it was solely for a cosmetic purpose. The PAT requested that claim 32 be reconsidered because it was directed to a cosmetic effect even if it would also achieve the same objectives as claims 33–35.[35]

These cases have also provided greater insight into the working of the exclusion for methods of medical treatment. The exclusion did not include methods of diagnosis or those that have a cosmetic effect. The statement in *Schering A G's Application* underscores the distinction that was constantly being made, albeit indirectly, between method of treatment *simpliciter* and a method of medical treatment. In that decision, it was stated that 'since 1914 it seems to have been accepted as axiomatic that there can be no patents for "medical" treatment'.[36] This clearly showed that the PAT was cognisant of the distinction it had made earlier since it placed emphasis on the word 'medical'. Therefore, the exclusion only related to methods of 'medical treatment' of the human body and not 'methods of treatment' thereof. That notwithstanding, the PAT thought it was illogical that a patent may be granted for new therapeutic drugs but not for methods of medical treatment.[37] This is important since it underscores the rationale for the exclusion that was later adopted by the UK courts, which was to ensure that patent law did not limit the actions of physicians when they treat their patients.

---

[33] *Oral Health Products Inc. (Halstead's) Application* [1977] RPC 612 (PAT).

[34] Ibid, at 615.

[35] The PAT in *Oral Health Products Inc. (Halstead's) Application* thought the claims might be allowable if they were drafted in such a way so as to limit it to the cosmetic effect although it doubted whether that could be achieved or not (at 616).

[36] *Schering A G's Application*, at 342 (emphasis in original).

[37] Ibid, at 343.

3 Treatment in Animals

The language of the courts and the PAT differed when they considered the patentability of methods of treatment of animals. They accepted a wider definition and, in the process, excluded all methods of treatment thereof. The Solicitor-General in *C & W's Application* stated, *obiter*, that if the process of removing lead were directed at animals to make them more marketable products, then *different* considerations would have to be applied.[38] Although the question was not answered either way, and because there was no mention of the other relevant considerations that might have been taken into account, the answer may be gleaned by applying the legal principle accepted therein by the Solicitor-General. If a 'new manner of manufacture' was defined as a 'machine or a process that can be used in making something that is, or may be, of a commercial value'[39] then the removal of lead from a herd of animals to make them vendible was within the ambit of the statute and therefore patentable.

The question whether medical procedure patents should be granted for animals continued to occupy the attention of the PAT. In *Canterbury Agricultural College's Application*,[40] the improvement in the quality and quantity of wool was not considered a method of medical treatment. However, the claim was concerned with a process for the *treatment* of animals and not the *medical treatment* thereof.[41] On that basis, therefore, the decision can be supported. The Examining Officer emphasised that the Patent Office had a long established practice of refusing patents for processes covering merely the treatment of animals, whether for the purpose of simply curing an illness or of increasing their commercial value, or of stimulating or altering a product of their metabolism.[42] However, the Solicitor-General in *C & W's Application* had not made such a sweeping generalisation. The Patent Office practice was related only to the claim for a method of medical *treatment* and the Solicitor-General had simply noted that with regard to animals, differing considerations would have applied. The remarks made in *Canterbury College Agricultural College's Application* suggested that the exclusion was wider than previously thought. Not only were methods of *treatment* excluded, but *any* process for the treatment of animals including the *medical* treatment thereof was similarly excluded. In *C & W's Application*, it was not stated that such considerations were also

---

38 *C & W's Application*, at 236.
39 Ibid.
40 [1958] RPC 85.
41 Ibid, at 86.
42 Ibid.

applicable to the treatment of humans, so one may limit the effect of such a sweeping statement by confining it only to the medical treatment of animals. Without a clear policy objective for the exclusion of methods of medical treatment, the Examining Officer was forced to make an analogy with patents for altering the climatic conditions of plants.[43] This is not surprising as the Examining Officer had accepted that *any* process for the treatment of animals irrespective of the objective would not be patentable.

The PAT in *Canterbury College Agricultural College's Application* rejected the suggestion made in *C & W's Application* that methods of medical treatment of animals were patentable notwithstanding that the legal basis on which that case rested had long since been discarded.[44] It is, therefore, the authority for the proposition that methods of treatment of animals were not patentable. The PAT in *United States Rubber Company's Application* reviewed some of the authorities and concluded that it would 'be difficult to say that on no reasonable view could the treatment of an animal be regarded as a manner of manufacture'.[45] Curiously, when discussing *C & W's Application*, the Examining Officer used the phrase *treatment* of animals; however, earlier in his judgment he had referred to methods of *medical treatment* of animals.[46] This case only confuses the issue of the appropriate scope of the exception as it excluded both 'treatments' and 'methods of medical treatment' of animals in different parts of the judgment.[47] In any event, the application was refused because there was no limitation of the subject matter covered by the patent but the PAT, nonetheless, pointed out that the patent might proceed to grant if the claims excluded the treatment of human beings. Therefore, the dicta concerning the patentability or otherwise of methods of medical treatment of animals were strictly *obiter*.

The decisions considered so far did not engage in any detailed examination why methods of medical treatment of animals were not patentable. In *Canterbury Agricultural College's Application*, there was no discussion of the merits or demerits of such an approach. More significantly, the exclusion was not based on any applicable legal principle. It is clear from the

---

[43] *N V Phillips' Gloelampenfabrieken's Application* (1954) 71 RPC 192 (PAT). It was held in that case that where one can isolate the alleged invention as a modification of the conditions under which the natural phenomena will pursue their inevitable course, it would be a misuse of language to hold that it discloses a manner of manufacture.

[44] *Schering A G's Application*, at 341.

[45] [1964] RPC 104, 107.

[46] Ibid.

[47] *Swift and Company's Application* [1961] RPC 129 (PAT) where the claim for a tenderising process where the enzyme is injected into the live animal to achieve the desired result was rejected.

judgment that the exclusion was derived solely from a blind acceptance that methods of treatment were excluded by the Patent Office and should, therefore, be excluded as a matter of law. This view was again accepted without hesitation in *Swift & Company's Application*[48] where the claim was for a method for tenderising meat, which included the injection of an enzyme into the live animal that was then distributed by the animal's heart and vascular system. The PAT simply held that the process in question was not a manner of manufacture.[49] The only reasoning employed may be gleaned from the rejection of the two grounds which had been accepted by the New Zealand courts for claims similar to those considered by the PAT. There, the method of treatment was held patentable because, first, the end result was vendible and, secondly, it had some economic significance.[50] Although important, the commercial value of the product should not determine the question of patentability.

On appeal, the Court of Appeal in *Swift & Company's Application* was hesitant to review the decision of the PAT on the question of patentability.[51] It accepted that the proper role of the Comptroller was to refuse applications, which, on no reasonable view, could it be said fell within the ambit of the Patents Act 1949. Lord Parker C.J. observed that 'having regard to the fully reasoned decisions of the High Court of Australia[52] and New Zealand[53] it was desirous to have a homogenous development of patent law. This meant that there was an error of law on the record'.[54] This raises the question as to the applicability of those two decisions to the future development of the law in this area. The Lord Chief Justice, regrettably, did not engage in any detailed discussion of the relevant principles.[55] The decision is fact specific and, therefore, cannot be held as deciding that methods of treatment for animals were patentable.

C THE RATIONALE FOR THE EXCLUSION

1 Introduction

An understanding of the *raison d' etre* of any legal doctrine is necessary for its consistent application. This is even more essential for the exclusions that

48 [1961] RPC 129.
49 Ibid, at 134.
50 Ibid.
51 *Swift and Company's Application* [1962] RPC 37 (QB).
52 *NRDC's Application* [1961] RPC 134.
53 *Swift and Company's Application* [1961] RPC 147 (NZCA).
54 *Swift and Company's Application* (QB), at 47.
55 *United States Rubber Application*, at 105.

are not found in the Patents Act 1977 (the 1977 Act) itself. In the cases that preceded the 1977 Act, there was hardly any discussion of the underlying arguments that may be made in favour of or against patent protection for methods of medical treatment. Without this framework with which to make this judicial determination of patent protection for methods of medical treatment, the courts merely muddied the waters in determining the rationale for the exclusion. It is submitted that mere articulation without appropriate reasoning was not a rational way to develop this area of the law.

2 A Question of Statutory Interpretation

(a) The statutory regime

In the period before 1977, the standard of patentability had to be derived from section 6 of the Statute of Monopolies which stated that:

> Provided also and be it declared and enacted that any declaration before mentioned shall not extend to any letters patent and grants of privilege, for the term of 14 years or under hereafter to be made of the sole working or making of any manner of new manufacture within this realm to the true and first inventor and inventors of such manufactures which others, at the time of making such letters or grant, shall not use, so as also they be not contrary to law nor mischievous to the state by raising prices of commodities at home or hurt trade or generally inconvenient.

The question was essentially whether a method of medical treatment was a 'manner of new manufacture'. Buttressed to this is the proviso that any such patent shall not be 'contrary to law not mischievous to the state by raising prices of commodities or hurt trade or generally inconvenient'. The courts have, on two occasions, and for two completely different reasons, had resort to the proviso as the basis for excluding methods of medical treatment from patent protection. These will be examined in due course. Long before the courts came to address the question of whether methods of medical treatment were patentable subject matter, they were addressing the meaning and scope of the Statute of Monopolies. It is not necessary, for present purposes, to trace that history and jurisprudence in any depth. However, the meaning that the courts gave to the section could have played a vital role when the question of methods of medical treatment arose for consideration. Consideration shall also be given to the approach in Australia as it had developed to 1977 to the extent that their jurisprudence provides a clearer understanding of the provision and insofar as its judicial decisions have been followed in the United Kingdom.

(b) The rise of the commercial object requirement[56]

The earliest case in relation to patenting methods of medical treatment did not adequately address the issue. The Solicitor-General in *C & W's Application*[57] excluded a claim for extracting lead from persons suffering from lead poisoning on the basis that it could not be used in the making of an object that was of commercial value.[58] The Solicitor-General stated that to be patentable, the invention must be 'a machine or a process that can be used in making something that is of commercial value'[59] which he thought was derived from the proviso to section 6 which stated that 'so as also they be not contrary to the law or nor mischievous to the State, by raising prices of commodities at home, or hurt of trade, or generally inconvenient'. The Solicitor-General had, therefore, derived, though the most literal interpretation possible, a hitherto unknown concept from the then 400-year-old statute and imposed it on UK patent law. As was succinctly stated by the Supreme Court of Israel in *The Wellcome Foundation Ltd v Plantex Ltd*,[60] '[t]he judgment by Lord Buckmaster in the matter of *C & W's Application* (1914) RPC 63 which serves as a cornerstone to the English doctrine of non-patentability of methods of therapeutic treatment of the human body, is based *mainly on a restrictive literal construction of the above definition*'.[61]

If one accepts that the definition of a manner of manufacture must include the making of an object of commercial value, then it would inevitably follow that methods of medical treatment would be excluded from patent protection since they are process patents which do not result in the making of an object. That reasoning will apply to all process patents because they do not result in the production of a tangible product. If, however, it could be shown that the process itself would be commercially viable then the required standard of patentability would have been met.[62] Methods of medical treatment were, therefore, excluded from patent protection on that limited basis and it formed, at that time, the then legal basis for the exclusion. The Solicitor-General thought immorality was irrelevant to the issue at hand and, therefore, it was not surprising that he sought another legal basis for the exclusion. The lack of engagement with the issue

---

56 Used interchangeably with 'vendible product' requirement.

57 The PAT in *GEC's Application* (1942) 60 RPC 1 (PAT), 4 reaffirmed the requirement that the patent must be for a vendible product.

58 *C & W's Application*, at 236.

59 Ibid.

60 [1974] RPC 514.

61 Ibid, at 538 (Kahn J.) (emphasis added).

62 Ibid.

of morality at this time, by the Solicitor-General, and the courts generally, will be considered in more detail below.

C & W's Application was considered by the Australian High Court in *Maeder v Busch*,[63] where Dixon J. had grave concerns about its rationale. He noted that there was a widening conception of manufacture over the years. The issue of whether methods of medical treatment were patentable, although not addressed at length, was considered by the court. It seemingly merely accepted the conclusion in *C & W's Application* but on the basis that methods of medical treatment did not result in 'the production or treatment of some object of mechanical utility so as to reflect a manual art or craft'.[64] Methods of medical treatment, Dixon J. stated, did not produce or aid the production of any article of commerce.[65] He was of the opinion that the patent in question, for forming waves in the human hair, was unpatentable as a method of treating the human body because it would always lack the artificial or mechanical element of an invention.[66] Although doubting the previous rationale for the exclusion as found in the United Kingdom, another was added which only complicated the legal rationale even further.

In *GEC's Application*,[67] Morton J. stated that '[a] method or a process is a manner of manufacture if it (a) results in the production of some vendible product or (b) improves or restores to its former condition a vendible product or (c) has the effect of preserving from deterioration some vendible product to which it is applied'.[68] The term vendible product was defined to include: vendible – 'utility in practical affairs' and product – 'an artificially created state of affairs'. The UK courts, most notably *GEC's Application*, as just observed, accepted without question the reasoning in *C & W's Application* that to be patentable the invention must be a machine or a process which can be used in making something of commercial value and did not apply the reasoning in *Maeder v Busch*. The legal rationale for the exclusion, at this point in both jurisdictions, rested on different approaches to the interpretation of section 6 of the Statute of Monopolies.[69]

---

[63] (1938) 59 CLR 684.
[64] Ibid, at 706.
[65] Ibid.
[66] Ibid, at 706.
[67] (1942) 60 RPC 1.
[68] Ibid.
[69] Pila, in 'Methods of Medical Treatment within Australian and United Kingdom Patents Law' (2001) 24 UNSW LJ 420, makes a similar observation.

(c) The demise of the commercial object requirement

It was not until the decision of the High Court of Australia in *National Research Development Corporation v Commissioner of Patents* ('*NRDC*')[70] that the commercial object requirement enunciated in *C & W's Application*, and applied in *GEC's Application*, saw its demise. The *NRDC* case was particularly important since it enlarged the categories of patentable subject matter because patent law 'has developed and necessarily must develop in a modern society'.[71] The court held that the term 'manner of new manufacture' should not be limited but that '[t]he word "manufacture" finds a place in the present Act, not as a word intended to reduce the question of patentability to a question of verbal interpretation, but simply as the general title found in the Statute of Monopolies for the whole category under which all grants of patents which may be made in accordance with the developed principles of patent law are to be subsumed'.[72]

The High Court of Australia in *NRDC* stated that in determining patentability under Australian law, and presumably UK law, the essential question that should always be asked was: 'Is this a proper subject of the letters patent according to the principles which have been developed for the application of s 6 of the Statute of Monopolies?'[73] The court, therefore, placed much emphasis on the spirit of the Statute.[74] Also, in answering the question whether an invention was a 'manner of manufacture' the court held that the invention must be 'a mode or manner of achieving an end result which is an artificially created state of affairs of utility in the field of economic endeavour'.[75] The court also stated that the 'process ... must be one that offers some advantage which is material, in the sense that the process belongs to a useful art as distinct from a fine art ... that its value to the country is in the field of economic endeavour'.[76]

Therefore, to be patentable, it was not essential that the use of the process should produce or improve a vendible product – it was sufficient that it had some commercial application including being part of the useful arts and some field of economic endeavour. This reasoning signalled the death knell of both previous legal justifications for the exclusion of methods of medical treatment by: (a) explicitly rejecting the vendible product requirement;

---

70 (1959) 102 CLR 252.

71 Ibid, at 277.

72 Ibid, at 269.

73 Ibid.

74 J. Pila, 'Methods of Medical Treatment within Australian and United Kingdom Patents Law' (2001) 24 UNSW LJ 420, 433.

75 (1959) 102 CLR 252 at 269.

76 Ibid, at 275.

and (b) accepting a test for patentability that was wider than the 'artificial or mechanical element' of the invention. The court, after an excellent theorising about the nature of patent protection under the Statute of Monopolies, stated that '[t]he exclusion for methods of surgery and other processes for treating the human body may well lie outside the concept of invention because the whole subject matter is conceived as essentially non-economic'.[77] At this juncture, the test for general patentability was reformulated by the court, but, in the process, it rejected medical procedure patents on the basis that they were essentially non-economic – a conclusion which seems at odds with the commercial reality of the practice of medicine.[78] What sphere do medical procedures form part of? Do physicians/surgeons not charge patients for the treatments that they deliver? Is this any less economic than other inventive areas? These questions were never answered by the court.

The PAT in *Schering A G's Application* rejected the learning in *C & W's Application*, and applied the reasoning in *NRDC*, stating that to be patentable it was *not* necessary for a process to result in the making of an object of value or be a process adapted to that end.[79] This undermined the legal logic of *C & W's Application* and meant that the issue of whether methods of medical treatment were patentable in the United Kingdom was no longer based on a questionable method of statutory interpretation. The commercial value of an invention would be important to determine whether the patentee would be able to receive an adequate return on her investment, but, as a substantive rule of law, it would have *prevented* the patenting of worthwhile inventions. However useful the test proved in the examination of patents, it could not now be a substitute for detailed scrutiny of the processing steps where the monopoly claimed made it necessary for them to be specified in some detail.[80] The acceptance of the reasoning in *NRDC* made it no longer possible for the commercial object requirement to form the basis of the exclusion for methods of medical treatment. The public policy justification – which had only just raised its ugly head – for the exclusion for methods of medical treatment that were considered in this case will be examined in more detail below.

One significant aspect of *Schering A G's Application* was that the economic rationale of the patent system was made a specific factor to be taken into consideration when determining the patentability of such inventions

---

[77] Ibid.

[78] A similar point is made by Pila, in 'Methods of Medical Treatment within Australian and United Kingdom Patents Law' (2001) 24 UNSW LJ 420.

[79] *Schering A G's Application* at 341.

[80] Ibid.

because of the considerable research effort that was put into the development of methods of medical treatment.[81] The reward function was made an important consideration for patents and, in particular, patents for methods of treatment. The courts had previously ignored such economic considerations and sometimes only made passing reference to it. For example, Whitford J. in *Schering A G's Application* stated that it was 'difficult to see any logical justification for the practice in relation to the processes for medical treatment, if the object of the system is in truth to give hope of a reward to people whose research and industry results in valuable products or processes'.[82] *Schering A G's Application*, therefore, embraced the classical theory of patent law, which saw the patent grant as a reward to inventors, indicating that there was some justification *for* patenting methods of medical treatment. However, the exact nature of that justification was not expanded upon. The court recognised that it was faced with a dilemma (between the patentability of drug therapies and the unpatentability of medical procedures) but was content to accept that the 1919 and 1949 Patents Act proceeded on the assumption that methods of medical treatment were outside the scope of patent law and, therefore, it should remain so.[83]

(d) Biological and biotechnological subject matter

After the demise of the commercial object requirement in *NRDC*, there was still some uncertainty in the decisions that followed. The PAT then borrowed heavily from the learning in cases that considered the patentability of biotechnological inventions and also the ambit of section 6 of the Statute of Monopolies. In *London Rubber Industries Ltd's Patent*,[84] the PAT, applying its understanding of the learning in *NRDC*, stated that the patent in question, which was for a method of birth control involving taking certain hormonal drugs at a specific time and in a specific order, was not patentable because 'it cannot be asserted with any reality that the human response to the ingredients so administered falls within any category of the useful arts'.[85] The usefulness or otherwise of the invention was dependent on the impact on the individual treated which itself was not, in the PAT's opinion, part of the useful arts. This reasoning was not elaborated further and there was no explanation why such responses were not part of the useful arts. Having failed to adequately address this issue, the PAT then

---

81 Ibid, at 339.
82 Ibid, at 343 (emphasis added).
83 Ibid.
84 (1968) RPC 31.
85 Ibid, at 34–35.

relied on its interpretation of the *NRDC* case to hold that methods of medical treatment were not patentable because 'the object is not to produce or aid in the production of any article of commerce'.[86] This uncertainty in the legal rationale for the exclusion of methods of medical treatment drove the courts to proffer other rationales for its exclusion from patent protection.

It was, therefore, no surprise that the courts were able to look towards the definition of 'new manner of manufacture' as it had been and was developing in relation to micro-organisms and other life forms. Most notably was the *NRDC* case where the High Court of Australia held that such biological subject matter would be the subject of patent protection if the technical invention of the claimed invention resulted in an artificial state of affairs which does not itself occur in nature. Although in *NRDC* it was expressly stated that methods of medical treatment 'may well lie outside the concept of invention because the whole subject matter is conceived as essentially non-economic', the courts and PAT did not embrace that reasoning. However, they relied on the other 'artificial' invention requirement, first articulated by Dixon J. in *Maeder v Busch*. This requirement was applied in *Neva Corporation's Application*[87] where the PAT refused a claim for a device which created a sound that had the physiological effects of inducing, in humans and animals, a state of reduced awareness and loss of pain and sensibility and held that it did not relate to a method of medical treatment. Although the application was, as Lloyd-Jacob J stated, 'framed in the form of a method claim and identifying the artificially contrived effect by this new manufacture and treatment may be observed', it was, nonetheless, held to be an excluded method of medical treatment.[88] The application was refused because it was thought that it would not attract a finding of validity based on the functions of the Comptroller of Patents and the PAT as enunciated in *Swift's Application*. The claimed subject matter, it was held, was 'an essay in the fine and not the applied arts'.[89] In the same way that the

---

86 Ibid.

87 [1968] RPC 481.

88 Ibid, at 486, citing *C & W's Application*.

89 *Neva Corporation's Application* at 485. The courts had now accepted that methods of medical treatment were not patentable subject matter. However, the PAT in *Palmer's Application* claimed that the alleged invention was a 'new mode of employing practically a person's art and skill' (at 601). The claim was for a painful non-lethal chemical irritant used as a defence against a human attacker. This reasoning would remove any barrier to patentability of methods of medical treatment if they were a new application of a person's art and skill. The PAT did not mean to state a test for patentability so wide that it would have undermined the already shaky foundation of the exception for methods of medical treatment.

human response to the sound was not considered a manner of new manufacture, so too in *London Rubber Industries Ltd's Application*, where the claim was in respect of a contraceptive method, the PAT held that it cannot be said that the 'human response to the ingredients so administered falls within any category of useful arts'.[90]

At about the same time as the *NRDC* decision, the English courts were already rejecting claims to the grant of a patent for the production of mutant strains of micro-organisms by electrical treatment on the basis that it was not a manner of new manufacture.[91] In *ex parte Swift & Co*,[92] the PAT held that although the claimed invention, relating to the modification of a known process of tenderising meat by the injection of an enzyme solution after death, produced a vendible end product, that alone was not sufficient to satisfy the requirements of a 'manner of manufacture'.[93] It was stated that the question, whether the end result was an artificial product having economic significance, must also be considered, but the reference to result alone cannot be exhaustive of the proper inquiry because many artificial products of economic significance were outside the scope of patent jurisprudence.[94]

According to the PAT, '[t]he real question must remain: Are the steps or stages which constitute the method artificial (in the sense of man-controlled) and operative in a useful art?'[95] The PAT held that the crucial step, the employment of the heart and vascular system of a living animal, was not patentable. On appeal to the High Court, Lord Parker C.J. observed that that conclusion was in conflict with the principle stated and the result in the *NRDC* case.[96] The court held that, in the absence of any English authority on the question, the PAT could not reasonably have held that there was no reasonable doubt as to the invention in question not being a manner of manufacture, contrary to the well-reasoned decision of the High Court of Australia and New Zealand.[97] The PAT's decision was therefore reversed. Although Lord Parker CJ did not directly engage the

---

Palmer's Application, it may be argued, accepted that the question of patenting methods of medical treatment was one of statutory interpretation albeit on different grounds than had been previously been accepted. On a remittal, the TBA accepted the application claim in a similar form to that considered.

90 [1968] RPC 31, 35.

91 *G E C's Application* [1961] RPC 21.

92 [1961] RPC 131.

93 Ibid, at 132.

94 Ibid, at 133.

95 Ibid.

96 *Ex parte Swift & Co* [1962] 1 All ER 610, 615.

97 Ibid, at 618.

question, there is an implicit acceptance that the requirement that the end result should be an artificial product having economic significance was good law.

These cases, most notably the *NRDC* decision, reshaped the jurisprudence and thinking of the term 'manner of manufacture' and, in the process, swept away traditional notions about the scope of the statute once accepted in *C & W Ltd's Application*. This meant that, for the first time, the previous legal basis was decisively rejected but at the same time it created a vacuum in the rationale for the exclusion, allowing the court to state, by a side-wind, that the exclusion for methods of medical treatment was essentially non-economic.

3 Patent Office Practice

The demise of the legal reasoning in *C & W's Application* meant that some other justification had to be found. Although the Solicitor-General in C & *W's Application* had based his decision on a dubious interpretation of section 6 of The Statute of Monopolies, he also observed that the Patent Office had refused the alleged invention on the basis that it was a method of medical treatment and that this was sound.[98] The Solicitor-General in *C & W's Application* had hinted that patents for methods of medical treatment for animals could be allowed. However, claims directed to the administering of mixtures to sheep to improve their wool yield were rejected in *Canterbury Agricultural College's Application*. The Examining Officer in that case stated that the remarks made in *C & W's Application* were *obiter*, and that it was the established practice of the Patent Office to refuse the grant of patents for processes covering the treatment of animals.[99] This exclusion, the Examining Officer emphasised, operated irrespective of whether the purpose was to increase their commercial value, to cure an illness or to alter or stimulate a product of their metabolism.[100] The Examining Officer in *Canterbury Agricultural College's Application* was not prepared to alter 'the practice' that had obtained for many years of not granting patents for processes covering merely the treatment of animals, except on the strongest possible grounds,[101] pointing out that such a practice had not been seriously challenged.[102] Although this statement was made in a case that dealt with methods of medical treatment for animals, it

---

98 *C & W's Application*, at 236.
99 *Canterbury College Agricultural College's Application*, at 86.
100 Ibid.
101 Ibid, at 87.
102 Ibid, at 86.

would not be an overstatement to argue that it could similarly form the basis for the exclusion of patents for methods of medical treatment of humans.

It was left to *Schering A G's Application*,[103] where the claim was for a method of contraception using certain pills, to put the question beyond doubt. Whitford J. observed that the *practice* of excluding methods of medical treatment from patent protection was well established and that this was either on the basis that 'such processes have never qualified as inventions, as "manner of new manufacture" within section 6 of the Statute of Monopolies, or on the basis that there is some other good ground for refusal'.[104] His Honour quoted the Solicitor-General in *C & W's Application*, stating that the Solicitor-General had merely endorsed what appeared to have been represented to him as being the Patent Office view on that case.[105] It was argued that *C & W's Application* did not establish that that was the Patent Office practice at the date; neither did it form the basis of the Solicitor-General's decision, nor were there any reasons to support the view that even at the date of the case it was a valid ground for refusal.[106] These statements do not assist in determining the rationale of the exclusion but showed that the courts were questioning the origins and legitimacy of Patent Office practice as the basis for the exclusion of methods of medical treatment from patent protection. Since *United States Rubber Company's Application*,[107] however, the courts accepted without question that Patent Office practice should be determinative of the issue. If the basis of the exclusion in English law was not a question of statutory interpretation, given the demise of the commercial object requirement in *C & W's Application*, and *C & W's Application* only indicated the Patent Office practice, what then was the basis for the exclusion?

The Court of Appeal considered this question in *The Upjohn Company (Robert's) Application*.[108] The court was at pains to point out that it was not asked to decide whether the method of treatment in question was patentable but to determine whether it was so obvious that it was not so

---

103 The court went on to point out that a contraceptive method was not a method of medical treatment.

104 *Schering A G's Application*, at 340. Lloyd-Jacob J. had accepted that the Patent Office had excluded methods of medical treatment for over 50 years citing *United States Rubber Company's Application* and *London Rubber Industries Limited's Patent*.

105 *Schering A G's Application*, at 341.

106 Ibid, at 341–342.

107 *United States Rubber Company's Application* [1964] RPC 104.

108 [1977] RPC 94 (CA).

capable, justifying its rejection by the Comptroller.[109] The claim included the use of a compound to reduce gastric secretion. Russel L.J., writing for the Court of Appeal, observed that the deliberations of the various committees and commissions that had considered revisions of patent law over the years had not resulted in a change in the view that methods of medical treatment were outside the scope of patent law.[110] Moreover, the court reasoned that this provided powerful support for the conclusion that the universally held view (that methods of medical treatment were not patentable) was correct in law.[111] A settled view of the law should not form the legal basis of the exclusion of methods of medical treatment from patent protection unless it is based on sound legal principle or policy. Without engaging in any discussion of the merits of the exception, the Court of Appeal asserted that it was '*well established* that a method of treatment of a human ailment with a known substance is not capable of being an invention under the statute ... '[112] The foundation for the justification still remained shrouded in mystery.

The cases that excluded methods of medical treatment from patent protection on the basis of Patent Office practice did not attempt to investigate or question why the Patent Office had that practice. One hint of the extent that this was the case can be gleaned from the statement made above in *Canterbury Agricultural College's Application* where it was stated that the practice had obtained for many years and that it was not ever seriously challenged. However, this takes us no further in explaining why the Patent Office refused to grant such patents and, as was stated in *Schering A G's Application*, '[t]here are no reasons given to support the view that even at the date of that case that [Patent Office practice] was a valid ground for refusal'.[113]

The grant of a patent by the Patent Office is distinct from its validity. Before 1800 the procedure for obtaining a patent in the United Kingdom was a simple one. However, by an Act in 1883 '[t]he office of Comptroller General of Patents and a staff of patent examiners were brought into being ... to carry out a limited form of examination; mainly to ensure that the specification described the invention properly, but without any investigation into novelty'.[114] The Patents Act of 1902 allowed a limited investigation

---

109 Ibid, at 96.

110 Ibid.

111 Ibid.

112 Ibid, at 98 (emphasis added).

113 *Schering A G's Application*, at 342.

114 The United Kingdom Intellectual Property Office Website, The Tudors and Stuarts.

into the novelty of the invention before a patent was granted.[115] This meant that patents that were refused by the patent offices were not based on the validity of the invention.

If the Patent Office practice referred to by the Solicitor-General in *C & W's Application* was that relating to the decisions of Examiners on application for patents for methods of medical treatment, then one needs to appreciate the role of the Examiners and the PAT within the general scheme of the Patents Acts in the period before 1977. In *ex parte Swift & Co*, it was stated that the function of the Comptroller-General and the PAT under section 6 of the Patents Act 1949 (the 1949 Act) was not only to decide whether an alleged new manner of manufacture is actually patentable, but also to refuse applications to proceed, which on no reasonable view could be said to be within the ambit of the Act.[116] Lord Parker C.J., speaking for a unanimous three member High Court, stated that must be the position when the scheme of the legislation is looked at as a whole and that it 'is for the High Court to determine actual patentability'.[117] The test was whether it was possible to say beyond a reasonable doubt that the process in question fell outside the ambit of the Act.[118] In *Virginia-Carolina Chemical Corporation's Application*[119] it was stated that since section 32(1)(d) of the 1949 Act 'permits the objection of no manner of manufacture to be raised in revocation proceedings, refusal [by the comptroller-general and the Patents Appeal Tribunal] is only appropriate in cases where a monopoly claim is plainly without justification'.[120]

Similarly, in the post-1977 period, patents must satisfy the stringent requirements of the 1977 Act for it to be patentable. However, this is not conclusive of the patent's validity, since there is the possibility that the patent may be revoked if it is not a patentable invention (1977 Act, s. 72(1)) or subject to infringement proceedings (1977 Act, s. 60). If this happens the patent is treated as not having ever been granted.

---

115 Ibid, The eighteenth and nineteenth centuries.
116 [1962] 1 All ER 610, 616–617.
117 Ibid, at 616.
118 *Re Cementation Co Ltd* (1945) 62 RPC 151, 153.
119 [1958] RPC 35, 37.
120 Ibid.

4 Ethical and Public Policy Grounds

(a) Morality: irrelevant?

The Solicitor-General in *C & W's Application* hastily accepted that the 'question of humanity' ought not to affect the decision in that case.[121] He pointed out that 'the medical profession do all in their power to discourage members of their body from obtaining protection for any discovery that has for its object the alleviation of human suffering' and that 'it is impossible to speak too highly of such conduct'.[122] However, the Solicitor-General thought that such factors were *irrelevant* in arriving at a conclusion upon the terms of the section of an Act of Parliament and that he had to exclude such considerations from his mind.[123] The ethical considerations and the concerns of the medical profession were not factors to be taken into account in determining the patentability or otherwise of methods of medical treatment. The Solicitor-General did not explain why it was impossible to speak highly of the 'conduct' of physicians patenting medical procedures. Was it ethically wrong to engage in such conduct? Or, was this conduct simply contrary to the medical profession's code of ethics? Such important and searching questions were not answered or even considered in *C & W's Application*.

This approach is certainly consistent with *A & H's Application* where the Assistant Comptroller refused to consider the relevance of moral considerations when determining patentability.[124] The comptroller had the power to 'refuse to grant a patent for an invention … of which the use would, in his opinion, be contrary to law or *morality*'.[125] Understandably, the Solicitor-General did not have regard to that provision since the question of morality, he thought, was not defined to include such ethical considerations. Whether morality had any role to play in patenting methods of medical treatment was the only issue for consideration in *A & H's Application*.[126] The question was whether the use of the contraceptive device was 'contrary to … morality' according to section 75 of the Patents and Designs Act 1907. The Solicitor-General avoided the issue, stating that he would 'express no opinion as to whether the use of these articles is consistent with morality'.[127] The Solicitor-General refused the claim on the

121 *C & W's Application*, at 236.
122 Ibid.
123 Ibid.
124 (1927) 44 RPC 298.
125 The Patent and Designs Act 1907, s. 75 (emphasis added).
126 (1927) 44 RPC 298.
127 Ibid.

basis that 'these are not articles for which … the Crown can be expected to exercise its discretion by way of granting a patent'.[128] This reasoning, however, does not explain *why* the Crown would not exercise its discretion in favour of granting the patent.

The rejection of any role for morality in determining whether patent protection should be granted for methods of medical treatment meant that yet another rationale had to be found. As explained above, the Solicitor-General in *C & W's Application* was able to invent the commercial product requirement as the legal justification for excluding methods of medical treatment from patent protection. This reasoning has been discredited and the practice of the Patent Office was expressly not relied on by the Solicitor-General. By the time *Schering A G's Application* was decided in 1971, *C & W's Application* was no longer the authority for the unpatentability of methods of medical treatment and could simply be confined to legal history.

(b) Morality: an emerging concept

In *Schering A G's Application*, the PAT, applying the Australian High Court decision of *NRDC*, rejected the commercial object requirement articulated in *C & W's Application*. The tribunal then buttressed this reasoning by stating that it 'was plainly arguable, upon *ethical* grounds, that there should be no patent protection in the medical field at all'.[129] This might have been a necessary step since the rejection of the commercial object requirement undermined the legal basis for the exclusion of methods of medical treatment in UK law and, since the PAT did not endorse the view expressed in *NRDC*, that methods of medical treatment are essentially non-economic, it was necessary to find some other basis for the exclusion. The reference to morality is significant as it is the first judicial acceptance that patents in the medical field, especially patents for methods of medical treatment, raise ethical and moral objections. The cases that followed *Schering A G's Application* made no attempt to elaborate on the ethical or public policy justifications for the exclusion of methods of medical treatment from patent protection. Any unwarrantable exploitation in the medical field, it was argued, was to be remedied by using compulsory licensing provisions found in section 41 of the 1949 Act.[130]

The distinction between products and substances used in the medical field, and methods of medical treatment, was made in *Schering A G's*

---

[128] Ibid.
[129] *Schering A G's Application*, at 340.
[130] Ibid.

Application. It was clear that patents could be granted for pharmaceutical products which meant that different public policy issues might be the reason for the distinction between the two. The Solicitor-General in *C & W's Application* thought that considerations of humanity and the concerns of the medical profession were irrelevant when determining the patentability of medical procedures. The patentability of pharmaceutical products, the PAT reasoned, was the result of the compulsory licensing provisions found in the 1949 Act which applied to substances or devices used in the production of medicine.[131] Presumably, there was no need to include methods of medical treatment because they were considered outside the scope of patent protection.[132]

In *Schering A G's Application*, it was pointed out that on a 'consideration of the terms of the statute ... claims to processes for medical treatment must be considered as excluded from the scope of the Act and the practice of the [Patent] Office'.[133] This represents a volte-face in the thinking of the PAT. Having pointed out that *C & W's Application* only indicated Patent Office practice,[134] and having rejected the *legal* basis on which that decision stood, it was surprising that the PAT came to that conclusion. It simply opined that '*whatever* ... the origin of the exclusion may be, in so far as it relates to processes of medical treatment of human beings to cure or prevent disease, it must be considered as *sound*'.[135] No reasoning was provided to justify that statement which showed that the court was not concerned in determining the *origins* of the exclusion because it thought the exclusion was sufficiently 'sound'. What was sound about the exclusion? Arguably, the PAT was referring back to the comment it had made earlier that there were strong ethical grounds for the exclusion of methods of medical treatment from patent protection. One cannot but reiterate the statement of the PAT that while the denial of patents for methods of medical treatment had been considered axiomatic,[136] the demise of the need for production of a commercial object made the logic of the exception unclear.

Schering A G's Application brought us only one step closer to determining the exact rationale for the exception. It confirmed that the reward

---

[131] Ibid.

[132] The Court of Appeal resorted to similar reasoning in *The Upjohn Company (Robert's) Application* [1977] RPC 94 (CA), 96–97.

[133] *Schering A G's Application*, at 344.

[134] His Lordship also indicated that the practice of refusing patents for methods of medical treatment was over 50 years old.

[135] *Schering A G's Application*, at 344 (emphasis added).

[136] Ibid, at 342.

function has an important role to play in determining patentability and, more specifically, it confirmed that patents for methods of medical treatment were not outside the scope of this economic analysis. It had, for the first time, recognised that ethical considerations were central to the question of patenting methods of medical treatment. There was not, however, any in-depth discussion of the nature of the ethical issues raised by medical procedure patents. This was surprising since the previous legal rationale – the commercial object requirement – was rejected. There was only a suggestion that this *might* be the rationale; not that it actually *was*. *Schering A G's Application* came much closer to accepting that morality had some role to play in the patenting of medical procedures than did *C & W's Application* where the Solicitor-General accepted that it had no role to play whatsoever. However, *Schering A G's Application* had, therefore, failed to offer a definitive answer to the question of the rationale for the exception and, in attempting to do so, it created more uncertainty. We were simply told that, based on the terms of the statute, methods of medical treatment must be considered as excluded without any discussion of the proper role and weight of any of the ethical considerations.

(c) Morality: one step closer to legal justification

Graham and Whitford JJ, who incidentally also decided *Schering A G's Application*, attempted to make sense of the exclusion of methods of medical treatment in *Eli Lilly & Company's Application*.[137] They accepted that it was legitimate to consider the proviso to section 6 of the Statute of Monopolies which prohibits inventions that are contrary to law or mischievous. However, it was made clear that one cannot outline in advance the inventions that were excluded by reason of the proviso.[138] It was then stated that '[t]he proviso at the end of the section can no more be ignored than can the earlier part of the section, and we are forced within the framework of this existing legislation to do the best we can in every case where the question of patentability arises'.[139] Although the court stated that it was legitimate to consider the proviso to section 6 it was not specifically applied to methods of medical treatment. The head note of the case does not suggest that the proviso to section 6 was the basis of the PAT's decision, contrary to statements in *Bristol-Myers Squibb v FH Faulding & Co*[140] and *Pfizer Inc v Commissioner of Patents*[141] that it formed that *ratio* of that

137 [1975] RPC 438 (PAT).

138 *Eli Lilly & Company's Application* [1975] RPC 438 (PAT), 444–445.

139 Ibid, at 445.

140 [2000] FCA 316 at [117].

141 [2004] NZCA 104 at [19].

decision. Had that been the case, it would have signalled a positive development in the law relating to patentability of methods of medical treatment by providing, for the first time, an explicit statutory basis for morality as the justification for the exclusion. However, later English courts did not embrace this as the best possible explanation for the exception. The PAT reiterated that the exception had long been established and that the 'reasons for such an exclusion *appear* to us to be based in *ethics* rather than *logic*'.[142] If, as the PAT suggests, the exclusion *appears* to be based in ethics rather than logic, then they must take a further step and make ethical considerations *the* basis for the exclusion. They must then articulate what those ethical considerations are to ensure a more coherent application of the exclusion.

This was, therefore, a lost opportunity to provide a moral juridical basis for the exclusion of methods of medical treatment from patent protection. The PAT simply observed that if there were to be any change of policy, which was thought sensible, it should 'be effectuated by legislation rather than by interpretation'.[143] The PAT must have been aware of the recommendations of the Banks Committee and the provisions of the then recently adopted European Patent Convention of 1973. The courts merely suggested that ethics could be a possible basis without explaining how this was so. It would have been much simpler for them to clearly indicate the role of ethical considerations in patenting methods of medical treatment.

(d) Morality: the legal justification

It was not until the decision of the High Court of Australia in *Joos v Commissioner of Patents*[144] that morality was explicitly recognised as the legal justification for the exclusion of methods of medical treatment from patent protection. The patent in issue was a claim for a cosmetic method of strengthening hair and nails. The claim was a patentable invention because it satisfied the test of being 'essentially economic' as articulated by the High Court of Australia in *NRDC*. The court went on to consider, *obiter*, whether methods of medical treatment were patentable. Barwick C.J. explained that methods of medical treatment were 'not the proper subject matter for the grant of a monopoly under the [Patent] Act' and that it was not necessary to 'discover and express its basis in law'.[145] He continued that

---

[142] *Eli Lilly & Company's Application*, at 445 (emphasis added).

[143] Ibid. The Court of Appeal in *The Upjohn Company's Application* thought that if the law in this regard should be changed it must be for the legislature to do so (at 98).

[144] (1972) 126 CLR 611.

[145] Ibid, at 619.

if he had to decide the question of whether patent protection should be provided for methods of medical treatment he would have thought that they were excluded by virtue of the phrase 'generally inconvenient', on public policy grounds, in the proviso to section 6 of the Statute of Monopolies.[146]

The link that was made between the exclusion of methods of medical treatment and morality in *Schering A G's Application* and the possibility that the term 'generally inconvenient' had any relevance to the exclusion of methods of medical treatment accepted in *Eli Lilly & Company's Application* was made explicit, albeit *obiter*, in *Joos v Commissioner of Patents*. It is surprising that *Eli Lilly & Company's Application* did not refer to *Joos v Commissioner of Patents* since it was decided two years after the decision in *Joos v Commissioner of Patents*. It is even more surprising that Whitford J., who decided *The Upjohn Company (Robert's) Application* at the PAT in rejecting the claim for a method of reducing gastric secretion in mammals by the systematic administration of certain compounds, did not expand on the possible marriage of the exclusion of methods of medical treatment and the proviso to section 6 of the Statute of Monopolies he had hinted at in *Eli Lilly & Company's Application*. On appeal to the Court of Appeal, the issue was not considered.[147] Although *Joos v Commissioner of Patents* was referred to in the decision of the Court of Appeal, it was remarkable that the legal basis for the exclusion derived from the term 'generally inconvenient' in the proviso was not mentioned. In light of this, Lockhart J in *Anaesthetic Supplies Property Limited v Rescare Limited*[148] stated that '[t]he English cases, particularly *Schering*, *Eli-Lilly* and *Upjohn*, do not provide a satisfactory basis on which to halt the development of the law relating to patentability and processes for medical treatment'.[149] If these cases were based on an explicit acceptance that the proviso to section 6 excluded methods of medical treatment from patent protection, they would have been more of an obstacle for Lockhart J. and he would not have dismissed them as summarily as he did.

The UK courts had not explicitly accepted ethics as the legal justification of the exclusion of methods of medical treatment from patent protection

---

146 Ibid, at 622.

147 *The Upjohn Company (Robert's) Application*, at 96.

148 (1994) 50 FCR 1.

149 Ibid, at [74]. An almost identical statement can be found in the judgment of Davison CJ, at first instance, in the case of *Wellcome Foundation Ltd v Commissioner of Patents* [1979] 2 NZLR 591 where he stated that '[t]he English cases – *Schering*, *Eli Lilly* and *Upjohn* do not provide a satisfactory basis on which to halt the development of the law relating to patentability of process for medical treatment' (at 621).

but increasingly recognised that it had some role to play. There was no attempt to articulate exactly the precise nature of the public policy considerations that underlie the exclusion of methods of medical treatment from patent protection. It is ironic that the only decision where the precise nature of the ethical consideration was delineated was *C & W's Application* which eschewed any reliance on morality or ethics. There, the Solicitor-General stated that 'the medical profession do all in their power to discourage members of their body from obtaining protection for any discovery that has for its object the alleviation of human suffering' and that 'it is impossible to speak too highly of such conduct'. Presumably, the Solicitor-General had in mind the medical profession's code of ethics which stipulates against patenting medical procedures.

(e) Morality: necessary or a hindrance?

Whether taking morality into account in determining patentability was appropriate will now be examined since the recognition of public policy as the basis for denying patentability has far-reaching implications, not only in the context of medical treatments, but all subject matter. In the context of public policy and ethics, the courts are not usually the place where such questions are resolved, and have neither the resources nor expertise to comprehensively examine all the arguments (especially the social and economic ones) that are made either way for patenting methods of medical treatment. Thus, arguably, such decisions should sensibly be left to Parliament.

If morality is to be accommodated by virtue of the proviso of section 6 of the Statute of Monopolies, it would give the Patent Office or the courts sufficient armoury to prevent the patenting of inventions that would be contrary to morality. It has been argued that such questions should not be dealt with by patent examiners and that patent law should be morally neutral.[150] Given the wide scope of the definition of patentable inventions, the exclusion based on morality should be narrowly construed, or, in other words, 'the power to refuse patents on the grounds of morality or public policy may need to be used cautiously'.[151] The issue of morality, it may be argued, is too broad a test to be used to determine whether or not a patent should be granted on an invention. The issue of morality may be better recast if it referred to the publication or the exploitation of the invention that would offend morality.

Where morality is a ground for refusing a patent, as is the case under Article 53(a) of the European Patent Convention (EPC), which excludes

[150] Cornish, Llewelyn and Aplin, *Intellectual Property*, p. 228.
[151] Ibid.

the patenting of inventions, the publication or exploitation of which would be contrary to '*ordre public*' or morality, it has been stated that a balancing exercise of the competing interests is to be undertaken. Therefore, in *HARVARD/Onco-mouse*,[152] where the issue was the patentability of a transgenic non-human mammal, the TBA stated that 'a careful weighing up of the suffering of animals and possible risks to the environment on the one hand and the invention's usefulness to mankind on the other'[153] needed to be carried out to determine whether the exclusion is applicable.

In *HOWARD FLOREY INSTITUTE/Relaxin*,[154] a decision of the TBA, the European Patent Office (EPO) had granted a patent in which claim 1 read as follows: 'A DNA fragment encoding human H2-preprorelaxin, said H2-preprorelaxin having the amino acid sequence set out in Figure 2'. On the issue of whether the grant of a patent for a human gene offends morality or *ordre public*, it was held that morality-based objections to the grant of patents should only occur 'in those very limited cases in which there appears to be an overwhelming consensus that the exploitation or publication of an invention would be immoral'.[155] Similarly, in *PLANT GENETIC SYSTEMS/Plant cells*[156] where the claim was for genetically engineered plants, the TBA held that 'inventions, the exploitation of which is not in conformity with the conventionally accepted standards of conduct pertaining to [the culture inherent in European society and civilization] are to be excluded from patentability as being contrary to morality'.[157] The TBA rejected the arguments against patent protection because it was not convinced that there was sufficient evidence to support the claim that the patent was contrary to morality.

D CONTRACEPTIVE METHODS

1 Introduction

The issue of whether contraceptive methods were methods of medical treatment has been a vexed one. They were initially excluded from the scope

---

152 (T 19/90) [1990] OJ EPO 476.
153 Ibid.
154 (T 272/95) [1995] EPOR 541.
155 Ibid.
156 (T 0356/93) [1995] EPOR 357.
157 Ibid.

of patent protection on dubious grounds.[158] The PAT was uncertain about the status of such methods until *Schering A G's Application*, where it was finally accepted that methods for contraception could not be considered as methods of medical treatment, so were, therefore, not excluded from patent protection. The issue then became a question of whether the pack claims, which contained the contraceptives, were allowable. The courts and PAT, although recognising that contraceptive methods were not methods of medical treatment, indicated that pack claims could be used to evade the exclusion of methods of medical treatment from patent protection.

Pack claims are process claims.[159] They involve the use of the various medicines in a particular way to achieve a given result and usually take the form of specified dosages of medicines or medication taken at various times of the day or at various periods. It may well be the case that the efficacy of a particular medicine is greatly improved by the use of the pack claim. Pack claims are, arguably, a species of treatment regimes for the therapeutic treatment of patients. The issue, broadly defined, was whether such treatment regimes were methods of medical treatment. Although the courts did not articulate the issue in such terms, it is clear that they sanctioned the use of such treatment regimes.

2 Whether a Method of Medical Treatment

The PAT had found itself engaging in legal gymnastics in *London Rubber Industries Limited's Patent*. The claim comprised the daily oral administration of oestrogen during the first part of the menstrual cycle and a progestogen during the second part of the cycle. The invention was for a regime that included taking the hormonal drugs which was only beneficial when taken in the prescribed manner set out in the claims. The question whether the claim was a method of medical treatment was not answered by the PAT.[160] The novelty of the claim, it is suggested, was in the taking of the various drugs sequentially at various times during the menstrual cycle. The

[158] This point was not argued in *A & H's Application* where it was held that the invention was not one that the Crown would exercise its prerogative to grant.

[159] Cf *Wellcome v Commissioner of Patents* (1980) 30 ALR 510 (HCA) 515.

[160] *London Rubber Industries Limited's Patent*, at 35. It made the analogy with apples and pears arguing, that apart from the unusual nature of the hormonal drugs, had those substances been apples and pears it would have been manifestly absurd to claim patent protection for putting them in the same bag.

PAT did not appreciate this and rejected the claim because it did not contain any *specific* directions to ensure the efficient administration of the drug.[161]

Without engaging in a discussion of whether a method of birth control could conceivably be considered a method of medical treatment, the PAT in *London Rubber Industries Limited's Patent* dived into an examination of the cases on methods of medical treatment. It observed that the claim related to a prescription of *medical treatment* to women and that the practice of the Patent Office was to refuse to grant patent for forms of *medical treatment* of the human body.[162] The claims would only be allowed if they excluded the *medical treatment* of humans.[163] Also, the question whether the claims amounted to a method of medical treatment was not argued because of a concession made by the applicant.[164]

The uncertainty was finally settled in *Schering A G's Application* where the PAT accepted that, although it was 'the practice for the past many years to refuse to exercise the royal prerogative to grant patents for inventions for contraceptive products',[165] that could not be a valid basis for refusal in light of section 102(1) of the 1949 Act, which expressly reserved the prerogative. The PAT reminded itself that the exception was *only* for methods of *medical* treatment of humans.[166] It emphasised that it would be 'extravagant to suggest that a contraceptive process could, as a matter of ordinary language, be described as a treatment of disease, and it may be argued whether it can be properly described as "medical" treatment'.[167] This was eminently sensible, as the purpose of contraception is to prevent pregnancy, not to cure or prevent any disease.[168]

3 Pack Claims

Since *Schering A G's Application*, the cases did not revolve around a consideration of whether a contraceptive method was a method of medical treatment. In *Organon Laboratories Ltd's Application*,[169] for example, it was taken for granted that the arrangement of pills on a card, for the prevention

---

161 *London Rubber Industries Limited's Patent*, at 35.
162 Ibid, at 34.
163 Ibid, at 35.
164 Ibid, at 33.
165 *Schering A G's Application*, at 340.
166 Ibid, at 342.
167 Ibid.
168 Ibid.
169 [1970] RPC 574 (PAT).

of conception, was patentable. The issue was whether a claim for the arrangement of a particular number of two types of pills, with instructions containing the dates on which they should be taken, was a new manner of manufacture. The PAT agreed that novelty might lie in the *manner* in which the pack or the cards were *arranged* and that patenting of the pack or the cards may be used to circumvent the unpatentability of new methods of treatment.[170] The novelty would, therefore, reside in the idea of creating an arrangement for that specific new method of treatment.[171] The arrangement was considered novel, although the idea that pills may be usefully arranged for a particular course of treatment was not.[172] However, if a claim did not contain specific instructions that taught the manner in which the pills were to be taken, as opposed to merely containing the product, it would be patentable.[173]

Therefore, patent protection was only available where there was a new method of arranging the pills pursuant to a new method of medical treatment. The patentee, arguably, would not have arranged the pills in that particular order without some knowledge of the new method of treatment. It was accepted that novelty may well lie in the application of that arrangement to that new method of treatment, rather than in the arrangement itself. This meant that the novelty of the pack claim was inextricably linked to the novelty of the method of treatment. It may be that the novelty was conferred *ex post* because one may conceive of a situation where the Z arrangement for X (new method of treatment) was similar to the Z arrangement for Y (old method of treatment). Would novelty not be conferred on the arrangement for X because it was also used for Y? The

---

170 Ibid, at 578.

171 In *L'Oreal's Application* [1970] RPC 565 (PAT) it was held that it was obvious, in light of prior art, to have a pack containing two components for use in a process for the treatment of human hair.

172 The High Court of Australia in *Wellcome v Commissioner of Patents* accepted that 'for there to be novelty in a package claim there must be an interaction between the container and its contents and the writing so that the instructions or directions are novel by virtue of the link with the process. Needless to say, *novelty is not often found in a package claim*' (emphasis added) (at 514).

173 *Ciba-Geigy AG (Durr's) Application* [1977] RPC 83 (Russell LJ). His Lordship stated that 'there seems to us to be *nothing inventive* about parcelling up the known material in any and every convenient package or container having written thereon the information that it can be used for the stated purpose in the stated *loci*. There is no interaction between the container with its contents and the writing thereon. The mere act of writing cannot make the contents of the container a manner of new manufacture. There is *nothing novel* in the mere presentation of information by ordinary writing or printing on a container' (emphasis added) (at 89).

PAT reasoning would suggest that the answer would be no. The novelty in the claim should be the *application* of Z arrangement for that X new method of treatment, irrespective of whether or not it was used before.

This preferred understanding of the issue stands in stark contrast to that accepted in *Organon Laboratories Ltd's Application,* where the TBA pointed out that the 'new method of treatment may give subject matter to a pack or a card of pills suitable for carrying out that method *providing* that there is something novel in the constitution of the pack or the card itself'.[174] It is difficult to appreciate why the *new* method of treatment would give subject matter to the pack when the pack itself *must* also satisfy the standard of novelty. The idea of using a particular arrangement of pills for a new method of medical treatment would be novel because the general public would not have used such an arrangement without the knowledge of the existence of the method of medical treatment. If the arrangement is old and the method of treatment new, the application will fail for want of novelty. It is suggested that there should be no further need to find novelty in the pack itself if the method of treatment is new. The requirement seems to be *inherent* novelty from the pack, itself not sufficient for patent protection and *derivative* novelty, which is only obtained from new methods of treatment.[175]

Whether the procedure involved in taking the pills was a method of medical treatment was not argued and was not an issue in *Organon Laboratories Ltd's Application*. To be patentable, the claim must contain specific instructions to enable the buyer to carry out the claimed invention effectively.[176] In *Dow Corning Corp. (Bennett's) Application*, the applicant discovered that the administration of certain compounds could alter the androgenic capacity in males. However, since the substances were well known, the reasoning in *Organon Laboratories Ltd's Application* was not applicable.[177] The cases in which the issue was considered were remarkably similar. The claims in *London Rubber Industries Limited's Patent* were directed to the timing of the hormonal drugs and to a pack containing the drugs in a specified numerical ratio; in *Organon Laboratories Ltd's Application*, to a package for the sequential taking of the pills; in *Schering A G's Application*, to the administration of the drugs in particular doses to achieve a particular result; and in *Dow Corning Corporation (Bennett's) Application*, to the dosage and method of administration of drugs.

---

174 *Organon Laboratories Ltd's Application*, at 578 (emphasis added).

175 *Blendax-Werke's Application* [1980] RPC 491 (Pat Ct), 502 (Graham J).

176 *Organon Laboratories Ltd's Application*, at 576. Cf. *Dow Corning Corp. (Bennett's) Application* [1974] RPC 235 (PAT).

177 *Dow Corning Corp. (Bennett's) Application*, at 239.

With the exception of *London Rubber Industries Limited's Patent,* none of these claims were rejected for being methods of medical treatment. However, such claims to specific doses of pharmaceutical substances raised issues relating to the novelty of pack claims. One can readily appreciate the novelty of pack claims because they indicate the manner in which the product is to be taken to achieve the desired result. The dosage requirement, however, raises another question altogether. These considerations are important as they beg the question of whether treatment regimes are excluded from patent protection. Patents for pack claims do not intrude on the activities of physicians because they are manufactured by pharmaceutical companies rendering moot some of the ethical objections that are made against patent protection for methods of medical treatment.

4 Setting Limits

The courts, although doubting the logic of the exclusion, felt impotent to change the law and thought it was sensible for Parliament to do so. It was, therefore, inevitable that they would have found some way of limiting the exclusion for methods of medical treatment. Although they accepted that contraceptive methods were not methods of medical treatment, they also made it clear that pack claims could be used to evade the exclusion of methods of medical treatment from patent protection. Graham J. in *Organon Laboratories Ltd's Application* stated that novelty could be conferred on pack claims when it was directed at a new method of treatment.[178]

The claim in *Blendax-Werke's Application* was for the application of two compounds sequentially to human teeth. The PAT was of the opinion that the mere placing of two ingredients, in two separate containers, in one pack, the ingredients being intended to be mixed together before use to produce a known compound, cannot *prima facie* amount to a manner of manufacture.[179] The court observed that the applicants were really trying to secure an extension of the protection that they already had for their process.[180] Accepting that his prior decision in *Organon Laboratories Ltd's Application* was correct, Graham J. observed that it was 'incomprehensible why an inventor who has invented a pack for use in process, which is unpatentable, cannot get a monopoly for the pack of articles which are useful in that process'.[181] This was a second endorsement of the usefulness of pack claims as a means of limiting the exclusion of methods of medical

178 *Organon Laboratories Ltd's Application*, at 576.
179 *Blendax-Werke's Application*, at 503.
180 Ibid.
181 Ibid, at 506.

treatment from patent protection. This reasoning is sound as it appreciates that the claims may be useful for the operation of the process itself and represents a pragmatic view of such claims.

E THE COMMONWEALTH

1 Introduction

The question whether patent protection should be available for methods of medical treatment is still a vexed one in Australia[182] and New Zealand.[183] They both still have the Statute of Monopolies[184] as their starting point for consideration of this question. In Australia the recent decision[185] on the matter has held that methods of medical treatment were patentable subject matter whilst the New Zealand courts have rejected this reasoning and held otherwise.[186] However, the courts in New Zealand have sanctioned the use of Swiss-type claims[187] notwithstanding the warning given by the Enlarged Board of Appeal of the European Patent Office (EBA) in *EISAI/Second medical indication* that its decision was based on the relevant statutory regime in question. An examination of recent cases in these jurisdictions

---

[182] See generally J. Pila, 'Methods of Medical Treatment within Australia and United Kingdom Patents law' (2001) 24 UNSW LJ 420; A. Feros, 'Patentability of Methods of Medical Treatment' [2001] EIPR 79; D. Kell, 'Expanding the Frontier of Patentability of Medical Treatment of the Human Body' [1995] EIPR 202; T.M. Martin, 'New Appellate Decision Clarifies Australian Law Concerning Patentability of Methods of Medical Treatment' (2000) J Pat & Trademark and Off Sco'y 645; P. Loughlan, 'Of Patents and Patients: New Monopolies in Medical Methods' (1995) 6 AIPJ 5.

[183] Y. Cripps, 'The Refusal of Patents for Methods of Medical Treatment: A Preference for Parliamentary Guidance' [1993] EIPR 173; A.W. White, 'Patentability of Medical Treatment *Wellcome Foundation's (Hitching's) Application*' [1980] EIPR 364; T. Syddall, 'Swiss-type Claims held valid in New Zealand' (1996) CIPA 420.

[184] See also *Darcy v Allen* (1602) 77 ER 1260 and J. Pila, 'The Common Law Invention in its Original Form' [2001] IPQ 209.

[185] *Bristol-Myers Squibb Company v FH Faulding & Co. Ltd* (2000) 97 FCR 524 (FCA).

[186] *Wellcome Foundation Ltd v Commissioner of Patents* [1983] NZLR 385 (NZCA).

[187] *Pharmaceutical Management Agency Ltd v Commissioner of Patents* [2000] 2 NZLR 529 (NZCA).

illustrates the continued problems that are faced by countries with such arcane patent laws.[188]

2 The Australian Approach

The Australian courts borrowed heavily from decisions of the UK courts because the origin of their patent laws is the same.[189] The Statute of Monopolies provided that the invention should be a new manner of manufacture. An invention would be considered as 'any manner of new manufacture ... not contrary to the law, nor mischievous to the state, by raising the price of commodities at home, or hurt trade, or generally inconvenient'. Therefore, decisions emanating from the UK courts would be regarded as persuasive authority.[190]

The Australian courts first dealt with patenting methods of medical treatment in *Maeder v Busch*,[191] where the claim was for a method of forming permanent waves on human hair. The invention was invalidated, as it did not satisfy the requirement of invention test in *C& W's Application*.[192] However, the judges doubted[193] the correctness of the vendible test[194] and a complete rejection of this requirement was achieved in *NRDC*. The court accepted a vague test for determining patentability, which was to ask whether the claim in question was one that was 'the proper subject of letters patent according to the principles which have been developed for the application of s. 6 of the statute of Monopolies?'[195] Applying this test, the court opined that methods of medical treatment 'may well lie outside

---

[188] See J. Pila, 'The Common Law Invention in its Original Form' [2001] IPQ 209 for a detailed historical account.

[189] *Maeder v Busch* (1938) 58 CLR 684 (HCA), *National Research Development Corporation v Commissioner of Patents* (1959) 102 CLR 252 (HCA), *Joos v Commissioner of Patents* (1972) 126 CLR 611 (HCA), *Wellcome Foundation v Commissioner of Patents* (1980) 30 ALR 510 (HCA), *The Wellcome Foundation Ltd (Hitching's) Application* (1980) RPC 305 (HCA), *Anaesthetic Supplies Pty Ltd v Rescare Ltd* (1994) 50 FCR 1 (FCA) and *Bristol-Myers Squibb v FH Faulding & Co. Ltd* (2000) 97 FCR 524 (FCA).

[190] *Swift and Company v Commissioner of Patents* [1960] NZLR 775 (NZCA), *Wellcome Foundation Ltd v Commissioner of Patents* [1983] NZLR 385 (NZCA) and *Pharmaceutical Management Agency Ltd v Commissioner of Patents* [2000] 2 NZLR 529 (NZCA).

[191] (1938) 58 CLR 684 (HCA).

[192] Ibid, at 699.

[193] Ibid, at 706–707.

[194] This requirement had been articulated in 1914 in *C & W's Application.*

[195] *NRDC*, at 269.

the concept of invention because the whole subject is conceived as *essentially non-economic*'.[196]

In 1972, when the court was confronted with the issue in the case of *Joos v Commissioner of Patents*, it held that a method of cosmetic treatment was patentable subject matter because of its commercial application. The court went on to suggest the exclusion of methods of medical treatment was based on public policy grounds.[197] These were not fully explored until the decision in *Anaesthetic Supplies Pty Ltd v Rescare Ltd* where the court had to determine whether an invention for a method of controlling sleep apnoea was patentable. The Federal Court of Australia accepted that once the reasoning based on vendible product was jettisoned there could be no valid distinction between a product for treating the human body and a method of treating the human body.[198] The court pointed out that no previous authority in Australia had explicitly excluded methods of medical treatment from patent protection and that the decisions of *Maeder v Busch*, *NRDC* and *Joos* had simply assumed the existence of the exclusion.[199]

The issue was most recently considered by the court in *Bristol-Myers Squibb v FH Faulding & Co Ltd*[200] where the claim was for a method of administering the anti-cancer drug taxol. The patent was invalidated for lack of novelty. However, the Federal Court of Australia went on to determine whether the claim, if valid, could have been infringed if it was for a method of medical treatment. The court accepted that the view of the majority in *Rescare* was preferable.[201] Two principal grounds fortified the court's decision. First, the court felt that it would be an 'insurmountable problem, from a public policy viewpoint, of drawing a logical distinction which would justify [patent protection] for a *product* for treating the human body, but deny patentability for a *method of treatment*'.[202] Secondly, the court emphasised the lack of legislative interference in regulating patents for the human body.[203]

This reasoning provides an alternative interpretation that the courts in the United Kingdom could have adopted to resolve the problem of patent protection for methods of medical treatment. The Federal Court of Australia has, however, failed to appreciate that patent protection for pharmaceutical products and methods of medical procedure patents raise different

---

[196] Ibid, at 275 (emphasis added).

[197] *Joos v Commissioner of Patents*, at 622.

[198] Lockhart J. quoting Davidson C.J. in *The Wellcome Foundation Ltd (Hitchings's) Application* [1980] RPC 305.

[199] *Anaesthetic Supplies Pty Ltd v Rescare Ltd*, at 125.

[200] (2000) 97 FCR 524 (FCA).

[201] Ibid, at 529.

[202] Ibid, at 530 (emphasis in original).

[203] Ibid, at 529.

ethical and public policy considerations. At the very basic level, there is a concern that patent protection for both will restrict access to essential health services and medicines. This is a valid concern but the debate is much wider than this. The patenting of medical procedures raises specific ethical issues relating to the medical practitioner and her relationship with her patients which, arguably, do not arise in the context of pharmaceutical products.

3 The New Zealand Approach

Although the courts in New Zealand initially excluded methods of medical treatment from patent protection, they proceeded to allow claims that were directed at the medical treatment of animals.[204] Diagnosis, however, was held to be patentable on the condition that the surgical steps were excluded from the claims.[205] The court in *Wellcome Foundation Ltd v Commissioner of Patents*[206] gave an authoritative answer to this question. The applicants in that case claimed patent protection for a method of treating meningeal leukaemia in the brain using known compounds for that specific new purpose. The court held that patent protection was not available for methods of medical treatment or for a new medical use of a known compound or substance.[207] Recently, in *Pfizer Inc v Commissioner of Patents*,[208] the New Zealand Court of Appeal unanimously reiterated that methods of medical treatment were unpatentable. The court thought that any reform in the law is better undertaken through the Parliamentary process, no doubt mindful of the current reform of patent law being undertaken there.[209] As Hammond J. said, the question of whether patents

---

[204] *Swift & Co. Application* [1960] NZLR 775 (NZCA).

[205] *Bio-Digital Sciences Incorporated's Application* [1973] RPC 668 (PAT). See *Stafford Miller Ltd's Applications* [1984] FSR 258 (Pat Ct) where court allowed patents for the treatment of lice.

[206] [1983] NZLR 385 (NZCA). However, in *Pharmaceutical Management Agency Ltd v Commissioner of Patents* [2000] 2 NZLR 529, Gault J., speaking for a unanimous Court of Appeal, pointed out that '[w]hat emerges from this is that it can no longer be said that a method of treating humans cannot be an invention. To the extent that the judgments in *Wellcome* express that view we *depart* from them. The exclusion from patentability of methods of medical treatment rests on *policy (moral) grounds*' (emphasis added).

[207] This case has been overruled in *Pharmaceutical Management Agency v Commissioner of Patents* on the patentability of second medical use patents. However, the learning with regard to methods of medical treatment is still the applicable law in New Zealand.

[208] [2004] NZCA 104.

[209] *Review of the Patents Act 1953: Boundaries to Patentability* March 2002.

should be granted for methods of medical treatment is 'a particularly difficult problem of *public policy* which lies well beyond the competence of this Court'.[210]

4 Second Medical Uses Patents in New Zealand

(a) Introduction

The issue of second medical use was a vexed one in some commonwealth jurisdictions.[211] It is instructive to see how the courts have been able to grapple with this issue especially in the jurisdictions that have maintained the exclusion for methods of medical treatment. The use of compound X for the treatment of Y ailment is a classic example of a method of medical treatment. This point was made in *EISAI/Second medical indication* where the EBA observed that use claims are indeed method claims and 'whether an activity is claimed as a method of carrying out the activity (setting out a sequence of steps) or as a use of a thing for a stated purpose (the sequence being implied) is … a matter of preference … and there is no difference of substance'.[212] The EBA also pointed out that a claim directed to the use of a substance or composition for therapy would conflict with Article 52(4) EPC as it would be for a method of medical treatment.[213]

(b) Finding an appropriate solution

The issue of second medical use arose in a decision that revolved around the question of whether a method of medical treatment for treating meningeal leukaemia in the brain was patentable.[214] The New Zealand Court of Appeal in *Wellcome Foundation Ltd v Commissioner of Patents*[215] held that methods of medical treatment were unpatentable under New Zealand patent law. The claim was for the use of known compounds for the treatment of leukaemia. The substances were also used to treat malaria. This was a classic example of a new use claim. Having rejected the argument that methods of medical treatment were patentable, Cooke J did not think that the application should fare any better if presented as a use claim.[216] It was made clear that 'there is

---

210 [2004] NZCA 104 [128].

211 In Canada the issue was based on the specific and complex statutory regime, which governs this area: *Tennessee Eastman Co v Commissioner of Patents* (1974) 30 DLR (3rd) 459.

212 *EISAI/Second medical indication* (G 05/83), at 245.

213 Ibid, at 246.

214 *Wellcome Foundation Ltd v Commissioner of Patents* [1983] NZLR 385.

215 Ibid.

216 Ibid, at 392 (Cooke J.).

much to be said for developing the law'[217] to allow patenting of first or subsequent medical uses of known substances. However, 'whether any significant innovative movement is justifiable … is *not a matter for the courts*.'[218]

The court distinguished the *NRDC case* on the basis that although the claim was directed to a new use of a known substance, namely a method of weed control by the application of known substances not previously used for that purpose, it was not directed to a first or even a second medical use.[219] McMullin J., however, opined that although the instant case can be distinguished from *NRDC* 'the logic for its extension to treatments of human complaints is nonetheless most persuasive'.[220] Indeed, Somers J. asserted that the opinion of the High Court in *NRDC* represented the law of New Zealand on the issue in question.[221]

The question, therefore, was whether this reasoning ought to be applied to methods of medical treatment. Although McMullin J. thought the application of the *NRDC* case was persuasive he did not apply it. Cooke J. noted that there was distinction between the discovery of a new drug from the discovery of a new use for an old one and the law should reflect that distinction.[222] This does not solve the problem that faced the court. The issue, as Somers J. saw it, was 'whether a claim for a new use of an old substance is ever patentable especially as in the instant case the claim was for a second therapeutic use of a known compound'.[223] Somers J. sought to distinguish the instant case by pointing out that the substance was previously used for malaria.[224] His Lordship was not persuaded by the argument that the new therapeutic use was the novel feature of the invention.[225] The fact that the new use was also a therapeutic one was not sufficient to derive novelty as the claim was seen as 'but a kind of therapy'.[226] This is reminiscent of EPO jurisprudence before *EISAI/Second medical indication* where it was thought that if one discovered a therapeutic purpose for a substance or composition then that fact foreclosed any attempt to patent a second medical use.

---

217 Ibid, at 398 (McMullin J.).

218 Ibid, (emphasis added).

219 *Wellcome Foundation Ltd v Commissioner of Patents*, at 397 (McMullin J.); at 400 (Somers J.).

220 *Wellcome Foundation Ltd v Commissioner of Patents*, at 397.

221 Ibid, at 400.

222 Ibid, at 389.

223 Ibid, at 399.

224 Ibid, at 397.

225 Ibid.

226 Ibid.

(c) EISAI/Second medical indication in a New Zealand Court

The EBA in *MOBIL/Friction reducing additive* had warned against using the reasoning in *EISAI/Second medical indication* outside the statutory context from which it was derived, observing that the *ratio decidendi* of that decision was 'essentially confined to the proper interpretation of Articles 52(4) and 54(5) EPC 1973 in their context'.[227] Similarly too, Aldous L.J. in *Bristol-Myers Squibb* made it clear that the decision in *EISAI/Second medical indication* was based on the interplay between Articles 52(4) and 54(5) EPC 1973.[228] This meant that *EISAI/Second medical indication* should not be used in a totally different context and statutory regime. However it was left to be seen whether the rationale that informed *EISAI/Second medical indication* could be similarly used in any context.

The New Zealand Court of Appeal in *Pharmaceutical Management Agency Ltd v Commissioner of Patents*[229] ignored these words of caution and applied *EISAI/Second medical indication* in a different context and statutory regime. The court was faced with its previous decision in *Wellcome Foundation Ltd v Commissioner of Patents* where it held that a new medical use of a known compound or substance was not patentable. The court accepted that methods of treating humans were inventions within the meaning of the statute, and that the purpose of the exclusion is to ensure that medical practitioners were not subject to restraints when treating patients.[230] The question, the Court of Appeal stated, was 'whether a discovery of a new pharmaceutical use can be protected without impinging on the activities of the medical practitioner in the practice of her diagnostic, therapeutic or surgical methods?'[231]

The court was satisfied that the Swiss-type claims achieved that objective.[232] It noted that the statutory regime under the EPC was different to what obtained in New Zealand. However, it was at pains to point out that the exclusion in Article 52(4) EPC was broadly similar to New Zealand law.[233] The court's reasoning in relation to Article 54(5) EPC 1973 is suspect. It accepted that Article 54(5) EPC 1973 covered first medical use of a known compound and that this did not 'create a situation different from

---

227 (G 02/88) [1990] EPOR 73, 84.
228 [2001] RPC 1, 17.
229 [2000] 2 NZLR 529.
230 Ibid, at 538.
231 Ibid.
232 Ibid, at 539.
233 *Wellcome Foundation Ltd v Commissioner of Patents* [1983] NZLR 385.

that which prevails in New Zealand'.[234] This statement is in stark contrast to the *ratio decidendi* of *Wellcome Foundation Ltd v Commissioner of Patents*, unless, however, the court is prepared to say that *Wellcome Foundation Ltd* did not stand for that proposition of law. The court made short shrift of this argument, alluding to various parts of the three judgments where vague references suggesting the opposite were made.[235] It is suggested that such an approach was not sufficient. It is true that the court in *Wellcome Foundation Ltd* did not engage in a detailed analysis of the issue and merely asserted that patent protection was not available for pharmaceutical uses of known substances but that is no reason to deny the *ratio* of the decision.

The use of a compound for treating a disease is a method of medical treatment. The court in *Wellcome Foundation Ltd* rejected the patentability of methods of medical treatment generally and, specifically, methods of medical treatments in that particular form. Therefore, the New Zealand Court of Appeal could not accept the *NRDC* decision without accepting the applicability of the reasoning therein to new uses of known pharmaceutical substances. It may be argued that the court in *Wellcome Foundation Ltd* appreciated that distinction but, nonetheless, thought that the answer would be without significance as the method would still have been an excluded one.

Article 54(5) EPC 1973 made a limited exception to the novelty requirement for the medical use of a known substance. Therefore, the court in *Pharmaceutical Management Agency* had to deny the reasoning in *Wellcome Foundation Ltd* to make the necessary analogy. The court was correct in applying the reasoning in *EISAI/Second medical indication* because it was confronted with a similar dilemma that faced *EISAI/Second medical indication*. This was a result of accepting that methods of medical treatment were unpatentable (Article 52(4) EPC/*Wellcome Foundation Ltd*) with the patentability of uses of known substances (Article 54(5) EPC 1973 (limited to medical uses)/general reasoning). The court was of the opinion that product claims for inventions arising from the discovery of the first pharmaceutical use of known substances were allowable[236] although it cites no authority for this proposition of law.

The court rejected the argument that the instant case could be distinguished because the provisions of the EPC dictated the actual result in

---

234 *Pharmaceutical Management Agency Ltd v Commissioner of Patents* [2000] 2 NZLR 529.

235 Ibid, at 541

236 Ibid.

EISAI/Second medical indication.[237] It was not persuaded that it was precluded from applying *EISAI/Second medical indication* by either authority or principle.[238] Heavy reliance was placed on the fact that Swiss-type claims were not product claims.[239] The court reasoned that if an exception could have been fashioned to deal with finding of new properties in substances of a class previously disclosed, so too can the courts recognise the inventiveness of new uses of known compounds, whilst at the same time avoiding interference with the practice of diagnosis and therapy.[240]

The court was satisfied that this would be achieved using the Swiss-type formulation as it is directed to use of a known compound in the manufacture of a medicament for a new therapeutic use. This would be sufficient to evade the exclusion for methods of medical treatment whilst protecting new uses of pharmaceutical products. Concerns about the infringement did not deter the court in applying this reasoning.[241] These concerns, the court explained, 'were more apparent than real'.[242] It was sensible to use the Swiss-type claim to circumvent the exclusion for methods of medical treatment. The novelty would lie in the new therapeutic purpose discovered. As such, it would provide sufficient incentive for research into new and further uses of known substances whether or not they have had a medicinal purpose.

(d) Conclusion

The question of second medical use patents is one that is varied and the issues intriguing. It involves a rethinking of traditional notions of the novelty requirement in patent law and is usually considered with the question of method of medical treatment. This is because a use of a substance or composition to treat a disease is a method of medical treatment. This was the dilemma that faced the court in *Wellcome Foundation Ltd* but it did not deal satisfactorily with the issues that were raised. The New Zealand Court of Appeal has applied *EISAI/Second medical indication* to a different statutory regime, reasoning that the issues were very similar and the result obtained under the EPC was equally applicable

---

[237] Ibid, at 544.

[238] Ibid.

[239] Ibid.

[240] Ibid, at 545.

[241] The court opined that the state of mind of the infringer or the purpose of the alleged infringer is not unknown to patent law (at 546).

[242] *Pharmaceutical Management Agency Ltd v Commissioner of Patents*, at 546.

in New Zealand. The approach is, therefore, consistent with the international trend of recognising the need for allowing novel first and subsequent medical uses of known compounds.[243]

5 Conclusion

The decisions from Australia and New Zealand are interesting insofar as they show that the jurisprudence in the United Kingdom could have gone either way on the question of whether patent protection should have been provided for methods of medical treatment. That the two jurisdictions concerned share a similar statutory origin is even more fascinating in light of the different conclusions arrived at by their courts. The courts in New Zealand, taking a more cautious approach, rejected the notion that patent protection should be available for methods of medical treatment, in line with the UK authorities on the issue. However, the court in Australia rejected UK authorities and held, to the contrary, that, in principle, methods of medical treatment are not excluded from patent protection under section 6 of the Statute of Monopolies.

F CONCLUSION

In the period before 1977, it was generally accepted that methods of medical treatment of humans were unpatentable, although the question of patenting medical treatment for animals remained uncertain. The decided cases did not provide a reasoned rationale for the exclusion of methods of medical treatment from patent protection. Whether the exclusion was based on Patent Office practice or public policy considerations were not addressed fully. However, in the period immediately preceding the 1977 Act, a vague notion of public policy was accepted as a possible justification for the exclusion, although this was not expanded upon.

The different approaches in the Commonwealth jurisdictions provided alternative approaches to the rationale for the exclusion, and showed that the judicial exclusion that was maintained in the United Kingdom before 1977 was not an inevitable consequence. The PAT was not entirely satisfied

---

[243] This approach was very similar to that taken by the Supreme Court of Israel in *The Wellcome Foundation Ltd v Plantex Ltd* [1974] RPC 514. The patent was for a use of a known chemical used for the treatment of gout. The court was of the opinion that a novel property of an old substance was patentable (at 536, Witkon J.). Kahn J. accepted this but opined that this should be limited to the first pharmaceutical use and not subsequent uses (at 539).

with the exclusion. The dissatisfaction became manifest when the court sanctioned and asserted that pack claims could be used to evade the exclusion for methods of medical treatment. Judicial deference, in light of continued uncertainty and disquiet about the rationale for the exclusion, were not significant enough to convince them to remove the judicially created exclusion of methods of medical treatment. The courts and PAT felt incompetent to interpret the law to provide patent protection for methods of medical treatment and asserted that, if there were to be any change, it should be made by the legislature.

9. United Kingdom Patents Act 2004

A INTRODUCTION

The new Patents Act 2004 (the 2004 Act), to ensure 'conformity of practice', has implemented the changes brought about by the revision of the European Patent Convention (EPC) in 2000, and has kept the exclusion as part of UK law.[1] A judicially created exclusion of methods of medical treatment from patent protection existed prior to the enactment of the Patents Act 1977 (the 1977 Act).[2] Now, in the post 1977 period, the courts in the United Kingdom are burdened with interpreting a specific legislative exclusion for methods of medical treatment.[3] They have accepted, with little hesitation and under the guise of conformity, the interpretation given by the Technical Boards of Appeal (TBAs) and the Enlarged Board of Appeal of the European Patent Office (EBA) of the European Patent Office (EPO) on the corresponding provisions of the European Patent Convention (EPC). This approach has been followed blindly for over 20 years.[4]

---

[1] Explanatory Notes to the Patents Act 2004 (Chapter 16, 2004) at para. 16. The ideas in this chapter have been derived, in part, from the following: E. Ventose, 'The *Byzantine* Logic of Patent Law Jurisprudence: Patent Protection for Dosage Regimes Revisited' (2009) JIPLP 415; and 'Patent Protection for Methods of Medical Treatment in the United Kingdom' [2008] IPQ 58.

[2] See J. Pila, 'Methods of Medical Treatment within Australian and United Kingdom Patents Law' (2001) 24 UNSW Law Journal 420.

[3] See generally, A. Feros, 'Patentabilty of Methods of Medical Treatment' [2001] EIPR 79; A. Horton, 'Methods of Treatment and Second Medical Use' (2000) Patent World 19 and D. Kell, 'Expanding the Frontier of Patentability of Methods of Medical Treatment of the Human Body' [1995] EIPR 202. The 'Examination Guidelines for Patent Applications relating to Medical Inventions in the UK Intellectual Property Office', June 2007 provides invaluable guidance in respect of the jurisprudence on methods of medical treatment in the United Kingdom and the European Patent Office.

[4] This approach is not surprising given the statutory obligation in s. 130(7) of the 1977 Act that the various sections, including s. 2, are 'so framed as to have, as nearly as practicable, the same effects in the United Kingdom as the corresponding provisions of the [EPC]'.

Little has generally been written on the exclusion in the United Kingdom.[5] This chapter aims to examine the application of the exclusion of methods of medical treatment by the UK courts. In order to achieve this, it will: first, compare and contrast the exclusion of methods of medical treatment under the 1977 Act with the exclusion as it existed prior to 1977; secondly, examine the current UK jurisprudence relating to the exclusion from patent protection of methods of treatment by: (a) surgery; (b) therapy; and (c) diagnostic methods; and, thirdly, explore the importation, into UK law, of the EPO rules relating to patent protection for second and further medical uses. Where the UK courts have not yet explored a particular exclusion, the approach of the EPO will be briefly outlined, indicating a possible approach to the interpretation of the exclusions that the UK courts might wish to adopt given their obligation under section 130(7) of the 1977 Act to achieve conformity with the jurisprudence of the EPO.

B COMPARISON WITH PRE-1977 LAW

1 A Brief History

As noted in the previous chapter, the exclusion for methods of medical treatment in the United Kingdom in the period before 1977 is said to originate from the decision of the Solicitor-General in *C & W's Application*.[6] In that decision, the Solicitor-General held that the claimed method, which was for removing lead from the human body, was not a 'manner of manufacture' as stated in section 6 of the Statute of Monopolies. The courts and the Patent Appeal Tribunal (PAT) were, nonetheless, initially preoccupied with determining the basis of the origin of the exclusion of methods of medical treatment from patent protection. They accepted, following in some instances the jurisprudence of Commonwealth countries, that the reasons might be: (a) a question of statutory interpretation;[7] (b) Patent Office practice;[8] and (c) ethical and public policy considerations.[9] By 1970, at least in the United Kingdom, the question relating to the origin of the exclusion seemed to have been answered on the basis that the

---

[5] See generally, Cornish, Llewelyn and Aplin, *Intellectual Property*, pp. 237–243.

[6] (1914) RPC 235.

[7] *Schering A G's Application* [1971] RPC 337.

[8] *The Upjohn Company (Robert's) Application* [1977] RPC 94.

[9] *Eli Lilly & Company's Application* [1975] RPC 438.

exclusion was firmly rooted in ethical and public policy considerations.[10] Once that question was settled, thereby entrenching the exclusion of methods of medical treatment from patent protection, the issue became one of delineating the parameters of the exclusion. The exclusion was thought to extend to the patenting of claims for, among other things: (a) a device used to inject a substance into a person;[11] (b) a method for repairing, sealing, filling and hardening tooth surfaces;[12] and (c) a method for inducing a state of reduced awareness in humans.[13]

However, the courts and the PAT still doubted the logic of the exclusion of methods of medical treatment from patent protection.[14] They made it clear that: (a) if the law was to change, it should be done by the legislature;[15] (b) the continued existence of the exclusion for methods of medical treatment lacked logic;[16] and (c) a change of policy would be sensible.[17] Notwithstanding these criticisms, the courts and the PAT not only applied the exclusion but thought that irrespective of the origins of the exclusion of methods of medical treatment from patent protection, it must be considered as sound.[18]

2 The 1977 Act

(a) Introduction

The legislature seemingly responded to the calls of the courts and the PAT with the passage of the 1977 Act, which proclaimed in its preamble that its function was to introduce a *new law of patents*. The exclusion for methods of medical treatment was not included in the provisions that dealt with the determination of whether or not a *thing* could be considered as an *invention*. Section 4(2) of the 1977 Act provided that '[a]n *invention* of a method

---

[10] *Pfizer Inc v Commissioner of Patents* [2005] NZLR 362. The Australian courts have, however, taken a rather different approach: see, for example, *Anaesthetic Supplies Pty Ltd v Rescare Ltd* (1994) 50 FCR 1 and *Bristol-Myers Squibb Company v FH Faulding & Co. Ltd* (2000) 97 FCR 524.

[11] *Palmer's Application* [1970] RPC 597.

[12] *Lee Pharmaceutical's Application* [1978] RPC 31.

[13] *Neva Corporation's Application* [1968] RPC 481.

[14] *Schering A G's Application*, at 344.

[15] *Eli Lilly & Company's Application*, at 444. This was reiterated by the Court of Appeal in *The Upjohn Company (Robert's) Application*, at 98. See generally, Y. Cripps, 'The Refusal of Patents for Methods of Medical Treatment – A Preference for Parliamentary Guidance' [1983] EIPR 173.

[16] *Schering A G's Application*, at 344.

[17] *Eli Lilly & Company's Application*, at 445.

[18] *Schering A G's Application*, at 344.

of treatment of the human or animal body by surgery or therapy or of diagnosis practised on the human or animal body *shall not be taken* to be capable of industrial application'. Thus, the question was no longer whether such methods were inventions, because section 4(2) specifically states that they can be inventions;[19] but inventions that are excluded from patent protection solely on the basis that they are incapable of industrial application. Inventions relating to methods of medical treatment, therefore, did not satisfy one of the salient requirements of a patentable invention, namely, of industrial application. The methods of medical treatment excluded from patent protection on that basis are: (a) methods of treatment of the human or animal body by therapy; (b) methods of treatment of the human or animal body by surgery; and (c) diagnostic methods practised on the human or animal body.

(b) Reformulation of the exclusion

The 1977 Act recast the exclusion for methods of medical treatment in the United Kingdom. It was based on the lack of industrial applicability, and, therefore, there was no longer any debate relating to the doctrinal basis for the exclusion. It introduced a firm legal foundation for the exclusion of methods of medical treatment in the United Kingdom. Interestingly, just six years prior to the enactment of the 1977 Act, the PAT in *Schering A G's Application* and subsequent decisions were beginning to accept a vague notion of public policy as the rationale for the exclusion of methods of medical treatment. The fact that there was now a firm legal basis for the exclusion did not prevent the courts, in the post-1977 period, from articulating what they considered to be the public policy rationale underlying the exclusion, which, they made clear, was to prevent any limitations on the actions of physicians when they treat their patients.

(c) Further reformulation of the exclusion

This search for an underlying public policy rationale for the exclusion, given the formulation of the exclusion as derived from Article 52(4) EPC, may no longer be necessary. The 2004 Act, which adopts the EPC 2000 position, has introduced a new section 4A into the 1977 Act, which provides that: 'A patent shall not be granted for an invention of – (a) a method of treatment of the human or animal body by surgery or therapy, or (b) a method of diagnosis practised on the human or animal body.' There is no mention of industrial applicability – methods of medical treatment are simply not patentable. The drafters of the EPC 2000 openly accepted

[19] If this were the case, the exclusion simply would have been placed in s. 1(1).

that it was undesirable to uphold the previous fiction of lacking industrial application as the basis for the exclusion because methods of medical treatment are excluded from patentability in the interests of public health (and presumably morality and ethics).[20] This reformulation of the exclusion for methods of medical treatment removes any doubt concerning the underlying public health rationale for the exclusion. If this is right, it would confirm: (a) the approach that was in its rather embryonic stage in 1971 when *Schering AG's Application* was decided; and (b) the opinion of the courts in the period after 1977 that has explicitly adopted such policy considerations as the rationale for the exclusion of methods of medical treatment from patent protection.

(d) Treatment of humans

In some respects, the exception found in section 4(2) of the 1977 Act is similar to the exclusion as it existed prior to 1977. The pre-1977 law was directed at methods of treatment for treating or curing diseases in humans (therapeutic treatment). The courts and the PAT had consistently maintained that the exclusion related only to methods of *medical* treatment and not all methods of treatment of humans.[21] This was indicated by the PAT's rejection of the view that methods of diagnosis[22] and cosmetic methods of treatment[23] are excluded from patent protection. Section 4(2) expanded the scope of the exclusion to include methods of treatment of the *human* body by: (i) therapy and (ii) surgery.

(e) Treatment of animals

The Solicitor-General in *C & W's Application* hinted that methods of medical treatment of animals were patentable noting that, with respect to animals, different considerations would have applied. This view was, however, rejected by later courts and the PAT which not only excluded methods of *medical* treatment of animals but also excluded from patent protection, all methods of treatment irrespective of their intended purpose. Section 4(2) of the 1977 Act expanded on the scope of the exclusion to cover methods of treatment of the *animal* body by: (i) therapy and (ii) surgery.

(f) Diagnostic methods

The courts and the PAT did not have many occasions to consider exhaustively the patentability of diagnostic methods. However, on one occasion,

---

20 Explanatory Notes to the Patents Act 2004 (c. 16) at para. 17.

21 *United States Rubber Company's Application*, at 106.

22 *Bio-Digital Sciences Incorporated's Application* [1973] RPC 668, 674.

23 *Oral Health Products Inc. (Halstead's) Application* [1977] RPC 612, 615.

in *Bio-Digital Sciences Incorporated's Application*,[24] the PAT had to consider the issue. In that decision, the claims related to a method of examination of cells for evidence of disease. The Superintending Officer held that the method of testing was 'not applicable to the improvement or control of manufacture'.[25] Graham J., agreed noting that the claim covered a method of testing under the 1949 Patents Act, but held that the 'object of the method is really to select samples which need further examination. It is in no sense a method of testing such as section 101 is directly contemplating'.[26] The court held that, whatever the position was before, the section makes it clear that 'methods of testing applicable to the improvement or control of manufacture should be regarded as a manner of manufacture within the Act'.[27] The claimed method was not considered as a method of medical treatment, only because 'it may in appropriate cases be a preliminary step leading to subsequent medical treatment if decided upon'.[28] Section 4(2) of the 1977 Act includes a section which provides for the exclusion of diagnostic methods practised on the human or animal body.

(g) Cosmetic methods

Given the aggressive way in which pharmaceutical companies explore the possibilities of finding new medical and non-medical uses of substances, it was inevitable that the issue of a non-medical uses, in particular cosmetic uses, of substances or compositions would find its way through the courts. In *Oral Health Products Inc. (Halstead's) Application*, claim 32 in the patent specification was for cleaning teeth which comprised contacting the teeth with an aqueous alkaline solution of N-monochloroglycine. Claims 33–35 were rejected by the Examining Officer on the basis that they related to a therapeutic treatment, namely the prevention of caries. Graham J. observed that the compounds were the same in all the claims and that the therapeutic effect would result even when the substance in claim 32 was used. His Lordship noted that there could hardly be a logical distinction between claims 33–35 and claim 32, because 'the method of claim 32, even if it covers and produces what has been called the cleaning or cosmetic effect of the new material cannot help also producing the curative effect'.[29] Graham J. was of the opinion that the Examining Officer ought to further consider claim 32; and, if possible, 'amend that claim in such a way as to

---

[24] [1973] RPC 668.
[25] Ibid, at 672.
[26] Ibid, at 671.
[27] Ibid, at 673.
[28] Ibid, at 674.
[29] *Oral Health Products Inc. (Halstead's) Application*, at 616.

limit it to what has been called the cosmetic effect, then I think it will probably be allowable'.[30] His Lordship was not, however, prepared to grant the patent in its wide form, so the claim was remitted to the Patent Office for further consideration in light of the judgment. The question whether cosmetic methods are patentable under the 1977 Act is still an open one.

C APPLICATION OF THE EXCLUSION

1 Ex Post Facto Rationalisation

In the period before 1977, the courts were unable to articulate with consistency an explicit rationale for the exclusion of methods of medical treatment from patent protection, but have now been able to clearly and confidently articulate what they believe was the proper rationale for the exclusion under the 1977 Act.[31] The Patents Court, sitting *en banc*, in *Wyeth's Application*,[32] for example, held that section 4(2) was 'not intended to exclude pharmaceutical inventions from patentability but has as its purpose to ensure that *the use in practice by practitioners of such methods of medical treatment in treating patients should not be subjected to possible restraint or restriction by reason of any patent monopoly*'.[33] Similarly too, Jacob J., at first instance, in *Bristol-Myers Squibb* opined that:[34]

> There is also the limited purpose of the exception to be considered. It is not so broad as to stop doctors using whatever they feel they need to treat patients. If that were the purpose then one would not allow patents for medicines or medical implements at all. *The purpose of the limitation is much narrower, merely to keep patent law from interfering directly with what the doctor actually does to the patient.* Patent monopolies are permitted to control what he administers to, or the implements he uses on, the patient.

In the Court of Appeal, Aldous L.J. shared a similar sentiment, observing that the section has a '*limited purpose* of ensuring that actual use, by

---

30 Ibid.

31 Neuberger J in *Visx v Nidex Co. Ltd* [1999] FSR 405 stated that '[t]he policy behind this provision is that the medical profession should be free to perform operations untroubled by considerations of whether what they are doing infringes a patent' (at 464–465).

32 *John Wyeth and Brothers Ltd's Application and Schering A G's Application* [1985] RPC 545.

33 Ibid, at 565 (emphasis added).

34 [1999] RPC 253, 274 (emphasis added).

practitioners, of methods of medical treatment when treating patients should not be subject to restriction or restraint by patent monopolies'.[35] Therefore, on the authority of both the Patents Court and the Court of Appeal, the rationale for the exclusion for methods of medical treatment was grounded in preventing any restraints on the activities of physicians when they treat their patients.

2 Inherent Contradictions

The question relating to the benefit of perpetuating the dichotomy between patent protection for products, substances and devices for medical purposes and the lack thereof for methods of medical treatment also continued under the new law. Jacob J., in *Bristol-Myers Squibb*, indicated that it could be readily appreciated that patent law would control the pharmaceutical substances the physician *administers* to or medical devices she *uses* on the patient, but not on what she actually *does* to the patient.[36] His Lordship noted that the thinking behind the exception was not particularly rational and that, if one accepted that a patent monopoly is a fair price to pay for the extra research incentive, then there was no reason to suppose that it would not also apply to methods of medical treatment.[37] These criticisms invoke one of the arguments made for patent protection of methods of medical treatment – that the patenting of some medical procedures might need the incentives of the patent system, although they raise some important public policy considerations, including those that are particular to the medical profession.[38] However, as Professor Cornish has pointed out: the 'exception is fixed in legislation and so is not just a matter of judicial determination'.[39] The exclusion, however, seems to be here for the foreseeable future.

3 Method of Treatment by Therapy

(a) Defining therapy

One of the first cases to consider the exclusion of methods of treatment under the 1977 Act had the major task of determining the thorny issue of

---

35 [2001] RPC 1, 21 (emphasis added). His Lordship continued by stating that '[t]he difficulty is to decide whether the restraint concerns a method of treatment as opposed to what is available for treatment'.

36 *Bristol-Myers Squibb* (CA) at 21.

37 Ibid (emphasis added). These views were reiterated by Jacob J. in *Teva Industries Ltd.*

38 This view mirrors that of the Federal Court of Australia in *Bristol-Myers Squibb v FH Haulding & Co. Ltd* at 530. See generally, A. Sims, 'The Case against Patenting Methods of Medical Treatment' [2007] EIPR 43.

39 Cornish, Llewelyn and Aplin, *Intellectual Property*, p. 243.

whether a method of treatment for *therapy* included either curative and preventative treatment, or only curative treatment. The claim in *Unilever Ltd's (Davis's) Application*[40] was for a method of immunising poultry against coccidiosis by adding a substance to their feed. After an exhaustive and rather lengthy survey of the various meanings given to the word 'therapy', Falconer J. accepted that it should be given its wider meaning that would include *both* curative and preventative treatment.[41] He noted that there was no intention by Parliament to use the word 'therapy' in two senses – one in relation to the medical treatment of humans, and the other in respect of animals.[42] Falconer J. was of the opinion that if the definition of therapy excluded preventative treatment then the decision in *Schering A G's Application*, which established that methods for the medical treatment of human beings to cure or prevent disease were not patentable,[43] would still be the applicable law.[44] This was because there was a presumption against a change in the existing law, and neither should one presume that a method of treatment for animals that was patentable under previous law should be so under the new law.[45]

(b) Application of the exclusion

In *Bristol-Myers Squibb*, the claims, which were in the Swiss-type form, related to a scheme for treating cancer and reducing neutropenia. This included the administration of the drug taxol to a patient over a period of three hours or less. It was well established that the drug taxol, which is a naturally occurring substance derived from the Pacific Yew tree, could be used as an anti-cancer drug. The claims, as outlined by the defendants' lawyers, included the use of taxol and sufficient medications: (a) to prevent anaphylactic reactions; (b) for manufacturing a pre-medicamentation for simultaneous, separate or sequential application; (c) for the administration of 135mg/m^2 up to 175mg/m^2 taxol over a period of three hours or less; and (d) as a means of treating cancer and simultaneously reducing neutropenia.[46] The claimants applied for a patent because they had discovered that a reduction in the time of infusion would reduce a condition called neutropenia, which causes a fall in the patient's white blood cells. Prior trials had not been able to strike the appropriate balance between the dosage given to

40 [1983] RPC 219.
41 Ibid, at 228.
42 Ibid, at 228–229.
43 *Schering A G's Application*, at 343–344.
44 *Unilever Ltd's (Davis's) Application*, at 228.
45 Ibid, at 229.
46 *Bristol-Myers Squibb* (HC), at 270.

patients and minimizing the resulting side effects of taxol. Bristol-Myers Squibb claimed that their scheme achieved that optimum balance.

Jacob J. was firmly of the opinion that the claimed method was not a method of medical treatment, but that it related simply to 'the manufacture of the medicines to be used in that treatment'.[47] The exclusion of methods of medical treatment from patent protection, in the opinion of Jacob J., only covers the activities of physicians when they treat their patients – not the products for use when they do so.[48] Jacob J. did not consider the question of whether the claim was actually for a treatment regime, having accepted that the claim was not actually a method of medical treatment. But, any reasonable reading of the claims would reveal that it seemed actually to relate to a treatment regime for that particular patient. The patient was to, first, take a cocktail of premedication; and, second, to be administered a dosage of taxol, which was made specifically for that patient, using a combination of the patient's weight and height measurements. Jacob J. noted that 'the premedication is separate from the taxol and the taxol is made up to be patient specific'.[49] In other words, the claim was 'directed at the use of taxol for making a medicamentation for administration (using premedication) under specified dosage and times'.[50] Jacob J. agreed with counsel that '[t]he claim is for the manufacture of what is administered to the patient but stops short of being a claim actually to administration'.[51]

In the Court of Appeal, Aldous L.J., however, drew a distinction between what is available for treatment (substances and compositions) and a method of medical treatment. His Lordship reasoned that the various steps necessary to ensure that the treatment was successful were intimately connected with the activities of the physician; for example, the pre medication was chosen by the physician and administered according to the physician's instruction.[52] Indeed, the very medicament necessary for treatment was actually produced inside the patient's body which meant that it was not, by any means, an invention, which 'can be made or used in any kind of industry' according to the dictates of section 4(2).[53] According to Aldous L.J., '[t]he actual medicament that is said to be suitable for treatment is produced in the patient under supervision of the medical team. It is

---

[47] Ibid, at 274.
[48] Ibid, at 273.
[49] Ibid.
[50] Ibid.
[51] Ibid.
[52] *Bristol-Myers Squibb* (CA), at 21.
[53] Ibid.

not part of a manufacture'.[54] Since '[e]verything that happens as described in claim 1 of the patent is, or ought to be, under the direction of the clinician',[55] the claim was held to be an excluded method of medical treatment contrary to section 4(2) of the 1977 Act. Aldous L.J. was convinced that the appellant's claim 'was an unsuccessful attempt to monopolise the new method of treatment by drafting it along the lines of a Swiss-type claim', which did 'not disguise its effect'.[56]

Buxton L.J. noted that the 'manufacture claimed is not the use of the active ingredient, paclitaxel, in the manufacture of taxol; but the mixing in the hospital pharmacy of taxol and other ingredients to produce the medium that is injected into the patient'.[57] For the purposes of the Swiss-type claim, it was only the second process that the appellant claimed was susceptible of industrial application. That 'assertion' was described by Holman J. as 'artificial' because it would scarcely have been made but for 'the need to demonstrate that the invention is not of a method of treatment'.[58] The mixing process, Buxton L.J. emphasised, was 'a long way away from anything that in normal parlance would be considered an *industrial* application',[59] and was 'in reality not a self-standing operation, but subordinate and incidental to the doctor's treatment of the patient'.[60] His Lordship concluded that the patent did not actually teach 'how to manufacture a drug for use in the treatment of the patient … but how to treat the patient', which meant that it was, therefore, an unpatentable method of medical treatment.[61] The form of claim used by the appellants, in effect, comprised a method of medical treatment which Buxton L.J. held was exactly the 'teaching that the Swiss-type claim is designed to avoid'.[62]

4 Methods of Treatment by Surgery

This exclusion has not been considered directly by the UK courts.[63] However, in *Unilever Ltd's (Davis's) Application*, Falconer J. stated, *obiter*, that:[64]

---

54 Ibid (emphasis added).
55 Ibid, at 30 (Holman J.).
56 Ibid, at 21.
57 Ibid, at 28.
58 Ibid.
59 Ibid (emphasis in original).
60 Ibid.
61 Ibid.
62 *Bristol-Myers Squibb* (CA), at 28.
63 *Visx v Nidex Co. Ltd*, at 465.
64 *Unilever Ltd's (Davis's) Application*, at 228.

> [S]urgery can be curative of the disease or diseased conditions, or prophylactic, that is, preventive of diseased conditions, as for example, where an appendix or tonsils may be removed before any diseased condition starts up, and surgery may even be cosmetic without being curative or preventive. So that the subsection it seems to me is saying that any method of surgical treatment, whether it is curative, prophylactic or cosmetic, is not patentable.

The interpretation of the exclusion for methods of treatment of the animal or human body by surgery at the EPO has been the subject of reconsideration by the EBA as a result of the recent referral to the EBA, by the TBA in *MEDI-PHYSICS/Treatment by surgery*, of three questions relating to the scope of the exclusion. As noted previously, the TBAs have accepted that second medical uses of surgical instruments are excluded from patent protection[65] but that a method of surgery, that involves the death of the subject, falls outside the scope of the exclusion.[66] However, there are some inconsistent decisions relating to whether the definition of surgery relates only to: (i) the nature of the intervention on the human or animal body[67] or (ii) the purpose of that intervention.[68] Also, there is some disquiet concerning whether a claim is an excluded surgical method solely because it (a) is directed primarily at a cosmetic purpose (where the therapeutic aspect of the claim is only incidental)[69] and (b) merely contains or recites a surgical feature. The EBA in *MEDI-PHYSICS/Treatment by surgery* has ruled on these issues, accepting that it was not necessary that a method be curative in purpose to amount to a surgical method; secondly, the inclusion of a surgical step in a multi-step method would exclude it from patent protection; and, thirdly, it is legitimate to use disclaimers to avoid the exclusion of surgical methods under Article 53(c) EPC but they need to conform with the other requirements of the EPC.

5 Diagnostic Methods

The courts in the United Kingdom have not yet considered the scope of this exclusion. However, there is an emerging jurisprudence relating to diagnostic methods in the EPO. The EBA in *CYGNUS/Diagnostic method*, to ensure consistency in the application of Article 52(4) EPC, clarified and

---

65 *CODMAN/Second surgical use* (T 0227/91) [1995] EPOR 82.

66 *SEE-SHELL/Blood flow* (T 182/90) [1994] EPOR 320.

67 Ibid. See also *GEORGETOWN UNIVERSITY/Pericardial access* (T 35/99) [2001] EPOR 169.

68 *THE GENERAL HOSPITAL CORPORATION/Hair removal method* (T 0383/03) at para. 3.

69 Ibid.

restated the definition of diagnostic methods that was to be used by the various TBAs when they apply the exclusion from patent protection of diagnostic methods practised on the human or animal body. Diagnostic methods were to comprise the following steps: (a) examination and data gathering; (b) comparison of the data with normal values; (c) recording any significant deviation; and (d) attributing the deviation to a particular clinical picture (the deductive medical or veterinary decision phase[70] or the diagnosis for curative purposes *stricto sensu*[71]). Any claimed method, to constitute a diagnostic method, must contain all of the four steps outlined above. The last step, step (d), is clearly a defining feature of a diagnostic method without which the claim would, at best, relate to diagnosis but not comprise a diagnostic method. So strict is that requirement that any claim which does not clearly outline the actual diagnosis, and only leads to intermediate results, would not be patentable.

The EBA in *CYGNUS/Diagnostic method* stated that, for a claim to be excluded from patent protection, any step of a technical nature, from the 'preceding steps which are constitutive for making a diagnosis for curative purposes',[72] must be practised on the human or animal body. The EBA emphasised that no specific type and intensity of interaction with the human or animal body was required;[73] the only requirement was that the performance of the step implied any interaction with the human or animal body necessitating its presence.[74] Recent decisions of the TBAs have clarified that, first, steps (b) and (c) would not usually be technical in nature and, therefore, in most cases, it was only with respect to step (a), which is usually of a technical nature, that it would be necessary to determine if it was practised on the human or animal body;[75] and, secondly, intermediate steps which form part of steps (a) to (c) are not to be examined to determine whether they are practised on the human or animal body, and are to be ignored for that part of the analysis.[76]

---

70 *BRUKER/Non-invasive measurement* (T 385/86) [1988] EPOR 357 at para. 3.3.

71 *CYGNUS/Diagnostic method* (G 01/04) at para. 5.

72 Ibid, at para. 6.4.1.

73 Ibid, at para. 3 of the Conclusion.

74 Ibid, at para. 4 of the Conclusion.

75 *THE AUSTRALIAN NATIONAL UNIVERSITY/Method and apparatus for early detection of glaucoma* (T 1197/02).

76 *BETH ISRAEL HOSPITAL ASSOCIATION* (T 0143/04) at para. 3.1.

D SECOND AND FURTHER MEDICAL USES

1 Introduction

The high expenditure of discovering new drugs, it has been argued, justifies the patents granted to the various pharmacological companies.[77] Without it, inventors would, arguably, not have the necessary incentive to conduct much-needed research, and society would be deprived of essential cures for various illnesses that such further research could provide.[78] Second medical use patents, according to the wording of section 2(6) of the 1977 Act, cannot be excluded from patent protection on the basis that they are incapable of industrial application. When a substance or composition is new, it can be claimed as a product, including all its known or unknown uses (even if used in an excluded method of medical treatment).[79] It is when the substance or composition has a known use that the exception begins to bite[80] because the claim would be for the product with that newly discovered therapeutic use. Such a claim would be incompatible with section 4(2) of the 1977 Act, which excludes methods of medical treatment from patent protection. The pharmaceutical industry lobbied for an exception to that general exclusion and the resulting compromise, by way of compensation,[81] was found in section 2(6) of the 1977 Act which allowed patent protection for a *new medical use* of an old substance or composition. Therefore, whilst section 4(3)[82] serves as an exception to the exclusion in section 4(2), section 2(6) is an exception to the standard novelty requirement to accommodate new medical uses of substances or compositions.

2 EISAI/Second Medical Indication

As was seen in Chapter 7, the question of whether Article 54(5) EPC 1973 included second and further medical uses was answered in the affirmative by the EBA in *EISAI/Second medical indication* which sanctioned claims

---

77 H. Suchy, 'Patent Protection for Second Medicinal Use' [1982] 6 EIPR 161.

78 Ibid, at 162.

79 1977 Act, s. 4(3).

80 Cornish, Llewelyn and Aplin, *Intellectual Property*, p. 216.

81 Base Proposal for the Revision of the European Patent Convention 2000 Article 54(5), Explanatory Remarks, para. 1.

82 Section 4(3) provides that s. 4(2) shall not prevent a product consisting of a substance or composition being treated as capable of industrial application merely because it is invented for use in any such method. Section 4(3) of the 1977 Act has, by virtue of the 2004 Act, become s. 4A(2) of the 1977 Act: see Explanatory Notes to the Patents Act 2004 at para. 18.

that were directed to the 'use of a substance or composition for the manufacture of a medicament for a specified purpose'.[83] Therefore, to be patentable at that time, a claim for a second or further medical use must have been in the Swiss form.

3 Doctrinal Issues

(a) Only first medical use protected

The cases that first considered the scope of section 2(6) of the 1977 Act extended patent protection only to the first medical use. The claim in *Sopharma S.A'.s Application*[84] related to the discovery that a substance and its salts were effective in treating cancer. The issue was whether the invention lacked novelty for the purposes of section 2(6) of the 1977 Act if that substance is not known in: (a) any method of medical treatment; or (b) the same method of medical treatment. In other words, the question was whether or not the existence of a known therapeutic use of a compound prevented the invention, consisting of that same compound for use in a method of treatment of cancer, from being taken to be new in accordance with section 2(6).[85] The Principal Examiner was of the opinion that 'a known substance can only be claimed for use in a method of medical treatment the *first* time that it is disclosed as being useful in medical treatment'.[86] He continued by stating that '[o]nce the use of the compound in a method of medical treatment has formed part of the state of the art, it *cannot then be claimed* a second time in respect of some new medical use'.[87] The Principal Examiner was convinced that that was the correct approach because his view was reinforced by: first, the observations made in the Consultative Document on Patent Law Reform; secondly, the actual wording of Article 54(5) EPC 1973; and, thirdly, the Minutes of the Munich Diplomatic Conference.[88] Therefore, the Principal Examiner concluded that 'the words "in any such method" in section 2(6) mean in *any* method of medical treatment and not merely the method referred to in the invention under consideration'.[89]

---

[83] [1984] OJEPO 581.

[84] [1983] RPC 195.

[85] Ibid, at 197.

[86] Ibid, at 197–198 (emphasis in original).

[87] Ibid (emphasis added).

[88] Ibid.

[89] Ibid, at 199 (emphasis in original). That view was reiterated by the same Principal Examiner in *Bayer AG (Meyer's) Application* [1984] RPC 11 at 12. See generally, A. White, 'Patenting the Second Medical Indication' [1985] EIPR 62.

(b) A matter of principle

It was only a matter of time before the issue of second medical use patents arose for further consideration by the courts in the United Kingdom. The Patents Court, sitting *en banc*, in *Wyeth's Application* had to decide whether the reasoning in *EISAI/Second medical indication* was applicable to similar provisions under the 1977 Act. The court had to consider a claim which related to a chemical compound that was not only effective in lowering blood pressure but also had the unexpected property of preventing diarrhoea. The issue, as the court saw it, involved a consideration of the 'allowability of claims directed to an invention based on the discovery of a second (or subsequent) pharmaceutical use of a known substance or composition, already known for a particular medical use (or particular medical uses), the new use being unconnected with the previously known use or uses and not being an obvious development'.[90] The court considered *Sopharma S.A'.s Application*, noting that 'we think it right to state that, in our judgment, in so construing section 2(6) in *Sopharma* the principal examiner was plainly correct and *Sopharma* rightly decided that the [claims under consideration] were rightly refused as lacking novelty'.[91]

The court was of the opinion that 'claims in the form of the [second medical use claims] are impermissible as contrary to section 4(2) of the [1977] Act and the principal examiner was right to refuse to allow [such claims]'.[92] It pointed out that sections 4(3) and 2(6) do not limit the type of pharmaceutical inventions that might be patented pursuant to both sections; and that, in particular, 'there can be no objections to the patenting in the Swiss form of claim of an invention directed to a second or subsequent medical use of a known pharmaceutical *if* the statutory requirement of novelty can be met'.[93] These arguments are unassailable if a rather simplistic textual analysis is applied. It must be appreciated that the EBA in *EISAI/Second medical indication* eschewed such reliance and made what seemed to most commentators to be a policy decision that patent protection should extend to second and further medical uses. The debate relating to the propriety or otherwise of that approach is now a sterile one in light of the explicit protection for second and further medical uses found in Article 54(5) EPC 2000.

(c) The desire to achieve conformity

The Patents Court in *Wyeth's Application* noted that, had the position to be decided only in accordance with the provisions under the 1977 Act, without

---

90 *Wyeth's Application*, at 556.
91 Ibid, at 558.
92 Ibid. This point was again reiterated at 559.
93 *Wyeth's Application*, at 565 (emphasis added).

regard to developments at the EPO, 'the better view would be that a claim in the Swiss form to an invention directed to the use of a known pharmaceutical to manufacture a medicament, not in itself novel, for a second or subsequent and novel medical use would not be novel as lacking the required novelty'.[94] After considering the decision of the EBA in *EISAI/Second medical indication*, the court felt that the Swiss-type claim would not be novel and, therefore, not patentable. The court opined that, had it been the intention of the legislature to provide protection for second medical use patents, it could have simply omitted the word 'any' from section 2(6).[95] However, the court informed itself of the requirement, under section 91(1) of the 1977 Act, to take judicial notice of decisions of any relevant convention court (interpreted to extend to decisions of the EBA of the EPO).[96] The court further noted that the approach adopted in *EISAI/Second medical indication* was, therefore, equally possible under the corresponding provisions of the 1977 Act. Therefore, the reasoning of the EBA in *EISAI/Second medical indication* was applied because of 'the desirability of achieving conformity', although the court thought it did not represent 'the *better* view'.[97]

(d) The current UK approach

(i) Reluctant application by Jacob J. It was clear that the claimed methods in *Bristol-Myers Squibb* were in the Swiss form of claim. Jacob J., before examining the nature of the claim, pointed out that 'an ordinary skilled man (to whom the [claim] is notionally addressed) would find it puzzling, unless he has been initiated in some *Byzantine logic of patent law and jurisprudence*'.[98] The Swiss form of claim, he pointed out, was 'trying to steer clear of two obstacles to patentability': first, the exclusion of methods of medical treatment from patent protection; and, secondly, the requirement for novelty.[99] Jacob J. considered the ratio of the decision of the EBA in *EISAI/Second medical indication*, noting that, even when a substance is old, the Swiss form of claim is 'said to confer novelty and yet not be a method of medical treatment'.[100] His Lordship further pointed out that the EBA was not at all concerned with questions relating to infringement,

[94] Ibid.
[95] Ibid.
[96] Ibid, at 567.
[97] Ibid (emphasis added).
[98] *Bristol-Myers Squibb* (HC), at 271 (emphasis added).
[99] Ibid.
[100] Ibid.

noting that there were serious difficulties with *EISAI/Second medical indication*.[101] The first was the lack of justification for the reasons why the manufacture of any medicament is rendered new because of the new use.[102] The second related to whether the addition of the purpose of the manufacture made the process any 'newer'.[103] These considerations, Jacob J. noted, were already canvassed by the court in *Wyeth's Application* which had followed *EISAI/Second medical indication* notwithstanding the serious reservations it had with that decision. Similarly, Jacob J. felt bound by *EISAI/Second medical indication* because of: (a) the desirability of achieving conformity accepted by the Patents Court in *Wyeth's Application*, and the House of Lords in *Merrell Dow*;[104] and (b) the need to avoid a fragmentation of the European system of patent law.[105]

Nonetheless, the question was whether the claimed method satisfied the requirements of the Swiss form of claim. Jacob J. held that the claim in *Bristol-Myers Squibb* was 'not a case of second medical use at all. The use is the same. *All you have new in the patent is more information about that use*. I think that is right'.[106] The new information that the old three-hour infusion regime caused less neutropenia 'does not more than give the skilled man yet another motive to use three-hour infusion with premedication'.[107] The claim was, therefore, not a second medical use claim.

(ii) Reaffirmation by the Court of Appeal As mentioned above, claim 1 of the Bristol-Myers Squibb patent specification was for the use of taxol and sufficient medications for manufacturing a medicament (over a period of about 3 hours or less) for treating cancer and simultaneously reducing neutropenia. The Court of Appeal in *Bristol-Myers Squibb* confirmed that the reasoning of the EBA in *EISAI/Second medical indication* was equally applicable under the provisions of the 1977 Act. Aldous L.J. accepted that the claim was not directed to a second medical use; and, since 'the medicaments in question were known to be suitable for treating cancer', 'the reasoning in *Eisai* does not apply'.[108] The claim, in His Lordship's opinion, actually related 'to the way that such a medicament was to be used'.[109] In

---

101 Ibid, at 272.
102 Ibid.
103 Ibid.
104 *Merrell Dow Pharmaceuticals v N H Norton* [1996] RPC 76.
105 *Bristol-Myers Squibb* (HC), at 273.
106 Ibid, at 277 (emphasis added).
107 Ibid, at 279.
108 *Bristol-Myers Squibb* (CA), at 17.
109 Ibid.

other words, the patent did not teach 'how to manufacture a drug for use in the treatment of the patient, which would be in the form at least of a Swiss-type claim, but how to treat the patient'.[110] Therefore, as mentioned above, the claim was simply an 'unsuccessful attempt to monopolise the new method of treatment by drafting it along the lines of the Swiss-type claim'.[111]

Buxton L.J. argued that it was far from clear that the wording of Article 54(5) EPC 1973 should be interpreted to mean 'as referring to any method *whatsoever*'.[112] His Lordship thought such an argument was unpersuasive[113] – if the intention of the drafters of Article 54(5) EPC 1973 was to exclude second medical use patents, they could have easily provided it in the form: 'provided that its use for any *other* method of treatment, etc., is not already comprised in the state of the art'.[114] Once that objection is excluded, Buxton L.J. continued, the conclusion of the EBA in *EISAI/Second medical indication* 'seems ... irresistible'.[115] His Lordship observed, however, that the use of the Swiss-type claims may seem to be 'merely a roundabout way of seeking to patent a medical process, and one that only doubtfully gives proper weight to the first sentence of Article 52(4)'.[116] However, Buxton L.J. was of the opinion that it was not open to the Court of Appeal 'to use such doubts as a reason for not applying *Eisai* at all'.[117]

The doubts concerning the decision of the EBA in *EISAI/Second medical indication* were not sufficient for the Court of Appeal to reject its reasoning.[118] The court accepted the reasoning of the EBA in *EISAI/Second medical indication* that it was necessary, by analogy with first medical uses, to allow patents for second and further medical uses. The consistent application of the principle in *EISAI/Second medical indication* meant that the novelty must lie in the end result at which the use is directed and not in the nature of the use itself.[119] This meant that 'the relationship between the first and second medical use must be of the same nature: the second medical use must be for an end-purpose distinctively different from the first, albeit also medical, purpose for which the substance was used'.[120]

---

110 Ibid, at 28 (Buxton L.J.). See also, Holman J. at 30.
111 Ibid, at 21.
112 Ibid, at 25 (emphasis in original).
113 Ibid.
114 Ibid (emphasis in original).
115 Ibid.
116 Ibid, at 26.
117 Ibid.
118 Ibid.
119 Ibid.
120 *Bristol-Myers Squibb* (CA), at 26 (Buxton L.J.).

However, '[i]f novelty can lie in the nature of use, rather than the end-result at which that use aims, then it is indeed the method of medical treatment on which patentability rests'[121] and that would offend section 4(2) of the 1977 Act.

All three members of the Court of Appeal agreed with Jacob J. that the claim was not directed to a second medical use, which meant that the learning in *EISAI/Second medical indication* could not be applied.[122] The claims in question were not for a new therapeutic use of taxol, but rather the same use (the treatment of cancer using the drug taxol in sufficient medications). The medicaments in *Bristol-Myers Squibb* were 'already known for treating cancer'[123] and were simply 'an improvement in the method of administering an existing treatment',[124] which did not satisfy the test in *EISAI/Second medical indication* that 'there must be a therapeutic application or purpose which was not only inventive but new'.[125] The only difference was in the manner of use (the infusion of the drug from over 24 hours to about three hours or less).[126] The product was a known one (taxol), the method of treatment was an old one (infusion) and the purpose (treating cancer) was also well known. One of the salient requirements of the Swiss-type claim – the new purpose – was completely non-existent. The only new aspect of the claim was the *manner* of use. The Court of Appeal, therefore, held that the reduction in the time of the infusion of taxol to three hours, as compared to 24 hours, was not a functional technical feature of the claim and, certainly, not a novel feature worthy of patent protection.[127] The reduction in neutropenia was the only effect of using reduced dosages of taxol over a shorter period. The purpose was still the same although the procedure was carried out in a more effective and efficient manner. The applicant simply sought to patent new information about the effectiveness of the use of taxol for treating cancer.

The Swiss-type claim is directed at the *manufacture* of the medicament, which meant that the claims in the patent specification must teach *how* the medicament was to be made. Indeed, the medicament in *Bristol-Myers Squibb* was 'manufactured' inside the patient – an event that could hardly

---

121 Ibid.

122 Ibid, at 17 (Aldous L.J.); at 27 (Buxton L.J.) and at 30 (Holman J.).

123 Ibid, at 17 (Aldous L.J.).

124 Ibid, at 27 (Buxton L.J.).

125 Ibid, at 30 (Holman J.).

126 The Court of Appeal noted that novelty was lost because the Winograd lecture contained clear and unmistakeable directions to carry out the three-hour infusion, which would have resulted in less neutropenia.

127 *Bristol-Myers Squibb* (CA), at 18.

be said to constitute a *manufacture* of the medicament in any sense of the word. The form of the claim cannot be determinative of the question, so regard must be had to: (i) the purpose of the exclusion of methods of medical treatment from patent protection, as interpreted by the EPO;[128] and (ii) the effect of the claim, when determining patentability.[129] The attempt by Bristol-Myers Squibb to patent a method of medical treatment under the guise of second medical use patent was thwarted. Medical use patents are exceptions to the exclusion of methods of medical treatment (also an exception to patentability) and should therefore be narrowly interpreted.

Although the Court of Appeal was quite equivocal that such treatment regimes were not patentable because they were effectively excluded methods of medical treatment, the issue arose again in *Teva Industries Ltd v Instituto Gentili SpA*.[130] In that decision, the claim was for a substance that contained an active ingredient taken orally for the treatment of urolithiasis and the inhibition of bone reabsorption. The patent, in the court's opinion, was 'for the preparation of a medicament which can be used in a weekly 70mg dosing regime',[131] 'rather than the known 10mg a day'.[132] The patent, which only taught that 'a particular dosage regime is new',[133] was sought because the dosage of once a week produced fewer adverse GI events and was more convenient for patients who would only have to fast and stay upright for 30 minutes once a week.[134] The defendants argued that the patent was an excluded method of medical treatment. Jacob J., at first instance, observed that, but for the decision of *Bristol-Myers Squibb* and despite the width of the claim, he would not have concluded that it was a method of medical treatment.[135] He pointed out that the monopoly covered the preparation of the dose to be administered to the patient, and not its actual administration.[136] The fact that the claim could cover the activities of a nurse or physician when they measured out the doses to be administered to the patient was immaterial because that would be an act of

---

128 Ibid, at 21.
129 Ibid, at 28 (Buxton LJ).
130 [2003] EWHC Civ 5; [2003] FSR 29.
131 Ibid, at [71].
132 Ibid, at [67].
133 Ibid, at [70].
134 Ibid.
135 Ibid, at [71].
136 Ibid.

preparation, not administration.[137] His Lordship grudgingly followed the 'principle' enunciated in *Bristol-Myers Squibb*, but concluded that:[138]

> the claim is in substance to a method of treatment of the human body by therapy. *I do so with regret*. For patents are provided to *encourage* research. If new and non-obvious improved methods of administration of known drugs for known diseases are not patentable in principle – even with the Swiss form claim, then there will be less of a research incentive to find such methods. Giving the exception a narrow scope, so that any preparation used in such a method is protectable if only by the artificial construct of a Swiss form claim, *would be a research incentive*. But I must follow the current state of interpretation of the exception in *Bristol-Myers*.

On appeal, the Court of Appeal,[139] applying *Bristol-Myers Squibb*, agreed with Jacob J. that the claim was for a method of medical treatment within section 4(2) of the 1977 Act and dismissed the appeal.

(e) Applying the requirements of the Swiss-type claim

Any Swiss-type form of claim must satisfy two indispensable requirements: first, a *manufacture of a medicament*; and, secondly, a *new therapeutic, surgical or diagnostic application* of that medicament. The use of a Swiss-type claim, arguably, enabled patentees to use section 2(6) to circumvent the exclusion of methods of medical treatment in section 4(2) by claiming *the manufacture* of the medicament.

(i) Manufacture of a medicament A claim for the preparation of a medicament is an invention for a process, which means that the exact manner of manufacture must be clearly delineated in the claims.[140] In *Monsanto v Merck*, Pumfrey J., at first instance, had to consider the ambit of the phrase 'preparing a medicament', as used in the claims in the patent specification. Pumfrey J. observed that these words 'are concerned with the step of preparation of the medicament as opposed to preparation of the active ingredient. Ex hypothesi, the active ingredient is outside the claim and is not present in the result of the preparation'.[141] The patent specification must provide sufficient instructions to enable the reader to make the

---

[137] Ibid.

[138] Ibid, at [80] (emphasis added).

[139] *Instituto Gentili SpA v Teva Pharmaceutical Industries* Ltd [2003] EWCA Civ 1545 at [59].

[140] *Monsanto & Company v Merck & Co. Inc* [2000] RPC 77, 92.

[141] Ibid, at 85.

medicament.[142] This, it has been emphasised, is evident from the use of the word *manufacture* in the Swiss-type claim.[143] It is not sufficient for the claim to describe how the medicament is to be used, in which case it would effectively be covering a method of medical treatment.[144] If the patent merely teaches how the invention is to be used then it will be a use claim *simpliciter*, and this type of claim is an excluded method of medical treatment.

(ii) New therapeutic application? The other distinct feature of the Swiss-type claim was that the claim must always indicate the new therapeutic, surgical or diagnostic application. As was seen in Chapter 7, the EBA, in *EISAI/Second medical indication*, was there dealing with the interaction of Article 54(5) EPC 1973 and Article 52(4) EPC, but its focus was only on therapeutic methods. This meant that its analysis related primarily to that exclusion and thus the full scope of the interaction of those two Articles cannot be gleaned by focusing on therapeutic methods, since Article 52(4) EPC (and now Article 53(c) EPC) has three exclusions, namely, therapeutic, surgical and diagnostic methods. The interpretation of that exclusion can neither focus only on one, nor can the interpretation of each import aspect relating to the other, since each has its own sphere of operation. This much was reiterated by the EBA in *MEDI-PHYSICS/Treatment by surgery* when it accepted that the nature of interventions excluded from patent protection as a method of treatment by surgery cannot focus on whether it is for a curative purpose, as this related to methods of treatment by therapy. With this in mind, most of the decisions in this area have focused on therapeutic methods, so, naturally, one of the requirements was that the Swiss form of claim must have a therapeutic purpose in order to satisfy the requirements of Article 54(5) EPC 1973, as interpreted by the EBA in *EISAI/Second medical indication*.

In relation to therapeutic methods, therefore, the novelty of the claim should reside not in the manner of use (since it would be either old or effectively a method of treatment) but in the new therapeutic purpose.[145] This could be achieved by showing that there is no connection between the new use and any old uses,[146] or that the claim is directed to a known medicament to treat an illness *not previously treated* by that substance.[147]

[142] See *American Home Products v Novartis* [2001] RPC 8.
[143] *Monsanto & Company*, at 85.
[144] *Bristol-Myers Squibb* (CA), at 28.
[145] Ibid.
[146] *Wyeth's Application*, at 566.
[147] *EISAI/Second medical indication* (G 05/83), at 248 (emphasis added).

The patentee must also show that the invention had been made, not that there was a mere possibility that it could be made.[148] Simply listing the possible medical uses would not suffice because the House of Lords has cautioned that patentees must not be allowed to monopolise every use of a product without providing the necessary support for the claims.[149] Second medical use claims must show how the claimed substance or composition is effective to achieve the new treatment; if this was not so (or not discernibly so), it would not be suitable for that treatment.[150] The specification in such claims must: (a) support the claims in respect of any substance or composition, forming part of a class, which are directed at a particular medical use;[151] and (b) provide, by way of description, enough material to enable the person skilled in the art to say that the medicament does actually treat the alleged condition.[152]

(f) Codification of EISAI/Second medical indication

Patent protection for first and second (and further) medical uses of substances and compositions has now been separately provided for in the 2004 Act. The rationale for the change was to 'simplify and clarify the manner in which patent protection may be obtained for such inventions'.[153] Section 2(6), which was originally thought to extend only to first medical uses of known substances and compositions, is retained in the same form in section 4A(3) of the 1977 Act. This provision states that, in the case of an invention consisting of a substance or composition for use in any such method, the fact that the substance or composition forms part of the state of the art shall not prevent the invention from being taken to be new if the use of the substance or composition in any such method does not form part of the state of the art. Interestingly, the Government's view was that the

---

[148] *Hoerrmann's Application* [1996] RPC 341, 345 applied in *McManus Application* [1994] FSR 558 and *Consultants Suppliers Ltd's Application* [1996] RPC 348, 352.

[149] *Biogen Inc. v Medeva plc* [1996] RPC 1, 52.

[150] *Pfizer Ltd's Patents* [2001] FSR 16 at para. 42. The court also made it clear that it did not matter that success involved the collaboration of the compound with other agents.

[151] See generally, B. Domeij, 'Patent Claim Scope: Initial and Follow-on Pharmaceutical Inventions' [2001] EIPR 326 and P. Marsico, 'The Chemical-Pharmaceutical Product Patent: Absolute Protection, General Formulas and Sufficiency of Description' [1990] EIPR 397. The rules in relation to selection patents are also applicable here: *American Home Products v Novartis*, at [34]. See generally, Cornish, Llewelyn and Aplin, *Intellectual Property*, pp. 188–89.

[152] *Prendergast's Applications* [2000] RPC 446. See also, *Imperial Chemical Industries Ltd (Richardson's) Application* [1981] RPC 609, 611.

[153] Explanatory Notes to the Patents Act 2004 at para. 19.

new provision only applies where 'the substance or composition is *first* used in a method of treatment or diagnosis'.[154]

In relation to second (and further) medical uses, the new section 4A(4) of the 1977 Act, which mirrors Article 54(5) EPC 2000, codifies the *EISAI/ Second medical indication* principle, providing for a simpler method of patent protection for second and further medical uses. It provides that, in the case of an invention consisting of a substance or composition of a specific use in any such method, the fact that the substance or composition forms part of the state of the art shall not prevent the invention from being taken to be new, if that specific use does not form part of the state of the art. The Government's explanation was that such claims are allowed only '[w]here the substance or composition is subsequently used in a method of treatment or diagnosis which is different from the method in which it was first used'.[155] It stated that the new section 4A(4) allows patent protection for the 'second or subsequent use of a substance or composition in a method of treatment or diagnosis by a direct claim in the form "Substance X for use in treatment of disease Y"'.[156] It further stated that 'the Swiss form of claim will still be possible, but inventions may now be claimed in the simpler form'.[157]

E DOSAGE REGIMES

1 Setting the Scene

The issue has arisen under the jurisprudence of the TBAs of the EPO, and most recently in the United Kingdom, whether dosage regimes are patentable. Essentially, the question revolves around whether they amount to an excluded method of medical treatment, in particular, a method of treatment of the human or animal body by therapy. Patents relating to dosage regimes usually claim, not the product itself, but, specifically, its administration to the patient, and may include, *inter alia*, the number of times it should be administered, or the times of day, or period during which administration should take place.

The issue of whether dosage regimes are patentable is in a state of flux at the EPO, with differing decisions of the TBA. Meanwhile, the British

---

154 Ibid, at para. 20 (emphasis added).
155 Ibid, at para. 21.
156 Ibid, at para. 22.
157 Ibid.

courts have not been silent.[158] Initially, following the lead of the EPO,[159] the Court of Appeal in *Bristol-Myers Squibb v Baker Norton Pharmaceuticals*[160] seemingly rejected the view that dosage regimes were patentable. However, through the persistent efforts of Jacob L.J. (at first instance in *Bristol-Myers Squibb* and again as first instance judge in *Teva*), the British position has come full circle with the subsequent decision of the Court of Appeal in *Actavis UK Limited v Merck & Co Inc*,[161] embracing patent protection for dosage regimes, in line with recent authority from the EPO.[162]

This section aims, first, to explore the role of second medical use patents in relation to the issue of patenting dosage regimes under the British Patents Act 1977 (before the changes made in 2004). It then analyses the decisions of the UK courts dealing with the issue. Finally, it critically analyses the Court of Appeal decision in *Actavis v Merck*.

A proper understanding of this issue is important if research is to determine the most efficient manner of administering drugs and drug therapies to patients. In such cases the court must navigate: (a) the unpatentability of methods of medical treatment; (b) the exception relating to novelty for 'first' medical uses of substances or compositions; (c) the extension of that exception to second and further medical uses by the EBA in *EISAI/Second medical indication* and (d) relevant public policy concerns, including public health considerations and the need for continued research and development in the medical field. It is unsurprising, therefore, that Jacob J. stated that 'an ordinary skilled man (to whom it is notionally addressed) would find [second medical use claims] puzzling, unless he had been initiated in some of the *Byzantine* logic of patent law and jurisprudence'.[163]

2 Introduction

As mentioned previously, second medical use patents, according to section 2(6) of the 1977 Act, cannot be excluded from patent protection on the

---

158 See Chapter 7.

159 *PROCTER & GAMBLE/Gastronintestinal compositions* (T 317/95) [1999] EPOR 528.

160 [2001] RPC 1. See A. Feros, 'Patentability of Methods of Medical Treatment' [2001] EIPR 79 and A. Horton, 'Methods of Treatment and Second Medical Use' (2000) *Patent World* 19.

161 [2008] EWCA Civ. 444; [2008] RPC 26. See F. Ch'en and I. Karet, 'Court of Appeal can overrule itself to follow the EPO: UK adopts EPO stance on second medical use claims' [2008] JIPLP 543.

162 *GENENTECH INC/Method of administration of IGF-I* (T 1020/03) [2006] EPOR 9.

163 [1999] RPC 253, 271.

basis that they are incapable of industrial application. When a substance or composition is new, it could be claimed as a product, including all its known or unknown uses. It is when the substance or composition has a known use that the exception applies,[164] because the claim would be for the product for that newly discovered therapeutic use. Such a claim would be incompatible with section 4(2) of the 1977 Act which excluded methods of medical treatment from patent protection. The pharmaceutical industry lobbied for an exception to that general exclusion and the resulting compromise, by way of compensation,[165] was found in section 2(6) of the 1977 Act, which allowed patent protection for a *new medical use* of an old substance or composition. Therefore, while section 4(3)[166] served as an exception to the exclusion in section 4(2), section 2(6) is an exception to the standard novelty requirement to accommodate new medical uses of substances or compositions.

3 Dosage Regimes: A First Look

The patenting of second medical use claims, particularly the Swiss form of claim, forms the backdrop against which patenting dosage regimes are decided, for it is armoured with such claims that patentees have sought to drive a coach and horses through the unpatentability of methods of medical treatment. As noted above, in *Bristol-Myers Squibb* Claim 1, which was in the Swiss form, was for the use of taxol and sufficient medications for manufacturing a medicament (over a period of about three hours or less) for treating cancer and simultaneously reducing neutropenia.[167] Jacob J. held that it was 'not a case of second medical use at all. The use is the same. *All you have new in the patent is more information about that use*. I think that is right'.[168] The new information that the three-hour infusion regime caused less neutropenia 'does no more than give the skilled man yet another motive to use three-hour infusion with premedication'.[169] The claim, in the opinion of Jacob J., was not, therefore, a second medical use claim.

---

[164] Cornish, Llewelyn and Aplin, *Intellectual Property*, p. 216.

[165] Base Proposal for the Revision of the European Patent Convention 2000 Article 54(5), Explanatory Remarks para 1.

[166] Section 4(3) provides that s. 4(2) shall not prevent a product consisting of a substance or composition being treated as capable of industrial application merely because it is invented for use in any such method. Section 4(3) of the 1977 Act has, by virtue of the 2004 Act, become s. 4A(2) of the 1977 Act: see Explanatory Notes to the Patents Act 2004, para. 18.

[167] Ventose [2008] IPQ 58, 75.

[168] [1999] RPC 253, 277 (emphasis added).

[169] Ibid, at 279.

However, any reasonable reading of the claim would reveal that it apparently related to a treatment regime for that particular patient because 'the patient was to, first, take a cocktail of premedication; and, second, to be administered a dosage of taxol, which was made specifically for that patient, using a combination of the patient's weight and height measurements'.[170] Jacob J. observed that 'the premedication is separate from the taxol and the taxol is made up to be patient specific',[171] which meant that the claim was 'directed at the use of taxol for making a medicamentation for administration (using premedication) under specified dosage and times'.[172] The claim, therefore, was 'for the manufacture of what is administered to the patient but stops short of being a claim actually to administration'.[173]

On appeal, the Court of Appeal had no doubt that the reasoning in *EISAI/Second medical indication* applied equally under the 1977 Act. Aldous L.J. considered that the claim was not directed to a second medical use; since 'the medicaments in question were known to be suitable for treating cancer', 'the reasoning in *Eisai* does not apply'.[174] Consequently, he reasoned that the claim actually related 'to the way that such a medicament was to be used'.[175] Buxton L.J. claimed that it did not teach 'how to manufacture a drug for use in the treatment of the patient, which would be in the form at least of a Swiss-type claim, but how to treat the patient'.[176] The claim was unashamedly an 'unsuccessful attempt to monopolise the new method of treatment by drafting it along the lines of the Swiss-type claim'.[177] However, he noted if 'novelty [of the claim] can lie in the nature of use, rather than the end-result at which that use aims, then it is indeed the method of treatment on which patentability rests',[178] which would offend the prohibition on patenting methods of medical treatments found in section 4(2) of the 1977 Act.

The Court of Appeal agreed unanimously with Jacob J. that the claim was not a second medical use; consequently, *EISAI/Second medical indication* could not be applied.[179] The claim in question was not for a new therapeutic use of taxol, because the medicaments were 'already known for

---

[170] Ventose [2008] IPQ 58, 66.
[171] [1999] RPC 253, 273.
[172] Ibid.
[173] Ibid.
[174] [2001] RPC 1, 17.
[175] Ibid.
[176] Ibid, at 28 (Buxton L.J.).
[177] Ibid.
[178] Ibid.
[179] Ibid, at 17 (Aldous L.J.); at 27 (Buxton L.J.) and at 30 (Holman J.).

treating cancer'.[180] The claimed method resulted in 'an improvement in the method of administering an existing treatment'[181] which did not meet the condition in *EISAI/Second medical indication* that 'there must be a therapeutic application or purpose which was not only inventive but new'.[182] As I have pointed out elsewhere:[183]

> The product was a known one (taxol), the method of treatment was an old one (infusion) and the purpose (treating cancer) was also well known. One of the salient requirements of the Swiss-type claim – the new purpose – was completely non-existent. The only new aspect of the claim was the *manner* of use.

The Court of Appeal, therefore, held that the reduction in the time of infusion of taxol to three hours, as compared to 24 hours, was not a functional technical feature of the claim and certainly not a novel feature worthy of patent protection.[184]

The decision in *Bristol-Myers Squibb* seemed quite equivocal that, under UK law, dosage regimes were not patentable.[185] Professor Cornish explains that as a result of *Bristol-Myers Squibb* 'more efficient or less harmful dosages in known treatment … still remain unpatentable', and that 'it is not within the "second medical use" exception to claim a medicament so formulated that it would release the drug taxol over three hours instead of 24, thus reducing its side effects'.[186] However, Jacob J., whose decision was overruled in *Bristol-Myers Squibb*, remained steadfast. He returned to the issue of patentability of dosage regimes in *Teva Industries Ltd v Instituto Gentili SpA*.[187] There, the patent, which only taught that 'a particular dosage regime is new',[188] was sought because the dosage of once a week produced fewer adverse GI events and was more convenient for patients who would only have to fast and stay upright for 30 minutes once a week.[189] As mentioned above, Jacob J. observed that, but for *Bristol-Myers Squibb*

---

180 Ibid, at 17 (Aldous L.J.).
181 Ibid, at 27 (Buxton L.J.).
182 Ibid, at 30 (Holman J.).
183 Ventose [2008] IPQ 58, 76–77 (emphasis in original).
184 [2001] RPC 1, 18.
185 The Intellectual Property Office accepted this view: Examination Guidelines for Patent Application relating to Medical Inventions in the UK Intellectual Property Office, June, 2007 at para. 111.
186 Cornish, Llewelyn and Aplin, *Intellectual Property*, p. 217.
187 [2003] FSR 498.
188 Ibid, at [70].
189 Ibid.

and despite the width of the claim, he would not have held that it was a method of medical treatment.[190]

4 Dosage Regimes: Reconsideration in Actavis

(a) Introduction

At issue in *Actavis v Merck*[191] was the question of whether dosage or treatment regimes are patentable in the United Kingdom. The Court of Appeal reversed its previous decision in *Bristol-Myers Squibb* that seemingly held that they were not.

(b) At first instance

At first instance, before Warren J., Actavis sought revocation of Merck's patent, which was in the Swiss form of claim and was for the use of finasteride for the treatment of baldness at a daily dose of 0.05 to 1mg.[192] Their argument was based on an earlier patent that described the use of finasteride, but only at 5mg daily, as part of a prostate enlargement treatment.[193] The patent also made reference to the use of finasteride as an anti-baldness treatment.[194]

Actavis persuaded Warren J. that the facts were indistinguishable from those underlying *Bristol-Myers Squibb*.[195] Warren J., accepting that as a judge at first instance he was bound by *Bristol-Myers Squibb*, held that to be patentable in the Swiss form of claim, the second medical use claim must evidence a specified therapeutic application (or purpose) that was, not only non-obvious, but also new.[196] Consistently with *Bristol-Myers Squibb*, Warren J. noted that novelty of the substance cannot lie in the method of use (for if so, it will be an excluded method of medical treatment), but must simply relate to a new therapeutic purpose.[197] It followed that a different dosage regime (even if new and non-obvious) cannot meet the novelty threshold required for second-medical use claims.[198] Warren J., nonetheless, decided the issue of obviousness in the patentee's favour.[199] Stripped to its

---

190 Ibid, at [71].
191 [2008] EWCA Civ. 444; [2008] RPC 26.
192 [2007] EWHC 1311 at [9].
193 Ibid, at [6].
194 Ibid, at [25].
195 Ibid, at [23].
196 Ibid, at [22].
197 Ibid, at [27].
198 Ibid.
199 Ibid, at [121].

essentials, the issue in *Actavis v Merck* was whether a claim in the Swiss-type form was acceptable under section 2(6) of the UK Patents Act 1977 (before the amendments under the 2004 Patents Act), where the only novel feature of that claim resided in the dosage amount of 0.05 to 1.0 mg of the medicament per day.

(c) The Court of Appeal

The Court of Appeal allowed the appeal by Merck on the question of novelty and patentability, dismissing the cross-appeal by Actavis in relation to obviousness.[200] In so doing, the Court of Appeal, surprisingly, held that second medical use claims (in the Swiss form of claim) do not need to evidence a new therapeutic application (that is an identifiable and different medical indication): novelty can lie in a new dosage regime (or other form of administration or treatment) of a known substance or composition for a known medical indication.[201] Jacob L.J. pointed out that, in line with previous UK authority, 'Swiss form claims have long been accepted in the UK', citing *Wyeth*,[202] *Bristol-Myers Squibb* at first instance, and *Bristol-Myers Squibb* in the Court of Appeal. The Swiss form of claim was examined in detail by Jacob L.J., who accepted the *ratio* of *EISAI/Second medical indication* that such claims must relate primarily to the new (second (or further)) medical purpose of the medicament,[203] the EBA was saying that 'the novelty of the process (i.e. use of X in the manufacture of a medicament for Y) comes from the "new therapeutic use" '.[204] Having accepted that statement as the *ratio* of *EISAI/Second medical indication*, Jacob L.J. proceeded to ask himself:[205]

> Does this mean only treatment of a different disease ("second medical indication" in a narrow sense), or does it also extend to a different method of using a compound for treatment of a particular disease when it was already known for use in treating that disease but by a different method?

It is uncertain how this question can be posed in light of what Jacob L.J. accepted as the *ratio* of *EISAI/Second medical indication*. His Lordship

---

200 Ibid, at [120].
201 Ibid, at [49].
202 [1985] RPC 545.
203 [2008] EWCA Civ 444 at [27].
204 Ibid.
205 Ibid, at [28].

thought 'that the latter should be the answer is fairly clear from policy', stating that:[206]

> Research into new and better dosage regimes is clearly desirable – and there is simply no policy reason why, if a novel non-obvious regime is invented, there should not be an appropriate patent reward. Such a reward cannot extend to covering the actual treatment but a Swiss form claim which specifies the new, inventive, regime is entirely in accordance with policy.

Importantly, Jacob L.J. also preferred the statement made by the EBA to the effect that, in principle, there will be no difficulty over the question of novelty where the medicament has novel technical features – for example, a new formulation, *dosage* or synergistic combination.[207] However, with all due respect to Jacob L.J., this statement was merely *obiter* – the EBA did not intend to dilute its holding that the novelty of Swiss-type claims resides solely in the new therapeutic (or surgical or diagnostic) use to which the old substance is put. Jacob L.J. then swiftly concluded that 'on the basis of *Eisai* alone we hold that Swiss form of claims are allowable where the novelty is conferred by a new dosage regime or other form of administration of a substance',[208] retreating from this startling holding by claiming that it is 'far from saying that in general just specifying a new dosage regime in a Swiss form of claim can give rise to a valid patent'.[209] Such claims, he continued:[210]

> On the contrary nearly always such dosage regimes will be obvious – it is standard practice to investigate appropriate dosage regimes. Only in an unusual case such as the present (where, see below, treatment for the condition with the substance had ceased to be worth investigating with any dosage regime) could specifying a dosage regime as part of the therapeutic use confer validity on an otherwise invalid claim.

Jacob L.J. was not the first to treat that statement by the EBA as the philosopher's stone, undetected by previous decisions of the TBAs until recently, or by courts throughout the Member States of the EPC which can convert the base metal of unpatentable subject matter into the gold of

---

206 Ibid, at [29].
207 Ibid, at [22].
208 Ibid, at [31].
209 Ibid, at [32].
210 Ibid.

patentability. He does not, however, explain how the trick is done.[211] Similarly, the TBA in *GENENTECH INC/Method of administration of IGF-I*[212] accepted that same statement of the EBA in *EISAI/Second medical indication* as allowing Swiss form claims, directed to the use of a composition for manufacture of a medicament for a specified new and inventive therapeutic (or surgical or diagnostic) application, where the novelty of the application might lie only in the dose to be used or the manner of application.[213] That was the first decision of the TBA to hold that dosage regimes were patentable under the EPC 1973. Consequently, Jacob L.J. thought that not only does the EPO take 'the same view about the effect of *Eisai* as us', but that there 'is now clear [EBA] authority holding, as we do, that it follows from *Eisai* that a novel dosage regime can confer novelty to a Swiss form claim'.[214] If that result follows from *EISAI/Second medical indication*, it scarcely would be necessary to pose the question at [28] (quoted above). Unsurprisingly, therefore, Jacob L.J. believed that *GENENTECH INC/ Method of administration of IGF-I* 'was hardly a new departure in some respects, even though it disapproved of certain earlier decisions'.[215] Jacob L.J. wholeheartedly embraced decisions of the TBA that followed *GENENTECH INC/ Method of administration of IGF-I*,[216] which did nothing more to explain why dosage regimes are novel using the Swiss form of claim. All they do is apply that decision without any explanation or elaboration. Not surprisingly, Jacob L.J. ignored some decisions of the EPO which had signalled that such dosage regimes were unpatentable,[217] observing that Swiss form of claims, whose novelty depends on a new treatment by a different dosage regime or method of administration, are treated as novel and not as claims to a method of medical treatment, has been accepted by the EPO, in Germany and even in New Zealand. In His Lordship's opinion, these developments meant that the 'position is settled'.[218]

(d) Obviousness

On obviousness, Warren J. held that, although treating androgenic alopecia with finasteride had been previously suggested, by the priority date the

---

211 A phrase borrowed from the judgment of Lord Hoffmann in *Lewis v AG of Jamaica* [2001] 2 AC 50, 88 where he used it in an altogether dissimilar context.

212 (T 1020/03), [2006] EPOR 9.

213 [2008] EWCA Civ 444 at [72].

214 Ibid, at [33].

215 Ibid, at [34].

216 Ibid, at [37]–[40].

217 For example, *PROCTER & GAMBLE/Gastrointestinal Compositions* (T317/95) [1999] EPOR 528.

218 [2008] EWCA Civ 444 at [44].

expectations of the person skilled in the art that this condition could successfully be treated had been reduced to a point where he would not even start investigating suitable doses.[219] Jacob L.J. upheld the inventiveness of the claim: although it seemed incredible, an invention which might be obvious on one date may later become non-obvious.[220] Obviousness, nonetheless, must be determined at the priority date of the invention claimed.[221] However, His Lordship noted that since it was standard practice to investigate appropriate dosage regimes of known substances or compositions with a view to ascertaining the most efficient and effective dose, the Swiss form of claims relating to dosage regimes would almost inevitably be obvious.[222]

(e) What did Bristol-Myers Squibb decide?

The next issue for the Court of Appeal in *Actavis v Merck* was whether it should 'follow such settled jurisprudence' ('that a new dosage regime is enough to confer novelty on a Swiss form of claim'[223]). Since the received understanding of *Bristol-Myers Squibb* stood in the way of so holding, the secondary question was what *Bristol-Myers Squibb* actually decided.[224] Jacob L.J. observed that many have interpreted *Bristol-Myers Squibb* as deciding that (a) a novel, non-obvious dosage regime specified in a Swiss form of claim cannot make it novel and (b) such a claim is to a method of medical treatment.[225] His Lordship also pointed out that there was widespread acceptance that that was what *Bristol-Myers Squibb* decided by: (a) the Opposition Division in relation to parallel designation of the Bristol-Myers Squibb patent itself; (b) the EBA in *GENENTECH INC/ Method of administration of IGF-I*; (c) Jacob J. in *Merck's Patents*;[226] (d) the UK Intellectual Property Office and (e) Warren J. in this case.[227]

It was necessary to find out what *Bristol-Myers Squibb* actually decided, because it was only if a clear *ratio* could be found in it that it could bind a subsequent Court of Appeal.[228]

Jacob L.J.'s views of the judgments in *Bristol-Myers Squibb* will now be analysed: Are his criticisms justified? Jacob L.J. was of the opinion that

219 [2007] EWHC 1311 at [121].
220 [2008] EWCA Civ 444 at [119].
221 Ibid, at [118].
222 Ibid, at [32].
223 Ibid, at [49].
224 Ibid, at [46].
225 Ibid, at [50].
226 [2003] FSR 29.
227 [2008] EWCA Civ 444 at [50].
228 Ibid, at [56].

Aldous L.J. in *Bristol-Myers Squibb* 'did not decide that for novelty, a Swiss form claim must specify a second medical use in the sense of a distinct and different medical condition'.[229] The only novel feature of the invention over the prior art was that, by administering taxol over a period of about three hours or less, as compared to the previous 24-hour infusion, neutropenia is reduced. That fact was central to the argument of Aldous L.J. in relation to novelty of the Swiss form of the claim in question. Notwithstanding that Aldous L.J. decided that the claim was a method of medical treatment, which did not diminish his central argument that the new dosage regime was not a novel feature for the purposes of the Swiss form of claim, because the claim was for 'a discovery *not a second therapeutic use* as considered in *Eisai*'.[230] It is accepted that Aldous L.J. 'did *not* decide that for novelty, a Swiss form claim must specify a second medical use in the sense of a distinct and different medical condition';[231] but, it seems clear, from the tenor of his judgment, that he accepted that as implicit from the decision in *EISAI/ Second medical indication*.

Even in relation to the methods of medical treatment point, Jacob L.J.'s analysis is deficient. Aldous L.J., in *Bristol-Myers Squibb*, stated:[232]

> The invention was the discovery that by changing the treatment from a 24-hour infusion to three hours a similar effect was obtained with less neutropenia. That was a discovery that a change in the method of treatment provided the result. The claim is an unsuccessful attempt to monopolise the new method of treatment by drafting it along the lines of the Swiss form claim.

Three points should be noted. First, Aldous L.J. was clear that it was the change of treatment from 24 hours to three hours that constituted the invention. Secondly, the invention was held to be a method of medical treatment. Thirdly, such treatment cannot be patented in the Swiss form of claim. Aldous L.J. stated that the claim contained specific instructions for the physician, and was patient-specific. This, however, does not diminish his previous holding that such a claim was a method of medical treatment – his views on the specificity of the claims merely confirmed a conclusion he had already made. Jacob L.J. held that 'the method of treatment point [was decided by Aldous L.J.] on a narrow ground indeed. It was that if in essence the claim is merely to a method of treatment it is bad'.[233] Jacob L.J.

229 Ibid, at [57].
230 [2001] RPC 1, 21 (emphasis added).
231 [2008] EWCA Civ 444 at [57].
232 [2001] RPC 1, 21.
233 [2008] EWCA Civ 444 at [59].

observed that the claim, in the instant case, was far from that at issue in *Bristol-Myers Squibb* because it 'is in its essence directed at the manufacturer' and that the doctor's only involvement will be in prescribing for the treatment of 'the 1mg pill made by an alleged infringer'.[234] Therefore, Jacob L.J. argued that he 'did not regard Aldous L.J.'s *ratio* as binding in its effect so far as the general case of dosage specific Swiss form claims or so far as this case is concerned'.[235] But, if as argued above, Aldous L.J. was stating a general principle, without basing his decision on the specific claims, Jacob L.J.'s conclusion must be wrong.

The judgment of Buxton L.J. received similar treatment.[236] Jacob L.J. quoted the following passage from the judgment of Buxton L.J.:[237]

> If the Board's analogy is to hold, therefore, the relationship between the first and the second medical use must be of the same nature: the second medical use must be for an end-purpose distinctively different from the first, albeit also medical, purpose for which the substance was used. That not only follows from the structure of the Board's argument, but also from the need to respect the exclusion of methods for treatment from patentability. If the novelty can lie in the nature of use, rather than in the end-result at which that use aims, then it is indeed the method of treatment on which patentability rests.

Some preliminary remarks must be made about this passage. First, Buxton L.J. was plainly articulating and applying what he considered to be the *ratio* of *EISAI/Second medical indication*, for he specified that 'the second medical use must be for an *end-purpose* distinctively different from the *first, albeit also medical, purpose* for which the substance was used'. If this does not mean that the second medical use must be for a different purpose than the first, what would?! Secondly, if the invention, as mentioned above, was for the use of the three-hour infusion (as compared to the previous 24-hour one), the invention related to the nature of the use. This means, therefore, that Buxton L.J. rejected that claim as a method of medical treatment: '[i]f the *novelty* can lie in the *nature of use*, rather than in the *end-result at which that use aims*, then it is indeed the *method of treatment on which patentability rests*'.

It appears that Buxton L.J. was accepting a two-pronged argument: (i) that the purpose of the second medical use must be different from the first medical use, and (ii) that dosage regimes clearly are methods of

---

234 Ibid.
235 Ibid, at [59].
236 Ibid, at [60]–[64].
237 [2001] RPC 1, 26.

medical treatment. But is this not what we all thought (and some of us still think) *Bristol-Myers Squibb* decided? Jacob L.J. was not convinced, as he rejected the first assertion on the basis that 'some sentences suggest that this is so. But others do not',[238] failing to provide any evidence for his assertion, while accepting that the words '"for a different therapeutic purpose" has a very wide meaning and could encompass a different treatment for a known condition'.[239]

Jacob L.J.'s analysis does not withstand scrutiny. After citing the sections from the passage quoted above, he concluded that Buxton L.J. was 'not laying down a "different medical condition" rule'.[240] This conclusion seems unsupported in light of the clear meaning of the words used by Buxton L.J. who left no doubt as to what he meant to convey. It is true that Buxton L.J. was at pains to point out the exceptional nature of the claims in question, the invention being for a method of medical treatment. Therefore one can hardly disagree with Jacob L.J.'s view that the *ratio* emerging from that statement was that 'the claim concerned was essentially to a method of medical treatment'.[241] However, importantly, Buxton L.J. pointed out:[242]

> But that merely underlines that what the patent teaches is not how to manufacture a drug for use in the treatment of the patient, which would be in form at least a Swiss form claim, but how to treat the patient: which is the teaching that the Swiss-type claim is designed to avoid.

Notwithstanding his previous assertions, Buxton L.J. made it abundantly clear that the claim did not show 'how to manufacture a drug for use in the treatment of the patient' which, in his opinion, and in line with *EISAI/ Second medical indication*, 'would be in form at least a Swiss-type claim'. The question arises as to whether a dosage or treatment regime *simpliciter* is a method of medical treatment. If it is, dosage regimes remain unpatentable, even with the Swiss form of claim (which, as argued above, it was hardly meant to accommodate). If it is not, there is little reason, in principle, why they must necessarily be in the Swiss form of claim. I am not altogether convinced that 'it seems clear that the EPO would not accept [Buxton L.J.'s views] as correct', as Jacob L.J. suggested, claiming further that the EPO 'accepts that any Swiss form of claim by its nature stops short of claiming a method of medical treatment – it does not monopolise the

238 [2008] EWCA Civ 444 at [63].
239 Ibid, at [63].
240 Ibid, at [64].
241 Ibid, at [73].
242 [2001] RPC 1, 28.

actual treatment of the patient'.[243] But it does. It is suggested that giving a patentee a monopoly over how the patient is to take a particular drug does not provide here: (a) a monopoly over the product (for the product is old); (b) a claim to any new use (for clearly in such cases the use is the same); or (c) the manufacture of the product (in which case, the novelty must lie in the new use (as outlined in (b)).

What such claims actually do is to provide the patentee with a monopoly over how the patient, the physician or any other person administers the drug. It is further suggested that a dosage regime might, perhaps, be the simplest method of treatment of the body, but that since it might be so it is reason enough for it to be excluded, rightly, from patent protection on the basis that it offends the prohibition on patenting methods of medical treatment. Jacob L.J. was convinced that the new dosage regime was 'not enough in our view to mean that the claim is in substance to a method of treatment'.[244] He then distinguished the instant case from *Bristol-Myers Squibb* on the basis that '[t]here is nowhere near the degree of involvement of medical personnel which turned the case in *BMS*'.[245] That might be true, but it matters little if one accepts that dosage regimes are, in principle, methods of medical treatment.

Why should the degree of detail matter in the determination of whether a claim amounts to an excluded method of medical treatment? Even if the claim is window-dressed as claiming 'the use of finasteride for the preparation of a medicament of the specified dosages',[246] it does not alter the fact that the substance of the claim is not for any new use, but for the 'specified dosages'. Jacob L.J. comes close to saying that, if the method of treatment 'is not aimed at and does not touch the doctor – [and] is directed at the manufacturer',[247] it is patentable. But there is no such gloss on the exclusion from patent protection of methods of medical treatment. If the claim amounts to a method of medical treatment, it is not patentable. The EBA in *CYGNUS/Diagnostic method*[248] clarified that whether a claim is considered as an excluded method of medical treatment should not depend on the participation of the medical practitioner. Again, Jacob L.J.'s view that 'every prescription medicine must be prescribed – that does not mean that they are all methods of medical treatment'[249] cannot be correct because:

243 [2008] EWCA Civ 444 at [73].
244 Ibid, at [75].
245 Ibid.
246 Ibid.
247 Ibid.
248 (G 01/04) [2006] EPOR 15.
249 [2008] EWCA Civ 444 at [75].

(a) it is usually the medicine (substance or composition) itself that is patentable; (b) where the claims mention the actual dosage regime, it was never really intended to be part of the monopoly claimed; and (c) the prescription could, arguably, be considered – at its lowest – a method of medical treatment–which practitioners have hardly ever sought to patent over the years.

In respect of Holman J., Jacob L.J. noted that his statement 'there must be a therapeutic application or purpose which is not only inventive but new',[250] 'is not clearly saying that there has to be a treatment of a different disease'.[251] His Lordship emphasised that it was 'the application which has to be new and inventive – and a novel dosage regime which is inventive would seem to satisfy Holman J.'s test'.[252]

(f) Which novelty?

Jacob L.J. thought that, if one examined Warren J.'s judgment on the various points raised, it would illustrate 'particularly vividly why it was unlikely that *BMS* actually decided that a Swiss form of claim whose difference from the prior art is only in the dosage regime lacks novelty'.[253] Warren J. concluded that the claim lacked novelty because the only thing that differentiated it from the prior art was the new dosage regime. This conclusion appeared to surprise Jacob L.J., who pointed out that 'no one has ever used finasteride for that purpose or ever given clear and unmistakable directions to do so'.[254] So although Warren J. thought that 'it may be novel to use it in the small dosage which it is now apparent can result in successful treatment',[255] he felt bound by the holding in *Bristol-Myers Squibb* 'that *that* novelty was not enough to count as novelty for the purposes of validity'.[256] If that conclusion is correct, Jacob L.J. stated, it meant that:[257]

> there are two kinds of novelty attacks possible against Swiss form claims. First there is what may be called the 'conventional' novelty attack – the well-known *General Tire* [1972] RPC 457 at 485–6 'clear and unmistakable directions test.' But also available would be a different test – one asks is the novelty of the claim

---

[250] Ibid, at [101].
[251] Ibid, at [65].
[252] Ibid.
[253] Ibid, at [66].
[254] Ibid, at [67].
[255] [2007] EWHC 1311 at [27].
[256] [2008] EWCA Civ 444 at [68] (emphasis added).
[257] Ibid, at [69].

> only due to a novel dosage regime? If that is so then it does not matter that no one has ever proposed that regime – the claim lacks novelty.

Jacob L.J. was convinced that 'that cannot be so – there is only one novelty test and it is the *General Tire* test' and it was impossible to 'conclude that the court in *BMS* was holding that there are two tests and certainly it was not clearly doing so'.[258] His Lordship then concluded by stating that 'we are not satisfied that [*Bristol-Myers Squibb*] contains a clear *ratio* that a Swiss form claim lacks novelty if the only difference between it and the prior art is a new dosage regime for a known medical condition'.[259] As noted above, Jacob L.J. further observed that, in any event, *Bristol-Myers Squibb* was distinguishable from the instant case, because 'even if *BMS* is right on this point, it cannot be extended to cover every case where novelty depends on a specified dosage regime'.[260] It is suggested that the issue is *not* that dosage regimes cannot be novel, but as Warren J. pointed out, the novelty of dosage regimes is simply *not* what is required for the purposes of the Swiss form of claim, and that must be correct, in light of the learning from *EISAI/Second medical indication*.

(g) Precedent

The Court of Appeal stated that, if it was wrong that *Bristol-Myers Squibb* did not evidence a clear *ratio*, it should recognise a further exception to the precedent rules laid down in *Young v Bristol Aeroplane Company*.[261] The Court of Appeal, therefore, ruled that it 'is free but not bound to depart from the *ratio decidendi* of its own earlier decision if it is satisfied that the EPO Boards of Appeal have formed a settled view of European Patent law which is inconsistent with that earlier decision'.[262] Therefore, the Court of Appeal, following *GENENTECH INC/Method of administration of IGF-I*, allowed the appeal and held that a new dosage regime was enough to confer novelty on a Swiss form claim.[263]

5 Conclusion

Actavis v Merck rejected the received learning of *Bristol-Myers Squibb* by, first, claiming that it contained no *ratio* to the effect that: (a) a novel,

---

[258] Ibid, at [70].
[259] Ibid, at [71].
[260] Ibid, at [75].
[261] [1944] KB 718.
[262] [2008] EWCA Civ 444 at [107].
[263] Ibid, at [84].

non-obvious dosage regime specified in a Swiss form of claim cannot make it novel and (b) such a claim is to a method of medical treatment.[264] Secondly, if it was wrong on that point, the Court of Appeal accepted that, since the EPO had a 'settled view' to the contrary, it was entitled (but not bound) to follow that view, even if it was inconsistent with *Bristol-Myers Squibb*. In this instance, it decided to follow *GENENTECH INC/Method of administration of IGF-I*.

In any event, since the decision in *Actavis v Merck* was based on Article 54(5) EPC 1973 (as enacted in section 2(6) of the Patents Act 1977), it will have little impact on patentees forwarding the future. If anything, it will provide some (*albeit* very limited) guidance to the EBA when it finally considers the similar question of whether patent protection is available for dosage regimes under Article 53(c) and Article 54(5) EPC 2000, pursuant to the referral to it by the TBA in *KOS LIFE SCIENCES INC/Dosage regimen*.[265] The EBA, which has now decided the referral, could have agreed with Jacob L.J. in *Actavis v Merck* that patent protection should be provided for dosage regimes, on the basis that: first, there is no difference, in substance, between patenting second medical uses under Article 54(5) EPC 1973, as explained by the EBA in *EISAI/Second medical indication*, and the new Article 54(5) EPC; and, secondly, the decision in *EISAI/Second medical indication* compels that result. Indeed, as was seen in Chapter 7, the EBA in *ABBOTT RESPIRATORY/Dosage regime* agreed with the conclusion of Jacob L.J. that patent protection is available for dosage regimes under the EPC, on the basis that the specific use in Article 54(5) EPC should not be confined only to a new disease, but to any new uses. However, for reasons fully argued in Chapter 7, the EBA might have simply got it wrong.

F CONCLUSION

The 1977 Act maintained the exclusion of methods of medical treatment from patent protection in the United Kingdom, albeit in statutory form. It heralded the halt to the quest to find a rationale for the judicially-created (if not accepted) exclusion which had engaged much of the time of the courts and the Patent Appeal Tribunal in the period before 1977. Although the exclusion was kept, its scope was widened to include methods of treatment of the human or animal body by therapy or surgery, and diagnostic

---

264 Ibid, at [50].
265 (T 1319/04).

methods practised on the human or animal body. The legal basis for the exclusion has been further reformulated by the 2004 Act, which has swept away the previous formulation of the exclusion as lacking industrial application. The UK courts have only considered the scope of the exclusion on a few occasions, particularly methods of treatment of the human body by therapy. However, the EBA and the Technical Boards of Appeal of the EPO have been busy reformulating the scope of the exclusions in the past 30 years. The UK courts have not lagged behind, and, where necessary, they have, however reluctantly, applied the EPO jurisprudence; in particular, that relating to second and further medical use patents. Their concerns relating to the doctrinal basis of second (and further) medical use patents have now been laid to rest with the explicit recognition of such patents in the EPC 2000, which now forms part of UK law by virtue of the 2004 Act.

10. United States of America

A INTRODUCTION

The courts and the US Patent and Trademark Office (USPTO) oscillated on the issue of patent protection for methods of medical treatment. Medical procedures were initially excluded from patent protection, but in 1954 the Patent Office Board of Appeal (US) (POBA) in *ex parte Scherer* decided affirmatively that they were not outside the scope of patent protection. The patenting of medical treatments continued unhindered, without posing any serious threat to the medical profession and health care, after the decision in *ex parte Scherer*. The issues only climaxed in the aftermath of the *Pallin v Singer*[1] litigation where one physician sought to enforce a patent for a method of medical treatment against another physician. The publicity given to this case in the media alerted the public to the possibility of patents negatively impacting health care. The legislators were quick to respond to what was perceived to be an upsurge in patents for methods of medical treatment. The Medical Procedures and Affordability Act 1996 (MPAA) was the resulting compromise that provided immunity to physicians and related health care entities against suits for patent infringement. The legislation, the drafters thought, achieved a proper balance between on the one hand, the public health considerations and, on the other hand, the economic incentives of the patent system.

Recently, however, there has been an upsurge in decisions relating to methods of medical treatment reaching the Federal Circuit, and indeed one missed opportunity in *Laboratory Corporation v Metabolite Labs* for the United States Supreme Court to finally decide the issue. This chapter will also examine this emerging jurisprudence of the Federal Circuit and the dissenting opinion in *Laboratory Corporation v Metabolite Labs* where the issue of whether methods of medical treatment are patentable subject matter under section 101 of the Patents Act has been considered. It will also examine the recent Supreme Court decision in *Bilski v Kappos* which rejected the test for patentability accepted by the Federal Circuit in *In re*

[1] 36 USPQ 2d 1050 (US DCDY 1995).

Bilski. Moreover, it will consider what approach the Federal Circuit might take in light of the order of the Supreme Court that it reconsider the decisions of *Prometheus v Mayo* and *Classen v Biogen*, both of which dealt with medical patents, in light of the Supreme Court's ruling in *Bilski v Kappos*.

B INITIAL JUDICIAL DETERMINATION

1 Introduction

The POBA initially held that methods of medical treatments were not protected under United States patent laws[2] but their decisions were not well reasoned. *Ex parte Brinkerhoff*[3] was based on a dubious legal analysis and the subsequent decisions did not strictly adhere to the supposed rule enunciated therein. The retreat from the *ex parte Brinkerhoff* decision was crystallised in *ex parte Scherer*[4] where the POBA expressly overruled *Brinkerhoff* to the extent that it held that methods of medical treatment were unpatentable subject matter. There was no consideration of the nature of the exclusion, or whether it only applied to methods of *medical* treatment or covered all methods of *treatment*. Similarly, there was no discussion as to whether the exclusion covered humans only, or whether it also extended to animals. It seemed that only methods for the medical treatment of humans were excluded from patent protection before the decision in *ex parte Scherer*. Diagnostic methods of treatment were, however, considered to be patentable subject matter.[5]

2 Initial Exclusion

The first case that dealt with the issue of patenting methods of medical treatments was decided just over 140 years ago. In *Morton v New York Eye Infirmary*,[6] the plaintiff sought to recover damages for infringement of a patent for an 'improvement in surgical operations' which used sulphuric ether in producing nervous quiet and insensitivity to pain, especially during operations. The District Court held that the process was a well-known one

---

[2] See, generally, I.J. Fellner, 'Patentability of Therapeutic Methods' (1946) 28 JPOS 90.

[3] (1883) reprinted in 27 JPOS 797 (POBA (1945)).

[4] 103 USPQ 107 (POBA (1954)).

[5] *Ex parte Kettering* 35 USPQ (POBA (1936)).

[6] (1862) 17 F Cas 879.

and that the discovery of the effect of increased quantities of the substance was not new. The patent, in the opinion of the District Court, 'simply furnishes evidence that it can be applied to at least one useful purpose; a fact quite independent of other elements necessary to make a discovery patentable'.[7] The discovery that increased quantities of the inhaled ethers could result in a complete insensitivity to pain was not sufficient to confer novelty on the claim. The invention was, therefore, for the use of an old substance (the ethers) in an old way (by inhalation) for inducing insensitivity in mammals (old purpose). The usefulness or otherwise of the invention could not be a substitute for satisfying the statutory requirement of patentability.[8]

The District Court did not determine that, as a matter of law, patents could not be granted for methods of medical treatment. The patent, as the court held, was 'nothing more, in the eye of the law, than the application of a well-known agent, by a well-known [method], to a new or more perfect use, which is [not] sufficient to support a patent'.[9] Indeed, the District Court proceeded on the basis that patent protection was available for methods of medical treatment. There was no discussion about the patentability of methods of medical treatment *per se* – the issue was whether the alleged invention satisfied the requirements for patent protection. The District Court was of the view that a discovery was not patentable *per se* but where the inventor had 'connected [the discovery] with some particular medium or mechanical contrivance' where it 'acts on the material world' she can secure its exclusive control with a patent monopoly.[10] The patentee would control the method by which she brought the discovery to some practical application. If the discovery is severed from its practical application the claim becomes 'a naked discovery and not an invention'[11] and would not be patentable. The applicant in the instant case had not found a useful way to embody the discovery in a useful object, so it was therefore not patentable.

---

7 Ibid, at 884.

8 Ibid, at 883.

9 Ibid.

10 Ibid.

11 Ibid. The court opined that '[e]very invention may, in a certain sense, embrace more or less a discovery, for it must always include something that is new; but it by no means follows that every discovery is an invention. It may be the soul of an invention, but it cannot be the subject of the exclusive control of the patentee, or the patent law, until it inhabits a body, *no more than can a disembodied spirit be subjected to the control of human laws*' (at 883).

One of the first POBA decisions that dealt with the issue directly was the 1883 decision of *ex parte Brinkerhoff*,[12] where it held that methods of medical treatment were not patentable subject matter. The claimed invention was for the use of surgical instruments for the treatment of the human body. The POBA emphasised that the applicant had already obtained a patent for the surgical instruments and that their sale should allow the purchaser the right to use them in any way that they desire.[13] It was weary of the patentee gaining secondary protection for his invention by patenting specific uses of the already patented surgical instruments. The POBA held that the patent was for 'discoveries which may in a majority of cases under certain conditions accomplish certain results, but no particular method or mode of treatment under all circumstances, and in all cases will produce upon all persons the same result'.[14] In other words, methods of medical treatment of certain diseases by physicians were not patentable because they could not provide 100 per cent certainty of curing any particular patient because of the vagaries of medical treatment.[15] The patentability of an invention should not be determined by a mathematical calculation of the success rate of the invention. This is especially so since it cannot ever be determined with any accuracy whether a particular result of any method of medical treatment would be the same in all cases.

There was no discussion about the propriety or otherwise of granting patents for methods of medical treatment in *ex parte Brinkerhoff*. The references to the human body were to simply illustrate the nature of the invention and to reiterate that no method of treatment could ever guarantee the same result for each patient. According to the POBA, patents for methods of medical treatment 'would have a tendency to deceive the public by leading it to believe that the method therein described and claimed would produce the desired result in all cases'.[16] The deception was presumably the perception that people would have that the invention could guarantee 100 per cent certainty of results when this could not conceivably be the case. The POBA held, on the 'authority' of *Morton v New York Eye Infirmary*, that the invention in *ex parte Brinkerhoff* could not be patented.[17] The invention was for a mode of treatment 'which must be treated as a discovery, and falls clearly … under the class of discoveries, held not to

---

[12] (1883) reprinted in 27 JPOS 797 (POBA (1945)).
[13] Ibid, at 798.
[14] Ibid.
[15] Ibid.
[16] Ibid.
[17] Ibid.

be patentable in the *Morton* case'.[18] The *Morton* case, it must be emphasised, simply reiterated that a discovery must have *some* practical application before it could be patented and was *not* based on the unpatentability of any particular class of inventions. It should not, therefore, be taken as the authority for the unpatentability of methods of medical treatment.

3 Another Approach to Ex Parte Brinkerhoff

The later District Court and POBA decisions merely paid lip service to the *ex parte Brinkerhoff* decision. The claim in *Dick v Lederle Antitoxin Laboratories*,[19] which post-dated *ex parte Brinkerhoff*, was for a method of securing scarlet fever toxin and injecting that toxin into the skin of a human being. The toxin was useful for the development of a skin test for susceptibility to scarlet fever, preventative immunisation and the production of an antitoxin. The District Court noted that the claims in question were the proper subject matter of patent laws, an art, based on the *Morton* precedent.[20] It was of the opinion that it was not necessary to engage in any discussion of whether methods of medical treatment were patentable, because the processes claimed by the plaintiff embraced methods claims, which were the proper subject of a patent.[21] In his dissenting opinion in *ex parte Scherer*, the Chief Examiner asserted that cases such as *Dick*, 'were concerned with a method of testing for susceptibility and not a claim to a medical treatment'.[22] Despite the decision of the POBA in *ex parte Brinkerhoff*, the District Court implicitly accepted that methods of medical treatment could, nonetheless, be patented. Similarly, in *ex parte Wappler*,[23] where the claims were for a method of shrinking living tissue, it was held that 'the invention in question was not excluded from patent protection, as they were not of the *types* that were excluded in *Morton* and *ex parte Brinkerhoff*'.[24] However, it was made clear by the POBA that the process satisfied the conditions found in the classic definition of a process given in *Cochrane v Deener*[25] and that the procedure outlined was sufficiently certain to avoid the criticism made in the *Brinkerhoff case*. Although not

---

18 Ibid.
19 43 F 2d 628 (DC SDNY (1930)).
20 Ibid, at 630.
21 Ibid.
22 *Ex parte Scherer*, at 111.
23 26 USPQ 191 (POBA (1934)).
24 Ibid (emphasis added). This case was also based on a misinterpretation of the *Morton case*.
25 94 U.S. 780 (1954).

disapproving the dictum in *ex parte Brinkerhoff*, the POBA ensured that its decision could withstand an *ex parte Brinkerhoff* challenge.

The *ex parte Brinkerhoff* case was discussed in *ex parte Kettering*[26] where the claims were for a process which involved subjecting the human body to the effect of a high frequency field to create a fever in the human body while keeping it dry at the same time. The POBA expressly stated that the *ex parte Brinkerhoff* case did not preclude the granting of a patent in the instant case, because the claims considered by the POBA covered a procedure that did not have the object of, or had any direct relation to the curing of any particular disease.[27] This was particularly startling since the POBA had already correctly pointed out that the ultimate purpose of the invention was the creation of fever in the human body *to cure* a disease.[28] The POBA accepted that the question of whether the disease can be cured depended, to a considerable extent, on the skill with which the treatment is applied and the response of the patient.[29] However, the POBA, ever fearful of the dictum in *ex parte Brinkerhoff*, stated that insofar as the production of fever is concerned, the results at which the process is aimed are sufficiently certain to avoid the limitation of *ex parte Brinkerhoff*.[30]

The courts did not embrace or consider the ethical considerations in determining the patentability of methods of medical treatment until the decision of the District Court in *Martin v Wyeth*,[31] where the patent was for a special form or kind of treatment for the disease, mastitis in milk cows. The District Court pointed out that 'instances of valid patents for a method of medical or surgical treatment have been rare indeed, although a few cases may be found in which therapeutic agents, such as aspirin, have been held patentable'.[32] It continued that there were previous cases that dealt with methods of medical treatment, namely a method of applying an inoculation against scarlet fever.[33] The District Court emphasised that '*Doctors and surgeons have seldom thought it desirable to try to patent their new procedures for human relief*'.[34] This indicated that the policy of the medical profession was not to encourage patents for methods of medical treatment. It explained that '*[t]he professional ethics of doctors and surgeons are more consistent with the widespread use of their medical and*

---

26 35 USPQ 342 (POBA (1936)).
27 Ibid.
28 Ibid.
29 Ibid.
30 Ibid.
31 96 F Supp 689 (DC DM (1951)).
32 Ibid, at 694–695.
33 Ibid, at 695.
34 *Martin*, at 695 (emphasis added).

surgical discoveries for the benefit of mankind than in obtaining a monopoly to control their discoveries for personal commercial advantage. In this respect it would seem also that public interest is here involved'.[35] The District Court recognised, for the first time, that patenting of methods of medical treatment raised ethical and public policy considerations. This rationale was not expanded upon or adopted in the cases that followed.

The District Court in *Martin* pointed out that 'a medical or surgical method may, if otherwise patentable, be placed in the category of an art and therefore within reach of the statute'.[36] This statement was inconsistent with the traditional understanding of *ex parte Brinkerhoff*, which was not cited in the judgment. The patent was invalidated because it involved the use of an old device for a new purpose. This conclusion was also surprising in light of the District Court's previous observation that the plaintiff's discovery of the new use met many of the objective tests for patent protection. *Morton* was referred to by the District Court, but the invention in the *Morton* case was directed at the use of an old substance in an old way to achieve the same purpose. The patent in *Martin* was found invalid for want of *required standard of invention.*[37] The *Morton* case was applied to invalidate the patent, although it, arguably, stood for a different principle.

4 Patent Protection Reasserted

Since there was no strict adherence to the learning in *ex parte Brinkerhoff*, it was time that the courts or the POBA either rejected or re-affirmed its reasoning. The issue then arose directly for consideration in *ex parte Scherer*, where the claim was for a method of injecting fluids into the human body in which the epidermis acts as a passive member. There, the POBA stated that '*the method claimed is of a character which would normally be regarded as within the field of patentable subject matter, except for the fact that that human body is the subject acted upon*'.[38] The question was whether the involvement of the human body prevented the invention from being patentable subject matter. It was stated, correctly, that the *Morton* case did not establish the principle that all methods involving the treatment of the human body were unpatentable,[39] and that the patent in the *Morton* case was invalidated for lacking novelty.[40] The POBA continued that 'no proper

35 Ibid (emphasis added).
36 Ibid.
37 Ibid, at 695–696.
38 *Ex parte Scherer*, at 109 (emphasis added).
39 Ibid.
40 Ibid.

inference that any and all medical or surgical methods are excluded from the field of patentable subject matter can be drawn from the opinion, and neither do the facts upon which the opinion is based warrant such a broad generalisation'.[41] It held that the uncertainty of results, which was one of the grounds on which *ex parte Brinkerhoff* was decided, was 'more appropriately considered under the utility requirement than as a freestanding reason for rejecting patents for methods of medical treatment'.[42] *Ex parte Brinkerhoff* was expressly overruled to the extent that it had held that methods of medical treatment were unpatentable subject matter.[43] If there was any uncertainty about whether or not *ex parte Brinkerhoff* was an authority for the unpatentability of methods of medical treatment, *ex parte Scherer* made clear that it was *never* such an authority, and if this was the *correct* interpretation of *ex parte Brinkerhoff*, then it should *no longer* be the case.

Geniesse, Examiner-in-Chief, dissented from the decision of the POBA, arguing that the asserted improvement was only useful as a method of treatment of the human body for a therapeutic purpose and was therefore not patentable.[44] He also pointed out that the decisions in *ex parte Kappler* and *ex parte Kettering* did not represent the unanimous opinion of the POBA and that there was no actual decision of a competent court accepting that methods of medical treatment of the human body were patentable.[45] Geniesse argued that the majority were in error in suggesting that the claimed process came within the acceptable definitions of processes previously accepted by the courts.[46]

Ex parte Scherer finally settled the question and accepted that methods of medical treatment were patentable subject matter in the United States. It was not until 1994, some 50 years later, that the next significant decision relating to methods of medical treatment emerged. In *Pallin v Singer*,[47] the action was for patent infringement on a surgical technique for use during cataract surgery in a manner that would allow the wound to be 'substantially self-sealing'. The court denied the defendant's plea for summary judgment because there were genuine issues of fact to be considered at trial.[48] A Consent Order was later declared which invalidated the patent

---

41 Ibid, at 110.
42 Ibid.
43 Ibid.
44 Ibid, at 111.
45 Ibid.
46 Ibid.
47 36 USPQ 2d 1050 (DC DV (1995)).
48 Ibid.

and stated that the plaintiff would take no action to enforce the patent against the defendants. There was much publicity about this case and it was the catalyst for the change in the law that was to follow.

C LEGISLATIVE INTERVENTION

1 Introduction

There was an enormous public outcry following the *Pallin v Singer* litigation. A coalition[49] of various interest groups led by the American Society of Cataract and Refractive Surgery quickly assembled to halt what they considered to be an insurgence of medical procedure patents. They lobbied Congress tirelessly to deal with the matter. The AMA criticised the patenting of medical procedures and issued a policy document that denounced the practice amongst physicians.[50] Before the final form of the legislation was agreed, there was considerable debate and rejections of various Bills that were introduced in the House of Representatives[51] and Senate[52] to deal with the matter. In the end, a compromise Bill[53] was agreed to, which became the MPAA.[54]

49 American Academy of Dermatology, American Academy of Ophthalmology, American Academy of Orthopaedic Surgeons, American Academy of Otolaryngology Head and Neck Surgery, American Association of Neurological Surgery, American College of Radiology, American College of Surgeons, American Institute of Ultrasound in Medicine, American Medical Association, American Society of Dermatologic Surgery, American Society of Plastic and Reconstructive Surgery, American Urological Association, Association of American Medical Colleges, Society of Cardiovascular and Interventional Surgery and Society of Vascular Technology.

50 'Ethical Issues in the Patenting of Medical Procedures' 53 Food & Drug LJ 341.

51 H.R. 1127, 104th Congress, 1st Session, H.R. 3814, 10th Congress, 2d Session.

52 S. 1334, 104th Congress, 1st Session which became the forerunner to the later H.R. 3610 104 Congress (1996).

53 H.R. 3610 104 Congress (1996).

54 MPAA, s. 287(c). See, generally, B.G. Alten, 'Left to One's Own Devices: Congress Limits Patents on Medical Procedures' (1998) 8 Fordham Intell. Prop. Media & Ent. LJ 837; S.L. Nichols, 'Hippocrates, the Patent-Holder: The Unenforceability of Medical Procedure Patents' (1997) 7 Geo. Mason L Rev 227; C.J. Katopis, 'Patients v. Patents?: Policy Implications of Recent Patent Legislation' (1997) 71 St. John's L Rev 329; W.W. Yang, 'Patent Policy and Medical Procedure Patents' (1995) 1 B U J Sci & Tech L 5; R.M. Portman, 'Legislative restriction on

2 Legislative History

Senator Frist tabled Senate Bill 1334 on October 18, 1995, seven months after the introduction of HR 1127.[55] The Senate Bill provided that it shall not be an act of infringement for a patient, physician, or other licensed health care practitioner, or a health care entity with which a physician or licensed health care practitioner is professionally affiliated, to use or induce others to use a patented technique, method, or process for performing a surgical or medical procedure, administering a surgical or medical therapy, or making a medical diagnosis.[56] This exclusion of liability for infringement did not apply to the use of, or inducement to use, such a patented technique, method, or process by any person engaged in the commercial manufacture, sale, or offer for sale of a drug, medical device, process, or other product that is subject to regulation under the Federal Food, Drug, and Cosmetic Act or the Public Health Service Act.[57]

Senate Bill 1334 was also the subject of intense debate during the congressional testimony of 19 October 1995.[58] It was argued that a case for the exclusion was not made and the 'right without a remedy'[59] effect of the Ganske/Frist compromise was contrary to one of the fundamental benefits of the American patent system, *viz* the right to exclusive use.[60] Opponents to the Bill declared that such a patent 'without a meaningful remedy against infringement is *like no patent at all*'.[61] The exclusion from patentability and the infringement liability section were considered discriminatory because they would 'achieve the result by discriminatory treatment based on the identity or profession of the infringer'.[62] The legislation, it was argued, may

---

Medical and Surgical Procedure Patents Removes Impediments to Medical Progress' 4 (1996) U Balt Intell Prop LJ 91; S.D. Anderson, 'A Right Without a Remedy: The Unenforceable Medical Procedure Patent' (1999) 3 Marq Intell Prop L Rev 117; W.E. Havins, 'Immunising the Medical Practitioner "process" Infringer: Greasing the Squeaky Wheel, Good Public Policy or What?' (1999) 77 Uni Det Mercy L Rev 51; W.B. Lafferty, 'Statutory and Ethical Barriers in the Patenting of Medical and Surgical Procedures' (1996) 29 J Marshall L Rev 891 and B.J. Meier, 'The New Patent Infringement Liability Exception for Medical Procedures' (1997) 23 J Leg 265.

55 142 Cong. Rec. S15291 (daily ed. 18 October 1995).

56 Senate Bill 1334, 104th Cong., 1st Sess. (1995).

57 Ibid.

58 142 Cong. Rec. S15291 (18 October 1995).

59 142 Cong. Rec. S11845–01 (30 September 1996) (letter by Dr. OG Hatch).

60 Ibid.

61 142 Cong. Rec. S11845–01 (30 September 1996) (letter by Senator Kirk) (emphasis added).

62 Ibid, S11847.

ultimately increase litigation over the meaning and effect of the legislation itself.[63] Senator Kirk observed that the exception in the Bill relating to the use of a composition of matter was problematic, including the section which provided that the exception did not apply unless the use 'directly contributes to achievement of the objective of the claimed method'.[64]

3 Nature of the Exclusion in Section 387(c)

(a) General

Senate Bill 1133 never became law but it formed the basis of House Bill 3610 which was enacted on 28 September 1996.[65] Section 287(c) of 35 USC attempted to provide a comprehensive answer to the issue of medical procedure patents by exempting physicians and medical health care entities from infringement liability. The exclusion was, therefore, a narrow one.[66] Section 287(c)(1) stipulates that the provisions dealing with infringement shall not apply against the medical practitioner or related health care entity with respect to such medical activity.[67] This exception was followed by another exception,[68] which excluded persons engaged in acts of commerce from benefiting from the immunity provided in section 287(c)(1) provided that such acts take place outside the physician's office[69] and is regulated by various Acts.[70]

A medical activity was defined as the performance of a medical or surgical procedure on the human body but did not include the use of a patented machine[71] or the practice of a patented use of a composition of matter in violation of the patent[72] or the practice of a patent in violation of a biotechnology patent.[73] The definition of 'medical activity' did not

---

63 Ibid.

64 142 Cong. Rec. S11845–01 (30 September 1996) (letter by Senator Hatch).

65 MPAA, s. 287(c). This section was s. 616 of House Bill 3610 which received a vote of 370 to 37 on 28 September 1996 and in the Senate passed with 84 to 15 (142 Cong. Rec. S11, 815 at S11, 816 (daily ed. 30 September 1996). This Bill was the result of a conference agreement and therefore was not subject to the usual amendment in the Senate. It could only get an up or down vote.

66 R.M. Portland, 'Legislative Restriction on Medical and Surgical Procedure Patents' (1996) U Balt Intell Prop LJ 91, 114.

67 MPAA, s. 287(c)(1).

68 MPAA, s. 287(c)(2).

69 MPAA, s. 287(c)(2)(A).

70 MPAA, s. 287(c)(2)(B). The Food, Drug, and Cosmetic Act, the Public Health Service Act, or the Clinical Laboratories Improvement Act.

71 MPAA, s. 287(c)(3)(B)(i).

72 MPAA, s. 287(c)(3)(B)(ii).

73 MPAA, s. 287(c)(3)(B)(iii).

include diagnostic methods as practised on the human or animal body as obtained in Article 53(c) EPC. However, a Bill introduced in the United States Congress by Representative Lynn Rivers, on 14 March 2002, is attempting to remedy this supposed deficiency.[74]

The medical practitioner must be a natural person licensed by the State[75] and includes someone acting under her direction in the performance of the medical activity.[76] The 'patented use of a composition of matter' does not include a claim for a method of performing a medical or surgical procedure on a body that recites the use of a composition of matter, if the use of that composition of matter does not directly contribute to achievement of the objectives of the claimed method.[77] The definition of body,[78] professional affiliation[79]and related health care entity is provided for, and the subsection is not retroactive.[80]

(b) Legislative intention

The conference report on section 287(c) provided some valuable insight into the legislative intent for the new law.[81] The objective of this section was to preclude the filing of civil actions for damages, or injunctive relief for the infringement of patents for medical procedures, against a medical practitioner licensed by the state or related health care entity.[82] The approach under the MPAA is to: first, *identify* the medical practitioner or related health care entity; secondly, decide whether a *medical activity* was performed; and, thirdly, determine whether the medical activity was *an infringement* of a patented procedure. This three-pronged approach will be used to explore the various aspects of this new legislation.

---

74 Genomic Research and Diagnostic Accessibility Act of 2002, HR 3967, 107th Congress, 2nd Sess. (2002).

75 MPAA, s. 287(c)(3)(C)(i).

76 MPAA, s. 287(c)(3)(C)(ii).

77 MPAA, s. 287(c)(3)(D).

78 MPAA, s. 287(c)(3)(A): 'the term "body" shall mean (i) a human body, organ or cadaver, or (ii) a nonhuman animal used in medical research or instruction directly relating to the treatment of humans'.

79 MPAA, s. 287(c)(3)(E): 'the term "professional affiliation" shall mean staff privileges, medical staff membership, employment or contractual relationship, partnership or ownership interest, academic appointment, or other affiliation under which a medical practitioner provides the medical activity on behalf of, or in association with, the health care entity'.

80 MPAA, s. 287(c)(4).

81 HR Conf. Rep. No.104–863 (1996).

82 Ibid.

(i) Defendant The section specifically exempts medical practitioners or related health care entities from actions for patent infringement.[83] A medical practitioner was defined as a natural person licensed by a State to provide medical activity,[84] or a natural person acting under the direction of the aforementioned in the performance of the medical activity.[85] A related health care entity includes an entity with which the medical practitioner has a professional affiliation, under which the medical practitioner performs a medical activity,[86] and includes, without limitation, an affiliation such as a nursing home, hospital, university, medical school, health maintenance organisation, group medical practice or a medical clinic.[87] Any person who was concerned with, or engaged in, the commercial exploitation and provision of pharmaceutical products and services would not be able to invoke the immunity provided in section 287(c)(1).[88] The activities excluded in section 287(c)(2) must be *directly related* to the commercial exploitation of pharmaceutical products, uses of substances or the provision of clinical or laboratory services (not being services provided in a physician's office),[89] or regulated under the various Acts.[90]

(ii) Medical activity A medical activity was defined as the performance of a medical or surgical procedure on a body,[91] but it did not cover a biotechnology patent.[92] The section created three exceptions to this definition namely: (a) the practice of a patented machine, manufacture, or composition of matter in violation of such a patent;[93] (b) the practice of a patented use of a composition of matter in violation of such a patent;[94] and

---

83 MPAA, s. 287(c)(1).
84 MPAA, s. 287(c)(3)(C)(i).
85 MPAA, s. 287(c)(3)(C)(ii).
86 MPAA, s. 287(c)(3)(F)(i).
87 MPAA, s. 287(c)(3)(F)(ii).
88 MPAA, s. 287(c)(2).
89 MPAA, s. 287(c)(2)(A).
90 MPAA, s. 287(c)(2)(B) namely the Federal Food, Drug and Cosmetic Act, the Public Health Service Act, or the Clinical Laboratories Improvement Act.
91 MPAA, s. 287(c)(3)(B).
92 MPAA, s. 287(c)(3)(B)(iii) provides that the term medical activity shall not include the practice of a process in violation of a biotechnology patent. The report expands this definition of a biotechnology patent to include a patent on a biotechnological process as defined by 35 U.S.C. S 103(b), as well as using those materials, where those materials have been manipulated *ex vivo* at the cellular or molecular level.
93 MPAA, s. 287(c)(3)(B)(i).
94 MPAA, s. 287(c)(3)(B)(ii).

(c) the practice of a process in violation of a biotechnology patent.[95] Given the wording of these provisions, it seems clear that the intention was to prevent the activities of physicians from being hindered by medical procedure patents. It is also instructive that the exception included the major areas of research in the medical field, namely, pharmaceutical products, new uses of substances and machines. These exceptions were able to appease the lobbyists that were opposed to various versions of the Bill as it went through Congress.

The medical activity *must* be practised *on* a body which includes the human body, organ or cadaver.[96] It is not immediately clear why the cadaver of the human body was included in this definition. If the rationale for the exclusion is to provide access to various forms of treatments for patients, then it seems unnecessary to apply this to cadavers. A patent could reasonably be granted to cover such a procedure but would be limited to human cadavers and not the live human body. Where the subject of the infringement action was a non-human, it must be directed at 'research or instruction directly relating to the treatment of humans'.[97] This subsection will raise interesting questions when determining whether a particular method of treatment of an animal is one that is *directly related* to the treatment of humans. The rationale for this curious formulation was, arguably, to cover medical research on non-humans which has the treatment of humans as their specific purpose. It seems, however, that where the medical research or instruction is not *directly related* to the treatment of humans, it will be patentable. This reading of the section is in line with the objective of the statutory provision which was to ensure that patents did not limit the actions of medical practitioners when they treat their patients. Therefore, the activities of veterinarians would not be covered by the provision as it concerns medical research or instruction relating to the treatment of animals.

(iii) Patented use of a composition of matter The most complicated aspect of the MPAA is determining what is excluded from the definition of 'a patented use of a composition of matter'. This was included as part of the two exceptions to the definition of medical activity found in section 287(c)(3)(B). Section 287(c)(3)(B) excludes: (i) the use of a patented machine, manufacture, or composition of matter in violation of such a patent or (ii) the practice of a patented use of a composition of matter in

95 MPAA, s. 287(c)(3)(B)(iii).
96 MPAA, s. 287(c)(3)(A)(i).
97 MPAA, s. 287(c)(3)(B)(ii).

violation of such a patent. In other words, a 'patented use of a composition of matter' and the practice of a patented use of composition of matter were not considered as medical activities. Section 287(c)(3)(D), therefore, limited the definition of a 'patented use of a composition of matter' by providing that it did not include a claim for a method of performing a medical or surgical procedure on a body that recited the use of a composition of matter, if the use of that composition of matter did not directly contribute to the achievement of the objective of the claimed method.[98]

The House Report explained that the use of a composition of matter in a claim 'will direct[ly] contribute to the achievement of the objective of the claimed method if it is itself novel or if it contributes to or is necessary to establish the non-obviousness of the claim as a whole'.[99] Therefore, to directly contribute to the achievement of the objective of the claimed method, the use of a composition of matter must either be: (a) novel or (b)(i) contribute to, or (ii) be necessary to establish the non-obviousness of the claim as a whole. This meant that a claimed activity, which recited the use of a composition of matter, will not be considered as a medical activity unless it is novel or contributed to the objective of the claimed method.[100] Uses of compositions of matter included: novel uses for drugs; novel uses of chemical or biological reagents for diagnostic purposes, novel methods for scheduling or timing of the administration of drugs; novel methods of combining drug therapies; and, novel methods for providing genetic or biological materials to a patient (including gene therapies).[101]

A use claim would be considered as 'a patented use of a composition or matter' if it directly contributed to the objectives of the claimed method. In other words, the contribution of the use claim to the objective of the claimed method as a whole was *sine qua non* of patentability. This objective would be achieved if the *use* was either novel or if it contributed to or was necessary to establish the non-obviousness of the claim. It was strange that the determination of whether a claim was a method of medical treatment was made dependent on the novelty of the use claim and its overall impact on the claimed method itself. The use of the word 'contribute' suggested that the threshold was a low one and, when juxtaposed with the requirement of 'necessity', it does indicate a real oddity. A claim where each method recited a 'use of a composition of matter', for example, a novel use of a drug for the treatment of diabetes that involves the administration of a drug at a particular time of the day and/or at a dose and/or with a

98 MPAA, s. 287(c)(3)(D).
99 HR Conf. Rep. No.104–863 (1996).
100 Ibid.
101 Ibid.

concomitant medicinal therapy, would not be construed as a medical activity. The novelty of the use claim was sufficient to overcome the exclusion of medical procedures from patent protection, which suggested that every new use of a pharmaceutical product could be tailored to come within the definition of 'medical activity', given the peculiar wording of this provision in section 287(c)(3)(D).

(iv) Hybrid claims Although not mentioned in the statute, the report identified what it termed a 'hybrid' claim which exists when a claim consists of a step that recites the use of a composition of matter and at least another step that is not directed to the use of a composition of matter.[102] In such circumstances, the test to be applied is two-pronged. One must, first, determine *the objective of the claimed method*, taking into account all the process steps outlined in the claim and then, secondly, determine *whether the steps, involving the use of the composition of matter alone or collectively, contribute to the achievement of the claimed method.*[103] For example, if the objective of the method were to treat cancer, it would be necessary to determine whether the *steps* comprising the use of the anti-cancer drug would *contribute* to the achievement of that aim (treating cancer). On that basis, treatment regimes that involve a novel use of a substance or composition would, therefore, be patentable.[104] The report stated that where 'individual steps involving uses of one or more compositions of matter … are *not novel individually* or *in combination with each other*, these uses may directly contribute to the achievement of the objective of the claimed method if, in combination with the steps that involve collectively obvious medical or surgical techniques, they produce a novel and non-obvious method'.[105] In other words, novelty could be achieved if the old use of the composition of matter is combined with surgical or medical procedures that produce a novel and non-obvious method.

The example given by the conference report was of a heart transplant using a conventional anaesthetic (old use) in a claim for a non-conventional surgical procedure (new technique) which it claimed would exclude the claim from the definition of medical activity (section 287(c)(2)(B)(ii)).[106] A novel medical procedure, *simpliciter*, would not be patentable. However, when combined with an old use of a patented composition or matter, it would not be regarded as falling within the definition of medical activity, so

---

102 Ibid.
103 Ibid.
104 Ibid.
105 Ibid.
106 Ibid.

patent protection would be available. This interpretation necessarily follows from an understanding of that subsection, when read in conjunction with subsection 287(c)(3)(D) (that the use should either be novel or contribute to the achievement of the non-obviousness of the claim), that a new procedure would confer novelty on a method that involved an old use of a composition of matter.

(c) Infringement

The defendant, in order to claim immunity from infringement of the patented medical procedure, must prove that he is a registered medical practitioner or works for a related health care entity. Section 271(a) provides that anyone who 'without authority makes, uses, offers to sell or sells any patented invention … infringes the patent'.[107] Similarly too, a person who 'actively induces infringement of a patent shall be liable as infringer'.[108]

4 Genomic Research and Diagnostic Accessibility Act

The aim of the then proposed and long buried Genomic Research and Diagnostic Accessibility Act (GRDA)[109] was 'to provide for non-infringing uses of patents on genetic sequence information for purposes of research and genetic diagnostic testing, and to require public disclosure of such information in certain patent applications'.[110] The GRDA was proposed because the 'interests of patients and the overall health care system in this country will be far better served if laboratories, universities, and the private sector are free to use patented information for the development of diagnostic tests'.[111] It may be argued that it has failed to achieve this because the proposed diagnostic immunity section relates only to genetic diagnosis and does not fall within the types of medical and surgical procedures usually associated with physicians. The latter are process patents and involve different arguments of policy and principle than those that are made for patents on the product *viz*. diagnostic testing.

---

[107] 35 U.S.C 271(a).

[108] 35 U.S.C 271(b).

[109] HR 3697 2002. See also the proposed Genomic Science and Technology Innovation Act 2002. More recently, another version of the GRDA has been proposed: Genomic Research and Accessibility Act 2007.

[110] HR 3697 2002.

[111] Statement by Rep Lynn Rivers, dated 14 March 2002, on the introduction of the GRDA into the United States House of Representatives.

The GRDA would, first, provide immunity for infringers for research on genetic sequences.[112] Secondly, it deals with diagnostic testing by providing that section 287(c)(2) of title 35, United States Code, would be changed by amending subparagraph (A) to read as follows: '(A) the term "medical activity" means the performance of a genetic diagnostic, prognostic, or predictive test or a medical or surgical procedure'.[113] The GRDA would broaden the definition of medical activity to include a genetic diagnostic, prognostic or predictive test. The provision would not cover diagnostic methods that are not genetic in nature. It then defined the term 'genetic diagnostic, prognostic, or predictive test' to mean 'any test, designed to detect disease, to predict the potential for a medical disorder, or to predict the effectiveness of therapeutics, which uses either an ordered listing of nucleotides comprising a portion of a human or human pathogen genetic code or the proteins encoded by such nucleotides'.[114] This definition would be inserted into the MPAA as subparagraph (F) after section 287(c)(3)(E).

It would also repeal section 287(c)(3) so that persons engaged in the commercial development, manufacture, sale, importation, or distribution of a machine, manufacture, or composition of matter or the provision of pharmacy or clinical laboratory services (other than clinical laboratory services provided in a physician's office), would now be granted immunity from patent infringement. However, these activities must be: (a) directly related to the commercial development, manufacture, sale, importation, or distribution of a machine, manufacture, or composition of matter or the provision of pharmacy or clinical laboratory services (other than clinical laboratory services provided in a physician's office), and (b) regulated under the Federal Food, Drug, and Cosmetic Act, the Public Health Service Act, or the Clinical Laboratories Improvement Act, in order to get immunity from patent infringement.[115]

The GRDA would apply retrospectively. Section 287(c)(4) of the MPAA provided that the subsection shall not apply to any patent issued on or whose earliest effective filing date is before 30 September 1996. However, the GRDA provides that '[n]otwithstanding section 287(c)(4) of title 35,

---

112 GRDA, s. 2 (1). 'It shall not be an act of infringement for any individual or entity to use any patent for or patented use of genetic sequence information for purposes of research. This paragraph shall not apply to any individual or entity that is directly engaged in the commercial manufacture, commercial sale, or commercial offer for sale of a drug, medical device, process, or other product using such patent for or patented use of genetic sequence information.'

113 GRDA, s. 3(a)(1).

114 GRDA, s. 3(a)(3).

115 GRDA, s. 3(b).

United States Code, the amendments made by subsection (a) shall not apply to any patent issued based on an application the earliest effective filing date of which is before the date of the enactment of this Act'.[116] The potential of this section for stifling research potential is vast and troubling. For example, this means that the BRCA1 gene patents (breast cancer gene patents) would not be available.[117] Not surprisingly, the biotechnology industry was vehemently opposed to the Bill.[118]

It seems clear that the GRDA is contrary to the spirit of the MPAA. The MPAA was a compromise Bill that followed the Ganske Amendment to House Bill 3814, which attempted to remove USPTO's funding for new medical procedures except as a necessary component of a patentable medical device or machine. The biotechnology industry made it clear that the Bill would 'undermine the patenting of gene therapy treatments'.[119] No intention to remove from patentability biotechnological processes or treatments derived from such processes could be found in the provisions of the MPAA. Indeed, the MPAA could be regarded as a classic case where industry lobbying had its greatest role because of the number of concessions made to the biotechnology industry. For example, section 287(c)(3)(B)(ii) provides that the term medical activity shall not include the practice of a process in violation of a biotechnology patent.

D THE CONSTITUTIONAL POWER

1 Introduction

The constitutional guarantee, by virtue of Article 1, Section 8, Clause 8, of the Constitution of the United States, provides that 'Congress shall have the power ... To promote the Progress of Science and useful Arts, by securing for limited Times to Authors and Inventors the exclusive Right to their respective Writings and Discoveries'. In furtherance of this clause, Congress enacted the Patent Act, and established the USPTO. To this end, section 101 of the Patent Act, 35 U.S.C., relating to inventions patentable,

---

116 GRDA, s. 3(c).

117 See generally S.J.R. Bostyn, 'The Critical Analysis of the (Non) – Patentability of Diagnostic Methods and the Consequences for BRCA1 Gene Type Patents in Europe' (2003) Bio-Science L R 111.

118 Letter to Rep Lynn Rivers by the Biotechnology Industry Organisation dated 21 March 2001 noting the chilling effect that HR3967 would have on biotech research and development and the huge investment in research and development that is necessary for the continued development of innovative life saving products.

119 142 Cong Rec H8278 (24 July 1996) (statement by Rep Dooley).

provides that 'Whoever invents or discovers any new and useful process, machine, manufacture, or composition of matter, or any new and useful improvement thereof, may obtain a patent therefor, subject to the conditions and requirements of this title'. The United States Supreme Court and The United States Court of Appeals for the Federal Circuit ('Federal Circuit') have, in the past, attempted to determine the scope of this section. Although the Supreme Court in *Diamond v Chakrabarty*[120] endorsed the view that patent protection extends to 'anything under the sun made by man',[121] subsequent decisions of the Supreme Court have been more cautious, explaining, as it did in *Diamond v Deihr*,[122] that '[e]xcluded from such patent protection are laws of nature, natural phenomena, and abstract ideas'.[123]

In recent years, the Supreme Court had avoided decisions concerning the scope of section 101 of the Patent Act, presumably, because it felt that its jurisprudence provided a clear statement of applicable legal principles, or that the recent pronouncements of the Federal Circuit had not gone too far astray from that jurisprudence for them to be reined in. Patentees have filed patents on the basis of current understandings of the law and, if the Supreme Court were to step in, without a significant reason to do so, it would unsettle the various patents that had been granted previously. Therefore, it was not surprising that in the last few years the Supreme Court has rejected a chance to review not only the scope of patent protection for diagnostic methods, but recently took another opportunity to reconsider various Federal Circuit decisions relating to patentable subject matter. In *Laboratory Corporation v Metabolite Labs*,[124] not only did the Supreme Court refuse to consider the issue of the scope of patent protection for methods of medical treatments, in particular, diagnostic methods, but, importantly, it refused to give a definitive answer whether such patents are allowable, suggesting they might be, with its approval of the Federal Circuit's decision. This section of this chapter will consider: first, diagnostic methods in the Federal Circuit before *Laboratory Corporation v Metabolite Labs*; secondly, diagnostic methods in the United States Supreme Court, with specific focus on *Laboratory Corporation v Metabolite Labs*; thirdly, diagnostic methods in the Federal Circuit after *Laboratory Corporation v*

---

120 *Diamond v Chakrabarty* 447 U.S. 303 (1980).
121 Ibid, at 308.
122 450 U.S. 175 (1981).
123 Ibid, at 185.
124 548 U.S. 926; 126 S. Ct. 2976; 165 L. Ed. 2d 990 (2006).

Metabolite Labs; fourthly, the standard for patentability in *Bilski v Kappos*;[125] and, fifthly, patent protection for diagnostic methods and other methods of medical treatment after *Bilski v Kappos*.

2 Diagnostic Methods in the Federal Circuit before Laboratory Corporation v Metabolite Labs

The Federal Circuit considered the issue of whether patent protection should be provided for diagnostic methods in the 1980s. In *In re Grams*,[126] it had to consider whether a claim for a method of diagnosing an abnormal condition in an individual was patentable under section 101.[127] The claimed method consisted of comparing and then measuring the levels of chemical and biological constituents in an individual to those of a normal set of parameters to determine whether the individual's condition was normal. The issue for the Federal Circuit was whether the claims, which included an algorithm for measuring the values, were excluded from patent protection.[128] It noted, quoting *In re Walter*,[129] that once a mathematical algorithm is extant in the claimed method, the claim as a whole must be analysed and, if the mathematical algorithm was implemented in a specific manner to define structural relationships between the physical elements of the claim or to refine or limit claim steps, it would be patentable under section 101.[130] The Federal Circuit also noted that the sole physical process step in claim 1 was performing the clinical tests on individuals to obtain data, but that step merely focused on the algorithm itself. As a result, it held that the claims were unpatentable under section 101 as being related to a non-statutory mathematical algorithm, and upheld the rejection of the patent by the District Court.[131] The Federal Circuit did not have to pronounce on the issue of whether the extant diagnostic method was patentable under section 101 (which never arose for discussion) since the claims included a subject matter ineligible for patent protection, namely, a mathematical method; and, therefore, the claim was rejected on that basis alone.

In the process of reasoning, the Federal Circuit in *In re Grams*[132] noted that the claim it was there considering was similar to the ones considered by

---

125 130 S. Ct. 3218; 177 L. Ed. 2d 792 (2010).
126 888 F.2d 835 (Fed. Cir. 1989).
127 Ibid, at 836.
128 Ibid, at 837.
129 618 F.2d 758, 205 USPQ 397 (CCPA 1980).
130 *In re Grams*, at 837.
131 Ibid, at 841.
132 888 F.2d 835, 840 (Fed. Cir. 1989).

the Federal Circuit in *In re Meyer*.[133] In *In re Meyer*, the invention was for a process and an apparatus for carrying out the process of testing a complex system and analysing the results of these tests. The process included: (a) dividing the complex system into a plurality of 'elements' and (b) associating a factor of function or malfunction with each of these elements.[134] In *In re Bilski*, the Federal Circuit characterised the claim in *In re Meyer* as a claim for a computerised method for aiding a neurologist in diagnosing patients.[135] The Federal Circuit in *In re Meyer* claimed that the invention was mainly concerned with replacing, in part, the thinking (mental) processes of a neurologist with a computer. It then asserted that the decisive question was whether that mental process was applied to physical elements or process steps in an otherwise statutory process, machine, manufacture, or composition of matter, in accordance with section 101.[136] The Federal Circuit, therefore, held that the claims were for a mathematical algorithm representing a mental process that had not been applied to physical elements or process steps and was, therefore, not limited to any otherwise statutory process, machine, manufacture, or composition of matter.[137] The claimed method was, therefore, not patentable.

In *In re Griffin*,[138] the claim was for a method for diagnosing an increased risk for thrombosis or a genetic defect causing thrombosis in the human body.[139] Although the issue in this decision was, not whether the claimed method was patentable under section 101, but, rather, whether it was invalid under section 102(g) of the Patents Act, the Federal Circuit still considered the meaning of such diagnostic claims. It simply noted that the preamble was directed to 'diagnosing an increased risk for thrombosis of a genetic defect causing thrombosis'.[140] The diagnostic method was indicated in the following: 'wherein the presence of said point mutation in said test nucleic acid indicates an increased risk for thrombosis or a genetic defect causing thrombosis'. Consequently, the Federal Circuit held that diagnosis is thus the essence of this invention; its appearance in the count gives 'life and meaning' to the manipulative steps.[141]

---

133 688 F.2d 789 (Fed. Cir. 1982). See also *In re Abele* 684 F.2d 902 (Fed. Cir. 1982).

134 Ibid, at 790.

135 *In re Bilsiki* 545 F.3d 943 at 1002 (Fed. Cir. 2008) (en banc).

136 Ibid, at 795–796.

137 Ibid, at 796.

138 285 F.3d 1029 (Fed. Cir. 2002).

139 Ibid, at 1031.

140 Ibid, at 1033.

141 Ibid.

3 Diagnostic Methods in the United States Supreme Court

The question of whether a diagnostic method was patentable arose directly for consideration by the Supreme Court in *Laboratory Corporation v Metabolite Labs.*[142] In that decision, the jury found that the claimant (LabCorp) had indirectly infringed the defendant's patent (the '658' patent). The 658 patent claimed a method for detecting cobalamin and folate deficiency. Both are B vitamins, and their deficiency can cause various illnesses in the human body, namely, vascular disease, cognitive dysfunction, birth defects and cancer. However, if this deficiency is detected at an early stage, vitamin B supplements can treat this deficiency. University Patents Inc developed a test which was able to identify the deficient vitamin and it formed the basis of the 658 patent, whose claims read as follows:

> 13. A method for detecting a deficiency of cobalamin or folate in warm-blooded animals comprising the steps of: assaying a body fluid for an elevated level of total homocysteine; and correlating an elevated level of total homocysteine in said body fluid with a deficiency of cobalamin or folate.

The 658 patent was eventually licensed to LabCorp, which originally performed total homocysteine assays, but then switched to a total homocysteine assay developed by another company. Metabolite sued LabCorp for infringement and succeeded in the District Court, which held that LabCorp had infringed the 658 patent, and that the claims at issue were not invalid.

On appeal, the Federal Circuit, accepting a broad construction of the patent, agreed with the District Court's conclusion that 'correlate' meant 'to establish a mutual or reciprocal relationship between'.[143] It noted that the mutual relationship was established when an elevated homocysteine level was present, whereas a reciprocal relationship was established when an

---

[142] 548 U.S. 124, 126 S. Ct. 2921, 165 L. Ed. 2d 399 (2006) (dismissing the writ of certiorari as improvidently granted). Twenty-one amicus briefs were filed, including the Intellectual Property Owners Association, I.B.M., the Public Patent Foundation, AARP, and the American Heart Association. See e.g., Brief of American Intellectual Property Law Ass'n as Amicus Curiae Supporting Respondent, *Lab. Corp. of Am. Holdings v Metabolite Labs., Inc*, 126 S. Ct. 2921 (2006) (No. 04–607) (mem.), 2006 WL 303907; Brief of American Heart Ass'n as Amicus Curiae Supporting Petitioner, *Lab. Corp. of Am. Holdings v Metabolite Labs., Inc*, 126 S. Ct. 2921 (2006) (No. 04–607) (mem.), 2005 WL 3561169.

[143] *Laboratory Corporation v Metabolite Labs*, at 1363 (Fed. Cir. 2004).

elevated homocysteine level was absent.[144] LabCorp argued that the claim should only cover a mutual relationship because 20 per cent of the assays correlated elevated levels of homocysteine to diagnose a B vitamin deficiency.[145] The Federal Circuit accepted that claim 13 was only infringed when the assays performed by LabCorp revealed elevated levels of homocysteine and that approximately 80 per cent of the assays LabCorp processed revealed unelevated levels of homocysteine.[146] However, the majority of the Federal Circuit vacated the jury's verdict that the assays resulting in unelevated levels of homocysteine infringed claim 13, and further vacated and remanded the jury's verdict on damages for recalculation based only on those infringing assays that demonstrated elevated levels of homocysteine.[147]

LabCorp petitioned the Supreme Court to review the decision of the Federal Circuit. The Supreme Court invited the government to brief on the following question:

> Respondent's patent claims a method for detecting a form of vitamin B deficiency, which focuses upon a correlation in the human body between elevated levels of certain amino acids and deficient levels of vitamin B. The method consists of the following: First, measure the level of the relevant amino acids using any device, whether the device is, or is not, patented; second, notice whether the amino acid level is elevated and, if so, conclude that a vitamin B deficiency exists. Is the patent invalid because one cannot patent 'laws of nature, natural phenomena, and abstract ideas'? *Diamond v Diehr*, 450 U.S. 175, 185 (1981).

The Solicitor-General, in his reply, accepted that claim 13 described more than a natural phenomenon, as it did not merely recite a natural relationship between elevated total homocysteine and deficiencies in the B vitamins, but also claimed a diagnostic method based on that relationship – assaying for total homocysteine in order to determine cobalamin or folate deficiency.[148] He claimed that whether the application of the natural relationship was patentable may depend on facts that were not well developed in the record, particularly because the validity of claim 13 under the natural phenomenon doctrine was not discussed by the lower courts.[149] The

144 Ibid.
145 Ibid.
146 Ibid.
147 Ibid, at 1364.
148 Brief for the United States as Amicus Curiae at 8, *Laboratory Corporation v Metabolite Labs*, 126 S. Ct. 2921 (No. 04–607), 2005 WL 3533248.
149 Ibid, at 9.

Solicitor-General stated that the natural relationship between elevated homocysteine and deficiencies in the B vitamins was an unpatentable 'principle in natural philosophy or physical science'.[150] Consequently, he urged the Supreme Court to deny the petition.[151] The Supreme Court rejected his advice and granted review only in respect of question 3 in the petition, namely:[152]

> Whether a method patent setting forth an indefinite, undescribed, and non-enabling step directing a party simply to 'correlat[e]' results can validly claim a monopoly over a basic scientific relationship used in medical treatment such that any doctor necessarily infringes the patent merely by thinking about the relationship after looking at a test result.

Notwithstanding that the Supreme Court had granted *certiorari* to decide the question of whether a method patent directing a party simply to 'correlate' test results can validly claim a monopoly over a basic scientific relationship such that any doctor necessarily infringes the patent merely by thinking about the relationship after looking at a test result, it decided not to rule on the question, but dismissed the writ as improvidently granted.[153]

Breyer J., along with Souter and Stevens JJ., dissented, arguing that the Supreme Court should have ruled on the question because those who engage in medical research, who practise medicine, and who, as patients, depend upon proper health care, might well benefit from this Supreme Court's authoritative answer.[154] He noted that the Federal Circuit agreed with the District Court that claim 13's 'correlating' step simply meant 'relating total homocysteine levels to cobalamin or folate deficiency, a deficiency in both, or a deficiency in neither'.[155] He further noted that the

---

[150] Ibid, at 10.

[151] Ibid, at 5.

[152] The exact questions were: 'The precise questions posed were as follows: 1. Whether liability can be imposed for willfully inducing patent infringement under 35 U.S.C. section 271(b) based solely on evidence that a party has disseminated a basic scientific fact to others. 2. Whether an express limitation in a patent claim can be ignored so as to allow the patent to cover the exact opposite of what was claimed. 3. Whether a method patent setting forth an indefinite, undescribed and nonenabling step directing a party simply to "correlat[e]" test results can validly claim a monopoly over a basic scientific relationship used in medical treatment such that any doctor necessarily infringes the patent merely by thinking about the relationship after looking at a test result' (Petition for Writ of Certiorari, Metabolite, 126 S. Ct. 2921 (No. 04–607), 2004 WL 2505526).

[153] *Laboratory Corporation v Metabolite Labs* 165 L. Ed. 2d 399 at 400.

[154] Ibid.

[155] Ibid, at 403.

Federal Circuit 'did not address LabCorp's argument that, *if so construed*, claim 13 must be struck down as an improper effort to obtain patent protection for a law of nature'.[156] The question for the court, Breyer J. further noted, was whether claim 13, as construed and applied by the Federal Circuit, was invalid in light of the 'law of nature' principle.[157]

Breyer J. noted that, as construed by the Federal Circuit, claim 13 provided those researchers with control over doctors' efforts to use that correlation to diagnose vitamin deficiencies in a patient. In his view, claim 13 was invalid no matter how narrowly one reasonably interpreted the 'natural phenomenon' doctrine.[158] Breyer J. asserted that there could be little doubt that the correlation between homocysteine and vitamin deficiency set out in claim 13 was a 'natural phenomenon', arguing that this was accepted by the Solicitor-General and the petitioners, and that even the respondents conceded as much.[159] The respondents argued that the correlation was patentable because claim 13 embraced a 'process' for detecting vitamin deficiency, with discrete testing and correlating steps.[160] Moreover, they claimed that claim 13 was a patentable 'application of a law of nature' because, considered as a whole, it, first, 'entails a physical transformation of matter', namely, the alteration of a blood sample during whatever test is used; and, secondly, 'produces a "useful, concrete, and tangible result"', namely, detection of a vitamin deficiency.[161]

These arguments were rejected by Breyer J. who argued that claim 13's process instructed the user to, first, obtain test results and, secondly, think about them. He asked why it should matter if the test results themselves were obtained through an unpatented procedure that involved the transformation of blood, replying that claim 13 was indifferent to that fact, because it told the user to use any test whatsoever.[162] Breyer J. continued that even if he were to assume (purely for argument's sake) that claim 13 met certain general definitions of process patentability, it still failed the main one under consideration, namely, the requirement that it not amount to a simple natural correlation, that is, a 'natural phenomenon'.[163] He argued that at most, respondents had 'simply described the natural law at issue in the

---

156 Ibid (emphasis in original).

157 Ibid.

158 Ibid.

159 Ibid.

160 Ibid.

161 Ibid, at 406, citing *State Street Bank & Trust Co v Signature Financial Group Inc* 149 F. 3d 1368, 1373 (Fed. Cir. 1998).

162 *Laboratory Corporation v Metabolite Labs* 165 L. Ed. 2d 399 at 406.

163 Ibid, at 406–407.

abstract patent language of a "process", but that they could not avoid the fact that the process was no more than an instruction to read some numbers in light of medical knowledge'.[164] Breyer J. explained that 'one might, of course, reduce the "process" to a series of steps, e.g., Step 1: gather data; Step 2: read a number; Step 3: compare the number with the norm; Step 4: act accordingly, but that one can reduce any process to a series of steps'.[165] The question, in his opinion, was what those steps embody, explaining that in the instant case, aside from the unpatented test, they embody only the correlation between homocysteine and vitamin deficiency that the researchers uncovered. That correlation, in his opinion, was an unpatentable 'natural phenomenon', and that nothing in claim 13 added anything more of significance.[166]

Breyer J. then considered special public interest considerations which he claimed reinforced his view that the Supreme Court should have decided the case, claiming that a failure to do so threatened to leave the medical profession subject to the restrictions imposed by this individual patent and others of its kind.[167] He continued that those restrictions may: first, inhibit doctors from using their best medical judgment; secondly, force doctors to spend unnecessary time and energy to enter into licence agreements; thirdly, divert resources from the medical task of health care to the legal task of searching patent files for similar simple correlations; and, fourthly, raise the cost of health care while inhibiting its effective delivery.[168] Breyer J. claimed that, even if he is wrong that the claimed invention is an unpatentable law of nature, it was still valuable for the Supreme Court to decide the case, because: first, doing so would help diminish legal uncertainty in the area, affecting a 'substantial number of patent claims'; secondly, it would permit those in the medical profession better to understand the nature of their legal obligations; and, thirdly, it would help Congress determine whether legislation is needed.[169]

4 Diagnostic Methods in the Federal Circuit after Laboratory Corporation v Metabolite Labs

The majority opinion of the Federal Court in *In re Bilski*[170] explained at footnote 27 that several Justices of the Supreme Court, in a dissent to a

---

164 Ibid, at 407.
165 Ibid.
166 Ibid.
167 Ibid.
168 Ibid.
169 Ibid.
170 545 F.3d 943 (Fed. Cir. 2008) (en banc).

dismissal of a writ of *certiorari*, expressed their view that a similar claim in *Laboratory Corporation v Metabolite Labs* was drawn to unpatentable subject matter.[171] They continued that there the claimed process only comprised the steps of: (a) 'assaying a body fluid for an elevated level of total homocysteine' and (b) 'correlating an elevated level of total homocysteine in said body fluid with a deficiency of cobalamin or folate'.[172]

Rader J., in dissent, pointed out the Federal Circuit's 'willingness to venture away from the statute follows on the heels of an oft-discussed dissent from the Supreme Court's dismissal of its grant of *certiorari* in [*Laboratory Corporation v Metabolite Labs*]'.[173] He noted that the dissent was 'premised on a fundamental misapprehension of the distinction between a natural phenomenon and a patentable process'.[174] Rader J. claimed that the distinction between 'phenomena of nature', 'mental processes', and 'abstract intellectual concepts' was not difficult to draw. He claimed that the fundamental error in the dissent in *Laboratory Corporation v Metabolite Labs* was its 'failure to recognize the difference between a patent ineligible relationship – i.e., that between high homocysteine levels and folate and cobalamin deficiencies – and a patent eligible process for applying that relationship to achieve a useful, tangible, and concrete result – i.e., diagnosis of potentially fatal conditions in patients'.[175] He noted that there was nothing abstract in that claimed method, asserting that testing blood for a dangerous condition was not a natural phenomenon, but a human invention.[176]

Further, he explained that the distinction was simple but critical, noting that a patient may suffer from the unpatentable phenomenon of nature, namely high homocysteine levels and low folate.[177] But the invention, in his opinion, 'did not attempt to claim that natural phenomenon; but instead claimed a process for assaying a patient's blood and then analyzing the results with a new process that detects the life-threatening condition'.[178] Rader J. said that 'the sick patient did not practise the patented invention, but instead the patent covered a process for testing blood that produces a useful, concrete, and tangible result: incontrovertible diagnostic evidence to

---

[171] Ibid, at 965.
[172] Ibid.
[173] Ibid, at 1014.
[174] Ibid.
[175] Ibid.
[176] Ibid.
[177] Ibid.
[178] Ibid.

save lives'.[179] In his opinion, the 'patent did not claim the patent ineligible relationship between folate and homocysteine, nor did it foreclose future inventors from using that relationship to devise better or different processes'.[180] Consequently, Rader J. held that, contrary to the language of the dissent, it was the sick patient who embodied only the correlation between homocysteine and vitamin deficiency, not the claimed process.[181]

He claimed that, from the standpoint of policy, the dissent in *Laboratory Corporation v Metabolite Labs* avoided the same fundamental question that the Federal Circuit did not ask or answer in *In re Bilski*, namely: 'Is this entire field of subject matter undeserving of incentives for invention? If so, why?'[182] In the context of the decision in *Laboratory Corporation v Metabolite Labs*, he claimed that that question was very telling: 'the natural condition diagnosed by the invention was debilitating and even deadly'.[183] Rader J. pointed out that before the invention featured in *Laboratory Corporation v Metabolite Labs*, medical science lacked an affordable, reliable, and fast means to detect this debilitating condition. Consequently, he claimed that 'denial of patent protection for this innovation – precisely because of its elegance and simplicity (the chief aims of all good science) – would undermine and discourage future research for diagnostic tools'.[184] In other words, he asked: 'does not Patent Law wish to encourage researchers to find simple blood tests or urine tests that predict and diagnose breast cancers or immunodeficiency diseases?' In that context, he explained, the Federal Circuit might profitably ask whether its decisions incentivise research for cures and other important technical advances.[185] Without such attention, he cautioned that the Federal Court inadvertently advised investors that 'they should divert their unprotectable investments away from discovery of "scientific relationships" within the body that diagnose breast cancer or Lou Gehrig's disease or Parkinson's or whatever'.[186]

The claim in *Classen Immunotherapies, Inc v Biogen Idec*[187] related to a method of determining whether an immunisation schedule affected the

---

[179] Ibid.

[180] Ibid.

[181] Ibid.

[182] Ibid.

[183] Quoting, see U.S. Patent No. 4,940,658, col. 1, ll. 32–40 ('Accurate and early diagnosis of cobalamin and folate deficiencies … is important because these deficiencies can lead to life-threatening hematologic abnormalities … Accurate and early diagnosis of cobalamin deficiency is especially important because it can also lead to incapacitating and life-threatening neuropsychiatric abnormalities').

[184] 545 F.3d 943 at 1014 (Fed. Cir. 2008) (en banc).

[185] Ibid.

[186] Ibid.

[187] 304 Fed. Appx. 866 (Fed. Cir. 2008).

incidence or severity of a chronic immune-mediated disorder in a treatment group of mammals, relative to a control group of mammals.[188] In the District Court,[189] Merck argued that the claimed methods were unpatentable because they involved 'thinking about' whether a vaccination schedule reduced the incidence of chronic disease and, therefore, sought to patent an abstract mental process about a natural phenomenon.[190] Classen, on the other hand, argued that they did not claim a scientific truth, but instead described a method for reducing the incidence of chronic immune-mediated disorders. The District Court stated that the correlation between vaccination schedules and the incidence of immune-mediated disorders is a natural phenomenon,[191] and that the issue was whether the claimed method simply described this correlation.[192] The District Court explained that the claimed method involved: (a) immunisation of a treatment group; and (b) a comparison of the incidence of chronic immune mediated disorders in the treatment group relative to a control group.[193] It further explained that, since the patent described only a general inquiry of whether the proposed correlation between an immunisation schedule and the incidence of chronic disorders existed, it was indistinguishable from the idea itself and that the applicant sought to patent an unpatentable natural phenomenon.[194] It, therefore, held that it was an attempt to patent an unpatentable natural phenomenon.[195]

It might be said that the difficulty with the District Court's decision in *Classen v Biogen* was that the judge made reference to both the natural phenomena and the mental process as the basis on which he decided that the claimed method was not patentable under section 101. At first blush, this argument seems attractive, but the point about the comparing/correlating claims is that the physician would have to go through the mental process of comparing the information and then determining that the correlation exists in the particular case under consideration. After examining the information gathered, the physician would then determine whether in light of that information a particular illness exists or, as in the case in *Classen v Biogen*, determine the optimal immunisation schedule for the

---

[188] Ibid, at 867.

[189] *Classen Immunotherapies, Inc v Biogen Idec*, 2006 U.S. Dist. LEXIS 98106 (D. Md., 16 August 2006).

[190] Ibid, at 13.

[191] Ibid.

[192] Ibid.

[193] Ibid.

[194] Ibid, at 14.

[195] Ibid, at 15.

patient. But, that determination is based on the physician observing and concluding (the mental process) that a particular correlation exists. In the classic diagnostic method claims, the physician would determine, given particular symptoms, that a particular disease exists – the correlation being the existence of these symptoms and the disease (natural phenomena). Therefore, the judge in *Classen v Biogen*, arguably, got it right insofar as he appreciated the distinction between the two even though he did not articulate it as such.

On appeal, the Federal Circuit, in light of its decision in *In re Bilski*,[196] affirmed the District Court's decision, clarifying that the claims were neither 'tied to a particular machine or apparatus' nor did they 'transform[] a particular article into a different state or thing'.[197] This is not surprising since the Federal Circuit had only recently revisited the issue of the patent eligible subject matter and the test for determining patentability under section 101 in *In re Bilski*. It, therefore, did not want to have to look at the issue again. But, the Federal Court's rejection of the patent, on the basis of its decision in *In re Bilski*, does not tell us anything about how it would have arrived at that conclusion in light of the two-pronged test it had only recently accepted therein.

In *Bilski*, the Federal Court had provided a 'definitive test' for determining whether a process is patent-eligible under section 101: a claimed process is directed to patentable subject matter if (a) 'it is tied to a particular machine or apparatus', or (b) 'it transforms a particular article into a different state or thing'.[198] Under the *Bilski* machine-or-transformation test, 'the use of a specific machine or transformation of an article must impose meaningful limits on the claim's scope to impart patent-eligibility' and 'the involvement of the machine or transformation in the claimed process must not merely be insignificant extra-solution activity'.[199] The question of whether this test is the *sole* test for determining patentability has now been considered by the Supreme Court and will be examined later.

In *Prometheus Laboratories, Inc v Mayo Collaborative Services*,[200] the claim was for a method of optimising therapeutic efficacy for treatment of an immune-mediated gastrointestinal disorder.[201] The main claim of the

---

196 545 F.3d 943 (Fed. Cir. 2008) (en banc).
197 *Classen*, at 867.
198 *In re Bilski*, at 953.
199 Ibid, at 961–962.
200 581 F.3d 1336 (Fed. Cir. 2009).
201 Ibid, at 1340.

invention was that the blood levels of certain metabolites of some thiopurine drugs used for treatment of immune-mediated gastrointestinal disorders correlate with toxic side effects of the thiopurine drugs.[202] The claims under consideration in this decision, at first blush, seem to be in similar terms to the ones considered by the Supreme Court in *Laboratory Corporation v Metabolite Labs*, insofar as they both relate to finding a correlation between two things. But, the result of that correlation differs – whereas in *Laboratory Corporation v Metabolite Labs*, the correlation enabled the medical practitioner to make a diagnosis, in *Prometheus Laboratories*, it provided information to the medical practitioner suggesting whether a more efficient dose should be used for the patient. Thus, the claim in *Laboratory Corporation v Metabolite Labs* was to a diagnostic method; whereas the claim in *Prometheus Laboratories* was to a method of finding out the optimum dosage regime for a patient.

The District Court held that the patents claimed the correlations between certain thiopurine drug metabolite levels and therapeutic efficacy and toxicity. It reasoned that the claims contained three steps, namely: (1) administration of the drug to a subject; (2) determination of the metabolite levels; and (3) a warning that an adjustment in dosage may be required.[203] The District Court explained the fact that the inventors framed the claims as treatment methods only did not render them patentable; rather, it found that the '"administering" and "determining" steps were merely necessary data-gathering steps for any use of the correlations' and that 'as construed, the final step – the "warning" step (i.e. the "wherein" clause) – is only a mental step'.[204] It noted that the 'warning step' did not require any *actual* change in dosage and that it was 'the metabolite levels themselves that "warn" the doctor that an adjustment in dosage *may* be required'.[205] It explained that the claims included 'only two active steps: "administering" the drug and "determining" metabolite levels, which are merely data-gathering steps; plus the additional mental step that the doctor be warned (by the metabolite levels) that an adjustment in dosage may be required. Therefore, the claims recite the correlations themselves'.[206] With this understanding of the claims, the District Court concluded that the claims recited the correlations between particular concentrations of 6-TG and 6-MMP and therapeutic efficacy or toxicity in patients taking AZA drugs.[207]

202 Ibid.
203 Invalidity Opinion, 2008 WL 878910 at 9.
204 Ibid.
205 Ibid (emphasis added).
206 Ibid, at 9–10.
207 Ibid, at 10.

The District Court also held that there was little doubt that the claimed correlations were 'natural phenomena'.[208] It explained that the inventors did not 'create' the correlation between thiopurine drug metabolite levels and therapeutic efficacy and toxicity, but, the correlation resulted from a natural body process, which the inventors conceded was found in the patient population.[209] It stated that the correlation between particular 6-TG and 6-MMP metabolite levels and therapeutic efficacy and toxicity was not an 'invention'; rather, '6-TG and 6-MMP are products of the natural metabolizing of thiopurine drugs, and the inventors merely observed the relationship between these naturally produced metabolites and therapeutic efficacy and toxicity'.[210] As a result, the District Court found that those correlations were natural phenomena and not patentable inventions because the correlations resulted from a natural body process.[211] In addition, the District Court held that '[b]ecause the claims cover the correlations themselves, it follows that the claims "wholly pre-empt" the correlations'.[212] It also held that the claims recited natural phenomenon – the correlations between thiopurine drug metabolite levels and therapeutic efficacy and/or toxicity – and that they 'wholly pre-empt' use of those correlations. Therefore, the District Court concluded that the claims were invalid under section 101.[213]

In the course of its reasoning, the District Court also examined the dissenting judgment of Breyer J in *Laboratory Corporation v Metabolite Labs*. It observed that the facts of the instant case were similar to those of *Laboratory Corporation v Metabolite Labs*, namely, that the patent claimed a method of measuring the level of an amino acid in the blood, called homocysteine which correlated with a deficiency in two vitamins, cobalamin and folate.[214] The District Court claimed that, although the dissent in *Laboratory Corporation v Metabolite Labs* did not have precedential value, it found Breyer J.'s reasoning persuasive, noting that the claims in the patents under consideration were clearly analogous to the claim in *Laboratory Corporation v Metabolite Labs*. It explained that the claim in *Laboratory Corporation v Metabolite Labs* comprised two steps, namely: first, assaying a body fluid for an elevated level of total homocysteine; and, secondly, correlating an elevated level of total homocysteine in said body

208 Ibid.
209 Ibid, at 11.
210 Ibid, at 15.
211 Ibid, at 11.
212 Ibid, at 17.
213 Ibid.
214 Ibid, at 11–12.

fluid with deficiency of cobalamin or folate.[215] The District Court reasoned that, first, the 'assaying' step in *Laboratory Corporation v Metabolite Labs* was akin to the 'administering' and 'determining' steps in the claims under consideration as both were necessary steps for any use of the correlations; and, secondly, *Laboratory Corporation v Metabolite Labs*'s 'correlating' step was akin to the 'wherein' clause in the claims under consideration as both recite the claimed correlation.[216] Therefore, it claimed that the same reasoning which led Breyer J. to conclude the correlation between elevated homocysteine levels and deficiency of cobalamin or folate was a natural phenomenon supported the finding that the correlation between thiopurine drug metabolite levels and therapeutic efficacy and toxicity was also a natural phenomenon.[217]

On appeal, the Federal Circuit noted that the issue before it was whether the claims met the requirements of section 101.[218] While noting that it had also been established that 'while a claim drawn to a fundamental principle – i.e., a law of nature, natural phenomenon, or abstract idea – is unpatentable', it accepted that 'an application of a law of nature or mathematical formula to a known structure or process may well be deserving of patent protection'.[219] They key issue for patentability, the Federal Circuit observed, was whether a claim was drawn to a fundamental principle or an application of a fundamental principle.[220] After examining the argument of the appellants, Prometheus, and the respondents, Mayo, the Federal Circuit ruled that it agreed with Prometheus the asserted claims were drawn to statutory subject matter and, therefore, reversed the District Court's decision.[221] It observed that the proper inquiry under section 101 was whether these methods met the Supreme Court's machine or transformation test articulated in *Benson* and *Diehr*, and applied in *Bilski*, and, if so, whether the machine or the transformation was central to the purpose of the claims.[222]

The Federal Circuit concluded the methods of treatment claimed in the patent fell within the realm of patentable subject matter because they 'transform an article into a different state or thing', and this transformation

---

215 Ibid, at 12–13.
216 Ibid, at 13.
217 Ibid.
218 *Prometheus Laboratories* 581 F.3d 1336 at 1341 (Fed. Cir. 2009).
219 Ibid, at 1342, citing *In re Bilski*, at 953.
220 *Prometheus Laboratories*, at 1342.
221 Ibid.
222 Ibid, at 1345.

was 'central to the purpose of the claimed process'.[223] The transformation, it explained, 'was of the human body following administration of a drug and the various chemical and physical changes of the drug's metabolites that enabled their concentrations to be determined'.[224] The Federal Circuit continued that since the claimed methods met the transformation prong under *In re Bilski*, it was not necessary for it to consider whether they also met the machine prong test.[225] It also stated claims were methods of treatment that were always transformative when a defined group of drugs was administered to the human body to remedy the effects of the illness.[226]

The Federal Circuit then distinguished *In re Grams* on the basis that, in that decision, the Federal Circuit had found that the process was not patentable, because the invention essentially claimed a mathematical algorithm, rather than any transformation of the tested individuals; in other words, the process was unpatentable because 'it was merely an algorithm combined with a data-gathering step', that is, performing a clinical test.[227] The Federal Circuit noted that the claims in *In re Grams* did not require the performing of clinical tests on individuals that were transformative – and thus rendering the entire process patentable subject matter – because the tests were just to 'obtain data'. In its opinion, both the patent and the Federal Circuit focused only on the algorithm rather than the clinical tests purported to be covered by the claims.[228] The Federal Circuit asserted that unlike the clinical test recited in *In re Grams*, the administering and determining steps in Prometheus's claimed methods were not 'merely' data-gathering steps or 'insignificant extra-solution activity'; they were, however, part of treatment regimes for various diseases using thiopurine drugs.[229] As a result, it concluded the claims were therefore not drawn merely to correlations between metabolite levels and toxicity or efficacy.[230]

The Federal Circuit held the steps preceding the 'warning' steps provided useful information to the physician for possible dosage adjustments to the method of treatment using the drugs for a particular patient.[231] Consequently, it held that the claims were directed to therapeutic methods of treatment which determined the optimal dosage level for a course of

[223] Ibid.
[224] Ibid.
[225] Ibid, at 1346.
[226] Ibid.
[227] Ibid.
[228] Ibid.
[229] Ibid.
[230] Ibid.
[231] Ibid, at 1349.

treatment, and that it comprised a series of transformative steps that optimised efficacy and reduced toxicity of a method of treatment for particular diseases using particular drugs.[232] In addition, the Federal Circuit held the claims covered transformative methods of treatment, not correlations; that they covered a particular application of natural processes to treat various diseases; and, that transformative steps utilising natural processes were not unpatentable subject matter.[233] Moreover, it reiterated, first, the claims did not pre-empt natural processes – they merely utilised them in a series of specific steps; and, secondly, because the claims met the machine-or-transformation test, they did not pre-empt a fundamental principle or all uses of these natural processes.[234] The Federal Circuit, therefore, concluded the claimed methods of treatment were patentable subject matter, which satisfied the requirements under *In re Bilski's* transformation prong for patent-eligible subject matter under section 101.[235]

5 Standard for Patentability in Bilski v Kappos

The Supreme Court has finally decided the case of *Bilski v Kappos*[236] where it had to clarify the standard of patentability under section 101. In *In re Bilski*, the Federal Circuit had held that a process was *only* patentable if it was, first, tied to a particular machine or apparatus or, secondly, it transformed a particular article into a different state or thing. It then reversed its previous decision in *State Street Bank & Trust Co v Signature Financial Group, Inc*[237] and, moreover, asserted *this* test – the 'machine-or-transformation test' – was the *sole* test for determining patentability under section 101. In *State Street Bank*, it had also held that claims to a process were eligible for patent protection as long as they produced a 'useful, concrete and tangible result'.[238] *That* test, the Federal Circuit in *In re Bilski* held, was 'insufficient to determine whether a claim is patent-eligible under section101',[239] preferring the 'machine-or-transformation test'.[240]

---

232 Ibid.

233 Ibid.

234 Ibid.

235 Ibid, at 1350. See *Ariad Pharmaceuticals Inc v Eli Lilly and Co* 560 F 3d 1366 (Fed. Cir. 2009) which related to diagnostic methods, but the decision focused on the requirement for sufficiency.

236 130 S. Ct. 3218; 177 L. Ed. 2d 792.

237 149 F.3d 1368, (Fed. Cir. 1998), cert. denied, 525 U.S. 1093 (1999). See also, *AT&T Corp v Excel Communications Inc* 172 F. 3d 1352, 1357 (Fed. Cir. 1999).

238 *State Street Bank*, at 1373.

239 *In re Bilski*, 545 F.3d at 960.

240 Ibid.

The Supreme Court in *Bilski v Kappos* had to consider the deceptively simple question of whether a patent can be issued for a claimed invention designed for the business world. Kennedy J., who delivered the opinion of the Supreme Court, noted that the patent application claimed a procedure for instructing buyers and sellers how to protect against the risk of price fluctuations in a discrete section of the economy.[241] The Supreme Court also had to consider whether the Federal Circuit was correct in ruling that the machine-or-transformation test was the *sole* test to be used for determining the patentability of a 'process' under section 101.[242] Applying that test, the Federal Circuit had held that the petitioners' application was not patent eligible.

The Supreme Court began its analysis with section 101, stating it specifies four independent categories of inventions or discoveries that are eligible for protection: processes, machines, manufactures, and compositions of matter.[243] Citing *Chakrabarty*, the Supreme Court observed that its precedents provide three specific exceptions to section 101's broad patent-eligibility principles, namely, 'laws of nature, physical phenomena, and abstract ideas'.[244] Even if the requirements of section 101 were satisfied, the Supreme Court accepted that the matter did not end there but that, in order to receive the Patents Act's protection, the claimed invention must also satisfy 'the conditions and requirements of this title', namely, novelty (section 102), non-obvious (section 103) and full and particular description (section 112). Since the claim was a 'process', the Supreme Court opined that section 101 must be read in light of section 100(b) which defines a 'process' as: 'process, art or method, and includes a new use of a known process, machine, manufacture, composition of matter, or material'.[245]

Quoting *Diamond v Diehr*,[246] the Supreme Court reiterated that it has 'more than once cautioned that lower courts "should not read into the patent laws limitations and conditions which the legislature has not expressed"'.[247] It observed that the words in the Patents Act, unless otherwise defined should be given their ordinary, contemporary, common meaning.[248] The Supreme Court explained that it had 'not indicated that the existence of the well-established exceptions to patentability, namely

[241] Ibid, at 799.
[242] Ibid.
[243] Ibid, at 800.
[244] Ibid, at 801.
[245] Ibid.
[246] 450 U. S. 175, 182 (1981).
[247] *Bilski v Kappos*, at 801.
[248] Ibid, citing *Diehr*.

laws of nature, physical phenomena, and abstract ideas, gives the Judiciary *carte blanche* to impose other limitations that are inconsistent with the text and the statute's purpose and design'.[249] By adopting the machine-or-transformation test as the sole test for what constitutes a 'process' (as opposed to just an important and useful clue), the Supreme Court held that the Federal Circuit violated the relevant statutory interpretation principles,[250] and that it incorrectly concluded the Supreme Court had endorsed the machine-or-transformation test as the exclusive test.[251] The Supreme Court, therefore, concluded its precedents establish 'the machine-or-transformation test is a useful and important clue, an investigative tool, for determining whether some claimed inventions are processes under section 101 and that the machine-or-transformation test is not the sole test for deciding whether an invention is a patent-eligible "process".'[252]

It then castigated the machine-or-transformation test as a relic of the Industrial age (where the inventions were grounded in a physical or other tangible form) and argued that it was doubtful whether that test should be the sole criterion for determining the patentability of inventions in the Information Age.[253] Citing amicus briefs, the Supreme Court continued 'the machine-or-transformation test would create uncertainty as to the patentability of software, advanced diagnostic medicine techniques, and inventions based on linear programming, data compression, and the manipulation of digital signals'.[254] It explained that it was 'important to emphasize that its decision was not commenting on the patentability of any particular invention, let alone holding that any of the above-mentioned technologies from the Information Age should or should not receive patent protection'.[255] The Supreme Court continued that 'this Age puts the possibility of innovation in the hands of more people and raises new difficulties for the patent law';[256] and, further, 'with ever more people trying to innovate and thus seeking patent protections for their inventions, the patent law faces a great challenge in striking the balance between protecting inventors and not granting monopolies over procedures that others would discover by independent, creative application of general principles'.[257] The

249 *Bilski v Kappos*, at 802.
250 Ibid.
251 Ibid.
252 Ibid, at 803.
253 Ibid.
254 Ibid.
255 Ibid.
256 Ibid.
257 Ibid.

Supreme Court then concluded that nothing in this opinion should be read to take a position on where that balance ought to be struck.[258]

The Supreme Court argued rather than adopting categorical rules that might have wide-ranging and unforeseen impacts, it resolved the instant case narrowly on the basis of its previous decisions in *Benson*, *Flook*, and *Diehr*, which showed the petitioners' claims were not patentable processes, because they attempted to patent abstract ideas.[259] All the nine Justices agreed with this conclusion. On the facts of the case, the Supreme Court, applying its previous precedents of *Benson*, *Flook*, and *Diehr*, held that the claimed method was not a patentable 'process', but merely an explanation of the basic concept of hedging, or protecting against risk.[260] It then concluded the concept of hedging, described in claim 1 and reduced to a mathematical formula in claim 4, was an unpatentable abstract idea, just like the algorithms at issue in *Benson* and *Flook*; and that allowing petitioners to patent risk hedging would pre-empt use of this approach in all fields and would effectively grant a monopoly over an abstract idea.[261] Indeed, in the Supreme Court's opinion, all the claims attempted to patent the use of the abstract idea of hedging risk in the energy market and then instruct the use of well-known random analysis techniques to help establish some of the inputs into the equation.[262]

6 Diagnostic Methods after Bilski v Kappos

(a) Introduction

The Federal Circuit's decisions in both *Prometheus v Mayo* and *Classen v Biogen* were also before the Supreme Court at the same time it decided *Bilski v Kappos*. The Supreme Court granted *certiorari* in both decisions, vacated the judgments, and remanded these two cases to the Federal Circuit for further consideration in light of its decision in *Bilski v Kappos*.[263] The question now is how the Federal Circuit would interpret *Bilski v Kappos* to determine whether the diagnostic method and therapeutic methods/dosage regimes at issue in these two cases, including the recent District Court

---

[258] Ibid.
[259] Ibid, at 806.
[260] Ibid, at 807.
[261] Ibid.
[262] Ibid.
[263] (ORDER LIST: 561 U.S.)

decision of *Association of Molecular Pathology v U.S. Patent and Trademark Office (AMP v USPTO)*[264] which also related to whether medical diagnostic methods are patent-eligible subject matter under section 101 of the Patents Act. This section will now consider how the Federal Circuit might apply the Supreme Court's decision in *Bilski v Kappos* to determine the issue of patentability in these decisions. The first two decisions have already provided guideposts for how the Federal Circuit might determine the issue, but, since they both applied the Federal Circuit's decision in *In re Bilski*, they are ripe for reconsideration, as mandated by the Supreme Court itself in light of its decision in *Bilski v Kappos*. This section will also consider, *inter alia*, whether methods of medical treatments and diagnostic methods, first, can be excluded based on the machine-or-transformation test; secondly, are abstract ideas; and thirdly, can be considered as unpatentable subject matter per se.

(b) Defining diagnostic methods

Typically, diagnostic methods, using the analysis of the EBA in *CYGNUS/Diagnostic method*, include: (i) the examination phase involving the collection of data; (ii) the comparison of these data with standard values; (iii) the finding of any significant deviation, that is a symptom, during the comparison; and (iv) the attribution of the deviation to a particular clinical picture, that is the deductive medical or veterinary decision phase. This is very similar to what Breyer J. said above, namely: (i) gather data; (ii) read a number; (iii) compare the number with the norm; and (iv) act accordingly. The differences between the two are: first, the EBA's step (i) is Breyer J.'s steps (i) and (ii); secondly, Breyer J.'s formulation does not have step (iii) of *CYGNUS/Diagnostic method*; and, thirdly, Breyer J.'s formulation does not have step (iv) of *CYGNUS/Diagnostic method*. It would seem that Breyer J.'s formulation is wider than that of *CYGNUS/Diagnostic method*, since it does not say exactly what one is doing the comparison for and, consequently, what further steps must be done with the information found. In a sense then, most of the decisions considered in this section are not strictly diagnostic methods, based on the definition accepted in *CYGNUS/Diagnostic method*. Such claims usually involve gathering and analysing data and comparing it to determine whether a particular correlation is satisfied. That correlation in the strict diagnostic method is the determination that a particular medical condition exists or whether a patient has a predisposition to that medical condition.

---

[264] US District Court, Southern District of New York, 09 Civ 415, 29 March 2010.

In *In re Grams*, the method was to determine if a particular abnormal condition existed in a patient. Similarly, in *In re Meyer*, the claimed method was for determining whether a malfunction existed in a patient and in *In re Griffin*, the claimed method was for diagnosing an increased risk for thrombosis or a genetic defect causing thrombosis. All of these methods would be considered diagnostic methods, since they all contained the steps necessary for making a diagnosis. The difference between the claims in *In re Grams* and *In re Griffin* was that, in *In re Grams*, the claim sought to find whether the patient had a particular medical condition, whereas, the claim in *In re Griffin* sought to determine whether the patient had a genetic defect causing thrombosis, or whether there existed in that patient an increased risk for thrombosis. *In re Griffin*-type claims are wider since they are not only able to tell whether the patient has a particular genetic disorder, but whether that patient is predisposed to having one. As such, they both essentially perform related but different functions of determining whether a patient has a particular illness or whether there is a strong possibility that he may develop it later. Therefore, it makes little difference, in terms of patentability, whether the patent claims a particular medical condition or a predisposition to that medical condition. Where a claim suggests a particular treatment for the patient, that further treatment would be an independent therapeutic method, not a diagnostic one.

The claimed method in *Laboratory Corporation v Metabolite Labs* was to determine whether the patient had cobalamin or folate deficiency, both or neither. This was a quintessential diagnostic method, as all four steps were extant in the claimed method. In *Classen v Biogen*, the claimed method was for determining the efficiency of an immunization schedule on a group of patients. This would not be considered as a diagnostic method, since the information gathered does not determine whether the patient is suffering from a particular disease, but, rather, whether the dosages need to be adjusted to better treat that patient for the disease already being treated. In *Prometheus v Mayo*, the claimed method was similar to the ones in *Classen v Biogen*, in that, it claimed a method for optimising the therapeutic efficiency of treatment of an immune-mediated gastrointestinal disorder. In both *Classen v Biogen* and *Prometheus v Mayo*, there were no steps (ii)–(iv) based on the decision of the EBA in *CYGNUS/Diagnostic method*. This was not surprising since the purpose of the information gathered was, not to determine whether the patient was suffering from an illness, as was the case in *In re Meyer*, *In re Grams*, *In re Griffin* (and at least predisposed to such an illness) and *Laboratory Corporation v Metabolite Labs*, but, rather, to determine whether the optimum dosage regime for that patient in respect of treatment already administered for an illness already ascertained. This necessitates an answer to the separate question of whether dosage or treatment regimes are patentable under section 101. In *Prometheus v Mayo*, the claimed method was not directed at the dosage regime at all, but how to determine whether a particular patient needed an adjustment in the dosage administered. In other words, it did not determine the actual dosage for the patient, but allowed the physician, based on the information provided, to determine a patient-specific dosage regime. This involved, first, administering the drug to the patient and, secondly, determining the levels of metabolite of the drug subsequent to administration. That level then would determine whether an increase or decrease in the amount of drug administered was necessary.

(c) Machine-or-transformation test

It will be remembered that the Federal Circuit, in *In re Bilski*, had asserted that the machine-or-transformation test was the sole test for determining whether a process is patentable under section 101. In *Bilski v Kappos*, the Supreme Court rejected that view asserting that that test was a useful one, or a clue to patentability of a process under section 101, and that it was not at all the sole test. Now that the machine-or-transformation test has been discredited, it means that the Federal Circuit's tortuous reasoning using the transformation part of the test in *Prometheus v Mayo* to find that methods of optimising therapeutic efficiency of treatment of an immune-medicated gastrointestinal disorder, needs to be revisited. The Supreme Court vacated the Federal Circuit's decision in *Prometheus v Mayo* and remanded it back to the Federal Circuit for reconsideration in light of the Supreme Court's decision in *Bilski v Kappos*. In *Prometheus v Mayo*, the Federal Circuit had held that the method in question transformed an article into a different state or thing, on the basis of the change which occurred in the human body following the administration of the drug. It must be pointed out that the claimed method itself must effect that transformation. However, the method in question was simply the process for determining an optimised treatment of the human body. In other words, it was directed at the process for making that determination whereby the physician was to make some observations concerning how effective certain dosages were. It was, therefore, not directed to the actual treatment of the patient for, if it were, it would be a method of treating the human body. Arguably, there was no transformation of the human body based on the claimed method that Prometheus sought to patent. It is even more inconceivable that the second part of the test could ever be satisfied in light of the requirement that the invention be tied to a particular machine or apparatus. As will be examined below, the Federal Circuit, on reconsideration, applied the machine-or-transformation test, in the same way it did in *Prometheus v Mayo*, in its recent decision of *Prometheus v Mayo (No. 2)* to find the claims at issue patentable.

Similarly, the Supreme Court also vacated the Federal Circuit's decision in *Classen v Biogen* and remanded it to the Federal Circuit for reconsideration in light of the Supreme Court's decision in *Bilski v Kappos*. The Federal Circuit in *Classen v Biogen* had found that the claimed method for determining appropriate dosages to be given to a treatment group, by comparing associated disorders to that of a controlled group, did not meet the machine-or-transformation test set forth in *In re Bilski*. The Federal Circuit gave no reasons why the claimed method did not meet that test, although the point is now moot in light of the Supreme Court's rejection of the machine-or-transformation test in *Bilski v Kappos*.

(d) Natural phenomena

In rejecting the machine-or-transformation test as the sole test for patentability, the Supreme Court in *Bilski v Kappos* did not articulate any specific test that should be used by the Federal Circuit to determine patentability under section 101, observing that guideposts are to be found in its precedents, namely, *Benson*, *Flook*, and *Diehr*. The Supreme Court observed that the Patents Act was intended to encompass new and unforeseen inventions, and that new technologies may call for new inquiries, even pointing out advanced diagnostic medicine techniques as one such technology. It specifically made it clear, however, that it was not commenting on the patentability of such techniques. This means that, to be patentable, the methods of medical treatment, including diagnostic methods, must not fall under the exclusions from patent protection for abstract ideas, for example: mathematical algorithms; natural phenomena; and laws of nature, according to an unbroken line of Supreme Court authority.

The question now is whether methods of medical treatment, in particular diagnostic methods, are abstract ideas, natural phenomena, or part of the laws of nature. It is clear they are not abstract ideas and do not cover the laws of nature. The more specific question which will now be addressed is whether diagnostic methods are natural phenomena. It will be remembered that Breyer J. accepted this in *Laboratory Corporation v Metabolite Labs* and the District Court judges in both *Prometheus v Mayo* and *Classen v Biogen* held the claimed methods were natural phenomena. In *Gottschalk v Benson*,[265] the Supreme Court noted '*Phenomena of nature*, though just discovered, *mental processes*, and abstract intellectual concepts are not patentable, as they are the basic tools of scientific and technological work'.[266] It then quoted its statement in *Funk Bros Seed Co v Kalo*

[265] 409 U.S. 63 (1972).
[266] Ibid, at 67 (emphasis added).

Inoculant Co[267] which reads: 'He who discovers a hitherto unknown phenomenon of nature has no claim to a monopoly of it which the law recognizes. If there is to be invention from such a discovery, *it must come from the application of the law of nature to a new and useful end*'.[268] The Supreme Court noted that, although, in *Funk Bros*, it was considering a product claim, that statement applied to process claims as well.[269] The Supreme Court in *Benson* noted that 'Transformation and reduction of an article "to a different state or thing" is the clue to the patentability of a process claim that does not include particular machines'.[270] This is apt where the process leads to the production of a particular thing, but it does not apply where the process leads to information, as with the case of diagnostic methods – the method simply tells us what disease the patient is suffering from. Clearly, this does not involve the transformation or reduction of an article, contrary to the holding of the Federal Circuit in *Classen v Biogen*.

In respect of the claimed method at issue in *Benson* for converting binary-coded decimal numerals into pure binary numerals, the Supreme Court held the 'mathematical formula involved here has no substantial practical application except in connection with a digital computer, which [meant that if granted] the patent would wholly pre-empt the mathematical formula and in practical effect would be a patent on the algorithm itself'.[271] What therefore does this say about patentability under section 101? If the claimed method embraces an unpatentable natural phenomenon, for example, it must have some substantial practical application outside the claimed method. If it does not, it would mean that the patent would wholly pre-empt the natural phenomena and would effectively be a patent on the natural phenomena itself. This prompts the necessary question of whether a diagnostic method contains or recites natural phenomena. As mentioned above, two Districts Court judges thought as much, and so did the dissenting Justices in *Laboratory Corporation v Metabolite Labs*.

In *Parker v Flook*,[272] the Supreme Court had to consider whether the identification of a limited category of useful, though conventional, post-solution applications of such a formula made a method for updating alarm limits, where the only novel feature was a mathematical formula, was

267 333 U.S. 127 (1948).
268 Ibid, at 130 (emphasis added).
269 *Benson*, at 68.
270 Ibid, at 70.
271 Ibid, at 71–72.
272 437 U.S. 584 (1978).

eligible for patent protection.[273] It noted that '[t]he line between a patentable "process" and an unpatentable "principle" is not always clear'.[274] The Supreme Court noted the 'notion that post-solution activity, no matter how conventional or obvious in itself, can transform an unpatentable principle into a patentable process exalts form over substance', observing that a 'competent draftsman could attach some form of post-solution activity to almost any mathematical formula'.[275] It therefore ruled that it was absolutely clear the respondent's application contained no patentable invention.[276] Although the Supreme Court in both *Benson* and *Flook* found that the claimed method was unpatentable, because it attempted to monopolise an algorithm, it was left to *Diamond v Diehr*[277] to articulate the circumstances in which a claimed method that includes an excluded subject matter will, nonetheless, still be patentable.

In *Diehr*, the question for the Supreme Court was whether a process for curing synthetic rubber, which included, in several of its steps, the use of a mathematical formula and a programmed digital computer, was patentable subject matter under section 101.[278] The Supreme Court, relying on its previous precedents, including *Benson* and *Flook*, noted the claimed method for a physical and chemical process for moulding precision synthetic rubber products fell within the section 101 categories of possibly patentable subject matter.[279] It continued that that conclusion was 'not altered by the fact that in several steps of the process a mathematical equation and a programmed digital computer are used'.[280] The Supreme Court then distinguished *Benson* on the basis that the claims were held unpatentable, because the 'sole practical application of the algorithm was in connection with the programming of a general purpose digital computer'.[281] It also distinguished *Flook* on the basis that 'the application sought to protect a formula for computing this number'.[282] The Supreme Court then concluded that, in contrast, the patentee in *Diehr* did not seek to patent a mathematical formula but only sought patent protection for a process of curing synthetic rubber. It continued that although the process admittedly employed a well-known mathematical equation, they did not

---

273 Ibid, at 585.
274 Ibid, at 589.
275 Ibid, at 590.
276 Ibid, at 594.
277 450 U.S. 175 (1981).
278 Ibid, at 177.
279 Ibid, at 184.
280 Ibid, at 185.
281 Ibid, at 185–186.
282 Ibid, at 186.

seek to pre-empt the use of that equation, but, rather, it sought only to foreclose from others the use of that equation in conjunction with all of the other steps in their claimed process.[283] The Supreme Court reasoned it was obvious one did 'not need a computer to cure natural or synthetic rubber, but if the computer use incorporated in the process patent significantly lessens the possibility of "overcuring" or "undercuring" the process as a whole does not thereby become unpatentable subject matter'.[284]

Citing *Benson* and *Flook*, the Supreme Court asserted that these decisions lent support to its conclusion that a claim drawn to subject matter, otherwise statutory, does not become non-statutory simply because it uses a mathematical formula, computer program, or digital computer.[285] It reiterated that it was 'now commonplace that an *application* of a law of nature or mathematical formula to a known structure or process may well be deserving of patent protection'.[286] The Supreme Court held that the claims were 'nothing more than a process for molding rubber products and not as an attempt to patent a mathematical formula'.[287] It was of the opinion that when 'a claim recites a mathematical formula (or scientific principle or phenomenon of nature), an inquiry must be made into whether the claim is seeking patent protection for that formula in the abstract'.[288] Relying on its previous decisions of *Benson* and *Flook*, the Supreme Court reasoned that 'a mathematical formula as such is not accorded the protection of our patent laws, and this principle cannot be circumvented by attempting to limit the use of the formula to a particular technological environment'.[289] In addition, it explained that insignificant post-solution activity will not transform an unpatentable principle into a patentable process.[290] If this were not the case, the Supreme Court said that it 'would allow a competent draftsman to evade the recognized limitations on the type of subject matter eligible for patent protection'.[291] It claimed that 'when a claim containing a mathematical formula implements or applies that formula in a structure or process which, when considered as a whole, is performing a function which the patent laws were designed to protect (*e. g.*, transforming or reducing an article to a different state or thing), then the

---

283 Ibid.
284 Ibid, at 187.
285 Ibid.
286 Ibid (emphasis in original).
287 Ibid, at 191.
288 Ibid.
289 Ibid.
290 Ibid, at 191–192.
291 Ibid, at 192.

claim satisfies the requirements of [section] 101'.[292] Consequently, the Supreme Court held the claim was not an attempt to patent a mathematical formula, but, rather, to be drawn to an industrial process for the moulding of rubber products.[293]

It will be recalled the EBA in *CYGNUS/Diagnostic method* held that 'as the deductive or veterinary decision phase, diagnosis for curative purposes in itself is an intellectual exercise, unless, as a result of developments in the field of technology, a device capable of reaching diagnostic conclusions can be used'.[294] It was, therefore, not surprising the EBA held that the deductive medical or veterinary decision phase, as an intellectual exercise, was not a patentable invention within the meaning of Article 52(1) EPC.[295] The EBA in *CYGNUS/Diagnostic method* has observed that 'diagnosis' included 'activities which are not normally practised on the body but predominantly involve *mental acts*, i.e. activities of a non-technical nature performed by a medical professional, such as the steps of comparing the data with normal values and recording any significant deviation and attributing the deviation to a particular clinical picture'.[296] Article 52(1)(c) EPC excludes from patent protection, *inter alia*, schemes, rules and *methods for performing mental acts*. Where the extent to which the final part of diagnostic methods requires the physician to think about whether a diagnosis can be made based on the information presented, it would be unpatentable in light of the requirement in *Benson* that, *inter alia*, *phenomena of nature*, though just discovered, and *mental processes* are not patentable, as they are the basic tools of scientific and technological work. In addition, the mental step the physician is required to make is a determination whether the patient is suffering from a particular disease, based on the systems which have been identified. Where it has been discovered that elevated levels of certain amino acids mean that there were deficient levels of vitamin B, there is no doubt, as Breyer J. held in *Laboratory Corporation v Metabolite Labs*, this correlation would be a natural phenomenon.

The question is whether this reasoning applies as a matter of principle to all diagnostic methods, or whether the patentability of each claimed method should be decided on a case-by-case basis to determine whether the natural phenomenon has some substantial practical application outside the claimed method itself. This, arguably, cannot be determined without considering each claimed method in the context of the applicable technology. It

292 Ibid.
293 Ibid, at 192–193.
294 *CYGNUS/Diagnostic method* (G 01/04) at para. 5.2.
295 Ibid, at para. 5.5.
296 Ibid, at para. 3.5.

is reasonable to assume that, if such a correlation is found, unless there are other correlations which determine whether that a particular illness or deficiency is present in the human body, it would not have any substantial use outside the context of making that diagnosis. It is possible to argue that the natural phenomena is only used in the diagnostic method; but, that matters little if its only or substantial application would be in that diagnostic method, meaning that the inventor would, effectively, have a monopoly on the natural phenomena itself. In such cases, there is hardly any way around this argument, unless other uses of those natural phenomena are available. Would it matter in such circumstances that the patentee's diagnostic method might be the only one such use of the natural phenomena, and that he would have a monopoly of that natural phenomena when used as a method of diagnosis?

In light of the above, it might be appropriate to consider how the Federal Circuit might consider the decision of the District Court in *AMP v USPTO*.[297] In that decision, one of the claimed methods was, essentially, for the identification of a predisposition to breast cancer based on 'analysing' or 'comparing' the BRCA1 and BRCA2 gene sequences.[298] The District Court pointed out that the claimed process was not limited to any particular method of analysis and did not specify any further action beyond the act of 'analysing'.[299] The District Court distinguished the decision of the Federal Circuit in *Prometheus v Mayo* on the basis that the determining step in that decision was found to be transformative because the action of determining the metabolite levels was itself construed to include the extraction and measurement of metabolite concentrations.[300] However, it argued that, in the instant case, the language of the claims was plain and that the ordinary meanings of 'analysing' and 'comparing' established that the claimed method was directed to 'the abstract mental processes of "comparing" and "analysing" gene sequences'.[301] The purpose of the claimed method, it continued, was to detect the germline alteration in the BRCA1 gene. The District Court held that the preparatory transformations relating to obtaining the DNA sequences could not be relied on to satisfy the requirements of section 101[302] and, even if the claims could be construed to

[297] US District Court, Southern District of New York, 09 Civ 415, 29 March 2010.
[298] Ibid, at 146.
[299] Ibid, at 137.
[300] Ibid, at 141.
[301] Ibid.
[302] Ibid, at 145.

include those transformations, it would still not satisfy the machine-or-transformation test in *In Re Bilski*.[303] Applying the decision of the Federal Circuit in *In re Grams*, it held that the isolation and sequencing of DNA from a human sample, even if incorporated in the claimed method, represented nothing more than data-gathering steps to obtain the DNA sequence information on which to perform the claimed comparison or analysis.[304]

In regard to the claim relating to comparing the growth rate of cells in the absence of potential cancer, the District Court held that it, arguably, recited certain transformative steps, such as the administration of the test compound.[305] However, it further held the essence of the claim was that it embraced an act of comparing cell growth rates and coming to the conclusion that a slower growth rate of the host cells was indicative of therapeutic cancer.[306] This, the District Court held, was the scientific method itself for which the claimed method sought patent protection.[307] As such, it held the transformative steps represented nothing more than preparatory, data gathering steps to obtain growth rate information which was not patentable under section 101.

(e) Applying Bilski v Kappos

(i) Relevance of the machine-or-transformation test Responding to the Supreme Court's request for it to reconsider its decision *Prometheus v Mayo* in light of the Supreme Court's decision in *Bilski v Kappos*, the Federal Circuit reconsidered the issue of patenting treatment or dosage regimes in *Prometheus v Mayo (No. 2)*.[308] The first thing the Federal Circuit pointed out was that the Supreme Court did not 'reject the machine-or-transformation test, but rather characterized the test as "a useful and important clue, an investigative tool, for determining whether some claimed inventions are processes under [section] 101"'.[309] In addition, it stated that the Supreme Court's decision in *Bilski v Kappos* 'did not undermine our pre-emption analysis of Prometheus's claims and it rejected

---

303 Ibid, at 147.
304 Ibid, at 146.
305 Ibid, at 148.
306 Ibid.
307 Ibid, at 149.
308 Federal Circuit decision on remand from the Supreme Court of the United States dated 17 December 2010.
309 Ibid, at 10.

the machine-or-transformation test only as a definitive test'.[310] In other words, the Supreme Court did not 'disavow the machine-or-transformation test'.[311] This paved the way for the Federal Circuit in *Prometheus v Mayo (No. 2)* to use its previous reasoning in *Prometheus v Mayo* which was based on the machine-or-transformation test. It claimed that, in light of the Supreme Court's decision in *Bilski v Kappos*, 'patent eligibility in this case turns on whether Prometheus's asserted claims are drawn to a natural phenomenon, the patenting of which would entirely pre-empt its use as in *Benson* or *Flook*, or whether the claims are drawn only to a particular application of that phenomenon as in *Diehr*'.[312]

(ii) Interpreting the claims Before examining the decision of the Federal Circuit in *Prometheus v Mayo (No. 2)*, it is necessary to have a firm understanding of what exactly Prometheus claimed in the patent specification. Three of the claims make it clear that the patent claimed a 'method of optimizing therapeutic efficacy' for treatment of a particular disease; others claimed a 'method of optimizing therapeutic efficacy and reducing toxicity' associated with treatment of a particular disease. Both claims related to a method of medical treatment but were not claims to actual methods of medical treatment. A method of treating a particular disease by using some drugs would be a method of medical treatment because the claimed method would be for *treating* the patient *using* that particular drug. This is not the case here where the claims concerned, not the actual treatment of the patient using 6-thioguanine, but, rather, a method of determining the optimal treatment of the patient by administering drugs to the patient, observing certain conditions, and then comparing those results with standard values. That information would then enable the physician to know whether to increase or decrease the dosage of the drug.

The Federal Circuit in *Prometheus v Mayo (No. 2)* seemed confused as to the exact scope of the claims. That question, arguably, was the most important one because only after you determine what the claims cover could you sensibly entertain a discussion of whether it fell within the scope of section 101. The Federal Circuit noted that the claimed method related to 'the treatment of a specific disease by administering specific drugs and measuring specific metabolites'.[313] It then spoke of 'the treatment methods claimed in Prometheus's patents'.[314] Confusingly, the Federal Circuit

---

310 Ibid, at 14.
311 Ibid, at 15.
312 Ibid, at 12.
313 Ibid, at 15.
314 Ibid, at 16.

pointed out that the 'asserted claims are in effect claims to *methods of treatment*' but then, later on in the same paragraph, said that 'Prometheus here claimed *methods for optimizing efficacy and reducing toxicity of treatment regimes* for gastrointestinal and non-gastrointestinal autoimmune diseases that utilize drugs providing 6-TG by administering a drug to a subject.'[315] More importantly, however, is its assertion that the 'invention's purpose to *treat the human body* is made clear in the specification and the preambles of the asserted claims'.[316] Although novelty is not a question to be considered when determining patent eligibility under section 101, it is instructive to note that if the claims were actually for a method of treating the human body using those drugs, then it would not be novel because the method was already known. What the patentee invented was a method of finding out how to make that medical treatment (treatment using particular drugs) more efficient by, first, increasing its chances of success and, secondly, reducing the associated side effects. It is clear that, when the wording of the claims is read in the context of what the patentee sought to achieve, there was no intention to claim merely a method of medical treatment.

The Federal Circuit claimed that, 'unlike the clinical test recited in *Grams*, the administering and determining steps in Prometheus's claimed methods are not "merely" data-gathering steps or "insignificant extra-solution activity"; they are part of *treatment regimes for various diseases* using thiopurine drugs'.[317] This cannot be correct, because the claimed method was not directed to a treatment regime at all – it merely provided a method by which that treatment regime could be *ascertained*. The treatment regime is the actual dosage that the patient would have to take. This was not found in the claims because it was not directed to a particular dosage regime, but to the method by which each individual dosage regime may be ascertained. In the last paragraph of its 23 page opinion, the Federal Circuit asked what it thought was the critical question, namely: what did the applicant invent? It replied by saying it was 'a series of transformative steps that optimizes efficacy and reduces toxicity of a method of treatment for particular diseases using particular drugs'.[318] This is not in line with its previous assertions that the claimed methods were for treating the human body or were methods of medical treatment. Moreover, this wording correctly puts the *invention* in its proper context – it related to a method of medical treatment but was not actually a method of medical treatment.

---

[315] Ibid (emphasis added).
[316] Ibid, at 17.
[317] Ibid, at 21 (emphasis added).
[318] Ibid, at 23.

(iii) Applying the machine-or-transformation test The Federal Circuit in *Prometheus v Mayo (No. 2)* held that, the machine-or-transformation test, 'as applied to the [Prometheus] claims ... leads to a clear and compelling conclusion, viz., that [they] pass muster under [section] 101. They do not encompass laws of nature or preempt natural correlations.'[319] It also held that 'Prometheus's asserted method claims recite a patent-eligible application of naturally occurring correlations between metabolite levels and efficacy or toxicity, and thus do not wholly preempt all uses of the recited correlations'.[320] It continued that, first, the 'steps involve a particular application of the natural correlations' and, secondly, the 'claims do not preempt all uses of the natural correlations; they utilize them in a series of specific steps'.[321] In addition, the Federal Circuit claimed that the 'inventive nature of the claimed methods stems not from preemption of all use of these natural processes, but from the application of a natural phenomenon in a series of steps comprising particular methods of treatment'.[322] Importantly, it held that '[o]ther drugs might be administered to optimize the therapeutic efficacy of the claimed treatment'.[323]

The Federal Circuit, therefore, reaffirmed its previous view that the treatment methods claimed in Prometheus's patents satisfied the transformation prong of the machine-or-transformation test, as they transform an article into a different state or thing and this transformation was central to the purpose of the claimed process.[324] The most crucial part of the reasoning of the Federal Circuit was its opinion that the transformation that occurred in the claimed method was 'of the human body and of its components following the administration of a specific class of drugs and the various chemical and physical changes of the drugs' metabolites that enable their concentrations to be determined'.[325] As a result, it held that there was no need for it to separately determine whether the claims also satisfied the machine prong of the test.[326] What, therefore, is the nature of this so-called transformation? If the claimed method was for a method of medical treatment, then the transformation identified by the Federal Circuit would have been correct because the transformation would be the effect in the human body that cures the patient. The invention, however,

---

319 Ibid, at 15.
320 Ibid.
321 Ibid.
322 Ibid, at 15–16.
323 Ibid, at 16.
324 Ibid.
325 Ibid.
326 Ibid.

was not for the method of treatment – it was for a method of finding the optimum treatment for a particular patient. The so-called transformation, if it exists, was not at all a central feature in the claimed method. The chemical reaction which took place in the human body did not transform anything worthy of patent protection under section 101 because the claimed method was not directed to that aspect of the drug – its ability to treat patients.

The Federal Circuit continued that, after administration of a drug such as AZA or 6-MP, 'the human body necessarily undergoes a transformation. The drugs do not pass through the body untouched without affecting it'.[327] The Federal Circuit claimed that the transformation was, in fact, the actual effect on the body after metabolising the artificially administered drugs, which was the sole purpose of administering the drugs. In other words, the drugs were administered to a patient, providing 6-TG, which was thought to be the drugs' active metabolite in the treatment of a disease.[328] This would have been correct if the claimed method was for a method of medical treatment whereby the patient was to take certain drugs to treat a particular ailment. That was not the object of the claimed method – for if it were, the claim would lack novelty because, as mentioned above, that fact was already known. What researchers sought to do, and Prometheus did successfully, was to find a way of determining the optimum dosage level of the drug. Usually, this would be applicable generally to everyone and the claimed method would indicate that a particular dosage would have the effect of increasing efficacy and decreasing the toxic side effects. However, in this case, there was not a particular dosage that would apply universally (and the patent did not claim a dosage regime) but the dosage would be patient specific after analysing the information derived from carrying out the claimed method. Contrary to this view, the Federal Circuit held that the administering step was not merely data-gathering but a significant transformative element of Prometheus's claimed methods of treatment that was sufficiently definite to confine the patent monopoly within rather definite bounds.[329] The administering step did not amount to a transformation as it related to a process by which the subject matter of the claimed method was to be achieved. It was a means to an end, not the end in itself!

After noting that not all the claimed methods contained the administering step, the Federal Circuit explained that this did not diminish the patentability of the claimed methods because the determining step was also

327 Ibid, at 17.
328 Ibid.
329 Ibid, at 18.

transformative and central to the claimed methods. In other words, '[d]etermining the levels of 6-TG or 6-MMP in a subject necessarily involves a transformation'.[330] It seems incredible, to say the least, that a step, directed at the reader of the specification or the person carrying out the invention, could amount to a transformation. The Federal Circuit did not show how the trick is done! It continued by noting that 'this transformation is central to the purpose of the claims, since the determining step is, like the administering step, a significant part of the claimed method'.[331] What is puzzling about this statement is why the importance of a step to a claimed method should mean that it is transformative. Should not that transformation be shown to exist irrespective of the nature or significance of the step in question? It is true that '[m]easuring the levels of 6-TG and 6-MMP is what enables possible adjustments to thiopurine drug dosage to be detected for optimizing efficacy or reducing toxicity during a course of treatment' but this involves no transformation in the ordinary sense of the word.

In respect of the requirement in *Flook*, as noted above, that the steps must not merely amount to insignificant extra-solution activity, the Federal Circuit held that the 'administering and determining steps are transformative and are central to the claims rather than merely insignificant extra-solution activity'.[332] It continued that the 'crucial error the district court made in reaching the opposite conclusion was failing to recognize that the first two steps of the asserted claims are not merely data-gathering steps'.[333] The Federal Circuit agreed with the District Court that the administering and determining steps gather useful data but claimed that 'it is also clear that the presence of those two steps in the claimed processes is not "merely" for the purpose of gathering data'.[334] The question then is what really was the function of those two steps in the claimed method? The Federal Circuit replied that the two steps 'are part of a treatment protocol, and they are transformative', claiming 'the administering step provides thiopurine drugs for the purpose of treating disease, and the determining step measures the drugs' metabolite levels for the purpose of assessing the drugs' dosage during the course of treatment'.[335] By the Federal Circuit's own admission, it is clear that the role of the two steps in the claimed method, although important, did not mean that they were transformative.

It then claimed that '[g]iven the integral involvement of the administering and determining steps in Prometheus's therapeutic methods, this case is

330 Ibid.
331 Ibid, at 19.
332 Ibid.
333 Ibid.
334 Ibid.
335 Ibid, at 19–20.

easily distinguishable from prior cases that found asserted method claims to be unpatentable for claiming data-gathering steps and a fundamental principle',[336] citing *In re Grams*. I am not altogether sure how *In re Grams* was distinguishable from the claims at issue. Both decisions considered the same type of claims. The Federal Circuit noted that in *In re Grams*, '[t]he claims did not require the performing of clinical tests on individuals that were transformative – and thus rendering the entire process patentable subject matter – because the tests were just to "obtain data"'.[337] On the contrary, the claimed method in *In re Grams* was to determine whether a patient suffered from a particular abnormality – that is a diagnostic method. From the information gathered, a conclusion could, therefore, be made as to whether the patient was suffering from a particular abnormality. In the instant case, however, the claim was to determine whether an increase or decrease in the dosage was appropriate for a particular patient. The claimed method did not determine the actual dosage required by the patient – that was to be done by the physician after analysing the information gathered from the claimed method. In the end, the Federal Circuit held that Prometheus's asserted method claims satisfied the pre-emption test as well as the transformation prong of the machine-or-transformation test.[338]

(iv) Natural phenomena The Federal Circuit was quick to point out, as noted above, that the claimed methods did not encompass laws of nature or pre-empt natural correlations – they involved a particular application of the natural correlations.[339] In other words, the 'method claims recite a patent-eligible application of naturally occurring correlations between metabolite levels and efficacy or toxicity, and thus do not wholly preempt all uses of the recited correlations'.[340] It was of the opinion that it did 'not view the disputed claims as merely claiming natural correlations and data-gathering steps'.[341] The Federal Circuit claimed that 'the administering and determining steps are not insignificant extra-solution activity, and the claims are therefore not drawn merely to correlations between metabolite levels and toxicity or efficacy'.[342] The essence of the claims was that the metabolite level, ascertained through carrying out the claimed method, correlated to the efficacy of the drugs and the toxic side effects of using the

336 Ibid, at 20.
337 Ibid.
338 Ibid, at 23.
339 Ibid, at 15.
340 Ibid.
341 Ibid, at 16.
342 Ibid, at 21.

drugs. It is that correlation that enabled the physician to determine whether an increase or decrease in the dosage of the drug was needed for a particular patient.

(v) Mental step In addition, the Federal Circuit agreed with the District Court that the final 'wherein' clauses were mental steps and, therefore, not patent-eligible per se.[343] It argued that the claims at issue were not 'simply to the mental steps' and that those subsequent mental steps do not, by themselves, 'negate the transformative nature of prior steps'.[344] The difficulty here is that, as was seen above, a critical element of the claimed method is the correlation that enabled the physician to determine, in respect of information derived from carrying out the test for each patient, whether an upwards or downwards change in the dosage was needed for that particular patient. More importantly, and in addition to this, is the part of the claimed method where the physician is to make a judgment, based on the results, as to whether the dosage for that particular patient should be increased or decreased. This was the basis of the claimed method – that is, a method of finding the dosage for each patient tested by, first, administering the drug to the patient and, secondly, determining the level of 6-thioguanine in the patient. This information is then processed by a physician (the mental step) based on the correlation (part of the laws of nature).

The Federal Circuit argued that, when viewed in the proper context, the final step of providing a warning based on the results of the prior steps did not detract from the patentability of Prometheus's claimed methods as a whole.[345] What then would be patentable? Based on the reasoning of the Federal Circuit, it would be the administration and determining aspect of the claim which, as stated above, are, by their nature, hardly, if ever, transformative. The Federal Circuit claimed that, 'contrary to Mayo's assertions, a physician who only evaluates the result of the claimed methods, without carrying out the administering and/or determining steps that are present in all the claims, cannot infringe any claim that requires such steps'.[346] Arguably, the essence of the invention was the ability of the physician, based on the information provided, to be able to determine what alterations, consequently, should be made to the patient's dosage regime. This is not transformation, plain and simple.

The Federal Circuit was of the opinion that, because the 'wherein clauses describe the mental processes used to determine the need to change

343 Ibid.
344 Ibid.
345 Ibid.
346 Ibid.

the dosage levels of the drugs, each asserted claim as a whole is drawn to patentable subject matter'.[347] Contrary to the view of the Federal Circuit, this is but one reason why the claimed method was not drawn to a patentable subject matter; the other was the claimed method embraced the correlation which is a natural phenomenon. Importantly, the Federal Circuit accepted that, '[a]lthough a physician is not required to make any upward or downward adjustment in dosage during the "warning" step, the prior steps provide useful information for possible dosage adjustments to the method of treatment using thiopurine drugs for a particular subject'.[348] This statement implicitly accepts the point made above that the real purpose of the claimed method was to determine whether a particular patient needed an adjustment in the drugs administered. Notwithstanding this, the Federal Circuit said that '[v]iewing the treatment methods as a whole, Prometheus has claimed therapeutic methods that determine the optimal dosage level for a course of treatment'.[349] If, as argued above, the claimed methods related to a method of determining whether adjustments were needed for specific patients, then the Federal Circuit cannot be correct in saying that they were 'treatment methods'.

7 Conclusion

The question of whether methods of medical treatment generally, and, more specifically, diagnostic methods, are patentable in the United States is in a state of flux. The diverging decisions of the Federal Circuit on the matter do not assist in providing any sound basis for the development of the law in this area. This is more so since the Supreme Court in *Bilski v Kappos* rejected the machine-or-transformation test, as the sole test for patent eligibility, that was used by the Federal Circuit in *Prometheus v Mayo* to hold patentable a so-called diagnostic method, but that same test was used by the Federal Circuit in *Classen v Biogen* to deny patent protection for a similar method. The Supreme Court then remanded both decisions back to the Federal Circuit for reconsideration in light of its judgment in *Bilski v Kappos*. The only court that has remained consistent on the issue is the District Court in both *Prometheus v Mayo* and *Classen v Biogen* which held that the claimed method was a phenomenon of nature. Both decisions relied on the dissent of Breyer J. in *Laboratory Corporation v Metabolite Labs* which had also held that similar claims were unpatentable

347 Ibid, at 22.
348 Ibid.
349 Ibid.

because they were phenomena of nature. The view that such methods are phenomena of nature makes sense in light of the content of such claims, and is fast gaining currency, and was seemingly accepted by the District Court in *AMP v USPTO*.

The Federal Circuit has reconsidered its previous decision of *Prometheus v Mayo* in light of the Supreme Court decision in *Bilski v Kappos*. In *Prometheus v Mayo (No. 2)*, it claimed that, although the Supreme Court said that the machine-or-transformation test was not the determinative test for patentability under section 101 of the Patents Act, it was still a clue to patent-eligibility. Therefore, applying that test, the Federal Circuit held that the claimed methods, for determining the dosage regime for patients, were patentable. This is certainly not the last word from the Federal Circuit on this issue in light of *Classen v Biogen* which will soon be reconsidered by it, and *AMP v USPTO*, the District Court decision which has been appealed. A decision by the Supreme Court in either of these cases seems inevitable.

E CONCLUSION

The courts in the United States and the USPTO have confronted this issue of whether patent protection should be provided for medical procedures for over a century. The question was always whether the legal requirements of patentability were met and, when medical procedure patents were rejected, it was usually on the basis that they were not new. They were not rejected on the ground that they were *incapable* of being patentable subject matter. *Ex parte Brinkerhoff* was the only case that held they were not patentable because of the uncertainty of the results of such treatments. The fallacy of that argument was made clear in *ex parte Scherer* which overruled *ex parte Brinkerhoff* to the extent that it had held that medical procedures were not patentable subject matter.

The courts did not question the availability of medical procedure patents on the basis that they may be contrary to public policy or unethical. The only case where this was hinted was *Martin v Wyeth* where Chesnut J. pointed out that '[*t*]*he professional ethics of doctors and surgeons are more consistent with the widespread use of their medical and surgical discoveries for the benefit of mankind than in obtaining a monopoly to control their discoveries for personal commercial advantage*. In this respect it would seem also that public interest is here involved'.[350] Although he rightly pointed out that a method of medical treatment raised some public health considerations, he did not proceed to provide any discussion of the issue.

---

[350] 96 F Supp 689 (DC DM 1951).

For over 50 years the legal position was settled and physicians and others alike patented medical treatments. The *Pallin v Singer* case served as the catalyst for various Bills that were introduced in Congress to exclude medical procedures from patent protection. This was achieved with the enactment of the MPAA which did not exclude medical procedures from patent protection. It maintained the status quo but provided immunity to physicians and related health care entities from patent infringement suits to ensure that they were not hindered in the treatment of patients. It also sought to address the concerns of the opponents to medical procedure patents by excluding new uses of pharmaceutical products, machines and biotechnological process patents from the scope of the Act. The MPAA attempted a compromise between patenting methods of medical treatment and the incentives of the patent system. Methods of medical treatment remained patentable whilst the remedies available to the patentee, *vis à vis* a medical practitioner or a related health care entity, were removed. A different route from that taken in Europe was adopted but the end result was the same *viz*. providing physicians with no patent restrictions on the methods of treatment that they use to treat their patients.

While there has been a resurgence of the issue of patenting methods of medical treatments, in particular, diagnostic methods, the United States Supreme Court has yet to finally pronounce on the issue. It missed an opportunity in the 2006 *Laboratory Corporation v Metabolite Labs* case where the minority argued that the insufficiency in the record of decisions of lower courts dealing with the issue should not have been a reason not to decide the matter. Subsequently, a plethora of Federal Circuit decisions dealt with the same issue, namely, *Prometheus v Mayo* and *Classen v Biogen*, but the Supreme Court in June 2010, vacated these decisions and remanded them to the Federal Circuit for reconsideration in light of its recent decision in *Bilski v Kappos*. The Federal Circuit, in *Prometheus v Mayo (No. 2)*, reconsidered and affirmed its reasoning in *Prometheus v Mayo*. Soon, it will have to consider the other remanded decision and the District Court's decision of *AMP v USPTO* which also relates to the question of whether medical diagnostic methods are patent-eligible under section 101 of the Patents Act. There is no question, therefore, that, in the foreseeable future, these questions will finally be decided by the Supreme Court, especially in light of the reasoning of the Federal Circuit in *Prometheus v Mayo (No. 2)*.

11. Conclusion

The examination of issues considered in the previous chapters has shown that the question of whether patents should be granted for methods of medical treatment is a policy decision since it involves some serious public health considerations. Initially, this was not appreciated by the courts in the United Kingdom but, later, they hinted that it might be the justification for the exclusion and, in the process, castigated the previous bases to legal history. But the European Patent Convention (EPC) 1973 contained the exclusion for methods of medical treatment in Europe in the form of Article 52(4) EPC, which was subsequently changed to Article 53(c) EPC 2000. What then formed the basis of the exclusion in each of those provisions, as a matter of statutory interpretation? The legislative history of the exclusion sheds little light on the reasons for it, but provides some insight into what the drafters meant in respect of the exclusions for therapeutic, surgical and diagnostic methods. Are the exclusions justified at all then? A comprehensive look at these considerations formed part of the matrix of arguments for and against patent protection considered in Chapters 2 and 3. The EPC jurisprudence relating to the interpretation of the exclusion informed Chapters 4–7. These chapters also considered new technologies in light of the medical treatment exclusion and other exclusions from patentability that might be implicated. The UK position was explained in Chapters 8 and 9, while Chapter 10 dealt with the issues relating to methods of medical treatment from a US perspective.

A JUDICIAL DETERMINATION OF THE EXCLUSION

1 The United Kingdom

The origin of the exception for methods of medical treatment in the United Kingdom is shrouded in mystery. The judicially created exclusion for methods of medical treatment in the United Kingdom was not based on any well-established rationale. The cases have, over time, adopted differing approaches to this question. It was first conceived as a question of statutory interpretation by the Solicitor-General in *C & W's Application* while accepting that Patent Office practice was to the same effect. The courts blindly applied this without any specific evidence that the Patent Office actually had the practice of not granting patents for methods of medical treatment. With the demise of the legal basis on which *C & W's Application* rested (the commercial object requirement), it was necessary for the courts to find some other rationale for maintaining the exclusion. It was hinted that the exclusion was based on ethics in *Schering A G's Application*. *Joos v Commissioner of Patents* made ethics/morality the legal basis of the exclusion by virtue of the proviso to section 6 of the Statute of Monopolies, whereas this was only hinted at in *Eli Lilly & Company's Application*. Therefore, the UK cases immediately preceding the Patents Act 1977 (the 1977 Act) began to accept a vague notion of public policy as the justification for the exclusion of methods of medical treatment from patent protection without proper articulation or explanation. The Patent Appeal Tribunal (PAT) was not entirely satisfied with the exclusion. The dissatisfaction became manifest when it sanctioned and asserted that pack claims could be used to evade the exclusion for methods of medical treatment. Judicial deference, in light of continued uncertainty and disquiet about the rationale for the exclusion, were not significant enough to convince them to remove the judicially created exclusion of methods of medical treatment. The courts and PAT felt incompetent to interpret the law to provide patent protection for methods of medical treatment and asserted that if there were to be any change, it should be made by Parliament.

2 Australia and New Zealand

The different approaches towards patent protection for methods of medical treatment in Commonwealth jurisdictions showed that the judicial exclusion maintained in the United Kingdom before 1977 was not inevitable. The decisions from Australia and New Zealand are interesting insofar as they show that the jurisprudence in the United Kingdom could have gone either way on the question of whether patent protection should have been provided for methods of medical treatment. That the two jurisdictions concerned share a similar statutory origin is even more fascinating, in light of the different conclusions arrived at by their courts. The courts in New Zealand, taking a more cautious approach, rejected the notion that patent protection should be available for methods of medical treatment, in line with the UK authorities on the issue. However, the court in Australia rejected the UK authorities and held that, in principle, methods of medical treatment are not excluded from patent protection.

3 The United States of America

The US courts have also had to grapple with a similar problem *viz.* determining whether methods of medical treatment were patentable subject matter. The Patent Office Board of Appeal (US) (POBA) in *ex parte Brinkerhoff* excluded methods of medical treatment from patent protection on dubious grounds but the courts continued to allow patents for medical diagnosis. However, in 1954, *ex parte Brinkerhoff* was overruled by the POBA in *ex parte Scherer* thereby allowing patents of methods of medical treatment. In 1996, the United States Congress acted quickly in enacting the Medical Procedures and Affordability Act 1996 (MPAA) on the heels of the *Pallin v Singer* case where one physician sued another for infringing a medical procedure patent. The MPAA provided immunity from patent infringement suits to physicians and medical health care entities. A comprehensive discussion of the rationale for excluding methods of medical treatment arose during the debates that preceded the passage of the MPAA in the United States. The immunity provided to physicians was based on the belief that patent protection would have dire consequences for the physician/patient relationship, and an increase in the cost of, and access to, health care.

While there has been a resurgence of the issue of patenting methods of medical treatments, in particular, diagnostic methods, the United States Supreme Court has yet to finally pronounce on the issue. It missed an opportunity in the 2006 case of *Laboratory Corporation v Metabolite Labs* where the minority argued that the insufficiency in the record of decisions of lower courts dealing with the issue should not have been a reason not to decide the matter. Subsequently, a plethora of Federal Circuit decisions dealt with the same issue, namely, *Prometheus v Mayo* and *Classen v Biogen* but the Supreme Court, in June 2010, vacated these decisions and remanded them to the Federal Circuit for reconsideration in light of its decision in *Bilski v Kappos*.

As mentioned before, the Federal Circuit has reconsidered its previous decision of *Prometheus v Mayo* in light of the Supreme Court decision in *Bilski v Kappos*. In *Prometheus v Mayo (No. 2)*, it claimed that, although the Supreme Court said that the machine-or-transformation test was not the determinative test for patentability under section 101 of the Patents Act, it was still a clue to patent-eligibility. Therefore, applying that test, the Federal Circuit held that the claimed methods, for determining the dosage regime for patients, were patentable. This is certainly not the last word from the Federal Circuit on this issue in light of *Classen v Biogen* which will soon be reconsidered by it, and *AMP v USPTO*, the District Court decision which has been appealed. A decision by the Supreme Court in either of these cases seems inevitable.

B EUROPEAN PATENT OFFICE JURISPRUDENCE

1 Legislative History

The discussions which took place during the negotiations of the EPC and the various working papers presented at them did not provide any evidence that policy based arguments featured significantly at any time preceding the acceptance of the final form of the EPC accepted in 1973. The drafters of the EPC 2000 have recently accepted that methods of medical treatment are excluded in the *interests of public health*. The previous position, which was proposed by Germany at the Munich Diplomatic Conference in 1973, excluded methods of medical treatment because they were deemed incapable of industrial application. The recent reformulation of the exclusion marks a significant shift in the thinking which puts the focus back on the public health rationale of the exclusion, without reliance on the previous dubious statutory basis of lacking industrial applicability. It is also in line with the reasoning of the Enlarged Board of Appeal of the European Patent Office (EBA), Technical Board of Appeal (TBA) and the UK courts that the rationale for the exclusion was to prevent patents from affecting the activities of physicians when treating their patients.

2 Therapeutic Methods

The TBAs accepted that the definition of therapy was not limited to the curing of diseases but covered any treatment which 'was designed to cure, alleviate, remove or lessen the symptoms of, or prevent or reduce the possibility of contracting any disorder or malfunction of the human or animal body', or prophylactic treatment aimed at maintaining health by preventing ill effects that would otherwise have arisen. As a result, they have held that contraceptive methods are not excluded from patent protection since they do not fall within that broad definition. They have exalted the principle that patents should be granted, and that the exclusion should be narrowly construed, ensuring that cosmetic methods are patentable even if they might incidentally have some therapeutic effect. With similar boldness, they have allowed patents for implantable devices in the human body only where there is no relationship between the device and the therapeutic benefit on the human body to which it is applied. The patenting of methods that involve animals for industrial purposes has proved troubling and the

TBAs still have to establish some clear rules relating to this. The potential for the exclusion to become an unruly horse has been tamed, ensuring that the exclusion only applies where it specifically relates to a therapeutic method of treatment.

In relation to claims that include a device implanted in the human body being a method of treatment of the human body by therapy, the TBAs have made it clear that: first, there should not be any therapeutic effect produced on the human body, that is with a view to maintaining or restoring the health of the human body or curing diseases; secondly, there should be no nexus or functional link between the device claimed and any therapeutic effect produced on the human body to which it is applied; and, thirdly, the claim must specifically only relate to the functional or technical features of the device claimed. If all these conditions are satisfied, the claimed method will not amount to an excluded method of treatment of the human or animal body by therapy, contrary to Article 53(c) EPC 2000. In respect of claims which have both a therapeutic and cosmetic treatment, the TBAs have articulated the following principles: First, if the two purposes are distinct and the patentee claims only the cosmetic indication, then patent protection should be available for the cosmetic indication. However, two conditions must be satisfied, namely, the therapeutic effect must either: (a) be incidental to the cosmetic effect; or (b) only arise in some instances (either in relation to the subject to which it is applied, or by its nature). Secondly, where the claimed method would always have a therapeutic effect, it would not be patentable notwithstanding the secondary cosmetic indication. In other words, the therapeutic effect should not be an inevitable consequence of carrying out the claimed method. Thirdly, to specifically exclude any therapeutic aspect of the claimed method from the ambit of the claims, applicants can use a disclaimer.

The exclusion of methods of medical treatment of the human or animal body by therapy does, in fact, include treatment of animals, but this was hardly considered in any of the decisions of the TBAs. However, from the handful of decisions that were found, the TBAs made it absolutely clear that no distinction should properly be made between the activities of a farmer and a veterinary practitioner when they carry out such treatment on animals. The interpretation given to the exclusion by the TBAs sits comfortably with the intention of the drafters of the EPC, insofar as it excludes purely therapeutic treatment of animals from patent protection, whereas treatments that are designed to increase the quantity or quality of the animal product are allowable. The TBAs have had to steer a course to ensure that the exclusion of methods of medical treatment from patent protection is not rendered meaningless since such treatments can be part of the farming industry, and, therefore, should fall outside the scope of the exclusion. Unsurprisingly, they have maintained that although the exclusion should be narrowly construed, it cannot be interpreted in such a way that medical treatments for use in commercial farming are allowable, whereas other medical treatments are not. Also, importantly, the exclusion from patent protection of methods for treatment of the human or animal body by therapy does not *per se* exclude gene therapy or stem cell therapy, although the subject matter very well may be considered under Article 53(a) EPC relating to morality or *ordre public*. The Biotech Directive has considered some of these issues and has spelt out that the patenting of these new technologies is without prejudice to the exclusions for methods of medical treatment in Article 53(c) EPC.

3 Surgical Methods

The previous decisions of the TBAs, arguably, allowed patent protection for such methods which did not have a curative purpose, but simply had a cosmetic or industrial purpose. However, the decision of the EBA in *MEDI-PHYSICS/Treatment by surgery* has now closed the gap in the jurisprudence of the TBAs. The EBA stated clearly that some methods, namely, uncritical methods involving only a minor intervention and no substantial health risks, when carried out with the required care and skill, while still adequately protecting the medical profession, would not be excluded from patent protection under Article 53(c) EPC. It explained that some invasive techniques, such as tattooing, piercing, hair removal by optical radiation and micro abrasion of the skin, which are now safe and of routine character, are nowadays generally carried out in non-medical, commercial environments such as in cosmetic salons and beauty parlours, and, as such, it is hardly still justified to exclude them from patentability.

There exists a significant limitation of the test(s) accepted by the EBA to determine whether a method should be regarded as a method of treatment by surgery, namely, whether that method includes an invasive step representing a substantial physical intervention on the body which requires professional medical expertise to be carried out and which entails a health risk even when carried out with the required professional care and expertise. The difficulty of, first, providing tests/guidelines which rest on such subjective criteria, secondly, dictating that the Examiners and TBAs take into consideration other criteria which, arguably, are too subjective and, thirdly, saying that other criteria are not foreclosed in determining what amounted to a method of treatment by surgery, means that the EBA has not conformed with its own self-professed aim of providing legal certainty.

The EBA, although declining to give a definitive and comprehensive definition of 'treatment by surgery', ruled that the definition of surgical methods does not embrace methods that are for a curative purpose, and that neither the ordinary reading nor the intention of the drafters of the EPC 1973 compels one to that conclusion. It asserted that the exclusion for surgical methods, and indeed the other medical treatment methods under Article 53(c) EPC, namely therapeutic and diagnostic methods, should not be applied to methods which are not excluded on one or more of the following: (a) in the interests of public health; (b) for the protection of patients; or (c) freedom of the medical profession to apply the treatment of choice to their patients – the so called 'new direction'. Importantly too, the EBA, agreeing with the established jurisprudence of the TBAs, reiterated that a claimed method is excluded under Article 53(c) EPC if it comprises or encompasses at least one feature defining a physical activity or action that constitutes a method step for treatment of the human or animal body by surgery or therapy. The EBA also formally accepted that disclaimers may be used in claims, in respect of the exclusions under Article 53(c) EPC, provided that they satisfy the requirements in *PPG/Disclaimer* and they conform to the requirements of Articles 83 and 84 EPC.

4 Diagnostic Methods

The EBA in *CYGNUS/Diagnostic method* clarified and restated the definition of diagnostic methods that was to be used by the various TBAs when they apply the exclusion from patent protection of diagnostic methods practised on the human or animal body. Diagnostic methods were to comprise the following steps: (a) examination and data gathering; (b) comparison of the data with normal values; (c) recording any significant deviation; and (d) attributing the deviation to a particular clinical picture (the deductive medical or veterinary decision phase or the diagnosis for curative purposes *stricto sensu*). To constitute a diagnostic method, a claimed method must contain all of the four steps outlined above; and, to be excluded from patent protection, at least one step of a technical nature must be practised on the human or animal body. The last step, step (d), is clearly a defining feature of a diagnostic method; without which the claim would, at best, relate to diagnosis but not comprise a diagnostic method. So strict is that requirement that any claim which does not clearly outline the actual diagnosis, and only leads to intermediate results, would not be patentable. The TBA, therefore, quite rightly, rejected the notion that the presence or involvement of the medical or veterinary practitioner was at all relevant to the question of whether a method was a diagnostic one. The definition given to diagnostic methods is now reflective of the nature of such a multi-step method, so all its constituent steps must be present in a claimed method to offend Article 53(c) EPC.

The TBAs have continued to reject patent applications relating to diagnostic methods for broadly the same reasons that they did before. The decisions that have followed *CYGNUS/Diagnostic method* have not found any significant difficultly in applying the principles enunciated therein, in particular, the four-pronged definition of diagnostic methods. However, the limitation that the diagnostic method must be practised on the human or animal body has been subject of further clarification by the TBAs. First, following *CYGNUS/Diagnostic method*, it was held that only steps of a technical nature in steps (a) to (c) were to be examined to determine whether they were practised on the human body. Secondly, it was also decided that steps (b) and (c) would not usually be technical in nature; therefore, in most cases, it was only with respect to step (a), which is usually of a technical nature, where it would be necessary to determine if it (step (a)) was practised on the human or animal body. Thirdly, it was decided that intermediate steps which form part of steps (a) to (c) were not to be examined to determine whether they are practised on the human or animal body and, consequently, are to be ignored for that part of the analysis.

The question of whether new technologies, such as genetic diagnostic testing, would offend the exclusion for methods of medical treatment have already been examined by the TBAs of the European Patent Office (EPO). Claims to diagnostic testing using the BRAC1 and BRAC2 genes have been held as not excluded from patent protection because they are not practised on the human or animal body. Although not excluded by Article 53(c) EPC, there is the additional question of whether they offend Article 53(a) EPC. The TBAs have held that that exclusion was not implicated with the patenting of genetic diagnostic testing, but it is doubtful whether these decisions will be the last word on the issue.

5 Second and Further Medical Uses

The EBA in *EISAI/Second medical indication* accepted the practice of the Swiss Federal Intellectual Property Office, which had sanctioned claims that were directed to the 'use of a substance or composition for the manufacture of a medicament for a specified purpose'. In order to secure patent protection, the Swiss-type claim, it was thought, must satisfy two criteria: (a) the manufacture of a medicament; and (b) a new therapeutic application. They are indispensable requirements of the Swiss-type claim and both have the functions of identifying novelty and defining the scope of the claim in question. The TBAs have made it clear that the principles deriving from *EISAI/Second medical indication* do not apply to second surgical uses of instruments or devices. However, they have expanded the subject matter covered by the Swiss form of claim to apply it to cases other than a new therapeutic purpose, thereby expanding the new medical indications that can satisfy the requirement of the Swiss form of claim. These new cases related to, first, a new class of subject to which the medicament was to be applied; and, secondly, a mode of administration or dosage or treatment regime. It was this second class of subject matter that was the subject of a recent referral to the EBA. If there was any doubt about the need of that incentive provided for by *EISAI/Second medical indication*, Article 54(5) EPC means that there is now a statutory basis for second (and further) medical uses under the EPC. Therefore, it will no longer be necessary to resort to the Swiss form of claim. The status quo as it relates to first medical uses is found in Article 54(4) EPC.

The EBA in *ABBOTT RESPIRATORY/Dosage regime* stated that where it is already known to use a medicament to treat an illness, Article 54(5) EPC does not exclude this medicament from patentability for use in a different treatment by therapy of the same illness. This conclusion should have been limited in its scope if it is accepted that Articles 54(4) and 54(5) EPC relate to three distinct methods, and that *EISAI/Second medical indication*, with its emphasis on a new illness to be treated, was there dealing with a method of treatment of the animal body by therapy. Therefore, given that the excluded methods differ in their interpretation and scope, as has recently been held by the EBA in *CYGNUS/Diagnostic method* and *MEDI-PHYSICS/Treatment by surgery*, the proper interpretation of Article 54(5) EPC must relate to that particular exclusion only. In any event, the EBA also might be incorrect to suggest that something else, other than a new illness to be treated, would suffice for the application of Articles 54(4) and 54(5) EPC. The EBA also held that patent protection was not excluded where a dosage regime is the only feature claimed which is not comprised in the state of the art. The aforementioned reading of Articles 54(4) and 54(5) EPC necessarily means that, in relation to the second question, a dosage regime would not be included in the subject matter covered by these provisions, since they do not relate to a new illness but, merely, to new methods of administration of an old substance to treat an old illness. In answering the third question, the EBA stated that, where the subject matter of a claim is rendered novel only by a new therapeutic use of a medicament, such claim may no longer have the format of a so called Swiss-type claim as instituted by the decision in *EISAI/Second medical indication*. The EBA, therefore, has confirmed that patent protection is available for dosage regimes under the EPC, signalling in the process that the specific use referred to in Article 54(5) EPC is not limited to the treatment of a new disease, and confirming decisions of the TBAs that have accepted other new applications as patentable under Article 54(5) EPC 1973. As such, patentees no longer need to use the Swiss form of claim to gain patent protection for second or further medical uses – as this is specifically provided for in Article 54(5) EPC. The EBA also ruled that applicants would have a three-month limit to comply with the new requirement discussed by the EBA in its decision.

6 The United Kingdom Courts

The UK courts have been able to apply the exclusion of methods of medical treatment without much difficulty. The 1977 Act maintained the exclusion of methods of medical treatment from patent protection in the United Kingdom, albeit in statutory form. It heralded the halt to the quest to find a rationale for the judicially-created (if not accepted) exclusion which had engaged much of the time of the courts and the PAT in the period before 1977. Although the exclusion was kept, its scope was widened to include methods of treatment of the human or animal body by therapy or surgery, and diagnostic methods practised on the human or animal body. The legal basis for the exclusion has been further reformulated by the 2004 Act which has swept away the previous formulation of the exclusion as lacking industrial application. The UK courts have considered the scope of the exclusion on a few occasions only, particularly methods of treatment of the human body by therapy. However, the EBA and the TBAs have been busy reformulating the scope of the exclusions in the past 30 years. The UK courts have not lagged behind, and, where necessary, they have reluctantly applied the EPO jurisprudence; in particular, that relating to second and further medical use patents. Their concerns relating to the doctrinal basis of second (and further) medical use patents have now been laid to rest with the explicit recognition of such patents in the EPC 2000 which now forms part of UK law by virtue of the 2004 Act.

The Court of Appeal in *Actavis v Merck* rejected the received learning of *Bristol-Myers Squibb* by first claiming that it contained no ratio to the effect that: (a) a novel, non-obvious dosage regime specified in a Swiss form of claim cannot make it novel; and, (b) such a claim is to a method of medical treatment. Secondly, if it was wrong on that point, the Court of Appeal accepted that since the EPO had a 'settled view' to the contrary, it was entitled (but not bound) to follow that view, even if it was inconsistent with *Bristol-Myers Squibb*. In this instance, it decided to follow *GENENTECH INC/Method of administration of IGF-I*. Needless to say that the EBA in *ABBOTT RESPIRATORY/Dosage regime* has agreed with the decision of the Court of Appeal and allowed patent protection for dosage regimes under the EPC.

C THE ARGUMENTS FOR AND AGAINST PATENT PROTECTION

1 Introduction

Any society that puts primacy on the health of its citizens would ensure that an appropriate balance is achieved between the arguments for and against patent protection of methods of medical treatment. The solution should be one that gives appropriate weight to the rights of patentees, whilst, at the same time, accommodating the ethical and public policy objections to patent protection for methods of medical treatment. Since methods of medical treatment are already excluded under current law, the burden of proof for a change in the law is a heavy one. It must be shown, and rather convincingly too, that the arguments made in favour of patent protection are sufficiently strong to outweigh the arguments against patent protection. Any balancing exercise would need sound empirical evidence to show the actual impact of patenting medical procedures on society generally. The examination of the issues and arguments shows that they are not that simple and need careful consideration before a firm view could be taken either way on the patentability of methods of medical treatment.

2 The Arguments against Patent Protection

The ethical justifications against patenting methods of medical treatment did not feature significantly in the pre-1977 case law in the United Kingdom. The arguments made against patent protection include the increase in health care costs, the decreased accessibility and quality of health care, the unwarranted limitation on physician autonomy, breach of the physician's fiduciary duty to act in the best interest of the patient, breach of the right to health, the breach of patients' right to privacy, the potential for abuse by the patentee and the limitations on access to medical research. There are possible implications for the traditional tenets of the medical profession, namely, the Hippocratic Oath and the sharing norm.

This question engages a discussion about the proper role of patents in society. In most countries, including the European Community and New Zealand, the balance has been struck in favour of excluding methods of medical treatment from the scope of patent protection. Medical procedure patents are still available in the United States but physicians and related health care entities are provided with immunity from patent infringement suits. However, the Federal Court of Australia has allowed patent protection for methods of medical treatment.

These ethical considerations are central to the issue of patent protection for methods of medical treatment. It is important that this is appreciated and appropriate weight is given to these arguments by legislators and the courts if or when they have to decide the issue of where the balance between the two arguments should lie.

It is arguable that the difference between the availability of patent protection for drug therapies and the lack thereof for medical procedures is one of direct control over the supply of the patented invention. In the case of pharmaceutical products, the patentee can limit supply and increase the price but, in most cases, it would not be in their interests to do so. Similarly, with methods of medical treatment, the patentee-physician can also restrict supply of the necessary or potentially life-saving procedure by denying others the right to use it or by not performing it herself – which would be contrary to the public good. The consequences for the public seem to be worse in the case of the medical treatment since the procedure/process is unlike a drug which can be manufactured and distributed to millions of people. One method by which this question of access to the medical treatment may be resolved is to subject it to a compulsory licensing regime if licences are not readily made available by the patentee. However, this too has limitations and, without empirical evidence concerning its economic impact on public health, one cannot come to a firm conclusion on whether it achieves an optimum balance.

3 The Arguments for Patent Protection

On the other side of the debate are the arguments that are made in favour of patent protection of methods of medical treatment. The right of the patentee to the product of his labour, based on either the labour theory of Locke or the personality theory of Hegel, might justify patent protection for medical procedures. However, the patent system has the economic rationale at its core. Various economic theories have been proffered to explain the patent system, namely: the incentive to innovate theory (the patent system provides the necessary incentive to innovate in research and development); the patent-induced theory (patent protection for inventions that were induced by the patent system); the prospect theory (the patent system allows a limited monopoly to enable the patentee to develop the technological possibility); and the rent dissipation theory (the patent system aims to reduce rent dissipation).

Most of these theories do not necessarily provide a sufficient account of the patent system. It has been argued that the incentives of the patent system may have some application to methods of medical treatment, including the SET method and treatment regimes. The incentives to innovate and invent theories, important as they are, do not prove conclusively that inventors need them to develop medical procedures. Without empirical evidence supporting the link between the incentives of the patent system and methods of medical treatment, a firm conclusion cannot be reached. As far as the United Kingdom's position is concerned, the arguments for patent protection would have to be overwhelming to convince the policy makers that a change is desirable; and, that decision is not one that can be taken without consideration of the consequences for the harmonisation of patent laws in Europe – the very reason for the establishment of the EPC.

4 Conclusion

When issues of policy are decided, it is usually done after an exhaustive consideration and examination of all the relevant factors. This book has attempted to highlight the various considerations that should be taken into account when deciding the issue of whether patent protection should be granted for methods of medical treatment. However, a balancing of these considerations will be possible when there is evidence showing the impact of patenting methods of medical treatment on society. The arguments are finely balanced and one should avoid coming to a firm conclusion on the issue without a full and expansive review of all the issues concerned. It was clear, as the various opinions of judges emphasised, that the issue is not as simplistic as is sometimes suggested.

Therefore, when the Supreme Court of the United States in *Diamond v Chakrabarty*[1] was confronted with the question whether a live, human-made micro-organism was patentable subject matter under their patent laws, it stated:[2]

> What is more important is that we are without competence to entertain these arguments – either to brush them aside as fantasies generated by fear of the unknown, or to act on them. The choice we are urged to make is a matter of high policy for resolution with the legislative process and after the kind of investigation, examination, and study that the legislative bodies can provide and the courts cannot. The process involves the balancing of competing values and interests, which in our democratic system is the business of elected representatives. Whatever their validity, the contentions now pressed upon us should be addressed to the political branches of Government, the Congress and the Executive, and not to the courts.

---

1 447 U.S. 303 (1980).
2 Ibid, at 318.

The Court of Appeal of New Zealand in *Wellcome Foundation v Commissioner of Patents*[3] pointed out that 'not only is there the question whether medical and surgical methods should be treated as a special subject in patent law – a question upon which the views of the medical professional bodies would seem to be among those deserving consultation – but there must be an economic question of particular importance for a country of the size of New Zealand, dependent to the extent that it is upon overseas manufacturers'.[4] It then referred to *Diamond v Chakrabarty* quoted above and refused the request by the appellant to allow patents for methods of medical treatment.

Similarly, in *Bristol-Myers Squibb Co v F H Faulding & Co. Ltd*,[5] Finkelstein J of the Australian Federal Court asked '[h]ow is a court able to resolve these competing contentions? *None of them are supported by evidence.* Some may not even be capable of proof. Even if evidence was called to make good the unsubstantiated assertions, on what basis is the court to decide how the public interest will best be served?'[6] He then referred to the same passage in *Diamond v Chakrabarty* quoted above and stated that 'I do not believe that in a controversial issue such as is raised by the present argument, I would be abandoning my responsibility as a judge to follow this approach and to hold that if public policy demands that a medical or surgical process should be excluded from patentability, then that is a matter that should be resolved by the Parliament'.[7] He continued that:[8]

> It is likely that few of the arguments admit of a definitive answer. *The area of controversy is great.* Public interest groups, medical and professional associations, medical scientists and the pharmaceutical industry, among others, would need to be approached and their views ascertained before a court could ever hope to arrive at a reasoned conclusion, if it could ever do so. Indeed a court might well be asked to take account of ethical and moral considerations to arrive at a decision. *This is not the function of a court on an issue such as this.* In my opinion, medical treatment and surgical process are patentable under the legislation and, if public policy requires a different result, it is for the Parliament to amend the 1990 Act.

In the same way that the courts refused to consider the question of whether patent protection should be provided for methods of medical treatment (for

3 [1983] NZLR 385.
4 Ibid, at 21.
5 (2000) FCA 316.
6 Ibid, at [140] (emphasis added).
7 Ibid, at [141].
8 Ibid, at [142].

example, in New Zealand in the case of *Wellcome Foundation v Commissioner of Patents*) or whether methods of medical treatment should be excluded from patent protection (for example in Australia in the case of *Bristol-Myers Squibb Co v F H Faulding & Co. Ltd*), neither would be appropriate to decide the issue within the pages of this book without a more comprehensive examination of all the views of interested parties and the evidence supporting the case either way. Indeed, it is ironic that, in both New Zealand and Australia, the decision was made to retain the status quo because of the lack of strong evidence supporting the case for change.

Bibliography

BOOKS

Beauchamp, T.L. and J.F. Childress, *Principles of Biomedical Ethics* (5th edn, Oxford University Press, Oxford 2001)

Bently and Sherman, *Intellectual Property Law* (3rd edn, Oxford University Press, Oxford 2008)

Cook, T. C. Doyle and D. Jabbari, *Pharmaceuticals, Biotechnology & the Law* (Macmillan Publishers Ltd 1991)

Cornish, W., *Intellectual Property: Omnipresent, Distracting, Irrelevant?* (Clarendon Lecture Series, Oxford University Press, Oxford 2004)

Cornish, W., D. Llewelyn and T. Aplin, *Intellectual Property: Patents, Copyrights, Trade Marks & Allied Rights* (7th edn, Sweet and Maxwell, London 2010)

Davis, J., *Intellectual Property Law* (Butterworths, London 2001)

Domeij, B., *Pharmaceutical Patents in Europe* (Kluwer Law International 2000)

Dworkin, R., *Taking Rights Seriously* (Duckworth, London 1996)

Harris, J.W., *Property and Justice* (Oxford University Press, Oxford 1996)

Hegel, G.W.F., *Philosophy of Right* (S.W. Dyde (tr) 1996)

Kaufer, E., *The Economics of the Patent System* (Harwood Academic Publishers, Switzerland 1989)

Locke, J., *Two Treatises of Government* (M. Goldie (ed) 1993)

Mill, J.S., *A Manual of Political Economy* (D Appleton & Co, New York 1901)

Porter, R., *The Greatest Benefit to Mankind: A Medical History of Humanity from Antiquity to the Present* (HarperCollins Publishers, London 1997)

Smith, A., *The Wealth of Nations* (2nd edn, J.E.T. Rogers (ed) Clarendon Press, Oxford 1880)

Vaver, D., *Intellectual Property Law* (Concord, Ont., Irwin Law 1997)

Waldron, J., *The Right to Private Property* (Clarendon Press, Oxford 1988)

ARTICLES IN BOOKS

Bentham, J., 'A Manual of Political Economy' in *The Works of Jeremy Bentham* (J Bowring edn 1962)

Palmer, T., 'Are Patents and Copyright Morally Justified? The Philosophy of Property Rights and Ideal Subjects' in *Information Ethics: Privacy, Property, and Power* (Adam D. Moore (ed), University of Washington Press, Seattle 2005)

Plant, A.S., 'The Economic Theory Concerning Patents for Inventions' in A.S. Plant, *Selected Economic Essays and Addresses* (Routledge & Kegan Paul Ltd, London 1974)

Spence, M., 'Justifying Copyright' in *Dear Images: Art, Copyright and Culture* (D. McLean and K. Schubert (eds), Ridinghouse, London 2002)

Vaver, D., 'Defining and Rewarding Invention: a Review and a Modest Proposal for Patent Law' in Mirfin & Smith (eds) *Essays for Colin Tapper* (Butterworths, London 2003)

ARTICLES

Agnovic, A., 'Stem Cell Patents on a Knife Edge' (2008) JIPLP 718

Alten, B.G., 'Left to One's Own Devices: Congress Limits Patents on Medical Procedures' (1998) 8 Fordham Intell Prop Media & Ent LJ 837

AMA Council on Judicial and Ethical Affairs, 'Ethical Issues in the Patenting of Medical Procedures' 53 Food & Drug LJ 341

Anderson, S.D., 'A Right Without a Remedy: The Unenforceable Medical Procedure Patent' (1999) 3 Marq Intell Prop L Rev 117

Baxter, W.F., 'Legal Restrictions on the Exploitation of the Patent Monopoly' (1966) 76 Yale LJ 267

Becker, L.C., 'Deserving to Own Intellectual Property' (1993) Chi-Kent L Rev 609

Beier, F.-K., 'Exclusive Rights, Statutory Licences and Compulsory Licenses in Patent and Utility Model Law' (1999) 30 IIC 251

Bostyn, S.J.R., 'The Critical Analysis of the (Non)-Patentability of Diagnostic Methods and the Consequences for BRCA1 Gene Type Patents in Europe' (2003) Bio-Science L R 111

Bostyn S.J.R., 'No Cure without Pay? Referral to the Enlarged Board of Appeal Concerning the Patentability of Diagnostic Methods' (2005) EIPR 412

Bradshaw, J., 'Gene Patent Policy: Does Issuing Gene Patents accord with the purposes of the US Patent System?' (2001) Willamette L Rev 637

Buchanan, A.E., 'The Right to Decent Minimum of Health Care' (1984) 13 Phil & Pub Aff 55

Burch, G.F., 'Ethical Consideration in the Patenting of Medical Processes' (1987) 65 Tex L Rev 1139

Ch'en, F. and I. Karet, 'Court of Appeal can overrule itself to follow the EPO: UK adopts EPO stance on second medical use claims' (2008) JIPLP 543

Chiapetta, V., 'Defining the Proper Scope of Internet Patents: If We Don't Know Where We Want to Go, We're Unlikely to Get There' (2001) Mich Telecomm Tech L Rev 289

Cohen, S.E., 'To Innovate or not to Innovate, That is the Question: The Functions, Failures and Foibles of the Reward Function Theory of Patent Law in Relation to Computer Software Platforms' (1998) 5 Mich Telecom & Tech L Rev 1

Cornish, W.R., 'Rights in Employee Inventions: The UK Position' (1990) 21 IIC 290

Cripps, Y., 'The Refusal of Patents of Methods of Medical Treatment – A Preference for Parliamentary Guidance' (1983) EIPR 173

Dam, K.W., 'The Economic Function of Patent Law' (1994) 23 JLS 247

De Carvalho, N.P., 'The Primary Function of Patents' (2001) JL Tech and Pol'y 25

De Smet, W., 'Patentability in the Area of Therapy and Diagnosis under Belgian Law' (1991) 22 IIC 888

Domeij, B., 'Patent Claim Scope: Initial and Follow-on Pharmaceutical Inventions' (2001) EIPR 326

Eisenberg, R.S., 'Proprietary Rights and the Norms of Science in Biotechnology Research' (1987) 97 Yale LJ 177

Fellner, I.J., 'Patentability of Therapeutic Methods' (1946) 28 JPOS 90

Feros, A., 'Patentabilty of Methods of Medical Treatment' (2001) EIPR 79

Fisch, A.M., 'Compulsory Licensing of Pharmaceutical Patents; An Unreasonable Solution to an Unfortunate Problem' 34 (1994) Jurimetrics J 295

Friedgen, K.A., 'Rethinking the Struggle Between Health and Intellectual Property: Proposed Framework for Dynamic Rather Than Absolute Patent Protection of Essential Medicines' (2002) 16 EMORYILJ 689

Gocyk-Farber, B., 'Patenting Medical Procedures: A Search for a Compromise between Ethics and Economics' (1997) 18 Cardozo L Rev 1527

Grady, M.F. and J.I. Alexander, 'Patent Law and Rent Dissipation' (1992) 78 Va L Rev 305

Griffin, M.T., 'AIDS Drugs and the Pharmaceutical Industry: A Need for Reform' (1991) 17 Am JL & Med 363

Halewood, M., 'Regulating Patent Holders: Local Working Requirements and Compulsory Licences at International Law' (1997) 35 Osgoode Hall LJ 243

Hart, S., 'Getting Back to Basics: Reinventing Patent Law for Economic Efficiency' (1994) IPJ 216

Havins, W.E., 'Immunising the Medical Practitioner 'process' Infringer: Greasing the Squeaky Wheel, Good Public Policy or What?' (1999) 77 Uni Det Mercy L Rev 51

Hettinger, E., 'Justifying Intellectual Property' (1989) 18 Philosophy and Public Affairs 31

Horton, A., 'Methods of Treatment and Second Medical Use' (2000) Patent World 19

Jain, N., 'To Patent or not to Patent: Gene Therapy in the European Union and the United States' (1996) Cardozo J Int'l & Comp L 103

Katopis, C.J., 'Patients v. Patents?: Policy Implications of Recent Patent Legislation' (1997) 71 St. John's L Rev 329

Kell, D., 'Expanding the Frontier of Patentability: Methods of Medical Treatment of the Human Body' (1995) EIPR 202

Kitch, E.W., 'The Nature and Function of the Patent System' (1977) 20 JL & Econ 265

Lafferty, W.B., 'Statutory and Ethical Barriers in the Patenting of Medical and Surgical Procedures' (1996) 29 J Marshall L Rev 891

Lancon, P., 'Patentability in the Field of Therapy and Diagnosis' (1991) 22 IIC 893

Laurie, G., 'Patenting Stem Cells of Human Origin' (2004) EIPR 59

Lee, D.S., 'Pharmaceutical Manufacturers: Players or Pariah in Health Care Reform?' (1993) 3 Kan J L & Pub Pol'y 89

Loughlan, P., 'Of Patents and Patients: New Monopolies in Medical Methods' (1995) 6 AIPJ 5

Maddren, C.A., 'AIDS Vaccines: Balancing Human Rights with Public Health' (2003) 17 Temp Int't & Comp LJ 277

Marsico, P., 'The Chemical-Pharmaceutical Product Patent: Absolute Protection, General Formulas and Sufficiency of Description' (1990) EIPR 397

Martin, T.M., 'New Appellate Decision Clarifies Australian Law Concerning Patentability of Methods of Medical Treatment' (2000) J Pat & Trademark and Off Soc'y 645

Meier, B.J., 'The New Patent Infringement Liability Exception for Medical Procedures' (1997) 23 J Leg 265

Merges, R.P. and R.R. Nelson, 'On the Complex Economics of Patent Scope' (1990) 90 Colum L Rev 839

Merges, R.P., 'Rent Control in the Patent District: Observations on the Grady-Alexander Thesis' (1992) 78 Va L Rev 359
Moufang, R., 'Methods of Medical Treatment under Patent Law' (1993) 24 IIC 18
Nichols, S.L., 'Hippocrates, the Patent-Holder: The Unenforceability of Medical Procedure Patents' (1997) 7 Geo Mason L Rev 227
Noonan, W.D., 'Patenting Medical and Surgical Procedures' (1995) 77 J Pat and Trademark Off Soc'y 651
Odell-West, A., 'A Proposal to Amend the Medical Exclusion within Patent Law to Provide for Patentability of Certain Methods of Treatment' (2007) EIPR 492
Odell-West, A., 'Protecting Surgeons and their Art. Methods for Treatment of the Human Body by Surgery under Article 52(4) EPC' (2008) EIPR 102
Odell-West, A., 'The Legacy of Myriad for Gene-based Diagnostic: a New Policy and Regulatory Option' (2009) JIPLP 267
Pagenberg, J., 'Appetite Suppressant' (with case comment) (1987) 18 IIC 258
Palmer, T.G., 'Are Patents and Copyrights Morally Justified? The Philosophy of Property Rights and Ideal Objects' (1990) Harv J Law & Publ Pol'y 817
Panchen, K.E., 'Patentability in the Field of Therapy and Diagnosis' (1991) 22 IIC 879
Pennant, P., 'Patentability of Medical Treatment' (1981) EIPR 64
Pila, J., 'Article 52(2) of the Convention on the Grant of European Patents: What did the framers intend?' (2005) 36 IIC 755
Pila, J., 'Bound Futures: Patent Law and Modern Biotechnology' (2003) 9 Bos UJSTL 326
Pila, J., 'Methods of Medical Treatment within Australian and United Kingdom Patents Law' (2001) 24 UNSW Law Journal 420
Pila, J., 'The Common Law Invention in its Original Form' (2001) IPQ 209
Portman, R.M., 'Legislative Restriction on Medical and Surgical Procedure Patents' (1996) U Balt Intell Prop LJ 91
Radin, M.J., 'Property and Personhood' (1982) 34 Stan L Rev 957
Reisman, J.M., 'Physicians and Surgeons as Inventors: Reconciling Medical Process Patents and Medical Ethics' (1995) 10 High Tech LJ 355
Rimmer, M., 'Myriad Genetics: Patent Law and Genetic Testing' (2003) EIPR 20
Rogers, D., 'Exclusion of Patentability of Diagnostic Methods Practised on the Human Body: Article 52(4) EPC' (2007) JIPLP 60
Rogers, D., 'Glaucoma Diagnostic Invention Ruling Puts Flesh on Bones of G 0001/04' (2007) JIPLP 7

Scassa, T., 'Patents for Second Medical Indications and their Potential Impact on Pharmacase in Canada' (2001) 9 Health Law Journal 23
Sims, A., 'The Case against Patenting Methods of Medical Treatment' (2007) EIPR 43
Smith, J.A., 'It's your move – No its not! The Application of Patent law to Sports Moves' (1999) U of Colorado Law Review 1051
Smither, R., 'Patent Protection for Inventions Relating to Medical Treatment of Humans and Animals' (CLIP London 1993)
Spence, M., 'Passing Off and the Misappropriation of Valuable Intangibles' (1996) LQR 472
Staaf, M. and R.J., 'Patents, Coprights and Trademarks: Property or Monopoly?' (1990) Harv JL & Pub Pol'y 911
Suchy, H., 'Patent Protection for Second Medicinal Use' (1982) 6 EIPR 161
Syddall, T., 'Swiss-type Claims Held Valid in New Zealand' (1996) CIPA 420
Tandon, P., 'Optimal Patents with Compulsory Licenses' (1982) 90 J of Pol Econ 470
Taylor, J.A., 'Medical Process Patents and Patient Privacy Rights' (1995) 14 J Marshall J Computer & Info L 131
Thomas, D., 'Patentability Problems in Medical Technology' (2003) 34 IIC 847
Thums, D., 'Patent Protection for Medical Treatment – A Distinction Between Patent and Medical Law' 27 (1996) IIC 423
Ventose, E.D., 'Exclusion of Methods of Treatment of the Human or Animal Body by Surgery from Patent Protection' (2007) JIPLP 574
Ventose, E.D., 'Patent Protection for Diagnostic Methods Under the European Patent Convention' (2007) 38 IIC 884
Ventose, E.D., '"Farming" out an Exception to the Exclusion of Methods of Medical Treatment under the European Patent Convention' (2008) EPIR 509
Ventose, E.D., 'Making Sense of the Decision of the Enlarged Board of Appeal in *CYGNUS/Diagnostic method*' (2008) EIPR 145
Ventose, E.D., 'No European Patents for Second uses of Devices or Instruments' (2008) EIPR 11
Ventose, E.D., 'Patent Protection for Surgical Methods Under the European Patent Convention' (2008) 39 IIC 58
Ventose, E.D., 'Patenting Treatment or Dosage Regimes under Articles 53(c) and 54(5) of the European Patent Convention 2000' (2008) JIPLP 540
Ventose, E.D., 'Patent Protection for Methods of Medical Treatment in the United Kingdom' [2008] IPQ 58
Ventose, E.D., 'Disclaiming Methods of Medical Treatment from Patent Protection Under the European Patent Convention' (2009) JIPLP 706

Ventose, E.D., 'In the Footsteps of the Framers of the European Patent Convention: Examining the *Travaux Préparatoires*' (2009) EIPR 353
Ventose, E.D., 'New Developments in Patent Protection for the Myriad's BRAC 1 Gene at the European Patent Office' (2009) JIPLP 771
Ventose, E.D., 'Patent Protection for Second and Further Medical Uses Under the European Patent Convention' (2009) SCRIPTed – A Journal of Law, Technology & Society 57
Ventose, E.D., 'The *Byzantine* Logic of Patent Law Jurisprudence: Patent Protection for Dosage Regimes Revisited' (2009) JIPLP 415
Ventose, E.D., 'Patent Protection for Therapeutic Methods under the European Patent Convention (2010) EIPR 120
Ventose, E.D., 'Patent Protection for Dosage Regimes under the European Patent Convention 2000' (2010) JIPLP 474
Ventose, E.D., 'The Enlarged Board of Appeal Rules on the Scope of the Exclusion from Patent Protection for Methods for Treatment of the Human or Animal Body by Surgery' (2010) JIPLP 393
Ventose, E.D., 'Patent Protection for Dosage Regimes in Europe: A Dissenting View' (2011) JIPLP 108
Ventose, E.D., 'Patenting Surgical Methods in Europe after *MEDI-PHYSICS/Treatment by surgery*' (2011) JIPLP 238
Verkey, E., 'Patenting of Medical Methods – Need of the Hour' (2007) JIPLP 104
Vogelsang-Wenke, H., 'Patenting of Stem Cells and Processes Involving Stem Cells According to the Rules of the European Patent Convention' (2004) 23 Biotechnology Law Report 155
White, A., 'Patentability of Medical Treatment Welcome Foundation (Hitching's Application)' (1980) EIPR 364
White, A., 'Patentability of Medical Treatment Claims – The Nimodipin Cases' (1984) EIPR 38
White, A., 'Patenting the Second Medical Indication' (1985) EIPR 62
Wojan, P.L., 'A Conflict of Rights: Intellectual Property under TRIPs, the Right to Health and AIDS Drugs' (2002) 6 UCLA J Int'l & Foreign Aff 463
Yang, W.W., Patent Policy and Medical Procedure Patents' (1995) 1 B U J Sci & Tech L 5

REPORTS, PAPERS AND THESES

Australian Law Reform Commission, *Report 99 – Genes and Ingenuity: Gene Patenting and Human Health* (Australian Law Reform Commission, Sydney 2004)

Case Law of the Boards of Appeal of the European Patent Office (5th edn, December 2006)

IPI (Intellectual Property Institute), *Patents for Genetic Sequences: The Competitiveness of Current UK Law and Practice* (2004)

New Zealand, *Review of the Patents Act 1953: Boundaries to Patentability* (March 2002)

Nuffield Council on Bioethics, *The Ethics of Patenting DNA: A Discussion Paper* (Nuffield Council on Bioethics, London 2002)

Machlup, F., *An Economic Review of the Patent System* (Study of the Subcommittee on Patents, Trademarks and Copyrights of the Committee of the Judiciary United States Senate 85th Congress Study No 15 1958) 21

Ontario Ministry of Health, *Genetics, Testing and Gene Patenting: Charting New Territory in Healthcare* (Ontario Ministry of Health, Toronto 2002)

Opinion of the Group of Advisors on the Ethical Implications of Biotechnology of the European Commission No. 7 (1996)

Philips, J. and F. Levere *The Exclusion of Surgical, Therapeutic and Diagnostic Inventions from Patentability Under Article 52(4) of the European Patent Convention* (Intellectual Property Institute 2008)

Spence, M. and M. Molineaux *The First Mover Monopoly: A Study on Patenting Business Methods in Europe* (Olswang and Oxford Intellectual Property Research Centre, Oxford University 2001)

The Examination Guidelines for Patent Applications relating to Medical Inventions in the UK Intellectual Property Office (2007)

The Examination Guidelines for Patent Applications relating to Biotechnological Inventions at the UK Patent Office (2009)

Index

Access to medical procedures 48–52
  case against patent protection 50
  control, question of 50–52
  demand and supply, dynamics of 51–52
  increased costs of health care 52–53
  meanings 49
  methods of medical treatment 48–50
Actavis v Merck 361–372
  Court of Appeal 362–364
  'different medical condition' 368
  distinct and different medical condition 366
  first instance 361–362
  novel technical features 363
  obviousness 364–365
  precedent 371
  which novelty? 370–371
Animals 101–112
  agricultural methods 102
  application by TBAs 103–104
  EBA 111–112
  ectoparasitic infestations of pigs 103–104
  immunostimulation 107–108
  incidental objectives 106–111
  increased meat production 108–109
  industrial application 101–106
  legislative history 104–105
  method of treatment by therapy 109–110
  reformulation of exclusion 106
  surgical methods 111–112
  therapy, meaning 110
Arguments against patent protection 41–70, 443–444
  access to medical procedures 48–52
  case against patent protection 50
  control, question of 50–52
  demand and supply, dynamics of 51–52
  increased costs of health care 52–53
  meanings 49
  methods of medical treatment 48–50
breach of patient's privacy 68–69
  disclosure 69
  right to privacy 68–69
code of ethics 61–62
compulsory licences 53–58
  Act of 1977 54–55
  case for 56
  costs, and 57
  intellectual property rights 53
  limitations 57–58
  meaning 53
  public health, and 55–56
emotive arguments 41–42
Hippocratic Oath 61–62
  methods of medical treatment 63–65
  specific to medical profession 63–64
incentive structures 66–68
  alternative 67
methods 43–45
pharmaceutical products 43–45
physician liberty and autonomy 58–60
  factors affecting judgment 59
physician/patient relationship 60–61
products 43–45
public health implications 45–58
rationale for exclusion 42
right to health 46–48

sharing norm 62–63
erosion of 65
methods of medical treatment 63–65
nature of 64–65
TRIPs Agreement 47
Arguments for and against patent protection 443–447
Arguments for patent protection 9–40, 444–445
balancing exercise 443
direct control over supply of invention 444
economic purpose 10
economic rationale 444
ethical justifications 443–444
incentive to disclose 11–13
Chamberlain family 12
methods of medical treatment 11–13
research, and 13
incentive to invent/innovate 14–23
breadth of medical science 22
cost-benefit analysis, and 22
cost of research, and 17
Gocyk-Farber on 21–22
high development cost inventions 20–23
methods of medical treatment 15–18
promotion of R&D 16
reward theory 14–15
SET Patent 18–20
utilitarian principles 14
liberty/autonomy 34–39
collaborative research efforts 38
Hegel on 36
Locke's theory of property 35–36
methods of medical treatment 38–39
property rights, justification for 36–37
Radin on 37
rights of creator of invention 39
prospect theory 23–26
Kitch on 23–24
limitation 24
methods of medical treatment 25–26
simple methods of treatment 26
treatment regimes 25–26
rationales 9–10
rent dissipation theory 27–31
Grady and Alexander on 27–30
methods of medical treatment 28–31
reward/desert 31–34
endocrine therapy 33
identity of creator 34
methods of medical treatment 33–34
philosophical difficulties 32
value of product to society 33–34
Australia
judicial determination of exclusion 434
public interest 446

Commonwealth
manner of new manufacture *see* Manner of new manufacture
Contraceptive methods 97–100
feminine hygiene device 99–100
LHRH composition 97
manner of new manufacture *see also* Manner of new manufacture
arrangement of pills on card 317–319
hormonal drugs 316
method of medical treatment, whether 316
pack claims 316, 317–320
process claims 316
royal prerogative 317
setting limits 320–321
method of treatment by therapy, whether 97–98
personal use 98–100
susceptible to industrial application, whether 98–100
Cosmetic methods 89–96
acceptable form of claim 95–96
anti-snoring means 94
appetite suppressant 91
cleaning plaque 93–94
industrial application 94–95
meaning 90

not patentable 93–94
patentable 90–92
Patents Act 1977 *see* Patents Act 1977
thenoyl peroxide 90
therapeutic use, and 91–92

Diagnostic methods 184–228
application of principles 208–218
consistency of approach 218
defining diagnostic methods 208–212
interaction with human or animal body 213
intermediate steps 216–218
methodological issues: early view 213
methodological issues: more recent view 214–216
no diagnosis 209
no diagnosis and not practised on body 210
only examination and data gathering phase present 210–212
practised on human or animal body 213
'applied to the human or animal body' 188–189
blood extraction method 193–194
broad approach 196–201
application of general principles 200–201
blood extraction method 199
defining diagnostic methods 196–197
medical practitioners, involvement of 197–198
mental acts 196–197
practised on human or animal body 198–199
ultimate responsibility of physician 198
defining 189–192
EPO jurisprudence 439–440
examination phase 193
four-pronged test 190–191
legislative history 187–189
medical practitioners, involvement of 192–194
narrow approach 189–196
new medical technology 218–228
EU Biotech Directive *see* EU Biotech Directive
genetic diagnostic testing 219–221, 223–227
methods of medical treatment 219–221
morality, and 222–223
ordre public 222–223
patent law, and 218–219
non-invasive measurement 191–192
Patents Act 1977 *see* Patents Act 1977
practised on human or animal body 194–196
reconciling two approaches 201–208
delineating scope of definition 204–205
diagnosing diagnostic methods 201–206
essential features of claims 205–206
first principles 202
intellectual exercise 203–204
medical practitioners, involvement of 206–207
multi-step approach 202–203
practised on human or animal body 207–208
rationale for exclusion 201–202
scope of exclusion 184–185
Disclaimers 168–182
cosmetic method with therapeutic effect 170–171
EBA, and 180–181
excluded method of medical treatment 174–175
flow measurement 171–172
form of admissible claim 175–178
higher level of abstraction 177–178
implications of using 178–180
importance of 169–170
issue 169–170
legal analysis 182
limiting scope of claims, and 172

methods of medical treatment, and 170–175
'non therapeutic', meaning 173–174
omission of step 181–182
surgical methods, and 168–182
use of 175–176
when allowed 175–176
wording of claims, and 171

Dosage regimes
Patents Act 1977 *see* Patents Act 1977

Enlarged Board of Appeal (EBA)
animals, and 111–112
disclaimers, and 180–181
MEDI-PHYSICS/Treatment by surgery, and 140–148
surgical methods, and 123–124, 136–138, 153
therapeutic methods, and 85–87

EU Biotech Directive 221–223
aim of 221
methods of medical treatments 221–222
morality, and 222–223
ordre public 222–223

European Patent Office (EPO)
jurisprudence 436–442
diagnostic methods 439–440
genetic diagnostic testing 224–227
legislative history 436
medical treatment 5–6
second and further medical uses 440–442
surgical methods 438–439
therapeutic methods 436–438
United Kingdom courts, and 442

Excluded surgical step 158–168
applicable national laws 161–162
diagnostic methods 160–161
existence of surgical steps in claim 159–161
insertion of device into human body 162–163
interaction with body 158
MEDI-PHYSICS/Treatment by surgery 165–168
method for conditioning gas 163
non-surgical steps, and 159–160
ratio legis 161–162
surgical steps defined as excluded surgical treatments 162–164
surgical steps not defined as excluded surgical treatments 164–165

Genetic diagnostic testing 223–227
challenges 228
EPO jurisprudence 224–227
morality, and 223–227
nucleic acid 224–226
ordre public, and 223–227
socio-economic consequences of patenting 226–227

Hippocratic Oath 61–62
methods of medical treatment 63–65
specific to medical profession 63–64

Judicial determination of exclusion 433–436
Australia 434
New Zealand 434
United Kingdom 433–434
PAT 434
United States of America 435–436

Manner of new manufacture 287–331
Australia 321–330
ethical considerations 324
law 299
public policy 323
vendible test 322–323
biological subject matter 301–304
biotechnological subject matter 301–304
commercial object requirement 297–298
Commonwealth 321–330
contraceptive methods 315–321
arrangement of pills on card 317–319
hormonal drugs 316
method of medical treatment, whether 316
pack claims 316, 317–320

process claims 316
royal prerogative 317
setting limits 320–321
diagnostic methods, and 291–292
deafness, and 290–291
demise of commercial object requirement 299–301
economic rationale of patent system 300–301
ethical grounds 308–315
extraction of lead 297
medicine, meaning 288
micro-organisms 302–303
morality: emerging concept 309–311
morality: legal justification 311–314
morality: necessary or hindrance, whether 314–315
morality, relevance 308
nature of exclusion 288–295
New Zealand 321–330
EISAI 327–329
new use claim 325–326
novelty 326
public policy 324–325
second medical indication 327–329
second medical use patents 325–329
Swiss-type claims 327,329
Patent Office Practice 287, 304–307
Act of 1977 307
contraception 305
Examiners, role of 307
improved wool yield 304–305
PAT, role of 307
procedure 306–307
reduction of gastric secretion 306
public policy grounds 308–315
rationale for exclusion 295–315
sound treatment 302–303
Statute of Monopolies 296
statutory interpretation 296–304
statutory regime 296
test for general patentability 300
treatment in animals 293–295
treatment in humans 289–292
vendible product 298
widening conception of manufacture 298
Medical treatment
EPO jurisprudence 5–6
future of medical patents 7–8
patent protection 1–2
arguments 2–5
direct control 5
public health, and 3–4
patentability 6–7
Medicine
meaning 288

New medical technology 112–116
DNA technology 113–114
gene therapy 113–115
germline gene therapy 114–115
somatic gene therapy 114–115
stem cell therapy 115
therapeutic cloning 113–115
New Zealand
economic rationale 446
judicial determination of exclusion 434
manner of new manufacture *see* Manner of new manufacture

Patent Appeal Tribunal
judicial determination of exclusion 434
Patent Office Practice, and 307
Patents Act 2004 332–373
basis of origin of exclusion, and 333–334
comparison with pre-1977 law 333–338
interpretation 332–333
revision of EPC, and 332
Patents Act 1977 334–338
Actavis v Merck see *Actavis v Merck*
animals, treatment of *see also* Animals 336
application of exclusion 338–344
defining therapy 339–340
ex post facto rationalisation 338–339
inherent contradictions 339

method of treatment by therapy 339–342
pharmaceutical inventions 338
taxol 340–342
Bristol-Myers Squibb, and 361–370
cosmetic methods 337–338
diagnostic methods 336–337, 343–344
dosage regimes 356–372
Actavis v Merck 361–372
issues for courts 357
second medical treatment 357–360
further reformation of exclusion 335–336
humans, treatment of 336
industrial application 335
invention 334–335
methods of treatment by surgery 342–343
new law of patents 334
reformulation of exclusion 335
second and further medical uses 345–356
applying requirements of Swiss-type claim 353–355
codification of EISAI/Second medical indication 355–356
current UK approach 348–353
desire to achieve conformity 347–348
doctrinal issues 346–356
dosage regime 352–353
EISAI 345–346
manufacture of medicament 353–354
new therapeutic application 354–355
novelty in end result 350–351
only first medical use protected 346
pharmaceutical inventions 347
principle, matter of 347
reaffirmation by Court of Appeal 349–353
reluctant application by Jacob J 348–349
second medical indication 345–346
Swiss-type claim 351–352
taxol 349–353
Public health considerations 433

Royal prerogative
contraceptive methods and 317

Second and further uses *see also* Second and further medical uses
claims allowable, whether 252–253
'compounds' 232
devices 246–254
dosage regimes 255–285
controversy over 255–256
decisions of TBAs 279–280
defining 280–281
differences between EPC 1973 and EPC 2000 281–282
end of Swiss type claims 282–283
EPC 1973 261–269
EPC 2000 259–261, 269
first medical uses 273–274
new technical effect 281
relationship with medical treatment exclusion 271–273
second and further medical uses 256–259
specific uses under EPC 2000 274–277
Swiss-type claims 277–279
EISAI 235–237
EPO jurisprudence, and 440–442
extending reach of EISAI principle 244–246
administration of vaccine to sero-postive pigs 244–245
initial exclusion 234–235
instruments 246–254
claims allowable, whether 252–253
recent changes 253
legislative history 230–234
new medical technology 285–286
not applicable to products which are not medicaments 251

not falling within ratio legis of ESAI/second medical indication 249–251
origin 234–237
Second and further medical uses *see also* Second and further uses
Patents Act 1977 *see* Patents Act 1977
reform of EPC 254–255
'substance' 232–233
Swiss-type claims *see* Swiss-type claims
treatment regimes 255–285
controversy over 255–256
decisions of TBAs 279–280
differences between EPC 1973 and EPC 2000 281–282
end of Swiss-type claims 282–283
EPC 2000 259–261
first medical uses 273–274
new technical effect 281
relationship with medical treatment exclusion 271–273
second and further medical uses 256–259
specific uses under EPC 2000 274–277
Swiss-type claims 277–279
SET patent 18–20
funding 19
Surgical methods 117–183
animals 121–122
biotechnology, and 122
broadening of definition 183
cosmetic methods 148–153
beautifying human body 150–151
EBA in MEDI-PHYSICS/ Treatment by surgery 153
purpose test 149–151
removal of excess hair 150
technical features of claims 151–153
tightening skin surface 151–152
defining 124–138
dental treatment 155–156
diagnostic method 154
disclaimers *see also* Disclaimers 168–182
EBA in CYGNUS/Diagnostic method 136–138
EBA, referral to 123–124
EPO jurisprudence 438–439
exception 131–132
excluded surgical step 158–168
applicable national laws 161–162
diagnostic methods 160–161
existence of surgical steps in claim 159–161
insertion of device into human body 162–163
interaction with body 158
MEDI-PHYSICS/Treatment by surgery 165–168
method for conditioning gas 163
non-surgical steps, and 159–160
ratio legis 161–162
surgical steps defined as excluded surgical treatments 162–164
surgical steps not defined as excluded surgical treatments 164–165
expansive definition 125
hair removal method 121
interpretive criteria 155–157
intervention on structure of organism 156–157
issues relating to 118
legislative history 119–123
MEDI-PHYSICS/Treatment by surgery 138–148
apparatus for skin resurfacing 142
broad or narrow construction of exclusion 143–144
decision of EBA 140–148
decision of TBA 138–140
hair removal method 142
legal analysis 146–148
literal interpretation 140–141
ratio legis of exclusion 141–143
redefining methods of treatment by surgery 144–146
treatment by therapy 141
medical practitioners, involvement of 153–155

narrow interpretation 126–127
non-insignificant 129–130
pericardial access 124
physician, role of 153–155
polarized 129Xe 123–124
purpose of intervention 132–136
ratio legis 132–134
relevance 134–136
reason for exclusion 117
significance 157
surgery, meaning 128–129
therapeutic treatment, and 130–131
travaux preparatoires 120
treatment, meaning 125–126
Swiss-type claims 237–244
acceptable form 242–244
adsorbent, use of 238–239
anti-tumoural agent 242–243
L (-) carnitine 241
manufacture of medicament 238–239
new therapeutic application 239–242
requirements 237–244
sea lice infestation 242
serotonin receptor 240–241

Therapeutic methods 71–116
animals *see* Animals
contraceptive methods *see* Contraceptive methods
cosmetic methods *see also* Cosmetic methods
defining 75–78
EPO jurisprudence 436–438
implantable devices 78–88
application 86
blood assistance method 84–85
EBA 85–87
need for functional link or nexus 79–80
not patentable 80–81
pacemaker 81–84
patentable 81–85
rapid acquisition resonance imaging 87
therapeutic effect 88
involvement of medical practitioners 88–89
legislative history 73–75
maintenance of health 77–78
medical treatments 73
methods of therapy 73–74
new medical technology *see* New medical technology
'physical methods' 74
restoration of health 77–78
scope of exclusion 75–77
therapy, meaning 74–75
treatment by therapy, meaning 72–73
Therapy
meaning 74–75, 75–76
Treatment by therapy
meaning 72–73
TRIPs Agreement 47, 54

United Kingdom courts
EPO jurisprudence, and 442
United Kingdom Patents Act 2004 *see* Patents Act 2004
United States of America 374–432
applying *Bilski v Kappos* 422–430
applying machine-or-transformation test 425–428
diagnosis for curative purposes 420
interpreting claims 423–424
mental step 429–430
natural phenomena 428–429
relevance of machine-or-transformation test 422–423
balancing of competing values and interests 445
constitutional guarantee 392–393
constitutional power 392–431
creation of fever in human body 379
diagnostic methods after *Bilski v Kappos* 412–430
analysis of gene sequences 421–422
defining diagnostic methods 413–415
mathematical formula 417–418, 419
laws of nature 416–417

machine-or-transformation test 415–416
natural phenomena 416–422
process for curing synthetic rubber 418–420
diagnostic methods in Federal Circuit after *Laboratory Corporation v Metabolite Labs* 400–409
diagnostic methods in Federal Circuit before *Laboratory Corporation v Metabolite Labs* 394–395
diagnostic methods in Supreme Court 396–400
'application of a law of nature' 399
'correlate', meaning 396–399
'natural phenomenon' 399–400
'process' 399
public interest considerations 400
658 patent 396
Dick 378
ex parte Brinkerhoff 378–380
ex parte Scherer 374, 375
Federal Circuit 394–395
algorithm 394, 408
diagnostic claims 394–395
diagnostic methods after *Laboratory Corporation v Metabolite Labs* 400–409
fundamental principle 407
machine-or-transformation test 404
mental process 403–404
phenomena of nature 401–403, 406
transformation 407–408
'warning' steps 408–409
Genomic Research and Diagnostic Accessibility Act 390–392
contrary to spirit of MPAA 392
immunity from infringement 391
reason for 390
research on genetic sequences 391
retrospective application 391–392
infringement 390
inhaled ethers 375–376
initial exclusion 375–378
initial judicial determination 375–382
involvement of human body 380–381
judicial determination of exclusion 434
legal requirements of patentability 431
legislative history 383–384
legislative intervention 382–392
MPAA 382
MPAA 432
medical or surgical method 380
nature of exclusion in section 387(c) 384–390
cadavers 387
defendant 386
hybrid claims 389–390
legislative intention 385–390
medical activity 384–385, 386–387
patented use of composition of matter 387–389
three-pronged approach 385
patent protection reasserted 380–382
POBA 374
professional ethics 431
public policy 431
section 1, Patent Act 392–393
Senate Bill 1334 383
Supreme Court
categories of inventions eligible for protection 410
diagnostic methods after *Bilski v Kappos* 412–430
machine-or-transformation test 410–411
process, test for 411
standard for patentability in *Bilski v Kappos* 409–412
surgical instruments 377
USPTO 374